SOVIET MILITARY DECEPTION
IN THE SECOND WORLD WAR

SOVIET MILITARY THEORY AND PRACTICE

Projected volumes by David M. Glantz

This series examines in detail the evolution of Soviet military science and the way the Soviets have translated theoretical concepts for the conduct of war into concrete military practice. Separate volumes focus on how the Soviets have applied and refined theory in combat and on how they have structured their forces to suit the requirement of changing times.

SOVIET MILITARY DECEPTION

IN THE
SECOND WORLD WAR

DAVID M. GLANTZ

FRANK CASS

First published 1989 in Great Britain by
FRANK CASS AND COMPANY LIMITED
Gainsborough House, 11 Gainsborough Road,
London E11 1RS, England

and in the United States of America by
FRANK CASS AND COMPANY LIMITED
c/o Biblio Distribution Centre
81 Adams Drive, P.O. Box 327, Totowa, N.J. 07512

Library of Congress Cataloging-in-Publication Data

Glantz, David M.
  Soviet military deception in the Second World War.

  Bibliography: p
  Includes index.
  1. World War, 1939–1945—Military intelligence—
Soviet Union. I. Title.
D810.S7G55   1989   940.54'12'37   88-16228
ISBN 0-7146-3347-X

British Library Cataloguing in Publication Data

Glantz, David M.
  Soviet military deception in the Second
  World War.
  1. World War 2. Military operations by
  Soviet Military Forces. Strategy.
  Deceptions
  I. Title
  940.54'12'47

  ISBN 0-7146-3347-X

Printed and bound in Great Britain by
A. Wheaton & Co. Ltd, Exeter

To my wife Mary Ann
without whose selfless support this
book could not have been written

In contemporary conditions, when at the same time the scale of war grows and reconnaissance capabilities also improve, it is very difficult to mask the preparations of large operations. However, to conceal their true scale, especially the direction of undertaken measures, the concept and direction of the main blow, and the beginning time of active operations . . . is a quite real mission, which must be at the center of attention of military theoreticians, all commanders, staffs, and political organs.

M.M. Kir'yan, *Vnezapnost' v nastupatel' nykh operatsiyakh Velikoi Otechestvennoi voiny* [Surprise in Offensive Operations of the Great Patriotic War], 1986

CONTENTS

LIST OF ILLUSTRATIONS

LIST OF MAPS

EXPLANATION OF
MAP TRANSLITERATIONS

All maps included in the text have been derived from German archival or Soviet sources.

German intelligence maps are simplified versions of those contained in the records of the German OKH, army groups, or armies. In some cases they are composites, reflecting the views of multiple German headquarters. For example, see the adjacent original intelligence maps of German OKH noting the estimated situation just prior to the Soviet L'vov–Sandomierz, Kovel', and Vistula–Oder offensives. Simplified versions reflecting the same data, which match similar simplifications throughout the text, follow on the next six pages.

The actual situation maps showing Soviet force dispositions on the eve of each operation are derived from multiple detailed Soviet sources verified by retrospective assessments by German intelligence which usually confirm the accuracy of Soviet accounts regarding Soviet order of battle and force deployments.

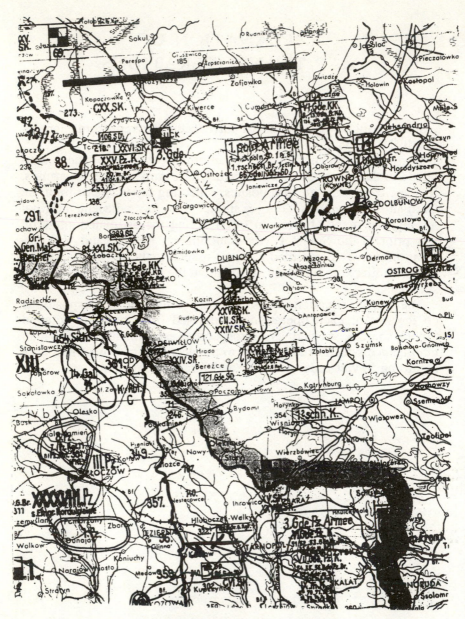

German *OKH Lage Ost*
12 July 1944
The Rava Russkaya Direction

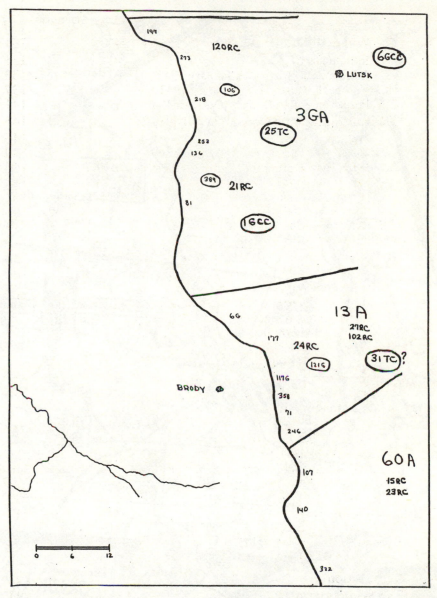

197
120RC
273
6GCC
⌀ LUTSK
106
218
3GA
25TC
252
136
389
21RC
81
1GCC

13 A
6G
27RC
102RC
177
24RC
31TC?
121G
BRODY ⌀
117G
358
71
246

60A
107
15RC
23RC
140

0 6 12

322

141. L'vov–Sandomierz, German intelligence assessment, Rava–Russkaya sector
12 July '44

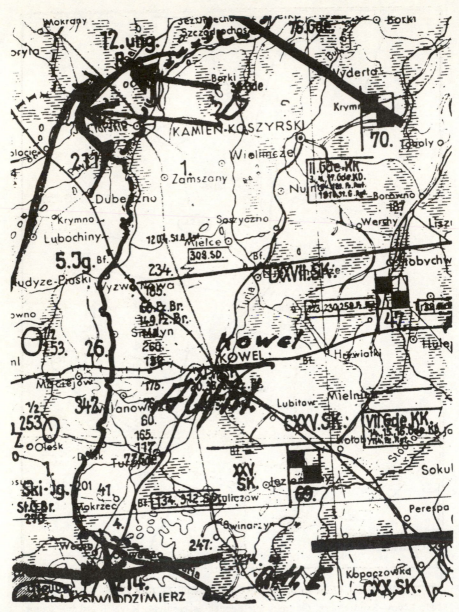

German *OKH Lage Ost*
17 July 1944
The Kovel' Sector

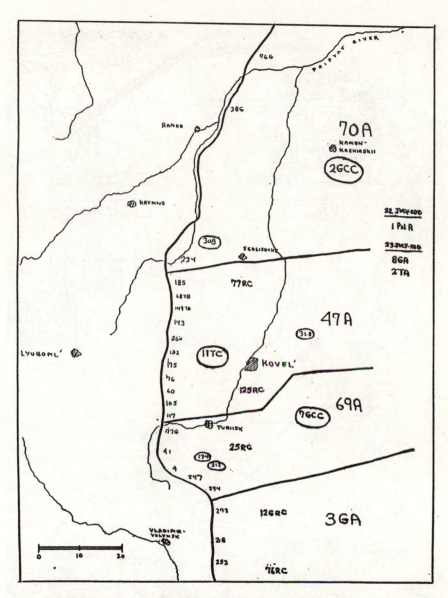

145. Lublin–Brest, German intelligence assessment, 17 July 1944

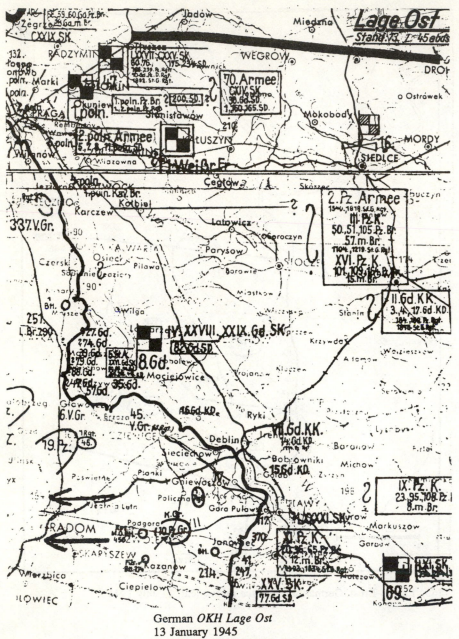

German *OKH Lage Ost*
13 January 1945
The Magnushev–Pulany Sectors

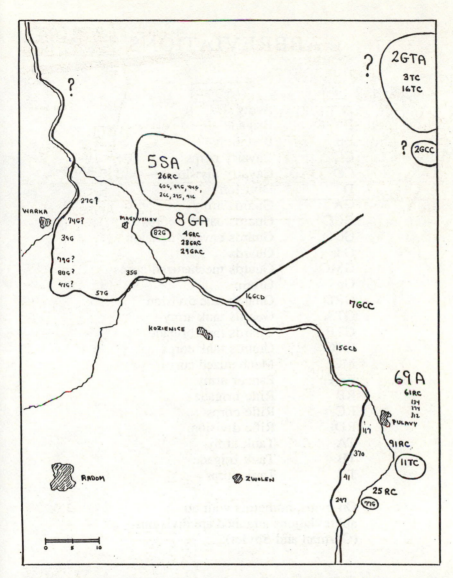

175. Vistula–Oder, German intelligence assessment, Magnushev–Pulavy sectors, 12 Jan. 1945

ABBREVIATIONS

A	Army
B	Brigade
Bn	Battalion
CC	Cavalry corps
CD	Cavalry division
D	Division
GA	Guards army
GCC	Guards cavalry corps
GCD	Guards cavalry division
Gds	Guards
GMC	Guards mechanized corps
Gp	Group
GRD	Guards rifle division
GTA	Guards tank army
GTB	Guards tank brigade
GTC	Guards tank corps
MC	Mechanized corps
PzA	Panzer army
RB	Rifle brigade
RC	Rifle corps
RD	Rifle division
TA	Tank army
TB	Tank brigade
TC	Tank corps

On maps, numerals with no
abbreviations attached are divisions
(German and Soviet).

PREFACE

Almost fifty years after the end of the Second World War, scholarly interest in its history appears to be as vigorous as ever. The approach of this important anniversary will, if anything, be marked by increased attention and the publication of a spate of new books. Despite this fact, both professional military historians and general readers are still poorly informed on the war as waged in Eastern Europe.[1] This is simply because the majority of relevant books published in the Western world focus on the campaigns in Italy and North Africa, the war in the Atlantic and Pacific, the invasion of northwestern Europe, and the strategic bombing of Germany. To the reader in the West, the part of the war with which he is so familiar may seem to have been fought on a gigantic scale. In actuality, though, the magnitude of the primarily land-based conflict between Communist Russia and Nazi Germany dwarfs that of the war on all other fronts combined.

There are four principal explanations for this relative ignorance and lack of interest in the war in Eastern Europe. First of all, the eastern and western fronts remained, for the most part, politically and physically separate for the duration of the war; what little coordination there was took place at only the very highest political and grand strategic levels. Consequently, the Western reader's direct and personal interest in such seemingly remote events continued to be weak. The same could probably be said of the Soviet reader's level of interest in the western theater of operations. Secondly, the traditional Soviet obsession with secrecy meant that the national archives could never be opened to Western historians (or for that matter to any non-official Russian historians). Furthermore, even if western historians were to gain access to the Soviet national archives or other primary source material, most would still be ill-equipped to overcome the language barrier. To date, few military historians have had the Russian language skills necessary to write a first-rate original history of the war in the East.

With the possible exception of works written from the perspective of one state fighting simultaneously on two fronts, most of the general historical surveys of the Second World War leave one with the impression that two separate, barely related wars took place. This is most characteristic of the military historians, who tend to specialize in either a particular professional dimension of the war (e.g., the war at sea, or strategic bombardment) or a specific campaign or battle (e.g., the Western Desert, Cassino, Normandy, the Battle of the Bulge). Diplomatic historians and those interested in grand strategy have of course devoted more time to the overall strategic attempts to coordinate the war effort as well as to the question of the Second Front between the Western Allies and the Soviet Union.

At this juncture, however, military historians need to take a much closer look at the war in general while examining how specific military operations in the East and West affected one another. The top priority in the years to come will be to write a unified history that links and correlates the events on both fronts. How, for example, did German preparations for the Battle of Kursk affect German strategic and operational planning on the Italian front? How did the invasion of Sicily or Normandy affect German operations on the Eastern Front? In what way did the Allied strategic bombing campaign benefit the Russians? In what form was the information obtained from ULTRA by the British passed on to the Soviet Union, and what was its practical value to the Russians? How did the Russians react to the news of Pearl Harbor and what, if anything, did Soviet intelligence know about the Japanese war plans? Such questions quickly reveal why it is now important to move from writing ethnocentric accounts of the Second World War to completing a truly comprehensive study of its history.

Yet before a thoroughly integrated history of the Second World War can be completed, much more must be learned about the war on the Eastern Front. Colonel David Glantz is one of the few Western historians who has drawn upon both Soviet and German primary and secondary sources to examine this subject in great detail. *Soviet Military Deception* is a pioneering, highly innovative work in which Col. Glantz shows that intelligence and deception played a central role in Soviet strategy and military operations throughout the war.[2] It should come as no surprise to the student of Soviet military affairs that deception was used continuously by the Red Army. More surprising, though, is the *scale* on which the Soviets employed deception in support of all their military operations as well as the fact that (as in the West) the Germans never found an effective way to counter it. Although recent studies have emphasized the scale on which the Western Allies successfully used deception on all fronts, it should also be evident by now that they did not have a monopoly on its use. What is even more fascinating, as it turns out with the publication of *Soviet Military Deception*, is the fact that Soviet and Allied deception operations tended to complement and perhaps even reinforce each other despite the lack of an overall deception plan.

In recent years, the publication of previously undisclosed details on ULTRA and the conduct of British deception operations radically changed some commonly accepted interpretations of operational decisions taken during the war. In light of Col. Glantz's study, many aspects of operational histories of the war in the East may have to be revised or modified, although this process may not be complete until the Soviet state archives are finally opened to scholars. It can only be hoped that the spirit of *glasnost* and possibly greater political and intellectual freedom in the USSR will also be accompanied by an increased readiness on the part of the Soviet government to cooperate with scholars. Indeed, a better understanding of the major Soviet contribution to the war effort might bring about an improvement in Soviet relations with the West and therefore support the *glasnost* policy itself.

In *Soviet Military Deception*, Col. Glantz is the first scholar to shed light on the extensive Soviet use of deception as well as on the learning process of the Soviet deceivers who, unlike their Western counterparts, are still anonymous. Although the Soviets have not published any detailed studies dedicated specifically to the use of deception during the Second World War, they refer to its use in almost all of their general histories. In doing so, they are trying to maintain a balance between the need to instruct their own military on the critical importance of deception – and the desire not to disclose too many of their methods to potential adversaries.

Col. Glantz's methodology in reconstructing the role of deception in Soviet military operations first involved a careful reading of all available Soviet literature on the "Great Patriotic War." In open literature he noted any references – whether direct or veiled – to the role of deception, the methods used to implement it, and the evaluation of its success. His second, quite original method involved the painstaking work of comparing German intelligence and order of battle maps used on the Eastern Front with Russian maps as published in the open Soviet literature. Discrepancies between the German and Soviet maps often indicated the success of certain Soviet deception operations. A similar technique was used by Roger Fleetwood Hesketh in his official report on the practice of deception in northwestern Europe.[3] Unlike Col. Glantz, Hesketh of course had access to the original British and German maps. Finally, Col. Glantz used a limited number of classified after-action reports written in the Soviet Union during the early phases of the war. These documents in part addressed the Soviet use of deception and the lessons learned from their earlier operations. In his analysis, Col. Glantz emphasizes the importance the Russians have always attached to the use of deception in their military and probably many of their political operations. It is of the greatest interest to see how the Soviet military has integrated deception into every level of planning. Col. Glantz convincingly demonstrates (as did, for example, Nathan Leites in his *Study of Bolshevism*) how the communist ideology makes the Russians more likely to resort to deception, as well as more likely to suspect its use by their opponents.

The recent revival of interest within the U.S. armed forces concerning the use of deception in support of all military operations makes the appearance of this volume seem all the more timely. In addition, this book will be indispensable for Western military and intelligence officers interested in becoming better acquainted with Soviet military doctrines and more specifically with the Soviet Union's use of *maskirovka* and *khitrost'*.[4] In view of the apparent success which the Soviets experienced with their deception operations in the Second World War, it stands to reason that the Soviet Union will continue to employ such methods in any future conflicts.

The fact that the Russians make extensive use of deception in war need not make them appear evil or cause Western military and intelligence officers to be paranoic. After all, as Sun Tzu observed, "All warfare is based on deception." Deception is a normal and essential part of warfare; and if this is not the understanding in the West, then much can be learned from the Russians. As much as deception is an integral part of war, it is nevertheless self-defeating and dangerous in peacetime, when it must be avoided if the objective is to create an atmosphere of trust and cooperation.[5]

U.S. Army War College   MICHAEL I. HANDEL
Carlisle Barracks,
June 1988

NOTES

1. This despite the existence of a number of excellent studies on the Eastern Front. Among these the most notable are:

   John Erickson, *The Soviet High Command 1918–1941*. London: Macmillan, 1962; U.S. edition Boulder, Co.: Westview Press, 1984.

   John Erickson, *The Road To Stalingrad*. London: Weidenfeld and Nicolson, 1975; U.S. edition New York: Harper and Row, 1975.

   John Erickson, *The Road To Berlin*. London: Weidenfeld and Nicolson, 1983; U.S. edition Boulder, Co.: Westview Press, 1983.

   Albert Seaton, *The Russo-German War 1941–1945*. London: Arthur Barker, 1971; U.S. edition New York: Praeger, 1971.

   B.S. Telpuchovski, *Die Sorwjetische Geschichte des Grossen Vaterlandischen Krieges 1941–1945*. Frankfurt-am-Main: Bernard Graefe, 1961. A one-volume English edition of this book has been published in Moscow as *Great Patriotic War of the Soviet Union 1941–1945: A General Outline*. Moscow: Progress Publishers, 1970.

   Alfred Philippi, Ferdinand Heim, *Der Feldzug gegen Sowjetrussland 1941–1945*. Stuttgart: W. Kohlhammer, 1962.

   Earl Ziemke, *Moscow To Stalingrad: Decision in the East*. Washington, D.C.: Center of Military History, U.S. Army, 1987.

   Earl Ziemke, *Stalingrad To Berlin: The German Defeat in the East*. Washington, D.C.: Office of the Chief of Military History, 1968.

2. Among Col. David Glantz's publications are:

   August Storm: The Soviet 1945 Strategic Offensive in Manchuria. Leavenworth Papers No. 7 (Ft. Leavenworth, Kansas: Combat Studies Insitute, 1983).

   August Storm: Soviet Tactical and Operational Combat in Manchuria, 1945. Leavenworth Papers No. 8 (Ft. Leavenworth, Kansas: Combat Studies Institute, 1983).

   The Soviet Airborne Experience. Combat Studies Institute Research Survey No. 4 (Ft. Leavenworth, Kansas: Combat Studies Institute, 1984).

   Forthcoming book:

   From the Don to the Dnepr: Soviet Offensive Operations December 1942 – August 1943 (London: Frank Cass, 1989).

3. For a discussion of the Hesketh Report see: Michael I. Handel (ed.), *Strategic and Operational Deception in the Second World War* (London: Frank Cass, 1987).

4. *Khitrost'* is a complementary term for *maskirovka*. While *maskirovka* means primarily all types of deception (active and passive), camouflage, concealment, etc. that are carried out by bureaucracies or organizations in general and are not specifically identified with a commander or a military leader, *khitrost'* is a concept that was widely used in the Soviet military literature in the 1930s and then disappeared from the Soviet military vocabulary until it was revived in the mid-1980s. It means the gift of cunning, guile, craft, wiles, or ruses and stratagem practiced as an art primarily as based on the "military genius" or talent of a specific commander rather than by an organization. It has been defined by V.N. Lobov in the *Military–Historical Journal (Voenno Istoricheskii Zhurnal)*, No. 3, March 1987, 18 as: "An

aggregate of measures, directed at the achievement of surprise in military operations and thereby, the creation of additional opportunities for victory with the least expenditure of forces, weapons, and time. The main components of military *khitrost'* are concealment and misleading the enemy."

5. See Michael I. Handel, *Military Deception in Peace and War* (Jerusalem: The Magnes Press, The Hebrew University, 1985, Jerusalem Papers on Peace Problems, No. 38, The Leonard Davis Institute for International Relations).

INTRODUCTION

As students of war and believers in dialectical materialism, modern Soviet military theorists appreciate the accelerated pace of contemporary war, and the potential impact of modern weaponry on its course and outcome. They realize the importance of time, the subtleties of political relationships, and the broadened spatial dimensions of global war. Above all, they understand the increased importance of surprise, particularly at strategic and operational levels, and the decisive effects it has on friend and foe. As a leading Soviet military theorist, Colonel V. E. Savkin, wrote in *The Basic Principles of Operational Art and Tactics* (1972):

> The ways and methods of achieving surprise are very diverse .... Depending on the concrete conditions of the situation, surprise may be achieved by leading the enemy astray with regard to one's intentions, by secrecy in preparation and swiftness of troop operations, by broad use of night time conditions, by the unexpected employment of nuclear weapons and other means of destruction, by delivering a forceful attack when and where the enemy does not expect it, and by employing methods of conduct and combat operations and new means of warfare unknown to the enemy.

Savkin's remarks, although based on history, reflect recent conclusions of Soviet military science regarding the importance of surprise in war.

Few nations have suffered as greatly from the consequences of surprise and deception as the Soviet Union. Few nations have labored so intensely to reap the benefits of surprise on the battlefield. The experience of surprise and deception has come to play a key role in contemporary Soviet military thought and practice.

This work surveys Soviet experiences with deception while attempting to achieve surprise during the Second World War. Because the means, deception (*maskirovka*), is closely connected with the end, surprise (*vnezapnost'*), it is impossible to deal with either topic without the other. While focusing on concrete deception measures, I will also be surveying changing Soviet attitudes toward success with surprise.

The growth and development of Soviet military art and science has been evolutionary, and heavily dependent upon experience. The structure and focus of this study reflect the extensive dimensions of Soviet military experiences in general with particular emphasis on surprise and deception. In the Second World War the Soviets conducted nearly 50 major strategic operations and over 140 *front* (army group) offensive operations. The fronts ranged upward to 500 kilometers with depths to 650 kilometers – each involving between 300,000 and 2.5 million men. In virtually all of these operations the Soviets attempted, with varying degrees of success, to achieve surprise through deception.

The scope of these efforts reflected the magnitude of those military experiences. As early as December 1941 at Moscow, the Soviets were able to mask the offensive employment of three armies totalling over 200,000 men. In November 1943, near Stalingrad, the Soviets secretly redeployed, concentrated, and attacked with major armored forces which encircled elements of two German armies. Just over a year later, in December 1943 west of Kiev, the Soviets secretly employed two tank armies and two combined armies to drive German forces irrevocably west of the Dnepr River. In the summer of 1944, in Belorussia Soviet deception measures concealed from German eyes the redeployment and subsequent offensive employment of two armies, a tank army, and several tank corps numbering over 400,000 men and 1,500 tanks. On the eve of the Vistula–Oder operation (January 1945), German intelligence failed to detect the presence of six Soviet rifle armies and one tank army and only tentatively detected another rifle army and two tank armies, a total force of almost one million men and over 2,000 tanks (about 40 per cent of the Soviet force used in the January offensive).

The ubiquitousness of Soviet deception, and the futility of attempting to understand strategic and operational deception from an examination of a few selected cases, require a comprehensive view of all operations – lest a critical segment of that deception be overlooked. A comprehensive view must also capture failure as well as success, for a review of successes only would belie the fact that successful deception is immensely difficult to achieve.

In my methodology I have relied as much as possible on Soviet sources, which are available, extensive, and accurate. Since the Soviets rely on experience to teach their officers, and are wedded by ideology to scientific methodology, they must treat their operations objectively. Thus, self-criticism operates in the military as else-where, and is a motivating force for accuracy in Soviet military studies.

In their works on deception, the Soviets have been selective in their coverage. They offer slices of their experiences – enough to educate but not enough to evidence the full scope of their efforts. To fill in the gaps and complete the mosaic, one must wade through hundreds of memoirs, campaign and operational studies, and unit histories. These efforts, however, do produce a comprehensive view of deception in its full scope.

Despite overall Soviet candor, I have used German sources to validate Soviet claims. For this I have relied on some secondary accounts and the operational records of German army groups, the high command in the East (OKH) and *Fremde Heere Ost* or German military intelligence (Foreign Armies East). These records generally confirm Soviet claims, and, at times, reflect even more success than the Soviets realized.

As is the case with most research on Soviet subjects, an absence of archival materials, and political-military sensitivities, preclude or inhibit examination of certain themes. In this case, I dwell on deception in terms of Soviet intent, the means used to realize that intent, and the results of those efforts. What emerges are patterns of deception based on concrete experiences. I have refrained from analysing the bases upon which the Soviets conducted and checked their deception efforts – specifically the patterns of intelligence which conditioned Soviet deception. Material on Soviet wartime intelligence exists. It is, however, either contentious, speculative, or difficult to obtain. Soviet archival materials, or secondary writing based on archival materials, are almost totally lacking. Secondary works on German intelligence only tangentially cover Soviet efforts. Speculation on such popularized themes as Soviet use of spy networks (such as Lucy) or Ultra materials abound, but are super-ficial in nature. Only a thorough analysis of *Fremde Herre Ost* records, *Abwehr* files, and British intelligence Ultra materials can begin to reveal the true nature and effectiveness of Soviet intelligence. Detailed study of Soviet deception indicates, however, that it was effective. Answers to those critical intelligence questions will be the subject of a future study.

This study, then, concentrates on the subject of Soviet military deception and provides a basis for further, more extensive research on Soviet intelligence. It demonstrates the extent of Soviet experiences with military deception and the degree to which the

Soviets have studied them. Above all, however, it emphasizes the importance the Soviets attach to military deception in a contemporary and future context. It would be folly for American military specialists to accord less attention to the subject.

CHAPTER ONE

THE THEORY OF *MASKIROVKA*

On 22 June 1941 German forces, spearheaded by four panzer groups, crossed the Polish–Soviet boundary and thrust deep into the Soviet Union. Capitalizing on surprise, in six months they had inflicted a shattering defeat on Soviet armies, and advanced over 800 kilometers along three strategic axes to the very outskirts of Leningrad and Moscow. By the time the offensive ground to a halt in the face of stiffened Soviet resistance and deteriorating winter weather, the Germans had destroyed a large portion of the peacetime Red Army, disrupted the Soviet military command structure, and forced the Soviets to initiate a drastic restructuring of their armed forces to insure their survival and promote achievement of ultimate victory.

The devastating consequences of this surprise left an indelible imprint on the work of Soviet military theorists. Although they had long appreciated the value of surprise in war and had studied its use, this was not enough to prevent the catastrophe of 1941. Consequently, during the heat of war Soviet military theorists again focused their attention on the role of surprise in combat and the techniques an army must master to achieve it. The wartime education was effective. By the last two years of war the Soviets had clearly mastered surprise at all levels of war. As a result, German armies experienced the same devastating effects of surprise as the Red Army had suffered in June 1941.

The lessons of the Second World War were not lost on Soviet military theorists in the post-war years. Intense investigation of the subject of surprise dominated Soviet military thought, particularly after Stalin's death. Improved communications and weaponry and the prospect of nuclear war placed a premium on the timeliness of offensive and defensive war preparations. Thorough Soviet study of the nature of the "initial period of war" has focused first and foremost on surprise and the means for achieving it. It has taught the Soviets that the achievement of surprise by friend, or the denial of surprise to the enemy, is indeed a major factor in achieving rapid victory or avoiding defeat.

Among the many factors contributing to the achievement of surprise, deception is undoubtedly the most important. The Soviet term for deception, *maskirovka*, is often translated into the simple English term camouflage.[1] This definition, however, belies the complexity of the Russian term. In fact, *maskirovka* covers a host of measures ranging from disinformation at the strategic level to the skillful masking of an individual soldier's foxhole. Officially the Soviets define *maskirovka* as:

> The means of securing combat operations and the daily activities of forces; a complexity of measures, directed to mislead the enemy regarding the presence and disposition of forces, various military objectives, their condition, combat readiness and operations, and also the plans of the command … maskirovka contributes to the achievement of surprise for the actions of forces, the preservation of combat readiness, and the increased survivability of objectives.[2]

Characteristically, the Soviets categorize *maskirovka* as strategic, operational, and tactical. At the strategic level *maskirovka* "is conducted by the high command and includes a complex of measures to protect the secrecy of preparations for strategic operations and campaigns, as well as disinformation of the enemy regarding the true intentions and operations of armed forces."[3]

Strategic *maskirovka* is the principal precondition for achieving strategic surprise, either during the initial period of war or during the course of war, and it contributes to the attainment of strategic aims. Successful use of surprise in the initial period of war

> allows the attacking nation to strike the enemy a heavy blow, to gain time for concentration and deployment of its remaining forces, to secure the initiative in operations, to deprive him of important strategic and economic regions by decisive advances, to disrupt or frustrate his organized conduct of mobilization, and to undermine the moral stability of his army and people."[4]

At the operational level *maskirovka* "is conducted by *front,* army, and fleet commanders and is undertaken to secure the secrecy of preparations for operations."[5] Operational *maskirovka* provides forces with the capability of dealing surprise strikes on the enemy which forces him to engage in combat in unfavorable conditions. Also, at the tactical level *maskirovka* is "undertaken by divisions, regiments, and battalions and on separate objectives in order to hide preparations for battle or the presence (disposition) of objectives."[6] Thus, by definition, *maskirovka* includes both active and passive measures designed to deceive and surprise the enemy.

Deception, in the Soviet view, permeates all levels of war. Since by Marxist-Leninist definition, war is but an extension of politics, deception also transcends war into the political realm – specifically into the period preceding the outbreak of war. Thus "experience demonstrates that to secure surprise blows, the government and military control organs of the aggressor states mobilize all methods and means of influencing the enemy, including political, diplomatic, and military acts, in order to hide from them the secret concept and timing for unleashed aggression."[7] Although written about hostile powers, this quote captures the essence of Soviet belief in the all-encompassing nature of deception. Since the state of war is a logical, if not inevitable, extension of peace, then the outcome of war depends in part on how a nation exploits conditions existing in the pre-war period. To be effective, deception designed to ensure victory or forestall defeat must be of constant concern in peacetime as well as wartime. This all-encompassing attitude is as much a product of Marxist ideology as it is a product of prudent military theory.

Marxism-Leninism is founded upon the truth of inevitable and predictable dialectical change.[8] The dialectic is deterministic. Based on economic, social, and political realities, the dialectical method describes a process of inevitable change resulting in the state of communism. To one who accepts the nature of the dialectical change, any and all measures that accelerate that process are desirable, if not essential. War, in its various forms, is a natural element of that process. Thus, deception is a legitimate tool to hasten change both in peace and war.

The dialectic, and the role of deception in it, assumes a moral character somewhat alien to Western democratic concepts which view deception as immoral, akin to lying. As a result Americans either resort to deception reluctantly, or do it poorly. Marxist-Leninist theory defines morality differently. Simply stated, morality is measured by the degree to which an action impells the dialectical process to its logical and desirable end. What assists in the achievement of socialism is moral. What does not is not. Hence deception in peacetime is a valid, if not an imperative, means for achieving political aims without resort to war. It is likewise a valid means for securing advantage in wartime.

Coexisting with this overall attitude toward the morality of deception and its relationship to historical change is the Soviet attitude toward the morality of war in general. To the Soviets there are "just" and "unjust" wars, and their justness is measured against the same scale as for measuring morality. Simply stated, "just" wars contribute to progress toward Socialism while "unjust" wars do not. The use of deception is justified in both cases, either in achieving "just" goals or in thwarting the actions of the "unjust."

Thus, Soviet attitudes toward war and historical change in general place an ideological as well as a practical emphasis on the art of peacetime and wartime deception. This study concentrates on Soviet experiences with deception only in the military realm.

CHAPTER TWO

PREWAR THEORY AND PRACTICE

The scope and sophistication of Soviet deception has evolved with
the changing nature of war. Before the Second World War the
Soviets were more concerned with the physical, rather than with the
more intellectual, aspect of deception at the strategic level. This
attitude was derived from the nature of the Soviet military establishment and the technological level of the Soviet state. Some nations
(for example Japan in 1904 and Germany in 1914) have been able to
use strategic deception at the onset of war, because their sophisticated military establishments permitted hasty but efficient
mobilization and rapid implementation of complex war plans in the
opening phase of hostilities. It was beyond the capability of the
Soviet Union, however, with its ponderous peacetime military
establishment and a cumbersome mobilization process, inhibited
by the immense size and the relative technological backwardness of
the Soviet state. Certainly the Soviets realized the potential benefit
of strategic deception. In their Civil War they had, on occasion,
achieved deception and enjoyed its benefits; but that had been done
with small forces employing limited weaponry. For example, they
had used secret rail movements to regroup large forces before major
offensives against the forces of Admiral Kolchak and Generals
Denikin, Yudenich and Wrangel. To do likewise against the most
efficient military machines of the more technologically advanced
Western powers was impossible.

This attitude was reflected in Soviet military regulations and war
plans. They focused on operational and tactical deception, but paid
only scant attention to strategic deception. However, as we shall
see, in their military theoretical writings of the inter-war period, the
Soviets displayed a growing realization that technological changes,
particularly the development of air and mechanized forces, offered
prospects for the conduct of more meaningful deception on a higher
level.

Soviet military writings during the 1920s concentrated on the, by then, classic realm of deception involving concealment of location and strength of offensive operations. They conceded that offensive intent and the timing of an offensive were more difficult to conceal.[1] Regulations and directives adopted a similar focus by limiting the impact of deception primarily to the operational and tactical levels of war. Thus, "in Soviet military art during the 1920s the theory of operational *maskirovka* [deception] was developed as one of the most important means of achieving surprise in operations."[2] The 1924 official directive for *front* and army commanders and field commands, *"Vyshee komandovanie"*, [Higher Commands], emphasizing the importance of operational *maskirovka*, pointed out that operational *maskirovka*, one of the basic means for achieving surprise, "must be based upon the principles of *aktivnost'* [activity], naturalness, diversity, and continuity and includes secrecy, imitation, demonstrative actions, and disinformation."[3]

In a more concrete vein, the 1929 *Field Regulations of the Red Army* enunciated the role of deception in achieving surprise:

> Surprise has a stunning effect on the enemy. For this reason all troop operations must be accomplished with the greatest concealment and speed. Rapidity of action combined with organization is the main guarantee of success in combat .... Surprise is also achieved by the sudden use for the enemy of new means of warfare and new methods of combat.[4]

Thus, while underscoring the importance of concealment, the regulation hinted of the impact of further technological developments in the realm of deception. For the first time the Soviets put forward the often ignored idea of achieving surprise through the use of new combat methods unforseen by the enemy. The remainder of the regulation referred only tangentially to deception by detailing the role concealment played in the successful conduct of maneuver. Concealment was achieved by:

a. confusion of the enemy by active operations of the covering force;
b. adaptation to the terrain, and camouflage;
c. performance of the maneuver swiftly and properly, particularly at night, in fog, and so forth, and;
d. keeping secret the preparations for the maneuver and its goal.[5]

The Soviet mechanization program undertaken in the 1930s widened the horizons of deception by increasing the speed and maneuverability of combat units and the importance of the time factor in the preparation and conduct of operations. Soviet military theorists first developed the theory of deep battle [*glubokii boi*] and subsequently the theory of deep operations [*glubokaya operatsiya*]. As a corollary for these theories the role of deception, as defined in regulations, expanded in scope and importance – but still only at the operational and tactical levels.

The *1935 Instructions on Deep Battle* and the *1936 Field Regulations* emphasized the growing importance of deception within the confines of the battlefield. The *Instructions* recognized that new weaponry and the tactics of deep battle had increased the importance of surprise. It articulated the bases of surprise as being "air superiority; mobility and maneuverability of forces; concealed concentration of forces; secret fire preparations; misleading of the enemy; use of smoke and technical *maskirovka*" and "the use of night."[6] While repeating the statements on the importance of surprise found in the 1929 regulations, the 1936 regulations added:

> surprise constitutes one of the essential elements of maneuver and success in battle. The present day implements of war which combine great fire and striking power with high mobility make it possible for the commander of larger units, by skillful sudden maneuver, to place his own forces in a favorable position with respect to the forces of an adversary and to force the latter to accept battle under unfavorable conditions.[7]

More importantly, the regulation emphasized the role of new weaponry and the potential for achieving technological surprise:

> Surprise action depends on concealment and speed, which are achieved by swift maneuver, *secret concentrations of forces*, concerted preparation of artillery concentrations, opening of surprise artillery fires, and by *launching unexpected infantry* (*cavalry*), *tank, and air attacks*.... Surprise is also achieved by the unexpected employment of new military weapons and new combat tactics.[8]

In 1937 Soviet theorists writing in the general staff journal, *Voennaya Mysl'* [Military Thought] demonstrated growing Soviet sophistication in the realm of deception, focusing on surprise in war and the role of *maskirovka* in achieving surprise. They drew principally on the experiences of the world war and Russian civil war but examined those experiences in the light of technological changes – primarily the mechanization of the Red Army and rise of air power. The articles demonstrated Soviet maturity on the subject and the degree to which the Soviets planned to integrate *maskirovka* practices into actual operational planning.

A. Vol'pe recognized the increased emphasis placed on surprise by Western theorists, noting, "Bourgeois, 'classical' military theory considers surprise as one of the basic 'eternal' principles of military art."[9] He summed up Western intent, stating, "In the end surprise has the aim of inflicting upon the enemy at a decisive point a blow by superior forces and unexpected means, when [his] forces are dispersed, when his reserves have not moved up, and when he neither expects nor is prepared to repulse the blow."[10] New technology had increased both the possibilities and consequences of surprise as evidenced by German development of armored and mechanized forces, air power, and an extensive road network for the use of deploying units. Vol'pe predicted, "Now the Maginot Line can be seized earlier than they think. Certainly, such an operation is far from easy, but not impossible."[11] While recognizing the importance of the tank and airplane, he stressed the necessity for employing both as part of a combined arms team to offset the probable development of anti-tank and anti-aircraft defenses. Such combinations promised greater maneuver on the battlefield and enhanced prospects for achieving surprise. Vol'pe also surveyed the role of technological surprise, citing the German U-boats as a prime example.

Quoting the 1936 *Field Regulations*, Vol'pe stressed the importance of operational *maskirovka*, in particular the role of secretly raised and deployed strategic reserves, the value of night operations, and the necessity for concealing main attacks. In all instances, secrecy, rapidity, and misleading the enemy were essential. While Vol'pe viewed secrecy as easy to achieve, principally through operational security and camouflage, rapidity was a more complex quality to achieve and more critical for surprise. It involved both mobility and maneuverability, the latter associated with skillful employment of aviation, mechanized forces, and cavalry. Vol'pe considered misleading the enemy to be "the most delicate of *maskirovka* means" requiring "the genius of a commander" and concluded that, above all, surprise and *maskirovka* required careful and skillful planning.[12] Quoting the earlier theorist, N.E. Varfolomeyev, he wrote, "The basic concept of *maskirovka* is established by the commander, who provides guiding orders of a general character concerning the order and means for realizing the concept."

He then repeated the precise measures that Varfolomeyev had recommended in his 1928 work *Voina i Revolutsiya* [War and Revolution]:

> On the basis of these [the commanders'] orders, the staff must fully work out the overall *maskirovka* plan. In it are defined:
>
> 1. the general aim of *maskirovka*;
> 2. the basic concept and basic means and devices of *maskirovka*;
> 3. the particular objectives of army executors with directives:
>   a. the sequence of fulfillment (devices, means, methods, and period of fulfillment);
>   b. coordination of work of separate parties;
>   c. succession of measures, and the relative importance of them or some of them;
> 4. the chief *maskirovka* measures, employed by troops – their importance in the total plan and in connection with measures of army scale.
>
> Executors plan their portions of the plan of operations and, having coordinated them with the staff, carry them out ...[13]

Vol'pe repeated Varfolomeyev's recommended assignment of orders and objectives, including:

1. To subordinate forces:
   a. concerning the order of movement (time of departure and arrival of the column, order for their variation by means of deviation from normal nature of composition, length, etc., routes and order of transportation);
   b. about the order of concentration (designated region, time of arrival, disposition of forces, and orders for technical *maskirovka*);
   c. concerning special measures to maintain military secrecy;
2. to army aviation – on organizing air cover for transport and concentration of forces;
3. to army cavalry – on organizing screening;
4. to engineer units:
   a. in the sphere of technical *maskirovka* – active (false fortifications and boundaries, false crossings, roads, airdromes, and warehouses, and false attacks and

defenses) and passive (covering sectors of supply roads, changing the appearance of railroad stations and approach routes, and concealing crossings);
in the realm of assisting troops by means of intensified supply of *maskirovka* materials, reinforcement by special *maskirovka* units, organizations, instructions, etc.;

5. to military supply services: false transport by rail, water, or truck roads with orders for the direction and time of that transport, and false concentrations;
6. to signal sources: the organization of radio maneuvers and radio *maskirovka*;
7. to political units: the dissemination of false rumors among the population and enemy forces, and the creation of the desirable mood among his forces;
8. to units struggling with hostile agents: strengthen counter-reconnaissance, strengthen surveillance of suspicious elements among the local population, and also orders relating to military censorship, and to changes in the order of individual treatment by means of dealings and movement in the sector near the front, particularly relating to regions in which work must be done to prepare the operation.[14]

To the recommendations of Varfolomeyev, Vol'pe added his own advice to: restrict severely the size of the planning circle; curtail publication of multiple documents; avoid stereotyped or patterned *maskirovka*; train routinely the habit of good *maskirovka*; and restrict the plan only to specialized measures. Above all, wrote Vol'pe, "The securing of surprise − is the personal function of the leader, who enlists to help him a minimum number of confidential agents. Only then can surprise count on success."[15]

Vol'pe's work and that of Varfolomeyev before him, were indicative of the detailed thought the Soviets accorded to operational *maskirovka* and surprise. It also represented an immense training challenge to those enjoined to implement *maskirovka* practices in the sprawling Red Army.

Three months after Vol'pe's article appeared, a more specific article by Gr. Pochter appeared in *Voennaya Mysl'* focusing on operational *maskirovka* and its relationship to surprise. Pochter accepted Vol'pe's judgements but added to them the "chief weapon of operational *maskirovka*," which he called "the art of operational-tactical deception [*obman*]."[16] He also drew on military experiences in Picardy, at Amiens, and in Palestine to delineate operational measures which, in combination, could produce false impressions in the enemy and conceal a force's operations. Focusing on the art of creating false indicators as the basic ingredient of operational *maskirovka*, he then cited the chief devices of operational *maskirovka*, which were:

a. demonstrative actions (sometimes in the form of offensive operations of comparatively large scale);
b. false march-maneuvers, and even false rail maneuvers;
c. false radio maneuvers, to impart great likelihood certainly combined with actual demonstrative movements, concentrations and operations of those or other separate units of forces;
d. proper *maskirovka*, that is hidden actual concentration of main forces and their actual regrouping (covered dispositions, night marches, sound and light *maskirovka*, etc.);
e. false rumors, false documents, prisoners, line-crossers and agents ("doubles"); and
f. erection of false engineer structures and construction of various false works (engineer and non-engineer, such as fake fodder purchases, release of quarters, etc.).[17]

Pochter stressed the vulnerability of *maskirovka* to enemy ground and air reconnaissance and, like Vol'pe, underscored the systematic nature of *maskirovka* and the necessity for careful planning. Separate single measures could produce occasional tactical successes; but only a carefully coordinated network of interconnected measures, focused on a specific aim, could yield operational surprise and achieve operational aims. Operational deception "must be based on a definite idea, flowing from the total operational decision and the characteristic conditions of the given concrete operation."[18] As such, specific missions would be assigned to specific parties, and *maskirovka* would be planned in timed phases to support the entire operation. *Maskirovka* means had to be suited to each specific end; but, throughout planning, patterns [*shablon*] had to be avoided. Pochter identified originality, flexibility, and credibility as the marks of superior *maskirovka* planning; but regardless of how well a plan was conceived or executed, planning staffs had to check its progress.

　　Pochter emphasized the practical aspects of operational *maskirovka*, sketching the inevitable variations present in a successful plan. He cited the importance of realism in demonstrations, feints and simulations, and argued for allocation of sufficient resources to lend them credibility. But he also realized the difficulties armies faced in modern times achieving both secrecy and rapidity in operations. Because "Night has become neither darker nor longer," "Forests have not become denser," and "False rumors are considerably easier to check," the movements of large armies with their immense technical equipment and rear services are more difficult to conceal.[19] However, Pochter cited the proliferation of rail lines and the emergence of road transport as a means for more flexibility and secrecy in moving those large forces. Tellingly, he stated, "The removal of surprise from maneuver has a real value only when time remains to anticipate and ward off a prepared blow." In other words:

> Neither the absoluteness nor 'purity' of surprise decides, but rather its beneficial operational action. The achievement of surprise – in general, surely not so much finally secures the secrecy of an operation (although to a large degree it does) as it gains time. The more possibilities open for realization of operational deception the more effective will be its results.[20]

The articles of Vol'pe and Pochter reflected the heightened concern of the Red Army High Command for the quickening pace of military-technological change and the looming threat of a remilitarized and resurgent Nazi Germany. Unfortunately, within the year, those who occupied the commanding heights of advanced military theory within the Red Army were purged and liquidated, effectively blocking any hope for immediate implementation of their theories.

While recognizing the importance of operational deception, theorists continued to discount the utility of deception at the strategic level, particularly deception designed to conceal the intent to launch an offensive. Illustrating this trend, the same year M. R. Galaktianov pointed out the difficulty involved in concealing major troop movements and hostile intentions. He hinted that it was only possible to mask the scale of such movements and stated, "The higher the mobility of the maneuvering mass, the more the effect of strategic surprise."[21]

Events in the Far East, Poland, Finland, and France in 1939 and 1940 were a vivid reminder to Soviet theorists of the role and importance of deception in war. The Soviets themselves had success with deception measures in September 1939 at Khalkhin–Gol where they assembled a large force under the future Marshal Zhukov and inflicted a disastrous defeat on a Japanese force of two divisions.[22] By using strict concealment measures the Soviets succeeded in concentrating a force double the size expected by the Japanese and containing a large armored contingent. The Soviets also used disinformation in the form of false troop concentrations and false defensive work to deceive Japanese planners about the location of the main Soviet attack.[23] In his memoirs, Zhukov underscored the importance of *maskirovka* stating,

> to achieve maskirovka and strict secrecy of planning the Military Soviet of the army group, simultaneously with planning for the upcoming operation, worked out a plan for operational-tactical deception of the enemy which included:
>
> - conduct of secret movement and concentration of forces arriving from the Soviet Union to reinforce the army group;
> - secret regrouping of forces and weapons, located in the defenses behind the Khalkhin–Gol River;
> - realization of secret movement of forces and material reserves across the Khalkhin–Gol River;
> - reconnaissance of jumping-off regions, sectors, and directions for attacking forces;
> - especially secret preparation of missions for all types of forces participating in the upcoming operation;
> - conduct of secret pre-reconnaissance by all types of forces;
> - disinformation and deception of the enemy to deceive him regarding our true intentions.
>
> By these measures we tried to create in the enemy the impression of the absence on our side of any preparatory measures of an offensive nature, to show that we were conducting broad measures to construct defenses and only defenses. To achieve this we decided to conduct all movement, concentration, and regrouping only at night when enemy aerial reconnaissance and visual observation in the region was limited.[24]

The Soviet main attacks, using the secretly assembled armored forces, succeeded in rapidly enveloping the Japanese defenders and destroying them. In Zhukov's words, "We considered the decisive factor in the success in the upcoming operation to be operational-tactical surprise, which would place the enemy in such a position that he could not resist our destructive blow and undertake maneuver."[25]

The events at Khalkhin–Gol accorded with contemporary Soviet military doctrine regarding deception. The deception measures at Khalkhin–Gol were essentially only tactical in scope, although they were imaginatively implemented, unlike the case later in 1939 when the Red Army performed poorly against the Finnish Army.

The 1939 *Field Regulation of the Red Army* further developed Soviet views on surprise and its relationship to *maskirovka..* Implicit in the new regulation was a belief that surprise could be achieved through secret planning and by deceiving the enemy regarding the location, position, combat readiness, and combat efficiency of one's forces.

The 1939 regulation recognized operational *maskirovka* as one of the primary means for achieving surprise and exhorted commanders at all levels "in all conditions of the situation, while not expecting special orders, to independently and continuously undertake all maskirovka measures for their units and their actions."[26] Specifically, the regulation required commanders to deceive the enemy by hiding the objectives of enemy reconnaissance, altering the appearance of potential enemy objectives; creating false (imitative) objectives; and using rumors and false movements for the purposes of disinformation. Further, it re-emphasized that *maskirovka* should be natural, continuous, and varied and avoid resort to repetitive patterns. Commanders were responsible for all *maskirovka* measures and each unit's chief of engineers would employ unit forces to conduct the *maskirovka* according to the plan worked out by the commander and his staff. The regulation focused special attention on *maskirovka* to foil enemy aerial reconnaissance.

In late 1939, however, when the Soviets attempted to launch a surprise war against the Finns to secure territories necessary to improve the defense of Leningrad, their tactics failed. Hastily mobilized, the Soviet forces planned a massive attack along multiple axes to catch the Finns by surprise. But the mobilization was chaotic, the attack poorly coordinated, and the forces were unprepared to perform their assigned tasks. Not only did the Soviets fail to achieve surprise, they suffered stunning and often disastrous defeats on virtually every axis of advance. Learning from this massive failure, the Soviets, in the spring of 1940, carefully prepared a new offensive incorporating more imaginative use of forces. This achieved the desired aims. The Germans also noted the Soviet failures of the fall, but failed to note that the Soviets had learned from those failures.

The German campaigns in Poland and France in September 1939 and May 1940 clearly demonstrated the potential for successful deception on a strategic scale, especially in the initial period of war. The lessons were not entirely lost on the Soviets.

In December 1940 key figures of the Red Army High Command met in Moscow to discuss contemporary military issues in light of the events of 1939 and 1940. Stalin chaired the lengthy session. During the meeting General Zhukov noted "that surprise in contemporary operations is one of the decisive factors of victory .... Having attached considerable importance to surprise, all means of *maskirovka* and deception of the enemy must be widely inculcated into the Red Army. *Maskirovka* and deception must run through the training and education of forces, commanders and staffs."[27] In his speech at the conclusion of the meeting Marshal S.K. Timoshenko took note of Zhukov's remarks. He surveyed the changing nature of war and underscored the increasing importance in combat of mobile groups of mechanized forces supported by aviation. Timoshenko argued that the use of *maskirovka* in an offensive involving a single frontal blow would be difficult, especially in a poorly developed theater of operations where the road net was poor. Conversely, *maskirovka* would be of use in an offensive which involved the mounting multiple attacks on a wide front. Finally he accepted Zhukov's judgement that "massive use of aviation and tanks demands especially thorough and artful organization of anti-aircraft defense, anti-tank defense, and use of *maskirovka* measures for all operating forces."[28] This appreciation of the emerging importance of surprise and *maskirovka* was underscored by substantial analysis of the events of the preceding two years.

Soviet critiques of German operations in France written in March 1941 displayed Soviet consternation over those events. One author writing in the *Military-Historical Journal*, noted:

> The allied command did not expect that the German Army's main attack would be inflicted on the left flank through Luxembourg and the Ardennes. Their intelligence was not able to discover in time the concentration of two German shock armies (6th and 9th) in the Ardennes Forest ... the French command, while expecting the offensive of the German Army, mistakenly calculated that, as in 1914, the

main attack of the German Army would be inflicted on the right flank.[29]

He assessed that "German disinformation and unsatisfactory intelligence work of the allies led to this mistake." Moreover the German Army, true to measures recommended in Soviet regulations, "having benefitted from the factor of surprise," developed the blow by massive use of aviation, armor, and airborne units, the new types of forces previously mentioned in Soviet regulations.[30]

A more pointed article appeared the same month in *Military Thought*, assessing the role of surprise in the German campaigns in Poland and France and concluding that deception had played a significant part in German achievement of surprise. The author, A. I. Starunin began with the admission that "It is natural that it is more difficult in contemporary conditions to realize operational surprise than it was in earlier wars," because "The presence of a large mass of aviation for the conduct of long-range air reconnaissance and the difficulty of hiding the concentration of modern armies, with their immense rears, lessens the possibilities for operational surprise." Nevertheless, Starunin argued that:

> The basic methods and means for achieving operational surprise in contemporary conditions basically remain as before: preserving the secrecy of the concept of the operation as long as possible, night movement and its concealment, the organization of diversions and all types of disinformation, rapid concentration of forces and development of maneuver, and the use of new technical means of struggle and combat and operational methods.[31]

To Starunin the recent German operations were striking examples of how surprise could be achieved in the challenging conditions of the initial period of war. In particular, he noted the Germans' imaginative surprise use of air power and airborne forces. Generalizing, he cited the essential objectives which must be attained in the initial period of war, including:

- gain air superiority to attack enemy objectives and protect your own;
- destroy enemy ammunition and fuel supplies and bases;
- inhibit or block enemy mobilization;
- create confusion in enemy rail movements during the period of strategic deployment;
- seize important regions and boundaries on enemy territory;

– destroy enemy covering forces and partially defeat deploying enemy armies on operational directions.[32]

He concluded that German operations had confounded contemporary use of "armies of incursion" which, in theory, were to initiate hostilities and seize important enemy objectives while the attacking nation's forces mobilized and prepared to follow the army of incursion. In Poland and France, Germany instead had "toppled that theory" by invading with the secretly concentrated mass of its armed forces supported by paralyzing air strikes.[33] Based on these experiences, Starunin concluded, "To achieve decisive success in the beginning period of war, exact organization of forces during concentration is necessary, since a mistake, allowed in the initial deployment, could hardly be corrected in the course of the entire campaign."[34]

Starunin noted the successful secret German maneuvers during the campaigns which had capitalized on initial successes and helped bring the operations to rapid successful conclusions. These maneuvers, for the first time, used massed armor which was the main contribution to German operational success. An additional footnote to the article, however, reminded the reader that France's military unpreparedness and corruption in ruling circles also conditioned the nation for defeat. Reflecting on the campaigns, it was apparent that German control of the air had permitted her forces "to achieve operational surprise relatively easily on any sector of the front."[35] German secret maneuver was obviously also a product of efficient peacetime training which had conditioned German forces to employ expertly night movements, regroupings, and concentration in new assault sectors. Starunin underscored three techniques used successfully by the Germans, and applicable to other armies, to conduct secret maneuver: efficient concealed marches, altering the configuration of their assault forces before the offensive, and rapid force movements, in particular by motor-mechanized and cavalry forces. "Thus, the possibilities of a deep flank blow in contemporary war have grown considerably; the more secretly the blow is prepared and the more rapidly it is fulfilled, the more chance of success."[36]

Ironically, both authors captured the essential nature of German successes in Poland and France. In doing so, they sketched out in detail the very techniques the Germans would use within three months against Soviet armies – with equally devastating effects as in the earlier operations.

Indirectly reflecting on operations in both Poland and France, the Soviet military theorist, S.N. Krasil'nikov, assessed the current role of *maskirovka* in modern operations:

> the rapid and hidden concentration of the army is a mission of first degree importance, since it hinders the enemy in undertaking operational counter-measures and consequently helps us secure the operational-strategic initiative.[37]

He also displayed a new realization of the strategic possibilities of deception, stating:

> measures for the operational masking of them [movements] have special importance in the period of concentration and deployment. External indicators along the front and in the sector of army concentrations must not display any kind of change noticeable to the enemy.[38]

Krasil'nikov outlined specific measures designed to effect the rapid and secret concentration of forces, all of which went far beyond the recommendations of earlier regulations. These included:

1. Air reconnaissance must be conducted with accustomed intensity and on usual directions.
2. Divisions located at the front must, under no circumstances, be changed for new ones before the completion of an operational deployment.
3. Radio transmissions must remain normal and can conform sometimes to the radio deception of the enemy (disinformation of a plausible character).
4. Secrecy of upcoming operations is maintained from forces and staff.
5. Regrouping and transfer of forces at night, gradually and in small columns.
6. Operational deception of forces in the forward region is organized by means of creating false orders about the arrival of forces in the forward area and the covering of the real disposition of forces and by a series of other *maskirovka* measures.
7. The starting positions for the offensive are occupied not earlier than on the eve of the offensive.[39]

Krasil'nikov's study anticipated many of the methods and techniques the Soviets would learn during wartime. Significantly, it captured the essence of changing warfare characterized by the introduction of large motorized and air forces. Thus Krasil'nikov concluded:

> The high level of motorization of modern armies creates a very real threat of sudden and rapid appearance close to the region of army concentration of large combined arms enemy formations, designated to disrupt the systematic character of our operational concentration of fresh forces, if it is discovered by the enemy.
>
> Therefore higher commands, undertaking an operational concentration of a new army on a direction not secured by a dense combat front, are obliged to put under strict observation all approaches from the enemy side to the concentration area ... with the aim of operational *maskirovka*, all movement of enemy forces in the concentration area must occur as far as possible only at night, and in the daytime there must be a strict routine in the region of deployed forces.[40]

In both a theoretical and practical sense, in 1941 the Soviets attempted to solve the problems so apparent in Soviet military performance in the war against Finland. The Timoshenko reforms sought to revitalize and reequip the Red Army force structure and capture in regulations military theory validated in the operations in 1939 and 1940. This included an expanding recognition of the importance of surprise and *maskirovka* in war at the strategic, as well as at lower levels. The 1941 *Field Regulations* recognized that "surprise stuns the enemy, paralyzes his will, and deprives him of the capability of rendering organized opposition."[41] It went on to specify the following means by which surprise could be achieved:

— secret preparations for an operation
— skillful selection of the direction of main blows (where the enemy least expects it)
— rapid and decisive preparation and conduct of the operation
— successful use of operational *maskirovka*.

It was one thing, however, to theorize about the achievement of surprise through *maskirovka*. It was another thing to develop in Soviet commanders a talent for carrying out such measures. The 1941 Soviet command cadre and staff was shaken by the purges of the late 1930s which had deprived the Red Army of its most experienced and creative practitioners of war. Those who remained were young, inexperienced, and understandably timid concerning innovation. Thus the 1941 theory of *maskirovka* remained just theory and was not translated into practice.

Ironically, the 1941 Regulations statement concerning surprise was prophetic. The German surprise attack of June 1941 stunned the Red Army, paralyzed its will (albeit briefly), and deprived it of the capability of rendering organized opposition. It would now take months of costly combat and experimentation for the Soviets to begin to develop skill in the employment of *maskirovka* in combat.

CHAPTER THREE

THEORY AND WAR EXPERIENCE

Despite the writings of Soviet military theorists on *maskirovka*, as the Second World War approached there remained a significant gap between the theory and practice of deception. As the events of June 1941 proved, the Soviets still lacked a serious appreciation of the nature and potential impact of strategic deception. Moreover the shock and chaos produced by Germany's surprise invasion ruled out constructive Soviet use of deception during the opening months of war. At the operational and tactical level ineptness and techno-logical backwardness hindered Soviet attempts to implement deception measures.

Remedies to Soviet problems soon began to flow from the very top of the Soviet command structure in the form of a series of instructions or directives. At first these were random and aimed at remedying specific ills in Soviet fighting techniques. In November 1942, however, the Soviets devised a system to amass and capitalize on war experiences in more organized fashion.[1] In subsequent months orders appeared pertaining to the planning and conduct of battle across the entire spectrum of war. By mid-1943 the techniques these orders mandated were absorbed by operating units and incorporated by the High Command into more substantial regula-tions.

During the early years of war the Red Army underwent a costly education of which the learning of deception techniques at every level was but one aspect. Early in the war Soviet *maskirovka* was tentative and largely ineffective. Red Army units soon learned that successful *maskirovka* was but one means for survival, an absolutely essential one in light of Germany's early dominance in armored and air warfare. The main early weaknesses, which persisted into the mid-war years, were an inability to master radio discipline and maintain communications security and the adverse effect of individual security problems on the secrecy of Soviet operational planning. On the positive side, the Soviets quickly learned camouflage techniques and were able to mask the movement of large forces when radio transmissions were not required. In addition, the Soviets severely limited the size of planning circles and adopted a system for sequential planning to provide a more secure planning environment. While these procedures improved the security of Soviet operational planning, they also had a negative impact on the performance of lower level units with limited planning time.[2]

The first wartime instruction concerning *maskirovka* was passed to Red Army units only four days after the German invasion. On 26 June 1941 the Red Army Military Engineer Administration issued instructions on operational *maskirovka* which repeated the contents of the 1936 regulation and exhorted Soviet commanders to undertake such operational measures as "conducting a series of secondary blows on a wide front before beginning operations on the main axis" and "strengthening the reconnaissance activity of all types of forces on secondary axes."[3] In addition, it instructed commanders to mask important operational objectives and create false objectives to confuse enemy air reconnaissance, making the planning and performance of such tasks the responsibility of the unit chief engineer.

Despite these instructions, Soviet operations in the summer of 1941 were fraught with "serious inadequacies in the preparation of offensives, to which the General Staff of the Soviet Army turned its attentions."[4] Hence, on 29 September 1941, the Chief of the General Staff dispatched a directive to *front* and separate army commanders highlighting the causes of these inadequacies and subsequent operational failures. The instructions noted that failures in offensive operations related directly to poor organization and faulty operational planning. Units often prepared for operations within the open view of the enemy without paying any attention to the attainment of surprise. Engineer measures were halfhearted and chiefs of engineers did not pay adequate attention to such measures. The directive went on to require commanders to pay special attention to masking their forces during the commander's reconnaissance and to hide from the enemy the location of their main attack.[5]

Subsequently, on 28 November 1941, a new *STAVKA* directive specified measures to improve Soviet *maskirovka* capabilities. The order designated *front* chiefs of engineers responsible for planning and conducting engineer measures to secure the operations of *fronts* and their component armies. The directive demanded "decisive elimination of indicated inadequacies" and made the chief of engineers responsible for "undertaking timely measures and sharply improving the *maskirovka* of forces and rear service units." It underscored to the military councils of *fronts* and armies the necessity for masking every operation and assigned specific commanders from the staff of *front* and army engineer forces who would be responsible for *front* and army level *maskirovka*.[6]

In the first year of war Soviet successes with deception were as much a product of the chaotic combat conditions produced by the rapid German advance as of improved Soviet security. During the German advance from June to October 1941 the Soviets were able to mobilize and commit to combat a series of new reserve armies. Initially, German intelligence generally kept up with the formation and commitment of these new forces, for they were in accordance with pre-war estimates. By the late summer and fall, however, the scale of Soviet mobilization began to surprise the German High Command. In addition, German intelligence began missing the scale and location of large-scale Soviet operational deployments (although German tactical intelligence was quite accurate and remained so throughout the war). The failure of German intelligence, and the corresponding success of Soviet deception, was manifested by the Soviet Moscow counter-offensive in December 1941 which was spearheaded by three armies, undetected by German intelligence. Later, in January 1942, the Soviets were able to mask offensive preparations in several sectors which contributed to the successful expansion of the Soviet counter-offensive. Although it did not achieve its desired end (the destruction of German Army Group Center), it did establish a future pattern for deception. By virtue of strict secrecy, the Soviets were able to conceal the movement and deployment of large army formations (aided in this fact by the depth of the German advance, bad weather – and perhaps most important – German over-confidence).

While the Moscow counter-offensive unfolded, the Soviets took advantage of harsh winter conditions and the strategic over-extension of German forces by conducting other surprise offensives. In the north, near Leningrad, the Soviets drove German forces back from their advanced positions in the Tikhvin area. In the Khar'kov area, the Soviet Southern Front struck westward and seized a sizable bridgehead across the Northern Donets River near Izyum, while in the south, in November and December, the Soviets achieved a dual success. In November they mounted a sudden attack on overextended German First Panzer Army and drove

German units westward from Rostov to the Mius River line. In December the Soviets mounted a surprise amphibious operation against German forces on the Crimean peninsula and obtained a lodgement at Kerch. *Maskirovka* played a role in each of these Soviet operational successes, but in each case German over-extension and unpreparedness for conducting operations in winter contributed to Soviet success.

Despite the success of Soviet deception at Moscow and else-where, throughout 1941 and 1942, the German High Command was able to identify the primary geographical arena of Soviet strategic concern while masking their own priorities. Soviet offensive operations conducted in early 1942 benefited somewhat from successful *maskirovka*, but Soviet misreading of German strategic intentions and poor operational techniques negated the positive effects of successful initial surprise. In the north, in February 1942, the Soviets conducted the Lyuban operation during which 2d Shock Army achieved surprise and considerable initial success. German countermeasures, however, negated that initial success and produced a Soviet operational disaster. Likewise, in May 1942 the Soviets launched a new operation from their bridgehead across the Northern Donets River south of Khar'kov. Although achieving considerable initial surprise through *maskirovka*. this new offensive was launched into the teeth of a major German buildup. Rapid German reaction combined with clumsy Soviet conduct of the operation to produce a fresh Soviet battlefield disaster.

Subsequently, in the summer of 1942, the renewed German offensive in southern Russia caught Soviet planners by surprise, although the Soviets adjusted well to this unpleasant reality. Throughout the 1942 German strategic offensive Soviet planners repeated their performance of late 1941 by marshalling under strict security measures a new array of reserve armies which they ultimately committed to battle in the Stalingrad region.

During the summer campaign Soviet deception measures improved in another regard, the secret formation and deployment of new type units.[7] In the spring and summer of 1942, the Soviets created first 15 new tank corps and five new tank armies. The *maskirovka* measures were so successful that German intelligence failed to note the creation of these forces. In the abortive Soviet offensive at Khar'kov in May 1942, the Soviets used two of their new tank corps, which German intelligence identified as brigades rather than corps. The same situation occurred in June and July when the Soviets committed to combat the first of their new tank armies.

Again the Germans identified them as brigades. Despite these intelligence failures, however, German forces were able to deal effectively with these new Soviet formations.

Throughout the summer and early fall of 1942 the Soviets mounted a series of operations across the front while they sought to parry the German thrust across southern Russia toward the lower Volga River region. The bulk of these operations were against German Army Group Center, poised west of Moscow. These operations, on a strategic direction along which the Soviets had originally intended to operate during the summer, were designed to improve the Soviet defensive positions west of Moscow and distract German forces from the main German thrust across southern Russia. The Soviets used *maskirovka* in these operations but with only limited success. German Army Group Center was the most difficult German command to deceive, probably because of their experience derived from the bitter fighting around Moscow in late 1941 and early 1942.

By the fall of 1942, more effective planning security and growing Soviet numerical superiority over the Germans improved Soviet operational *maskirovka*. A series of *STAVKA* orders and General Staff directives addressed the area of planning security. These sharply limited the size of planning circles for each operation, prohibited the preparation of orders in multiple copies, and required orders be transmitted orally, whenever possible. In addition, these orders tightened up secrecy in the security services of the front and rear.[8] The shifting correlation of forces also assisted the Soviets in achieving a greater degree of surprise. Marshal Zhukov wrote, "Our superiority over the Germans was manifested in the fact that the Soviet Armed Forces began to keep secret their intentions, to conduct large scale disinformation, and to mislead the enemy. Hidden regroupings and concentrations permitted the realization of surprise attacks on the enemy,"[9] such as the launch, in November 1942, of the Stalingrad counter-offensive. Although there had been indicators of a future Soviet offensive, its scale and location and the nature of units available came as a surprise for the Germans. Much of the German surprise was due to improved Soviet planning security and *maskirovka*. For the first time, the Soviets had undertaken a major effort at the highest level to mislead the Germans about their strategic intentions. This effort included *STAVKA* orders directing only defensive preparations around Stalingrad and orders for offensive operations elsewhere. Although the Germans were not totally misled, operationally the Soviet *maskirovka* measures succeeded. The encirclement of German Sixth Army at Stalingrad resulted.

Throughout the winter of 1943, as Soviet armies advanced across southern Russia toward the Dnepr River, Soviet commanders continued to attempt to use deception. The Soviet strategic intent was clear to the Germans, nor was there any major attempt by the Soviets to mask those intentions. The *maskirovka* which occurred did so at the operational level and took the form of attacks whose persistence and abandon amazed the Germans.

During the period immediately following the encirclement of German Sixth Army in Stalingrad the Soviets capitalized on German preoccupation with the fate of beleaguered Sixth Army and general operational chaos in German ranks to conduct a series of operations using successful *maskirovka*. In mid-December the Soviets concealed preparations for their attack across the middle reaches of the Don River against Italian Eighth Army (Middle Don Operation). Then, the Soviets masked the movement of 2d Guards Army into the region southwest of Stalingrad in their successful efforts to block German attempts to relieve the German force encircled at Stalingrad (Kotel'nikovo Operation).

While German forces in the Stalingrad region reluctantly withdrew westward under heavy Soviet pressure, the Soviets used *maskirovka* to prepare and conduct operations against Hungarian and German forces defending further north along the Don River in the Voronezh region. In the ensuing operations (Ostrogozhsk–Rossosh' and Voronezh–Kastornoye) a Hungarian army was virtually destroyed, and German Second Army severely mauled as the front shifted westward toward Khar'kov and Kursk.

Actually, during this period, the Soviets were themselves victimized by self-deception. The frantic nature of these Soviet offensives was conditioned by a belief that German forces were actually hastening to withdraw from their overextended position in southern Russia.[10] Consequently, renewed German counter-attacks in the Donbas and around Khar'kov inflicted serious (though temporary) defeat on overextended and over-optimistic Soviet commanders.

After March 1943, along the Eastern Front, a lull in action set in which endured until heavy fighting resumed in July. During this period the Soviets analysed war experiences and adjusted their force structure and doctrine based on that analysis. They systematized measures imposed by the 1941 and 1942 orders and directives and incorporated them into instructions and regulations governing the use of all types of forces in all conditions of combat. Meanwhile, the *STAVKA* continued exhorting all units to create and maintain an air of secrecy when planning, regrouping forces prior to, and conducting operations.

On 8 April 1943, the *STAVKA* issued a directive to all *front* and army chiefs of staffs requiring them to implement stricter secrecy measures when regrouping forces and preparing for operations. The directive stressed the need for tighter security in the forward area and reminded subordinate commanders and staffs about headquarters security and the security of communications lines. It required all commands except artillery, air reconnaissance, and tank units in battle to use code tables and coded maps in all telephone and radio transmissions. The code tables were to be changed not less than once every 24 hours and cipher keys were to be transmitted only by courier.

To impose planning security the directive restricted planning to a limited group of officers and commanders approved by the higher command. Operational plans were to be written by hand in only two copies with one copy going to the *STAVKA* and the other retained by the commander "sealed up in a secret depository."[11] Orders generated by the plans were to be distributed in person and issuance of the complete order was forbidden. Individual orders to lower level commanders were sent by courier or by cipher with one copy going by cipher to the General Staff.

During regrouping of forces and preparation for an operation, radio stations were forbidden to operate in the new attack region, while in the former combat regions, radio stations would continue operations using old codes and procedures. Reports about ongoing regrouping were made only in cipher and were not included in periodic operational summaries.

The Soviet 1943 *Field Regulation* incorporated the demands of earlier directives and required orderly conduct of *maskirovka* planning and *maskirovka* measures during an operation. It stipulated the contents of the operational *maskirovka* plan which accompanied each and every operational plan. It also identified missions to be accomplished in each stage in the planning and conduct of operations and battles and specified the nature, timing, and location of *maskirovka* measures. Finally, the regulation designated the party responsible for implementing the *maskirovka* plan. Commanders were ordered to pay constant attention to *maskirovka* throughout the operation, conceal force deployments, and check that concealment by air and ground observation and aerial photographs.[12]

The salutary effect of the new regulation and earlier directives became evident by mid-1943. Moreover, Soviet commanders had learned by hard example the perils of ignoring *maskirovka*. Soviet talent for *maskirovka* immeasurably improved as commanders employed measures stipulated in the regulations. The Soviets also harnessed their experience operating at night and across prohibiting terrain to enhance the effects of *maskirovka*. Earlier in the war German dominance of the air and control of traffic arteries had forced the Soviets to operate cross-country and under the cloak of darkness. In 1943, when German air dominance began to fade, the Soviets tapped their earlier experiences to reinforce their *maskirovka* capabilities. In fact the most successful Soviet force regroupings took place under the cloak of darkness and in areas the Germans neglected to observe because they thought them impassable.

Other factors assisted Soviet *maskirovka* efforts after mid-1943. The correlation of forces shifted decisively in the Soviet's favor, granting the Soviets the strategic and operational initiative. With the initiative in Soviet hands and with clear and growing force superiority, secret maneuver of forces and the selection of concealed attack directions became an easier process since the Soviets could choose multiple points of attack. Simultaneously, German physical intelligence collection capabilities diminished as German loss of air superiority increasingly limited German air reconnaissance. Soviet security measures in the rear area snuffed out the work of German agents; and, as the front moved westward, the number of Soviet prisoners of war and line-crossers measurably decreased, reducing the amount of intelligence available through interrogation. Tighter Soviet planning security and improved Soviet communications discipline compounded the difficulties of German intelligence, which was made more difficult by an increasing Soviet tendency to engage in disinformation by the production and release of false plans and orders and deliberate line-crossers bearing false information for the Germans. As German operational defeats mounted it became increasingly difficult for German intelligence to gain an accurate picture of Soviet force posture, in particular in the Soviet strategic and operational rear.

On the other hand, German communications intelligence skills improved as the number of radio direction finding units increased. German skills at identifying Soviet tactical units had been good early in the war and would remain a German strength. Yet for brief periods Soviet *maskirovka* could even confound German communications intelligence. German archival materials, which indelibly record what the Germans could and could not see, vividly attest to this fact.

The dilemma of both Soviet planners and operators who sought solace in *maskirovka* and German defenders who strained to observe an increasingly murky battlefield was best described as follows:

> Experience showed that even when one succeeded in fully concealing the concept of an operation, to carry out a whole series of measures to hide concentration of forces, to completely avoid disclosure to the enemy of the preparations for a large operation was difficult, especially if the flow was to occur across a broad front. In 1941–1942 measures to achieve surprise sought limited aims – to hide the concept of the operation and the concentration of the shock group. From 1943, when large forces were concentrated in a narrow sector of the front to penetrate an enemy defense, to content oneself with only these measures was already impossible. The enemy, by all types of ground reconnaissance, succeeded in discovering the preparations; and, since they were conducted in a narrow sector, it was not difficult to determine the direction of the main strike. On the other hand, with the increase in Soviet army forces and when we had the strategic initiative it became, in some measure, easier to achieve strategic surprise and more difficult to achieve operational and, in particular, tactical surprise in penetrating a strong enemy defense.

Measures for operational *maskirovka* became "an integral part of every offensive operation."[13] From mid-1943, the Soviets and Germans engaged in a deadly cat-and-mouse game. German intelligence collection skills were pitted against Soviet *maskirovka* skills. The gruesome stake in the fatal game would soon become apparent.

There was little strategic deception about initial Soviet intent in Soviet operational planning in mid-1943 during the German Kursk offensive. Soviet forces were clearly and deliberately on the strategic defensive. However, unknown to German intelligence, the Soviets included in their defensive planning, plans for a large-scale counter-offensive scheduled to begin when the German offensive tide began to ebb, and extensive plans for the conduct of strategic and operational diversionary operations. At Kursk, the Soviets engaged in large scale *maskirovka* measures to cover their intentions to launch these counter-strokes, including radio deception (the establishment by radio of false large-scale troop concentrations) and camouflage measures for actual troop concentrations. While the radio deception failed to achieve all its objectives, the active measures succeeded, and the Soviet July 1943 Orel and August 1943 Belgorod–Khar'kov counter-offensives came as a surprise for the Germans.[14] Again, although the Germans accurately assessed future Soviet intentions, they misassessed the timing, scale, and focus of the attacks and paid dearly for this mistake by suffering a series of major defeats which forced German forces to withdraw westward to the Dnepr River line.

In the autumn of 1943, while Soviet forces advanced along a broad front from Smolensk in the north to the Black Sea coast in the south, German intelligence correctly assessed that the Soviet main effort would be in the Ukraine. Consequently, German forces contained Soviet armies along the Dnepr River and in limited bridgeheads south of Kiev and south of Kremenchug. After a month of stalemate, a major Soviet strategic deception operation produced a break. By utilizing a variety of deceptive measures including dummy radio nets, mock-up tanks, and night movements, the Soviets secretly shifted an entire tank army (3d Guards) from the Bukrin area south of Kiev into a bridgehead across the Dnepr River in the Lyutezh area north of Kiev. There, 3d Guards Tank Army joined 38th Army in launching a surprise operation which drove German forces from the Kiev region. The Germans had insufficient forces available and were unable to parry the Soviet offensive thrust before it had established a major bridgehead west of Kiev.[15] Extensive Soviet diversionary activity along the front contributed to this strategic deception.

Meanwhile, across the front from the Baltic to the Black Sea, in late August, the Soviets conducted a series of operations, pressed back the faltering Germans, and distracted German attention from the Soviet main strategic thrust. Most of these operations involved Soviet *maskirovka* with varying degrees of success. The pre-eminent concern of Soviet commanders and planners was to mask their regrouping of forces and conceal the point of main effort. As in 1942, the Soviets had great difficulty masking their offensive intent in the central portion of the front opposite German Army Group Center. Here they failed to conceal offensive preparations during the early stages of the Smolensk operations and likewise suffered a similar reverse in the Sevsk area west of Kursk. Once the offensives began to unfold, however, the Soviets in both regions scored some *maskirovka* successes, most notably by secretly shifting armies from one sector to another. In October 1943 3d Shock Army masked preparations for an offensive northeast of Vitebsk which caught the Germans by surprise, secured Nevel', and carried Soviet troops forward into a salient threatening the key city of Vitebsk from the north.

Further south, in November Soviet forces took advantage of German preoccupation with events along the Dnepr River at Bukrin and Kiev to launch a surprise offensive (Gomel'—Rechitsa) into southern Belorussia, through the northern extremities of the Pripyat marshes. There credit for success belonged to 65th Army which artfully concealed its offensive preparations.

The Soviets also used *maskirovka* successfully in southern Russia at Novorossiisk along the Black Sea coast and in their drive to clear the Donbas, which began in September in the Melitopol' region. There, after initial failures, the Soviets secretly shifted 51st Army from the Southern Front's right flank to its left flank, in so doing finally breaking the German grip on Melitopol' and forcing the Germans to withdraw westward across the Dnepr River and into the Crimea. Subsequent Soviet tactical *maskirovka* successes gained for them footholds across the Dnepr River near Zaparozh'ye.

Along with these successful examples of operational deception, the Soviets also suffered failures in deception (some apparently deliberate), most notably along the Mius River in July 1943 and along the Northern Donets River in the Izyum region in July and August 1943 where poor Soviet radio security undercut the aims of the deception measures. In both instances the Germans adjusted their forces and halted the Soviet offensives after only minor gains. In both July failures, however, the Soviet attacks drew critical German reserves from other more important sectors of the front.

Ironically, or purposely, the Soviets have written very little about their most successful *maskirovka* effort in late 1943. The case becomes apparent from a day-to-day review of German operational records. In the latter stages of the Kiev operation, while the Germans attempted to compress and eradicate the Soviet bridgehead west of Kiev, the Soviets, while parrying the German counterstroke, created a massive concentration of forces near Brusilov, west of Kiev. In the course of three weeks, the Soviets redeployed into the area three new armies, including one tank army, and concentrated them for a new attack. Simultaneously, the Soviets regrouped and concentrated the forces of four armies already operating in the region. The Germans failed to detect most of the Soviet regrouping and the Soviet attack (Zhitomir—Berdichev operation) achieved almost total surprise.

By the end of 1943, Soviet deception operations had progressed from random attempts to secure operations, usually by passive deception measures, to a comprehensive and more active program of strategic and operational deception. Whereas early in the war no effective formal deception plans had existed, by late 1942 specific staff agencies within each headquarters were required to prepare specific deception plans to accompany normal operational plans.[16] Soviet deception successes during this period occurred primarily at the operational and tactical level. In 1941 and 1942 attempts at strategic deception were still crude and, hence, went largely unrealized. Cumulative operational successes did sometimes produce strategic results, in particular at Moscow. By mid-1943, Soviet strategic deception had become more coherent. The Stalingrad operation involved significant use of rudimentary strategic deceptive measures. Planning for the Kursk operation produced a well-thought-out strategic *maskirovka* plan using both extensive passive measures and active diversionary operations, all sequenced with devastating effect. The Kiev success demonstrated Soviet capabilities to orchestrate *maskirovka* "on the march" with only limited planning but with equally devastating effect.

During 1944 and 1945 the strategic initiative fell clearly into Soviet hands, permitting the Red Army to select the form and means for conducting the war. Consequently, the scale and scope of Soviet deception expanded to encompass overall offensive intent, the region of operations, as well as the form and timing of the attack. Improved technology (principally armor and communications equipment), growing Soviet domination of the air, and improved Soviet technical expertise made possible large-scale strategic deception and more efficient deception at all lower levels of command. Growing sophistication of deception became evident in early 1944.

Simultaneously, the Red Army incorporated lessons learned in the realm of deception into a wide range of new regulations. The 1944 *Regulation for Penetration of a Positional Defense* articulated the most pressing problem for Soviets planners stating:

> The difficulty of securing the concentration of large masses of forces in the penetration sector and the requirement of fulfilling a large volume of engineer work, demands the safe protection by military aviation and the most careful working out of measures for operational and tactical *maskirovka*.[17]

The basic 1944 *Field Regulations* demonstrated the expanded understanding of *maskirovka* derived from wartime experiences. The opening section of the regulation declared:

> Surprise dumbfounds the enemy, paralyzes his will, and deprives him of an opportunity to offer organized resistance.
>
> Surprise is achieved:
> — by leading the enemy astray and by keeping the plan of upcoming actions in strictest secrecy;
> — by the concealment and swift regrouping of forces and of the concentration of overwhelming forces and weapons in the decisive locations;
> — by the surprise [unexpected] attack of aircraft, cavalry, and motorized tank units;
> — by surprise [unexpected] opening of annihilating fires and the beginning of swift attacks.
>
> Surprise is also achieved by employing methods of fighting that are new for the enemy and weapons unknown to him.
>
> The enemy will also strive for surprise.[18]

The regulation then outlined specific measures for deception, underscoring the importance of those measures for achieving operational and tactical success, specifying the contents of deception plans, and delineating the staff responsibilities for implementing those plans. It declared:

> *maskirovka* is a mandatory form of combat support for each action and operation. The objectives of *maskirovka* are to secure concealment of the maneuver and concentration of troops for the purpose of delivering a surprise attack; to mislead the enemy relative to our forces, weapons, actions, and intentions; and thus force him to make an incorrect decision.[19]

Unlike previous regulations, that of 1944 specified that an enemy was to be misled:

— by concealing real objects from enemy reconnaissance and observation;
— by changing the external appearance of objects;
— by setting up dummy objects and by feints;
— by spreading false rumors;
— by sound discipline and by artificial noises;
— by masking the operations of radios, by setting up dummy radio nets, and by radio deception.[20]

TDAE—C*

The regulation reiterated that successful *maskirovka* was based on the principles of "naturalness, diversity, continuousness, and activeness [*aktivnost'*] of *maskirovka* measures."[21]

Drafting the overall *maskirovka* plan was the responsibility of appropriate staff, in accordance with the commander's concept of the operation. The plan was to articulate general missions during each phase of planning and conducting the operation, specific *maskirovka* measures by time and location of their execution, and officers responsible for the execution of the plan. However, planned feints and the spreading of false rumors were to be accomplished only under the direct orders of army and *front* headquarters as outlined in the army and *front maskirovka* plan.

The Soviets demonstrated their heightened awareness of *maskirovka* and the care they evidenced in addressing the subject by issuing a regulation on the subject. The 1944 *Manual on Operational Maskirovka* drew upon the vast range of war experiences, enunciated basic Soviet views on *maskirovka*, and contained special instruction regarding its proper employment. It declared that success in an operation depended on concealed preparations and delivery of a surprise attack. It was not enough, however, to rely on secrecy to deceive the enemy concerning one's offensive intentions. It was also necessary to create false objectives, conduct feints and demonstrations, and engage in an active disinformation program. Thus "given identical forces and other equal conditions he who outwits the enemy emerges as the victor."[22] The manual went on to provide *front* and army level planners basic guidance in the formulation of their respective plans for operational *maskirovka*.

Armed with these new regulations and manuals and guided by the experience of three years of war, the Soviets were more capable of carrying out effective deception in the final two years. *Maskirovka* became even more effective at the strategic level and involved far more active *maskirovka* measures than had earlier been the case.

From late December 1943 into early 1944, the Soviets concentrated their offensive efforts in southern Russia as they drove to clear the Ukraine of German forces. There was little attempt by the Soviets to mask their strategic intentions, but what surprised the Germans was the Soviet intention and ability to operate right through the period of thaw [*razputitsa*]. Previously, as if by mutual consent, both sides had halted operations in late February and March as the soil turned to a deep, gluey mass which inhibited effective operations.

In late January 1944, however, the Soviets launched a series of successive and then simultaneous *front* operations from Korosten (west of Kiev) to the Black Sea. To the Germans' consternation, the Soviets ultimately committed six tank armies and a cavalry-mechanized group to spearhead these operations which endured through early June, pushing German forces toward the Polish borders and into Bessarabia. While abstaining from the use of *maskirovka* as a strategic means to achieve surprise, in this period the Soviets relied instead on deceiving the Germans as to the location, form, and timing of their offensives. In addition, the Soviets resorted to extensive *maskirovka* at the operational and tactical levels with mixed success.

In January 1944 the Soviets also employed *maskirovka* in the Leningrad region to cover redeployment of forces for the Novgorod–Luga operation. The resulting surprise offensive drove German forces from the Leningrad area, liberated Novgorod, and opened a series of operations which ultimately drove German forces back into the Baltic states. Late in the same month, the Soviets conducted a major deception operation designed to mask the redeployment of 5th Guards Tank Army prior to the Korsun–Shevchenkovsky operation, but they achieved only limited success. As the Soviets began their spring offensives in the Ukraine, they resorted to *maskirovka* to conceal the redeployment of their armored and mechanized forces. They achieved their most notable success in the Proskurov–Chernovitsy operation of March and April 1944 as 1st Guards and 4th Tank Armies raced through the German rear area to the Rumanian border.

As the spring offensive ebbed, the Soviets undertook one of their most successful strategic deception operations, one which was disastrous for the Germans. Using a variety of active and passive *maskirovka* measures, the Soviets sought to convince German planners that the focus of offensive efforts would continue against German forces in south-eastern Europe and in the Baltic region. In reality, the Soviets intended to conduct a major strategic redeployment of forces and then strike German Army Group Center defending in Belorussia. The ensuing deception operation, orchestrated by the *STAVKA*, involved extensive radio deception, rumors, false orders, feints, and massive movement of forces under cover of extensive passive *maskirovka* measures. As a result of these efforts, the Germans concentrated all available operational reserves in south-eastern Poland, thus depriving the real Soviet target, German Army Group Center in Belorussia, of virtually all of its armored and mechanized forces.

The Soviet offensive destroyed three armies of German Army Group Center. Then, having advanced all the way to Riga, East Prussia, and Warsaw on the Vistula River line, the Soviets suddenly shifted their strategic emphasis southward in July and August. In rapid succession they delivered devastating blows against German Army Northern Ukraine defending south-eastern Poland (L'vov–Sandomierz operation, July) and against Army Group South Ukraine, defending Rumania (Yassy–Kishinev operation, August), both of which had just dispatched a significant portion of their armies' reserves northward to assist the remnants of Army Group Center. In both operations the Soviets made extensive use of operational *maskirovka* with good effect.

In the fall of 1944, after driving German forces from Belorussia and Rumania, Soviet forces sought to weaken the flanks of German forces in the East by severing German communications with their forces in the Baltic region and by driving to Budapest in the Danube Basin, on Germany's vulnerable southern flank. In one of the best examples of a concealed movement of major forces, in October 1944 the Soviet command secretly shifted forces from the Riga area to the south and opened a surprise attack in the Shaulyaya area which propelled Soviet forces to the Baltic Sea near Memel', severing communications of German forces in the Baltic with those in East Prussia and Poland. At the same time, in Hungary the Soviets conducted a series of offensives which culminated in a December 1944 operation to encircle Budapest. Soviet success in the Hungarian operations involved use of operational and tactical *maskirovka*, secret movement of armored forces, and secret regrouping of forces in close proximity to the enemy. Such was the case in December 1944 when 4th Guards and 46th Armies mounted their final successful drive to encircle Budapest.

In early 1945, as Soviet forces operated on a narrowing front from the Baltic Sea to the Danube River, it became increasingly difficult for the Germans to detect which sector posed the greatest danger. In fact, the Soviets deliberately sought to remain active on all fronts. Soviet strategic *maskirovka* was effective enough to attract German attention to Hungary and the critical Danube Basin where it appeared the Soviets would continue their drive into Austria and the soft underbelly of the German Reich. Consequently, as German forces concentrated their defensive (and offensive) efforts in Hungary, Soviet forces prepared and unleashed devastating offensives against German forces in East Prussia and Poland. They crushed three German army groups and propelled Soviet forces to the Baltic Coast and across the Oder River to within 60 kilometers of Berlin.[23]

Both the East Prussian and Vistula–Oder operations occurred in regions where the geography and configuration of the front lines made it relatively easy to predict where the focus of the offensives would fall. In addition, by January 1945 it was apparent to the Germans that the Soviets planned to conduct new large-scale offensives. Thus, operational *maskirovka* was indeed a difficult task for the Soviets. Despite these adverse conditions, the Soviets in January conducted their most successful *maskirovka* planning of the war and perhaps the most relevant for the contemporary situation.

In East Prussia the Soviets successfully masked the movement of 5th Guards Tank Army from the Riga area to its new area of operations north of Warsaw. This secret movement plus other redeployments and artful tactical *maskirovka* paved the way for rapid Soviet penetration of German defenses along the Narev River and decisive exploitation by 5th Guards Tank Army to the Baltic Sea near Elbing, pinning German forces in East Prussia against the Baltic Sea in the Konigsberg area.

South of Warsaw the Soviets used extensive *maskirovka* measures to conceal their preparations for the Vistula–Oder operation. By creating false operational concentrations of armor and by conducting extensive secret regrouping of forces while effectively concealing force deployments in the forward area, the Soviets were able to inject indecision into the German command concerning where the principal blows would occur. More important, the Soviets were able to conceal a major portion of their force build-up. The ensuing Soviet offensive was almost twice as powerful as the Germans expected. It smashed German defenses and carried all the way to the Oder River before its momentum ebbed. At the end of the operation the Soviets were able to again secretly regroup their forces and shift the offensive toward the flanks in the direction of Pomerania and Silesia.

During the preparation period for the long-awaited Berlin offensive, the Soviets engaged in *maskirovka* to deceive the Germans as to the point of Soviet main effort and to cover the rapid redeployment of twenty-eight armies, half of them over distances of from 300 to 800 kilometers. In the Berlin operation, however, the set-piece nature of the operation mitigated against the achievement of spectacular *maskirovka* successes.

As the incessant series of Soviet offensives in early 1945 moved toward the final defeat of German forces around Berlin, the Soviets were already contemplating a strategic offensive of even grander scale against Japanese forces in Manchuria. Acting in their own political interests and, coincidentally, responding to U.S. requests for assistance, the Soviets planned a major strategic redeployment of forces into the Far East after the final defeat of Germany. The reinforced Soviet Far Eastern Command would then strike at the Japanese Kwantung Army, occupy Manchuria, and prepare for possible joint U.S.–Soviet operations against Japan. Given the potential collapse of Japan, Soviet planners realized the operation had to be a rapid one, in their view complete within 30 days.

The severe time constraints on the operation, the size of and the terrain in the projected theater of operations, and the number (700,000) and dispositions of Japanese forces in Manchuria dictated that maximum deception be used by the Soviets both during the strategic redeployment of forces and during the operation itself. The Soviets faced the same problem as Germany had faced in June 1941, the necessity to win quickly in an "initial period of war."

The Soviets used extensive *maskirovka* measures including false orders, night movement, and a host of passive concealment and camouflage techniques. They also took maximum advantage of poor weather conditions and planned for large-scale attacks in terrain considered unsuitable by the Japanese. These deception measures achieved their objective. Japanese planners underestimated Soviet strength by over 30 percent and assessed that the Soviet invasion would take place at least a month after it actually occurred. The Soviets completed destruction of the Kwantung Army and occupied Manchuria in just over 15 days.

At the war's end, the Soviets had extensive experience with *maskirovka*, both as victim and as employer of deception. The complexity of those experiences reflected the difficulty and vast scope of operations on the Eastern Front as a whole. To judge the efficiency of Soviet planners and operators in this shadowy form of war, it is necessary to look in some detail at Soviet operational experiences.

In researching the theme of *maskirovka* the futility of attempting to cite representative cases becomes readily apparent. The comprehensiveness of real strategic *maskirovka* requires examining virtually all major and some minor operations. Like a puzzle, the mosaic of *maskirovka* is incomplete when pieces are missing. Invariably the missing piece completes the picture, and without it the whole loses meaning. This truth sabotaged my original selective intent, multiplied my work, but provided answers to questions which would have otherwise gone unanswered. The resulting cases bear witness to the complexity and comprehensiveness of *maskirovka* and coincidentally provide a sobering indication of maturing Soviet appreciation of and talent for *maskirovka*.

CHAPTER FOUR

THE PRACTICE OF *MASKIROVKA*
The First Period of War
(1941–November 1942)

At the beginning of the war, Soviet forces overcame the influence of the factors of the surprise attack of German-Fascist forces. They were forced to conduct defensive operations and try, first of all, to seize from the enemy the strategic initiative. Offensive operations primarily took the form of counter-attacks and counter-strokes. In these conditions, the concept of contemplated operations was worked out during the course of the defense, was simple, and the missions to forces were established before their full concentration. The basic means for achieving surprise was the rapid working out of a concept and the formulation of missions in accordance with complex conditions, the concealed concentration of forces and means for counter-attacks and counter-strokes, the use of the enemy's open flanks for the delivery of surprise flank attacks, and the extensive use of night operations.

> M. M. Kir'yan,
> *Vnezapnost' v nastupatel'nykh operatsiyakh Velikoi Otechestvennoi voiny* [Surprise in Offensive Operations of the Great Patriotic War], 1986

INTRODUCTION

The first eighteen months of the Second World War was a difficult period for Soviet forces. Struck hard by the surprise German offensive, the Soviets suffered disastrous defeats and catastrophic losses as they sought to halt the German juggernaut and restore equilibrium to the Eastern Front. The initial German attack shattered defending Soviet forces and forced the Soviets to throw into conflict freshly mobilized, but largely untrained, new armies to fight alongside veteran units hastily dispatched from the extremities of the Soviet Union. The opening months of war laid bare the true state of the Red Army. It was a large, but cumbersome force led by a command cadre representing the survivors of the years of bloody purges. These survivors ranged from competent to bumbling, but they shared one general characteristic – a tendency to avoid innovation and creativity on the battlefield. Armed with a relatively advanced theoretical doctrine, they were scarcely able to convert that doctrine into real battlefield practice. Moreover, the German attack caught the Red Army in the midst of a force structure reorganization and reequipment program. Large mechanized forces which began to form in early 1941 existed in form but not in substance, nor were they equipped with the modern weaponry due to come into the inventory by late 1942.

The German attack crushed that force structure, undermined the confidence of Soviet commanders at every level, and severely tested the validity of Soviet military doctrine. From the initial days of war the Soviet High Command and political leadership had the onerous task of rebuilding the force structure, restoring the confidence of the officer corps, and validating or correcting doctrine while fighting for its very survival as a nation. In this task it succeeded, although at tremendous cost.

In December 1941 the Soviets had halted the first German strategic offensive on the outskirts of Moscow. In late 1942 the Soviets again halted a German strategic offensive on the banks of the Volga River. While these great battles at Moscow and Stalingrad were epic in proportion and monumental in their own right, Soviet victories there did not occur in isolation from other events. In fact, they represented the culmination of hundreds of defensive and offensive battles elsewhere that gave shape, context, and meaning to what occurred at Moscow and Stalingrad. In the days, weeks, and months of combat before and between those great battles, the Red Army reconstructed itself; discovered a new command leadership, for the most part educated on the battlefield; and developed new strategic, operational, and tactical concepts for use on the battlefield. Leadership and combat skill finally emerged, forged by combat and the intimidating threat of death if failure ensued.

In two years of war the Red Army had to learn how to survive on the defensive and launch periodic offensives. In a practical sense the army learned how to plan and conduct operations of every scale. Much of that learning was done by experiencing combat and by learning from that experience. One very small but critical aspect of that education regarded *maskirovka*. The Soviets developed an appreciation for operational secrecy and deception regarding Soviet offensive intent.

The educational process was slow, for although Soviet *maskirovka* theory in 1941 was sound, the ability of the Red Army to implement that theory was weak. The ineptitude of Soviet commanders and staffs compounded the problem posed by the fact that the initiative was in German hands. Only when the Germans lost the initiative could the Soviets begin to practice rudimentary operational *maskirovka*.

ROSTOV, NOVEMBER 1941

Soviet offensive opportunities in 1941 were often a product of circumstances, the most fortuitous of which were German propensities to overextend themselves, and, for the Soviets, the salutary effect of winter weather on German forces unprepared for the rigors of operations in a hostile climate. German armies on every front in the fall of 1941 strove to achieve objectives beyond their reach (see map 1). While German forces knocked at the gates of Leningrad and surged forward from Vy'azma and Bryansk toward Moscow, German Army Group South set out eastward across the seemingly endless steppes of southern Russia. German forces crossed the Dnepr River into the Donbas, and approached the Mius River, seeking the natural limits to an offensive whose forward drive had produced a momentum of its own. As the wet weather of October gave promise of the impending cold of winter, Field-Marshal Edwald von Kleist's First Panzer Army (First Panzer Group until 6 October), spearheading Army Group South's eastward thrust, crossed the Mius River and secured a bridgehead on its east bank near the mouth of the river. By 4 November von Kleist's panzers (13th, 14th, 16th, and SS "Leibstandarte Adolf Hitler" Panzer Divisions and SS "Viking" and 60th Motorized Divisions) had crossed the river on a broad front, secured Taganrog, and poised themselves for a thrust into the great bend of the Don River or toward Rostov.

The Soviet High Command, faced with critical situations near Leningrad and a growing threat to Moscow, urged the Southern Front to undertake offensive action to halt the German drive short of Rostov and prevent any German reinforcements from being sent northward to reinforce the German drive on Moscow.[1]

Marshal S.K. Timoshenko, commander of the Southwestern Direction [in essence a TVD – theater of military operations], which consisted of the Southwestern and Southern Fronts, wished to launch an offensive but required additional forces to do so. The Southern Front's 9th and 18th Armies were stretched thin trying to hold the German advance along the Mius River, and the newly formed 56th Separate Army was similarly hard-pressed to defend the approaches to Rostov. Hence, Timoshenko appealed to the *STAVKA* for reserves with which to conduct the counter-attack. A race developed between German forces pushing toward Rostov and Soviet attempts to gather reserves and launch the attack before the Germans achieved their objective. The race clearly developed to the Soviet advantage, for as von Kleist advanced ever deeper, his flanks weakened and were more vulnerable to a Soviet counter-stroke. The Soviets, however, were not aware of this weakness. Although an order to 16th Panzer Division had fallen into Soviet hands, that order specified the timing but not the location of the main German thrust. On 5 November the Germans resumed their offensive, and it finally became apparent their objective was Rostov. So informed, Timoshenko and General Ya. T. Cherevichenko, Southern Front commander, planned to mount a counter-attack.

Timoshenko's initial plan was to use one division (99th) released by 18th Army, a cavalry corps from 9th Army, and several tank brigades, supported by the bulk of Southern Front aviation, to counter-attack through the growing gap between 9th and 18th Armies as they were pressed back by the German advance. Cherevichenko was pessimistic over the prospects for carrying out such a regrouping, but Timoshenko remained confident of his plan and sought forces from the *STAVKA* to implement it.[2] At his urgings the *STAVKA* assigned to him the newly formed 37th Army which consisted of four weak rifle divisions (4th, 176th, 218th, 253d). This measure proved critical, for the German attack's progress had forced immediate commitment to battle of the 99th Rifle Division and one tank brigade. Timoshenko thereafter steadfastly refused to relinquish control of any more of his reserves as he went about assembling his counter-attack force.

Timoshenko's counter-attack was planned by Major General A. I. Antonov, at that time attached to the Southern Front.[3] Antonov's most important task was to assemble the counter-attack force and maintain a cloak of secrecy around those movements. To facilitate Antonov's task, the *STAVKA* abolished the Bryansk Front (further north) and gave two of its armies (3d and 13th) to Timoshenko's Southwestern Front to enable it to release fresh

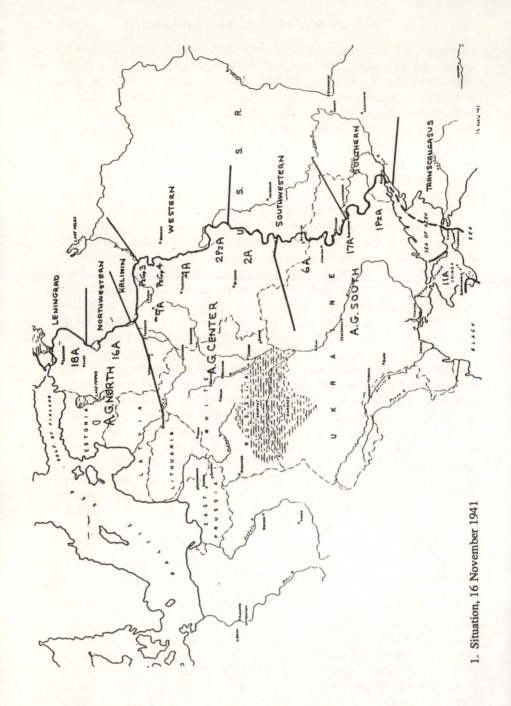

1. Situation, 16 November 1941

forces for the Southern Front. On 10 November, Timoshenko shifted two rifle divisions (216th, 259th) and a tank brigade from the Southwestern to the Southern Front, the first step in creating a Southern Front reserve. Two days later Antonov revealed his initial counter-attack plan which involved the use of 37th Army, one rifle division and one cavalry division of 9th Army, and two rifle divisions of 18th Army in an attack against the left flank of the advancing German force. These assault forces would concentrate for the attack from 11–15 November and commence the attack on 16 November.

Antonov's plan sought to achieve surprise, halt the German drive on Rostov, and alter the direction of the *front* attack should the need arise. Therefore the *STAVKA* approved it. The most difficult challenge was to assemble counter-attack forces secretly, in particular General A.I. Lopatin's 37th Army. (37th Army consisted of six rifle divisions [51st, 96th, 99th, 216th, 253d, 295th], three tank brigades [2d, 3d, 132d], four artillery regiments, and four anti-tank artillery regiments.) Two divisions of 37th Army and those of 9th and 18th Armies were already in the region. The remaining divisions had to be moved a considerable distance to 37th Army's assembly area in a very short period of time. Since it was clear that two divisions of the Southwestern Front (216th, 295th) could not make the move in time, they would be thrown into battle as they arrived. The remaining four divisions would attack as planned. Despite difficulties, the four divisions reached their assembly areas covered by a tight cloak of secrecy. Some supporting units (one tank brigade and an anti-tank artillery regiment) were also unable to assemble on time. Although Cherevichenko delayed the operation for one day, an angry *STAVKA* forced him to launch the attack on 17 November, albeit with only four rifle divisions and two tank brigades.

The successful assembly of even this abbreviated force required *maskirovka* skill on General Lopatin's part. To deceive the Germans, Soviet units on the German left flank constructed heavy fortifications to demonstrate defensive intentions.[4] Although the region was open and virtually treeless, the Soviets masked their movements by traveling at night under severe blackout conditions and by camouflaging all men, material, and vehicles. The army was assigned 12 sapper battalions to support the engineer *maskirovka* measures; but, due to the extensive work necessary, infantry units had to assist. Throughout the preparation period, heavy rains, fog, and low visibility hindered Soviet troop assembly, but also curtailed German aerial reconnaissance.[5]

The Soviet counter-attack surprised von Kleist's overextended forces. Nevertheless, he continued his advance and secured Rostov. Ultimately, however, the pressure of 37th Army's counter-attack and 56th Separate Army's attacks on Rostov forced the Germans to withdraw on 2 December to the Mius River line.

The Soviets clearly achieved surprise at Rostov. German intelligence material attests to that surprise as do the journal comments of German Army Chief of Staff Franz Halder. The war journal situation maps of Army Group South and First Panzer Army illustrate the degree of surprise the Soviets achieved (see maps 2 and 3). On 17 November, the day before the Soviet counter-attack, German intelligence noted the presence of two 37th Army divisions (51st and 99th) but not the remainder of 37th Army. First Panzer Army detected one additional Soviet division (253d) on 19 November and the remainder of the army the following day, too late to shift forces to forestall the successful Soviet attack.

Halder optimistically recorded the progress of von Kleist's advance throughout early November, noting First Panzer Army's "good progress" on 18 November. The next day, as the Soviet counter-attack began, Halder wrote, "Kleist's attack on Rostov is making good headway. The enemy is trying to check Kleist's southward drive by a flank attack from the east, but without success."[6] On 20 November Halder recognized greater Soviet success stating that the continuation of the attack on Rostov went well, but, "On the northeastern front of *First Panzer Army* (XIV Corps)," there was "hard fighting and threat of an enemy breakthrough."[7] The following day Rostov fell, but that success was marred by Halder's notation, "North of Rostov heavy fighting against the numerically far superior and apparently well-led enemy, who is attacking in tightly integrated groups, each several Divs. strong. It seems there is no immediate danger ..."[8] Further optimism the next few days that Kleist could handle the Soviet attack gave way to the news on 28 November that, "Under pressure of the concentric attacks by an overwhelmingly superior enemy Kleist is evacuating the city of *Rostov* and the area to the north."[9]

It is debatable whether Soviet surprise at Rostov was a result of efficient *maskirovka* or other conditions. Bad weather had an adverse impact on German intelligence collection and assisted the concealment of Soviet intentions as did the overextension of German units, their overconfidence, and their fixation on the objective of Rostov. It is also clear that Soviet planners sought to mask troop movements and offensive preparations. Even if these measures were limited, the success of the counter-offensive was a lesson to the Soviets regarding what efficient *maskirovka* could achieve in the future.

MOSCOW, DECEMBER 1941

The first major Soviet attempt to employ large-scale *maskirovka* to cover preparations for offensive operations occurred in the Moscow region in November and December of 1941, while German forces were straining to overcome the last vestiges of Soviet resistance and seize Moscow. Accordingly, Soviet planners were driven as much by desperation and circumstances as by a conscious well-planned effort to deceive and defeat German forces. They were unwittingly assisted by the German command which maintained an optimistic tone and continually depreciated the Soviet ability to generate and deploy fresh reserves. On 18 November the German Army Chief of Staff, General Franz Halder, wrote:

> Field Marshal von Bock shares my deep conviction that the enemy, just as much as we do, is throwing in the last ounce of strength and that victory will go to the side that sticks it out longer. The enemy, too, has nothing left in the rear and his predicament probably is even worse than ours.[10]

This typified German attitudes through the end of November and into December 1941. On 2 December Halder again wrote, "Overall impression: Enemy defense has reached its peak. No more reinforcement available."[11] Meanwhile, between three and seven days before, elements of three new Soviet armies had been deployed into the Moscow region.[12] Just three days before Halder's comment, the *STAVKA*, in coordination with the Western Front, had approved a plan to use these and other Western Front armies in a general counter-offensive against German forces lying exhausted on the northern and southern approaches to the Russian capital.

The Soviet counter-offensive, ordered by Stalin and planned by General Zhukov, commander of the Western Front, envisioned the use of these three new armies as shock groups to spearhead the new offensive. Deployment of the new armies into the forward area had begun on 24 November and continued until early December, ready for the designated attack date of 6 December.[13] Soviet *maskirovka*

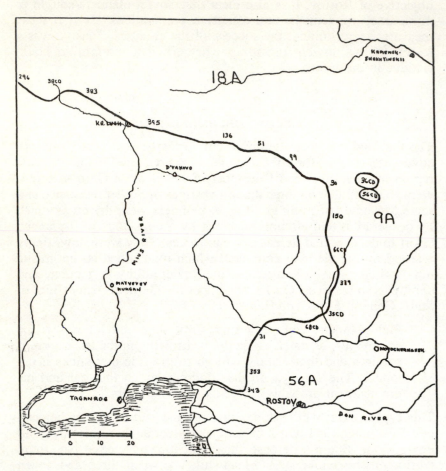

2. Rostov, German intelligence assessment, 17 November 1941

measures associated with the Moscow counter-offensive in general, and the movement of the three armies in particular, were neither systematically planned nor part of any well-organized strategic deception plan. Yet specific aspects of planning and deployment did have seemingly positive results, in particular the improved Soviet ability to cover large troop movements. Because of this and poor German intelligence, the Moscow counter-offensive came as a distinct surprise for German Army Group Center and the German High Command.

Soviet planning for the Moscow counter-offensive was completed

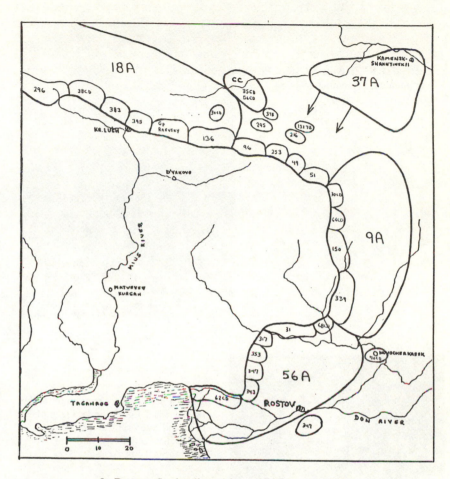

3. Rostov, Soviet dispositions, 17 November 1941

in only six days and with the utmost secrecy. Only select individuals
within the *STAVKA* and Western Front headquarters knew of the
plans, and even army commanders knew only their portion of the
plan. Soviet resort to sequential planning (step by step through
various levels of command), which endured in the future, improved
the secrecy of operational planning but limited the preparation
period of subordinate headquarters. In the Moscow operation,
however, it prevented disclosure of the plans to German intelligence.

Deployment of 1st Shock, 10th and 20th Armies, as well as other

1. General G.K. Zhukov, Western Front
    commander, December 1941

2. General M. Ye. Katukov, commander
    1st Guards Tank Brigade, December,
    1941 and later 1st Tank Corps,
    3d Mechanized Corps and
    1st Guards Tank Army

units into their attack positions, took place in strict secrecy (see map 4). The troops were required to observe strict light and camouflage discipline, and all movement occurred at night under absolute radio silence. The Soviets made every effort to camouflage supply depots, rail lines, and roads along deployment routes. Weather made the task of covering forward movement much easier.[14]

It was particularly difficult for the Soviet Western Front to hide the regrouping and concentration of Lieutenant General V.I. Kuznetsov's 1st Shock Army.[15] That army, created by the *STAVKA* on 20 November 1941 at Zagorsk, moved its lead elements into the Moscow region on 25 November. (Formed originally as 19th Army, it was renumbered on 23 November.) Immediately, the deteriorating defensive situation north of Moscow required commitment of a portion of the army into combat. On 27 November two brigades (29th and 50th) of 1st Shock Army and advanced units of 20th Army erected defenses along the Volga–Moscow canal and conducted a series of local counter-attacks which ultimately halted the advance of German Third Panzer Group. Meanwhile, the parent armies prepared in maximum secrecy for commencement of the Moscow counter-offensive.

1st Shock Army consisted of six rifle brigades (29th, 44th, 47th, 50th, 55th, 56th), two naval rifle brigades (71st, 84th), eleven separate ski battalions, two tank battalions, and supporting artillery. Offensive preparations by this and other attacking armies took place while army units still fought on defense. *Maskirovka* measures, although implemented by inexperienced personnel, were assisted by the bad weather and heavy snowfall.

While 1st Shock and 20th Armies prepared for the offensive in close proximity to the enemy, 10th Army had to deploy forward a considerable distance from the area south of Ryazan' before it could participate in the counter-offensive.[16] In some instances divisions had to travel up to 115 kilometers to their jumping-off positions east of Mikhailov. Thereafter, the army was to attack via Mikhailov and Novomoskovsk into the flank of General H. Guderian's Second Panzer Army. 10th Army received its orders on 5 December for its 6 December attack. At the time army divisions were already enroute to their jumping-off area, each responsible for its own reconnaissance and security. To conceal their movement, divisions marched at night across the snow-covered region. 10th Army went into combat from the march, relying on its movement, the bad weather, and crude *maskirovka* measures to produce a degree of surprise. Time was so pressing that only the three right flank divisions

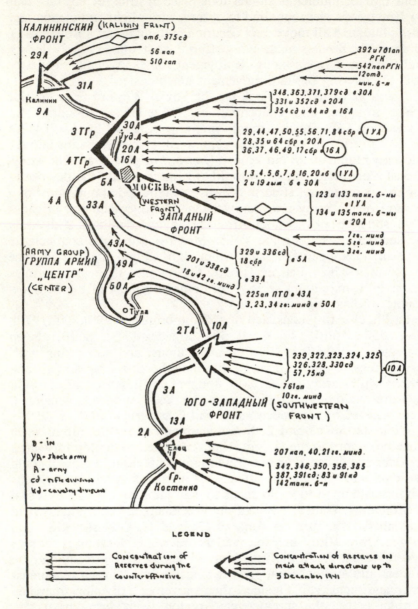

4. Moscow, Soviet regrouping of forces, November–4 December 1941

reached their jumping-off positions at the appointed time. The remaining four divisions continued to move and joined the offensive from the march. General F.I. Govorov, commander of 10th Army, later noted:

> It was difficult to judge what the enemy knew about 10th Army: its concentration, force or intentions. It was natural to think that he knew not a little, since his units had for several days conducted combat reconnaissance and for nearly a week our divisions had been unloading from trains ...[17]

These rudimentary *maskirovka* measures, plus the preoccupation of German forces with their own increasingly overextended situation, prevented German detection of Soviet redeployment.

German intelligence was, however, not entirely unaware. On 27 November, three days after the Soviet reserve armies began their redeployment, Halder wrote:

> The Right Flank of Second Panzer Army is confronted with an enemy concentration; a similar concentration is reported by Second Army. New forces have made their appearance in the direction of the Oka River, at which Second Panzer Army is aiming its thrust. The situation is not clear ...
>
> The enemy is apparently moving new forces also against the attacking wing of A Gp Center northwest of Moscow. They are not large units, but they arrive in an endless succession and cause delay after delay for our exhausted troops.[18]

Two days later Halder noted questioningly, "On the front of Fourth Army ... there is some talk that the enemy is preparing for an attack? ... Further east [of Second Panzer Army], the enemy movements to Ryazan from the south are continuing."[19] The casual note of Soviet troop movements, however, was lost in the general optimistic tone of Halder's notes.

Meanwhile Army Group Center evidenced similar optimism on 4 December: "The combat power of the Red Army cannot be so highly regarded to consider that the enemy presently located in front of the army groups can launch a major counter-offensive."[20] The following day Army Group Center and the German High Command noted on their intelligence maps only seven Soviet armies operating within the Soviet Western Front. Nowhere on the maps did the 1st Shock, 10th or 20th Armies appear (see maps 5 and 6).[21]

After his capture at Stalingrad, Field Marshal F. Paulus noted to

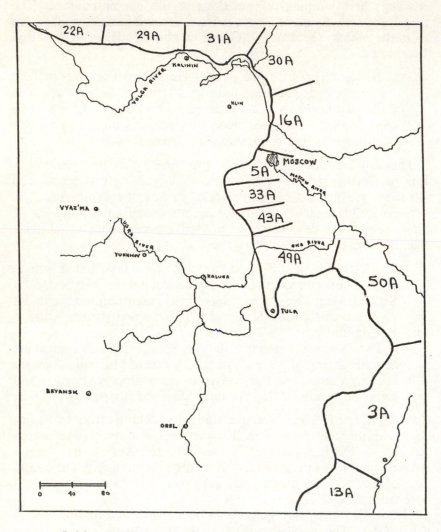

5. Moscow, German intelligence assessment, 4 December 1941

his captors, "The German Armed Forces High Command did not have intelligence about the preparations of the Soviet counter-offensive around Moscow."[22]

On 5 December the new Soviet offensive began, spearheaded by the three undetected armies. Within a week German forces were hard pressed to withdraw their forces from the Moscow region in

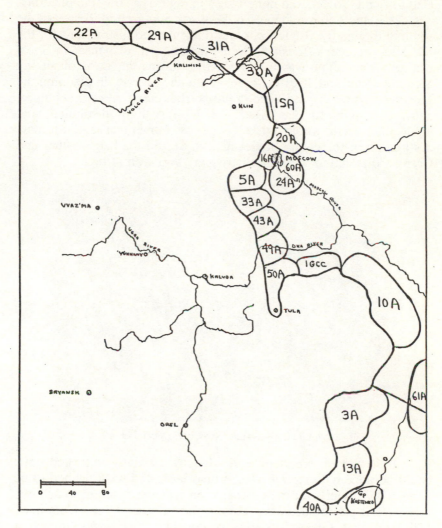

6. Moscow, Soviet dispositions, 4 December 1941

good order. Belatedly, on 8 December Halder noted, "Northwest of Moscow, Twentieth Russian Army has been in action since 6 December."[23]

Though the German forces were surprised by the ferocity of the Soviet Moscow counter-attack, it is by no means clear that the surprise was the result of an efficient Soviet *maskirovka* plan.

Certainly the Soviets did not engage in cohesive strategic planning. Attacks in the Leningrad area to the north and around Rostov in the south, although the Soviets cite them as planned distractions for the Moscow counter-offensive, were actually a response to local conditions and in no way weakened the German intention of seizing Moscow. Additionally, the Soviet haste and secrecy in planning the Moscow operation militated against the creation of a comprehensive *maskirovka* plan. Radio discipline, light discipline, and night movement masked the scope of movement and ultimate destination of relocating Soviet forces. So did the bad weather and German distraction with the distressing situation at hand.

3. Soviet infantry assault, Moscow, December, 1941

At best, Soviet experiences at Moscow partially indicated what could be done with *maskirovka*. It also indicated what needed to be done. The Soviet's ultimate frustration was their failure to achieve their strategic objectives. This spurred the High Command (*STAVKA* and General Staff) to consider a broader range of *maskirovka* measures that could contribute to even greater success in future operations. Moscow was only the first lesson in a long combat education.

MOSCOW, JANUARY 1942

In December 1941 the Soviet High Command had struck at German forces at the culminating point of the German offensive, when they felt German forces were reaching the point of exhaustion. This calculated aspect of Soviet motivation was tinged with a note of desperation on the part of the *STAVKA*, for there was no place for Soviet forces to withdraw without abandoning Moscow, the symbol of Russian power, to the Germans. Thus a certain abandon had characterized the counter-offensive which, in part, explained the huge human cost of the effort. This curious combination of calculation and desperation took its toll on German forces which had felt, and desperately hoped, that victory was near after six months of unexpectedly hard fighting.

The pressure of the Soviet attack collapsed the German front in several sectors and, for the first time in the war, German generals experienced the frightening prospect of losing control of the situation. In the end, the harsh winter conditions which had weakened German offensive capabilities also took a toll on the advancing Soviets. Ill equipped for mobile operations and lacking a supply system adequate to support such a major effort, the Soviet forces' advance ground to a halt in late December. By then Army Group Center found itself deployed in a huge salient jutting eastward toward Moscow from Kalinin in the north to Kirov in the south. All along this strategic sector German units clung for dear life to their defenses waiting for the Soviet offensive impulse to expire.

In ordinary circumstances it would have certainly been time for the Soviets to halt their forces, replenish and reequip their units, and consolidate their gains. But these were not ordinary times. The *STAVKA* and Stalin sensed imminent victory. Having invested major reserves in heavy and costly combat, the *STAVKA* felt it was now time to reap the ultimate reward – the destruction of Army Group Center. It appeared that only a final blow need be struck to accomplish that goal.

In early January the *STAVKA* ordered the Northwestern, Kalinin, and Western Fronts to mount fresh offensives fueled by the commitment of fresh *STAVKA* reserves. These new operations would develop on a broad front from Lake Seliger in the north to Mosal'sk in the south. Deep Soviet thrusts would cut into both flanks of Army Group Center, unite at Vyaz'ma, and entrap the Germans, while other Soviet forces would strike hammer blows directly at German positions west of Moscow. An additional deep strike from the north would penetrate the forests near Toropets and cut German communication lines west of Smolensk.

Such was the Soviet grand design. Fueled by unbridled optimism and remnants of that earlier desperation, in most instances the

Soviets bothered little to conceal their intent since German intelligence had an easy time keeping track of those Soviet forces which had been engaging them since early December (see maps 7 and 8). The Soviets had learned from their December operations that in sectors where combat was heaviest or where the Germans were weakest, concealed offensive preparations were indeed possible. They were also possible in regions which the Germans considered unsuited for combat operations. The Soviets had also learned that it was possible to conceal regrouping of forces within portions of the front.

Armed with their experiences of December, the Soviets set about planning a new wave of offensive operations. This time they sought to conceal their preparations, primarily on the Germans' north flank where they intended to commit another fresh reserve army.

Toropets–Kholm

On the northern flank of the proposed offensive the *STAVKA* ordered the Northwestern Front to attack with 3d and 4th Shock Armies from the Ostashkov region toward Toropets, Velizh, and Rudnya and, in cooperation with the Kalinin Front on its left flank, to penetrate south to cut the road running west of Smolensk.[24] On 2 January the Northwestern Front commander, Lieutenant General P.A. Kurochkin, issued implementing orders to his 3d and 4th Shock Armies. The armies were to concentrate between Dolmatikha on Lake Seliger to Selishche on Lake Volga on roughly a 70 kilometer front, less than half of which comprised frozen lakes. The two armies would thrust southwest and south toward Toropets and Smolensk. On the two shock armies' left flank 22d Army would occupy a secondary sector and further east, on the Northwestern Front's left flank, the 39th and 29th Armies would conduct the main attack of the Kalinin Front southward through Rzhev toward Sychevka and Vyaz'ma.

Kurochkin ordered his two army commanders to conceal their offensive preparations and surprise the overextended German forces in the region. The severe winter weather and difficult terrain conditions, which inhibited offensive preparations, also contributed to successful *maskirovka*. Winter temperatures dropped as low as minus 30 degrees centigrade, and snow cover ranged from 70 cms to 1.5 m. General A.I. Yeremenko, commander of 4th Shock Army, accurately described the terrain in the Northwestern Front's offensive sector:

The terrain, which consisted basically of forests, swamps and lakes was difficult for forces to operate in. Besides that, there were many rivers. In the northern and central parts of the region, namely where the army operated, the terrain was 85% forest covered, the territory around the river sources was a forest reserve, and the forest was protected from any wood-cutters by the strictest laws. Here no cuttings had been made.[25]

Both commanders, Yeremenko of 4th Shock Army and Lieutenant General M.A. Purkayev of 3d Shock Army, strove to exploit that terrain in their *maskirovka* planning. Yeremenko had assumed command of 4th Shock Army on 25 December, the same day that the army dropped its former designation (27th Army). While retaining a portion of 27th Army units, Yeremenko received from the *STAVKA* reserve four rifle divisions and ten ski battalions to use in the new offensive. Initially, the army consisted of eight rifle divisions, three rifle brigades, three tank battalions, and ten ski battalions.[26]

The 249th Rifle Division (of former 27th Army) covered the forward deployment of remaining 4th Shock Army units providing an opaque shield behind which Yeremenko could implement his *maskirovka* planning. The 249th was well suited for this task, for it was composed of experienced border guard troops who had served before the war and in the initial phases of the war. Yeremenko assigned the 249th the additional mission of reconnaissance, for the Soviet intelligence picture in that sector was fragmentary at best.[27]

Yeremenko's operational plan called for a main attack by two rifle divisions through Peno and Andreapol' to Toropets with one rifle division covering each flank. An additional rifle brigade was echeloned behind the left flank, one rifle division and two rifle brigades were in second echelon, and one rifle brigade was in reserve. The tank battalions reinforced the main attack force. The *front* commander, however, modified Yeremenko's plan by requiring him to launch an attack on his right flank, in support of 3d Shock Army's thrust. Ultimately, Yeremenko deployed for a main attack with three rifle divisions in first echelon (249th, 332d, 334th) backed up by a rifle brigade (21st) and a second main thrust on the right by one rifle division (360th) and a reinforced ski battalion backed up by a rifle brigade (48th). One rifle division (358th) and one rifle brigade (51st) were in reserve.[28] To confuse the Germans, Yeremenko planned to commence his attacks at night over a period of three days beginning on 8 January.

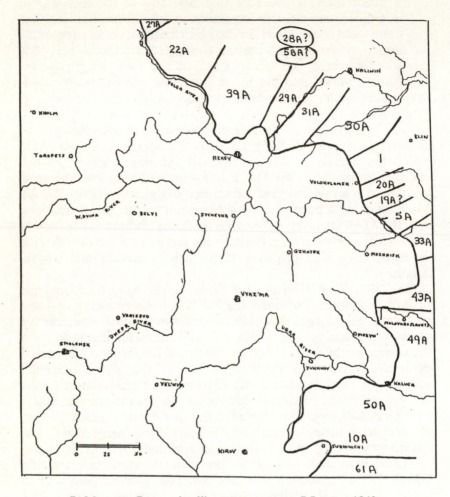

7. Moscow, German intelligence assessment, 7 January 1942

During planning for the operation, Yeremenko instituted strict *maskirovka* measures to maintain operational secrecy. Operational planning was restricted to the chiefs of army forces and services, and unit commanders knew only of those plans that pertained to their army units. At times this produced overlapping work and confusion, particularly regarding rear services support, since rear service personnel learned of the actual attack sectors only on the eve of the attack.[29]

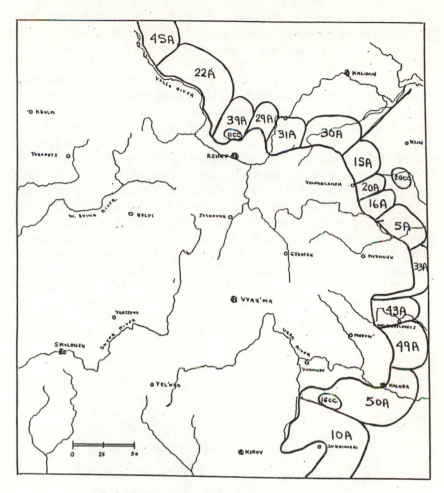

8. Moscow, Soviet dispositions, 7 January 1942

Yeremenko used the 7–10 days prior to the offensive to move his units forward and deploy them for combat, an especially difficult task in light of the terrain and the fact that the nearest railroad was 40 kilometers from the immediate army assembly area. Despite the difficulties, troop deployments were completed by the evening of 7 January.

Special attention was paid to maintaining the secrecy of force redeployments. Four rifle divisions (332d, 334th, 358th, 360th) were transported from the Moscow area to Ostashkov by truck; the rifle brigades, artillery, and tank units by rail; and the ski battalions on foot. The Northwestern Front and 4th Shock Army staffs created special groups to coordinate troop movements into the concentration areas. All movement by rail or road occurred at night, and final movement into jumping-off positions took place only 24 hours prior to the attack. These movement control measures were so severe that some second echelon units arrived late in their assembly areas.[30] Frontal aviation sought to disrupt enemy air reconnaissance. At the last minute, Yeremenko's shock groups replaced the covering units of the 249th Rifle Division in forward attack positions.

German documents attest to the efficiency of Yeremenko's *maskirovka* measures (see maps 9 and 10). German situation maps of 8, 9, and 10 January portray the 249th Rifle Division of 27th Army as defending in the Ostashkov–Lake Volga sector backed up by a cavalry division (46th), which actually was located further east in 39th Army's sector, and by the 334th Rifle Division. Thus German intelligence detected two rifle divisions and a cavalry division in a sector where five rifle divisions and four rifle brigades had concentrated for an attack. Well after the attack commenced, the Germans still failed to note the Soviet redeployments. On 12 January the Germans recognized the presence of the 332d Rifle

4. Soviet tank and infantry assault, Moscow, January 1942

Division. On 16 January, eight days after the Soviet attack, German intelligence maps noted the redesignation of 27th Army as 4th Shock Army. Only by 24 January did the German intelligence picture mature enough to recognize all 4th Shock Army units. By that time the Soviet attack had penetrated well into the German rear area.

3d Shock Army also carefully masked preparations for its offensive. General Purkayev had assumed command of the army (formerly 60th Army) on 25 December in the Moscow area. After deployment to the Lake Seliger area, his army consisted of three rifle divisions (23d, 33d, 257th), six rifle brigades (20th, 27th, 31st, 42d, 45th, 54th), one tank battalion, and six ski battalions.[31] Operational planning and the forward deployment of 3d Shock Army was similar to that of 4th Shock Army and terrain and time constraints on planning were almost identical. Purkayev organized his attack with three rifle divisions (23d, 33d, 257th) and one rifle brigade (20th) in first echelon, three rifle brigades (27th, 31st, 45th) in second echelon, and two rifle brigades (42d, 54th) in reserve.

Purkayev, like Yeremenko, successfully deceived German intelligence. On 10 January German intelligence noted two divisions (23d, 33d) of Soviet 27th Army operating where Purkayev's entire army was deployed. German intelligence noted the existence of 3d Shock Army on 16 January, and between 16 and 24 January it identified the remaining portion of Purkayev's actual force. By this time Purkayev's and Yeremenko's forces were almost 100 kilometers into the German rear area.

In the Toropets–Kholm operation the Soviets capitalized on bad terrain and weather to implement effective *maskirovka* measures. They were assisted by German preoccupation with what they thought were the most critical sectors of the front, namely those facing the Kalinin, Moscow, and Kaluga regions – where the bulk of German forces were deployed. The nature of the terrain and the paucity of German forces defending it probably contributed to the faulty German intelligence picture. But so did Soviet *maskirovka*, for ultimately the Germans identified the attacking Soviet units in time to halt the Soviet drive short of Smolensk but only after the Soviets had created a large salient in their rear.

It is interesting to compare the German intelligence picture in this sector with that in areas adjacent to 3d and 4th Shock Army. On 4th Shock Army's left flank, near Rzhev, the Soviets deployed 22d Army's three rifle divisions (179th, 186th, 178th) on an extended front, and 39th Army with six rifle divisions (361st, 373d, 355th,

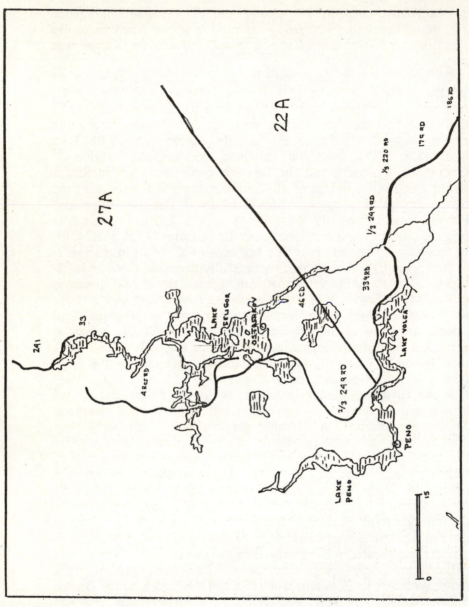

9. Toropets–Kholm, German intelligence assessment, 8 January 1942

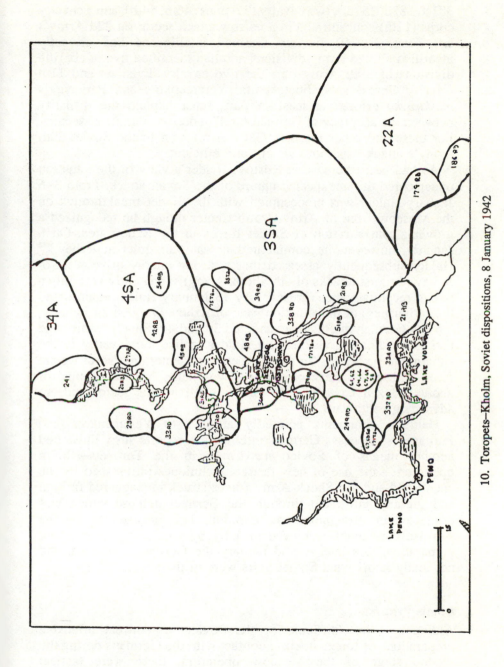

10. Toropets–Kholm, Soviet dispositions, 8 January 1942

381st, 183d, 357th), two cavalry divisions (46th, 54th), and a cavalry corps (11th) concentrated in a narrow attack sector on 22d Army's left flank. By 10 January German intelligence had correctly identified all 22d Army divisions and had identified five of six rifle divisions of 39th Army plus the two cavalry divisions and 11th Cavalry Corps' subordinate units. Yeremenko's and Purkayev's *maskirovka* efforts, at least in part, must explain the disparity between the accuracy of German intelligence work in these sectors. For these and other reasons, German reaction to the Soviet 39th Army's attack was more violent and efficient.

As had been the case at Rostov, Halder's view of the situation underscored the unexpected nature of the Soviet attack. From 3–6 January Halder was preoccupied with the Soviet breakthrough on the Moscow front of Army Group Center though he recognized a growing concentration of Soviet forces in the Rzhev area. On 8 January, however, he commented it was "all quiet at Rzhev."[32] Halder subsequently assessed that a strong enemy drive west of Rzhev (the first attacks of 4th Shock Army) "apparently was only a strong reconnaissance thrust."[33] By 13 January Halder again noted the seriousness of the situation west of Rzhev. Only on 24 January, the day German intelligence detected 3d and 4th Shock Armies and their subordinate divisions, did Halder realize the severity of the situation as he wrote, "In the gap between Center and North we are faced with a full stage offensive. Two enemy 'assault groups' of about a dozen Divs have broken through in this sector and are advancing southward."[34]

Halder's comments pointedly attested to Yeremenko's and Purkayev's success. German intelligence reports also illustrated another means of Soviet *maskirovka* in the Toropets–Kholm operation – the use of new tactical techniques unforeseen by the enemy. 3d and 4th Shock Army forces struck in staggered fashion and literally infiltrated through the German defense which was organized in strongpoint configuration. This only reinforced the surprise the Soviets achieved initially by concealing their attack preparations. As late as mid-January the German commands did not really know what Soviet units were in their rear.

Rzhev–Vyaz'ma

Although it was difficult for the Soviets to conceal offensive preparations of forces in close contact with the Germans during the second stage of the Moscow operation, there were tactical instances, involving Soviet 20th Army, where Soviet *maskirovka* measures succeeded.

Before the 10 January offensive, 20th Army deceived the Germans regarding the location of the main Soviet assault.[35] 20th Army was to conduct the Western Front main attack on the *front* right flank supported by 1st Shock and 16th Armies. It was to penetrate German defenses west of Volokolamsk and advance to Shakhovskii to link up with the Kalinin Front's 39th and 29th Armies and destroy surrounded elements of German Ninth Army and Third Panzer Army. 20th Army, after a two week pause to regroup and resupply, had to penetrate relatively strong German defenses with two rifle divisions, seven rifle brigades, and three tank brigades. Major General L.M. Dovator's 2d Guards Cavalry Corps was to exploit the attack. 20th Army planned to deceive the Germans as to the location of the main attack by firing an artillery preparation at 0800 10 January where two rifle brigades of the army were to make a supporting attack. One hour later a new artillery preparation would precede the Red Army main attack in a different sector. The false artillery preparation disoriented the Germans and, after the real one and one-half hour preparation, 20th Army forces successfully (but slowly) penetrated the German tactical defenses.

On a second occasion, in mid-February 20th Army again used *maskirovka* to spur on a flagging offensive. During the period 10–19 February 1942, 20th Army simulated a false concentration of forces on its right flank opposite German forces defending along the Lama River. The Soviets used false guns and tanks, decoy tank engine noise, and radio signals imitating assembling units; and the army operations department arranged for deceptive radio transmissions to simulate a false concentration. Similar deceptive measures took place on secondary directions across the front, and numerous campfires were lit in false concentration areas. The Germans shifted forces to the regions of false concentrations and conducted numerous air sorties over the area.[36]

During January 1942 the Western Front commander ordered use of passive *maskirovka* measures to augment the active deception. Combat units were moved from the front to the rear where offensives were being prepared. In other sectors troops moved forward, radio transmissions increased, false batteries and tank and vehicle mock-ups were implaced, new roads were laid, reconnaissance intensified, tank concentrations were formed, and air reconnaissance increased.[37] Other *front* commanders issued similar orders.

During the Moscow operations and elsewhere on the Eastern

Front, Soviet *maskirovka* efforts were crude and intermittent. 3d and 4th Shock Armies' performance at Toropets and 20th Army's actions along the Lama River were exceptions to the rule. As one Soviet analyst noted:

> However, the skill to achieve surprise and to use original means of tricking the enemy were not worked out immediately by commanders, and forces still for a long time were not trained for strict observation of *maskirovka* discipline. Measures to trick the enemy often turned out unconvincing and primitive, and the effect was inconsiderable.[38]

LYUBAN, JANUARY 1942

After their success in the initial stages of the Moscow counter-offensive, in January 1942 the *STAVKA* ordered Soviet forces all along the Eastern Front to join the offensive. While Soviet forces were resuming offensive operations in the Moscow region, other Soviet *fronts* from the Baltic to the Black Seas prepared and conducted offensives of their own (see map 11). The Soviets intended to apply maximum pressure on the Germans, prevent reinforcement of Army Group Center, and ultimately destroy the army group.

In the Leningrad area the Soviets sought to break the German stranglehold on the city and, if possible, drive German forces back into the Baltic states. Urged on by the *STAVKA*, the Leningrad and Volkhov Fronts planned a two-front operation with thrusts from Leningrad proper and across the Volkhov River to encircle and destroy German forces southeast and east of Leningrad.

The *STAVKA* concept for the operation, issued on 17 December 1941, called for Leningrad and Volkhov Front forces to converge on Lyuban and destroy German forces located in the salient east and southwest of Leningrad. The Volkhov Front (consisting of 4th, 59th, 2d Shock, and 52d Armies) was to attack westward through German defenses along the Volkhov River to the Lyuban area, then advance northwestward to join the Leningrad Front forces and encircle German forces.[39]

General K. A. Meretskov, Volkhov Front commander, decided to make his main attack with 59th and 2d Shock Armies to penetrate German defenses near Spasskaya Polist' and exploit to link up with the Leningrad Front's 54th Army. His forces were to concentrate by 24 December and attack on 7 January.[40] To conceal the assembly of

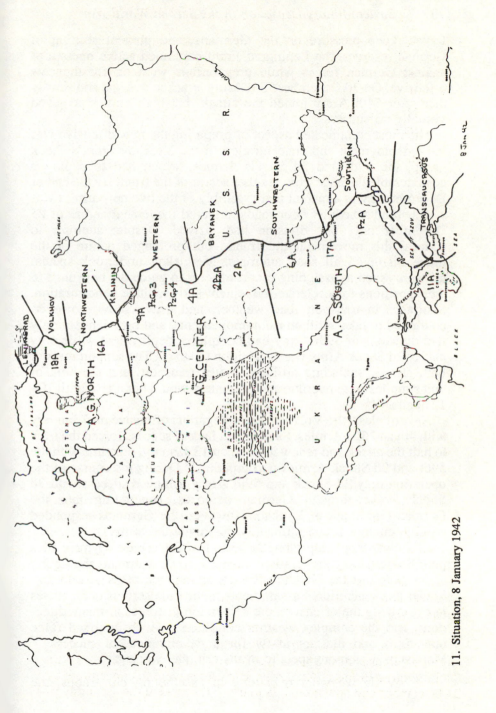

11. Situation, 8 January 1942

forces, keep pressure on the Germans, and prevent shifting of German reserves, the Leningrad Front continued active operations against German forces while preparations went on for the new offensive. On 20 December 55th Army attacked at Mga, and shortly thereafter 54th Army joined the attack, but both armies achieved virtually no success.

The most complicated aspect of preparing the new offensive was the redeployment and concentration of the Volkhov Front's shock group, the 59th and 2d Shock Armies, which had to deploy a considerable distance from another sector of the front. By the end of December it was apparent that assembly of the two new armies was well behind schedule. Poor roads hindered movement and as of 25 December only one division had arrived. Despite attempts to conceal this movement, the frantic but prolonged nature of the move disrupted all such attempts. Meretskov undertook special measures such as assigning escort officers to guide the new units to their positions to accelerate movement and facilitate concentration. Shortages in transport, bad weather, and heavy snow, however, continued to take a toll on troop movements; and by 7 January only five divisions of 59th Army had completed deployment while only half of 2d Shock Army was in position to attack. The support units of both armies, including artillery, motor transport, and the bulk of unit supplies were overdue and ultimately would not arrive until 10–12 January.[41]

Nevertheless, the Volkhov Front began its offensive on 7 January with 4th and 52d Armies. Subsequent lack of success forced the *front* to halt the attack and renew it again on 13 January, this time with the 59th and 2d Shock Armies participating.[42] During the course of the operation only 2d Shock and 59th Army achieved success; and 2d Shock broke through German defenses, penetrating into the German rear south of Lyuban. However, the Germans responded rapidly, encircled, and ultimately destroyed the army.

It is clear that the prolonged period of force redeployment plus poor Soviet attack preparations revealed to the Germans the timing and location of the Volkhov Front's attack (see maps 12 and 13). Soviet post-operational assessments noted "the serious deficiencies in organizing the offensive, the dispersion of forces in many directions, and the complex weather conditions, which inhibited force operations and did not allow for a development of success."[43] Meretskov was more specific in his critique, writing:

While we were over-long in assembling our troops, the

Germans were organizing their defenses. Their reconnaissance not only discovered the *front* was preparing an attack, but also fairly accurately established the direction of our main blow. Here is what we read in the captured January war diary of Army Group North: "Intelligence reports clearly indicate that the enemy's main blow will be delivered against the frontage of the 126th Infantry Division and the right flank of the 215th Infantry Division. Moreover, large scale preparations for offensive operations have been observed in the vicinity of the Gruzino and Kiriski bridgeheads, as well as on the army's northeastern sector, on either side of Pogostye."[44]

German intelligence records confirm Meretskov's judgement, as did Halder, who recorded in his diary on 7 January, after several days of quiet in the north: "In Army Group North an attack on Chudovo must be expected soon according to deserter reports. Shifting of forces to the Ladogo front across the lake."[45] With this information in their possession, the Germans regrouped their forces and reinforced units in the Lyuban area, in particular their XXXIX Motorized Corps. Additionally, the Germans reinforced their defenses along the Volkhov River. All of these measures contributed to the rapid German response to the Soviet attack and their encirclement of 2d Shock Army. During the operation, subsequent Soviet attempts to regroup also met with failure.

Soviet *maskirovka* failures in the Lyuban operation were typical of those experienced by Soviet commanders during the winter offensive of January 1942. Staff organization was poor, troop experience minimal, and virtually all offensives were hastily planned. In addition, dismal weather conditions, treacherous roads, and poor communications delayed and hampered timely assembly of forces. Ensuing Soviet haste in driving tired forces forward made adherence to strict and skillful *maskirovka* measures simply a folly.

BARVENKOVO–LOZOVAYA, JANUARY 1942

While Soviet *fronts* were conducting offensive operations in the Leningrad and Moscow regions, the *STAVKA* ordered its forces operating in southern Russia to do likewise. Already, in December, the Southern Front had sought to capitalize on its victories around Rostov by attacking the left flank of First Panzer Army in the

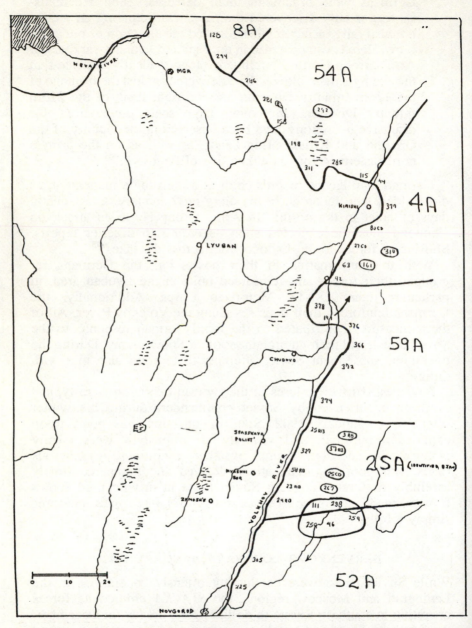

12. Lyuban, German intelligence assessment, 12 January 1942

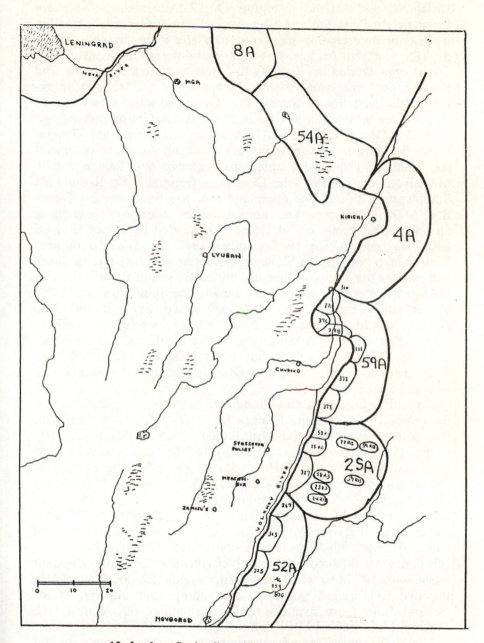

13. Lyuban, Soviet dispositions, 12 January 1942

Lisichansk and Artemovsk region. On 22 December the Southern Front's right flank 6th and 12th Armies struck German forces but made only imperceptible gains although later joined in the attack by the 18th and 37th Armies west of Voroshilovgrad. Here, also, poor Soviet organization, an inability to adjust to winter conditions, and Soviet failure to conceal offensive preparations and troop redeployments hindered Soviet forces. The Germans were able to move fresh forces into action in time to block the Soviet offensive.

On 25 December, the *STAVKA* appointed Lieutenant General R. Ya. Malinovsky, former commander of 6th Army, to command the Southern Front with orders to organize and launch a new offensive in cooperation with Lieutenant General F. Ya. Kostenko's Southwestern Front. The commander of the Southwestern Direction, Marshal Timoshenko, coordinated the operation by creating an operational group on 14 December, headed by Major General I. Kh. Bagramyan. On 19 December 1941 the *STAVKA* ordered Timoshenko "to strike a blow against German Army Group South and liberate the Donbas" by a combined assault of the left flank of the Southwestern Front and right flank of the Southern Front.[46] The Southwestern Front's 6th Army, supported by 21st and 38th Armies, would advance to secure Khar'kov while the Southern Front's 57th and 37th Armies would strike southwest and south into the Donets Basin. The 9th Army would remain in reserve behind 57th Army, under Southwestern Direction control. The attack was to begin on 12 January.

Difficult winter conditions hindered offensive preparations and the extensive regrouping of forces necessary to carry out the plan. Bagramyan noted, "We could fulfill the mission in only one circumstance: if our offensive was a surprise for the Germans, both tactically and operationally."[47] The problem was achieving surprise in such harsh conditions. Major General K. S. Moskalenko's 6th Army (the largest in the Southwestern Front), from 5 to 12 January, had to truncate its front lines from a width of 120 kilometers to 55 kilometers by turning over two rifle divisions and one cavalry division on its left flank to 59th Army and by concentrating its remaining three rifle divisions and three newly received rifle divisions in its new main attack sector.[48] Meanwhile, 6th Army conducted local attacks to improve its forward positions. (To complicate matters, Major General A. M. Gorodnyansky took command of 6th Army on 12 January, but accepted Moskalenko's plan.)

The challenge of secretly regrouping was even greater for the Southern Front. It had to shift two armies (9th and 37th) a distance of over 100 kilometers from its left flank to its right flank, and had to integrate into its composition the 57th Army, assigned on 3 January from the *STAVKA* reserves. The *STAVKA* directed the *front* to employ strict *maskirovka* measures to conceal its offensive preparations.[49]

Bagramyan's operational group supervised Southern Front planning. Both Timoshenko and Malinovsky emphasized the necessity to conceal the regrouping movements and the main attack direction, partly through strict movement security and partly by using radio disinformation to portray false Soviet intentions to attack from the left wing of the Southern Front. To assist Bagramyan, the *STAVKA* dispatched fresh materials derived from Soviet experiences during the December offensive around Moscow.

Front Chief of Staff Major General Antonov supervised planning and implemented measures similar to those he had used during the Rostov counter-offensive. He restricted the size of the planning group, instituted strict sequential planning, limited the number of copies of the plan, forbade the creation and use of any notes or written information concerning those plans, and severely restricted all communications traffic. During the day the army group either conducted or simulated movements of large forces to the south where signal units simulated a false concentration of forces, and engineer units used mock-up tanks and other engineer means to reinforce the false image.[50]

The Southern Front regrouped at an agonizingly slow pace. 9th and 37th Armies turned over their left flank sectors to 56th Army and moved north to occupy new positions. Actual 9th and 37th Armies' movements to the north were conducted at night, under severe blackout conditions, although bad weather and the poor road net delayed the ultimate concentration of forces into their attack positions. (A severe seven day blizzard inhibited 37th Army movements but did prevent the Germans from carrying out air reconnaissance.) An extensive road guards system helped direct traffic northward, and strict security concealed activity at all rail stations and road junctions. 37th Army's rail movement, which would normally have taken 10 hours to complete, actually took 38–50 hours. Ultimately the army deployed into positions between 57th and 12th Armies. 57th Army had deployed forward from the rear into positions between Izyum and Krasnyi Liman. At the same time 9th Army deployed into *front* second echelon positions south of Sviatovo, behind 57th Army. Compounding the complexity of these movements 1st, 5th, and 6th Cavalry Corps regrouped to reserve positions in their respective *fronts*, and the Southern Front headquarters displaced from Kamensk, on the *front's* south flank, northward to Starobel'sk. The apparent difficulties in regrouping forced the *STAVKA* to accede to the Southwestern Direction's request to postpone the start of the offensive until 18 January.[51]

While seeking to regroup secretly and conceal the area of the main attack, the Soviets also adopted new attack means to conceal the time of attack. By early 1942 the Soviets usually preceded their attack with an artillery preparation. Noticing this, the Germans would leave forward trenches unmanned until the artillery preparation had ended. Then German infantry would reoccupy the trenches and greet the advancing Soviet infantry. On this occasion Soviet forces commenced barrage fire on enemy trenches, then after 10 minutes, began scattered methodical fire. The German infantry left their cover and occupied forward positions in expectation of the infantry assault. Instead, they were hammered by a new barrage on their forward positions. The Soviets repeated this procedure several times at different intervals. Finally the artillery of all neighboring units on the flanks of the Soviet shock group opened fire to support the penetration.[52] The infantry assault followed at 0500 on 18 January.

These operational and tactical measures permitted the Soviets to achieve a considerable amount of surprise. Lieutenant General A.F. von Bechtolzheim, Chief of Staff of German Sixth Army's XXIX Army Corps, later commented on the efficiency of Soviet regroupment *maskirovka*, stating:

> Air reconnaissance had detected baffling rail movements in the Kupjansk area east of Khar'kov, but the enemy in this season of long nights managed to conceal its concentrations to such an extent that no indicators of enemy troops behind the front lines had filtered out. Rail movements pointed rather to an attack on Khar'kov north of Balaklaya .... It was a complete surprise, therefore, for the German command when the organized Soviet attack broke loose in the small hours of January 18th in two wedges at Izyum proper where the Soviets had regained a small bridgehead on the southern bank of the river and at Savintsy.[53]

Halder's diary confirmed von Bechtolzheim's judgements. On 16 January Halder noted, "In AGp-South, the enemy is apparently closing up for an attack between IV Corps and the area north of

Khar'kov."[54] The following day Halder laconically acknowledged an attack against the left wing of Seventeenth Army and against Sixth Army had begun. Finally, on 19 January, Halder recognized the gravity of the situation, stating:

> On the northern front of Seventeenth Army and in some sectors of Sixth Army the enemy has now opened his full scale offensive, which earlier indications [radio intercepts] had linked with Khar'kov. The most critical spot is the boundary of Seventeenth and Sixth Armies. We shall go through trying days before this crisis is resolved.[55]

German intelligence records indicate the degree of surprise the Soviets achieved (see maps 14 and 15). On the night of 18 January the Germans had detected three to four of 57th Army's six divisions and three to four of 37th Army's six divisions but was uncertain as to the armies' presence. None of 9th Army's units were recognized, and the Germans thought that army and 37th Army were still in the south. More important, German intelligence had not detected two of the three Soviet cavalry corps and Soviet concentration for the assault. They finally recognized 57th and 37th Armies' presence on 20 January and 30 January, respectively.

Soviet concealed offensive preparations for the Barvenkovo–Lozovaya operation were particularly effective in light of the weather obstacles which had to be overcome. This was probably due to the growing experience of the Southwestern Direction and *front* commanders, Timoshenko and Malinovsky, and the, by now, proven staff work supervised by the efficient Antonov who would soon find himself serving on the General Staff in Moscow. Soviet *maskirovka* measures were still crude, but there was more systematic deception planning and even attempts at disinformation, through the use of false communications and dummy assembly areas. Unfortunately for the Soviets, within several months the fruits of that success evaporated in the Khar'kov disaster of May 1942.

KHAR'KOV, MAY 1942

As spring approached on the Eastern Front, both sides sought to seize the initiative and achieve strategic goals unrealized in 1941 (see map 16). The Germans intensely examined strategic questions and argued about what strategic military goals Germany should strive to realize in 1942. Simultaneously, the Soviet High Command sought to divine German strategic intentions and resume active

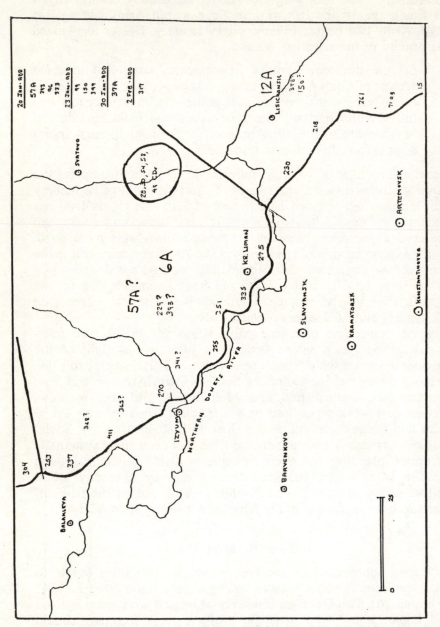

14. Barvenkovo–Lozovaya, German intelligence assessment, 18 January 1942

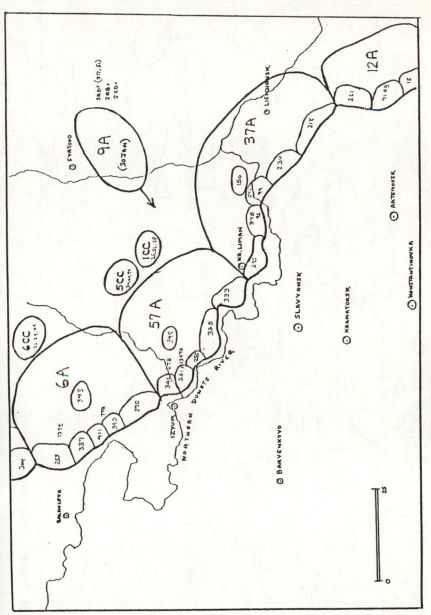

15. Barvenkovo–Lozovaya, Soviet dispositions, 18 January 1942

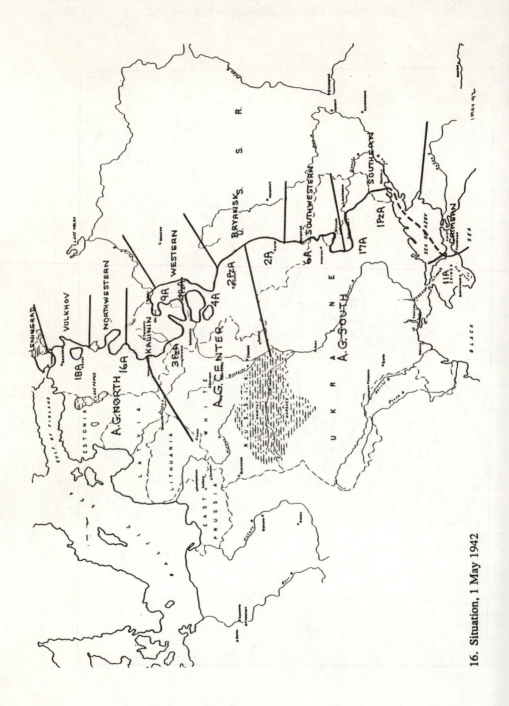

16. Situation, 1 May 1942

operations to maintain the initiative which had passed into their hands in December 1941.

Ultimately Hitler defined German strategic intentions but not without vociferous arguments from elements of the German High Command. Hitler decided that Germany would resume the strategic offensive in early summer, but unlike the offensive of 1941 which had unfolded in three axes, that of 1942 would thrust across southern Russia into the economically valuable Caucasus region. Thereafter, with Soviet defensive strength weakened and her economic base undermined, German armies would loosen the Soviet grip on Leningrad. This was basically the concept of Operation "Blau," the strategic drive which would end in disaster at Stalingrad. Within a few months the Germans would begin a major strategic deception of their own designed to reinforce the impression in the Soviets' minds that the focus of German strategic efforts would occur on the Moscow axis.[56]

The Soviet High Command and Stalin, transfixed by the traumatic ebb and flow of combat in the Moscow area in late 1941 and early 1942, allowed the Moscow axis to dominate their attention and plans for the summer of 1942. Zhukov recalled:

> Stalin believed that in the summer of 1942 the Germans would be able to carry out large scale offensive operations simultaneously in two strategic directions – most likely at Moscow and in the south of the country .... Of the two directions where, as Stalin believed, the enemy could attempt strategic operations, he was above all concerned about the Moscow direction where over 70 German divisions operated.[57]

While Chief of the General Staff, General B.M. Shaposhnikov, argued for the cautious conduct of a strategic defense, Stalin demanded active limited offensive activity to pre-empt German action or distract them from their principal aim. Consequently, Stalin ordered offensives to be conducted in the Khar'kov sector, in the Crimea, and on less important directions. Meanwhile, Stalin concentrated the bulk of Soviet strategic reserves in the Orel–Kursk sector to defend the southwestern approaches to Moscow.[58] The then Chief of the Operations Department of the General Staff, General A.M. Vasilevsky, recalled, "The largest group of German forces (more than 70 divisions) were located on the Moscow direction. That provided the *STAVKA* and General Staff the basis to presume that, with the beginning of the summer period, the enemy would try to deliver the decisive blow against us, namely on the

Central direction. That opinion, as was well known to me, was shared by the commanders of the majority of the *fronts*."[59] By 15 March the *STAVKA* concept for 1942 operations was complete. It envisioned the conduct of an active strategic defense, a build-up of reserves, and then a resumption of the decisive offensive on the Moscow–Smolensk direction. Thus, while the German High Command prepared to initiate a major strategic offensive in southern Russia, the *STAVKA* implemented a strategic defensive with supporting operational thrusts, also in the south. Both sides would implement deception plans to support their offensive intentions.

The Soviet Southwestern Direction received orders to prepare a major spring offensive in the Khar'kov region. On 30 March Stalin and the *STAVKA* enunciated the concept of the operation which called for a two-pronged attack by the Southwestern Front to secure Khar'kov, while the Southern Front would secure the southern flank of attacking Soviet forces.[60] Marshal Timoshenko, commanding both the Southwestern Direction and the Southwestern Front, was to plan the attack along with his chief of staff, Bagramyan, who recalled:

> From the point of view of strategy and operational art the intention of our High Command to undertake the Khar'kov operation in May 1942 was correct since it was based on the firmly held *STAVKA* view, that with the beginning of the summer campaign, Hitler's High Command would strike the main blow on the Moscow direction, with the aim of capturing the capital of our country – and against the forces of the Southwestern Direction simultaneously as a secondary attack by limited forces .... Personally I also firmly held that opinion, which turned out to be mistaken.[61]

Bagramyan noted that the Khar'kov operation, in addition to securing that important city, would also divert German forces from the critical assault on Moscow.

On 10 April the Southwestern Direction command presented its draft operational plan to the *STAVKA*. The plan called for a two-stage offensive against German forces defending Khar'kov. In the first stage, over a period of three days Soviet forces would penetrate German defenses north and south of Khar'kov to a depth of 20–30 kilometers. Subsequently, in the second stage, Soviet forces would encircle and destroy German forces in the Khar'kov area.

The Southwestern Front was to conduct the offensive with one shock group (28th and part of 21st and 38th Armies) rupturing German defenses near Volchansk and a second shock group (6th Army and Group Bobkin) penetrating German defenses west of Izyum. The 9th and 57th Armies of the Southern Front would cover the southern flank of the operation.[62] On 16 April Timenshenko issued orders for large scale regroupment and concentration of forces for the 4 May offensive.

The elaborate plan called for a substantial regrouping of forces under stringent security and *maskirovka* measures. The South-western Front had to concentrate its armies into attack positions, form and deploy the new 28th Army, and integrate into its structure numerous units from the *STAVKA* reserve. In addition, on 17 April the *STAVKA* ordered the *front* to create three new tank corps from tank brigades already assigned to the *front*.[63] This difficult task of creating a command and control and logistical structure for the tank corps was especially critical since these corps were to spearhead the Soviet exploitation operation. In addition, the Southern Front had to shift forces from its center and left flank to its right flank in order to fulfill its mission of covering the southern flank of the South-western Front while it conducted the operation.

The regrouping effort, which began after mid-April, was hindered by the *razputitsa* – the thaw which turned the soil into mud to a considerable depth. This problem and *maskirovka* requirements (night travel in blackout conditions) slowed the entire process and ultimately forced postponement of the offensive until 12 May.

Soviet participants in the Khar'kov operation have severely criticized the regrouping process and the efficiency of *maskirovka* measures. Because much of the regrouping force had to traverse the front laterally, the Germans detected Soviet movement. The limited preparation time exacerbated the problem by forcing hasty and often careless movement and control over regrouping forces was also lax. General Moskalenko, 38th Army commander, noted the complexity of the move stating:

> But the *front* staff and we also, in the command and staffs of the armies, did not take matters in our own hands. We did not create a single regrouping plan and did not give clear orders regarding the order and priority of crossing bridges, the conduct of road marches, the organization of air defense on the march and in concentration areas, and finally about the observation of *maskirovka*.[64]

Consequently, movement was slowed, the secrecy of those

movements was compromised, and many planned preparations were not fulfilled in time. As a result:

> Even worse was the fact that the regrouping of large masses of forces to their appointed penetration sectors occurred without required organization and secrecy. Therefore, no one was surprised that the German-Fascist command divined our plans. Having divined them, he hurriedly undertook measures to strengthen the defenses in threatened sectors .... Thus the prepared operation was not unexpected or a surprise for the enemy.[65]

Bagramyan, who was responsible for planning the operation, said little about the success of *maskirovka*. Instead he candidly highlighted the overall problem of the Soviet offensive, stating:

> Comparing the plans of both sides it is necessary to underscore one very important factor in order to understand that the Soviet High Command intended on the southern wing in the summer campaign to limit its offensive operations to missions of an operational nature, that is, to improve somewhat the position of its forces in the southwest strategic direction. Hitler's High Command decided to accomplish there a large scale strategic mission with long range aims.[66]

Although the Soviets admit to a major failure at Khar'kov in May 1942, both in terms of the strategic intelligence misjudgement and poor operational and tactical *maskirovka*, examination of German records and accounts provides evidence of some Soviet success amidst the large-scale disaster.

German intelligence picked up clear indicators of Soviet movement as early as mid-April. Halder, in his diary, noted on 17 April, "In south, opposite Kleist's front confused movement and radio silence."[67] Again on 22 April he wrote, "The movements opposite *Kleist's Group* continue. Opposite Sixth Army the enemy is shifting forces southward," presumably into the Izyum bridgehead; and he repeated that judgement on 24 and 26 April.[68] On 4 May Halder reported Soviet forces concentrating in the northwestern corner of the Izyum salient as well as attack preparations in the Volchansk sector.[69] The diary of Field Marshal Fedor von Bock, commander of Army Group South, also reflected German expectations of a Soviet attack in the Khar'kov region. As early as 8 May he expressed his fear "that the Russians may forestall us with their own attack" and noted that Sixth Army projected such an attack both at

Volchansk and Khar'kov. He also mentioned increased Soviet movements in and around the Izyum salient although "whether this is indicative of an intention to attack is not yet clear."[70] Two days later he recorded Soviet reconnaissance probing attacks in the Volchansk and Slavyansk sectors.

Yet, if German intelligence detected Soviet intent to attack, the scope of that attack clearly caught the Germans by surprise. Both Halder and von Bock evidenced alarm at the offensive's rapid progress, enough alarm to cause von Bock to suggest the conduct of immediate counter-attacks at the expense of aborting the initial stages of German Plan "Blau," a step vehemently rejected by Hitler. Von Bock recorded on 12 May, "In the afternoon it became clear that the break on VIII Corps' [6th Army] front had assumed serious proportions .... In the evening enemy armored forces were within twenty kilometers of Khar'kov."[71] Halder echoed von Bock's remarks writing, "The enemy ... has scored considerable initial successes," which, by the next day, he termed, "Grave crisis south of Khar'kov."[72] Lieutenant General M.F. von Bechtolzheim remembered the conditions prior to the Soviet attack a bit differently. He and the other corps chiefs of staffs attended a party given by Sixth Army's chief of staff in Khar'kov on the evening of the 11th. Early the following morning:

> Everybody in Khar'kov was aroused by a tremendous rumbling of artillery on the east. While the German forces at Slavyansk and Taranovka were still assembling and preparing their counterattack on the Izyum pocket, Marshal Timoshenko struck full blast at Khar'kov .... With hitherto unequalled concentrations of armor (400 tanks in a given area), the Soviets attacked in two wedges ...[73]

In part, German surprise over the ferocity and strength of the Soviet drive was a product of the failure of German intelligence to detect the full scale of Soviet force concentrations. German intelligence did not realize the Soviets had created new tank corps and deployed two of these corps into the salient. German intelligence still thought the largest Soviet armored formation was the separate tank brigade.[74]

German intelligence records indicate that on the evening of 11 May most assembled Soviet rifle units had been identified and concentration of those forces was evident (see maps 17 and 18). Some confusion still remained, primarily concerning Soviet armored forces. The Germans detected six of eleven Soviet tank

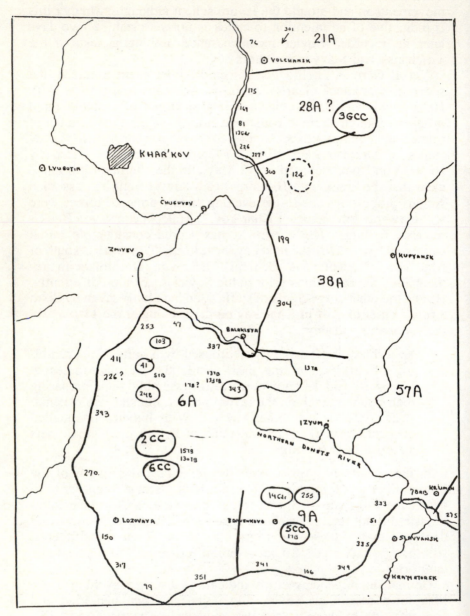

17. Khar'kov, German intelligence assessment, 11 May 1942

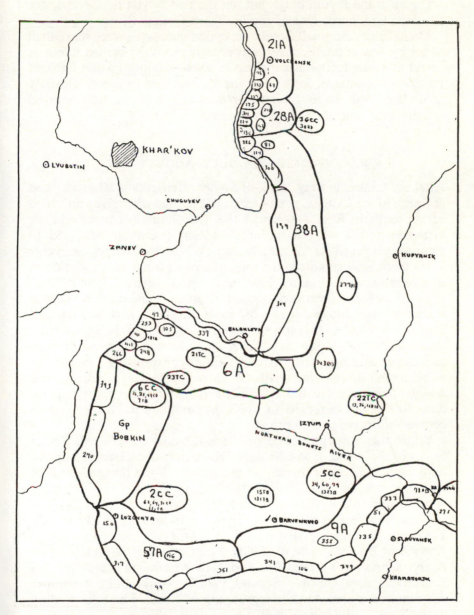

18. Khar'kov, Soviet dispositions, 11 May 1942

brigades in the Izyum bulge but not the two Soviet tank corps, nor the third tank corps east of the Northern Donets River.

On balance, the small Soviet deception successes were more than offset by Soviet intelligence failures to determine German intent or detect German forces assembling in great strength on the flank of the Soviet offensive. In the ensuing week, German forces virtually annihilated the large Soviet force which had, at first, moved triumphantly out of the Izyum salient.

RZHEV–SYCHEVKA, JULY–AUGUST 1942

After the failure, in May 1942, of Soviet offensives at Khar'kov and at Kerch in the Crimea, a new series of German offensives unfolded across southern Russia (see map 19). The Germans concealed their offensive intent with a major deception operation designed to simulate preparations for an advance on Moscow. Although events in southern Russia indicated a major German force concentration in that area, especially after late June when German Plan "Blau" began to unfold, German deception efforts prompted the Soviets to maintain large forces on the Moscow direction. In late June and July, as the Soviets began a strategic withdrawal in the south, their forces in the central region of the front undertook offensive activity to pressure German Army Group Center and force the Germans to weaken their drive in the south. The Soviet offensives in the central region ultimately created conditions for Soviet deception operations in the fall designed to mask preparations for their massive counter-offensive at Stalingrad.

While this strategic game of cat-and-mouse developed, Soviet forces of the Western and Kalinin Fronts prepared offensive operations against German forces in the Rzhev, Vyaz'ma and Bolkov regions west and southwest of Moscow. *Maskirovka* played a considerable role in these operations, but with mixed results.

These new Soviet offensive efforts began inauspiciously in July 1942 with an unsuccessful operation by the Western Front's 61st Army near Bolkhov. The plan called for General P.A. Belov's 61st Army, supported by the 10th and 16th Armies, to attack toward Bolkhov against German Second Panzer Army. Quite naturally, this required a considerable regrouping of forces which, according to the Soviets, did not go well:

> The regrouping and movement of forces to jumping-off positions was conducted without serious *maskirovka*. A series

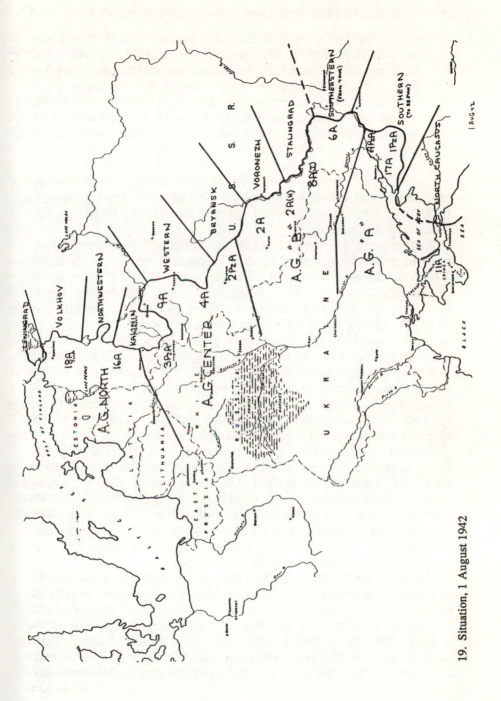

19. Situation, 1 August 1942

of formations shifted during the daytime which could not remain unnoticed by the enemy. Units of the 149th Rifle Division on the march and units of the 350th Rifle Division during movement forward into jumping-off positions were discovered and subjected to heavy artillery fire. While suffering heavy casualties, they could not occupy their jumping-off positions on time. The movement of tanks to assault positions was also poorly masked.[74]

These failures plus poor *maskirovka* of artillery deployments revealed Soviet attack intentions to the Germans. Thus, although 61st Army had clear numerical superiority over the Germans, the attack failed miserably.

Further north the Soviet Kalinin and Western Fronts prepared an even larger scale offensive against German forces in the Rzhev–Vyaz'ma salient to tie down German Army Group Center units, prevent reinforcements from being sent south, and disrupt Army Group Center plans to attack the Toropets salient.[75] On 16 July the *STAVKA* ordered the two *fronts* to conduct joint operations to clear German forces from the region north of the Volga River near Rzhev and east of Vyaz'ma around Zubtsov, Pogoreloye and Gorodishche. After two weeks of preparations, on 28 July the Kalinin Front's 29th and 30th Armies were to strike against Rzhev. Then on 31 July the Western Front's 20th and 31st Armies would join the attack from the east. Two tank corps (6th and 8th) and one cavalry corps (2d Guards) would support the Western Front force.

General I.S. Konev, Kalinin Front commander, ordered 30th Army to make the main attack on Rzhev while 29th Army struck along the Volga River toward Zubtsov. General Zhukov, commander of the Western Front, ordered 31st and 20th Armies to combine their efforts on an axis south of Zubtsov. Three days after 31st and 20th Armies' attack, on 3 August the 5th Army would join the offense followed several days later by 33d Army. *Front* artillery assets would relocate to support each offensive.[76]

The two *front* commanders and their staffs implemented a variety of measures to deceive the Germans. They used the usual means to cover regrouping and concentration of forces, and the Western Front also attempted to simulate a false troop concentration to distract German attention from the main attack sector. This involved creation of a false concentration of forces in 43d, 49th, and 50th Army sectors southward in the Yukhnov region and construction of a false anti-tank defense region on the boundary between 49th and 50th Armies.[77]

Zhukov's *maskirovka* plan was the first to require the conduct of a specific *maskirovka* operation. *Front* headquarters designated two staffs to supervise the operation, one in the 43d and 49th Armies' sectors, the other in 50th Army's sector, and specific units to carry out the *maskirovka* preparations (four *maskirovka* companies, three rifle companies, 122 vehicles, nine T-60 tanks, anti-aircraft machine guns, 11 RB5 and RB radios). These units constructed 833 mock-up tanks, vehicles, guns, fuel tanks, and mobile field kitchens. Together the *maskirovka* forces and equipment simulated rail unloading and movement and concentration of tank and motorized rifle columns into the assembly and concentration areas. Meanwhile, false radio nets passed messages from these false units to and from higher headquarters.

Since earlier attempts at simulating false unit movements had failed because German aerial reconnaissance had detected the inert nature of the mock-up equipment even if emplaced and moved at night, on this occasion real tanks and vehicles participated in the ruse to give it life and real movement. The real vehicles also laid multiple tracks to simulate actual column movements. When attacks by enemy air occurred, personnel ignited inflammables or used bottles of burning fuel to simulate real fires while returning the fire of the aircraft.[78]

Because of the *maskirovka*, German air strikes intensified against the false region of concentration and against the railhead where the false columns simulated unloading (Myatlevo), while at two other railheads 22 kilometers away the real tank corps were unloading unhindered by German aviation. The Germans also shifted critical reserves into the Yukhnov region in the expectation of a Soviet attack (three panzer and one motorized division of XXXX Panzer Corps).[79]

In the Western and Kalinin Fronts' actual attack sectors, regrouping occurred at night under strict light discipline. Maximum use was made of the heavy forests to conceal movement along the front and into the main attack areas. Lieutenant General M.A. Reiter's 20th Army required considerable regrouping to conduct the operation.[80] 20th Army was to attack in the sector of 31st Army's 251st Rifle Division. Reiter received from the *STAVKA* as reinforcements one rifle corps (one rifle division and four rifle brigades), three rifle divisions, three tank brigades, and other support units. On the eve of the operation the 251st Rifle Division of 31st Army (with its sector) reverted to 20th Army control while the three left flank rifle brigades of 20th Army reverted to 5th Army control. Before redeployment all forces participating in the attack remained in the deep army rear. Thereafter army main forces redeployed to the army's extreme right flank where the main attack would occur (the sector of 251st Rifle Division).

To conceal the redeployments all movement occurred at night beginning on the evening of 1 August. The 251st Rifle Division conducted reconnaissance for the upcoming operation while reconnaissance occurred elsewhere to confuse German intelligence. In general, all sectors conducted activities at a normal intensity. General Reiter, his chief of staff and chief of artillery personally inspected the designated attack sector. As one Soviet analyst noted:

> Therefore 20th Army delivered its main attack not from its sector but from the 251st Rifle Division sector "leased" from 31st Army which was given to 20th Army only on the eve of the operation.[81]

On 31 July and 1 August heavy rains inundated the region. Consequently, although the Kalinin Front commenced operations on 30 July, Zhukov postponed the Western Front offensive until the morning of 4 August. Deploying units left some units in place forward but moved the remainder into concealed temporary locations in the rear.

On 4 August the Western Front assault began. In two days the 20th and 31st Armies advanced up to 40 kilometers into the German defenses. By the time the offensive ground to a halt on 23 August, Soviet forces had pushed 60 kilometers into the Rzhev–Vyaz'ma salient. The Soviets credit that success to the surprise achieved by 20th and 31st Armies.

Halder's notations bear out Soviet claims. On 18 July Halder referred to Soviet simulated attack preparations in the Yukhnov sector, stating, "In *Center*, no new developments. Something seems to be brewing on the supply road in Fourth Army Sector."[82] This was along the front of Soviet 49th and 50th Armies, where Zhukov's simulation was occurring. The following day he noted, "Concentrations opposite the Yukhnov salient, which foreshadow attacks. Increased railroad traffic east of Sukhinichi salient, the purpose of which is not clearly understood."[83] After several days characterized as quiet, on 23 July Halder said attack appeared imminent in several sectors. But again, things quieted down. As late as 29 July Halder recorded, "Otherwise all quiet. No important developments in Center and North."[84]

This relative calm ended on 30 July with the news that heavy enemy attacks "with partly fresh troops" had occurred at Rzhev resulting in a penetration of 6 kilometers. But on the following day Halder said "the enemy attacks" were beaten off. Finally on 4 August Halder recorded the results of the expanded Western Front attack stating, "Very heavy penetration on the eastern front of Ninth Army in direction of Zubtsov (the enemy is apparently attacking with seven Inf. Divs. and one Armd. Brig., supported by ample artillery)."[85] While noting the major attack, he gave no indication that two Soviet tank corps would soon join the battle.

The German historian and former officer, K. Tippel'skirch, credited Soviet deception for the limited Soviet successes in the operation and for preventing transfer of units southward. He wrote, "The penetration was successfully averted when three panzer and several infantry divisions, which had already prepared to transfer to the southern front, were halted and introduced at first to localize the enemy and then for a counter-attack."[86]

German intelligence reports also attested to the Soviet *maskirovka* success (see maps 20 and 21). The Germans failed to detect the concentration of either 31st or 20th Armies and recognized the presence of 6th and 8th Tank Corps only on 8 August, days after they had been committed to combat.

Soviet successes around Rzhev were only episodic. On several occasions in the fall Soviet Western Front forces attempted to conduct new offensives to distract German attention and forces from the south. At best Soviet *maskirovka* measures in most of these instances were poor. In November 20th Army attacked in a narrow sector toward Sychevka. The inactivity of neighboring armies permitted the Germans to pinpoint Soviet attack preparations. The same occurred in December southeast of Rzhev when newly arrived tank units openly advertised their presence and gave away Soviet intentions to attack.[87] All of those attacks, however, did serve the purpose of preventing reinforcement of German forces in the south.

The operations at Rzhev and Vyaz'ma demonstrated what *maskirovka* could accomplish. They also underscored the fact that Soviet commanders still applied these measures unevenly. Within the context of the Stalingrad operation the diversionary nature of these operations presaged similar operations on a larger scale in 1943 – operations in support of the Soviet Kursk counter-offensive.

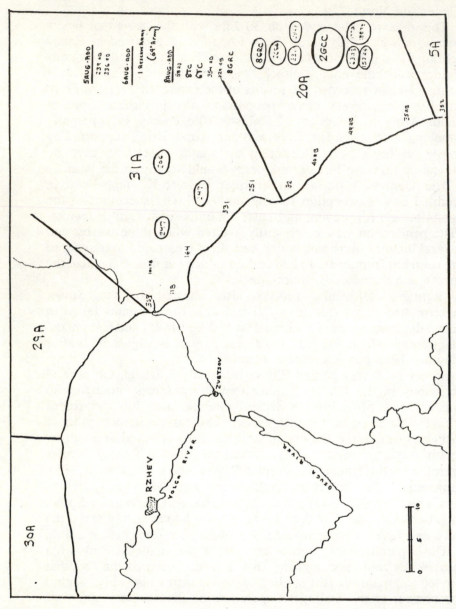

20. Rzhev–Sychevka, German intelligence assessment, 3 August 1942

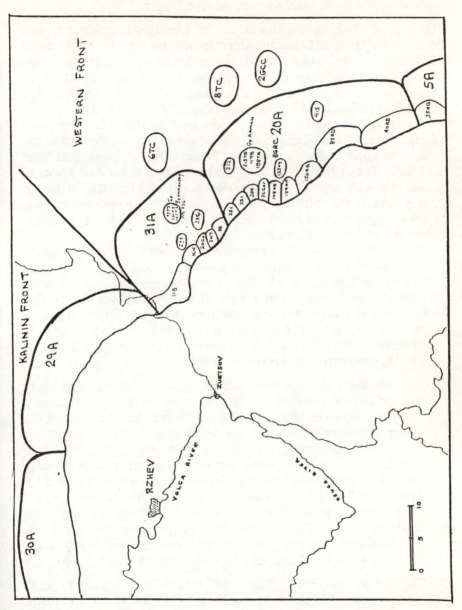

21. Rzhev–Sychevka, Soviet dispositions, 3 August 1942

SINYAVINO, AUGUST 1942

In August 1942 Soviet forces in the Leningrad region renewed offensive activity to break the German hold on the city, to pin down German reserves, and to contribute to Soviet success in the south. The Sinyavino offensive drew upon *maskirovka* experiences in the failure at Tikhvin (November 1941) and the limited success during the initial stage of the Lyuban operation (January 1942).

The Leningrad and Volkhov Fronts were to attack German positions in the Schlusselberg–Sinyavino salient which extended to the shores of Lake Ladoga and cut off Soviet forces in Leningrad from the main Soviet front line. The Volkhov Front's 8th Army was to make the main attack due westward north of Mga and 2d Shock Army would exploit from second echelon to link up with forces from the Leningrad Front's Neva Operational Group which was to attack eastward across the Neva River.

The Volkhov Front, commanded by General K.A. Meretskov, sought to deceive the Germans in several respects. First, it chose to attack in the least trafficable area, a swampy region where German weakness would compensate for the difficulty in movement. Unlike previous offensives the Soviets concentrated their forces in a very narrow attack sector (16 kilometers). Second, Meretskov and his staff ordered diversions and false movements to simulate an intent to attack elsewhere. Meretskov recalled:

> Throughout August we carried out sham tactical maneuvers to make the Germans believe that we were concentrating a large number of troops in Malaya Vishera situated east of the upper reaches of the Volkhov and they got the impression that we were planning an operation in the Novgorod area. Moreover, we took advantage of troops being dispatched to the Southern Front by entraining some of the troops bound for the Sinyavino area. First the troop trains moved toward Moscow, then they were turned toward Tikhvin, reaching it via Vologda and Cherepovets. The troops were transported in closed cars marked "fuel," "food," or "fodder." Tanks were loaded on open carriages and covered with hay.[88]

The Volkhov Front Chief of Operations, Colonel V.Y. Semyonov, and Chief of Staff, Major General G.D. Stelmakh, included in the operational plans secondary (diversionary) strikes to be delivered by other Volkhov Front armies further south along the front to distract German attention from the Mga sector.[89] In addition, false troop concentrations were formed in the Novgorod sector on the Volkhov Front's left flank.

Regrouping for the operation required the *front* to move 13 rifle divisions, eight rifle and six tank brigades, and more than 20 artillery regiments. All regrouping occurred at night, and all dislocating units left radio stations and staff elements in their former locations to simulate unit locations. In new assembly areas all radio traffic was forbidden, and even wire communications were kept to a minimum. Deploying units paid special attention to avoiding detection by German air reconnaissance which Meretskov claimed "acted very efficiently."[90]

In the designated attack sector units carried out extensive defensive measures to conceal attack intentions and specific *front* resources were assigned the task of implementing the *maskirovka* measures. One rifle battalion, a platoon of the 30th *Maskirovka* Company, seven vehicles, tractors, and rail equipment were responsible for simulating the false concentration region in the Novgorod sector. These units formed five commands to do the actual imitative work.[91] Included in their task was the conduct of extensive false rail traffic. Stringent secrecy cloaked all operational planning. *Front* permitted no written order or directive at any level, and all orders were given orally and in person.

The Volkhov Front completed offensive preparations by 27 August, although severe weather and terrain conditions prevented full concentration of all units. Meanwhile, attacks from Leningrad, begun on 19 August, had stalled but seemed to divert German attention from the Mga sector.

Meretskov noted that the Germans finally detected his preparations on 26 August and the following day dispatched numerous reconnaissance planes over his positions. Before the Germans could react, however, on the morning of 27 August, Meretskov launched his offensive. Meretskov later learned from German prisoners that German intelligence had, in fact, discovered Soviet preparations on 26 August and planned a reconnaissance in force on the 28th. Consequently, the Soviet attack took the Germans by surprise and ultimately drove 10 kilometers into the German defense. In subsequent weeks Soviet attempts to expand the offensive failed, and the Germans by October counter-attacked and liquidated the Soviet penetration. Meretskov attributed final German success to Soviet weakness and the fact that the Germans shifted units from other sectors of the front into the Leningrad area.[92] Candid Soviet critiques of the operations take Soviet commanders and staffs to task for numerous planning deficiencies. Deception at Sinyavino did not play a critical role.[93]

German reports seem to substantiate Meretskov's claims and substantiate the success of his *maskirovka* plan (see maps 22 and 23). Halder noted the Leningrad Front's attack on 19 August, and subsequently its failure. On 25 August he recorded, "very heavy rail traffic toward our front. The enemy is moving his Hqs forward, toward the Volkhov Front."[94] The following day, 26 August, he judged, "The Russians will soon strike south of Lake Ladoga," confirming Meretskov's fears that his attack preparations were finally detected. Two days later Halder recognized that "a very distressing penetration" had occurred south of Lake Ladoga. He reflected uncertainty over Soviet aims by adding that there were "Also preparations for an attack on the Volkhov Front."[95]

Thus Sinyavino represented, like other operations in 1942, a partial Soviet success in the complicated task of deceiving the enemy. As was the case elsewhere, the Soviets consciously knew what to do and did it with improved efficiency. However, other conditions contributed to their failure to achieve full success.

CONCLUSIONS

In the fall of 1942 German and Soviet forces prepared for the culminating struggle along the Don and Volga Rivers in southern Russia. All along the front, under *STAVKA* guidance, Soviet forces strove to conceal their intention to challenge German forces in the Stalingrad region. The Soviet High Command issued its *ne shagu nazad* [not a step back] order and gathered its forces to launch what it hoped would be the climactic and decisive battle against Army Group South. Meanwhile it drew upon the experiences of the previous eighteen months of combat to mask its offensive preparations and deceive the Germans about the location of the offensive.

It was no coincidence that several of the key Soviet planners at the *STAVKA* level were those who had used *maskirovka* effectively in prior months. Zhukov, former Western Front commander and now a *STAVKA* coordinator, brought with him the experience of conducting *maskirovka*, first at Moscow in 1941 and 1942 and then at Rzhev in July 1942. Soon General Antonov, one of the architects of successful *maskirovka* at Rostov and Barvenkovo–Lozovaya, also joined the General Staff.

Since the *STAVKA's* appreciation of the value of *maskirovka* had increased, the Soviet High Command closely examined the experiences of the previous year. In November 1942 the Soviets created a mechanism to collect, process, and analyse war experiences as a prelude to the issuance of new orders and regulations governing the conduct of battle. The first two war experience volumes related to all aspects of operations which had taken place in 1941 and 1942 and included a critique of *maskirovka* practices during operations in the winter and spring of 1941 and 1942.[96]

The studies focused first on the necessity of concealing regroupment and concentration of forces for the offensive, particularly in the main attack sector, stating:

> In order to conceal the fact of regrouping and of occupation by the troops which were to take part in the attack of the departure position, combat security and reconnaissance was carried out by elements of the units which were previously in contact with the enemy.
>
> The infantry occupied its departure position not long before the time for the launching of the attack ...[97]

Regarding the exploitation of meteorological conditions, the volume stated:

> It is best to launch the assault in the darkness of night or in snowstorms .... The wide use of night attacks during the past winter as a rule proved favorable for our forces, even when the relationship of strength between us and the enemy was not in our favor ...[98]

It recommended that artillery preparations for an offensive be masked by a variety of measures including:

- movement by night into firing positions
- registration over a period of two days, with a limited number of guns to prevent revelation of true artillery positions
- firing by specially designated weapons from reserve or false firing positions
- camouflage and engineer preparation of outposts and firing positions verified by higher headquarters personnel
- use of traffic control personnel to avoid confusion or mistakes during movement.[99]

The war experience analysis focused also on secret use of mobile forces, cavalry and armor alike. It recommended "the cavalry should take the enemy by surprise, and the cavalry which is to be

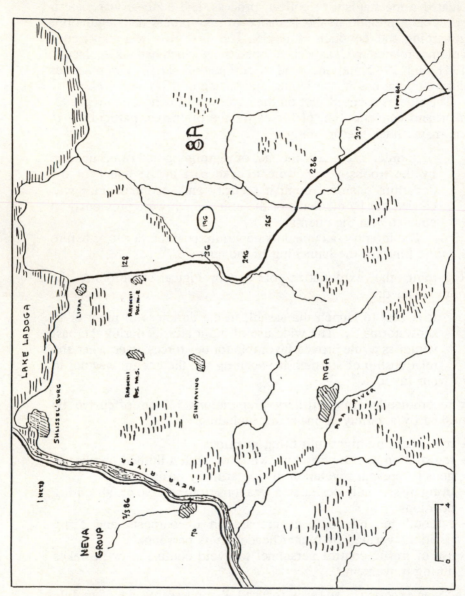

22. Sinyavino, German intelligence assessment, 31 August 1942

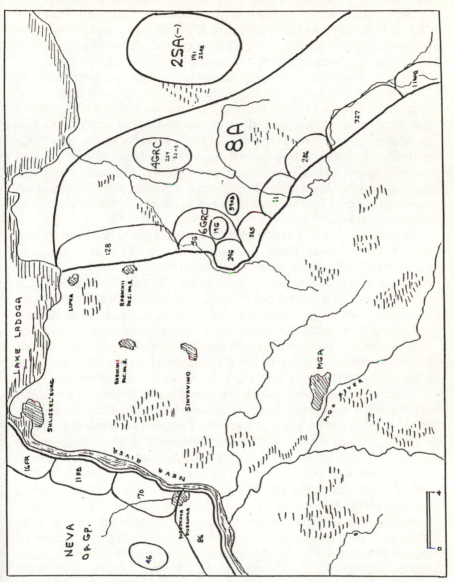

23. Sinyavino, Soviet dispositions, 31 August 1942

used against the enemy rear should be brought up to the front in secrecy; in particular, it should be concealed from enemy air observation."[100] Since surprise was "the decisive element in all types of tank corps operations," the critique recommended it be attained "by camouflage, by concealing one's positions and moves, by moving at night, and by preventing enemy air reconnaissance from observing the area in which the tank corps is disposed."[101]

By late 1942 the mass of *maskirovka* experiences permitted the Soviets to derive basic norms pertaining to the size and quantity of units to be devoted to the task and the time necessary to implement the measures. Experience demonstrated that at least one rifle company, three tanks, three anti-aircraft machine guns, and three anti-aircraft guns were required to create a false unit [regiment] concentration. Thus, a major *maskirovka* operation required dedication of considerable force assets. Specific time requirements were determined for the production of *maskirovka* materials such as mock-up tanks and guns.[102]

Prior to the fall of 1942 Soviet operational plans had on occasion included *maskirovka* plans (in particular the Western Front), but most *maskirovka* plans were only formulated and implemented on the basis of separate written or oral orders. By late 1942, however, it was apparent that formal operational and tactical *maskirovka* plans were necessary to guarantee any measure of success. Thus, at both army and *front* level the *maskirovka* operation became an integral part of each operational plan and the responsibility of a special staff working under the army or *front* operational directorate (a special *maskirovka* staff or one provided by the chief of engineers).[103]

The Soviets seldom resorted to strategic *maskirovka* in 1941 and early 1942. The strategic benefits of surprise achieved by the Soviets at Moscow occurred more as a result of combat conditions than as a conscious effort by the Soviets to implement strategic regrouping under the cloak of strategic *maskirovka* measures. In early 1942 it was the Germans who succeeded to a considerable extent in deceiving the Soviets regarding their strategic intent with disastrous consequences for the Soviets in southern Russia. By mid-1942, however, the Soviets began to engage in strategic *maskirovka* associated with Soviet plans to conduct a strategic counter-stroke in the south against increasingly overextended German forces. Early Soviet attempts in the summer and early fall to distract German attention from the south by offensive actions in the center and north by late fall turned into a conscious Soviet plan to demonstrate offensive intent in the center in order to cover Soviet offensive preparations in the south. This involved secret transfer southward of major forces critical for the successful conduct of the impending Soviet counter-offensive.

Operationally the Soviets made significant strides in *maskirovka*. In short, they learned what needed to be done although they were not always able to meet that need. Thus:

> The experience of force operations showed that when commanders devoted serious attention to *maskirovka*, as a rule success accompanied them; and on, the other hand, when the enemy succeeded in discovering our plans, then the forces often suffered great losses and did not fulfill their assigned missions. During the organization of an offensive every commander had imposed on himself as a duty to prepare a deeply thought out *maskirovka* plan to deceive the enemy, to avoid patterns in these plans and to demonstrate all kinds of resourcefulness.[104]

Operationally and tactically, Soviet skill at achieving surprise through *maskirovka* improved. Soviet commanders and staffs tightened planning security through Draconian security and strict use of sequential planning by small planning groups. They increasingly sought to hide the direction of the main attack by both *maskirovka* and by choosing unlikely places to attack. They began to appreciate the benefits of concealing the timing of an attack even when unable to conceal intent. Soviet forces skillfully used darkness and bad weather to conceal attack preparations even though those conditions often hindered the effectiveness of the ensuing attack. Although some commanders attempted radio *maskirovka*, Soviet communications training would have to improve significantly for those measures to be effective. Likewise, even improved *maskirovka* discipline in armor, artillery, and infantry units could not counter effective German aerial reconnaissance, which quite often sounded the alarm over upcoming Soviet operations. That problem would be solved only when Soviet airmen could sweep the skies of German aircraft.

Candidly a Soviet analyst admitted, "Without exact observance of these requirements, measures for operational *maskirovka* did not achieve their aims."[105]

In late 1942 Soviet forces were in the midst of an education in planning and conducting war, in *maskirovka* as well as in hundreds of other subjects. They were also on the eve of the first real test of that education – a test on how to prepare and conduct large scale offensive action – a test conducted around Stalingrad.

CHAPTER FIVE

THE PRACTICE OF *MASKIROVKA*
The Second Period of War
(November 1942–December 1943)

Soviet forces, enriched by military experience, improved the means of achieving surprise. It became more and more difficult for the enemy to be able to guess the intentions of the Soviet command. Assessments of conditions on the Soviet–German front, issued by the German command intelligence directorate [Foreign Armies East], more often indicated that difficulty ....

The mission of deceiving the enemy from 1943 was resolved by conducting more active operational *maskirovka* (along with passive) and also by finding new means of secret movement of formations into departure positions, of clearance of mine-fields, of the conduct of registration fire, artillery security, etc.

M. M. Kir'yan,
Vnezapnost' v nastupatel'nykh operatsiyakh Velikoi Otechestvennoi voiny [Surprise in Offensive Operations of the Great Patriotic War], 1986

INTRODUCTION

After eighteen months of often unpleasant combat experience, in the late fall of 1942 the Red Army prepared its second strategic counter-offensive, which it hoped would produce major victories. Armed with this experience, equipped with new *maskirovka* regulations issued in late 1942, and more extensive means to conduct systematic *maskirovka*, the Soviets had every reason to expect success. There was no more important place or time to begin reaping success than in the southern Soviet Union in the fall of 1942 where events set in motion in June were reaching a culminating point. As in early 1942, *maskirovka* would play a major role in the outcome.

In June 1942, following a series of operational failures resulting from Soviet attempts to seize the initiative, the German Army

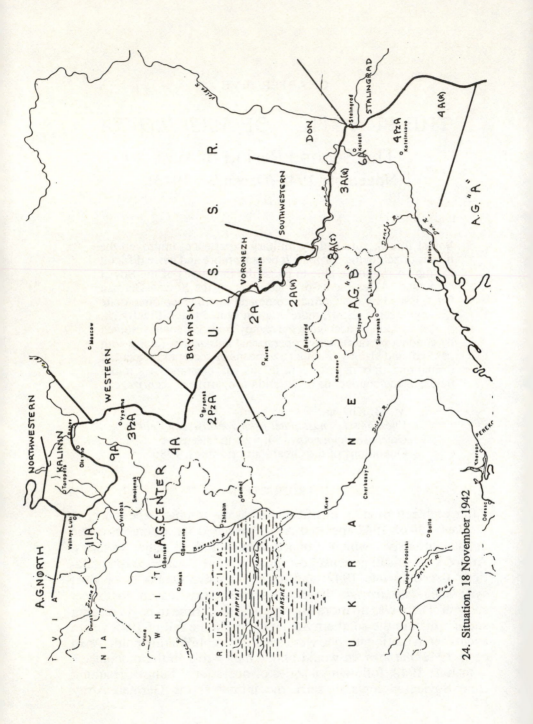

24. Situation, 18 November 1942

started a second strategic offensive across the southern Soviet Union. Its forces swept forward to the Don River at Voronezh and then swung south toward Stalingrad and past it into the Caucasus (see map 24). The Red Army resisted the German advance with a series of counter-attacks in the Voronezh region, along the upper Don River, and on the approaches to Stalingrad proper. It also adopted a deliberate defensive strategy involving the systematic withdrawal of forces before they were threatened with encirclement and a conscious decision to conduct a deliberate defense in the city of Stalingrad, preparatory to launching a strategic counter-offensive. Unlike the situation in 1941, in late 1942 the Soviets retained the planning initiative and avoided the hasty reactive planning of the Moscow days. By November 1942 German forces were locked in a bitter and costly struggle for Stalingrad, a struggle which consumed German operational reserves, forced the Germans to deploy extensively allied forces, and rely on those forces for protection of the long German flanks extending into the Stalingrad area.

As in late 1941, in the summer and fall of 1942 the *STAVKA* carefully raised and deployed reserve armies and formed new armored forces (tank armies and mechanized corps) for use in a major counter-stroke in the Stalingrad region. It also undertook a concerted attempt to capitalize on war experiences (by now systematically collected, analysed, and converted into orders for every level of command, among which were directives for more thorough *maskirovka* measures). A directive of Red Army engineer forces dated 9 November 1942 spoke of recurring operational-tactical deficiencies in Soviet *maskirovka* practices and recommended a series of remedies. This directive specifically stated:

– false objectives and concentrations of forces are seldom used and are unsystematic, and during the erection of false objectives matters are often limited to the construction of only one type of dummy and no reserves are used to animate them, as a consequence of which reactive measures of the enemy are absent, aside from scattered reconnaissance flights, which establish the fact of false objectives;
– of all rear area objectives only command posts of *front* and army staffs are well camouflaged;
– roads, used as the basic routes for transport and evacuation, are in no fashion masked by vertical covers from ground observation,

and therefore the enemy is capable of conducting mortar and artillery fire not only on transport but also on vehicles;
– the chiefs of engineer forces, in spite of the *STAVKA* orders of 28 November 1941 in a majority of cases do not participate in the formulation of operational plans conducted by *fronts* and armies, as a consequence of which camouflage security of the operation is absent and camouflage units are not used as they are supposed to be.[1]

The directive ordered units to take corrective action and made chiefs of engineers and individual *front* and army commanders responsible for such corrections. In addition, it specifically required greater efforts at disinformation. The November directive became the focal point of Soviet deception efforts for the Stalingrad counter-offensive.

STALINGRAD, NOVEMBER 1942

Planning for the Stalingrad operation was more deliberate than it had been at Moscow. Starting on 13 September, it intensified as the attack date (19 November) approached.[2] The Soviets conducted planning in the greatest secrecy and integrated into the strategic plan measures both to deceive the Germans about the location and timing of the attack, and to cover the scope of offensive prepara- tions. Future Marshal A.M. Vasilevsky, then a representative of the *STAVKA* involved in planning for the Stalingrad operation, wrote:

> The Commander in Chief [Stalin] introduced conditions of strictest secrecy into all initial preparations for the operation. We were ordered categorically to tell no one anything about the operation, even members of the State Defense Commit- tee. Stalin gave notice that he himself would speak to whomever was necessary about such preparations. G.K. Zhukov and I could pass to the commanders of the *fronts* only that which directly concerned each of them and not a word more. I dare say that, under such conditions, a similar measure of caution would be fully warranted.[3]

Only the *front* commanders were acquainted with the operational plans, but they did not become actively involved with their develop- ment until November. To secure the offensive the official decision to form an additional *front* (Southwestern) was implemented in late

October. *Front* commanders were to concern themselves only with the defensive operation. Vasilevsky wrote:

> I was ordered to familiarize the commander of Stalingrad Front forces, A.I. Yeremenko, with the counter-offensive plan, in order to hear his opinion but did not enlist him in practical work in preparing the offensive until November, having left before him the basic and singular mission at that time of defending Stalingrad.[4]

The General Staff also restricted the size of the planning circle. It forbade correspondence relating to the operation between the General Staff and the *fronts* and between *fronts* and armies. All co-ordinating for the offensive was to be accomplished personally through contact of *STAVKA* representatives (G.K. Zhukov, A.M. Vasilevsky, and N.N. Voronov) with *fronts* and armies. Voronov wrote:

> With the purpose of keeping offensive preparations secret, it was forbidden to publish any written, printed, and graphic documents. At first, a very limited number of generals and officers were acquainted with the new combat missions. This, of course, made preparation for the operation very difficult, and made us plan our work by each *front* and then by each army. In my case, the number of officers who could be entrusted with such an important secret was also quite limited.[5]

Within corps and divisions all instructions were verbal and directed only to those who would carry the orders out.

The *STAVKA* attempted to deceive the Germans as to the location of the Soviet counter-offensive.[6] In mid-October 1942 it ordered *fronts* in southern Russia to engage only in defensive operations. Detailed written instructions specified the establishment of defensive boundaries, construction of engineer obstacles, and the preparation of populated areas for all round strongpoint defense.[7] Simultaneously, throughout the summer and fall of 1942, the *STAVKA* ordered the Kalinin and Western Fronts in the Moscow region to prepare active offensive operations against German Army Group Center in what they hoped the Germans would perceive as a renewal of Soviet actions that had terminated in April 1942. As a result, the Soviets launched the Rzhev–Sychevka Operation (30 July–23 August), which achieved only limited gains but drew 12 new German divisions into Army Group Center. The Soviet feint and subsequent Soviet build-up west of Moscow had the desired effect. A 29 August 1942 assessment by the Eastern Intelligence Branch of the German Army High Command (OKH) concluded that the Russians would have considerable offensive potential in the fall in both Army Group Center's and "B's" sectors, but:

> that the Russians would be more eager to remove the threat to Moscow posed by the forward elements of Army Group Center and would, therefore, most likely exploit the salients at Toropets and Sukhinichi for converging attacks on Smolensk, with the objective of destroying the Ninth, Third Panzer, and Fourth Armies.[8]

The *STAVKA* ordered this activity to continue into the fall to reinforce German fears of strikes against Army Group Center and, for that matter, against any sector that could detract from German strength at Stalingrad. According to Vasilevsky, in October the *STAVKA* assigned Zhukov the task of preparing diversionary operations of the Kalinin and Western Fronts while Vasilevsky coordinated the Stalingrad operation.[9] Zhukov, later wrote:

> According to the Supreme Command plan, the energetic operations our forces undertook in the summer and autumn of 1942 in the western direction against the Nazi Army Group "Center" were to disorient the enemy to make the German command think that it was precisely at this point, and nowhere else, that we were getting a major winter operation ready ... by early November the Nazi Army Group "Center" had received reinforcements, including 12 divisions.[10]

A focal point of Soviet strategic deception was the Rzhev salient where Soviet forces postured for an attack and kept German intelligence perplexed over when that attack would occur. The August Rzhev operation had prompted the 29 August German intelligence estimate. Moreover, according to one German analyst, "The penetration succeeded in both preventing the transport of three panzer and several infantry divisions which had already been prepared to move to the southern front which were now held up and introduced at first to localize the penetration and then for counterattacks."[11] In the following two months OKH noted the Soviet build-up west of Moscow and judged that a Soviet offensive would begin after the fall rains, two to three weeks after 16 October.[12]

On 29 October both German Ninth Army and Foreign Armies East agreed that the Soviets would launch a major offensive against

Ninth Army from both sides of the Rzhev salient. Ninth Army estimated the attack could be ready in a few days.[13] Interestingly enough, for German intelligence "this indication of a gathering of enemy forces was but one of many all over the Army Group Center front early in November. Everywhere Russian movement quickened." Responding to these conditions, on 6 November Gehlen issued an appreciation which stated, "Before the German east front the point of main effort of the coming Russian operation looms with increasing distinction in the area of Army Group Center."[14] While Western and Kalinin Front armies prepared and implemented their plans for diversionary operations, armies adjacent to those participating in the Stalingrad operation engaged in smaller scale deceptions to help cover the large-scale offensive preparations along the Don River.

General F.J. Golikov's Voronezh Front defended the front along the Don River north and south of Voronezh on the right flank of the Stalingrad shock group. During the first half of November Golikov's armies engaged in disinformation operations. Lieutenant General K.S. Moskalenko, commander of 40th Army, described his army's role, stating:

> We had to imitate construction of crossings across the Voronezh River, regrouping of forces and the concentration of infantry and artillery, and also a tank corps on our right flank. All this, it was understood must convince the enemy command of preparations for an operation in our sector of the front. To me, it became clear: an offensive would soon begin somewhere not far from us. But where?[15]

Thus, from August through early November Soviet armies all along the front played their role in a massive disinformation plan designed to distract German attention from the Stalingrad region.

Strenuous Soviet *maskirovka* measures within the *fronts* and armies of the Stalingrad region also contributed to confounding German intelligence assessments. The chief intention of Soviet *maskirovka* was to cover the forward deployment of the immense forces needed to conduct a successful offensive, complicated by a limited transportation network and restricted bridgeheads south and west of the Don River, out of which the offensive would have to be launched. *Maskirovka* would have to cover the forward deployment of over 300,000 men; 1,000 tanks; and 5,000 guns and mortars with immense amounts of ammunition, fuel, and other supplies.

A 25 October directive from Vasilevsky to the commanders of the

Don and Southwestern Fronts set the standards for the *maskirovka* effort:

a. All marches will be conducted only at night, placing the units in concealed positions for day time rest;
b. Movement will be covered by aviation and anti-aircraft units .... the necessity for camouflage of each operation will be assigned to the Military Council of the Front (Army), and development and execution of a decision will be achieved for the camouflaging, based upon the utilization of operational and engineering camouflage measures and misinformation of the enemy; separate commanders, who will be personally responsible for camouflage on a *front* and army scale, will be allotted from the personnel of the staffs of the engineer troops of the *fronts* and armies ...[16]

Following these instructions, the Southwestern Front began masking the forward deployment of 5th Tank Army and 21st Army into restricted bridgeheads south of the Don River at Serafimovich and Kletskaya. They built 22 bridges (five false) across the Don, concealing the approaches with vertical covers. They also camouflaged the crossings, command points and *front* and army headquarters. German aircraft bombed the false bridges but left the functional bridges intact. As the attack date of 19 November neared, the Soviets used smoke to cover armor units crossing the Don. On 19 November extensive smoke screens covered the crossing by 26th Tank Corps into the Serafimovich bridgehead.[17] At army level, engineers constructed simulated concentrations of artillery and tanks to deceive German artillery and air observation. With the assistance of road guards and traffic controllers, all movement within armies was carried out at night under strict light discipline. Skillful camouflage and the use of loudspeakers to cover engine noises facilitated the secret forward deployment of three Soviet tank corps (1st, 26th, 4th) into the bridgeheads.

The Stalingrad Front conducted active offensive operations between 29 September and 4 October to secure enlarged bridgeheads for the future offensive and to distract German forces from the defensive actions at Stalingrad proper. Subsequently the Stalingrad Front moved two mechanized corps, one cavalry corps, five air defense artillery regiments, a tank brigade, two rifle divisions, and seven artillery divisions into its bridgeheads west of the Volga River. The night movements here and at Stalingrad proper involved the passage across the river of 160,000 men; 10,000 horses; 430 tanks; 600 guns; 14,000 vehicles; and 7,000 tons of ammunition, most undetected by German intelligence.[18]

The forces of the Don Front undertook similar extensive measures to cover preparations. *Front* commander K.K. Rokossovsky recalled:

> Much was done in order to deceive the enemy. We tried to convince him that we were about to attack in the area between the rivers and conducted more operations here. In the remaining sectors of the front, intensified operations for the erection of foxholes, fortifications, etc., were simulated. Any movement of troops into those regions, from where they were to operate, was carried out only at night, with the observance of all camouflage measures.[19]

65th Army commander General P.I. Batov wrote:

> Concentration and regrouping of forces was conducted exclusively at night. Some formations and units of the troops even moved in an opposite direction to deceive the enemy. At the Kletskaya bridgehead, in spite of intensified reconnaissance flights by German aviation, we managed to concentrate the basic mass of our troops and equipment in time. In this region, the rumble of mortars was not audible in the daytime, movement of ground forces was forbidden, and everything died down.[20]

Similar camouflage measures occurred in the air forces supporting all three Soviet *fronts*.

As well as using disinformation on a strategic scale and extensive operational and tactical *maskirovka*, the Soviets used more subtle methods to cover their intent to attack and create an impression of defensive intent. *Front*, army, and divisional newspapers echoed the by then familiar slogan, *Ne shagu nazad* ["Not a step back!"] and added a host of exhortations to Soviet troops to hold fast in every sector and make the Germans pay a heavy price in blood for every offensive effort. At the same time, the newspapers talked of plans to seize other objectives elsewhere and periodically mentioned the feats of fictitious units and commanders.

The extensive Soviet *maskirovka* measures achieved considerable success (see maps 25 and 26). The greatest feat was in masking the scale of the offensive. While numerous indications of Soviet offensive intent surfaced, they did not convey to German intelligence the magnitude of the Soviet offensive. As at Moscow,

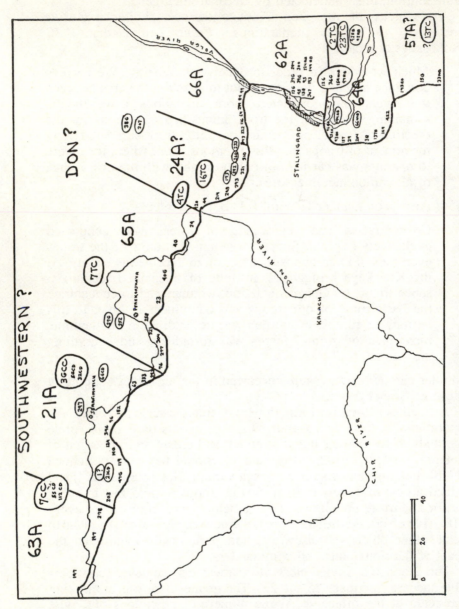

25. Stalingrad, German intelligence assessment, 18 November 1942

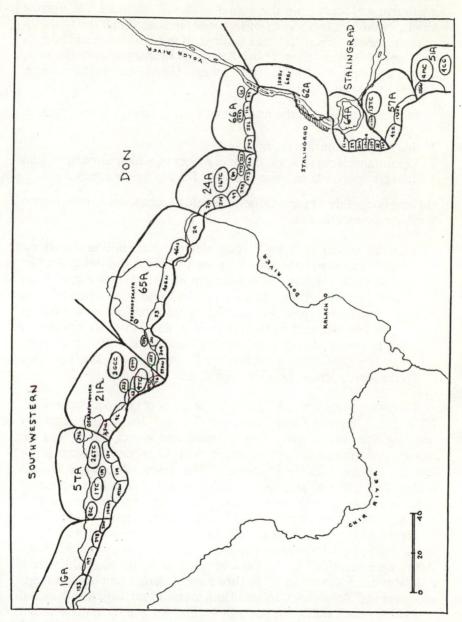

26. **Stalingrad, Soviet dispositions, 18 November 1942**

German optimism and even overconfidence tended to distract intelligence officers from the actual evidence. German intelligence reports in the last two weeks of October "indicated that the build-up opposite Army Group 'B' was limited to the Serafimovich bridgehead opposite Rumanian Third Army."[21] Rumanian concern was, in fact, growing. On 29 October, General Dmitrescu of Third Army reported to Army Group:

1. Marked increases in the number of Don crossings in the Russian rear;
2. Statements from deserters;
3. Continuous local attacks, the sole object of which must be to find the soft spots and to pave the way for the major attack.[22]

On receiving this report, General Paulus, commander of German Sixth Army recollected:

> I went myself to Army Group Headquarters in Starobielsk on November 9 and submitted a report with the following details: three new infantry formations with some tanks had been identified in the Kletskaya area, and one new armored, one new motorized, and two new infantry formations were thought to be concentrated in the same area; and in the Blinov sector the presence of two new infantry formations with a few tanks had been definitely established. A major enemy attack, it was considered, could be expected at any moment.[23]

Army Group responded by moving a support group and the weak XXXXVIII Panzer Corps to back up the Rumanians and by ordering intensified air reconnaissance and direct air attacks on Soviet concentrations. However, on 31 October, Eastern Intelligence Branch (OKH) reported, "The level of activity in the bridgehead did not presage a major attack but rather appeared more and more to indicate that only local attacks were expected."[24]
Indicators of a Soviet build-up against Army Group "B" mounted in early November to a level sufficient to raise concern within the army group. By 10 November two rifle divisions of Soviet 5th Tank Army were identified in the Serafimovich area, although the parent unit was still assumed to be further north (carried on German maps southwest of Yefremov). In addition, German intelligence detected a possible new *front* headquarters (the Southwestern) to go with the already detected Don Front north of Stalingrad.[25] Meanwhile XI Army Corps, Fourth Panzer Army, and XIV Panzer Corps reported

Soviet movements into and concentration at bridgeheads facing their positions.[26] While Army Group "B" had concluded by mid-November that an offensive was in the offing against Third Rumanian and Fourth Panzer Army, the Eastern Intelligence Branch of OKH clung to its optimistic view, noting on 6 November that the Soviet main effort was certain to come against Army Group Center and that the offensive on the Don would come later. It reiterated this view on 12 November in an assessment claiming conditions were too obscure for a definite prediction, but qualified the assessment by stating:

> However, an attack in the near future against Rumanian Third Army with the objective of cutting the railroad to Stalingrad and thereby threatening the German force farther east and forcing a withdrawal from Stalingrad must be taken into consideration.[27]

The branch added that, "There are not sufficient forces available for the enemy to develop broad operations."[28] Chief of the German General Staff, Colonel-General Kurt Zeitzler, echoed this view:

> The Russians no longer have any reserves worth mentioning and are not capable of launching a large scale offensive. In forming any appreciation of enemy intentions, this basic fact must be taken fully into consideration.[29]

Despite these predictions, on 19 November Soviet forces launched an offensive which penetrated Rumanian and German defenses, encircled Sixth Army, and inflicted the most disastrous defeat on German forces since the creation of the Wehrmacht.

In a 29 November Directive, Zeitzler paid tribute to Soviet *maskirovka* efforts in the operation:

> Distinctive characteristics of the Russian preparations for the offensive: good concealment of all units taking part in the operations, and especially tank formations .... It is well known to all the Russian capacity to hide masterly preparations for an offensive from our reconnaissance and observation ...[30]

To the Soviets, Stalingrad represented a turning point [*perelom*] in their military operations in the Second World War, first and foremost because they achieved their first unqualified strategic success on the battlefield. Their success with *maskirovka* was even

5. Soviet troops attack during the Stalingrad counteroffensive, November, 1942

more remarkable, for their record of deception prior to November 1942 was generally poor.

Zhukov later wrote about the Soviet *maskirovka* plan:

> Our superiority over the Germans was felt in that the Soviet Armed Forces learned to preserve in deep secretiveness the intentions to execute disinformation on a large scale and to deceive the enemy. Secret regrouping and concentration of forces allowed us to realize surprise blows on the enemy.[31]

At Stalingrad the Soviets first experimented with rudimentary techniques for strategic deception. They made conscious efforts to simulate offensive preparations in other sectors of the front. While German troop adjustments in reaction to this attempted deception were minimal, the German OKH became transfixed by Soviet intentions in Army Group Center's sector. This, plus high command preoccupation with the bitter fight for Stalingrad proper, distracted them from undue concern over the vulnerable flanks of Army Group "B." If Soviet strategic *maskirovka* measures were rudimentary, they certainly indicated the potential value of such activities if carried out on an even larger scale. Soviet planning in the future was to demonstrate that increased Soviet appreciation, with more devastating effects for the Germans.

In the operational and tactical realm, Soviet *maskirovka* feats reaped even greater harvest. The virtually airtight planning secrecy and the extensive camouflage measures successfully covered the forward deployment of large Soviet combat forces, producing destructive, paralyzing surprise to the German and Rumanian forces when the assaults began. Before the Germans could regain their balance, major damage had been done and could not be repaired. Although Soviet *maskirovka* did not eradicate all offensive indicators, it blurred their intention, obscured the timing and form of the attack, and certainly masked its scope. From these experiences the Soviets learned the relative importance of the latter two effects which, if achieved, almost negated the necessity for concealing ultimate intent. In subsequent operations the Soviets would continue to attempt to hide intention, timing, form, and scope of offensives, but they would concentrate on the latter three with increasing success.

THE AFTERMATH OF STALINGRAD, DECEMBER 1942

Background

Careful Soviet preparations of the Stalingrad counter-offensive paid immense dividends. Within seven days after commencement of the operation Soviet forces had surrounded German Sixth Army and a portion of Fourth Panzer Army at Stalingrad. At the same time, however, the operational success posed new challenges to Soviet planners. The bag of German forces encircled at Stalingrad exceeded Soviet expectations, and its destruction required greater resources than the Soviets had originally intended. Commitment of the bulk of the Don and Stalingrad Fronts to the mission of destroying German forces at Stalingrad left the task of blocking any German attempts to relieve Sixth Army to the Southwestern Front and a small portion of the Stalingrad Front.

In early December those relief attempts loomed more menacing. The Germans assembled forces for two such attempts, one mounted by LVII Panzer Corps from the Kotel'nikovo region southwest of Stalingrad and the other by XXXXVIII Panzer Corps from the Tormosin region west of Stalingrad. To block these relief forces the Soviets deployed 51st Army on an extended front covering the Kotel'nikovo approach and 5th Tank Army along the Chir and Don Rivers opposite German forces west of Stalingrad. Separate cavalry corps filled the gap between the two armies. It was clear that neither force could resist a concerted German relief effort without considerable reinforcement. The principal reinforcement available in the Stalingrad region was 2d Guards Army, the last of the Soviet reserve armies.

The *STAVKA* decided first to conduct a major operation (Saturn), spearheaded by the Southwestern Front, across the Don River against Italian Eighth Army and German/Rumanian Army Detachment Hollidt, to crush German defenses along the middle Don, penetrate deep in the German rear to Rostov, and hence preempt German relief attempts at Stalingrad. The *STAVKA* ordered 2d Guards Army to reinforce the Southwestern Front. Events at Stalingrad, however, disrupted that plan. German strength at Stalingrad forced the *STAVKA* to commit 2d Guards Army to assist the assault on encircled German Sixth Army. The *STAVKA* then truncated Operation "Saturn" into "Little Saturn," a shallower envelopment of Italian Eighth Army and Army Detachment Hollidt by the Southwestern Front. "Little Saturn," if successful, still promised to divert at least one of the German relief attempts.

In mid-December as the Soviets were completing preparations for "Little Saturn" and "Koltso" (the reduction of Stalingrad) the Germans began the relief operation from Kotel'nikovo. The *STAVKA* reacted by dispatching 2d Guards Army from the Stalingrad area to the southwest to reinforce Soviet 51st Army, now being severely pressed on the Kotel'nikovo approach by LVII Panzer Corps, whose attack had penetrated to the Aksai River, halfway to the Stalingrad perimeter.

In the ensuing Middle Don and Kotel'nikovo operations the *STAVKA* and participating *fronts* and armies engaged in extensive *maskirovka* to cover large but hasty offensive preparations in an extremely fluid situation. In both cases *maskirovka* contributed to ultimate Soviet success.

Middle Don, December 1942

The concept of Operation "Saturn" originated on 25 November when representative of the *STAVKA* Vasilevsky met with the Southwestern Front commander Lieutenant General N.F. Vatutin and others.[32] It involved the use of 1st Guards and 3d Guards Armies to strike converging blows from the Don River and Chir River toward Millerovo and then exploitation by 2d Guards Army toward Rostov. The *STAVKA* approved the concept on 2 December and ordered the attack to begin on 10 December. Events at Stalingrad, however, diverted 2d Guards Army and delayed "Saturn" until 14 December, although the objectives remained unchanged. After the 12 December German attack from Kotel'nikovo, plan "Saturn" became "Little Saturn" with a start date of 16 December.

"Little Saturn" called for a penetration of Italian defenses south of the Don River by the concentrated forces of 6th Army and 1st Guards Army. Thereafter four tank corps (17th, 18th, 24th, 25th) would exploit deep to seize German airfields and sever communications routes in the Millerovo and Tatsinskaya areas. Further east a shock group of 3d Guards Army would strike westward across the Chir River. Its mobile group (1st Guards Mechanized Corps) would exploit, link up with the tank corps, and ultimately seize Morozovsk. As a result, Italian Eighth Army and Army Detachment Hollidt would be destroyed and XXXXVIII Panzer Corps at Tormosin would be forced to abandon its relief attempt toward Stalingrad.

Planning time for "Little Saturn" was extremely short. *Front* and army commanders began planning on 2 December and corps and division commanders received their orders on 5–6 December. A considerable number of units had to regroup for the attack, including three rifle divisions, one rifle brigade, one tank corps, and seven artillery and mortar brigades assigned by the *STAVKA* to 6th Army and five rifle divisions, three tank corps, one mechanized corps, and six tank, and sixteen artillery and mortar regiments assigned to reinforce the Southwestern Front.[33]

A cloak of tight secrecy surrounded all operational planning and the regrouping and concentration of forces for the attack. Only key personnel knew the contents of the operational plans, and the *front* distributed all orders orally or by liaison officer. Commanders and chiefs of staffs wrote all documents by hand in a single copy; and the Soviets prohibited telephone and wire communications and permitted radio operators only to receive transmissions.[34]

All movement into assembly areas occurred at night or during fog or snowstorms, and the *front* commander mandated strict light discipline. Tank forces occupied their departure areas 7–10 kilometers from the front and mechanized corps 20 kilometers, no earlier than four days before the offensive. Units spent from one to six days in departure areas. There they used maximum camouflage and occupied trenches and dugouts already concealed by forces which had previously occupied the area. On the evening of 16 December the mobile corps began crossing the Don River and concentrated in jumping-off positions. Concentration of reserves was completed by 12 December, and regrouping by 15 December. Specially designated engineer-sapper units helped conceal forces in departure areas and jumping-off positions.[35]

In these areas spoken commands, smoking, talking, and light signals were prohibited and specially selected officers supervised observation of these prohibitions. The Soviets also concentrated air defense assets to prevent enemy air reconnaissance over the most critical sectors.[36]

To further deceive the Germans, armies within the *front* arranged for movement and reconnaissance on secondary directions where the enemy could observe it. Under Vasilevsky's and Zhukov's supervision the Voronezh Front to the north created a false concentration of forces opposite German defenses to distract Army Group "B" from Soviet attack preparations occurring further south. From 7 to 20 December 40th Army engaged in attack preparations in the Storozhevoye bridgehead, simulating the intention of attacking toward Korotoyaka. 40th Army cut lanes through barbed wire obstacles, cleared minefields from a false penetration region, and assembled forces for an offensive. Commanders conducted personal reconnaissance near the front in full view of the enemy, and engineers worked on roads to the front.[37]

Further south Lieutenant General P.L. Romanenko's 5th Tank Army began diversionary operations across the lower Chir River. On 7 December 5th Tank Army's 1st Tank Corps, and later other units, crossed the Chir and struck XXXXVIII Panzer Corps forcing the Germans to commit 11th Panzer Division to incessant counterattacks which occupied the German corps's attention for almost two weeks. The diversion prevented XXXXVIII Panzer Corps from mounting a relief effort toward Stalingrad and assisting beleaguered Italian forces to the northwest.

Reconnaissance for "Little Saturn" began on 10 December and lasted until 15 December. The extended period was designed to confuse the Germans over the timing of an attack. In fact, it revealed Soviet attack intentions; and by 16 December the German command had dispatched local reserves into the area (two infantry divisions and one understrength panzer division). German intelligence, however, failed to recognize the full threat to their forces defending along the Middle Don River (see maps 27 and 28). Transfixed by 5th Tank Army's operations across the Chir and the Stalingrad relief efforts, it detected only two of the four Soviet tank corps concentrated near Verkhnyi Mamon, failed to note the existence of 1st Guards Mechanized Corps, and missed the formation and concentration of 3d Guards Army. It assessed the Soviet build-up in the area as tactical and limited in scope.

Thus, despite some German adjustments, the Soviet attack came as a surprise; in particular, its scale and intensity. Within three days Soviet mobile forces were exploiting southward toward Tatsinskaya. The offensive destroyed Italian Eighth Army and a significant portion of Army Detachment Hollidt, and forced German XXXXVIII Panzer Corps to abandon its defense along the lower Chir River.

The Soviets have credited that success to *maskirovka*:

> As a result of our precautionary measures, the enemy failed to notice or learn anything certain about the grouping of our forces and to pinpoint our main thrust line. Although the enemy was in possession of some information on our preparations for the offensive and was taking measures for its repulsion, our precautions ... preserved the element of surprise as to time, direction and power of the thrusts delivered by the Red Army.[38]

Manstein substantiated the Soviet view:

> On 15 December there were obvious signs of an enemy attack being prepared in front of the left wing of the Don Army Group and the right wing of Army Group B, and the following day local attacks were launched. Initially it was not entirely clear whether the enemy was following his frequent practice of feeling out the front prior to a decisive breakthrough, or whether he was seeking to prevent us from transferring any forces from this sector of the battlefield east of the Don. Then, however, our radio monitors identified a new army (Third Guards) which implied that a breakthrough with some such far-reaching objective as Rostov was impending.[39]

The 3d Guards Army Manstein referred to had been formed on 5 December from units of 1st Guards Army's left wing and *STAVKA* reinforcements. German intelligence finally detected the army on 18 December. In the "Little Saturn" offensive the Soviets reinforced the surprise achieved in their earlier Stalingrad offensive and demonstrated what *maskirovka* could do against an overextended and increasingly distraught enemy. After 16 December only one more threat existed to the successful Soviet destruction of German

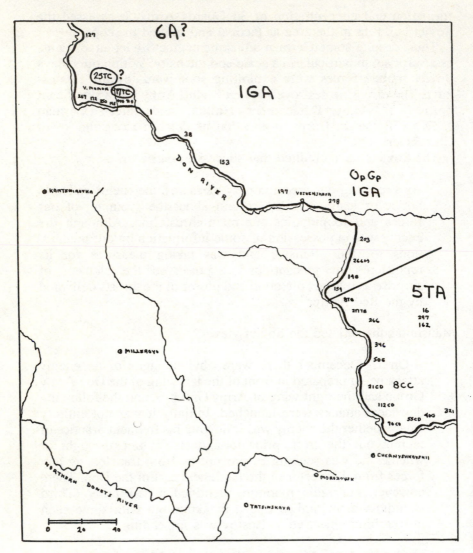

27. Middle Don, German intelligence assessment, 17 December 1942

Sixth Army. This threat materialized along the Aksai River, southwest of Stalingrad.

Kotel' nikovo, December 1942

On 12 December German LVII Panzer Corps (6th Panzer, 23d Panzer, 15th Air Force, 5th Cavalry, 8th Cavalry and Rumanian 1st,

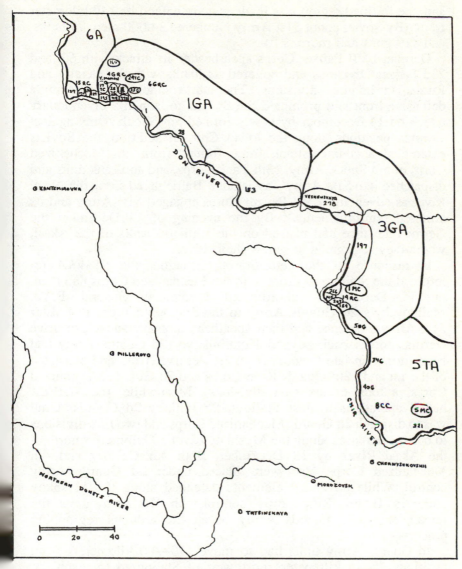

28. Middle Don, Soviet dispositions, 17 December 1942

2d, 18th Infantry Divisions) began operations from the Kotel'-nikovo area northeast toward the Aksai River and Stalingrad.[40] The German thrust confronted the defenses of Soviet 51st Army which covered the southwestern approaches to Stalingrad. 51st Army's three rifle divisions, two cavalry divisions, one tank corps, and one fortified region was inadequate to defend its 140 kilometer front. (By Soviet count 51st Army numbered 34,000 men, 79 tanks, and 419 guns and mortars.[41])

German LVII Panzer Corps spearheaded its attack with 6th and 23d Panzer Divisions and covered its flanks with the cavalry and Rumanian infantry divisions. The attack cracked 51st Army's defensive front and prompted the Soviets to launch a diversionary attack on 14 December by newly formed 5th Shock Army against German positions along the lower Chir. In addition, the Soviets assembled a counter-attack force formed from 4th Mechanized Corps of 5th Shock Army, 13th Tank Corps, and anti-tank units and dispatched it to 51st Army's assistance. Battle raged along the Aksai River as advancing LVII Panzer Corps engaged 51st Army and its armored reinforcements.[42] By the evening of 14 December the German advance had paused on the northern banks of the Aksai, where they regrouped to renew their drive.

In response to the deteriorating situation, the *STAVKA* reinforced the Stalingrad Front with 6th Mechanized Corps and then, on 15 December, subordinated Lieutenant General P.Ya. Malinovsky's 2d Guards Army to the Stalingrad Front to bolster 51st Army's defense and then spearhead a counter-attack to drive German forces back beyond Kotel'nikovo (2d Guards Army had been formed in late October from 1st Reserve Army and consisted of the 1st and 13th Guards Rifle Corps and 2d Guards Mechanized Corps, a total of six rifle divisions). Meanwhile, the *STAVKA* halted operations against Stalingrad.[43] Initially 2d Guards Army was to dispatch 2d Guards Mechanized Corps and two rifle divisions to occupy defenses along the Myshkov River 30 kilometers north of the Aksai River by 18 December. Both 4th Cavalry and 4th Mechanized Corps also were placed under 2d Guards Army control. While advanced elements defended along the Myshkov under 1st Guards Rifle Corps' control with 51st Army units, the remainder of 2d Guards Army began the arduous regrouping process.

2d Guards Army units had to move 170–200 kilometers from positions 75–95 kilometers northwest of Stalingrad to reach the Myshkov area. Hasty planning and movement was necessary if 2d Guards Army was to prevent the Germans from reaching and crossing that last river barrier on the approach to Stalingrad. Frosty weather and almost constant blizzards hindered the move although they provided a measure of concealment. Units marched only at night or under cover of the bad weather and averaged a movement rate of 40–50 kilometers per day to meet their required deployment time of 18–20 December.[44]

All 2d Guards Army planning occurred in maximum secrecy. Malinovsky planned only on his map, and the *front* commander and Vasilevsky approved those plans in person. All orders to corps and lower commanders were delivered orally.[45] By 18 December 1st Guards Rifle Corps' lead divisions closed into defenses along the Myshkov River. Two days later, when the German LVII Panzer Corps launched new assaults with its newly arrived 17th Panzer Division, 2d Guards Army's main force arrived and deployed for combat. For three days fighting raged along the Myshkov River. On 23 December the deteriorating situation north of the Don in Eighth Italian Army sector forced Army Group Don to shift 6th Panzer Division from LVII Corps to assist the beleaguered German defenders near Tatsinskaya and Morozovsk. This loss and growing Soviet strength along the Myshkov River forced LVII Panzer Corps to cease its march toward Stalingrad. Four days later, on 23 December, 2d Guards Army unleashed its assault and with 51st Army began pushing LVII Panzer Corps back to the Aksai River.

Manstein, commander of Army Group Don, recounted that after 27 December, "Two Soviet armies (Fifty-first and Second Guards, consisting of three mechanized, one tank, three rifle and one cavalry corps) were identified on the northern and eastern fronts of Fourth Panzer Army."[46]

It is clear that early in the relief attempt German forces over-estimated the strength of Soviet forces facing LVII Panzer Corps, for Soviet 51st Army was a weak one whose four rifle divisions were barely over 50 percent full. Subsequently, however, German intelligence did not detect the full scale of Soviet reinforcement, in particular the rapid movement southward of 2d Guards Army (see maps 29 and 30). Had it done so earlier, it would have realized the futility of the relief attempt, which, if it had progressed with full abandon, would likely have resulted in the loss of a major portion of LVII Panzer Corps. Thus, the German decision to end the relief attempt on 24 December was an intelligent one, even if not based on "hard" intelligence.

On the Kotel'nikovo direction, as elsewhere in the Stalingrad offensive, the Soviets displayed a new-found ability to move large forces great distances relatively undetected by German intelligence. Early in the operation, German failures could be credited to a fixation on the fighting at Stalingrad proper and a high-level preoccupation with the fate of Army Group Center. After the

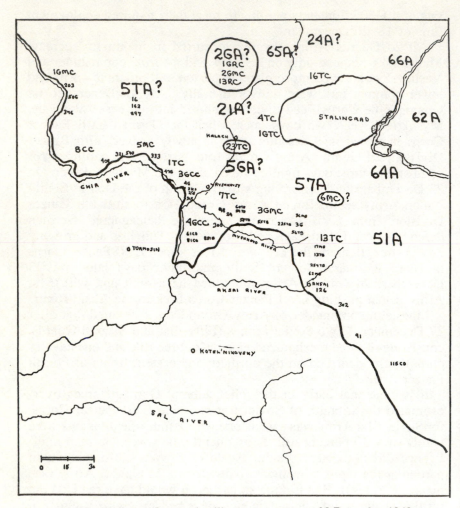

29. Kotel'nikovo, German intelligence assessment, 23 December 1942

encirclement of Sixth Army, the deteriorating situation contributed to German intelligence lapses. Yet at Stalingrad, unlike at Moscow a year before, this time a major reason for these German failures was improved Soviet *maskirovka*, in terms of active diversionary activity, secret planning, disinformation, movement security, and basic troop *maskirovka* discipline. In that regard Stalingrad boded ill for the future; and future operations would, to an increasing degree, be characterized by similar German failures and Soviet successes.

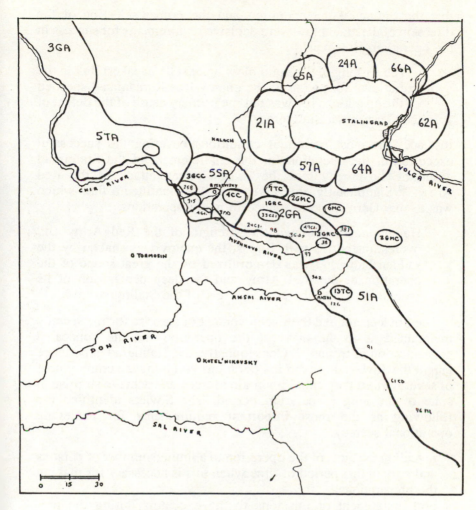

30. Kotel'nikovo, Soviet dispositions, 23 December 1942

The Lessons of Stalingrad

In the months after the operation had ended, the Soviet General Staff analysed data relating to the Stalingrad experiences.[47] Ultimately that analysis and analysis of subsequent operations occurring in the winter of 1942, provided the basis for its 1943 *Field Regulation* and other operational and tactical directives.

In their analysis of war experiences the General Staff singled out surprise and *maskirovka* as key ingredients of victory, emphasizing

TDAE—F*

that the timing of the operation and the proper selection of the direction of the main blow were decisive requirements for success in the operation. However:

> The striking of the main blow against the weakest link in the operational formation of the enemy [the Rumanians] speeded up the operations but was not the primary cause of the defeat of the Germans at Stalingrad.[48]

Instead, "the most important conditions ensuring the successful execution of the operation for the encirclement of the Stalingrad group of the enemy was the *sudden* counterattack of the Red Army."[49] Significantly, the Soviet analysts identified a flaw which was to mar German performance in many operations:

> Having underestimated the strength of the Red Army and overestimated his own forces, the enemy was shaken by the sudden blow and was demoralized by the great scope of the operation of the Red Army and the deep penetration of its mobile units into the strategic rear of the Stalingrad group.[50]

The Soviets credited their achievement of surprise to "the secrecy maintained as to the aims of the operation and the concealed concentration of troops."[51] Consequently, the Stalingrad experience taught the Soviets that even in operations involving the employment of several *fronts* they could maintain secrecy and achieve surprise in spite of the long preparation period. The Soviets identified the following as the most important requirements for achieving operational secrecy:

— revealing the aims of the operation to a limited number of persons and only in that period of time when this is necessary for making the preparations;
— oral assignment of missions to the executors during the preparatory period to the extent necessary for them to carry out their missions, with gradual broadening of orientation in proportion as the moment of action approaches;
— concealed concentration of troops and means of reinforcement in the area designated, the forbidding of movement in the daytime and careful camouflaging of troops in the areas of concentration;
— careful organization of the headquarters commandant's service in the areas of the concentration of troops, the prevention of the penetration into the afore-mentioned areas of persons not connected with the given large units (or small unit);

- forbidding the concentrated troops to conduct reconnaissance with their own forces, leaving for this purpose, at their disposal, sufficiently strong reconnaissance units, and also organs of combat security from the troops previously operating in the area;
- successful radio silence of the attacking units, especially of tanks, carried out on a large scale;
- movement and engineer preparations only at night;
- extremely careful feeling out of all the front by ordinary actions of shock detachments (of up to regimental size) separated by long time intervals to determine weak areas of the front;
- renunciation of artillery fire for adjustment;
- intensification of air attacks against enemy supply bases and command and control for many days prior to the beginning of the attack.[52]

All of these measures would become common practice as the Red Army prepared and conducted subsequent operations. They provided a base of knowledge upon which future planners could, and would, build.

THE WINTER CAMPAIGN, JANUARY–FEBRUARY 1943

Introduction

After frustrating German attempts to relieve encircled Sixth Army the *STAVKA* ordered its *fronts* in the southern Soviet Union to undertake a series of operations simultaneous to the destruction of the encircled force (see map 31). The *STAVKA* intended to apply maximum pressure on German forces and those of her allies by a series of successive *front* operations to collapse German defenses on the entire southern wing of the Eastern Front. The earliest of these operations were well-planned, but as time passed each successive operation became more hasty in nature. The last series of operations, in early February, were literally planned and conducted from the march. Planning time for the earlier operations was sufficient for the Soviets to engage in detailed *maskirovka* planning. Later operations were characterized by poor *maskirovka* as increasingly overtaxed and exhausted Soviet units sought to deliver that last blow required to produce German collapse.

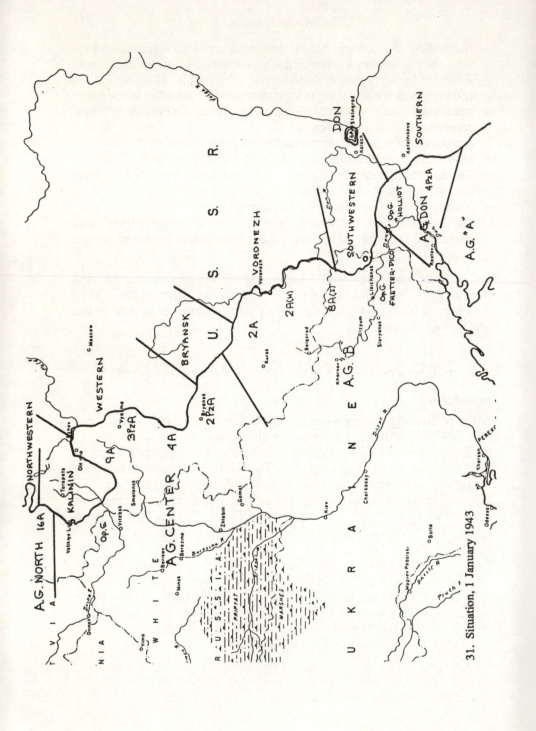

31. Situation, 1 January 1943

Ostrogozhsk–Rossosh', January 1943

The first of this series of *front* operations occurred shortly after the Southwestern Front's destruction of Eighth Italian Army. It sought to capitalize on the confusion within German Army Group "B," whose right flank had virtually been destroyed in the "Little Saturn" operation. The *STAVKA* ordered the Voronezh Front to strike the center of Army Group "B's" defenses, a sector manned by the Second Hungarian Army and German forces deployed along the Don River from Voronezh to Kantemirovka. The Voronezh Front, which had played a secondary, diversionary role in support of its left flank neighbor, the Southwestern Front, during operation "Little Saturn", would now have its chance to wreak destruction on German forces in the southern Soviet Union.

On 21 December the *STAVKA* ordered Lieutenant General F.I. Golikov's Voronezh Front to prepare and conduct an operation to destroy German forces in the Ostrogozhsk–Rossosh' area and clear German forces from the rail line between Liski and Kantemirovka. The Southwestern Front's 6th Army would cooperate with the attack. Prior to the operation the *STAVKA* reinforced the Voronezh Front's existing armies (38th, 60th, 40th, 18th Rifle Corps) with 3d Tank Army (two tank corps, one tank brigade, and two rifle divisions), 7th Cavalry Corps, three rifle divisions, and 4th Mechanized Corps, and appointed Zhukov and Vasilevsky to supervise preparations for the operation. Three shock groups would conduct the offensive: General K.S. Moskalenko's 40th Army from the Storozhevoye bridgehead south of Voronezh, Major General P.S. Rybalko's 3d Tank Army from south of Novaya Kalitva, and Major General P.M. Zykov's 18th Rifle Corps from the region southeast of Liski. Virtually all of the forces of the left flank and center of the Voronezh Front (90 percent of rifle forces and artillery, 100 percent of armor) concentrated in these three attack sectors (250 of 450 kilometers).[53] The shock groups of 40th Army and 3d Tank Army would penetrate German defenses and link up southwest of Ostrogozhsk to entrap major elements of Army Group "B" (Soviets planned to encircle 14 of 22 enemy divisions in the region).

All commands involved in the operation implemented extensive *maskirovka* plans to conceal attack preparations and mislead the Germans regarding the location of the main attacks. All planning was subject to the same stringent control measures that had been used in the Stalingrad operation, including limitations on the number of planners and strict document controls.

The large scale regroupment necessitated by the plan required the Soviets to direct considerable energy to concealing troop movements. An elaborate regroupment plan controlled all unit movements. All movement occurred at night, and a specific staff monitored movement and directed the work of a large group of traffic regulators. By early January all regrouping within the *front* was completed.[54] Movement of *front* reinforcements proved more difficult in light of the limited transport means and deep snow.

The operations order required Rybalko's 3d Tank Army to move its personnel, equipment, and 493 tanks a distance of 130–170 kilometers from its railhead to the Kantemirovka area after a 9–15 day rail trip over a 25 day period from the area just south of Plavsk. 3d Tank Army began concentrating at Kantemirovka on 4 January and completed the process on 13 January (causing the 3d Tank Army's offensive to be delayed until 14 January).[55] Ultimately, 371 tanks completed the move. From 7 to 13 January 3d Tank Army prepared for the offensive in maximum secrecy. Rifle divisions conducted reconnaissance with one reinforced rifle battalion each. These battalions assumed unit designations of the 350th Rifle Division, a division which had been in position a long time and was assigned the task of covering the deployment of 3d Tank Army. In 40th Army's attack sector the redeployment process was also difficult and, because of transport problems, 4th Mechanized Corps arrived too late to participate in opening phases of the operation.[56]

The Voronezh Front created a comprehensive plan for operational *maskirovka* described by General Golikov:

> In order to conceal the plan of our operation and deceive the fascists we conducted a series of measures. The plan of misinformation included: false regroupings of troops in weakened sectors; transport and unloading of repair tanks and mock-ups at railroad stations adjacent to passive sectors; massive demonstrations of an approach to the forward edge of these sectors of false *chasti* [regiments] and the conduct of false exercises by them; a show of artillery reinforcement in these sectors by means of the widespread use of "roving" guns and M-13 and M-20 rocket launchers; the conduct of false reconnoitering; the "loss" of directives and leaflets with the missions of the attack on Voronezh and Pavlovsk; active maneuver by radio facilities through the Front zone; clearing of roads in

false directions; movement in daylight of troop columns toward passive sectors, etc.

It was our purpose to show the enemy that our passive defense sectors were not only not being weakened, but conversely reinforced, and that we were contemplating active operations there.

At the same time, we accomplished careful camouflage of our assault forces. Nearly all of the *soyedineniya* [divisions] designated in the composition of the assault groups had to carry out difficult marches of 200–350 kilometers. In daylight, they used the roads leading to the passive sectors of the forthcoming offensive, and at night they used roads which entered the regions of actual concentration. In this total zone, there were also *chasti* which were not taking part in the offensive. They served only as objects of misinformation – by day, they went to the forward edge, and at night they returned. And they did this several times.

It is necessary to add to what has been said that our weak forces, located in the passive sectors, conducted demonstration offensive operations at a whole series of points. Thus, the 270th Rifle Division, occupying a 65-kilometer front, launched an attack on the Alpine Corps at the same time as the 3d Tank Army. Our *podrazdeleniya* [battalions] also conducted demonstrative offensive operations from the direction of Liska station. All of this, taken together, made it possible for us to deceive the enemy once and for all as to our intentions.[57]

The *front maskirovka* plan required Moskalenko's 40th Army to employ imitative deception to confuse the Germans regarding the location of its main attack. In December Moskalenko had employed such a plan in conjunction with Operation "Little Saturn." From 7 to 20 December 40th Army had postured for an attack in the Storozhevoye bridgehead sector against Korotoyaka and Svoboda.[58] This distracted Army Group "B's" attention from the real Soviet main attack east of Novaya Kalitva. After the Southwestern Front's 16 December attack Moskalenko changed the focus of his deception measures, this time to deceive the Germans into believing the Soviet attack would emanate from the Voronezh region.[59] Moskalenko ordered the construction of ice bridges across the Don River at Voronezh and the organization of troop movements into the Voronezh region, in particular at night.[60] He used a reserve regiment, a second echelon division, and army reserves under a special group from the army staff to implement his plan. These units conducted actual movement to and from the front lines. As a result "the enemy believed in the intention of Soviet forces to take Voronezh. One must say that there was nothing surprising in this. The *STAVKA* actually planned to liberate that city in the near future. But it was decided to first destroy the enemy along the Don."[61]

While the Soviets were implementing measures to fix German forces in the Voronezh area they also simulated attack preparations in the Liski and Pavlovska sectors of 18th Rifle Corps. As a result, Army Group "B" moved a reserve corps consisting of the 26th, 168th Infantry and the 1st Hungarian Panzer Division, into that sector while maintaining a large force opposite Voronezh.[62]

Just before the new offensive began, the Soviets conducted deceptive reconnaissance in 40th Army's sector just as in 3d Tank Army's sector. Reconnaissance began on 12 January when the advanced battalions of the shock group replaced units covering their forward deployment. Shortly thereafter assault division main forces deployed into forward positions.

These measures worked. German attention remained riveted to the Voronezh and Liski areas where they deployed their main strength (see maps 32 and 33). The Germans assessed that the Soviets had deployed portions of two rifle divisions, one rifle brigade, and one tank brigade in the Storozhevoye bridgehead, when, in fact, there were almost three times as many troops there.[63] German intelligence failed to note the redeployment of 3d Tank Army from the region east of Kursk to its new attack positions north of Kantemirovka and the concentration of Soviet 18th Separate Rifle Corps east of Liski. The commander of the Italian III Alpine Corps later stated:

> We were poorly informed about the condition of Russian forces, about their composition, and the quality of their defense, rather we knew nothing. We did not suppose that the Russians were preparing an offensive, and therefore did not pay special attention to those important questions.[64]

40th Army commenced its offensive on 13 January, joined the following day by other *front* shock forces. By 18 January the northern and southern shock groups united, encircling the bulk of Second Hungarian Army and a number of German divisions. Fresh from this victory the *STAVKA* ordered a new offensive, this time against German Second Army defending at Voronezh.

Voronezh–Kastornoye, January 1943

The destruction of Hungarian Second Army left German Second Army (consisting of 10 German and two Hungarian divisions) defending a vulnerable, if not untenable, salient jutting eastward to the Don River at Voronezh. Although Second Army's northern flank and center seemed stable, the defeat of forces on its southern flank made its position perilous. Second Army was opposed in the north by the Bryansk Front's 13th Army and the Voronezh Front's 38th Army, on its center along the Don River by the Voronezh Front's 60th Army and, on its open southern flank by 40th Army, then just completing destruction of Hungarian Second Army.

On 18 January Vasilevsky submitted a plan to the *STAVKA* for the encirclement and destruction of German Second Army by attacks from the north by Major General N.P. Pukhov's 13th Army and from the south by Moskalenko's advancing 40th Army, spearheaded by Major General A.G. Kravchenko's 4th Tank Corps. The two armies were to unite west of Kastornoye and, supported by 38th and 60th Armies, destroy encircled elements of German Second Army. This was to be the first of the winter *front* offensives launched in part by forces already on the march.[65] The following day the *STAVKA* approved the plan, and on 21 January Vasilevsky issued orders to Lieutenant General M.A. Reiter the Bryansk Front commander and Golikov of the Voronezh Front. The 40th Army was to complete its destruction of Hungarian forces by 21 January, regroup, and commence the new attack on 24 January. On 25 January Lieutenant General I.D. Chernyakhovsky's 60th Army and on 26 January Pukhov's 13th Army and Lieutenant General N.E. Chibisov's 38th Army would join the attack. By 30 January the four armies were to have destroyed German Second Army and driven its remnants westward to the Tim River near Staryi Oskol.[66]

Although the position of the German Second Army was already becoming untenable, and, in fact, German forces ordered a withdrawal from Voronezh just before the Soviet offensive, the Soviets, nevertheless, developed a *maskirovka* plan and maintained strict planning secrecy.[67] Security measures in 13th Army were particularly strict.[68] Only a limited number of officers formulated the army operations plan, all necessary documents were prepared by hand in only one copy, and individuals received orders

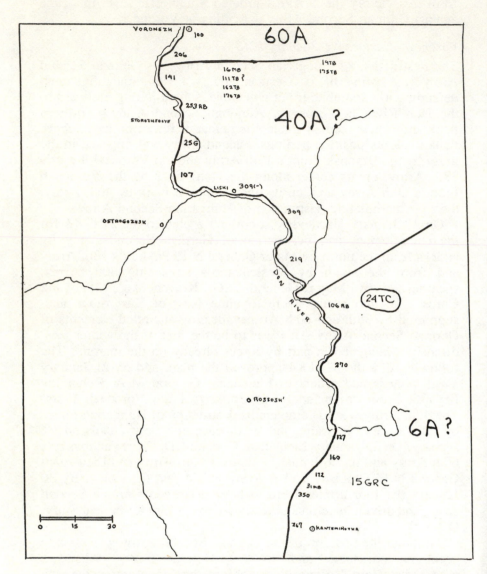

32. Ostrogozhsk–Rossosh', German intelligence assessment, 13 January 1943

concerning only their activity and responsibilities. In exercises and war games prior to the offensive, division commanders were familiarized with the overall plan only to an extent required by the exercise. All exercise documents were secured under lock and key

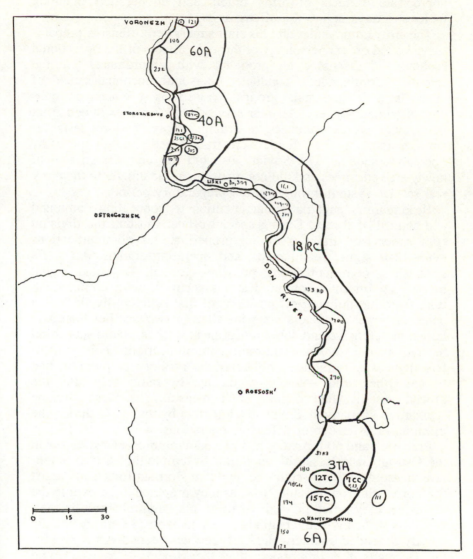

33. Ostrogozhsk–Rossosh', Soviet dispositions, 13 January 1943

by the army staff and only the army commander and chief of staff had access to these documents. Notes pertaining to any aspect of operational planning were encoded, and commanders issued orders to subordinates orally and on a map prepared by the army staff. Officers of the army operations department personally provided appropriate extracts of army orders and cooperation planning tables two days before the offensive began.

The army commander and his staff supervised offensive preparations, issued orders personally or through officers of the operational section, and discussed all problems with subordinates "on the terrain." Commanders conducted personal reconnaissance of attack sectors in small groups dressed as privates or non-commissioned officers. All rear service units were excluded from operational correspondences regarding supply; and requests for supplies (shelter, fuel, food) were transmitted through the army operations section. The Soviets also hid the unit designation of newly arrived forces and did not incorporate the units into the army rear service system throughout the preparatory period.

Headquarters paid particular attention to concealing command and control of forces. During special officer musters the division staff supervised training in the proper use of communications tables, call signs, coded maps, and operating signals. All staffs established communications priorities for all technical signal means. To improve communications security, wire communications from the jumping-off positions of first echelon divisions to a depth of three kilometers were installed in two parallel lines and buried in defensive and communications trenches. Radio sets could receive but not transmit, and radio communications between artillery units was forbidden until after the artillery preparation had begun. Other units could communicate by radio only after the ground assaults had begun. Such measures as these became standard in virtually all Soviet headquarters by mid-1943 during the planning of offensive or defensive operations.

Both 38th and 60th Armies had played a minor *maskirovka* role in the Ostrogozhsk–Rossosh' operation by employing active defensive measures in their sectors to tie down German forces and assist the Voronezh Front assault. Now, as they prepared to go over to the offensive, they relied on 40th Army to play a similar role in their behalf. 40th Army would begin its new attack on 24 January into the weakly defended southern flank of German Second Army to give the Germans the impression that the Soviet offensive would materialize only from the south and to distract the Germans from 13th and 38th Armies' offensive preparations. At the same time 38th Army demonstrated offensive intent on its left flank against the rear of the German Voronezh bridgehead. 38th Army's simulation forced German forces in the Voronezh sector to withdraw westward across the Don River on 25 January.[69]

Meanwhile, further south 40th Army completed destroying encircled Hungarian Second Army and from 21 to 24 January regrouped its units. This involved transferring a 22 kilometer sector on 40th Army's right flank along with two rifle divisions and two tank brigades to 60th Army. 40th Army then received from *front* reserve two rifle divisions, one rifle brigade, and 4th Tank Corps which had arrived too late to participate in the Ostrogozhsk–Rossosh' operation. By 24 January 40th Army had turned on its axis 90 degrees from a western and southwestern posture to a northern and northwestern orientation and was prepared to resume its offensive.[70]

German intelligence was aware of the deteriorating situation on Second Army's right flank but failed to detect 13th and 38th Armies' offensive preparations (see maps 34 and 35). German forces reacted to the former threat and abandoned Voronezh but, in so doing, suffered an even worse reverse when the unexpected assaults from the north began.

Bryansk and Voronezh Front armies attacked as planned from 24 to 26 January and within days encircled two of three corps of Second German Army which then engaged in a costly battle to break out of encirclement westward. Although marginally contributing to the almost foreordained success of Soviet forces at Kastornoye, *maskirovka* measures displayed a sophistication not evident in subsequent Soviet operations during the winter of 1943.

Postscript – The Donbas and Khar'kov

Although the Soviets displayed considerable skill at tactical and operational *maskirovka* during and after the Stalingrad offensive and had standardized *maskirovka* procedures to a considerable extent, the efficacy of those measures depended to a large degree on thorough planning. Thoroughness was a direct product of available time. Thus where planning time was short or non-existent, *maskirovka* tended to be sloppy or was neglected altogether. This became apparent in the frantic Soviet drive across southern Russia in late January and February 1943.

Before the Voronezh–Kastornoye operation was finished, the *STAVKA* ordered all of its operating *fronts* in the south to conduct simultaneous offensive operations in the hope that German Army Group "Don" would collapse (see map 36). Such a collapse would result in destruction of that army group and of Army Group "A"

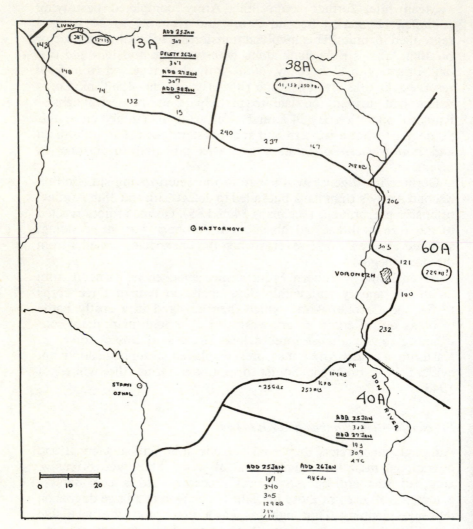

34. Voronezh–Kastornoye, German intelligence assessment, 24 January 1943

which still occupied extended though hard-pressed positions in the Caucasus.

While the Soviet Southern Front drove German forces back toward Rostov, the *STAVKA* ordered the Voronezh and South-western Fronts to strike the junction of Army Groups "B" and Don southeast of Khar'kov. The grand design of the *STAVKA* echoed the offensive abandon evident in early 1942. The Voronezh Front

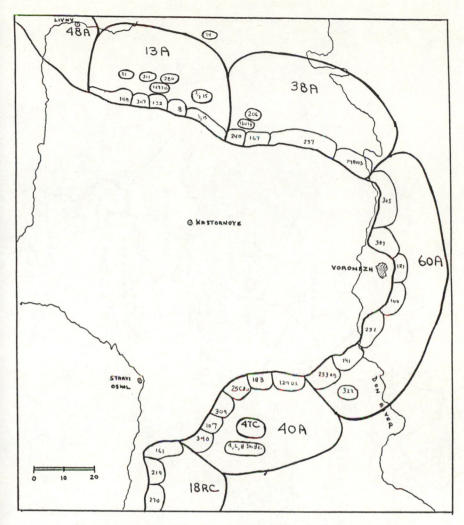

35. Voronezh–Kastornoye, Soviet dispositions, 24 January 1943

was to seize Kursk, Belgorod, and Khar'kov and, if possible, push toward the Dnepr River southeast of Kiev. The Southwestern Front was to advance westward toward Izyum and then swing south across the Northern Donets River, occupy Zaporozh'ye and bridgeheads across the Dnepr, and ultimately reach the Sea of Azov near Melitopol' thus entrapping Army Group Don and isolating Army Group "A" in the Kuban area.

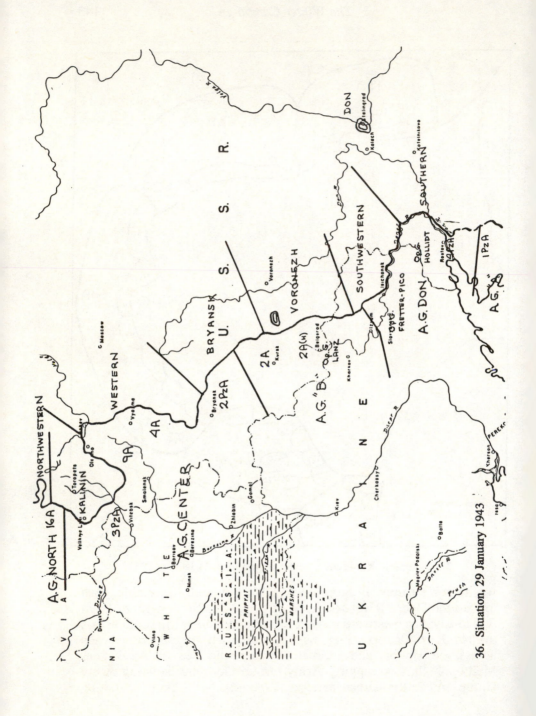

36. Situation, 29 January 1943

This grand design for a new and larger Stalingrad was fueled by *STAVKA* optimism that the Germans were nearing collapse and by a woeful over-estimation of their own force capabilities. The new offensives (later named the Khar'kov and Donbas operations) began in late January, from the march and without extensive planning. Although Soviet units individually observed basic *maskirovka* tenets, it is doubtful Soviet *front* and armies planned active deception operations on the scale of those used at Stalingrad. Moreover, the hasty preparations and regrouping militated against the effectiveness of passive *maskirovka* measures. Consequently, German intelligence kept track of Soviet force movements, even though at the outset of the operation the Germans could do little to counter the rapidly developing Soviet offensives.

Soviet forces swept westward to Kursk and through Khar'kov, across the Northern Donets, and toward the Dnepr River in the rear of Army Group Don.[71] While they advanced, unit strength eroded because of the skillful German defense and the debilitating effects of time and distance on forces operating at the end of long and tenuous supply lines. The Germans reacted by holding firmly to positions along the shoulders of the penetration and by rapidly shifting large forces from the Caucasus through the Rostov "gate" into the Donets Basin (Donbas) to counter the exploiting Soviet forces.

In one of the clearest cases of self-deception on the Eastern Front, the Soviets permitted their optimism and over-confidence to cloud their judgement. Soviet intelligence detected the large scale German redeployment of armored forces westward but steadfastly interpreted that movement as a German withdrawal to new defensive positions along the Dnepr River. Consistently, the *STAVKA* and the *front* commands clung to their optimistic view as they spurred their advancing forces on, even as Soviet lower level commanders began to suspect and fear the worst.

By mid-February the Germans had contained the Soviet advance west of Kursk and short of Poltava, but Soviet forces were nearing the Dnepr River on a broad front north and south of Dnepropetrovsk. By this time Field Marshal Manstein of Army Group Don had nearly completed orchestrating a regroupment which was about to bring to bear the force of three panzer corps against the flanks of advancing Soviet forces. Soviet army commanders' warnings went unheeded as message after message from the *STAVKA* and Southwestern Front headquarters urged their forces on. Soviet intelligence continued to misinterpret the clear evidence of major

German troop concentrations south of Khar'kov and in the Donbas. Only on 23 February, days after the devastating German counter-stroke had begun, did the air of unreality enveloping the *STAVKA* and Southwestern Front headquarters evaporate. By then it was too late. By the end of February Soviet forces were reeling back to the Northern Donets River after heavy losses. Subsequently, in early March, Manstein mauled the Voronezh Front and seized Khar'kov and Belgorod before Soviet reinforcements and the spring thaw brought operations to a halt.

The events of February and March had a sobering effect on the Soviet High Command. Once and for all, it ended the Soviet tendency to launch offensives designed to succeed at all costs – offensives like those conducted in the winter of 1942 and 1943. It prompted a period of sober reflection on the part of the Soviets, a period which endured to July 1943. That period was probably the most productive in the entire war for the Soviets in terms of force reorganization and the analysis and inculcation of war experience into Red Army combat theory and practice. In the late spring and early summer of 1943 the Soviets created the basic force structure which would endure until war's end and drafted the directives and regulations which incorporated lessons learned at Stalingrad and during the winter. Subsequent Soviet combat performance at Kursk and thereafter attested to the effectiveness of that Soviet study and analysis. In the realm of *maskirovka* the legacy of that analysis soon became clear.

THE KURSK STRATEGIC OPERATION, JULY 1943

Prelude

After the three month wave of almost constant Soviet offensives had ended in the setbacks of February and March 1943, an operational lull set in on the Eastern Front (see map 37). During the lull German planners pondered ways to regain the strategic initiative in the East by capitalizing on the victories of March. Although the Germans considered several offensive plans, all in the south, their attention and that of Hitler was inexorably drawn to the Kursk Bulge, which seemed to be a ripe target for envelopment. If the Soviets chose to defend it, it offered the opportunity to bleed the Red Army white in a relatively small sector without subjecting German forces to arduous operations over long distances, which had been the Germans' Achilles' heel in the past.

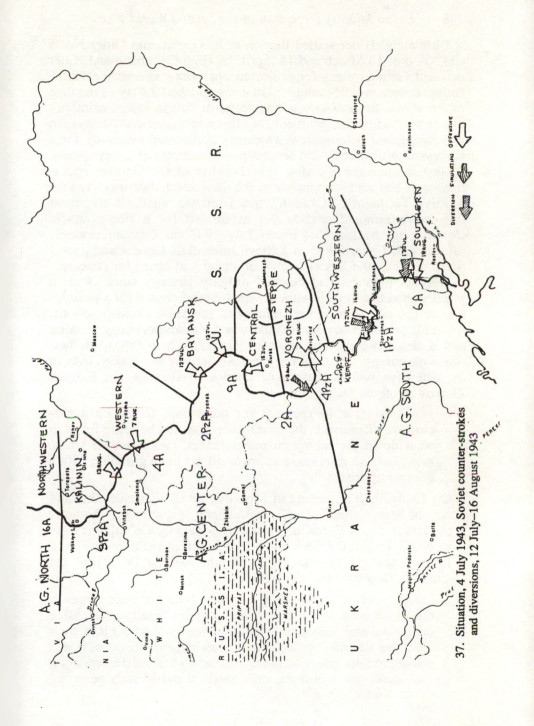

37. Situation, 4 July 1943, Soviet counter-strokes and diversions, 12 July–16 August 1943

Ultimately, Hitler settled the issue. In Operational Order No. 5 and No. 6 of 13 March and 15 April the High Command and Hitler outlined German plans for projected operations against the Kursk Bulge, codenamed "Citadel."[72] Hitler established 3 May as the date of the attack. Immediately a long series of delays began, primarily associated with the problem of force preparation. Delays in regrouping and fielding new weaponry considered necessary for a successful offensive forced several postponements of the operation. At last, despite the growing apprehension of the German operations staff and some commanders, the final attack date was fixed for 5 July. To launch "Citadel," the Germans amassed the most impressive armored armada yet assembled for a single attack. Considering the fact that up to July 1943 no German strategic offensive had ever failed to achieve immediate tactical and operational success, the Soviet High Command had cause for concern.

STAVKA planners had debated military strategy since German planners had begun their work in April. Stalin argued for a resumption of the offensive in the summer to pre-empt German actions, while his principal advisors (Zhukov and Vasilevsky) urged caution and a defensive posture until the Germans had expended their offensive energy. Then, they argued, Soviet forces could go over to the offensive with a reasonable chance of success. On 8 April Zhukov wrote to Stalin:

> I consider it inexpedient for our troops to launch a pre-emptive offensive in the near future. It would be better for us to wear down the enemy on our defenses, knock out his tanks, bring in fresh reserves, and finish off his main grouping with a general offensive.[73]

On 12 April, at a meeting in Moscow, Zhukov, Vasilevsky, and Chief of the General Staff's operations department, Antonov argued their case with Stalin. Armed with messages of support from *front* commanders, the three convinced Stalin of the necessity for a defensive strategy. General S.M. Shtemenko, 1st Deputy of the Operations Department, later wrote:

> Ultimately it was decided to concentrate our main forces in the Kursk area, to bleed the enemy forces here in a defensive operation, and then switch to the offensive and achieve their complete destruction. To provide against eventualities, it was considered necessary to build deep and secure defenses along the whole strategic front, making them particularly powerful in the Kursk sector.[74]

Stalin's general defense plan directed that the Voronezh and Central Fronts defend the Kursk Bulge, flanked on the north by the Bryansk Front and on the south by the Southwestern Front. In the rear Stalin created a large strategic reserve, the Steppe Military District, which would ultimately become the Steppe Front. Since Soviet planners were uncertain throughout April of the direction of the main German thrust, which they assumed would be against Kursk or south of Khar'kov, the *STAVKA* ordered all five *fronts* to erect strong defenses. Initially, the reserve armies of the Steppe Military District, formed around the nucleus of 5th Guards Tank Army, assembled in the Liski area east of Khar'kov, a location from which they could deploy to meet either German thrust.

After some uncertainty in early May when Stalin again considered a pre-emptive assault, the *STAVKA* by mid-May settled firmly on the defensive plan. As reported by Zhukov:

> The final decision concerning the deliberate defense was accepted by the *STAVKA* at the end of May and beginning of June 1943 when it became known, in fact in all its details, about the German intention to strike the Voronezh and Central Fronts a strong blow by the use of large tank groups and new "Tiger" tanks and "Ferdinand" assault guns.[75]

Maskirovka During the Strategic Defense

For the first time in the war the *STAVKA* formulated a general strategic defense plan incorporating broad *maskirovka* measures which assisted in the strategic defense and concealed preparations for offensive operations.

The *STAVKA* directive assigned defensive missions to all *fronts* but, at the same time, incorporated into the defense two major counter-strokes, one to begin during the German offensive and the second to follow shortly after the German offensive had ended. Never before had the Soviets planned counter-strokes so soon in a defensive operation. The *STAVKA* also ordered strict *maskirovka* measures to cover the assembly and redeployment of the strategic reserve – the Steppe Military District. Accompanying the defense and preceding the major counter-strokes, the Soviets ordered *fronts* in other sectors to undertake diversionary offensives of their own timed to drain German operational reserves away from the point where the counter-strokes would occur. The Soviets also planned to deliver against the concentrated German forces, once that concentration had been detected, major pre-emptive air and artillery counter-preparations to disrupt the final stage of German deployment.

The missions assigned to Soviet *fronts* reflected these extensive plans. The Voronezh and Central Fronts were to erect substantial defenses within the Kursk Bulge and, while concealing as much of their forces and preparations as possible, would meet and defeat the main German assaults on Kursk from the north and south. The Steppe Front was to displace secretly northward to occupy assembly areas east of Kursk, back up the two forward *fronts*, prepare to repulse German penetrations, and launch a major counter-stroke on the Belgorod–Khar'kov axis after the defensive phase at Kursk had ended. The Bryansk Front and left wing of the Western Front were to support the Central Front's defense and prepare to undertake a major counter-stroke against German forces at Orel as soon as the Central Front had halted the German advance. The Southwestern and Southern Fronts were to prepare diversionary attacks in the south. Zhukov described the purpose of the diversionary attacks, stating, "In order to tie down enemy forces and forestall maneuver of his reserves, individual offensive operations were envisioned on a number of directions in the south of the country, and also on the northwestern direction."[6] The most important diversions would occur in the Donbas and along the Mius River.

Thus, Soviet strategic planning involved a deliberate planned defense incorporating several broad strategic *maskirovka* measures. First, while the defense operations unfolded, large troop concentrations would form in secrecy and prepare to launch a massive counter-stroke against German forces at Orel and to back up the Kursk defenders. Within days after the Kursk defenders had halted the German advance a second regroupment, conducted under massive security measures, would take place preparatory to the conduct of a second massive counter-stroke toward Belgorod and Khar'kov. During the interval between the first and second counter-strokes, the Southern and Southwestern Fronts would conduct diversionary offensives across the Northern Donets and Mius Rivers into the Donbas. Preparations for these offensives would occur during the German offensive phase, and it was all the better if the Germans detected those offensive preparations (which they obviously did). The defense plan also included a pre-emptive artillery and air strike and extensive defense preparations within the Kursk bulge, concealed to as great an extent as possible. All of these

6. Advancing Soviet armor, Kursk, July, 1943

7. Advancing Soviet armor, Kursk, July, 1943

measures were dependent upon Soviet intelligence, which was remarkably accurate regarding German intentions at Kursk.[77]

Zhukov and Vasilevsky supervised the preparation and conduct of the Kursk defense. *Front* and army commanders in the Kursk bulge exerted tremendous efforts to create a deeply echeloned and firepower intensive defense while attempting to ensure the secrecy of those preparations. *Maskirovka* was extensive. Building upon the experiences of earlier operations the Central, Voronezh, and Steppe Front staffs prepared detailed *maskirovka* plans which included the concealment of preparations, creation of false troop concentrations, simulation of false radio nets and communications centers, construction of false air facilities and false aircraft, and the dissemination of false rumors along the front and in the enemy rear area.[78] These plans emphasized secret movement of reserves, hidden preparations for counter-attacks and counter-strokes, and concealed locations of command posts and communications sites.

To conceal the deployment of 7th Guards Army into the area east of Belgorod and to insure radio security throughout the Voronezh Front all radio transmissions were prohibited. All sets could receive transmissions, but these were sent from armies and corps only in short 10–15 second bursts. All acknowledgements were then sent by wire communications. To maintain communications security all radio call signs were changed daily, and frequencies changed five times a month. When 7th Guards Army deployed into 69th Army's sector (in June), all orders to that army passed through 69th Army communications. In addition, the chief of staff of each *front* controlled the flow of all written correspondence to the army and corps staffs and determined who would work on each required project.[79]

To deceive extensive German air reconnaissance conducted in June and early July, *front* and army commanders established 15 false airfields, complete with mock-up aircraft, runways, control towers, and aircraft shelters and installed numerous mock-up tanks to simulate armored assembly areas (829 tank mock-ups in the Voronezh Front sector alone). German aircraft responded by bombing these false airfields nine times. The Soviets also prepared false gun positions along and in the depths of the front.[80] Every effort was made to make false assembly areas appear as "active" by using combat units and *maskirovka* units to simulate vehicle movement. In some army sectors the defenses included false first defensive positions in front of actual defenses to deceive the Germans into firing their preparation on unoccupied positions.

Concentration of forces into initial defense positions and all regrouping was conducted at night under strict blackout conditions. Fires were prohibited. Daytime preparations for movement included the staking out of routes and the establishment of a network of road guides. The engineers prepared concealed positions for deploying forces at night two days prior to their occupation. The Soviets emplaced minefields and obstacles in concealed locations and camouflaged them to blend in with the terrain. Similar care was taken to conceal communications lines and centers and defensive trench systems.

Movement by rail occurred only at night and increased during bad weather. Troops and equipment unloaded on the approaches to rail stations rather than at the stations themselves. Army supply services established depots in forests, ravines, and small populated places to make German aerial detection difficult.

Front and army commanders labored to hide command and observation posts by camouflage, radio deception, and by restricting the flow of visitors to each point. Lieutenant General P.I. Batov of 65th Army (Central Front) forbade his army staff to receive any visitors except subordinate division commanders, their deputies, or their chiefs of staff. The heads of all other army departments placed representatives in nearby villages where they conducted their business. All movement, on foot or by vehicle, was forbidden near command posts during the day, and at night only blackout movement was allowed, only by vehicles with special permits.[81] Lieutenant General I.M. Chistyakov of 6th Guards Army directed his subordinate units to create a system of false observation points manned by experienced reconnaissance personnel.[82]

Lieutenant General I.S. Konev's Steppe Front played an important part in both the defensive and offensive phases of the Kursk operation. In particular his forces generated a major portion of the element of surprise. Konev described the situation:

> Did the enemy know about the organization of a firm defense in the rear of our fronts? He knew. And that played a positive role. The enemy thought that we were preparing only for defensive battle. Possessing a huge number of tanks and SP guns of a new type, the Germans hoped that it was impossible to stop them.
>
> Thus as the enemy prepared, we prepared. The main thing was not to conceal the fact of our preparations, but rather the force and means, the concept of battle, the time of our counter-

offensive, and the nature of our defense. Very likely it was the only unprecedented occasion in military history, when the strong side, having the capabilities for offensive action, went over to the defense. The future course of events affirmed that in the given instance the most correct decision was made.[83]

This situation accorded the Steppe Front a critical role in the operation, and *maskirovka* played a considerable role in that *front's* success.

On 5 July 1943 Konev issued a special *maskirovka* directive which cited earlier deficiencies and mandated stricter *maskirovka* discipline.[84] Konev ordered army and corps commanders to implement specific *maskirovka* measures including: camouflage of troops, defensive lines, depots, and all critical objectives; plans to deceive the enemy regarding key objectives by the construction of false objectives, supply points, and unit concentrations; plans for erection of a false air defense network complete with dummy gun positions; and plans for the use of reconnaissance units to assist in camouflaging work and to check *maskirovka* efforts.

Throughout the preparations the *STAVKA* repeatedly reminded Konev of his responsibilities. An order of 9 July (after commencement of the German offensive) renamed Konev's force the Steppe Front, ordered his armies "to deploy in accordance with the verbal orders given by the General Staff" and "complete the movement of forces only at night."[85]

All of these *maskirovka* measures contributed to German underestimation of the resilience of the Soviet defenses, although some senior German commanders like Model and Manstein had reservations concerning the wisdom of the attack. General G. Schmidt, commander of 19th Panzer Division noted, "We knew too little about the strengthening of the Russians in this region [Oboyan and Korocha] prior to the beginning of the offensive .... We did not assume that there was even one fourth of what we had to encounter ..."[86]

General F. von Mellenthin observed:

> The penetration of the Russian positions, covered by large minefields, at the very beginning of the offensive proved more difficult for us than we had assumed. The horrible counterattacks, in which huge masses of manpower and equipment took part, were an unpleasant surprise for us .... The most clever camouflage of the Russians should be emphasized again. We did not manage to detect even one minefield or anti-

tank area until such time as the first tank was blown up by a mine, or the first Russian anti-tank guns opened fire.[87]

German intelligence detected most Soviet units in the forward defenses and most of the Soviet armor in tactical and operational reserve (see maps 38–41). It did not identify Soviet forces in the depths, in particular the second echelon armies. Nor did it grasp the coherency and strength of the Soviet defenses.

Defensive operations at Kursk commenced several hours before the German attack when the Soviets conducted their pre-emptive counter-preparation. At 0220 hours Zhukov reported to Stalin that his "symphony" of heavy artillery and multiple rocket launchers had begun.[88] Zhukov assessed the impact of the counter-preparation:

> Then, it was difficult to understand and determine immediately the results of the counter-preparation, but the insufficiently organized and non-simultaneous offensive begun by the Germans at 0530 bespoke of serious losses which were caused by our counter-preparation. Prisoners taken during the battle said that our counter-preparation was unexpected and that artillery, especially, suffered and almost all communications systems and observation and command and control systems were destroyed.[89]

Since the Soviet fire struck a broad area rather than specific targets, the Germans were able to avoid mass casualties.

Thereafter, the operation unfolded, first according to the German plan and, then, in accordance with the Soviet timetable. German assaults struck the Central and Voronezh Front's main defense sectors on 5 July.[90] As fighting raged in both sectors, the *STAVKA* implemented its strategic plans. On 7 July it ordered the Southern and Southwestern Fronts to begin preparations for offensives to commence on 17 July. Two days later the *STAVKA* ordered Konev to move his Steppe Front into positions from which it could support the two forward *fronts*. Almost simultaneously, it ordered the Bryansk and Western Fronts to make final preparations for their assaults on German positions around Orel.

Throughout the defensive phase of operations the Soviets still engaged in active *maskirovka* designed to conceal the movement of tactical and operational reserves. For example, the Voronezh Front tasked its Chief of Engineers with creating a false armored concentration near Sazhnoye to cover the redeployment of 2d Guards Tank Corps from that sector to another area. From 9 to 12

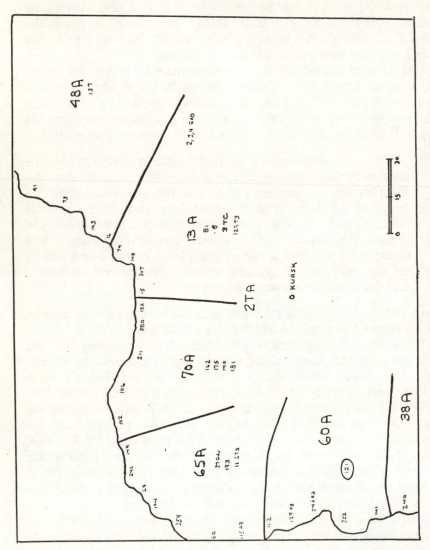

38. Kursk, German intelligence assessment, northern sector, 5 July 1943

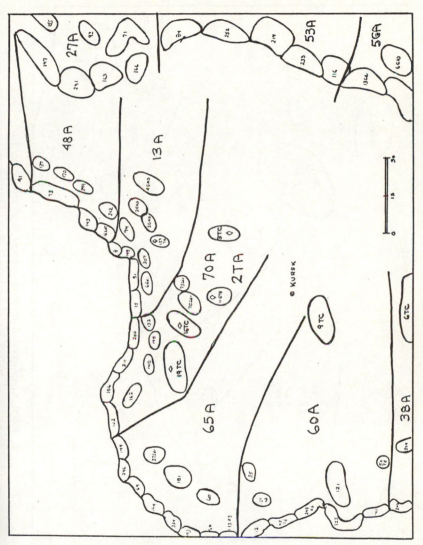

39. Kursk, Soviet Central Front dispositions, 5 July 1943

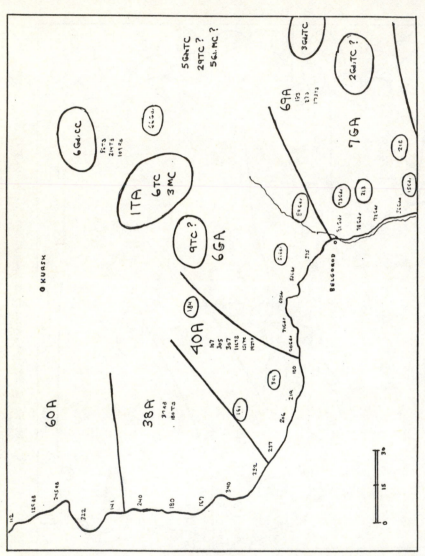

40. Kursk, German intelligence assessment, southern sector, 5 July 1943

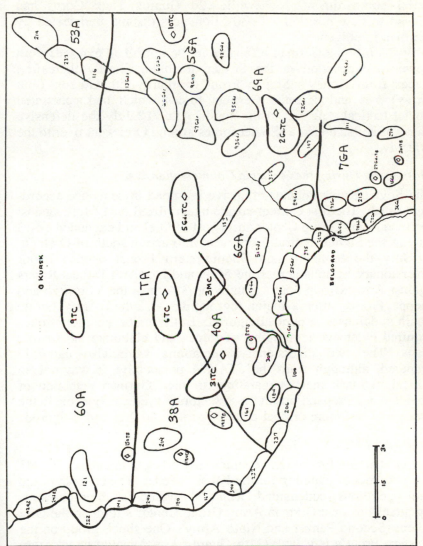

41. Kursk, Soviet Voronezh Front dispositions, 5 July 1943

July a team of 35 men from the 5th Engineer Brigade built 105 mock-up tanks to simulate the concentration, then cut tank tracks into the ground by hand to "animate" the area. Enemy aviation detected the concentration, bypassed it with its armor, and subjected it to heavy aerial bombardment. Meanwhile, 2d Guards Tank Corps had moved to new positions 20–30 kilometers distant, undetected by German intelligence.[91]

By 12 July the German offensive in the north had expired, worn down to exhaustion in the Soviet defenses. Shortly thereafter, forces from Konev's Steppe Front (primarily 5th Guards Tank Army) met and defeated German forces which had penetrated Soviet tactical defenses in the south. After 12 July the defensive phase of Kursk ended as Soviet forces around Orel went over to the offensive.

Maskirovka During the Strategic Counter-offensive

The Soviet Kursk counter-offensive unfolded in sequence according to plan. The first counter-stroke materialized on 12 July against German Army Group Center northwest of Orel and expanded on 13 July as the Soviet Central Front went into action south of Orel. On 17 July the Southern and Southwestern Fronts opened major diversionary assaults across the Mius and Northern Donets Rivers against Army Group South. Finally on 3 August the Voronezh and Steppe Fronts, after a major regrouping, assaulted Army Group South's defenses around Belgorod. Both major counter-strokes required extensive regrouping of forces and elaborate *maskirovka* plans. The two diversionary operations were also carefully prepared, although from the *STAVKA* perspective it was not so critical to mask their preparation. In fact, German detection of Soviet attack preparations in those sectors played a major role in the success of the more critical counter-strokes at Orel and Belgorod.

Orel, July 1943

Soviet planning for the Orel counter-stroke began in late April 1943 as an adjunct of planning for the Kursk defense. The concept of the Orel operations (codenamed "*Kutuzov*") called for three converging attacks against German Army Group Center's force in the Orel salient (Second Panzer and Ninth Army). One shock group on the Western Front's left flank (11th Guards Army) would attack from the north, two shock groups of the Bryansk Front (6th Army; and 3d and 63d Armies) would attack from the east, and one shock group of the Central Front (13th and 70th Armies) would attack from the south. The attack was timed to occur when German forces concentrated in the southern portion of the salient and attacking Soviet forces around Kursk had been brought to a halt. The Western and Bryansk Fronts would commence their assault first, followed by other forces of the Western Front, and finally the Central Front armies. Final adjustments to offensive plans and regrouping and concentration of forces occurred in the first few days of July after Soviet intelligence determined the German Kursk assault would begin between 3 and 6 July.[92]

Bagramyan, commander of 11th Guards Army, the Western Front's shock group, regrouped and concentrated his army in a 16 kilometer main attack sector on his left flank, leaving a single division to defend in the remaining 22 kilometers of his army's sector. He concentrated three rifle corps (nine rifle divisions) backed up by two tank corps (1st and 5th) in the main attack sector. Later Bagramyan wrote:

> The command and staff of the army undertook all possible measures to maintain secrecy in operational preparations and to deceive the enemy. The commandant's service functioned very precisely both in regions designated as jumping-off positions for the offensive in an engineer sense, and in concentration areas in the army rear as well as on all roads from the rear to the front.[93]

Bagramyan's *maskirovka* efforts continued defensive work in progress since early April, and sought to prevent effective German aerial reconnaissance. Armies of the Bryansk Front undertook similar precautions while the Central Front used the heavy combat underway north of Kursk to conceal its offensive preparations.

Soviet *maskirovka* efforts at Orel were generally passive in nature, designed to conceal offensive concentrations. Above all, the Soviets relied on the heavy combat occurring on the north face of the Kursk salient to distract the Germans from the activity brewing on their flank.

German intelligence failed to detect Soviet attack preparations, in particular the formation of offensive concentrations in each Soviet army sector (see maps 42 and 43). It identified the arrival of a new army (16th) but did not realize that army's role (or its new designation – 11th Guards). The Germans also missed the forward deployment of Soviet armored units (5th Tank, 1st Tank, and 1st Guards Tank Corps).

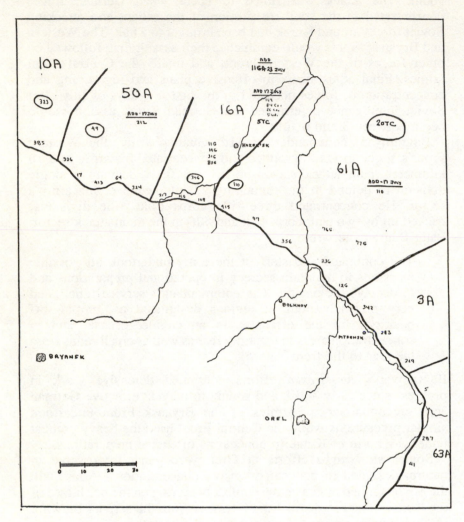

42. Orel, German intelligence assessment, 12 July 1943

Izyum–Barvenkovo, July 1943

No sooner had the German offensive begun at Kursk than Soviet forces elsewhere along the Eastern Front began to play their role in the strategic game of "cat and mouse." The *STAVKA* plan had

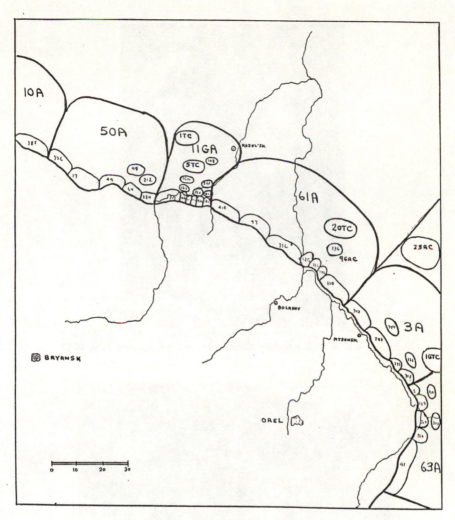

43. Orel, Soviet dispositions, 12 July 1943

stipulated: "as soon as the Kursk battle unfolded several neighboring *fronts* would go on the offensive in order that Hitler's High Command would not be able to strengthen its forces on the Kursk direction."[94] Accordingly, the Southwestern Front was to begin an attack across the Northern Donets River on Barvenkovo, and the

8. General K.K. Rokossovsky, Central Front Commander, July, 1943

9. General P.A. Rotmistrov, 5th Guards Tank Army Commander, July, 1943

Southern Front was to attack across the Mius River toward Stalino.[95]

On 7 July, two days after the German offensive had begun at Kursk, the *STAVKA* ordered General R.Ya. Malinovsky, commander of the Southwestern Front, to begin preparing for an attack on 15 July. Malinovsky was to attack First Panzer Army from bridgeheads across the Northern Donets River in the Izyum area with the joined flanks of 1st Guards and 8th Guards Armies and advance toward Barvenkovo and Krasnoarmeiskoye. 3d Guards Army would launch a supporting attack from the area north of Lisichansk toward Artemovsk. The 23d Tank and 1st Guards Mechanized Corps, serving as the *front's* mobile group, would exploit the penetration toward Stalino to join with Southern Front forces and encircle Army Group South forces in the Donets Basin. Malinovsky kept 12th and 46th Armies in *front* reserve.[96] The Southwestern Front had eight days to prepare the offensive.

Late on 7 July Malinovsky assigned missions to Colonel General V.I. Kuznetsov and Colonel General V.I. Chuikov, the commanders of 1st Guards and 8th Guards Armies. Chuikov later wrote, "In order to hide our intentions the word 'offensive' was not used in operational documents, in radio transmissions, and in oral orders to all subunit commanders. Only defense, defense ..."[97] Since his forces were near full strength, it was only necessary to

10. Soviet troops assault under cover of regimental artillery, Kursk, July, 1943

conceal regroupment and concentration for the attack. This should have been an easy process for by Chuikov's own admission, "The natural conditions were favorable for hidden movements."[98] The area along the Northern Donets River was heavily forested, and the forests were bisected by numerous roads.

Chuikov ordered army second echelon and rear service forces, not participating in the attack, to occupy the army secondary sector and to construct even heavier defenses. The army also implemented *maskirovka* practices expected of an experienced army. As the course of the offensive indicated, all turned out to no avail. The question remained, "Why was deception unsuccessful and why did the Soviets fail to achieve any measure of surprise?"

In his memoirs, published in 1980, Chuikov directly addressed the issue stating, "What occurred? Why in the middle of the day were our attacks smothered everywhere, in spite of the fact that the enemy had suffered greater losses?" In Chuikov's words,

> German officer prisoners pointed out that offensive preparations of the *front* were well known roughly after 12 July, that is, five days before its beginning. The directions of our main attacks were also approximately known. Surprise was not achieved, although it seemed we observed all precautionary measures.[99]

In this work Chuikov gave no explanation for the failure to achieve surprise. Later he noted that after the attacks had failed,

> The *STAVKA* demanded the offensive [continue]. At the time we could not weaken our pressure even for a moment. To the north an intense battle raged with forces of the Western, Voronezh, and Central Fronts. Therefore the army staff again ordered the forces to attack .... Battle did not cease for even an hour. We widened the bridgehead with difficulty and repulsed enemy counter-attacks, but it was already apparent that our offensive was swallowed up.[100]

Malinovsky ordered commitment of 23d Tank Corps in 1st Guards Army's sector, but when that assault failed he cancelled orders for commitment of 1st Guards Mechanized Corps. Finally on 27 July the *STAVKA* agreed with Malinovsky that the offensive be halted. In an earlier work Chuikov had provided an explanation for the failure to achieve surprise. Prefacing his explanation with the words "Here is how a minor front episode could completely crumble our intention of achieving surprise," Chuikov related how troops from a rifle division [74th Guards] bathed in the Northern Donets River and were taken prisoner and interrogated by German intelligence.[101] Chuikov asserted that subsequently captured German documents revealed that these prisoners had given away the Soviet intention to attack only minutes before the attack had begun.[102] Chuikov's explanation is not credible, for the Germans had detected Soviet attack preparations as early as a week before, right after they had begun. German intelligence had detected the concentration of Soviet units east and west of Izyum and, on 16 June, assessed that 62d (8th Guards) Army and the two Soviet mobile corps would soon approach the Northern Donets River (see maps 44 and 45). These offensive indicators were sufficient to cause First Panzer Army to call for reinforcements. By 14 July German Army Group South had dispatched XXIV Panzer Corps southward from the Khar'kov area to deal with the new threat. That corps's commitment to combat limited Soviet gains and ultimately thwarted the attack.[103]

What had ultimately been thwarted? In essence, a Soviet diversionary effort, although the Soviets would accept gains wherever they could achieve them. And what was the cost to the Germans? At a point when operational reserves were needed at Orel and would soon be needed at Belgorod, the Germans sent a full panzer corps south to the Izyum area. That, in essence, is the purpose of a diversionary attack. Within about two weeks after the termination of the Izyum operation, on 13 August the Southwestern Front resumed its offensive, this time with requisite forces and proper procedures, although again without spectacular results.

Mius River, July 1943

While the Southwestern Front prepared its operations south of Izyum, Tolbukhin's Southern Front prepared for operations across the Mius River against Sixth Army of German Army Group South. On 7 July the *STAVKA* ordered Tolbukhin to attack in the *front* central sector with 5th Shock, 2d Guards, and 28th Armies, while 51st and 44th Armies supported on the flanks. After 5th Shock and 28th Armies had penetrated German defenses near Dmitriyevka, 2d Guards Army would advance from second echelon, exploit to Stalino, and link up Southwestern Front forces. To strengthen Lieutenant General Ya. G. Kreizer's 2d Guards Army, Tolbukin assigned him two mechanized corps (4th Guards, 2d Guards) to spearhead his exploitation.[104]

Regrouping for the offensive within 7–8 days was an arduous task

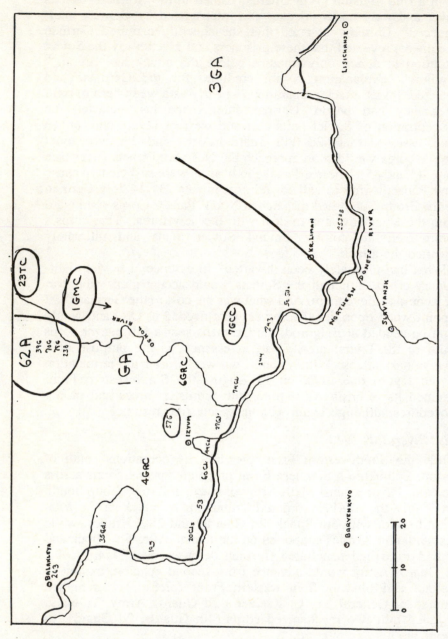

44. Izyum–Barvenkovo, German intelligence assessment, 16 July 1943

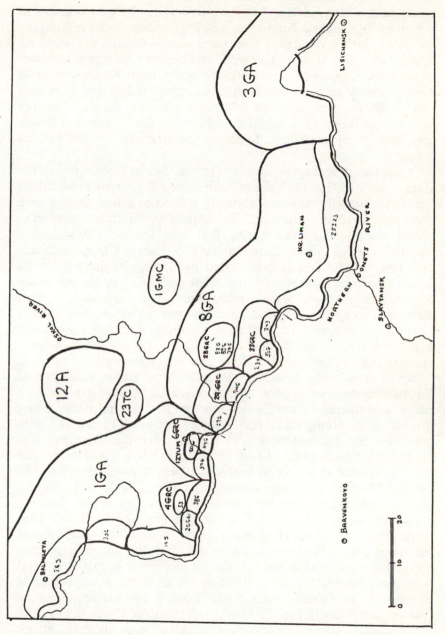

45. Izyum–Barvenkovo, Soviet dispositions, 16 July 1943

requiring the movement of about 90,000 men and considerable equipment. Since *maskirovka* was particularly difficult because of the short July nights, Tolbukhin permitted much of the regrouping to occur during daylight. The same round-the-clock operations applied to supply transport as well. The largest regrouping task was moving the 2d Guards Army 50 kilometers from Krasnodon to its new assembly area, a process that began on 10 July and took four days.[105] By the evening of 14 July regrouping was finished, and the forces were prepared to begin the offensive. On 17 July 5th Shock and 28th Army assaulted, followed the next day by 2d Guards Army.

In a situation analogous to that at Izyum, Soviet forces crossed the river, established a bridgehead, committed their two mechanized corps, but then the advance abruptly ground to a halt against well prepared German defenses. Subsequently, German reinforcements shifted from the north, first 23d Panzer Division and ultimately II SS Panzer Corps and XXIV Panzer Corps contained and smashed the Soviet bridgehead by 3 August, driving Soviet forces eastward across the Mius. That same day to the north the Soviets launched the second great Kursk counter-stroke, against German forces near Belgorod, forces now deprived of most of their operational reserves. In just short of three weeks the Southern Front would again attack, this time with a great deal more success because that action would no longer be diversionary.

Soviet *maskirovka* measures along the Mius River, according to German reports, were poor at best. German observers picked up major movements in the Soviet rear on 10 July, primarily using ground observation, since bad weather between 11 and 14 July prevented air reconnaissance.[106] By 11 July the Germans had identified the main point of concentration as being the Dmitriyevka region. German reports cite such examples of carelessness as: 2d Guards Mechanized Corps deploying forward with its lights on, guns and infantry moving forward in broad daylight, artillery openly registering near Dmitriyevka, and small groups of officers with maps in hand reconnoitering main attack sectors. The same reports recounted poor Soviet communications discipline which permitted analysis of radio traffic and location of all Soviet headquarters and unit designators. All these indicators led to German identification of virtually all Soviet forces, including the forward deployed 2d Guards Army. On 15 July 2d Guards Mechanized Corps in the clear (un-encoded) ordered reconnaissance to begin on its main attack direction. Late on 14 July the Germans reported a halt in Soviet movement which led them to conclude that preparations for the attack were complete. Subsequent air reconnaissance on 15 July confirmed the main Soviet concentration areas. Final Soviet command adjustments on 16 July, such as forward movement of *front* headquarters and the remaining armored forces, were duly recorded by the Germans.

The German intelligence picture on the evening of 16 July was close to reality (see maps 46 and 47). Intelligence identified every major Soviet force facing them across the Mius River with the exception of 28th Army. It did, however, identify many of the divisions of that army. Consequently, by 16 July, German Sixth Army forces had regrouped to meet the expected assault. 16th Panzer Grenadier Division in army group reserve deployed forward, and 23d Panzer Division in reserve on the army left moved into positions in close proximity to the projected Soviet main attack sector. The Germans were so aware of Soviet attack preparations that they held map exercises on 11 July to prepare a variety of countermeasures.

In fact, the Soviet offensive materialized in just the fashion Sixth Army had predicted, and with predictable results, just as had the attack further north along the Northern Donets River.

The Southern and Southwestern Fronts and their component armies were experienced combat organizations, commanded by effective commanders. They were subject to the same regulations that governed the use of other Soviet forces. Within the context of improving Soviet *maskirovka* techniques, the Mius and Izyum operations were aberrations. Here, at a time when Soviet *fronts* elsewhere over a considerable period successfully masked major portions of their force, the Germans had a crystal clear picture of what was going to occur. The explanation for these aberrations rests in the strategic context in which the operations occurred. Viewed out of context, the two operations were mere clumsy and unsuccessful sideshows. In context, however, the operations were essential cogs in a strategic plan without which the plan might have failed. As one Soviet observer pointed out:

> It is necessary, however, to understand that the Southern Front offensive was an important help to our forces in the Kursk Bulge: the enemy was not only unable to take one division from the Mius front in order to strengthen his forces at Kursk, but he was even forced to temporarily transfer to the Mius River his tank corps from Khar'kov.[107]

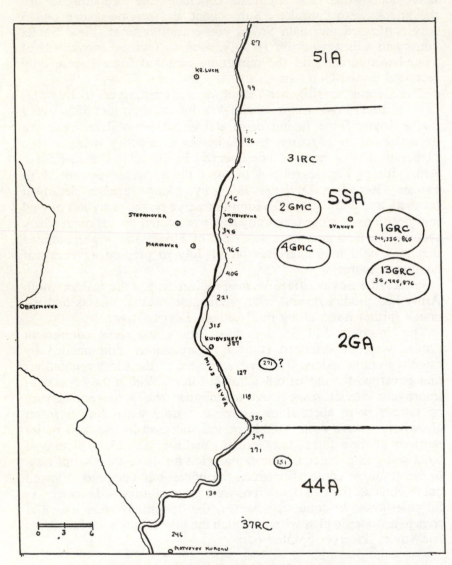

46. Mius River, German intelligence assessment, 16 July 1943

The success of Soviet counter-strokes in the Kursk area, the center of gravity of Soviet strategic plans, depended on the defeat of German Fourth Panzer Army and Army Detachment Kempf defending in the Khar'kov–Belgorod area. In mid-July, although

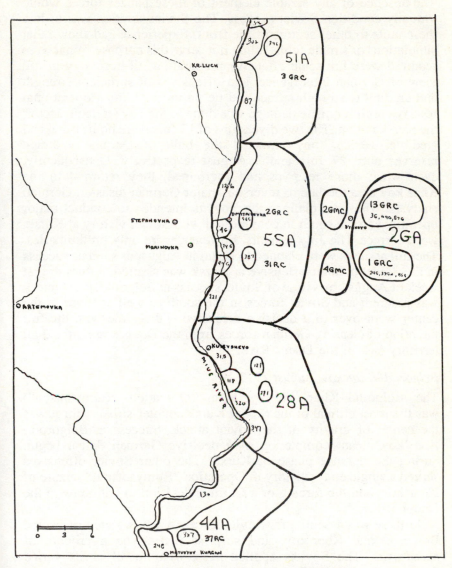

47. Mius River, Soviet dispositions, 16 July 1943

beaten at Kursk, the Germans retained a significant, if shaken, operational reserve consisting of II SS Panzer Corps, XXIV Panzer Corps, and XXXXVIII Panzer Corps, which, if employed as a body, could frustrate any Soviet attempt to achieve operational success.

The absence of any sizable element of these panzer forces would virtually condition Soviet success. The Soviet solution was to lure these units to other sectors of the front. Experience had shown that simulations or simple feints might not serve this purpose. What were required were full scale offensive preparations, if necessary in full view of German intelligence, and offensives of sufficient strength and credibility to both attract and tie up those German operational reserves until requisite damage was done in the key strategic sector, the Kursk region. The two diversions of 17 July were both strong and credible. Hence, they attracted the bulk of German strategic reserves until 27 July and 3 August respectively. Consequently, even when those reserves had regrouped, they returned to the Khar'kov area too late to reverse a major German disaster. German analysts, who later claimed the Soviets intended to conduct major operations in the south in conjunction with Soviet victory at Kursk, were correct. The July assaults, however, were only preliminaries. The full assaults were planned to begin in August as soon as success in the Soviet counter-offensive at Kursk was assured. After the first week of August, by virtue of Soviet success at Belgorod, that victory was assured; and Soviet forces in the south as well as those in the center went over to a decisive offensive – this time with the full intention of clearing German forces from the Donbas region and all territory east of the Dnepr River.

Belgorod–Khar'kov, August 1943

The Belgorod–Khar'kov Operation (Operation "Rumyantsev") was the most critical of the Soviet Kursk counter-strokes, for it was the center of gravity of the Soviet attack. Success at Belgorod–Khar'kov meant completion of a decisive German defeat begun during the defense phase of Kursk. The other Soviet offensives served a single end – victory in Operation "Rumyantsev," seizure of Khar'kov, and the forcing of a German decision to withdraw to the Dnepr River.

Surprise was essential for Soviet forces to achieve victory around Belgorod and Khar'kov, and surprise had to be a product of *maskirovka*. The Soviets applied *maskirovka* in all of its varied forms to deceive the Germans regarding the timing, strength, form, and location of the major Soviet counter-stroke. The Soviets had developed a general concept for a major counter-stroke toward Belgorod and Khar'kov during their initial planning for the strategic defense at Kursk. Unlike Operation "Kutuzov" (Orel operation), the Soviets did not draft specific plans for "Rumyantsev" until the outcome of the Kursk defense had been decided. Meanwhile the *STAVKA* amended and refined the concept of the operation.

On 24 July the *STAVKA* notified the Voronezh and Steppe Fronts to begin detailed preparations for the liberation of Belgorod and Khar'kov. Thereafter Vatutin and Konev, the *front* commanders, assembled and regrouped their forces and, with the assistance of *STAVKA* representative Zhukov, worked on specific plans to implement the *STAVKA* concept.[108] The *STAVKA* concept called for the Voronezh and Steppe Fronts to attack German positions around Belgorod and advance toward Bogodukhov and Valki in order to split German Fourth Panzer Army from Army Detachment Kempf and then envelop and destroy German forces in the Khar'kov area. As the operation developed, and as Soviet forces approached Khar'kov the Southwestern Front's 57th and 1st Guards Armies would join the assault. Subordinate headquarters had ten days to prepare the offensive, which was set to commence on 3 August.

Vatutin and Konev, after intense negotiations with Zhukov, decided to launch their main attack north and northwest of Belgorod on 3 August with their joined flanks. Four armies (5th Guards, 6th Guards, 53d, 69th) and a portion of a fifth (7th Guards) would begin the offensive, and late on the first day two tank armies (1st and 5th Guards) would begin the operational exploitation. Other armies along the flanks of the main attack would join the offensive on a time-phased basis to expand the strength and scope of the blow.

Soviet planners deliberately timed the attack to achieve surprise. Both sides had suffered huge casualties during the defensive fighting at Kursk. Thus the Germans assumed the Soviets would require a considerable period to regain sufficient strength to undertake a major offensive. Manstein on 1 August indicated he expected Khar'kov would be the next Soviet target. However, he believed the Soviets would require several weeks to make necessary force adjustments and regroup. On 2 August Manstein decided to wait for more definite signs of an impending offensive before pulling back to the original German defense lines from which they had launched their 5 July offensive.[109] In the meantime Manstein's operational reserves remained in the Donbas region.

Manstein's judgement should have been correct. Soviet armies of the Voronezh Front had suffered casualties of up to 30 percent in the defensive fighting. Armored units like 1st Tank Army and 5th Guards Tank Army had lost over 50 percent of their strength. What he had not reckoned with was Soviet intent to capitalize on timing to achieve surprise – specifically to attack with understrength forces and with hastily rebuilt tank armies.

To compensate for the weakness of specific armies the Soviets engaged in a hasty but massive regrouping effort to generate strength on the Belgorod–Khar'kov direction far in excess of German estimates. This regrouping involved extensive shifting of forces between Vatutin's and Konev's fronts, the insertion of new and fresh armies into their offensive formation (27th, 47th Armies), and the assembly of new *STAVKA* reserves (like 4th Guards Army).

The Soviets also sought to deceive the Germans regarding the form of the attack by eschewing a complicated double envelopment of the Belgorod–Khar'kov salient (which Stalin thought was too complicated for his tired troops and commanders to carry out) in favor of a direct strike against the nose of the salient. Hence, Stalin ordered concentration of a huge infantry, artillery, and armored force in a narrow sector north and northwest of Belgorod. This force was to strike directly toward Belgorod and then southwest through the center of the salient.

The *STAVKA* also ordered extensive use of *maskirovka* to deceive the Germans regarding where that main attack would occur. To prepare for Operation "Rumyantsev," *front* and army staffs developed extensive *maskirovka* plans which specified intent, measures, forces, resources, and timing, as well as the person responsible for control and implementation. Strict secrecy and security surrounded all operational and tactical planning. Engineer and line units concealed regroupment and concentration of forces by using all natural and artificial means of concealment, and specially detailed staff officers supervised the maintenance of *maskirovka* discipline. Engineer units allocated to each *front* prepared concealed march routes and positions for various types of combat units, prepared dummy concentration areas, and assisted the Voronezh Front in creating a major false concentration area.[110]

Steppe Front engineers assisted units to deploy, camouflaged troop assembly positions, created dummy positions, and built or repaired numerous roads and bridges across the Northern Donets River and its tributaries. This included construction of 22 secret underwater bridges complete with camouflaged approaches and many false bridges.[111]

The engineer *maskirovka* plan called for creation of three false tank company or battalion concentration regions in each rifle corps and ten false artillery positions in each rifle division.[112] Assisted by the engineers, the Soviets established a movement plan to mask regrouping and resupply of forces which involved extensive use of camouflage, strict traffic control, and movement primarily at night and in inclement weather. Signal units supported the *maskirovka* effort by creating dummy radio nets to conceal Soviet command and control. Command posts were dispersed and masked, and separate elements of each headquarters conducted their business at these dispersed locations. All communications lines, the primary means of command and control, were dug in and camouflaged. Signal units also took part in the Voronezh Front's simulation of a false concentration area.

The most creative aspect of *maskirovka* planning was a major ruse the Voronezh Front conducted to deceive the Germans regarding the location of its main attack (see map 48). This involved the simulated assembly of a large rifle force (two rifle corps), a tank army, and several tank corps in the Sudzha region on the Voronezh Front's right flank.[113] Between 26 July and 6 August the 38th Army (commanded by Major General K.S. Moskalenko until 3 August and thereafter by Lieutenant General N.E. Chibisov) carried out the simulated concentration of forces deep in its rear.[114] The *front* assistant commander General I.F. Nefterev, supervised the operation with a specially organized staff.[115] Moskalenko employed one rifle division (340th), an engineer-sapper battalion (260th), an engineer-mine company, and an engineer-*maskirovka* company in the simulation. He assigned to them seven radio stations, 18 trucks, eight tanks, 20 rail cars, 450 mock-up tanks, and, from 29 to 31 August, two–three aircraft. In addition, regular ground forces and aircraft, including a tank regiment and two sapper battalions, participated to make the simulation more "active."[116] During a preparatory period (27–28 July) 38th Army simulated reconnaissance and assembly of forces for an attack, including radio deception measures. Later (2–4 August) 38th Army ordered three divisions (240th, 180th, 167th) to attack after full preparation. Meanwhile, the 340th Rifle Division and attached units created the false concentration area in the rear.[117]

Under the 340th's supervision, assigned engineer units constructed 215 mock-up artillery pieces and an additional 250 mock-up tanks to "animate" the railroad unloading station at Lokinskaya. Two regiments of the division simulated the concentration of rifle forces near Sudzha by daytime marches throughout the area and by occupation of assembly areas constructed by the engineers.[118] The

Замысел оперативной маскировки войск Воронежского фронта
(28 июля — 6 августа 1943 г.)

48. Belgorod–Khar'kov, Soviet deception plan

38th Army staff organized special shuttle trains that conducted numerous daily runs from the rear into the forward railhead at Lokinskaya. Anti-aircraft units traveled with the trains and engaged German aircraft while the engineer-*maskirovka* company employed smoke screens to cover loading and unloading at the station.

Meanwhile the engineer battalion and engineer-mine company (a total of 180 men) worked constantly on building, deploying, and moving artillery mock-ups and dummy soldiers. Four teams prepared specific calibres of guns, and the fifth worked on the dummies. Artillery mock-ups were then shipped to the point of employment while tank mock-ups arrived by rail in assembled form. Once assembled, the teams employed artillery mock-ups in positions prepared by engineers and then camouflaged each piece.

This elaborate work attracted the attention of German aerial reconnaissance and enemy bombers, and reconnaissance aviation conducted 244 sorties over the area and dropped an estimated 1000 bombs on the false concentration region.[119] It also attracted the attention of German intelligence which, although it did not positively identify a tank army in the area, detected enough signs of a pending offensive to shift a panzer division (7th) and an infantry division (7th) into the Soviet 38th Army sector prior to the real Soviet attack on 3 August. This left only two German panzer divisions (19th, 6th) to back up German infantry northwest of Belgorod which, on 3 August, were inundated by a virtual torrent of Soviet infantry and armor. The German intelligence picture on the evening of 2 August was confused, especially regarding the location of 5th Guards Tank Army (see maps 49 and 50). In addition, the Germans failed to detect the forward deployment of 27th Army or the concentration of 5th Guards and 6th Guards Armies. In short, Soviet dispositions did not presage a major attack.

The Soviet offensive began on 3 August. Within two days Belgorod had fallen, and Soviet forces had begun an operational exploitation toward Khar'kov. Without significant operational reserves, the Germans were hard pressed to stop the Soviet advance. Slowly, over the ensuing days, those reserves arrived in the Khar'kov area; and the Germans committed them in piecemeal fashion to slow the Soviet advance. The damage, however, had already been done. On 23 August Khar'kov fell to Soviet forces, and at the end of the month German forces began a long withdrawal to the Dnepr River line.

Postscript

Maskirovka played a major role in the outcome of the Soviet strategic defensive at Kursk. The Soviet decision to incorporate specific offensive operations within the context of defensive operations surprised the Germans, in particular since this had not occurred before in so rapid a fashion. A former staff officer of Army Group Center later wrote:

> The force, and most of all the penetrative might of the Russian counter-offensive begun on 12 July in the northern and eastern sectors of the Orel Bulge, proved a cruel surprise for us .... In essence, it was incomprehensible that the Russians proved capable of accomplishing an offensive in the summer, and moreover with such success.[120]

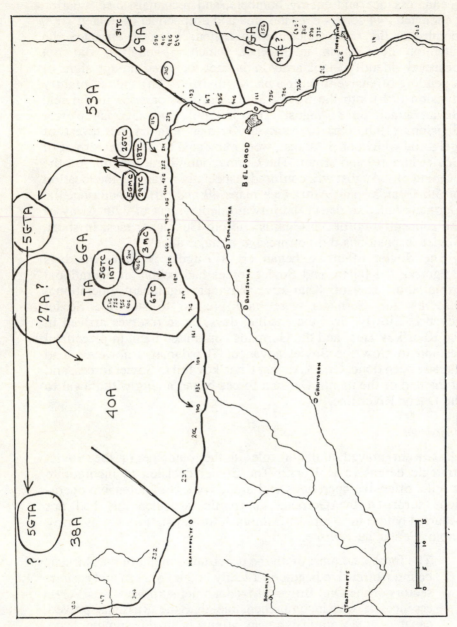

49. Belgorod–Khar'kov, German intelligence assessment, 2 August 1943

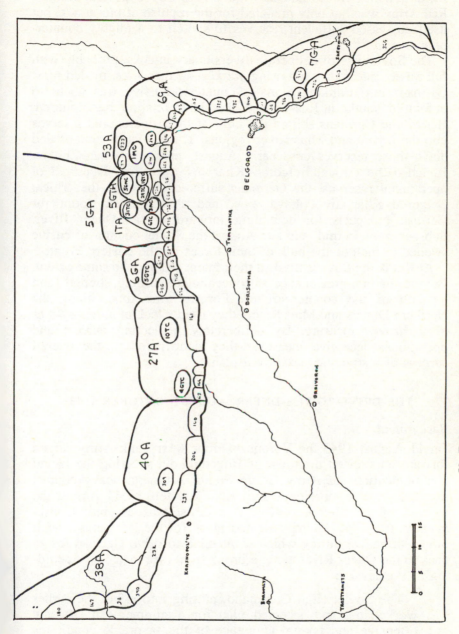

50. Belgorod–Khar'kov, Soviet dispositions, 2 August 1943

Field Marshal Keitel added: "We in no way expected that the Red Army was not only prepared for the repulse of our attack, but itself possessed sufficient reserves to switch to a mighty counter-offensive ..."[121]

The Soviet use of deliberate diversionary attacks, probably with full Soviet intent to avoid using *maskirovka* measures, misled most Germans into thinking a major counter-offensive was about to unfold in southern Russia, and this interpretation has endured. Hence, the Germans shifted the bulk of their operational reserves into the Izyum and Mius River regions. The Soviet diversions tied down those reserves until early August, precisely when Zhukov launched the critical Belgorod–Khar'kov operation. Deprived of operational reserves, the Germans suffered defeat on the critical Belgorod–Khar'kov–Poltava axis, and that spelled doom for German prospects for defending forward of the Dnepr River. Subsequently, in mid- and late August the Soviet counter-offensive swelled to include the bulk of their forces on the Eastern Front.

At Kursk the Soviets masked their intent to attack to some extent. But they had far greater success concealing the timing, strength, and location of the counter-strokes. For the first time, along the Northern Donets and Mius Rivers they used a lack of *maskirovka* as a *maskirovka* measure. By deliberately neglecting tactical and operational deceptive measures they contributed to the overall success of a strategic *maskirovka* plan.

THE DRIVE TO THE DNEPR, AUGUST–OCTOBER 1943

Background

On 11 August 1943 the Voronezh Front's 1st Tank Army surged forward and seized the town of Bogodukhov, severing the lateral communications of Army Group South. Although heavy combat raged for twelve more days until Khar'kov fell, by 11 August the success of the Belgorod–Khar'kov thrust was assured. Consequently, the *STAVKA* implemented plans for the late summer–fall Soviet offensive during which it intended to drive German forces back to the Dnepr River along a broad front (see map 51). According to Vasilevsky:

> The Soviet High Command, putting into effect the earlier worked out and accepted plan for a summer–fall strategic offensive and taking advantage of the favorable conditions resulting from Kursk, decided without delay to widen the

11. Armored advance, August, 1943

12. Armored advance, August, 1943

offensive front of our forces on the southwestern direction. The Central, Voronezh, Steppe, Southwestern, and Southern Fronts were given the mission to destroy the main enemy forces on one of the central sectors and all of the southern wing of the Soviet–German front, to liberate the Donbas, the left bank of the Ukraine and Crimea, to reach the Dnepr, and to secure bridgeheads on its right bank .... Simultaneously, operations were prepared to the north and south. The main forces of the Western Front and the left wing of the Kalinin Front planned to inflict defeat on 3d Panzer and 4th Field Armies of German Army Group "Center" and reach Dukhovshchina, Smolensk, and Rosslavl' in order to drive his front lines a greater distance from Moscow to create better conditions for the liberation of Belorussia, and deprive the fascists of the capability to transfer forces from there to the south, where the main objective of the campaign would be decided. The North Caucasus Front, in cooperation with the Black Sea fleet and Azov flotilla, was to clear the Taman peninsula and secure a bridgehead at Kerch. Thus, the *STAVKA* planned to conduct a general offensive on a front from Velikie Luki to the Black Sea.[122]

The timing of this series of offensives and their duration was as follows:

Smolensk – 7 August–2 October
Donbas – 13 August–22 September
Left Bank of Ukraine – 23 August–30 September
Chernigov–Pripyat – 26 August–10 October
Bryansk – 1 September–3 October
Novorossiisk–Taman – 9 September–9 October
Melitopol' – 26 September–5 November

At Stalin's insistence, the summer–fall offensive would consist of numerous frontal blows delivered across a broad front. (Zhukov argued for conduct of envelopments in more limited but critical sectors of the front, such as the Donbas.)[123] No two blows were to be simultaneous. Instead the timing was staggered to support the main thrust toward Kiev. Vasilevsky described the reason for the time-phasing:

They would cover one another with regard to time, by appearing successive only within the overall concept. That forced the enemy to divide his resources and throw them from

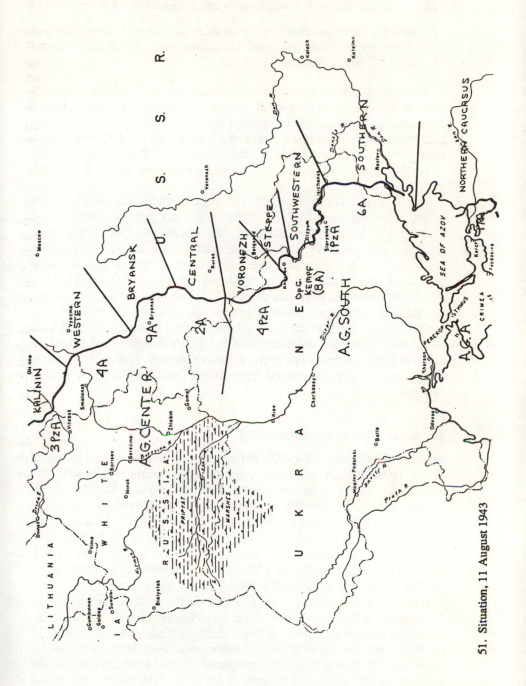

51. Situation, 11 August 1943

one sector to another, trying to shut off a front where here and there there were gigantic breaches made by Soviet forces through his defenses.[124]

To control the massive Soviet offensive, the *STAVKA* assigned representatives to groups of *fronts* operating on each major strategic direction. Zhukov supervised the Voronezh and Steppe Fronts on the critical Kiev direction, Vasilevsky did likewise in the south with the Southwestern and Southern Fronts, and General N.N. Voronov coordinated the *fronts* participating in the Smolensk operation.

The *STAVKA* concept capitalized on the staggered nature of the assaults to deceive the Germans regarding attack timing and priority of effort. In addition, the offensive simultaneously hindered the Germans' ability to shift forces and exploited the situation when the Germans did shift reserves. The broad front form of attack compounded the German problem of establishing defensive priorities and made it difficult for the Germans to detect Soviet concealed operational regroupings, although by attacking on a broad front, the Soviets inevitably dispersed their effort and failed to achieve decisive concentrations by which Zhukov had hoped to achieve decisive results in more selective sectors. During the operations the Soviets employed operational *maskirovka* with mixed success.

Smolensk, August–September 1943

In June 1943, the *STAVKA* informed the Western and Kalinin Front commanders of their part in the summer–fall strategic offensive – either to defeat the 40 German divisions in their sector or prevent their transfer to the critical southwestern direction. They would complete the liberation of the Smolensk region, occupy Smolensk and Rosslavl', and secure bridgeheads from which to launch future offensives into Belorussia.[125] Throughout the operations they would coordinate closely with Soviet forces operating on the Orel–Bryansk and Belgorod–Khar'kov directions.

General V.D. Sokolovsky's Western Front and General A.I. Yeremenko's Kalinin Front were to strike concentric blows converging on Smolensk, the former through Spas–Demensk toward Rosslavl' and the latter through Dukhovshchina. Since these operations would strike the best prepared German defenses on the Eastern Front, to foster planning security "all orders regarding attack preparations by the fronts were to be received directly in the *STAVKA* and General Staff."[126]

The *STAVKA* provided strategic reserves consisting of 21st and 68th Armies, 5th Mechanized Corps, 5th Artillery Penetration Corps, and numerous support units to the attacking *fronts*. On the eve of the operation the Western Front consisted of nine armies (31st, 5th, 10th Guards, 33d, 49th, 10th, 50th, 68th, 21st), one air army, one mechanized corps (5th), and one cavalry corps (6th Guards) and the Kalinin Front consisted of four armies (3d Shock, 4th Shock, 43d, 39th), one air army, and 3d Guards Cavalry Corps.[127] On 3 August Stalin visited the Western Front and underscored his concerns, primarily with concealing the massive offensive preparations.

Sokolovsky planned to conduct the Western Front main attack with four armies (10th Guards, 33d, 68th, 21st) supported by 5th Mechanized and 6th Guards Cavalry Corps in a 16 kilometer sector along the Yukhnov–Rosslavl' highway with two armies (10th Guards and 33d) in first echelon backed up by the remainder of the shock group. A supporting attack by 10th Army from the Kirov area would assist the main shock group in destroying German Fourth Panzer Army units in the Spas–Demensk region. On Sokolovsky's right flank, 31st and 5th Armies would attack toward Dorogobuzh in co-ordination with adjacent Kalinin Front forces to protect the northern flank of the Western Front's main attack. Two weaker armies (49th and 50th) on the Western Front's left flank would first defend and then join the attack as it progressed. As the offensive developed, 68th and 21st Armies in *front* second echelon and the two mobile corps, would spearhead the advance on Rosslavl' and Smolensk.

Yeremenko ordered 39th Army to make the Kalinin Front's main attack toward Dukhovshchina and Smolensk supported by elements of 43d Army on its right flank. The remainder of his *front* would defend in a broad secondary sector.

Secret regrouping and concentration of both *fronts'* forces were essential if the offensive was to achieve its ends. This required sound *maskirovka* planning for those forces making the main attack and for the second echelon 68th and 21st Armies. 10th Guards Army had to move 160 kilometers from the Gzhatsk area and then deploy into the interval between 5th and 33d Armies. In addition, all shock group armies had to incorporate significant reinforcements while they were conducting extensive internal regrouping and positioning reinforcing artillery. The Kalinin Front's 39th Army was reinforced by a rifle corps, and two mechanized and one tank brigade displaced up to 160 kilometers to support its attack.

Both fronts implemented detailed *maskirovka* plans to cover their extensive preparations. Yeremenko recalled:

> Concentration of our forces began in the second half of July and continued rather intensively. Regrouping and occupation of jumping-off positions was done in secrecy from both enemy air and ground observation. The weather was unfavorable with almost uninterrupted rain which, in fact, greatly hindered the fulfillment of our missions. However, the rainy, gloomy weather played a definite positive role since the enemy was not capable of conducting air reconnaissance.[128]

Sokolovsky's Western Front *maskirovka* plan involved creating a false concentration of forces in 50th Army's sector and on the left flank of 10th Army. 10th Army masked its preparations well. It moved at night 25–30 kilometers from its assembly area to its jumping-off positions using strict *maskirovka* discipline supervised by army headquarters personnel.[129] The army commanders used aircraft flights to mask the sounds of armor deploying forward. Single guns of in-place artillery units registered for artillery units deploying forward. To deceive the Germans the army constructed false artillery and anti-tank firing positions from which it conducted periodic fires, and three rifle divisions conducted reconnaissance up to 6 August in quiet sectors of the front where no offensive action was planned. In response, German units reinforced those sectors and laid additional minefields. These measures distracted the Germans from the real 10th Army attack preparations near Kirov. A German radio message intercepted on 6 August reported, "No noticeable enemy movement on the road east of Kirov."[130]

Despite these local successes, "Western Front measures to achieve surprise were not noted for their special effectiveness."[131] German forces detected Soviet preparations, in particular force regrouping and concentration in several of the main attack sectors. At the end of July German air reconnaissance, in spite of bad weather, reported those concentrations; and consequently, the Germans reinforced key sectors of their defense with reserves from the Orel region (including 18th and 25th Panzer Grenadier Divisions, 2d and 9th Panzer Divisions, and the 36th and 262d Infantry Divisions) (see map 52). Additional reserves followed after the 7 August Soviet offensive began.[132]

A German intelligence assessment for the end of July noted:

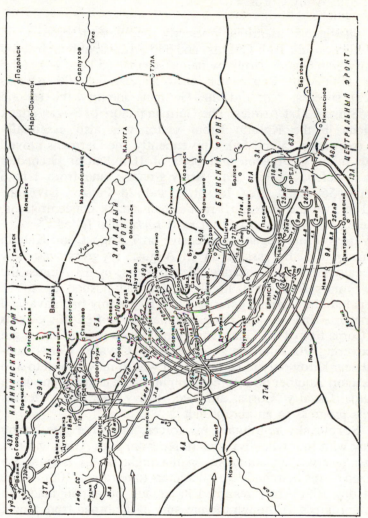

52. Smolensk, German force regrouping, 1–31 August 1943

The latest information from air reconnaissance again affirms the developing impression about the enemy and bears witness to the increasing armed strength in the sector of the internal flanks of 12th and 9th Army Corps and also 39th Panzer Corps and 27th Army Corps.[133]

German intelligence identified correctly the Western Front main attack sectors of 5th, 10th Guards, and 33d Armies, although it did not identify 10th Guards Army by name (see maps 53 and 54). It did not detect 10th Army's concentration which explains 10th Army's subsequent success. Nor did the Germans identify the second echelon 68th and 21st Armies. The German picture of Soviet attack preparations in the Kalinin Front sector was also essentially accurate (see maps 55 and 56). Consequently, the Germans moved the 246th Infantry Division and parts of 18th Panzer Grenadier Division to defend against 39th Army's attack, and from 1 to 6 August the 56th and 36st Infantry, and 2d Panzer Divisions deployed to face the Western Front's main attack concentrations. Thus, the extensive Western Front *maskirovka* plan failed.[134]

The Western Front began its offensive on 7 August, and Kalinin Front units joined the assault on 13 August. Progress was slow against heavy German resistance. Nevertheless, by 13 August the Western Front's four main attack armies had pushed up to 16 kilometers into the German defenses; and 10th Army had advanced 25 kilometers. That day the *front* commander shifted 6th Guards Cavalry Corps from 10th Guards to 10th Army's sector. In a night march covering 70 kilometers 6th Guards Cavalry Corps concentrated near Kirov only to be notified it was to move north to 33d Army's sector. Another 60 kilometer night march ensued, but when 6th Guards Cavalry Corps attacked, heavy German defenses brought its progress to an abrupt halt.[135]

Again Sokolovsky regrouped his forces, this time reinforcing 10th Army with four rifle divisions (three from 50th Army and one from *front* reserve). In addition, on the night of 12 August 5th Mechanized Corps marched 130 kilometers to reinforce 10th Army. The next day 10th Army resumed its assault but again made no significant progress. Although the pressure of the broad front attack forced the Germans to abandon Spas–Demensk, by 20 August the Soviet advance had expired only 10–40 kilometers into the German defenses. Much of the Soviet difficulty in this first phase of the Smolensk operation was due to the loss of surprise and subsequent German shifting of reserves. The Kalinin Front's attack suffered the same fate (for the same reason), and its attack stalled after minimal gains of up to 5 kilometers.

STAVKA representative Voronov in his report on the operation cited the main problem of the assault, stating, "1. The enemy, without a doubt, knew about our offensive preparations and implemented a series of measures to counter it."[136]

In late August the *STAVKA* developed plans to renew the drive on Smolensk, this time concentrating on the Yel'nya rather than the Rosslavl' area. Sokolovsky ordered 10th Guards, 21st, and 33d Armies, reinforced by 2d Guards Tank, 5th Guards Mechanized, and 6th Guards Cavalry Corps, to conduct the *front* main attack on 28 August toward Yel'nya and Smolensk while the flank armies provided support and conducted diversions. From 20 to 27 August the *front* carried out extensive regrouping of over 70 units and "despite the large scale of regrouping, Western Front forces ... succeeded in accomplishing it secretly and unnoticed by the enemy."[137]

The Soviets not only intended this new operation to invigorate the drive toward Smolensk but also intended for it to serve as a diversion for the Soviet operation along the main attack direction toward Kiev. For, despite logistical difficulties which inhibited the mounting of this new Western Front offensive:

> conditions on the southern wing of the Soviet–German front, where our forces, while overcoming stiff opposition, were developing the offensive, demanded the containing of his forces on other directions, to deny him the capability to transfer any divisions from the western to the southwestern or southern directions.[138]

STAVKA representative Voronov arranged diversionary activity to facilitate a successful Western Front attack. While the Western Front prepared for its 28 August attack, on 23 August Voronov ordered the Kalinin Front to renew its offensive toward Dukhovshchina. The ensuing unsuccessful attack drew German forces from the Yel'nya area, and even after the Western Front had attacked on 28 August, Voronov required the Kalinin Front to continue its futile operations until 7 September. In addition, Western Front's 49th and 10th Armies simulated attack preparations along the Warsaw–Moscow road on the Rosslavl' direction.[139] German intelligence identified the Soviet rifle forces facing them but assessed the Soviet point of main effort south of where it actually was (see maps 57 and 58). It also failed to identify the three Soviet mobile corps. The

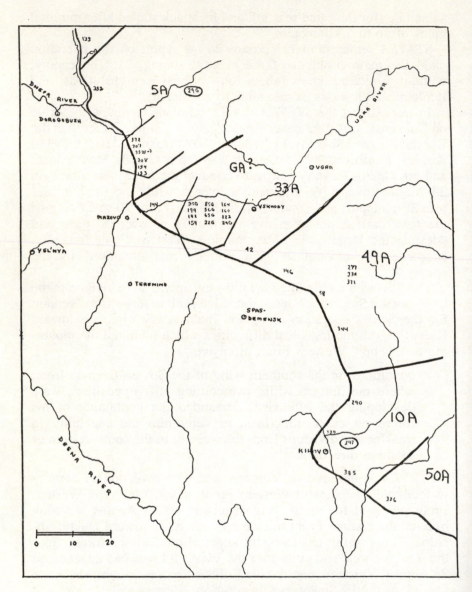

53. Smolensk, German intelligence assessment,
Spas–Demensk sector, 6 August 1943

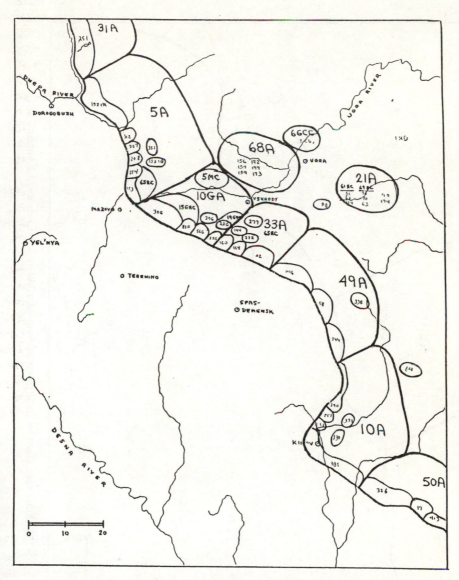

54. Smolensk, Soviet dispositions, Spas–Demensk sector, 6 August 1943

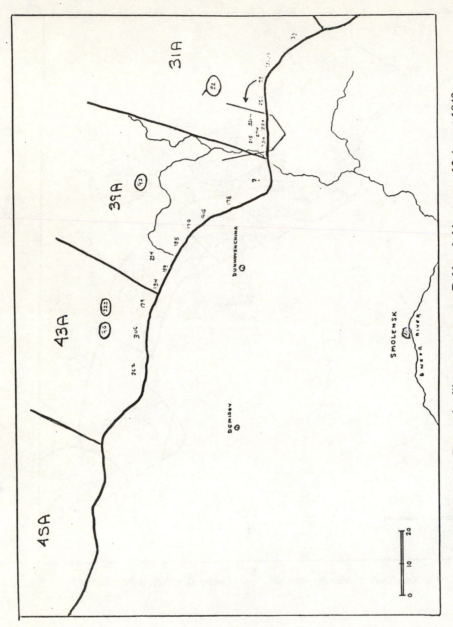

55. Smolensk, German intelligence assessment, Dukhovshchina sector, 12 August 1943

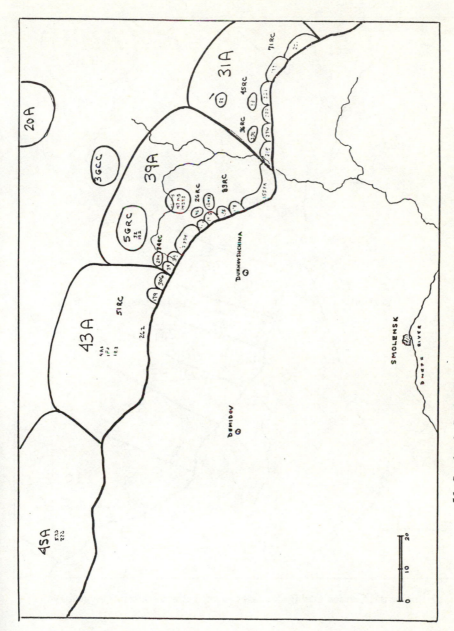

56. Smolensk, Soviet dispositions, Dukhovshchina sector, 12 August 1943

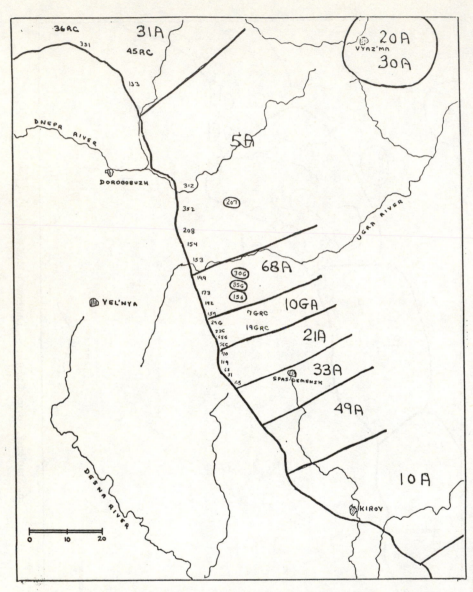

57. Smolensk, German intelligence assessment, Yel'nya sector, 27 August 1943

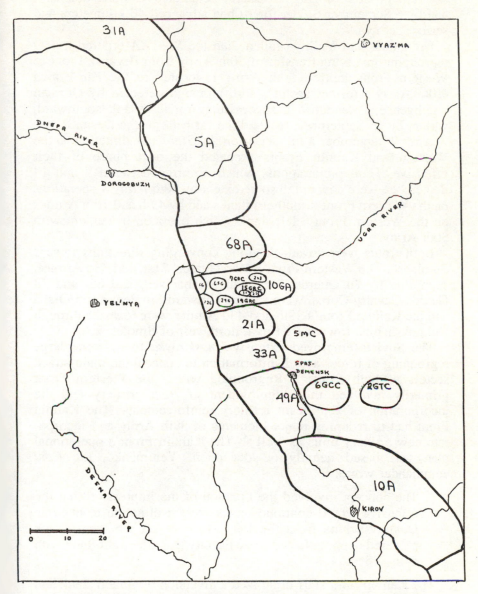

58. Smolensk, Soviet dispositions, Yel'nya sector, 27 August 1943

Western Front's 28 August assault penetrated German defenses, and by 6 September Soviet forces had advanced 40 kilometers and seized Yel'nya.

No sooner had Yel'nya fallen than the *STAVKA* ordered a new regrouping involving transfer of 50th Army from Bryansk Front to Western Front control. 50th Army re-located to the Kirov area (10th Army's former sector); and, although detected by German intelligence, it launched a successful surprise assault southward, which, by 15 September, reached the far bank of the Desna River.

After 7 September a lull set in on the Smolensk direction as the Western and Kalinin Fronts prepared the next phase of their offensive. Their preparations, which occurred between 7 and 14 September, were covered to some extent by 50th Army's operations on the Western Front's southern flanks and by 49th and 10th Armies on the Western Front's left flank which operated in tandem with 50th Army.

Both fronts were to attack along converging directions toward Smolensk. The Western Front's 10th Guards, 21st, and 33d Armies, supported by 2d Guards Tank, 5th Mechanized, and 6th and 3d Guards Cavalry Corps, were to attack toward Smolensk and Orsha and the Kalinin Front's 39th and 43d Armies were to strike through Dukhovshchina toward Rud'nya, northwest of Smolensk.

The Soviets employed extensive *maskirovka* to hide the large regrouping of forces and disinformation to conceal the main attack sectors of both *fronts*.[140] Regrouping within the Western Front primarily involved the redeployment of *front* artillery and the incorporation of significant artillery reinforcements. The Kalinin Front had to redeploy major elements of 39th Army and incorporate new artillery units as well.[141] The Kalinin Front's operational plan was based heavily on deception. Yeremenko, the *front* commander wrote:

> The concept involved the creation of the impression that the offensive would continue on its present direction to encircle Dukhovshchina from the left, when in fact the main attack prepared to encircle and seize the city from the right flank with 84th Rifle Corps.[142]

The Kalinin *front* staff organized a diversion on its left flank and concealed actual attack preparations on its right flank. The disinformation plan involved 39th Army. While the army's 5th and 83d Rifle Corps on the left flank regrouped, formed false concentrations, and conducted active reconnaissance, the 84th and 2d Guards

13. General A.I. Yeremenko, Kalinin Front commander, September, 1943

Rifle Corps on the army right flank engaged in extensive defensive work.[143] Army smoke generating units helped to simulate troop movements from the army right to the left flank. In addition, *front* ordered 43d Army, on 39th Army's right flank, to begin its attack one day before the attack of 39th Army to draw off German reserves.[144] As a final measure, on the eve of the offensive Soviet aircraft, by design, struck German defensive concentrations opposite the false Soviet concentration areas. The progress of the offensive demonstrated the effectiveness of these measures.

To conceal the direction of the Western Front's main attack, its left wing armies (10th and 49th) conducted similar diversionary operations along the Desna River which proved even more effective because of previous Soviet gains in those sectors. German intelligence failed to detect Yeremenko's shift of forces to his right flank (see maps 59 and 60). It did, however, detect most of the Western Front's attack preparations near Yel'nya although it identified the

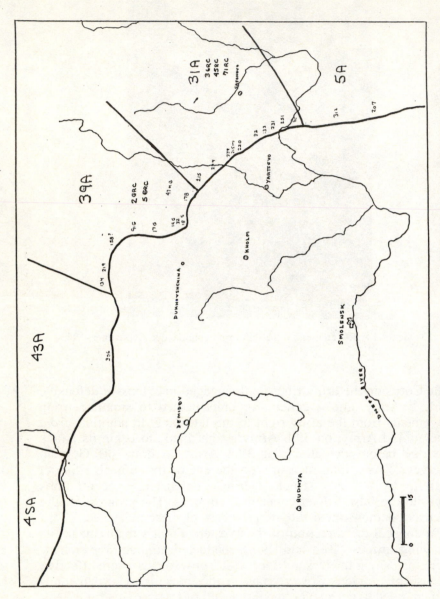

59. Smolensk, German intelligence assessment, Dukhovshchina sector, 12 September 1943

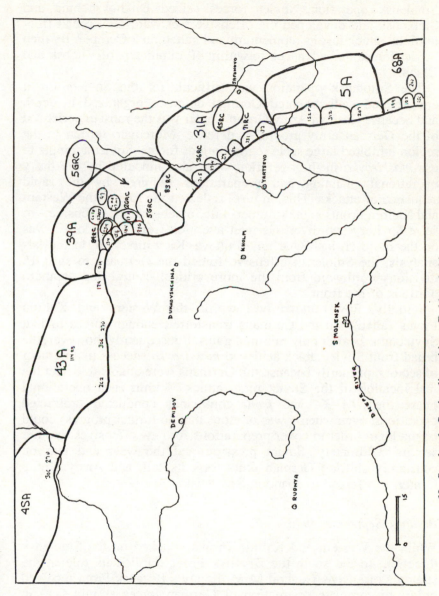

60. Smolensk, Soviet dispositions, Dukhovshchina sector, 12 September 1943

focal point of Soviet mobile forces as south, rather than north of the city (see maps 61 and 62). In this third, and last, phase of the Smolensk operation, Soviet forces seized Dukhovshchina and Smolensk and developed the offensive westward on a broad front until the attack lost its momentum and halted on 2 October. By then Soviet forces had advanced to within 40 kilometers of Vitebsk and Orsha.

The Smolensk operation was difficult for the Soviets for it encountered well prepared German defenses organized in depth and because German Army Group Center was the most experienced of the German army groups in defense. Moreover, terrain in the region inhibited large scale regrouping of forces. Soviet attempts to use *maskirovka* in the operation were also hindered by the hasty operational planning and preparations required by the rapid sequence of attacks. This, in turn, reflected the role of the Western and Kalinin Fronts in the summer–fall Soviet strategic offensive – to seize territory and divert German attention from Soviet offensives on the more critical Khar'kov–Poltava–Kiev direction. In the last analysis, the Smolensk offensive forced the Germans to shift 16 divisions northward from the more critical central and southern portions of the front.

Initially, Soviet *maskirovka* within the Western and Kalinin Fronts failed, and the Germans transferred enough forces to halt Soviet attacks after only minimal gains. Subsequently, however, the broad front Soviet attack achieved *maskirovka* success in a number of sectors, primarily because the Germans were unable to detect the real location of the Soviet main attack. Within each operational phase the *STAVKA* and *front* commands conducted protracted operations, even when it was obvious that no further progress could be made, in order to cover preparations for new offensives in other sectors. Ultimately, Soviet pressure and the wear and tear on constantly shifting German units took its toll, and Army Group Center was forced to abandon Smolensk.

Bryansk, September 1943

While the Western and Kalinin Fronts attacked on the Smolensk direction, to the south the Bryansk Front fulfilled its role in the strategic offensive. General M.M. Popov's Bryansk Front received orders to complete destruction of German forces around Orel in coordination with the Central Front and then to mount an offensive of its own on the Bryansk direction. Like its neighboring *fronts* to the north, Popov's *front* was to advance on Bryansk and also prevent redeployment of German forces southward.

Because of the heavy fighting required to liquidate the German Orel salient, the Bryansk Front delayed its new offensive until 1 September. On 16 August the *STAVKA* ordered Popov to:

> continue the offensive, reach to Desna River, secure Bryansk and seize a bridgehead [across the Desna] for use in developing the offensive in the Gomel direction.[145]

The *STAVKA* transferred 50th Army from the Western to the Bryansk Front raising the *front's* strength to five armies (50th, 3d, 11th, 11th Guards, 63d). Popov ordered 50th Army to regroup and move to the area south of Kirov, to attack in cooperation with 3d and 11th Armies against the left flank and center of German forces defending east of Bryansk, and subsequently, attack westward through the forested area east of the Desna River. On the *front* left flank 11th Guards and 63d Armies would cooperate with Central Front forces in an advance on Chernigov.[146]

The timing of the operation was designed to deceive the German defenders. On 1–2 September 63d and 11th Guards Army would attack on the *front's* left flank to distract German attention from preparations on the *front's* right flank. From 3 to 5 September remaining *front* forces would conduct reconnaissance. When German forces were fully occupied elsewhere, 50th Army would strike the German left flank near Kirov and cut into the German rear.

Popov's initial plan required Lieutenant General I.V. Boldin's 50th Army to regroup, penetrate German defenses, and advance southwest in cooperation with the westward thrust of 3d and 11th Armies. Several factors disrupted that plan. The enemy defenses (four infantry divisions) in 50th Army's new attack sector were strong and anchored on difficult, swampy terrain. The Germans also detected 50th Army's redeployment and further strengthened the defenses.[147]

Consequently, Popov decided to capitalize on the success achieved by the Western Front's 10th Army which had penetrated German defenses west of Kirov during early stages of the Smolensk operation. Popov requested *STAVKA's* permission to shift 50th Army northward into 10th Army's sector and then suddenly strike southward with 50th Army along the Desna River directly into the German rear.[148] The *STAVKA* approved Popov's proposal and ordered 10th Army to transfer part of its sector to 50th Army along

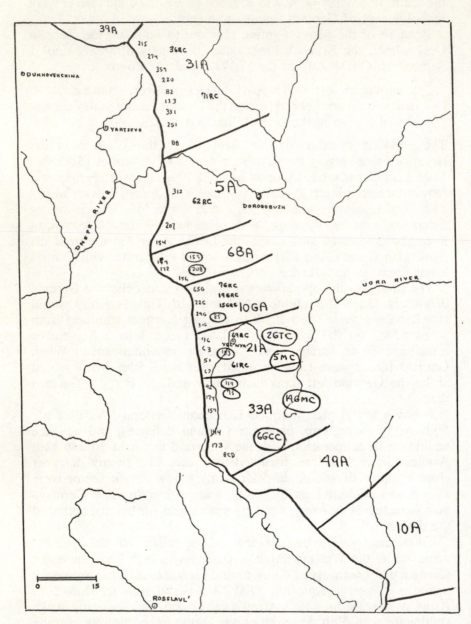

61. Smolensk, German intelligence assessment, 14 September 1943

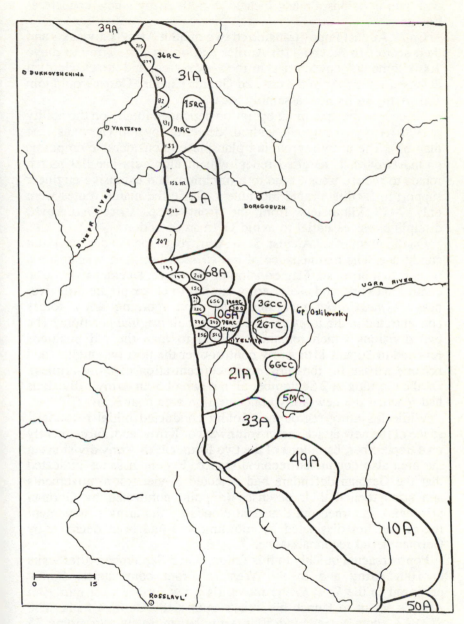

62. Smolensk, Soviet dispositions, 14 September 1943

with two divisions already located in 50th Army's new concentration area.

On 29 August Popov transferred two of 50th Army's divisions and their sectors to 3d and 11th Armies and ordered the army to move 100 kilometers, concentrate in the Kirov area, and attack German defenses southwest of the city. 2d Guards Cavalry Corps would join 50th Army in its new assembly area.

Success in the upcoming operation depended totally on the ability of 50th Army to regroup without detection by the Germans (see map 63). The army regrouping plan placed considerable emphasis on *maskirovka*. It required redeployment along six parallel march routes to reduce transit time to a minimum and extensive engineer support to facilitate rapid movement. Since the march routes were only 7–13 kilometers from the front lines, strict *maskirovka* discipline was essential to avoid German detection.

On the night of 29 August, 50th Army regrouped under black-out conditions. The maintenance of *maskirovka* discipline was ensured by constant army staff supervision of the move, an extensive traffic control network, and use of army aircraft to check on the effectiveness of *maskirovka* measures. The next morning army forces concentrated in the forests to the rear of their original positions. The two divisions which remained behind to man the old positions reverted to 3d and 11th Army control over the next two nights (and became a base for the subsequent concentration of those armies). On the morning of 2 September all but two of 50th Army's divisions had reached the new army concentration area near Kirov.[149]

While his army regrouped, Boldin conducted initial reconnaissance of the new attack sector southwest of Kirov; and, subsequently on 4 September, battalions of the two former 10th Army divisions in the area also conducted reconnaissance. Reconnaissance indicated that the German defenders had detected Soviet troop movements and strengthened their defenses (a point confirmed by German prisoners). It turned out that dust clouds on the army's movement routes had not dissipated by morning and had been detected by German aerial reconnaissance.[150]

Popov reacted quickly to this failure. On 5 September, after visits to 10th Army and to the Western Front commander, Popov proposed to the *STAVKA* he move his army further west into 10th Army's sector to launch his attack against the German flank. The *STAVKA* again agreed, and 50th Army began a new regrouping 35 kilometers to the northwest. This time 50th Army would attack

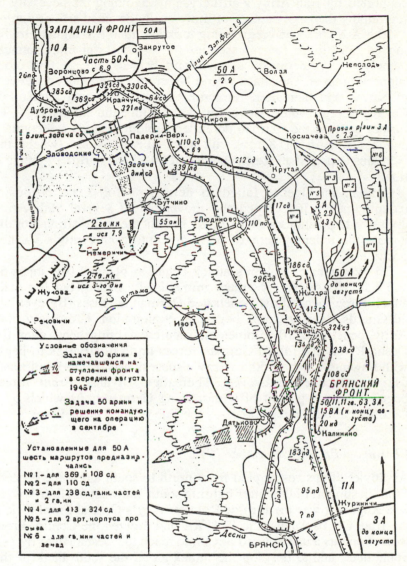

Перегруппировка войск 50-й армии и решение командующего на операцию (сентябрь 1943 г.)

63. Bryansk, 50th Army regrouping, 29 August–6 September 1943

supported by 10th Army's artillery, thus avoiding the necessity of regrouping the large number of more easily detected artillery units.

50th Army's second regrouping took less than two nights. Boldin moved only those forces essential for a successful initial attack, namely two rifle divisions, one tank brigade, and a few other supporting units. The attack would begin on 7 September northwest of Kirov, and thereafter, remaining army forces and 2d Guards Cavalry Corps would move forward to join the offensive.[151] To further confuse the German defenders Boldin planned a secondary attack southeast of Kirov with two rifle divisions (where the Germans expected an attack) preceded by a heavy artillery preparation.

German intelligence failed to detect the full scale of Soviet redeployments. It recorded the movement of several 50th Army divisions to positions west of Kirov but not the entire army. Nor did it note the redeployment of 3d Army into 50th Army's vacated positions.

On 7 September Boldin's attack began as planned (see maps 64 and 65). His secondary attack immediately stalled, but his main attack force successfully penetrated German defenses. By evening, 2d Guards Cavalry Corps began an exploitation. Ultimately 50th Army penetrated 70 kilometers, secured a bridgehead over the Desna River, and forced German forces north of Bryansk to begin withdrawing. Much of 50th Army's success was due to its ultimate use of effective *maskirovka*. Thereafter, Bryansk *Front* forces began a general pursuit of withdrawing German units which by 3 October carried Soviet forces to the line of the Dnepr River.

Chernigov–Pripyat, September 1943

As Soviet offensives rippled from north to south along the Eastern Front in support of the bitter fighting south and west of Khar'kov, in late August it was the turn of Rokossovsky's Central Front to join the fray. On 16 August the *STAVKA* had ordered the Central Front to continue its attack toward Sevsk, to reach the Desna River by 1–3 September, and to develop the attack along the south bank of the river through Konotop toward Chernigov. Preparations for the 24 August attack were to be completed by 20 August.

Rokossovsky's Central Front consisted of five armies (13th, 48th, 65th, 60th, 61st), one tank army (2d), one tank corps (9th), and one mechanized corps (7th Guards), most of which had been severely worn down in heavy fighting at Kursk and Orel. Rokossovsky ordered 65th and parts of 48th and 60th Armies to advance on Sevsk, covered on the right flank by 13th Army, and on the left flank by 60th Army. 2d Tank Army would exploit through 65th Army on the second day of the operation.[152]

Rokossovsky's plan required extensive regrouping of forces and movement of 2d Tank Army, 13th, and 48th Armies, 19th Rifle Corps of 65th Army, 9th Tank Corps, and the 4th Artillery Penetration Division distances of between 60 and 200 kilometers. All movement had to be completed by 20 August.[153] Complicating this task, supplies and equipment expended at Kursk required replenishment; and the route of projected *front* operations, which traversed several major rivers, required assignment of engineer-bridging units to the *front*. These difficulties forced postponement of the attack until 26 August.

Regrouping units used three march routes, and time constraints forced them to move during both day and night. *Front* initially provided a traffic control system and checked the *maskirovka* efficiency of units which moved into 65th Army's concentration area. Army and unit staffs supervised all other movements.

The *front maskirovka* plan incorporated a disinformation program to deceive the Germans regarding the main attack location and required use of other *maskirovka* measures to mask regrouping and concentration of forces for the attack. Lieutenant General I.D. Chernyakhovsky's 60th Army was to simulate preparations for a *front* main attack toward Rylsk on the *front's* left flank. 60th Army trucks dragged large branches to create dust clouds along roads into 60th Army's sector while Soviet security forces captured German agents in the rear area and used their radio transmitters to send false messages concerning Soviet offensive intent.[154]

Since, however, the regrouping time was excessive, the Germans were able to detect both the movement and its direction. As early as 20 July German aircraft bombed Soviet units and continued the attacks several times a day throughout the preparation period. These attacks failed to inflict major casualties because in the preceding months Rokossovsky had ordered 65th Army to construct a series of alternate jumping-off positions for use in attacks either toward Bryansk or Sevsk. Troops used these alternative positions for dispersed defense against air attack.[155] In addition, the *STAVKA* representative supervising the operation (General G.A. Vorozheikin, deputy commander of the Soviet Air Force) and the 16th Air Army commander concentrated all *front* fighter aviation units over 65th Army and used new radio locators to direct the

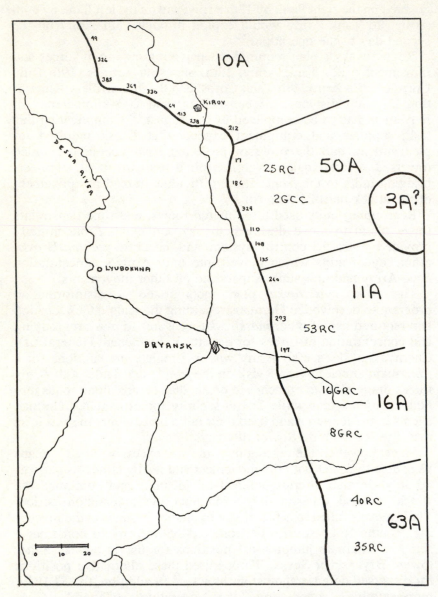

64. Bryansk, German intelligence assessment, 6 September 1943

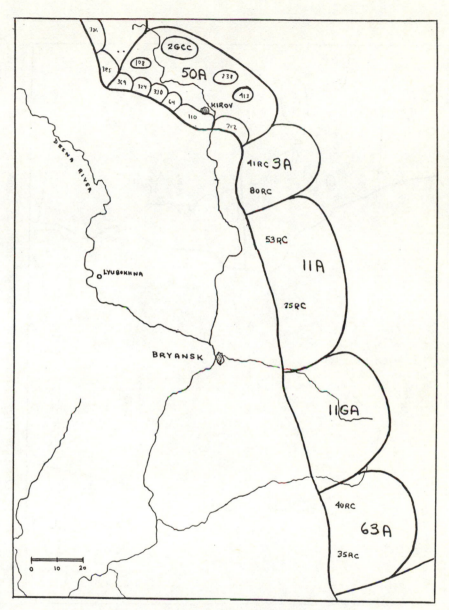

65. Bryansk, Soviet dispositions, 6 September 1943

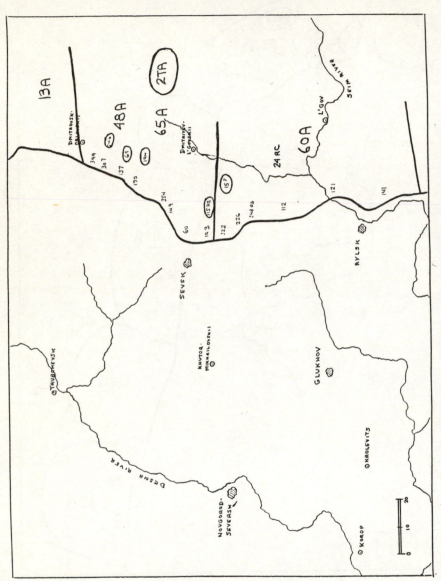

66. Chernigov–Pripyat, German intelligence assessment, 25 August 1943

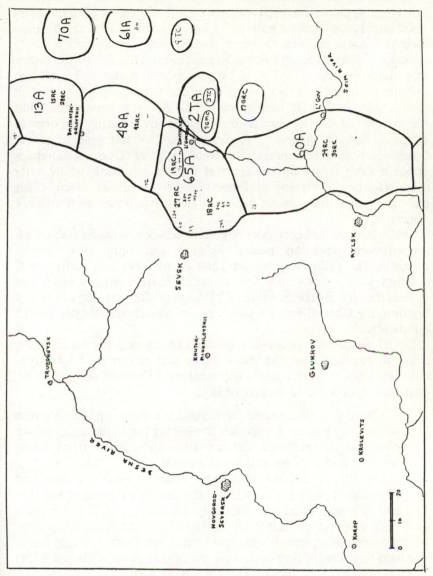

67. Chernigov–Pripyat, Soviet dispositions, 25 August 1943

aircraft. Rokossovsky also reinforced 65th Army with three anti-aircraft artillery divisions to provide denser air defense.

Despite these adjustments, German Second Army detected Soviet movement, correctly determined the location of the Soviet main attack, and moved new units into the Sevsk area to reinforce their defenses. In fact, German intelligence constructed a fairly accurate picture of Soviet force dispositions on the eve of the attack (see maps 66 and 67). By 26 August Ninth Army had sent two infantry divisions and two panzer divisions to the Sevsk area. Soviet accounts claim that German agents in the Soviet rear contributed to the failure of Soviet secret movements by sending reports to German Second Army.[156] A fortuitous but unforeseen result, however, was a commensurate weakening of German defenses opposite 60th Army on the Central Front's left flank where only three German divisions defended a 90 kilometer front. This ultimately militated against initial Soviet misfortunes on the Sevsk direction.

On 26 August Rokossovsky began his attack toward Sevsk, which immediately produced heavy fighting and only slow Soviet progress. The following day 2d Tank Army went into action; and, although the Soviets seized Sevsk, their offensive bogged down just west of the city. By the evening of 31 August, after four days of heavy fighting, the Central Front's shock group had advanced only 20–25 kilometers.[157]

On 27 August Rokossovsky decided to regroup his forces once again to capitalize on the more successful advance of Chernya-khovsky's 60th Army against the weakened German defenses (see map 68). According to Rokossovsky:

> Without encountering any strong enemy opposition, the 60th Army pushed far ahead. Exploiting the initial success, we hastened to reinforce Chernyakhovsky's army from Front reserve, and sent in additional aircraft ....
> On 29 August, the 60th Army carried Glukhov. We had obviously found a weak spot in the enemy's defenses, and this had to be exploited without delay. I decided to shift the Front's main effort to the left flank. We quickly carried out a regroup-ing maneuver, transferring the 13th Army from the right flank, and thrusting it into action on the boundary of 65th and 60th, and bringing up the 2d Tank Army as well.[158]

On 30 and 31 August 9th Tank Corps and two rifle divisions regrouped from *front* reserve, covered on their 100 kilometer march

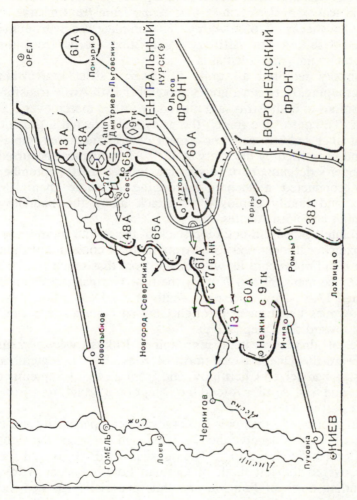

Маневр войск Центрального фронта в ходе Черниговско-Припятской операции

68. Chernigov–Pripyat, Central Front regrouping, 31 August–10 September 1943

by 16th Air Army which also shifted its bases forward to support the new main attack on the *front* left flank.[159] Further north, on the evening of 31 August, 2d Tank Army and 13th Army disengaged from combat. 2d Tank Army passed into *front* reserve, and 13th Army began a 320 kilometer march to new positions on 65th Army's right flank. Rokossovsky ordered 61st Army from *front* reserve to reinforce the attacks of 65th Army. To complete the regrouping Rokossovsky shifted 4th Artillery Penetration Corps from the Sevsk sector to the *front* left flank.

Rokossovsky required all units to observe strict *maskirovka* during regrouping. Between 1 and 3 September 13th Army transferred its positions to 65th Army and moved by forced march over 100 kilometers. To control the march the army staff created a graphic movement plan and stringent movement control measures implemented and controlled by the army staff.[160] All movement occurred at night under strict *maskirovka* discipline. From 8 to 10 September the army conducted a second regrouping of more than 100 kilometers and finally deployed to attack along the boundary between 60th and 65th Armies.

German intelligence did not keep track of the Soviet regrouping. On 10 September it identified 13th Army on the Central Front right flank, and it did not record its withdrawal from that sector until 12 September (see maps 69 and 70). By the time German intelligence had detected 13th Army's presence south of the Desna, both 13th and 60th Armies had broken through German defenses and were advancing toward the Dnepr River.

Because of this successful regrouping, Rokossovsky's *front* surged toward the Dnepr River north of Kiev. By 21 September Soviet forces had seized Chernigov, and from 22 to 24 September 13th, 60th, and 61st Armies forced the Dnepr on a broad front from Loyev to north of Kiev.

By rapid concealed maneuver Rokossovsky compensated for the earlier *front* failure to deceive the Germans, and collapsed the right flank of German Second Army. The subsequent drive toward the Dnepr uncovered the left flank of German Fourth Panzer Army, then defending north of Poltava, and thus materially assisted the Voronezh and Steppe Fronts on the strategic main attack direction.

Left Bank of Ukraine, August–September 1943

On the strategic main attack direction the Soviet Voronezh and Steppe Fronts, under Zhukov's supervision, sought to complete the Belgorod–Khar'kov operation and develop the offensive on both sides of Poltava to the Dnepr River. In late August heavy confused combat raged near Akhtyrka, Bogodukhov, and Khar'kov as the Germans threw into battle reserves shifted primarily from the south. The close, continuous nature of the fighting prevented extensive planning and, hence, the creation of elaborate *maskirovka* plans. Nevertheless, in the latter stages of the Belgorod–Khar'kov operation the Soviets were able to shift secretly large forces either laterally or from reserves and commit them into combat by surprise. These Soviet successes were a product of routine Soviet security and *maskirovka* measures and German preoccupation with the heavy and confused combat.

Late in the Belgorod–Khar'kov operation the *STAVKA* and *front* commands began committing their operational reserves to combat, in particular 47th Army and 4th Guards Army.[161] 47th Army, which German intelligence recognized as being somewhere in the Soviet rear, went into action on 16 August north of Akhtyrka. German intelligence failed to detect the army's presence for several days, even after it had thoroughly smashed German defenses and penetrated deep into the German rear. A similar situation occurred in the area east of Akhtyrka where on 20 August the Soviets committed 4th Guards Army against a German counter-attack. German intelligence failed to note the presence of that army throughout the duration of the operation. From 19 to 21 August the Soviets extensively regrouped their forces between Akhtyrka and Bogodukhov, but German intelligence picked up only a fraction of these moves. By 27 August the front had temporarily stabilized south of Kotel'va.

Meanwhile Konev's Steppe Front secured Khar'kov on 23 August and struggled southward toward Lyubotin and Merefa. Earlier, on 12 August, the *STAVKA* had ordered Konev to cooperate with the Voronezh Front and advance via Krasnograd to the Dnepr River in the vicinity of Dnepropetrovsk.[162] Konev's armies, however, had been severely weakened in the battle for Khar'kov and, hence, struggled for days to seize their initial objectives of Lyubotin and Merefa. Throughout this period Konev engaged in deception to convince the Germans his strength was greater than it was. The focal point of this *maskirovka* was Lieutenant General R. A. Rotmistrov's 5th Guards Tank Army. To conceal the weakened state of the army (50 tanks on 28 August), Rotmistrov organized his remaining tanks into several brigade-size detachments. He ordered each brigade to simulate by radio means a tank or mechanized corps headquarters. The only combat-effective

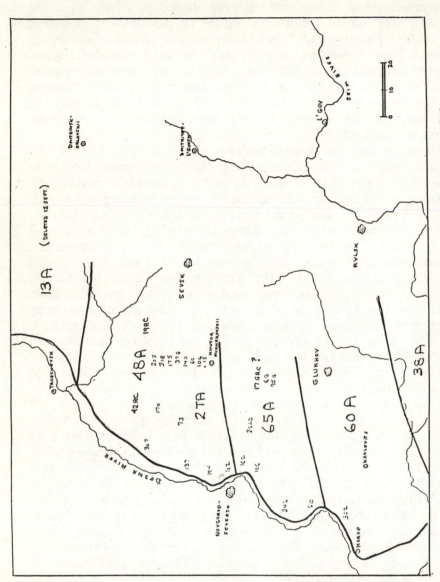

69. Chernigov–Pripyat, German intelligence assessment, 10 September 1943

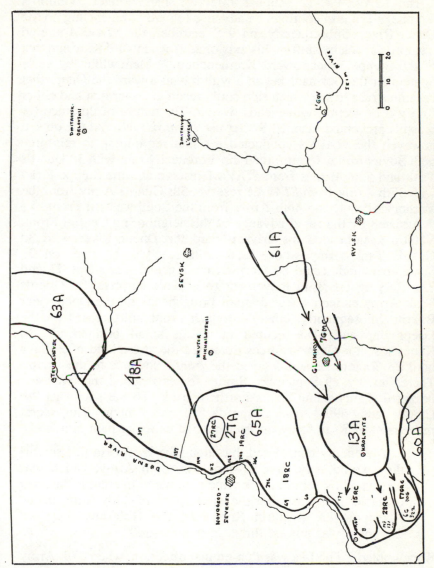

70. Chernigov–Pripyat, Soviet dispositions, 10 September 1943

brigade cooperated with 53d Army attacks on Merefa while the remaining units simulated the presence of a full tank army.[163]

The *STAVKA's* 12 August directive had ordered Vatutin's Voronezh Front to continue its advance toward Kremenchug on the Dnepr River. Subsequently, on 9 September, the *STAVKA* altered Vatutin's attack by shifting his axis of advance toward Kiev and that of the Steppe Front toward Kremenchug.[164] Meanwhile, by early September the Germans began a withdrawal toward the Dnepr that became a race to see which side could reach the river first and either fortify it or secure bridgeheads over it. The nature of this race (or pursuit) prevented planned Soviet use of *maskirovka*. At the outset, however, the *STAVKA* conducted a secret regrouping to reinforce both Soviet *fronts*. It reinforced the Voronezh Front with 3d Guards Tank and 52d Armies from *STAVKA* reserve and the Steppe Front with 37th Army from *STAVKA* reserve, 5th Guards Army from the Voronezh Front, and 46th Army from the Southwestern Front.

Assisted by the rapid advance of the neighboring Central Front, Vatutin spearheaded his drive toward the Dnepr River with 3d Guards Tank Army whose lead units reached the river on 21 September, undetected by German intelligence (see maps 71 and 72). Relying on rapid movement to achieve surprise, 3d Guards Tank Army elements seized small bridgeheads on the Dnepr near Bukrin. Subsequently, other Voronezh Front units closed on the Dnepr line and also secured numerous small bridgeheads. In Konev's sector German forces defended the stronghold of Poltava until 23 September and delayed the *front's* advance to the Dnepr. Thereafter, by 29 September Soviet forces reached the river and besieged Kremenchug on its northern bank. To the southeast 7th Guards and 69th Armies approached the Dnepr. The secret movement of 37th Army, in *front* second echelon, paid dividends:

> The enemy considered that along the Dnepr [in this sector] they would only have to deal with 69th Army, which was weakened by former battles and not able to overcome the river obstacle. Not expecting the appearance of 37th Army in the Kutsevolovka–Mishurin Rog area, the Hitlerites supposed that there was no real threat in this sector.[165]

Konev noted, "The fact was that on that direction, when 37th Army was introduced, the Germans had deployed only the remains of two infantry divisions."[166]

37th Army reached the banks of the Dnepr on 27 September and organized an assault crossing the following night protected by 69th

Army units. To deceive the Germans, Lieutenant General M. Sharokhin, the 37th Army commander, employed *maskirovka* and planned his assault to occur at night, without an artillery preparation.[167] At 0400 28 September the assault commenced, and by day's end 37th Army had consolidated its positions and was able to repulse German counter-attacks. German intelligence missed the presence of 37th Army until it was too late (see maps 73 and 74). The success of 37th Army, and 7th Guards Army further south, provided the Steppe Front with bridgeheads from which to launch future operations toward Krivoi Rog.

Thus, by the end of September Voronezh and Steppe Front forces had closed on the Dnepr and had begun the arduous task of seizing and enlarging bridgeheads across that formidable obstacle.

Donbas–Melitopol', August–September 1943

Within days after the Soviets had terminated their July diversionary attacks along the Northern Donets and Mius Rivers, the Southwestern and Southern Fronts began planning for key roles in the Soviet summer–fall counter-offensive. Having played a secondary yet critical role in the Kursk strategic operation, the *fronts* would now take full part in a strategic operation of considerable consequence. The successful commencement of the Orel and Belgorod operations required that supporting attacks be conducted in the north, and created conditions conducive to the final destruction of German forces in the south, in particular in the Donbas and Kuban regions. To that end the *STAVKA* initiated in full its summer–fall strategic operation by ordering the Southwestern and Southern Fronts "to speed up the destruction of German 1st Panzer and 6th Armies and to liberate the Donets basin."[168] Subsequently, the Southwestern Front was to advance to Zaporozh'ye on the Dnepr River, and the Southern Front would develop the offensive into the Northern Tavria and clear the region between the lower Dnepr River and the Crimean peninsula.

Malinovsky's Southwestern Front received orders to strike from the Izyum area toward Pavlograd to cut off German escape routes to the Dnepr, while Tolbukhin's Southern Front plunged across the Mius River toward the northeast and southwest to cooperate with the Southwestern Front's assault, seize Stalino, and also encircle German forces around Taganrog. Subsequently, the Southern Front would advance westward toward the lower Dnepr River and Crimea. The *STAVKA* underscored the high priority it accorded operations on the main strategic direction around Khar'kov by

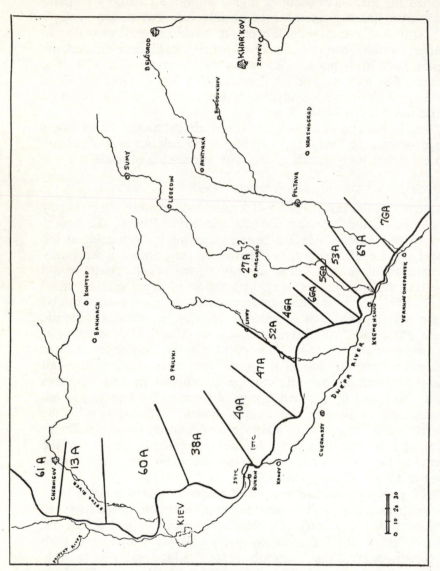

71. Along the Dnepr, German intelligence assessment, 22 September 1943

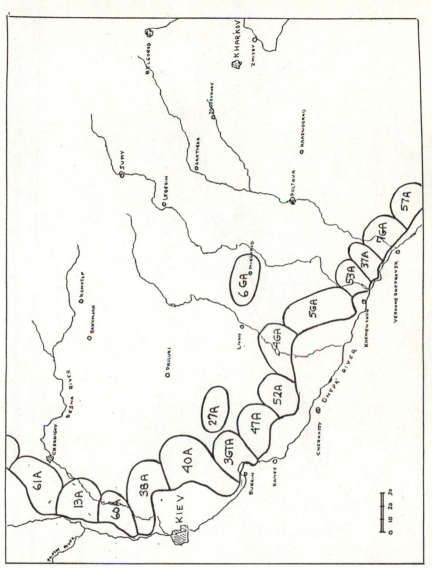

72. Along the Dnepr, Soviet dispositions, 22 September 1943

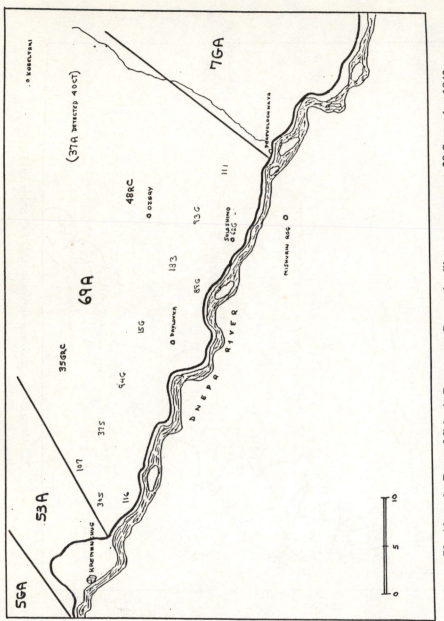

73. Along the Dnepr, Mishurin Rog sector, German intelligence assessment, 29 September 1943

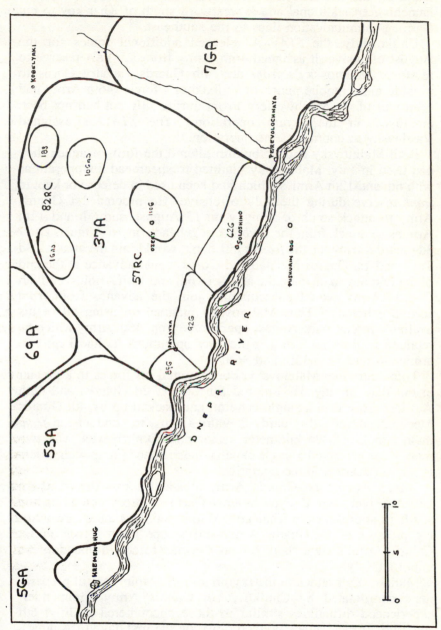

74. Along the Dnepr, Mishurin Rog sector, Soviet situation, 29 September 1943

requiring the Southwestern Front to assist the Steppe Front by launching an additional attack westward south of Khar'kov to cut German communication lines to the southeast.[169]

Unlike July, the *STAVKA* released additional forces for the August offensive. It assigned 46th Army from *STAVKA* reserve to reinforce Malinovsky's *front* and 4th Guards Cavalry Corps to provide more mobile punch to Tolbukhin's force. (46th Army had been part of the Southwestern Front during July but had not been employed in the Izyum operation.) The *STAVKA* assigned Vasilevsky to coordinate the operation.

Both Malinovsky and Tolbukhin altered the form of attack they had used in July. Malinovsky planned to spearhead his operations with 6th and 12th Armies which had been used in defense or kept in *front* reserve during the July offensive. He ordered 1st Guards Army to attack south of Zmiyev on 13 August, and 6th and 12th Armies to attack from the Izyum bridgeheads on 16 August. Later 3d Guards Army, on the *front's* left flank, would join the attack. 23d Tank and 1st Guards Mechanized Corps would advance at the end of the first day to develop the attack of 6th and 12th Armies, and 8th Guards Army would subsequently join the advance from *front* second echelon.[170] Thus Malinovsky planned on using all of his available forces in the August operation except 46th Army which he retained in *front* reserve. (In the July operations he had kept two armies in reserve − 12th and 46th.)

Tolbukhin, like Malinovsky, concentrated his forces to a greater extent than in July. He ordered 5th Shock, 2d Guards, and 28th Armies, arrayed in a single echelon and backed up by 4th Guards Mechanized and 4th Guards Cavalry Corps, to conduct the *front* main attack in a 25 kilometer sector near Dmitriyevka. The two mobile corps formed a single cavalry-mechanized group with orders to exploit success in the operation.

On 13 August 1st Guards Army attacked across the Northern Donets River near Zmiyev against German forces defending the southern approaches to Khar'kov. Within ten days the overwhelming pressure of 1st Guards Army and Steppe Front forces on 1st Guards Army's right flank forced German forces to abandon the important city.

Malinovsky's attack in the Izyum sector, despite careful preparations coordinated by Chuikov, 8th Guards Army commander, experienced difficulties similar to those encountered in July. 6th and 12th Armies' attack bogged down on the first day (16 August). On 22 August Malinovsky ordered Chuikov's 8th Guards Army together with 23d Tank and 1st Guards Mechanized Corps into action.[171] On 28 August, after suffering heavy losses and only minimal gains, Malinovsky ceased his attack in the Izyum sector. Subsequent commitment of 46th Army south of Zmiyev and 3d Guards Army on Malinovsky's left flank failed to dislodge the German defenders. About all that could be said of Malinovsky's offensive was that it prevented German force redeployments to other critical sectors.

Chuikov, who planned operations in the Izyum sector, described planning as "correct" and explained the *maskirovka* failure as follows:

I do not tire repeating the sage maxim of Aleksandr Vasil'evich Suvorov, a classic of Russian military art, "To surprise – means victory." Surprise – it is the main thing in such types of battles. Before my eyes an affirmation of those words unfolded in practice.

Our forces rose up and dashed toward the enemy positions. The artillery roared, and shells tore into the enemy's second line of defense, but from safe cover the enemy opened destructive machine gun and artillery fire on our forces. Our artillery had not suppressed his firing means.

Were conditions conducive for the surprise offensive of 6th and 12th Armies on 17 August? No. The offensive was conducted from a secured bridgehead. The enemy must have expected this development of events and the introduction of fresh forces, since a blow through Barvenkovo to the south would be mortally dangerous to him.

The approach of 6th and 12th Armies to the Northern Donets was undoubtedly discovered by the enemy, and their crossing of the river and replacement of 8th Army indicated the approximate time of the offensive. In such conditions the specific time of attack played no role. Here the established stereotype helped the enemy considerably – the beginning of the artillery offensive.[172]

Chuikov protested the commitment of 8th Guards Army into the welter of unsuccessful battle. Repeating the arguments of July, Vasilevsky said "confidentially" to Chuikov:

conditions to the north of us, in the Voronezh and Steppe Fronts zone of action, and our offensive on Khar'kov demands that we not lose time and we commit all forces so that we can draw off as many divisions as possible from Khar'kov. And even if we do not draw them off, at least we will not give Manstein the ability to take any of his units from our part of the front. If we attract one or two German tank divisions – it will be the best contribution to the defeat of the enemy in the south.[173]

On the eve of 8th Guards Army's attack Chuikov noted:

Surprise, it is a contradictory thing. Both a shelled bridge-head and offensive after offensive against it. I strive to have the army occupy its jumping-off positions secretly. How do you figure it? Only that the German command, having beaten off the attacks of 6th and 12th Armies, considered that we would not introduce yet another army into battle on that bridgehead. That calculation, certainly was not remarkable, but it was the only hope he gave us.

Interestingly enough, our blow turned out to be a surprise for the enemy. German officer prisoners later confirmed this and this affirmed the success of the offensive.[174]

On the eve of the new Soviet attack, German intelligence identified 6th and 8th Guards Armies in the bridgehead, as well as divisions from 12th Army (see maps 75 and 76). It did not detect 3d Guards Army's westward regrouping. The Germans were aware of an impending assault, although the scale of the assault and its persistance, surprised them. The terrain and deep German defenses militated against any rapid Soviet success.

Manstein confirmed the serious impact of Malinovsky's offensive on the German position along the Northern Donets, stating, "22 August was a day of crisis .... First Panzer Army had brought another attack to a standstill, but it too was coming to the end of its strength."[175]

Further south, on 18 August Tolbukhin attacked across the Mius River with massive forces deployed forward. Extensive *maskirovka* measures concealed the formation of the huge concentration. German intelligence failed to note Soviet concentration for the new offensive (see Maps 77 and 78). It assessed that 2d Guards Army was in the rear licking its wounds of July as were the two Soviet mechanized corps. As at Belgorod, German intelligence under-estimated the recuperative power and persistance of the Soviets. The massive nature of the Soviet attack mitigated the adverse effects of poor *maskirovka*. Within two days the Soviets had committed their mechanized forces and torn a deep hole in German defenses. By 31 August Army Group South ordered Sixth Army to fall back, a process which accelerated on 15 September when Army Group South received new orders to withdraw to the line of the Dnepr River and Melitopol'.

Maskirovka contributed only marginally to surprise in these two operations. Soviet offensive intent was clear as were the locations and general timing of the attacks. Whatever success the Soviets achieved resulted from the form of the attack, massive and single echelon, and from their introduction of a fresh army (8th Guards) into an area where two armies had already failed. Hence the Soviets achieved some success in concealing the scale of the attack.

By 21 September Soviet forces in the Donbas again faced German prepared defenses running from east of Zaporozh'ye south along the Molochnaya River to Melitopol' on the Sea of Azov. Two days later Vasilevsky, still *STAVKA* representative in the south, submitted a plan for an offensive to penetrate German Sixth Army's defenses. The original plan called for 5th Shock, 44th, and 2d Guards Armies to make the Southern Front's main attack on the *front* right flank and for 28th Army to conduct a supporting attack just south of Melitopol'. 51st Army, in *front* reserve, would develop the attack in the north. Tolbukhin also formed two mobile groups to exploit success and positioned both groups in the north. Group "Hurricane" consisted of 11th Tank and 5th Guards Cavalry Corps and Group "Blizzard" was composed of 19th Tank and 4th Guards Cavalry Corps.[176]

On 26 September Tolbukhin began his offensive, but it immediately stalled. Tolbukhin regrouped and attacked again on 9 October with 2d Guards and 51st Armies north of Melitopol' and with 28th Army south of the city. While the northern attack again failed, 28th Army penetrated 7 kilometers to the southern outskirts of the city. Consequently, on 11 October Tolbukhin ordered 51st Army, 19th Tank, and 4th Guards Cavalry Corps to regroup, march south, and reinforce 28th Army's attack on the morning of 12 October.[177]

Overnight 54th Rifle Corps of 51st Army conducted a rapid 35 kilometer march without prior reconnaissance of march routes but under strict *maskirovka* discipline.[178] Nevertheless, the bulk of the corps occupied its new positions at the designated time without detection by German intelligence (see maps 79 and 80). As a result of the new attack German defenses south of Melitopol' crumbled, and after a ten day battle the city fell. Ultimately, after a new Soviet attack on 24 October, German forces began a withdrawal to the lower Dnepr River and the Crimea.

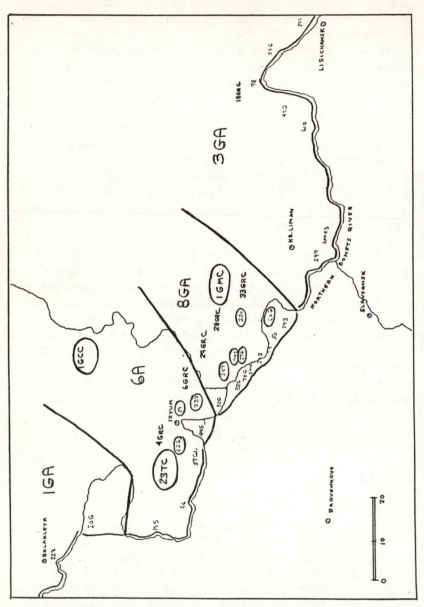

75. Donbas, Izyum sector, German intelligence assessment, 15 August 1943

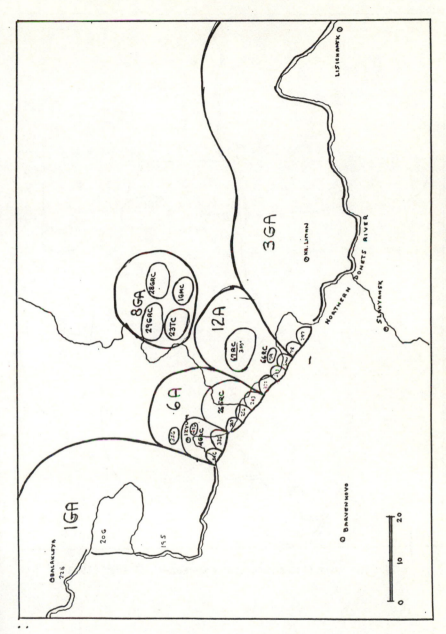

76. Donbas, Izyum sector, Soviet dispositions, 15 August 1943

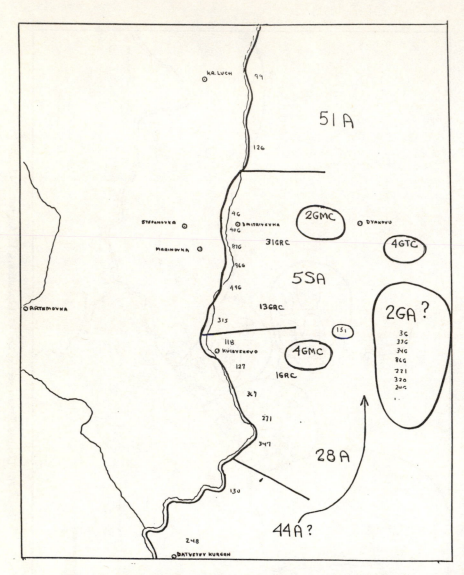

77. Mius River, German intelligence assessment, 17 August 1943

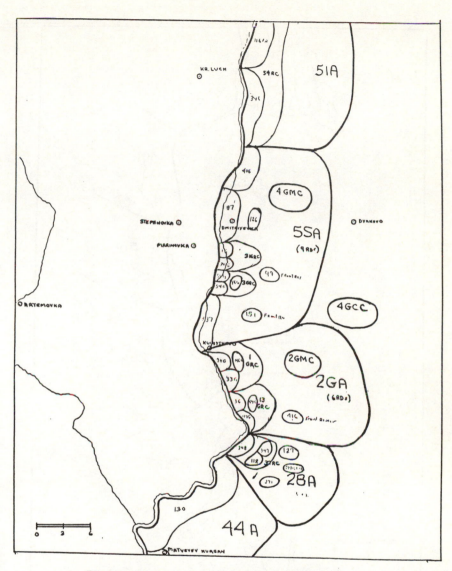

78. Mius River, Soviet dispositions, 17 August 1943

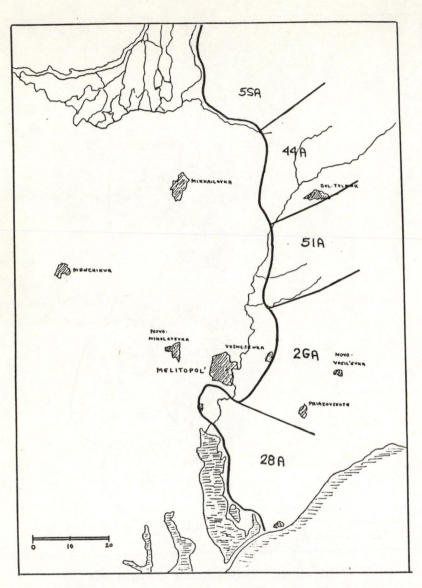

79. Melitopol', German intelligence assessment, 12 October 1943

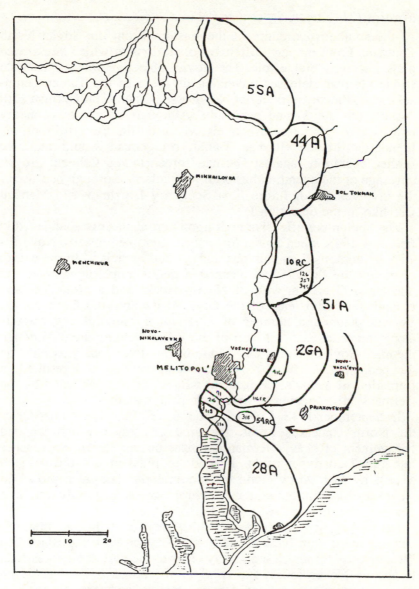

80. Melitopol', Soviet dispositions, 12 October 1943

Novorossiisk–Taman, September 1943

At the southern extremity of the Eastern Front the Soviet North Caucasus Front prepared offensive operations in which *maskirovka* played a considerable role. The Soviet objective was to penetrate strong German defenses traversing the base of the Taman peninsula, seize the key port city of Novorossiisk, and clear German 17th Army from the Taman peninsula. Although clearly a secondary operation in relation to events elsewhere on the Eastern Front, the liquidation of the German Taman bridgehead would facilitate further operations against German forces in the Crimea. (Soviet coverage of the operation has been particularly thorough because of the involvement of future First Secretary Brezhnev and Marshal Grechko in the operation.)

The September offensive built upon partial successes achieved in February 1943, when Soviet forces had attempted to seize Novorossiisk by combined amphibious and ground assault.[179] In the earlier operation the Soviets had planned a major amphibious assault at Yuzhnaya Ozereika, west of Novorossiisk, and a ground assault around the harbor east of the city. To deceive the Germans the Soviets planned a number of diversionary amphibious assaults along the coast east and west of the actual landing area. Although the main Soviet assaults failed, one of the diversionary assaults on the peninsula south of Novorossiisk succeeded and resulted in formation of a Soviet bridgehead which, though contained by the Germans, still threatened the city from the south.

In September 1943, Colonel General I.E. Petrov, commander of the North Caucasus Front, prepared an attack which avoided engagement of heavy German defenses on the eastern approaches into the Taman peninsula. Instead he planned a multi-pronged assault by 18th Army along the mountainous coastal approach to Novorossiisk from the east and an amphibious assault directly into Novorossiisk harbor (see map 81).[180]

On 30 August Petrov ordered 18th Army to conduct an amphibious operation with light forces in cooperation with the Black Sea Fleet directly through Tsemesskaya Bay to the port of Novorossiisk, to occupy Novorossiisk, and continue the attack to the west. 18th Army created two ground assault groups and one amphibious assault group. The eastern ground force (reinforced 318th Rifle Division) was to attack along the eastern shore of the bay and cooperate with the 1339th Rifle Regiment which would strike the

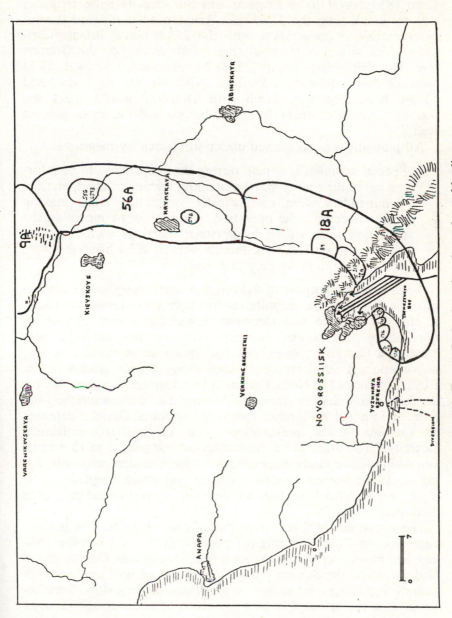

81. Novorossiisk–Taman, Soviet deception plan and actual landings

rear of German defenses by amphibious assault. The second ground force (83d Naval Rifle Brigade and 8th Guards Rifle Brigade) was to attack from the Myskhako bridgehead northward toward Novorossiisk in cooperation with the 255th Naval Infantry Brigade which would conduct an amphibious assault on the German rear. The amphibious group (255th Naval Infantry Brigade, 393d Separate Naval Infantry Battalion, 290th NKVD Regiment, and 1339th Rifle Regiment, 318th Rifle Division) would attack the rear of German defenses from the harbor and the main port as well.[181]

All planning was conducted under strict security measures:

> Special attention was paid during the preparation to disinformation of the enemy and maintaining secrecy of the operation. Commanders were catagorically prohibited from making notes concerning the operation. All questions concerning the operation were settled by personal meetings with the commander and staff. All documents were done by hand and were known only to those they concerned.[182]

To conceal the purpose of the large, but necessary, concentration of ships to convoy the amphibious force, *front* headquarters created a plan to deceive the Germans regarding Soviet objectives. Specifically, the Soviets openly prepared for landings near Yuzhnaya Ozereika (where they had failed seven months before) and conducted naval reconnaissance along a wide stretch of the Black Sea coast. The North Caucasus Front issued a written plan for the false amphibious operation.[183] Meanwhile, to the north the *front* ordered 56th and 9th Armies facing the principal German defenses to simulate attack preparations and display reconnaissance "activity." The Black Sea Fleet conducted war games on 13 August simulating future landing operations on the Crimean peninsula. All the while the Soviets carried out their real attack preparations at night and undertook to prevent German air reconnaissance over Tsmesskaya Bay.[184]

The actual amphibious force trained only at night. The landing boats occupied their jumping-off position precisely when the artillery and naval preparation commenced. Throughout the last phase of deployment the Soviets masked the noise of boat engines with aircraft flights over the assembly areas and landing sites. Simultaneous with the landings at port facilities, bombers struck German communications facilities inland to disrupt enemy command and control in the landing area.[185]

These Soviet measures surprised the German defenders. One critic noted:

> On the night of 10 September, when the amphibious force was on the way to Novorossiisk the enemy displayed no activity. He conducted methodical artillery fire on the Kaberdinki area, fired off rockets over our forward area at Myskhako, and twice conducted a searchlight search of the sea near Yuzhnaya Ozereika. It could be seen that the fascists knew nothing about the approach of the amphibious force to Novorossiisk, and if he was concerned, it was with the Yuzhnaya Ozereika area.[186]

German records substantiate the success of Soviet *maskirovka* around Novorossiisk. Army Group "A's" war diary contained an entry on 24 August which warned of a possible amphibious assault in the Ozereika region simultaneous with ground operations.[187]

The Soviet surprise amphibious assault began at 0300 10 September against the port facilities in Novorossiisk and was followed quickly by 18th Army's two ground attacks. By 15 September Soviet forces had penetrated well into the city, and at 1000 16 September the Germans abandoned it. Meanwhile, on 11 and 14 September 9th and 56th Armies struck German defenses in the north. By 3 October the Taman peninsula was cleared of German forces.

Postscript

By early October the Soviet summer–fall offensive had run its course. In the north Soviet forces had penetrated almost to the borders of Belorussia; in the center they had reached, and, at places, crossed, the Dnepr River; and in the south they had cleared the Donbas and Taman areas and were threatening the Crimea. They had accomplished these feats by conducting almost simultaneous operations across the entire extent of the Eastern Front.

The Soviets focused their offensive on what they perceived to be the most critical sector – the Khar'kov–Poltava–Kiev direction – for defeat of Germans there would render German defenses in the south untenable. To support their thrust to Kiev the Soviets mounted a series of supporting offensives to tie down German forces and prevent German reinforcement of the critical Khar'kov region. The Soviets carefully staggered the timing of supporting offensives to confuse German intelligence regarding their intentions. Most important, they expected the supporting attacks to achieve specific objectives, thus they were not solely of a diversionary nature as they had been in July. To a greater extent than at Kursk, supporting attacks were designed to provide specific assistance to the Soviet Voronezh and Steppe Fronts on the main attack direction. Thus 60th Army of the Central Front cracked open German defenses south of Chernigov and paved the way for the Voronezh Front's drive to the Dnepr River at Kiev. Likewise, the Southwestern Front's 1st Guards Army and 46th Army assisted the Steppe Front in breaking the German grip on Khar'kov.

The Soviet offensives in the south developed successfully, though not without repeating some of the frustrations experienced in July. In essence, the stiff German resistance in the Donbas justified the Soviet decision to concentrate its main effort further north.

In the summer–fall strategic offensive the Soviets engaged in strategic *maskirovka* only to the extent of trying to confuse the Germans regarding the location and strength of the main attack. Because of continuous close combat neither intent nor timing could be concealed. However, by shifting strategic reserves (in particular between the Central, Steppe, and Voronezh Fronts) they were marginally able to confuse the Germans regarding the strength of some of the thrusts. Throughout the operations the Germans placed more importance on events in the south than in the center (due partly to Hitler and German recollection of the post-Stalingrad offensive).

Maskirovka played a larger role at the operational and tactical level (as it would tend to do in the future when Soviet armies were on the march). Most Soviet forward progress was a product of the secret regrouping of armies within *fronts* (i.e. 50th Army of the Bryansk Front, 60th Army of the Central Front, and 51st Army of the Southern Front), between *fronts* (3d Guards Tank Army), or from *STAVKA* reserve (37th Army and 46th Army). Even at this level, the Soviets experienced marked difficulties, in particular in the Smolensk and Donbas regions where German forces occupied well-prepared defenses and used practiced intelligence techniques. Although *maskirovka* provided victory in key sectors, the Soviets still had much to learn. Meanwhile, the Soviets drew upon the lessons of the summer and fall as they prepared to overcome the next major obstacle to their continued advance, the Dnepr River.

ACROSS THE DNEPR, NOVEMBER 1943

Background

The forward lunge of Soviet forces, which began across the broad expanse of the Eastern Front in late August and September 1943 from Velikie Luki south to the Black Sea, by the end of September had propelled Soviet *fronts* to the eastern borders of Belorussia, the Dnepr River, and the lower Tavria (see map 82). The hard-pressed German army sought desperately to restore a coherent defense line midst the rapidly deteriorating situation. Quite naturally, the attention of German commanders focused on terrain features whose presence could act as a backbone for new defenses. Along the critical central and southern portions of the front the Dnepr and Sozh Rivers were natural barriers where German forces might make their next defensive stand. In late September, German forces raced for sanctuary on the western banks of these rivers, often scarcely hours ahead of their Soviet pursuers. In isolated sectors Soviet forces won the race and were able to insert small units into cramped but nevertheless threatening enclaves on the far bank. For the most part, however, the Germans successfully erected defenses on the west bank of the rivers; cordoned off those small Soviet bridge-heads; and tried, usually in vain, to eradicate them.

By 1 October Soviet forces in the north reached a line running from west of Velikie Luki southward, east of Vitebsk and along the Sozh and Dnepr Rivers, past Kiev to Melitopol'. German forces clung to bridgeheads on the eastern bank at Gomel' and Zaporozh'ye while the Soviets held tenaciously to tenuous footholds on the west bank at numerous locations, but most threateningly near Chernobyl', north of Kiev; at Bukrin, south of Kiev; and at Mishurin Rog, between Kremenchug and Dnepropetrovsk. The Soviet High Command understood that a summer–fall offensive could not be brought to a fitting end without achieving a major breach in these river obstacles, bridgeheads from which new and more powerful offensives could be launched in the winter of 1944.

At the end of September and beginning of October the *STAVKA* assigned new missions to its forces:

> The forces of the northwestern direction were expected to destroy the defending enemy group and prevent their withdrawal to Dvinsk and Riga. On the western direction it was planned to destroy the central enemy group, reach the line

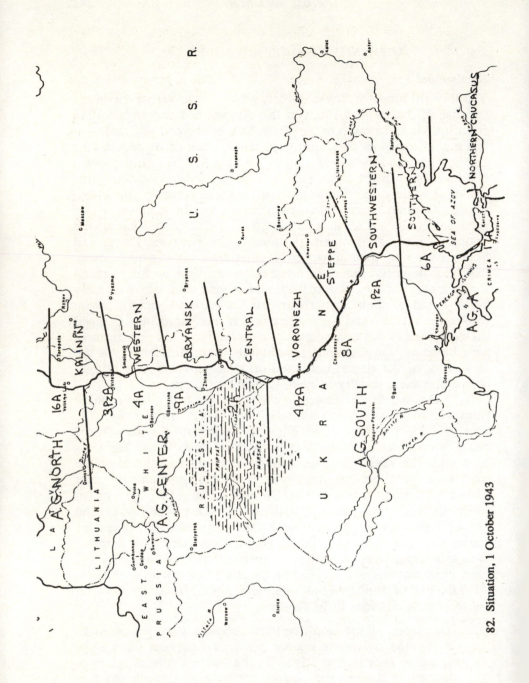

82. Situation, 1 October 1943

Vil'no, Minsk, Slutsk, Sluch' River and liberate regions of the Pre-Baltic and eastern Belorussia. The *fronts* of the south-western direction were to liquidate the Hitlerite bridgeheads on the Dnepr, inflict defeat on their southern group, and reach the line Mogilev–Podol'sk, Rybnitsa, and Kherson.[188]

As had been the case in the drive to the Dnepr, the main direction remained that of Kiev, where the Voronezh Front was to undertake the principal role. Its forces, in cooperation with the Central Front's left wing, were to liquidate the fascist group in the Kiev region, liberate the capital of the Ukraine, and then develop the offensive on Berdichev, Zhmerinky, and Mogilov–Podol'sk.[189] The Steppe Front would cooperate with the Voronezh Front along the Dnepr and attempt to enlarge its bridgehead at Mishurin Rog. Meanwhile the Southern and North Caucasus Fronts would eradicate German bridgeheads east of the Dnepr River, in the Tavria, and on the Taman Peninsula.

By early October most Soviet *fronts* and their German opponents had been in almost constant combat since early July. Exhaustion had taken its toll on both sides. Now the Soviets sought to capitalize on momentum generated in their strategic offensive by selecting the proper place and time to concentrate their exhausted forces and achieve decisive penetrations across the defensive river barriers so critical for the outcome of future operations.

Soviet critics noted the Soviet problem:

> The subsequent course of events demonstrated that not all missions assigned to *fronts* were successfully fulfilled in 1943. The penetration of the enemy defensive lines demanded considerable forces and weaponry which the *fronts* were clearly lacking in the concluding operations of 1943.[190]

This situation made success in operations even more dependent on careful planning and skillful *maskirovka*.

Nevel', October 1943

To support Soviet efforts to cross the Dnepr on the Kiev direction, Soviet *fronts* on the northwestern direction received orders to continue the arduous drive which had begun east of Smolensk in early August. In light of the Western Front's armies' weakened condition, the burden of the new offensive rested on the Kalinin Front's well-rested right flank armies, which during the Smolensk operation had rested fitfully on a front from Velikie Luki to Velizh.

Now in early October they were called upon belatedly to contribute to Soviet offensive efforts.

In late September the *STAVKA* worked out a plan to destroy German forces in the central sector of the Eastern Front from Vitebsk to Gomel'. Yeremenko's Kalinin Front was to penetrate German defenses on a narrow front and seize the critical city of Nevel' on the boundary of German Army Groups Center and North. The Western Front would strike directly at Orsha and Mogilev to tie down German reserves, and the Central Front, after cooperating with the Voronezh Front in seizing Kiev, would wheel northwest and attack toward Zhlobin, Bobruisk and Minsk. Other *fronts* to the north (Leningrad, Volkhov and Northwestern) were to remain as active as possible to fix German forces in their sectors.

Yeremenko decided to attack on 6 October from the *front's* right flank toward Nevel' with 3d and 4th Shock Armies. To divert German attention from the *front* main attack, Yeremenko ordered his left flank 39th and 43d Armies to conduct diversionary attacks westward toward Vitebsk on 2 October.[191] Yeremenko's plan depended for success first and foremost on the ability of 3d Shock Army to concentrate its forces rapidly and secretly, and to conduct a sudden well-coordinated attack. *Front* and army headquarters began planning the upcoming operation on 23 September and allotted two days (4-5 October) for necessary regrouping.

Lieutenant General K.N. Galitsky, commander of 3d Shock Army, planned to attack on a 4 kilometer front with two divisions (357th and 28th) and then exploit to seize Nevel' by committing a division (21st Guards) and tank brigade from second echelon. He retained one division (46th Guards) and two rifle brigades (100th, 31st) in reserve. On the remaining 100 kilometers of front, Galitsky deployed two understrength rifle divisions (178th, 185th), one rifle brigade (23d), and two fortified regions. On Galitsky's left flank two divisions of 4th Shock Army would cooperate in the assault and cover 3d Shock Army's flank.[192] Rapid seizure of Nevel' was critical, for the city controlled lateral communications between the two defending German army groups.

Yeremenko's *front* offensive plan capitalized on the heavily wooded, swampy, and lake strewn terrain east of Nevel' to both mask attack preparations and hinder German efforts to respond to the attack before the damage was done. The *front* diversionary attack on the left flank would further distract German attention from events further north. While preparing the surprise attack, *front* headquarters adhered to a strict regimen of secrecy and document control.

Galitsky's plan, which was approved on 27 August, incorporated extensive *maskirovka* measures designed to cover the regrouping and concentration of forces in his main attack sector.[193] Galitsky, his chief of staff, and member of the Military Council (political officer), developed the concept of operation. Subsequently, the chiefs of forces and services, the chief of operations department, and two operations department assistants helped formulate the plan. They prepared all necessary documents by hand in a limited number of copies.

Galitsky also ordered diversionary action in his army's sector. Units deployed in the 100 kilometer defense sector formed one–two battalion detachments, which were to conduct local attacks along the front to fix enemy units and mask the actual attack sector. Regrouping, which began on 3 October, involved movement of large forces into the main attack sector on the army left flank. Army staff officers closely supervised all movements, which occurred at night along numerous forest roads prepared by army sapper units and physically covered in key sectors by engineer units to prevent detection by German aerial reconnaissance, which was limited in any case by bad weather. All movement occurred in a strict time sequence. Radio communications was prohibited during regrouping and *front* and army headquarters relied on wire and messengers to convey messages. Fighter aviation provided air cover for troop movements and for the creation of forward supply depots as well.

Simultaneously with the concealed movements of 3d Shock Army, 39th Army to the south deliberately carried out similar movements in more open fashion to lend credibility to the diversionary assaults east of Vitebsk. This, in fact, is where the Germans assessed the attack would occur.[194]

By 5 October 3d Shock Army forces had closed into their new concentration areas. Division and regimental commanders conducted their reconnaissance; and battalion, company, and platoon commanders personally inspected the routes their units would use into jumping-off positions. Engineers physically concealed the approach routes.[195] After dark on 5 October first echelon rifle divisions, artillery units, and one tank brigade moved forward and by 0300 had occupied their jumping-off positions, only 300 meters from German defensive lines.[196]

At 1000 6 October Galitsky's army attacked, and within hours he committed his second echelon into the 28th Rifle Division's sector, where the greatest progress had been achieved. By 1530 that division, led by tanks of the 78th Tank Brigade, penetrated over twenty kilometers and captured Nevel'. According to the chief of 3d Shock Army's operations department:

14. A tank unit works out its mission on a map, Fall 1943

The combined attack of infantry and tanks turned out so decisive and unexpected that the enemy was fully demoralized and could not render serious opposition in the city .... Generals and officers located in the army observation point received word that the city was captured but could not immediately believe it .... In order to avoid a mistake and misunderstanding we sent the commander of the 78th Tank Brigade an inquiry and soon received a repeat report that Nevel' was actually secured by the mobile group.[197]

German records attest to the effectiveness of Galitsky's plan and verify the comments of the chief of 3d Shock Army's operations section. Ziemke described the situation as follows:

At the end of September and during the first few days of October the Germans lost track of the Kalinin Front's troop movements. Bad weather prevented aerial reconnaissance, and the Russians first changed their radio traffic patterns and then maintained radio silence.

Early on 6 October four rifle divisions and two tank brigades of Third Shock Army attacked the 2d Air Force Field Division, the left flank division of Third Panzer Army, and ripped through. Probably somewhat startled by their success, for the 2d Air Force Field Division had not merely given way but had fallen apart under the first assault, the Russians hastily loaded a guards infantry division on trucks and tanks and dispatched it northwest behind the Army Group North flank toward Nevel'. Before the Germans could form a clear picture of what had happened at the front the Russians were in Nevel'. The surprised garrison, after putting up scattered resistance, retreated out of town early in the afternoon.[198]

German intelligence on the evening of 5 October noted a concentration of Soviet forces around Velikie Luki but did not detect the concentration of 3d Shock and 4th Shock Armies southeast of Nevel' (see maps 83 and 84). Soviet *maskirovka* measures totally deceived German intelligence.

Subsequently, Soviet forces widened the penetration into a large salient but could not expand it west of Nevel'. Nor could the Germans, however, expel Soviet forces from the area and restore the critical communications lines. The new salient would pose a continuing threat to German forces defending near Vitebsk. A combination of successful Soviet active and passive *maskirovka* measures, which took advantage of the nature of the terrain, produced success in the Nevel' operation.

Gomel'—Rechitsa, November 1943

On the right flank of German Army Group Center, the Soviets followed up on the 1st Ukrainian Front's seizure of Kiev in early November by mounting an attack toward Zhlobin and Bobruisk in southern Belorussia. [On 20 October the Soviets had renamed some of their *fronts*: 1st Baltic (Kalinin), Belorussian (Central), 1st Ukrainian (Voronezh), 2d Ukrainian (Steppe), 3d Ukrainian (Southwestern), 4th Ukrainian (Southern). The Karelian, Leningrad, Volkhov, and Western Fronts retained their former designations and the Bryansk Front was dissolved. Its armies passed to the Belorussian and 1st Ukrainian Fronts.] A 1 October *STAVKA* directive ordered Rokossovsky's Central Front:

While delivering the main blow in the general direction of

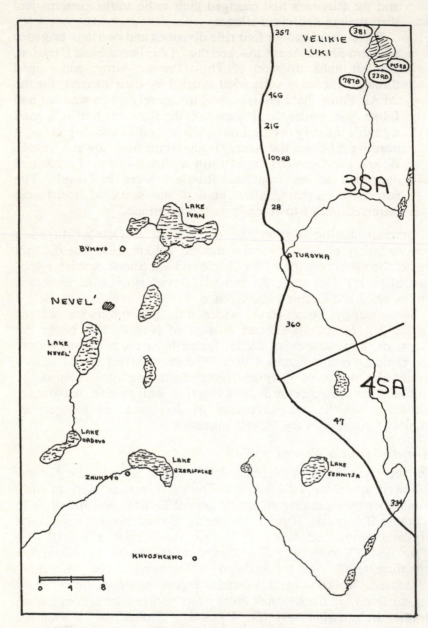

83. Nevel', German intelligence assessment, 5 October 1943

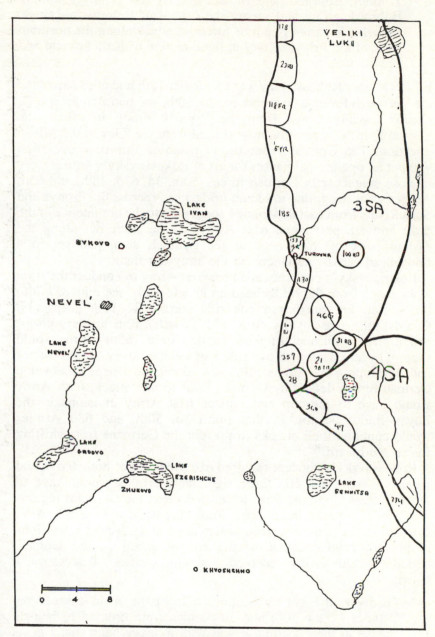

84. Nevel', Soviet dispositions, 5 October 1943

TDAE—J

Zhlobin, Bobruisk and Minsk, destroy the enemy Zhlobin–
Bobruisk group and secure the capital of Belorussia–Minsk.
Detach a separate group of forces to attack along the northern
bank of the Pripyat River in the direction of Kalinkovichi and
Zhitkovichi.[199]

By 10 October Rokossovsky was to transfer 13th and 60th Armies to
the Voronezh Front and receive the 3d, 50th, and 63d Armies and 2d
Guards Cavalry Corps from the Bryansk Front. In effect, the
Central Front's orientation now shifted from the Kiev to the Minsk
direction. The Central Front began planning this new operation
without an operational pause, for all of Rokossovsky's armies were
in close contact with German forces. 50th, 3d, 63d, 48th, and 65th
Armies were struggling to secure bridgeheads across the Pronya and
Sozh Rivers from east of Mogilev southward to the confluence of the
Sozh and Dnepr Rivers. 61st Army, whose front ran along the
eastern bank of the Dnepr to the Lyubich area, had seized a
bridgehead across the Dnepr on the army left flank.

Rokossovsky's concept called for 61st Army to conduct the *front*
main attack from the bridgehead on its left flank (see map 85). Into
this sector, he transferred one rifle corps, two tank corps (1st
Guards, 9th), one cavalry corps (7th Guards), four artillery corps,
and a sizable number of *front* support units. 65th Army would
support by attacking with two rifle corps in the Loyev–Radul' sector
and developing the attack northwest along the Dnepr to envelop
German forces defending Gomel'. Prior to this attack, 65th Army
would have to regroup and replace 61st Army divisions in the
Loyev–Radul' sector. Further north 3d, 50th, and 63d Armies
would continue their attacks to prevent the Germans from shifting
forces southward.[200]

Rokossovsky's concept required extensive use of both active and
passive *maskirovka*. His three right flank armies would have to
remain active along the Sozh River to deceive the Germans regarding Soviet attack intentions. Thus Lieutenant General A.V.
Gorbatov's 3d Army received orders to conduct "active operations
to prevent reinforcement of the enemy group in the Gomel'
region."[201] 50th Army received a similar mission. Rokossovsky
noted:

> To divert the enemy's attention from the main assault, on
> October 12 the 50th and 3d Armies were ordered to launch
> attacks in their sectors. It was with a heavy heart that I gave
> them their missions, fully aware of the scarcity of means at

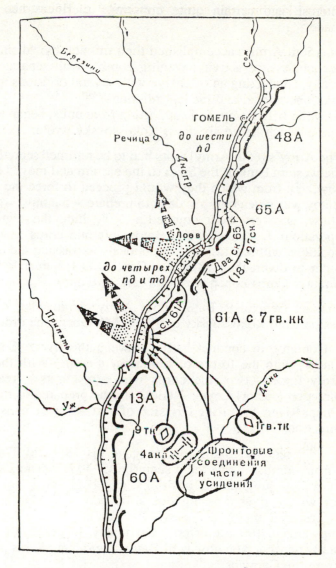

Перегруппировка войск Центрального фронта в
Гомельско-Речицкой операции

85. Gomel'–Rechitsa, Central Front regrouping, 8–14 October 1943

Boldin's and Gorbatov's disposal, but it was in the common interest, and certain quite conscious sacrifices had to be made.[202]

3d and 50th Armies accomplished their mission by: "disinformation; reconnaissance activity; waging combat with separate units; and, finally, conducting an offensive with several divisions to fulfill particular operational and tactical missions."[203]

Meanwhile 65th Army, and supporting *front* units, began a major regrouping which lasted six days. Rokossovsky wrote:

> The Army's [65th Army] units had to be returned secretly from the western bank of the Sozh to the eastern and moved to their new area from which they would proceed to force the Dnepr. Batov was given only six days to prepare – the most we could allow, as every hour counted .... To hide the regrouping operations from the nazis, Batov left one corps in the old positions with the task of continuously harrassing the nazis in order to divert their attention. General D.I. Samarsky's 19th Infantry Corps coped with this task brilliantly.[204]

Lieutenant General P. Batov, 65th Army commander, received his mission from Rokossovsky early on 7 October. The order read:

> Continue to conduct battle between the rivers [Sozh and Dnepr] with the forces of Samarsky's corps. With the main army force – two rifle corps with army units – reach the direction [sector] Loyev–Radul' and be prepared to force the Dnepr River. 55th Rifle Division of 61st Army defends in that direction.[205]

The order required Batov to disengage his 18th and 27th Rifle Corps from combat, move them secretly 35–40 kilometers at night to occupy new jumping-off positions, and begin an attack on 15 October with a river crossing operation across the Dnepr River against prepared enemy defenses. (Reinforcing *front* units had to move upwards of 100 kilometers.) Obviously, success in the operation totally depended on how well Batov could conceal his preparations from the Germans.

Batov's 18th and 27th Rifle Corps (six divisions) abandoned their old positions after darkness on 8 October leaving one division (246th) to cover the regrouping and fill the vacant corps' defensive sector until it was reoccupied by the adjacent 19th Rifle Corps. Subsequently, 19th Rifle Corps ran vehicles, with headlights shining, up and down the roads to the rear and lit bonfires throughout the corps' sector to simulate large force concentrations. Meanwhile, units in the bridgehead continued to use the radio call signs of 18th and 27th Rifle Corps.[206] Batov created a tight system of traffic control to guide the moving columns and conceal them during the daylight hours and implemented a smoke screen plan to cover deployment (see Appendix 1). The deploying units closely coordinated with the 55th Rifle Division, in whose sector Batov's corps moved, to learn about the terrain, the nature of enemy defenses, and the habits of the 55th Rifle Division. Wherever possible the new units used the 55th Rifle Division's supplies, ammunition, food, roads, trench system, and existing communications system.

Batov and his staff arrived before his deploying units, coordinated with the 55th Rifle Division and 61st Army commanders, and conducted personal reconnaissance of the region.[207] Late on 9 October Batov's lead regiments closed into the rear of 55th Rifle Division positions while that division continued carrying on its normal activities. Follow-on corps units assembled in the forests to the rear where they planned and prepared for the river crossing. When regrouping had been completed the corps' main force assembled 5–6 kilometers from the river and second echelon units 6–8 kilometers to the rear. Finally the 55th Rifle Division withdrew, replaced by the lead regiments of Batov's two rifle corps' first echelon divisions.[208] Throughout the Central Front's sector regrouping and concentration were complete by late evening on 14 October. Later, the units occupied final jumping-off positions awaiting the artillery preparation which would cover their assault river crossing.

To the north three days before, at dawn on 12 October, Gorbatov's 3d Army and Boldin's 50th Army had assaulted across the Sozh and Pronya Rivers and by 14 October had advanced only 3 kilometers.[209] They had, however, attracted German attention which was already fixed on containing another Soviet penetration in German defenses to the south near the mouth of the Pripyat River in the Voronezh Front's offensive sector.

The German intelligence picture on the evening of 14 October was inaccurate (see maps 86 and 87). It failed to note the Soviet regrouping of 48th, 65th, and 61st Armies and the creation of a massive concentration north and south of Loyev. German intelligence also failed to detect the presence of the Soviet mobile forces in the region.

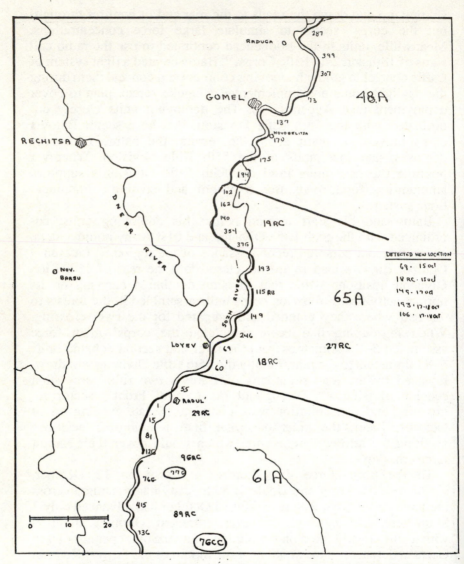

86. Gomel'–Rechitsa, German intelligence assessment, 14 October 1943

At 0600 15 October Rokossovsky's assault began. 61st Army made little progress, but Batov's 18th and 27th Rifle Corps crossed the Dnepr and secured a bridgehead 18 kilometers wide and 13 kilometers deep in the Loyev sector before the Germans halted their advance. Batov had achieved surprise due to his careful

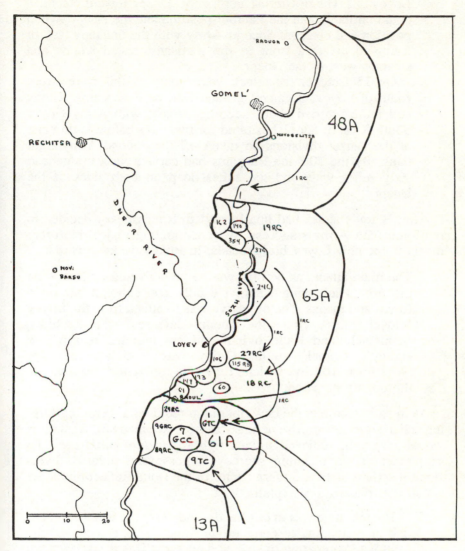

87. Gomel'–Rechitsa, Soviet dispositions, 14 October 1943

maskirovka preparations and the diversionary measures employed
by Rokossovsky. Ziemke described the German dilemma, stating:

> By that time [9 October] more trouble was brewing further
> south. While Second Army [German] was occupied with its
> flanks, Rokossovsky had built a strong concentration south of

Loyev .... There a thrust across the Dnepr toward Rechitsa could outflank both the Panther position and the Dnepr switch position and confront Second Army with the unhappy task of trying to create a front in the partisan-infested woods and swamps west of the Dnepr.

On 15 October the attack began on a 20 kilometer front south of Loyev. It gained ground fast, partly because Kluge, still more worried about keeping contact with Army Group South [west of Kiev], hesitated for two days before letting one of the panzer divisions be taken off the Second Army right flank. By the 20th the Russians had carved out a bridgehead sixty miles wide and ten miles deep on both sides of the Dnepr.[210]

After Batov's attack had finally stalled, Rokossovsky decided to reinforce 65th Army's success by concentrating major reinforcements in the new Loyev bridgeheads. In Rokossovsky's words:

The main attack, as before, was to be delivered by troops on the front's left wing where we duly concentrated our main forces and means. The objective was to attack from the Loyev bridgehead, penetrate the enemy defenses, take Rechitsa, Vasilevichi and Kalinkovichi and cut into the rear of the enemy's Gomel' group. D-day was tentatively set for November 10, by which time the operation was to be thoroughly prepared.[211]

As in early October, the new operation required a secret regrouping and a degree of surprise to be successful (see map 88). Again this would have to be achieved under a tight regimen of *maskirovka*. To supplement strict planning secrecy Rokossovsky ordered diversionary activity in the northern sector of the front. Reflecting on the situation, Rokossovsky explained:

The initiative was in our hands, and we could well afford the risk of pretending to concentrate forces on one sector of the front while preparing to strike on another. This is just what we did. I.I. Fedyuninsky's 11th Army together with V.Y. Kolpakchi's forces [63d Army] continuously attacked the enemy north of Gomel', drawing his attention to the area while we prepared the main attack on the Loyev sector.[212]

3d and 50th Armies also kept up their diversionary attacks north of Gomel'.

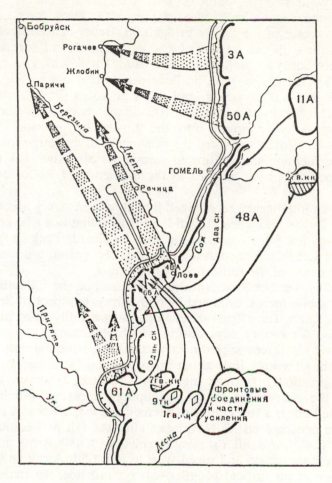

Маневр войск Центрального (Белорусского)
фронта в ходе Гомельско-Речицкой операции

88. Gomel'–Rechitsa, Central Front regrouping, 27 October–9 November 1943

Meanwhile two rifle corps of 48th Army were replaced by 11th Army units and shifted south to join 65th Army forces in the northern sector of the Loyev bridgehead. Batov concentrated 65th Army forces in the center of the bridgehead and received as reinforcements two tank corps (1st Guards and 9th), two cavalry corps (2d, 7th Guards), an artillery penetration corps (4th), *front* engineer and artillery units, and one rifle corps (95th) from 61st Army. This massive force moved 100 kilometers over a period of 14 days across two bridges into the Loyev bridgehead.[213] *Front maskirovka* measures covered the movement of this large force and requisite fuel and ammunition to sustain the offensive. The results of the new offensive attested to the efficiency of Rokossovsky's plan.

German intelligence recognized that all of 65d Army had moved into the Loyev bridgehead but did not realize that two rifle corps of 48th Army had joined them, along with 1st Guards Tank Corps (see maps 89 and 90). Although the Germans recognized a threat, they were unaware of the full scope of that threat.

On 10 November Rokossovsky struck; and on the following day Soviet mobile forces, followed by 65th Army, approached Rechitsa from the south. The offensive developed successfully along multiple directions for twenty days during which Rokossovsky constantly regrouped his forces secretly, in particular his mobile corps. The Soviets have written little about this operation (as is the case with many operations). German intelligence records, however, vividly record the success of these regroupings, most of which were conducted under a strict cloak of secrecy and *maskirovka*. A notable example occurred on 22 November after the fall of Rechitsa. 1st Guards Tank Corps, after seizing Rechitsa with 48th Army units, on 14 November turned and raced west to join 65th Army units on a thrust across the critical Mogilev–Mozyr rail line, the main communications route of Army Groups Center and South. 9th Tank Corps units, 1st Guards Tank Corps, and 65th Army's 19th Rifle Corps attacked by surprise across the rail line on 22 November and raced along the south bank of the Berezino River almost to Parichi, 40 kilometers south of Borisov.[214] Ziemke described the German surprise:

> In the meantime, Rokossovsky had prepared an unpleasant surprise. Early on 22 November, after a quick regrouping undetected by the Germans, he launched a thrust into the Ninth Army center south of Propoysk. It dealt Ninth Army a

sudden, staggering blow. The next day he pushed a strong spearhead into the gap between Second and Ninth Armies south of the Beresina and cut the railroad that ran north from Kalinkovichi.

The Ninth Army front around Gomel had by then become a giant, raging, tactically useless bulge ...[215]

The Soviet Gomel'–Rechitsa offensive finally ended on 30 November with Soviet forces lodged in a salient pointed dangerously close to Bobruisk. In the course of the operation German forces had to abandon the line of the Dnepr south of Zhlobin and the city of Gomel'.

Kiev, November 1943

The Soviet offensive thrusts in the north around Nevel' and in the center at Rechitsa were, of course, secondary in importance. They served the greater Soviet end which was, in November, penetration of the Dnepr River line, the liberation of Kiev, and the creation of credible bridgeheads south of the river. By the end of September 1943 the main force of the Soviet Army (the Central, Voronezh, Steppe, Southwestern, and Southern Fronts) had concentrated on the southwestern and southern directions. They had liberated the Donbas and left bank of the Ukraine, reached the Dnepr River on a 700 kilometer front from Loyev to Zaporozh'ye, and secured twenty-three small bridgeheads on the river's far bank. The most important bridgeheads along the Dnepr were those at Bukrin and Mishurin Rog. The Voronezh Front had secured the bridgehead at Velikii Bukrin, south of Kiev, in late September and had tried, in vain, in conjunction with a surprise airborne assault, to expand it. Despite repeated failures to break out through a cordon of German forces, Vatutin had been able to move significant forces into the bridgehead. Further south German forces were able to contain but not eliminate the Steppe Front bridgehead at Mishurin Rog. The *STAVKA* decided to make the Bukrin bridgehead its priority target.

On 29 September the *STAVKA* ordered the Voronezh Front:

having concentrated its main forces on the Kiev direction, in cooperation with the left flank of the Central Front, to liquidate the enemy group in the Kiev region; liberate the capital of the Ukrainian republic; to reach the line Stavishche, Fastov, Belaya Tserkov; and, having firmly secured its flank

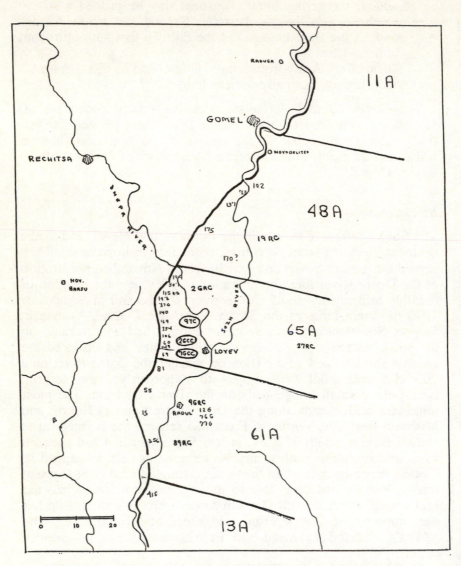

89. Gomel'–Rechitsa, German intelligence assessment, 9 November 1943

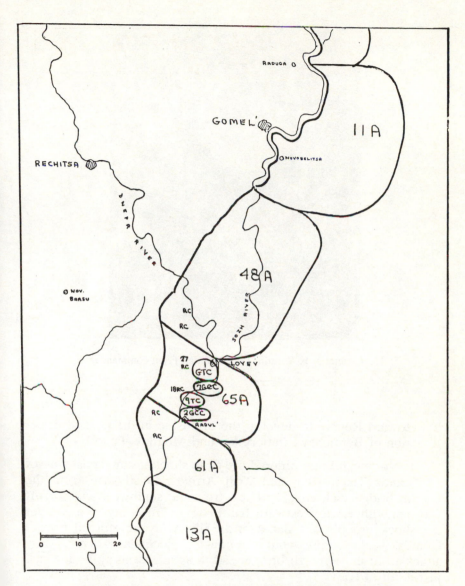

90. Gomel'–Rechitsa, Soviet dispositions, 9 November 1943

15. General N.F. Vatutin, 1st Ukrainian Front commander

toward Rovno, to develop the offensive in the general direction of Berdichev, Zhmerinka, and Mogilev–Podol'sk.[216]

The Voronezh Front ordered the *front* shock group, consisting of 3d Guards Tank, 40th, and 27th Armies, to advance from the Bukrin bridgehead, envelop Kiev from the southwest and cut off German withdrawal westward from Kiev. 47th Army would cover the shock group's left flank; and 38th Army, reinforced by 5th Guards Tank Corps, would conduct a secondary diversionary attack from the Lyutezh bridgehead, a small, swampy bridgehead just north of Kiev.

This initial plan failed badly. German defenses thwarted repeated Soviet attempts to break out of the Bukrin bridgehead and inflicted heavy losses on the attacking Soviet forces. Very simply, German attention was fixed on the Bukrin region; and the Soviets could not achieve surprise. While the bitter battle raged at Bukrin, however, 38th Army, north of Kiev, steadily enlarged its bridgehead without attracting significant German attention. Consequently, the 1st Ukrainian Front shifted its attention north (on 10 October the Voronezh Front was renamed the 1st Ukrainian Front). On 13 October the *front* military council dispatched an appreciation to the *STAVKA* which read:

> At the present time at a bridgehead 20–30 kilometers immediately north of Kiev the 38th Army of Chibisov is overcoming the enemy and pursuing him. We have a full possibility to develop further success on the southwestern direction: however, we do not have reserves for that. We also have the possibility to develop success from 60th Army's bridgehead [further north], but also do not have the force.[217]

Vatutin met with his staff on 22 October and recommended shifting his *front* main effort to the Lyutezh region on the right flank. With Military Council endorsement, Vatutin requested *STAVKA* approval of his plans and asked for one tank army as reinforcement.[218]

The *STAVKA* denied Vatutin's request for additional forces but approved Vatutin's recommendation for an attack north of Kiev. A 24 October *STAVKA* directive recognized the reasons for the Bukrin failures and stated: "The *STAVKA* orders the 1st Ukrainian Front to regroup its forces with the aim of reinforcing the right flank, while having the immediate mission of destroying the enemy Kiev group and securing Kiev."[219] To support Vatutin's new offensive the *STAVKA* ordered Rokossovsky's Central Front and Konev's Steppe Front to continue offensive activity and tie down German forces on their fronts. The *STAVKA* ordered Vatutin to transfer Rybalko's 3d Guards Tank Army northward in such a manner "that it is unnoticed by the enemy."[220]

Vatutin's plan involved secretly moving major *front* forces and concentrating them at Lyutezh while continuing to simulate offensive activity in 13th Army's sector to the north near Chernobyl' at the mouth of the Pripyat River and in the old *front* offensive sector at Bukrin. The plan required two major regroupings. The first and smaller involved the southerly movement and concentration of 60th and 13th Armies (just assigned to Vatutin's *front*) in small bridgeheads west of the Dnepr River and along the mouth of the Pripyat River. 13th Army was to conduct diversionary attacks north of the Pripyat while 60th Army joined the main attack from Lyutezh. The larger regrouping involved movement of 3d Guards Tank Army,

23d Rifle Corps, 4th Artillery Penetration Corps, and other *front* units 200 kilometers from the Bukrin area to the Lyutezh bridgehead.[221] These forces would then cross the Dnepr River and join the 38th Army assault which was originally planned for 1 or 2 November and later delayed until the 3d. The required regrouping had to be completed within six days and had to be kept secret if the new assault was to avoid the same fate as experienced by Soviet forces at Bukrin. All of these forces would join 38th Army in a 20 x 30 kilometer bridgehead which was swampy and half covered by forest.

Once assembled for the attack 38th, 60th, and 3d Guards Tank Army, supported by 1st Guards Cavalry Corps and 2d Air Army, were to penetrate German defenses north of Kiev and encircle the city from the west. Southward, in the Bukrin bridgehead, 40th and 27th Armies were to attack on 1 November to penetrate German defenses; divert German attention from the Lyutezh attack; and, if possible, advance westward in concert with Vatutin's main strike force. Prior to 1 November all *front* units received orders to adopt a temporary defensive posture necessary to replenish and refit units so heavily damaged in the heavy fighting at Bukrin. This order simulated both a major pause in operations and Soviet intent to shift the focus of the offensive to the south and north (in the Steppe and Central Front's sectors).

Meanwhile, the major regrouping effort commenced on the evening of 26 October under the direct supervision of Assistant Front Commander, Colonel General A.A. Grechko, who later wrote:

> On the night of 26 October we began regrouping. Under cover of heavy rain we secretly withdrew tank, rifle, artillery and engineer units from their positions in the Bukrin bridgehead. Having crossed to the left bank of the Dnepr, they secretly concentrated in designated areas; and, having waited for the following night, they began their march along the line of the front to the region of the Lyutezh bridgehead.[222]

As the regrouping progressed, 38th Army received considerable reinforcement. The 23d Rifle Corps, 21st Rifle Corps staff, 7th Artillery Penetration Corps, 3d Guards Mortar Division, 21st Anti-Aircraft Division, and many separate brigades deployed into wooded areas of the Lyutezh bridgehead together with tons of fuel and ammunition to sustain 38th Army's offensive.[223]

The most challenging task was the movement of 3d Guards Tank Army from Bukrin to Lyutezh in the allotted time (see map 91). At

16. From left to right, General A. A. Ypishev, commissar, 38th Army;
General K. S. Moskalenko, commander 38th Army; and General K. V.
Krainyukov, commissar of the 1st Ukrainian Front. Kiev operation,
November, 1943

1800 25 October, Lieutenant General P.S. Rybalko, 3d Guards
Tank Army commander, received a directive from Vatutin which
read:

> With the onset of darkness on 25 October 1943, begin the
> withdrawal of units from the Bukrin bridgehead to the east
> bank of the Dnepr using all available crossings .... By the end
> of 30 October 1943 concentrate in the vicinity of Svarom'ye,
> Vysshaya, Dubechnya, and Lebedev farm in readiness to
> begin a crossing of the Dnepr .... Make the march in absolute
> secrecy, move only at night observing *maskirovka* measures
> both during movements and at halts .... Categorically prohibit
> radio transmission. Conduct no telephone conversations
> concerning the move. Transfer tanks, incapable of moving and
> with poor running gear to 40th Army in place. Bear in mind
> that you will receive new tanks at the new assembly location in
> order to bring the army up to strength .... Submit march plan
> by 1000 hours on 26 October.[224]

After receiving his orders, Rybalko clarified the mission,
estimated the situation, issued warning orders, and at 0600 26
October signed the march order. His plan called for a transfer of his

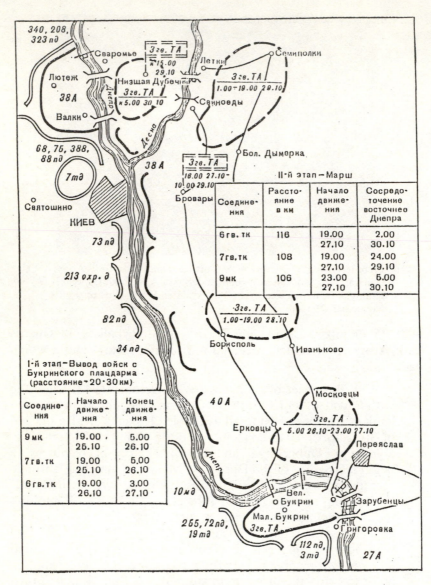

340, 208, 323 пд

Сваромье

3гв. ТА к 15.00 29.10

Летки

Семиполки

Лютеж

38 А

Низщая Дубечня

3гв. ТА 1.00–19.00 29.10

3гв. ТА к 5.00 30.10

Валки

Свиноеды

68, 76, 388, 88 пд

7 тд

Святошино

38 А

Бол. Дымерка

3гв. ТА 18.00 27.10– 10.00 29.10

II-й этап — Марш

Соедине- ния	Рассто- яние в км	Начало движе- ния	Сосредо- точение восточнео Днепра
6 гв. тк	116	19.00 27.10	2.00 30.10
7 гв. тк	108	19.00 27.10	24.00 29.10
9 мк	106	23.00 27.10	6.00 30.10

КИЕВ

Бровары

73 пд

213 охр. д

82 пд

34 пд

3гв. ТА 1.00–19.00 28.10

Борисполь

Иваньково

I-й этап — Вывод войск с Букринского плацдарма (расстояние ~ 20·30 км)

Соедине- ния	Начало движе- ния	Конец движе- ния
9 мк	19.00 25.10	5.00 26.10
7 гв. тк	19.00 25.10	5.00 26.10
6 гв. тк	19.00 26.10	3.00 27.10

40 А

Московцы

3гв. ТА 5.00 26.10–23.00 27.10

Ерковцы

Переяслав

10 мд

Вел. Букрин

Мал. Букрин

3гв. ТА

Зарубенцы

Григоровка

265, 72 пд, 19 тд

112 пд, 3 тд

27 А

План перегруппировки 3 гв. ТА к лютежскому плацдарму

91. Kiev, 3d Guards Tank Army regrouping, 26 October–2 November 1943

sector to 40th Army, the assembly of 3d Guards Tank Army across the Dnepr by 0300 27 October, and a subsequent march to the Kiev area at an anticipated march rate of 100 kilometers per night.[225] Rybalko later described his attempts to conceal the move, writing:

> To conceal the withdrawal of tank formations from the Bukrin bridgehead and their transfer to the new concentration region, strict *maskirovka* measures were used. Command points of formations and several radio stations were left on the bridgehead. All of these continued their usual work, while disinforming the enemy. In place of tanks withdrawn from positions we constructed mock-ups of wood and earth. Mock-up guns were placed in firing positions. The movement of tanks and trucks for the designated march was permitted only at night and under strict light discipline. Strict *maskirovka* also occurred in the new concentration region. The unfavorable weather during the days of our movement facilitated the maintaining of secrecy of our preparations for the new offensive. By our efforts we deceived the enemy, having forced his aviation in the course of the week to bomb our abandoned positions.[226]

The first night Rybalko's river crossing ran into difficulties which threatened to force him off his timetable. Thus, under cover of fog and smoke generated by *front* engineer units, he continued movements throughout the next day. By 0600 28 October the entire army had assembled east of the Dnepr.

Movement from assembly areas east of the Dnepr northward began on 27 October just as lead tank army units had finished crossing the Dnepr. Because of the bleak weather, units moved during the day as well as the night along two principal routes, supervised by traffic control officers designated by the army. After assembling his army east of Kiev, Rybalko moved his tanks into the Lyutezh bridgehead on the nights of 31 October and 1–2 November (31 October – 110 tanks, 1 November – 185 tanks, 2 November – the remainder).[227] Thereafter 3d Guards Tank Army formed in the northern sector of the Lyutezh bridgehead and prepared to support 38th Army's offensive.

Throughout the regrouping, tank corps established command-ants services to monitor the observation of *maskirovka* measures by subordinate units. Sequential assignment of missions and the limited number of personnel who received orders contributed to planning security. Extensive use of smoke covered the movement and protected bridges from enemy bombing (only six of 1000 bombs dropped on the bridge during this period hit their target).[228]

Through these efforts, 3d Guards Tank Army, with over 300 tanks, disengaged from combat, traveled 200 kilometers within 10–40 kilometers of the front, conducted three major river crossings, and concentrated for an attack without the Germans detecting the scale of its movement. (3d Tank Army moved a total of 345 tanks and self-propelled guns, 500 tractors, 3500 vehicles, and 250 guns.)

Meanwhile, in the Bukrin bridgehead Soviet units deceived the Germans by studiously continuing normal activities. Artillery fired in the usual pattern, radio stations continued normal transmissions, and units strengthened their defenses and conducted reconnaissance. According to plan the Soviets planted rumors of preparation for a new offensive which involved, in particular, the refitting of 3d Guards Tank Army and the billeting of new tank units in the Kiev and Pereyaslav–Khmel'nitsk area east of Kiev.[229] In support of this rumor campaign rifle battalions with tanks conducted exercises near the front within the Bukrin bridgehead while false traffic movements during the day and night continued in the bridgehead and to and fro across the river. Within the bridgehead the rear service units of the 206th and 307th Rifle Divisions, as part of the *maskirovka* plan, constructed mock-up huts and dugouts complete with smoke, and at night these units lit bonfires simulating troop concentrations. In addition, division and 27th and 40th Armies' engineers built tank and artillery mock-ups to create false concentrations of tank and artillery battalions and false fortifications and trenches.[230]

While Soviet forces in the Bukrin bridgehead fulfilled their *maskirovka* tasks, 38th Army simulated the intent to launch limited attacks westward rather than southward (where the real attack was to occur).

On 3 November Vatutin unleashed his attack north of Kiev and caught German forces unaware. The following day 3d Guards Tank Army went into action, and within two days it had severed German communications lines west of Kiev and was racing to the southwest toward Fastov. The Soviet offensive developed rapidly until 11 November when German reserves dispatched from the Bukrin area began arriving to stem the advance. Thereafter, heavy combat raged for over a month near Fastov, Zhitomir, and Korosten as German forces tried in vain to snuff out the significant Soviet bridgehead west of the Dnepr.

German intelligence records and accounts attest to the effectiveness of Soviet *maskirovka* at Kiev. On 11 October German Foreign Armies East correctly assessed the Soviet intent to exploit the gains made in the summer and fall offensive by improving their position for renewal of the offensive in the winter. Gehlen expected Soviet offensive activity in the south against Sixth Army and by the Voronezh and Steppe Fronts along the Dnepr, probably in the Kiev and Krivoi Rog regions.[231] After the unsuccessful Soviet attempts to break out of the Bukrin bridgehead Foreign Armies East qualified their view, stating:

> After the unsuccessful October battles on the Bukrin bridge-
> head the main events in November will develop in the
> Melitopol' and Krivoi Rog regions. There Soviet forces will try
> to close the circle around Sixth and First Panzer Armies. A
> second blow can be delivered on Pskov or Dvinsk–Riga with
> the aim of shattering the German northern flank.[232]

Thus, in general, Foreign Armies East recognized the main Soviet direction of attack was to the southwest. Constant activity else-where, however, generated uncertainty in German high-level circles, a product of Soviet strategic deception efforts.

At the operational level Army Group South was clearly deceived regarding the location and timing of the Soviet Kiev offensive. A 30 October assessment stated:

> The deployment of the 3d Guards Tank Army can be expected
> in the area north of Kiev or possibly south of Kiev in order to
> form a new main effort for a surprise attack. However, there
> are no clear indications yet for the latter possibility.[233]

The previous day Eighth Army intelligence picked up Soviet movement east of the river but not its actual scale. On 31 October Army Group South assessed:

> In the area around Kiev, it now seems that there are also parts
> of other tank units withdrawn from the Lyutezh area in order to
> be reconstituted. After this has been accomplished, one has to
> expect further offensive operations to build bridgeheads in the
> Kiev area. We have still no indication in which direction 3d
> Guards Tank Army might be deployed.[234]

After adhering to this view on 2 November, on 3 November, the day of the Soviet assault, Army Group South reported:

> The main effort seems to be undoubtedly north of Kiev where,

according to SIGINT, the deployment of 3d Guards Tank
Army is to be expected. Enemy actions from the Pereyaslov
area are believed to be intended to tie down German forces and
for deception.[235]

Throughout this period Fourth Panzer Army intelligence noted the
transfer of 3d Guards Tank Army to positions east of Kiev but did
not detect the army's presence west of the river until 5 November by
which time the Soviet army was well into the German rear.
Meanwhile Eighth Army assessed the presence of 3d Guards Tank
Army in its sector but east of the Dnepr up to 8 November. The
German intelligence picture on the evening of 2 November vividly
underscored the Soviet *maskirovka* success (see maps 92 and 93).
German intelligence underassessed the threat from the Lyutezh
bridgehead by almost 40 percent regarding rifle forces. More
important, it totally missed the looming armored threat. German
intelligence finally identified 3d Guards Tank Army as being west of
the river on 8 November, as it plunged into the German operational
depths. In retrospect Manstein confirmed the confused German
view, stating:

> At the beginning of November the enemy again attacked the
> northern wing of the Army Group, Fourth Panzer Army's
> Dnepr Front, with strong forces. It was not clear whether this
> was an offensive with far reaching aims or whether the enemy
> first intended to win the necessary assembly space west of the
> river.[236]

It was, of course, the former; and the damage done by Soviet
deception could not be repaired. Within several weeks the Soviets
again conducted a major offensive masked by even more extensive
deception in order to continue the offensive on the main (southwestern) direction.

Krivoi Rog and Nikopol', November 1943

STAVKA directives of late September 1943 had accorded the
Voronezh and Steppe Fronts a primary role in the closing stages of
the summer–fall offensive. Initially, they urged both Vatutin and
Konev forward and provided them with sufficient reserves to breach
the line of the Dnepr. While Vatutin's armies focused their efforts
on the Bukrin bridgehead throughout October, Konev sought to
enlarge his small bridgehead at Mishurin Rog, southeast of
Kremenchug. His objectives were Krivoi Rog and Nikopol' in the

militarily and economically valuable great bend of the Dnepr River. German forces tenaciously defended the Dnepr bend and several critical bridgeheads on its east bank (notably Zaporozh'ye and Nikopol') stiffened by Hitler's insistence that these regions be held at all cost. Hence, as the Soviet offensive developed, it was understandable that German reserves would gravitate into the lower Dnepr region and make Soviet progress there that much more difficult. Consequently, the Soviets ultimately were able to punch through German defenses further northwest of Kiev where the Soviet's offensive priority remained. Thus, throughout October the Krivoi Rog was a major Soviet target in its own right, but by November its role shifted to that of a secondary objective in support of more important efforts the Soviets were making around Kiev.

The same general relationship characterized operations of the Steppe, Southwestern, and Southern Fronts. In October all conducted operations of near equal importance as the latter two *fronts* cleared Germans from east of the Dnepr. When the Southwestern Front reached the Dnepr and the German strongpoint at Zaporozh'ye in early October; and the Southern Front raced west from Melitopol', cleared the Tavria, and reached the Dnepr and the northern border of the Crimea; both *fronts* assumed the secondary role of assisting Konev's Steppe Front in its attack on Krivoi Rog from the north. Simultaneously, Southwestern (soon 3d Ukrainian) Front beseiged Zaporozh'ye, and the Southern (soon 4th Ukrainian) Front struck the German bridgehead at Nikopol' to eradicate the bridgehead or to occupy the attention of the ten German divisions which defended it.

On 29 September the *STAVKA* ordered Konev to attack Kirovograd and Krivoi Rog and cut off German withdrawal routes westward from the Dnepr bend. Attempts to enlarge the bridgehead's flanks by attacks across the Dnepr failed, forcing Konev to shift major forces from other sectors of the front into the existing bridgehead which was held by 37th and 7th Guards Armies. (The bridgehead was 40 kilometers wide and 6–12 kilometers deep.)[237] On 7 October Konev received *STAVKA* permission to move 5th Guards and 57th Armies into the bridgehead along with significant supporting forces. He also requested 5th Guards Tank Army and 7th Guards Mechanized Corps from *STAVKA* reserve. The regrouping of forces took four to five days and was conducted under strict *maskirovka* measures. 5th Guards Army moved 100 kilometers laterally along the front into the bridgehead. 5th Guards Tank Army's task was even more arduous, for it was refitting in the

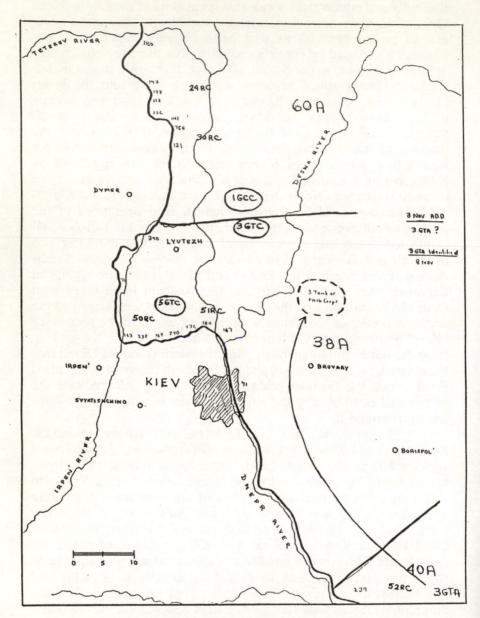

92. Kiev, German intelligence assessment, 2 November 1943

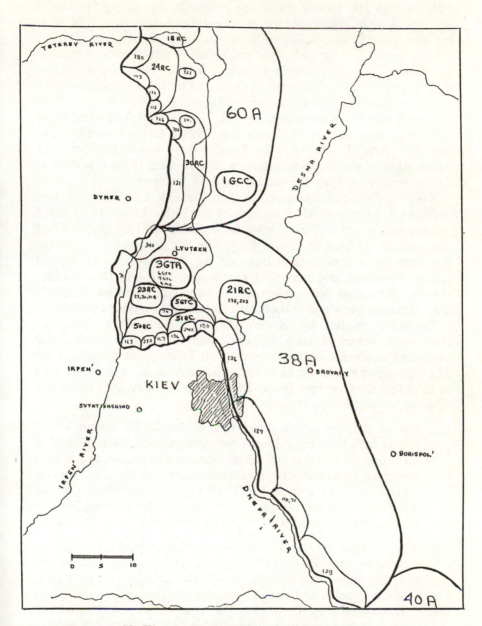

93. Kiev, Soviet dispositions, 2 November 1943

Poltava area 200 kilometers in the rear. All regrouping "occurred secretly at night. Therefore the enemy did not succeed in discovering the concentration of our forces and their preparations for the offensive and did not undertake corresponding measures to repulse our attack."[238] Konev simply noted, "Measures were used to conduct a regrouping of forces of the *front* and material to support them during a short period and concealed from the enemy."[239]

On 11 October Konev ordered 5th Guards and 37th Armies to spearhead the attack on 14 October, supported on the flanks by 57th and 53d Armies. 5th Guards Tank Army would exploit after penetration of the German defenses. Regrouping delays, however, forced Konev to delay the attack until 15 October.

Konev's forces attacked on 15 October and penetrated German defenses to a depth of 60 kilometers by the 19th. The *front* continued to advance against stiffening resistance and, by 24 October, reached the western outskirts of Krivoi Rog. The day before, the neighboring 46th and 8th Guards Armies of the Southwestern Front had joined the attack and occupied Dnepropetrovsk and Dneprodzerzhinsk. Thereafter heavy German counter-attacks threw Konev's lead elements back and forced him to end his October offensive.

Repeated attacks by Konev's and Malinovsky's *fronts* in November achieved only limited gains, and the bridgehead expanded westward toward Kirovograd. Throughout the action the *STAVKA* urged Konev on as much to assist Vatutin in the Kiev area as to defeat the Germans in the Dnepr bend. Konev later noted the relationship of his and Vatutin's offensive:

> I think that the active operations of the 2d Ukrainian Front, which inflicted heavy losses on Army Group "South" and at the same time tied down large German forces, did not permit their transfer to the Kiev direction against the forces of the 1st Ukrainian Front and, in the final analysis, contributed to the achievement of victory by Soviet forces in the Kiev region and the creation there of a strategic bridgehead.[240]

It was difficult for the Soviets to conceal preparations for the offensive across the Dnepr River in Konev's sector because the Mishurin Rog situation was analogous to Bukrin in Vatutin's sector. Large German forces had already assembled when Konev mounted his 15 October attack. Thereafter the German force grew. Moreover, there was no Lyutezh bridgehead for Konev to use as a second choice for his offensive.

Despite Soviet difficulties, German intelligence was not able to

17. Soviet troops crossing the Dnepr River during the Kiev operation, November, 1943

keep track of Soviet regrouping (see maps 94 and 95). It did not detect 5th Guards Army's move into the Mishurin Rog bridgehead until 16 October. Nor did the Germans note 7th Guards Army's concentration in the bridgehead or 5th Guards Tank Army's approach to the river. It identified the Soviet tank army on 18 October after the Soviets had committed it to combat.

Manstein affirmed the success of the *STAVKA maskirovka* plan, the effectiveness of Konev's regrouping, and its impact on German Dnepr defenses as a whole. Manstein first stated:

> The Army Group had to continue to regard its northern wing as the more decisive of the two, for if the enemy were to succeed in finally smashing it, he would be at liberty to execute an extensive outflanking movement against both Southern Army Group and Army Group A. In fact, however, he diverted his main efforts in October to attaining a success on the Dnepr bend itself. This ... compelled the Army Group to accept a decisive battle there.[241]

Manstein identified the Steppe Front as the most active throughout October, relegating Vatutin's efforts at Bukrin to a secondary position. Hence, Manstein used his armored reserve (XXXX Panzer Corps) to smash Konev's spearheads at Krivoi Rog. Thereafter Manstein suggested a strike with the panzer corps south from Nikopol'. Throughout this period, by his own admission, Manstein ignored his original operational premise that the northern wing was the more important. Manstein said, "One should never for a

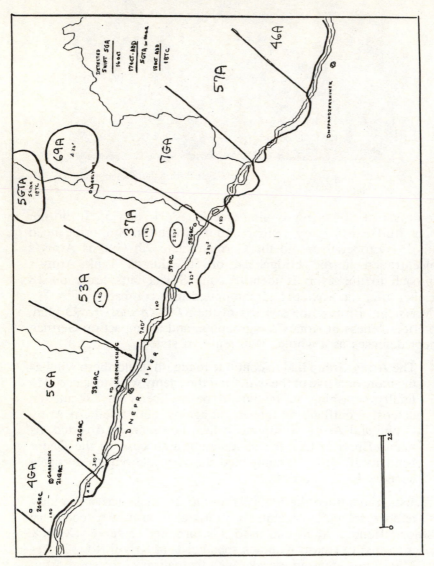

94. Krivoi Rog, German intelligence assessment, 14 October 1943

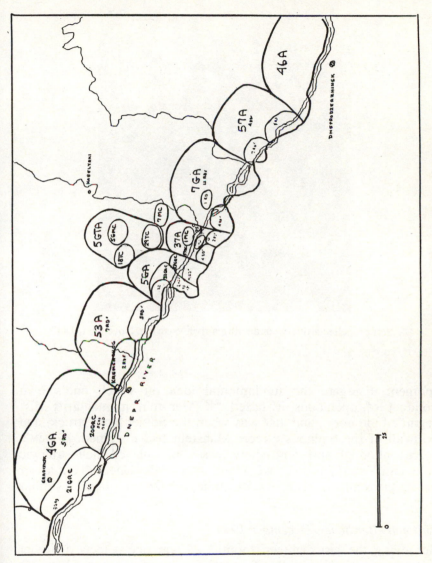

95. Krivoi Rog, Soviet dispositions, 14 October 1943

18. Self propelled artillery conducting a river crossing, November, 1943

moment disregard the fundamental idea on which one's own conduct of operations is based."[242] Manstein momentarily disregarded the north, and that was when the Soviet blow struck, and with all of the ominous effects Manstein had imagined. Konev's forces, although suffering heavy losses, had played their strategic role; and Vatutin's forces were free west of the Dnepr. To a lesser extent the Southern Front and its threat to Nikopol' played a similar role.

Zhitomir–Berdichev, December 1943

Surveying the last eighteen months of war one detects a Soviet reticence to speak candidly of deception in its full scope. Slices are laid bare in detail – an operation here and a sector there, but rarely do those cases reveal the true extent of either the scale of deception or deception's results. The Soviets reveal enough to educate in *maskirovka* but not enough to elucidate the scope of the *maskirovka*. Examination of intelligence records, however, reveals the truth and unveils the scope and effect of Soviet deception efforts, if not the means by which the Soviets achieved it. An excellent example is the Zhitomir–Berdichev operation which the Soviets prepared for during the late (defensive) stage of the Kiev operation. The Soviets have written little about deception in the operation. An examination of the records, however, reveals an immense gap between what German intelligence knew of those preparations and the actual scope of those preparations. The obvious conclusion is that Zhitomir is one of those cases the Soviets do not wish to discuss openly.

Although the Zhitomir operation was the first of the long series of offensives the Soviets collectively call the winter strategic offensive, preparations for the operation went on during the waning stages of the Kiev operation. Therefore it represents something of a transitional operation between the two major strategic offensives – summer–fall and winter.

The Soviets decided to launch the Zhitomir–Berdichev operation during the course of the Kiev operation, and the nature of the Kiev operation shaped the intent and form of the subsequent operation. Soviet forces in the Kiev operation had sought to create and then enlarge their strategic bridgehead in the direction of Berdichev and Vinnitsa while expanding the flanks of the bridgehead whenever possible, primarily toward and beyond Korosten, Zhitomir, and Belaya Tserkov. The initial Soviet thrust from Kiev penetrated beyond Fastov and to Zhitomir before the Germans halted the advance after 11 November.

The Germans then began a series of counter-attacks with XXXXVIII Panzer Corps to defeat Soviet forces and eradicate the bridgehead. The first counter-attacks, against Soviet 3d Guards Tank Army south of Fastov, halted the Soviets but failed to throw them back. On 12 November XXXXVIII Panzer Corps began a second counter-attack northward between Zhitomir and Fastov, which thrust first toward Brusilov and then westward toward Zhitomir. By 20 November the Germans had recaptured Zhitomir and turned northeast toward Radomysl'. Meanwhile the Soviets seized Korosten in the north. On 20 November XXXXVIII Panzer Corps swung east and marched on Kiev via Brusilov. By 25 November the Germans had seized Brusilov but heavy losses had forced curtailment of this drive. After a major regrouping, on 5 December XXXXVIII Panzer Corps again struck the Soviet flank north of Zhitomir, this time advancing toward Malin. Again the German drive made progress but, by 15 December, ultimately faltered short of the town as the Soviets shifted reserves from left to right to counter the German thrust. Failing to make decisive progress against the Soviet flank at Malin, on 17 December XXXXVIII Panzer Corps again regrouped, this time further west, to strike the Soviet flank near Korosten. On 19 December the fourth German counter-stroke struck Soviet units southeast of Korosten; but again, after three days of heavy fighting, the German attack ground to a halt after heavy losses.

The four German counter-attacks had steadily carried the center of combat activity northwest away from the original center of gravity of the Soviet assault. While the German focus shifted northwest, the Soviets maintained their focus on the original main attack direction – the Kiev–Brusilov–Berdichev direction. It was here, in the Brusilov region, that the Soviets patiently prepared their new offensive, while German attention shifted further to the northwest.

The Soviets conducted a strategic regrouping and concentrated large attack forces in the Brusilov sector while heavy combat was raging along the front to the northwest. In fact, that combat became a major element in the Soviet plan to deceive the Germans regarding the location and timing of the new offensive. The ferocity of fighting in the Kiev operation, to a considerable extent, masked Soviet intent to resume major offensive operations after such heavy fighting and losses.

In mid-November the *STAVKA* began assembling strategic reserves in the Kiev area. 18th, 1st Guards, and 1st Tank Armies, and 4th Guards and 25th Tank Corps all received orders to move into the 1st Ukrainian Front's sector across the series of new bridges hastily constructed across the Dnepr River at Kiev. When these units reached Kiev, the *STAVKA* strictly forbade their use in defensive combat which raged in the 1st Ukrainian Front sector. Ultimately the *STAVKA* permitted Vatutin to use one rifle corps (94th) of 1st Guards Army and 4th Guards and 25th Tank Corps in the heavy defensive fighting. Other units either occupied well-camouflaged defensive positions in 1st Ukrainian Front's rear area west of Kiev or concealed themselves in assembly areas near the city.[243]

By 24 November the 1st Ukrainian Front consisted of seven combined arms armies (1st Guards, 13th, 18th, 27th, 38th, 40th, 60th) and two tank armies (1st, 3d Guards), although some of these units were still en route. Only five combined arms armies and one tank army were engaged in active defensive operations. The remaining forces, secretly assembled and concentrated, would spearhead the new offensive.

A 28 November *STAVKA* directive ordered Vatutin to prepare the blow. It read, in part:

> 1. The available force of Nikolayev [codename for Vatutin] is insufficient to carry out a serious counter-offensive and destroy enemy forces. It is necessary, therefore for Nikolayev to go rapidly over to a firm defense in order to wear down enemy forces by artillery and aviation when he attempts an offensive or separate attacks ....
>
> 2. With the arrival of Leselidze [18th Army], Katukov [1st Tank Army], and other forces, it is obligatory to organize our offensive, with the aim of destroying enemy forces and reaching the Northern Bug. The counter-offensive must be organized as soundly and carefully as was done at Belgorod.[244]

The next day Vatutin ordered his armies to go on the defensive and block enemy advances toward Kiev. Meanwhile Vatutin and *STAVKA* representative Zhukov planned the new offensive. The plan required 1st Guards, 18th, and 38th Armies and 1st and 3d Guards Tank Armies to make the *front* main attack on 24 December in the center of the *front* sector toward Brusilov and Vinnitsa. Two days later 60th Army and 4th Guards Tank Corps would conduct a secondary attack in the Malin sector toward Radomysl', and 13th Army, with 25th Tank and 1st Guards Cavalry Corps, would strike at Korosten and Novgorod–Volynsk. Later 40th and 27th Armies would conduct secondary attacks on the *front's* left flank toward Belaya Tserkov.[245] The *STAVKA* approved the plan, and on 16 December, while the Germans prepared for their fourth counter-thrust in the Korosten area, Vatutin prepared directives for his subordinate units. The German counter-stroke played straight into Soviet hands.

The Soviet offensive plan called for elaborate *maskirovka* operation to conceal offensive intent, the location of the offensive, and the extensive regrouping. The 28 November *STAVKA* order and subsequent *front* orders concealed Soviet intent by requiring all units to go on the defense. Consequently, all along the front, but, in particular, from the Dnepr River to Malin, Soviet forces built elaborate defensive positions across the front and in the depth. Newly arrived 1st Guards Army units manned the deeper positions.

Thus reinforcements sent to participate in the new offensive initially contributed to the creation of a false defensive image. Meanwhile the *STAVKA* ordered the 2d and 4th Ukrainian Fronts to remain active in the Krivoi Rog and Nikopol' sectors further south.

To deceive the Germans regarding the main attack sector the Voronezh Front conducted active demonstrations in the Korosten and Bukrin areas. Near Korosten 13th and 60th Armies simulated offensive preparations. On 10 December 13th Army received responsibility for the Korosten area and took command of two of 60th Army's rifle corps operating in the region. 60th Army, in turn, concentrated in the Malin sector and was reinforced by 4th Guards Tank Corps. With only minimal reinforcement and by a re-shuffling of unit subordinations, the two armies simulated a major offensive concentration.[246] Mellenthin, in his work *Panzer Battles*, noted:

> The Russian Command had, in fact, been concentrating their forces for a massive offensive from Melini toward Zhitomir, and our attack with three panzer divisions must have seemed to them an instance of classical audacity.[247]

This was the impression the Soviets wished to create, for the real "massive" Soviet force concentration near Brusilov continued to grow almost entirely unnoticed. 38th Army commander, Moskalenko claimed the Soviets monitored German radio transmissions associated with the fourth counter-offensive and adjusted accordingly.

The secret Soviet regrouping and concentration at Brusilov began on 20 November when 1st Guards Army units began arriving east of Kiev. Two days later the army's three rifle corps crossed the river and occupied defensive positions east of Radomysl' and Brusilov with strict orders to avoid combat. Intense fighting east of Radomysl' forced the *STAVKA* on 24 November to release 94th Rifle Corps for active defense in that sector. The 74th and 107th Rifle Corps, however, remained uncommitted.

On 26 November, 3d Guards Tank Army received orders to begin disengaging its corps and assembling them west of Kiev. That day 6th Guards Tank Corps withdrew from the Brusilov sector. Three days later, on 29 November, lead elements of 18th Army arrived in the Kiev area from Novorossiisk which they had departed from on 17 November. The same day 1st Tank Army units began arriving at Daritza, east of Kiev. By 4 December, 18th Army and 1st Tank Army had crossed the Dnepr and occupied assembly areas west of Kiev. By this time 9th Mechanized Corps had withdrawn from combat into 3d Guards Tank Army assembly area, leaving only one corps (7th Guards Tank Corps) of that tank army in combat. On 5 December 18th Army completed assembling west of Kiev, and on 20 December 1st Guards Tank Army completed its movement into assembly areas.[248]

On 19 December Vatutin began a massive internal regrouping of his forces. Two combined arms armies (18th, 1st Guards) and two tank armies (1st, 3d Guards) deployed forward into the sector previously defended by 38th Army and a portion of 60th Army. This was done in stages up to the evening of 22 December when 7th Guards Tank Corps finally joined 3d Guards Tank Army in attack positions. The final concentration also involved massive lateral movement of forces into new attack positions. Moskalenko, commander of 38th Army, cryptically noted:

> The terrain in the sector of 38th Army was open and the enemy could discover the regrouping of forces and detect the intentions of our commands. Fortunately, that did not happen. To a considerable measure that was because the regrouping of forces, conducted according to orders from 20 to 23 December, occurred at nighttime. Besides that, strict *maskirovka* discipline was established.[249]

Moskalenko then underscored Soviet success, stating:

> We received a clear affirmation during the offensive that our regrouping of front forces near Brusilov was not discovered and picked up by the enemy command. In the army staff we kept a reconnaissance map of the enemy, showing his orders concerning the grouping and position of our forces. It is necessary to say that it corresponded in part to reality, but only up to the regrouping. Changes which occurred in the position of our forces in the last days, it did not contain. This would be revealed by our unlikely but decisive destruction of the enemy tank divisions and the impetuous movement of front forces best of all demonstrated the surprise of our offensive for the enemy.[250]

In fact, German intelligence records noted little of the Soviet regrouping or preparations for the attack at Brusilov (see maps 96 and 97). Intelligence detected large Soviet concentrations near Malin and Korosten, but up to 24 December failed to note the assembly of 1st Guards Tank Army and 18th Army in the Kiev area. German intelligence tentatively located 1st Guards Army headquarters west of Kiev but identified none of its subordinate units. Even worse for German fortunes, Soviet attack preparations from 20–23 December also went undetected. Hence three worn down panzer divisions (8th, 19th, 25th) had to face the massive Soviet assault while XXXXVIII Panzer Corps conducted an irrelevant operation east of Korosten.

On 24 December Soviet forces attacked, smashing the three German panzer divisions. Within two days Soviet tank armies were in the German operational rear area and heading for Berdichev. Belatedly XXXXVIII Panzer Corps raced south to block their advance.

Manstein later noted:

> I received the first reports of the start of an enemy attack on both sides of the Kiev–Zhitomir road while I was visiting 20th Panzer Grenadier division ... to attend the Christmas celebration of its regiments. At first the news did not sound any too serious, the only area where things looked at all precarious being that of 25 Panzer Division south of the road. However, the evening situation reports which I saw on arriving back at our headquarters in Vinnitsa indicated that the enemy was attempting a large-scale breakthrough toward Zhitomir.[251]

Manstein later described the attacking force:

> In the next few days the following intelligence report emerged: 1 Ukrainian Front in the Kiev sector had concentrated very powerful forces west of the town for a broad breakthrough along and south of the Zhitomir road. In the main assault group were Thirty-Eighth, First Guards and First Tank Army .... Within the next five days Eighteenth Army was identified.[252]

Thirty years later, 3d Guards Tank Army's participation in the attack remained undetected. German intelligence finally recognized the Soviet forces opposing them, but only four to five days after the Soviet offensive commenced; and, even then, they were unaware that 3d Guards Tank Army had participated in the initial assault.

The Soviet *maskirovka* plan for the Zhitomir–Berdichev operation was one of the most extensive ones yet conducted and one of the most successful, when measured against what German intelligence was able to discover.

Strategically, the Soviet diversions in the south (at Krivoi Rog, Nikopol', and Bukrin) had little impact, for Manstein by mid-November knew which sector was the most critical. The strategic regrouping, however, was very successful, for the Germans never detected it. Operationally within the 1st Ukrainian Front Vatutin's deception plan diverted German attention from the most critical sector of the front and concealed the final operational and tactical stages of the large-scale regrouping and the concentration of those regrouped forces in the Brusilov area. While the Soviets have been reticent to discuss what precise *maskirovka* techniques they used, the plan probably called for implementation of the same measures used earlier, only, in this case, with much more precision and, hence, impact.

Postscript

The nature of combat in October and November 1943 militated against the successful Soviet use of strategic *maskirovka*. The focus of Soviet offensive efforts on the Dnepr River front from the Pripyet River to Dnepropetrovsk was dictated by both military necessity and precedent. Since July 1943 the Kursk–Poltava–Kiev direction had been preeminent and would remain so into the winter.

During October and November Soviet operations on the front's central sector played a distinctly reduced strategic role. By October the slow and costly drive via Smolensk to the eastern borders of Belorussia had run its course. Earlier the Soviets considered these attacks important in their own right, although secondary in a strategic sense. They not only fixed German forces, they were major diversions which distracted German attention from the south-western direction. By October, however, efforts in the central region were less significant. The Nevel' operation was bothersome to the Germans but essentially local. The Gomel'–Rechitsa operation disrupted German inter-army group communications but was contained short of Minsk. Its geographical location along the northern reaches of the Pripyat swamps deprived it of strategic significance. Thus neither of these operations was capable of contributing to strategic deception.

The Soviet offensives in the south, across the Dnepr at Mishurin Rog and west of Melitopol' in the Tavria were of greater significance, for they posed a real threat to German strategic interests in the south, in particular because of the store Hitler placed on retaining the region in the Dnepr bend. Here the Soviets engaged in strategic *maskirovka* by capitalizing on the German concern for maintaining a continuous front along the Dnepr. Practicing deception along the Dnepr front was a formidable task for geography and military realities obstructed its use. The Soviets possessed a limited

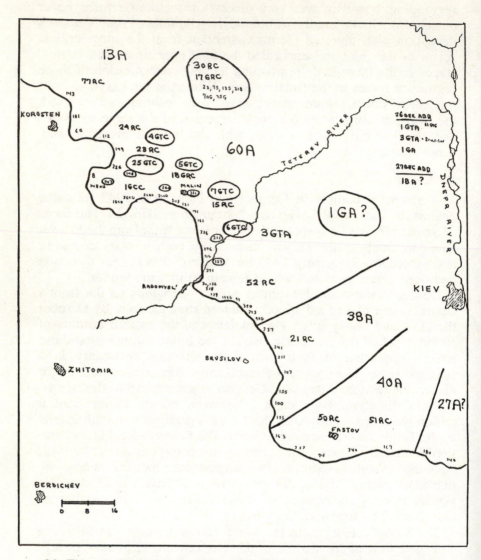

96. Zhitomir–Berdichev, German intelligence assessment, 23 December 1943

number of bridgeheads across the Dnepr, only two of which the Soviets initially considered suitable for use as platforms for expanded offensives – those at Bukrin and Mishurin Rog. Both sides realized this. Hence, the Germans constructed defenses around each, which made success difficult to achieve even if the

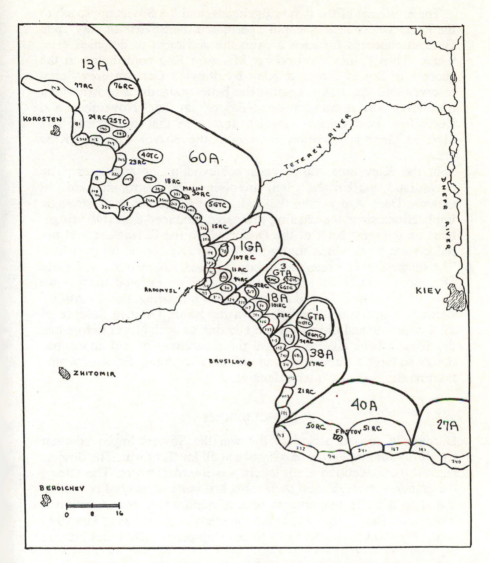

97. Zhitomir–Berdichev, Soviet dispositions, 23 December 1943

Soviets secretly moved additional forces into them. This was apparent in the case of Mishurin Rog where Konev's 2d Ukrainian Front succeeded in secretly regrouping forces only to have his attack fail after limited operational gains.

The existence of the two bridgeheads, and the Soviet approach to the lower Dnepr near Nikopol', permitted the Soviets to play upon German concerns for each area to the detriment of defenses elsewhere. Thus Konev's actions at Mishurin Rog contributed to the success of Soviet forces at Kiev by drawing German operational reserves into the area – against the better judgement of Manstein. Similarly, Soviet attacks on Nikopol' in late November and December fixed critical German forces in that bridgehead and diverted German attention from both the Krivoi Rog and Kiev areas.

In the Kiev area the Soviets achieved major successes. The operational *maskirovka* plan, involving the regrouping of 3d Guards Tank Army into the Lyutezh bridgehead, had strategic implications since the ensuing offensive produced a sizable bridgehead on the west bank of the Dnepr which the Germans could not reduce and from which future major offensives could be launched. The secret Soviet strategic regrouping in late November and early December, combined with the successful operational *maskirovka* plan of Vatutin's 1st Ukrainian Front preceding the Zhitomir–Berdichev operation, spelled doom for future German defense of the Dnepr line and ultimately the Ukraine as well. Never before had the Soviets been able to conceal the redeployment and concentration of so large a force. It was an ominous beginning for what would become the Soviet winter offensive.

CONCLUSIONS

During the second period of the war the Soviets improved their capability for employing *maskirovka* at all levels of war. The Soviets learned that deception at all levels was interdependent. The fate of the grandest strategic design or most brilliant operational deception rested on the effective employment of hundreds of mundane lower level tasks. Hence, they exploited the many experiences of late 1942 and early 1943 and used them to develop better techniques later in the year.

Strategic deception in a systematic, conscious sense had been absent in 1941 and most of 1942. The Soviets employed a crude, though partially effective, strategic *maskirovka* plan in the Stalingrad operation. During the winter of 1943, however, deception faded when the Soviets resorted to almost deliberately uncontrolled offensive operations across a broad front in southern Russia. The disasters which ensued were sobering and resulted in a conscious

Soviet effort to employ more effective strategic deception in the summer of 1943. In the Kursk strategic operation the Soviets displayed hitherto unprecedented maturity in deception. In fact, it was so effective it became a model for future efforts. After Kursk, with the strategic initiative firmly in Soviet hands, strategic deception became a major weapon in the Soviet arsenal. They made limited use of strategic deception in late 1943 but would do so with greater frequency in later years.

Operational *maskirovka* improved immeasurably in frequency and quality. Centralization of *maskirovka* planning and the requirement for all headquarters to prepare *maskirovka* plans for every operation made deception systematic and subject to quality control. The *STAVKA* determined the concept and objectives of *maskirovka* for multi-*front* operations and supervised the planning and conduct of *maskirovka* directly through its representatives. *Front* commanders did likewise for single *front* operations. At army level and below commanders bore specific responsibility for carrying out their portion of the operational *maskirovka* plan and for developing similar plans within their subordinate units.

Front and army staffs worked out operational *maskirovka* measures, forces and equipment to prepare them, the timing of the measures, and the persons responsible for supervising their conduct. Subordinate headquarters prepared similar plans in support of the operational *maskirovka* plan. The very fact plans were prepared provided a standard for future improvement if the plan failed, which it often did.

The most detailed operational *maskirovka* planning was conducted at army level. The army plan sought to fulfill the higher level concepts by designating specific measures to fulfill specific objectives and by assigning performance of these measures to individual units. At division level the commander formed a staff or operational group to supervise *maskirovka* planning and its conduct. Specialists from all branches and types of forces participated, all working in tight secrecy.

In the second period of war, specific *maskirovka* techniques became more routine in all operations. These included night regrouping and movement, night preparation of assembly areas, evacuation of the civilian population from a 25 kilometer sector to the rear of the front, advanced registration of artillery, covering of redeployment by in-place units, use of radio simulation or deception, secret rail movement of tanks and artillery, use of smoke in massive amounts to cover both real or false movements, extensive creation of mock-up assembly areas, and the simulation of false movements and assembly areas for large units. In general, the Soviets shifted from random individual use of disinformation to the use of a complex set of measures to produce a desired effect in accordance with an established plan. Most of these measures, however, were employed only in the preparatory period of an offensive. The Soviets still had to learn how to carry out deception during an operation.

Soviet critiques of *maskirovka* practices used at Kursk and in later operations provided a guidepost for improvement as evidenced by these lessons derived from experiences in the Kursk counter-offensive:

> The experience of the Soviet troops' counter-offensive showed that the success of the operation depended a great deal on its covert preparation. It was necessary to keep the purpose of the operation in secrecy, deceive the enemy as to the nature of the forthcoming actions of our troops, and covertly conduct regroupings and concentration of the *chasti* and *soyedineniya*.
>
> All operational camouflage measures should stem from the purpose of the operation and comprise an integral part of the decision of the Front (Army) commander and the plan of the operation. During organization of the offensive, each commander should have a well-thought-plan for *maskirovka* and for deception of the enemy. The methods and means of misinformation of the enemy should be varied, demonstrating their resourcefulness.
>
> For the designation of a false region of concentration of a rifle division and tank corps, as experience showed, it is advisable to allocate rifle and tank companies, an artillery battery, dozens of vehicles, 20–30 gun mock-ups, 60–80 vehicle mock-ups, and 10–12 field kitchen mock-ups.
>
> The approach of troops, occupation of initial position, and deployment of artillery should be conducted at night, with the observance of strict light and sound camouflage discipline.
>
> In sectors of the Front far removed from the direction of the main attack, it is necessary to organize the false approach of troops, operation of radio stations and scout searches, set up false batteries, install vehicle mock-ups, make the tracks of new roads, and simulate the concentration of troops and intensified activity of reconnaissance aviation.[253]

German records attest to the improvement in Soviet *maskirovka* in 1943. A 1 July 1943 report by Foreign Armies East entitled, "An Evaluation of the Situation in Front of Army Group South and Center," read in part:

> In recent months, the Red Army has gone to even greater lengths to camouflage their radio communications. After the first of this year, when it had already become impossible to determine the number of formations from Russian secret radio transmissions, even greater limitation of radio transmissions took place for some time, especially those of mobile formations which were in reserve .... In this connection, it was now impossible to establish permanent changes in the enemy situation.[254]

German army operational intelligence records bear mute testimony to this emerging truth. While German intelligence could still track and detect Soviet tactical units with remarkable accuracy, the Soviet operational rear blurred significantly. Even more disturbing, to a greater extent than before, Soviet commanders could move these units forward without immediate detection.[255] The failure to locate these units often prevented rapid reaction to deal with imminent threats. In 1944 this problem would grow as German intelligence began to lose its ability to detect tactical units as well, at least where Soviet commanders chose to hide them. This growing gap between German intelligence estimates and reality was largely the product of improved Soviet *maskirovka*.

CHAPTER SIX

THE PRACTICE OF *MASKIROVKA*
The Third Period of War (1944)

In 1944 and 1945 there was, in fact, not one *front*, or even army operation, in which preliminary measures for the achievement of surprise were not planned. They became more organized and more carefully planned and carried out. The cases of unsuccessfully conducted measures to secure the secrecy of preparations for an offensive and disinformation of the enemy were sharply reduced.

In 1944 the large scale use in the Soviet armed forces of a new means of conducting a campaign – the execution of consecutive strategic operations on various directions across the front ... was a surprise for the enemy. The Hitlerite command, disoriented on the strategic situation ... did not know where to expect the next blow and was forced to conduct large scale strategic regrouping, throwing its reserve from one sector to another. However, it could not save its situation. Reserves transferred to threatened sectors were usually too late.

> M.M. Kir'yan,
> *Vnezapnost' v nastupatel'nykh operatsiyakh Velikoi Otechestvennoi voiny* [Surprise in Offensive Operations of the Great Patriotic War], 1986

INTRODUCTION

In July 1943 Soviet forces had seized the strategic initiative on the Eastern Front by their planned counter-offensive at Kursk. They maintained the initiative by conducting active operations across the central and southern portions of the front throughout the late summer and fall and capped their offensive successes in November by seizing significant bridgeheads across the Dnepr River barrier – the vaunted German "Eastern Wall." In the course of six months Soviet forces eased the German stranglehold on Leningrad, cleared the Kalinin and Smolensk regions to the eastern extremities of

Belorussia, occupied and pierced the Dnepr River line, and isolated German forces in the Crimea.

As a result of its losses, the German Army was no longer capable of conducting even limited strategic offensives. It could, however, still conduct a credible defense, if the Soviets permitted it to do so. The principal Soviet task in 1944 was to maintain the strategic initiative and avoid the specter of positional war, which, some Germans hoped, could deny the Soviets victory by bleeding her armies white, destroying the Soviet's will to prevail.

The *STAVKA* realized it had achieved success in 1943 by applying pressure to German forces along the entire Eastern Front and collapsing German defenses in specific sectors. This had been a costly solution to the strategic problem in terms of casualties, and a continuation of that strategy in 1944 across the same extensive front could produce a diffusion of military efforts, continued heavy losses, and possible stalemate. Deputy Chief of the General Staff Shtemenko, described *STAVKA* strategic planning in mid-December 1943:

> The simultaneity of offensives of the Soviet Armed Forces on the entire front from the Baltic to the Black Sea, which had been characteristic of the autumn plan of 1943 was now in essence, impossible. Military reality forced us to abandon use of simultaneous offensives and replace them with powerful consecutive operations more suitable to the new situation, or as was then said and written, strategic blows.[1]

Large German forces still existed near Leningrad, in Belorussia, on the right bank of the Ukraine, and in the Crimea. Destruction of any of these groups in rapid fashion would require a tremendous concentration of effort, although the absence of large German strategic and operational reserves eased the Soviet problem somewhat. However, the Germans did possess reserves in corps and division strength which, if used properly, could thwart Soviet offensives in a particular operational sector.

Shtemenko articulated the Soviet solution to the strategic dilemma:

> In order to pierce the enemy front, fracture it over a wide area, and prohibit its restoration, Soviet strategy had to, in its turn, provide for the creation of groups of forces more powerful than the Germans. Every such group had to take on a vividly pronounced shock character through the future increased role

of tanks, artillery and aviation. This required large masses of reserve formations and large units which would permit us to create a decisive superiority of forces on chosen sectors in a short time and by surprise. In order to disperse the enemy reserves, it was more expedient to alternate our operations by time and conduct them in regions far apart from one another.[2]

For such a strategy to succeed, while avoiding the large casualties of earlier years, the *STAVKA* had to improve its ability to shift strategic reserves secretly from one sector to another. It had shown a propensity for doing so as early as 1941 when it had employed reserve armies deployed from the deep rear. By 1943 the Soviets had improved their capability to shift armies laterally across the front in secrecy. As late as 1943, however, the Soviet ability to deploy these armies secretly into forward positions was still limited. In instances when the Soviets secretly planned and employed effective *maskirovka*, they succeeded. Where they did not, they failed.

To implement a strategic plan such as the one envisioned by the *STAVKA* in late 1943, it was absolutely essential to employ effective strategic, operational, and tactical *maskirovka*.

THE WINTER STRATEGIC OFFENSIVE

Background

During the winter offensive the *STAVKA* planned to conduct operations across the entire front in staggered fashion.[3] It sought to clear German forces from the Leningrad region and develop the offensive in southern Russia to liberate as much of the Ukraine as possible, and the Crimea. The main strategic offensive would occur in the south where the bulk of Soviet reserves were deployed (see map 98). There the 1st, 2d, 3d, and 4th Ukrainian Fronts were to destroy German Army Groups South and "A."

Soviet offensive activity would commence almost simultaneously against the German northern flank in the Leningrad area and from the Dnepr bridgeheads. On the northwestern direction the Leningrad, Volkhov and 2d Baltic Fronts would strike Army Group North and drive German forces back to the eastern border of former Estonia. On the southwestern direction the 1st and 2d Ukrainian Fronts would attack Army Group South and drive it toward the Carpathians while the 3d and 4th Ukrainian Fronts drove German forces from the Krivoi Rog and Nikopol' regions of the eastern

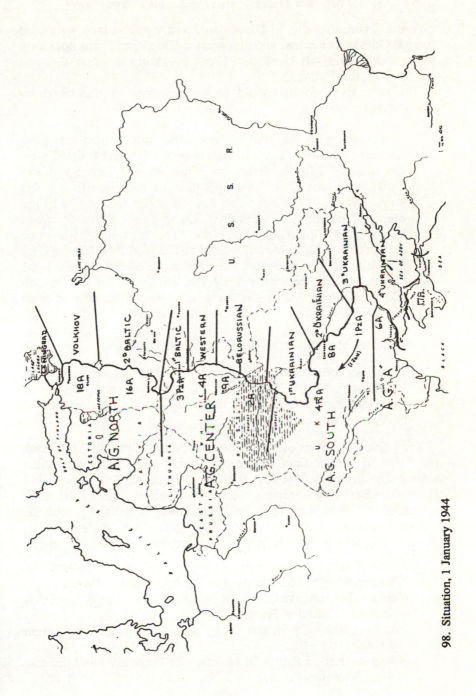

98. Situation, 1 January 1944

Ukraine. Thereafter the 3d Ukrainian Front would attack westward toward Odessa in tandem with 1st and 2d Ukrainian Front operating to the north, and 4th Ukrainian Front operating to clear German forces from the Crimea.

The offensive would unfold in three stages as described by Shtemenko:

> According to the plan of campaign, the earliest offensive (January 12th) was to be launched by the Second Baltic Front. On January 14th it would be joined by the Leningrad and Volkhov Fronts. This joint operation of the three fronts was known as the "1st blow." Ten days later (on January 24th) the main offensive, in the Ukraine, was to begin. Our operations here were designated the "2d blow." The "3rd blow" was to be delivered in March–April, when Odessa would be liberated by the Third Ukrainian Front, after which the enemy forces in the Crimea would be crushed by the onslaught of the Fourth Ukrainian Front. After this the plan envisaged an offensive on the Karelian Isthmus and in Southern Karelia.[4]

Shtemenko reiterated the purposes of Soviet strategy:

> This system of alternating blows at widely separated targets fully justified itself. The enemy was forced to swing his forces from one sector to another, including the distant flanks, and thus lost them bit by bit.[5]

The principal Soviet offensive on the southwestern direction took the form of ten distinct operations, some sequential and some almost simultaneous. The first, which began in late December 1943 (Zhitomir–Berdichev), represented both a culmination of the Kiev operation to secure a strategic bridgehead across the Dnepr and the commencement of the new strategic offensive. Subsequently, through the winter, Soviet forces conducted nine more operations as follows:

Kirovograd – 5–16 January 1944 (2d Ukrainian Front)
Korsun–Shevchenkovsky – 24 January–17 February 1944 (1st and 2d Ukrainian Fronts)
Rovno–Lutsk – 29 January–11 February 1944 (1st Ukrainian Front)
Nikopol'–Krivoi Rog – 30 January–29 February 1944 (3d and 4th Ukrainian Fronts)

Proskurov–Chernovitsy – 4 March–17 April 1944 (1st Ukrainian Front)

Uman–Botoshany – 5 March–17 April 1944 (2d Ukrainian Front)

Bereznegovataya–Snigirevka–6–18 March 1944 (3d Ukrainian Front)

Odessa – 26 March–14 April 1944 (3d Ukrainian Front)

Crimea – 8 April–12 May 1944 (4th Ukrainian Front)

While the Soviets were conducting their main "blows" into the Ukraine and a secondary "blow" in the Leningrad region, forces on other directions would engage in limited offensive action. On the northwestern direction Soviet forces were to distract German attention and forces from the Leningrad area and then capitalize on Soviet success at Leningrad by advancing to the border of the Baltic states. Forces on the western direction were to mount limited objective attacks into eastern Belorussia.

The *STAVKA*'s objectives were twofold. First, it sought to mask to as great a degree as possible the direction of the main strategic thrusts, a difficult problem, for geography and prior offensive operations made their intentions obvious. Second, and more important, the Soviets hoped to shift forces secretly between *fronts* operating on main strategic attack directions to achieve surprise and keep German forces off balance. *Maskirovka* would play a role in the initial operations and then as operations developed into the depths.

Leningrad–Novgorod, January 1944

Planning for the "first blow" began in September 1943, almost four months before the operation commenced. Because of the long planning time, the Soviets developed two offensive variations, Operation "Neva 1," predicated upon a German withdrawal from Leningrad and "Neva 2," which postulated the necessity for conducting a full penetration operation to clear the Leningrad region of German forces. Between 9 and 14 September the Leningrad and Volkhov Fronts outlined proposed offensive schemes to the *STAVKA*, and on 29 September the *STAVKA* ordered the *fronts* to begin preparations for the new offensive. Throughout the fall, the *fronts* husbanded their resources and incrementally planned for both versions of the offensive. Two realities necessitated the long planning time and flexible plans. First, the bulk of military reinforcements, equipment, and supplies were flowing south in support of ongoing and future operations on the main strategic direction. Second, Soviet planners realized that at any point the Germans could begin withdrawing from Leningrad to the "Panther" defense line they were constructing along the eastern borders of the Baltic states.

The *STAVKA* concept required the Leningrad and Volkhov Fronts "to destroy German Eighteenth Army, liberate the Leningrad region, and prepare to conduct successive offensive operations to liberate the Soviet Baltic republics."[6] The Leningrad Front's 2d Shock, 42d, and 67th Armies and the Volkhov Front's 8th, 54th, and 59th Armies were to strike simultaneous blows against the flanks of German Eighteenth Army south of Leningrad and east of Novgorod, and develop the offensive toward Kingisepp and Luga to destroy German forces and reach the Luga River. Subsequently Soviet forces were to advance on Narev and Pskov north and south of Lake Chud. Further south the 2d Baltic Front was to destroy German Eighteenth Army forces north of Nevel', tie down Sixteenth Army units to prevent reinforcement of Eighteenth Army, and join in the advance toward the Baltic states.[7]

General L. A. Govorov's Leningrad Front planned two attacks, one by 2d Shock Army eastward out of the Oranienbaum bridgehead and the second by 42d Army from south of Leningrad, which would converge to create a continuous front south of Leningrad. Thereafter the two armies would advance west toward Narva while a portion of 42d Army struck southwest toward Luga to link up with the Volkhov Front's 59th Army and encircle German Eighteenth Army. General K. A. Meretskov's Volkhov Front would make its main attack north of Lake Il'men' with 59th Army, which would penetrate German defenses north and south of Novgorod and advance toward Luga to link up with Leningrad Front forces.[8]

The success of both *fronts* depended largely on their ability to concentrate forces secretly in key sectors and to divert German attention from the real offensive sectors. Earlier failures had demonstrated how difficult it was to achieve success against prepared defenses in such difficult terrain without skillful concealed regrouping of forces. Thus Govorov, Meretskov, and their subordinate army commanders developed *maskirovka* plans to maintain planning secrecy, distract the attention of the Germans, and conceal the regrouping.

Both *front* commanders restricted their planning circles, established security controls over preparation of documents and communications, and engaged in strict sequential planning. On 16 and 17 October Meretskov alerted his army commanders to the possibility of German withdrawals and gave them general attack orders. When it became clear the Germans would defend, on 31 December Meretskov ordered 59th Army to prepare a penetration operation.[9] In the interim Meretskov field trained his armies, providing them strong indications that an offensive was forthcoming. Prior to 31 December *front* issued no written orders or directives. Instead, all information concerning offensive preparations was delivered orally to specific responsible parties.[10]

Govorov's staff developed a deception plan incorporating diversionary activity and false attack preparations in 67th Army's sector east of Leningrad and ordered Lieutenant General I.I. Fedyuninsky's 2d Shock Army to conceal its main attack by simulating an attack out of the western portion of the Oranienbaum bridgehead. 67th Army's deceptive artillery measures included the firing of a false artillery preparation.[11] Fedyuninsky planned his main attack in a 10.5 kilometer sector on the left center of his *front*. There he massed three rifle corps (of eight rifle divisions) and most of his artillery while defending the remaining 43 kilometers of his *front* with one fortified region and three naval infantry brigades. To deceive the Germans, he simulated a major troop concentration on his right flank complete with false radio nets.[12] Detached rifle battalions from two rifle divisions and a naval infantry brigade conducted daylight marches, built campfires in concentration areas, drove vehicles about at night with their headlights on, reinforced forward infantry positions, and conducted pre-offensive reconnaissance. Artillery batteries occupied false offensive firing positions, and tanks from an army tank brigade and regiment simulated heavy armor activity in the rear. 13th Air Army units reinforced the deception by conducting reconnaissance flights and heavy night bombing over German positions opposite the false concentration area and by concentrating fighter aircraft over the false concentration area.

To further confuse German intelligence the Soviets conducted reconnaissance throughout the entire *front* sector, particularly in simulated attack areas.[13] To insure the success of the deception, on 13 January two fully reinforced battalions of 2d Shock Army's 196th Rifle Division moved westward, in full view, into the false concentration area. That evening, in darkness and under blackout conditions, the battalions returned to their parent unit to participate in the next day's assault. 42d Army concealed its preparations by concentrating its forces either in heavily wooded areas or in population centers near the southern outskirts of Leningrad.[14]

To supplement active deception measures, passive *maskirovka* was particularly strict in the real concentration areas where significant numbers of forces regrouped and concentrated for the attack. German Eighteenth Army responded to the *maskirovka* by deploying two SS divisions (Polizsa and Nordland) to reinforce existing German forces opposite the false Soviet attack sector, leaving just one air force field division and one infantry regiment to defend against the real Soviet attack.

Meretsov also developed an elaborate deception plan for the Volkhov Front and, in particular, 59th Army. Lieutenant General I.T. Korovnikov's 59th Army planned to deliver the *front* main attack from a bridgehead over the Volkhov River 30 kilometers north of Novgorod with the reinforced 6th and 14th Rifle Corps (seven rifle divisions) and a secondary attack south of Novgorod across the ice of Lake Il'men' to strike Novgorod's communications in the rear with a special operational group consisting of one separate rifle brigade, a rifle regiment, a ski battalion, and two airsleigh battalions. On 59th Army's extended right flank the 150th Fortified Region defended a 30 kilometer sector backed up by 2d Rifle Division.[15] Meretskov deployed his *front* reserve behind 59th Army to exploit the army's success after Novgorod had fallen. Meretskov's other armies (54th and 8th) prepared to join the attack once 59th Army's attack had succeeded.

Meretskov's *front maskirovka* plan required 8th and 54th Armies to simulate offensive preparations from 1 to 7 January between Mga and Chudovo (where attacks had occurred so often before). The two armies organized radio and telephone disinformation, conducted actual force movements, simulated false assembly areas, and carried out intensive offensive field training. Meretskov used the headquarters and radio nets of 4th Army, which had been dissolved in November 1943, to "animate" the deception in 8th and 54th Armies' sector.[16] False offensive preparations in 54th Army's sector peaked 5–6 days before the real offensive. Forces occupied jumping-off positions, officer groups conducted reconnaissance, observation balloons were sent aloft, and air reconnaissance intensified. The army staff deliberately passed orders over telephone lines which they knew were monitored by the Germans, engineers cut lanes through minefields, and line rifle units intensified their movement.

General Korovnikov's 59th Army deception plan involved creating a simulated diversionary attack and concealing preparations for a real army secondary attack to occur in a region where the Germans were confident no attack would occur. The simulated 5–6 day diversion unfolded in two phases on 59th Army's right flank. During the first three-day phase the 2d Rifle Division and small units from the army's 112th Rifle Corps simulated regrouping and concentration in the region southwest of Chudovo on 59th Army's right flank. The second two-day phase involved disinformation concerning preparations for an impending attack. Throughout the entire period the army simulated regrouping from the left to the right flank, erected mock-up tanks and artillery, and moved vehicles to create the false impression of new concentration areas, deliberately used poor light discipline and engine sounds to animate the concentration, reinforced forward positions, and employed army engineers and signalmen in normal offensive preparations.[17]

Just days before the attack, the army conducted "corps exercises" focused on destruction of the Chudovo strongpoint; and circulated to troop units special written instructions relating to the nature and importance of the strongpoint in the certainty that they would fall into German hands. Finally, on 13 January 59th Army conducted intense reconnaissance on its right flank.

Meanwhile 59th Army prepared its real secondary attack in utmost secrecy. *Front* headquarters had planned the operation in September and had kept it secret from 59th Army for four months. *Front* supervised training of the units involved in the operation (225th, 372d Rifle Divisions, 58th Rifle Brigade, and specialized units) in areas remote from the front and moved those forces forward 24 hours before the attack.

Meretskov described the preparations:

> A very important role was played by the southern group which forced Lake Il'men'. We had planned this manoeuvre in September and the Front HQ kept quiet about it for four months. On my instructions no information was handed down to the 59th Army lest news of the forthcoming operation should filter through to the enemy. The Front HQ itself trained the team of guides which was to escort the Army across the lake and prepared the necessary maps. Initially, the 58th Separate Infantry Brigade, which had been transferred to the area of Lake Il'men', received orders to cover the left flank of the 225th Infantry Division that was to envelop Novgorod from the

north. I did not even tell Chief of Logistics L.P. Grachev anything. Later I learned that he had transferred and carefully camouflaged a quantity of ammunition "just in case" to Lake Il'men'. I dispatched the order to cross the lake to Commander of the 59th Army Lieutenant-General I.T. Korovnikov only on the night before the attack.

Under cover of darkness and a strong blizzard, Major-General T.A. Sviklin's group covered tens of kilometres across the ice, secured a beachhead approximately 25 square kilometres in area on the western bank of the lake, routed the battalions of Estonian and Lithuanian fascists and reached the line of the Veryazha River. On the following day the group cut the road between Novgorod and Shimsk thus creating a threat to German communications from the south.[18]

The ultimate test of planning security and the validity of the deception plan itself was the Soviet ability to conceal the wholesale regrouping of forces necessary to conduct the offensive. Within Govorov's Leningrad Front this meant the secret transfer of 2d Shock Army *in toto* into the Oranienbaum bridgehead. In November 2d Shock Army moved across the Finnish Gulf by boat under periodic air and artillery fire. To transport the 30,000 men, almost 100 tanks, hundreds of guns and vehicles, and thousands of tons of supplies in November, the Leningrad Front created an operational group headed by the *front's* chief of rear services and the commander of the Kronstadt naval defense region. The Baltic Fleet provided transport.[19]

All transport to the Oranienbaum port took place at night or in bad weather under blackout conditions, and unloading occurred before dawn. 2d Shock Army's command cadre arrived on 7 November, and the remainder of the army followed between 5 and 20 November and again after 24 December when transport aircraft also assisted in the movement. Movement continued up to 21 January, well after the Soviet offensive had begun. While 2d Shock Army deployed into the Oranienbaum bridgehead, massive amounts of *front* artillery were transferred from the Mga–Sinyavino area into the Oranienbaum area and west of the Neva River to support the 42d Army attack. All of this movement also had to be masked. Regrouping within the Leningrad Front resulted in the concentration of 72 percent of the *front's* rifle units, 68 percent of its artillery, and all of its armor into 2d Shock and 42d Armies' sectors.[20] Ultimately the regrouping involved movement of 53,797 men, 2300 vehicles and tractors, 211 tanks, 677 guns, and 30,000 tons of supplies.[21]

Regrouping was less extensive in Meretskov's Volkhov Front, nevertheless it resulted in the concentration of about 50 percent of *front* rifle and artillery strength and 100 percent of *front* armor in 59th Army's sector.

Final movement of forces into attack positions took place over three nights in 2d Shock Army's sector and four nights in 42d Army's sector. 59th Army units deployed forward in a similar period, with armored units moving into the Volkhov bridgehead, 4 kilometers from the front lines, late on 11 January. Tank units moved forward to support the infantry assault during the *front's* artillery preparations.

It is clear that Soviet *maskirovka* in the Leningrad–Novgorod operation succeeded to a considerable extent. German forces around Leningrad had a long successful record of countering Soviet offensives, and, up to late 1943, no Soviet offensive had seriously threatened German defenses in the area. German defensive strength had, however, eroded since considerable forces had been shifted southward to Army Group North's right flank to deal with the Soviet October offensive around Nevel'. In September the Germans had prudently begun work on the "Panther" position, a defense line through Narva and Pskov along the shores of Lakes Peipus and Pskov. Hitler, however, refused to authorize a withdrawal to those positions.

By November German intelligence had detected a Soviet buildup in the Oranienbaum bridgehead; but the High Command, and in particular Hitler, believed "the Russians had lost so many men in the fighting in the Ukraine that they might not try another offensive anywhere before the spring of 1944."[22] Moreover, German intelligence noted the presence of no new units in Oranienbaum. This meant "while an offensive sometime in January appeared a near certainty, the longer Eighteenth Army's intelligence officers looked, the closer they came to convincing themselves it would be cut in a modest pattern of the three earlier offensives around Leningrad."[23] Colonel General Georg Lindemann, commander of Eighteenth Army, on 10 January rated the build-ups in the Oranienbaum and Novgorod areas as modest, at least in terms of reserves. He went on to predict that without reserves the thrusts could not go very deep and would most likely be stopped.[24]

German intelligence detected 2d Shock Army's presence in the Oranienbaum bridgehead, but they detected only a fraction of the

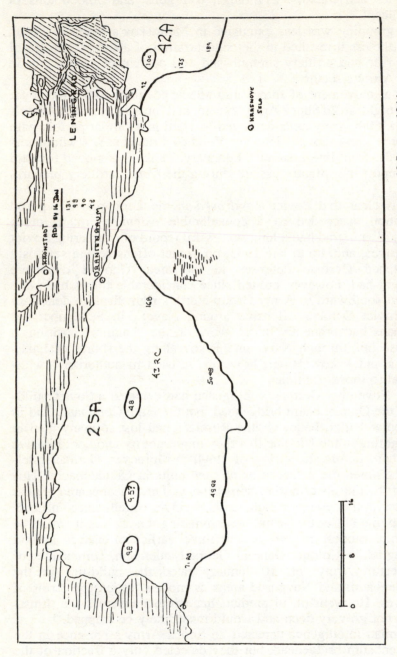

99. Leningrad–Luga, German intelligence assessment, Oranienbaum sector, 13 January 1944

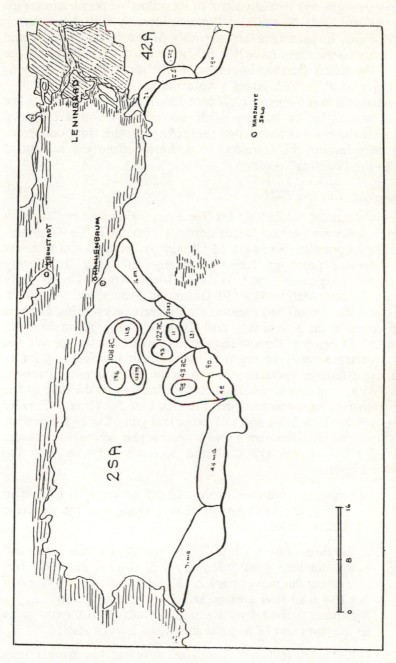

100. Leningrad–Luga, Soviet dispositions, Oranienbaum sector, 13 January 1944

army's strength and virtually none of its offensive preparations (see maps 99 and 100). Nor did intelligence identify 59th Army attack preparations, in particular the assembly of the force which would assault across the ice of Lake Il'men' (see maps 101 and 102). On the eve of the attack German intelligence still identified 4th Army as being deployed on 59th Army's right flank.

Lindemann and German intelligence indicators were wrong. The Soviet attacks on 14 January made considerable initial progress; and, after the Soviets committed their reserves, the front collapsed, ultimately forcing the Germans to withdraw from the Leningrad area to the "Panther" position.

Kirovograd, January 1944

In early January, while the 1st Ukrainian Front struggled with counter-attacking German forces north of Vinnitsa in the Zhitomir–Berdichev operation, Konev's 2d Ukrainian Front sought to break the stalemate north of Krivoi Rog by enlarging its already substantial lodgement south of the Dnepr River. Up to early January Konev, Malinovsky (3d Ukrainian Front), and Tolbukhin (4th Ukrainian Front) had focused their efforts on crushing German Sixth Army in the Krivoi Rog and Nikopol' areas, but to no avail.

On 20 December Konev requested permission to go on the defensive temporarily to regroup and refresh his forces prior to resuming offensive operations toward Krivoi Rog in early January. The *STAVKA* consented, established 5–7 January as the date of the new offensive, and soon reinforced Konev with 5th Guards Cavalry Corps and 400 new tanks and self-propelled guns. On 29 December, in light of the 1st Ukrainian Front's spectacular offensive progress west of Kiev, the *STAVKA* altered Konev's mission with the following order:

> In connection with the successful offensive of 1st Ukrainian Front forces, the *STAVKA* VGK in a change of the directive ... of 9.12.43 orders:
>
> 1. 2 Ukrainian Front, while firmly holding its lines on its left flank, not later than 5 January will resume the offensive, delivering the main attack on Kirovograd with the force of not less than four armies, including one tank army ....
> 2. Simultaneously deliver a secondary attack with two armies in the direction of Shpola and Khristinovka station.[25]

The *STAVKA* order required Konev to re-orient his army ninety degrees from a southerly to a westerly direction and concentrate on the Kirovograd direction. At this time Zhukov was responsible for coordinating the actions of 1st and 2d Ukrainian Fronts and Vasilevsky the 3d and 4th Ukrainian Fronts.

Konev formed two shock groups to strike north and south of Kirovograd. The northern group, consisting of 5th Guards Army and 7th Mechanized Corps, and the southern group, consisting of 7th Guards Army and 5th Guards Tank Army, were to penetrate German defenses and envelop the city from the north and east. 52d, 4th Guards, and 53d Armies would tie down German forces on the *front's* northern flank, where, by coincidence or by design, 5th Guards Tank Army's 8th Mechanized Corps and 53d Army were still in heavy combat with German forces.[26] The *front* directive issued, on 2 January, ordered armies to regroup, concentrate, and attack on 5 January.[27] Rifle forces regrouped on the night of 2–3 January and occupied jumping-off positions on the evening of 4 January. During the concentration 5th Guards and 7th Guards Army's sectors shrank from 30 to less than 15 kilometers.[28] On 3 January 5th Guards Tank Army's 29th Tank Corps moved 50 kilometers westward into assembly areas in the rear of 7th Guards Army. That evening 18th Tank Corps followed. The Germans detected the daylight movement of 29th Tank Corps, and, on 4 January, German artillery pounded the corps' assembly area. Later that day 30 German bombers struck near the corps' positions.[29]

Despite this lapse of *maskirovka*, the remainder of Konev's force operated within a strict *maskirovka* plan which combined normal planning security measures and restriction on all communications except by wire.[30] Although the hasty regrouping had necessitated daylight movement, Konev hoped that the rapidity of the shift together with active operations in 53d Army's sector, 20 kilometers north of Kirovograd, would compensate for *maskirovka* deficiencies and produce surprise. Soviet sources mention no use of active deception other than 53d Army's and 8th Mechanized Corps' operations, which served as a diversion for Konev's main offensive.

On 5 January Konev began his offensive; and, although 7th Guards Army made only limited progress, 5th Guards Army and 7th Mechanized Corps ruptured German defenses north of Kirovograd. Konev quickly detached 8th Mechanized Corps from 5th Guards Tank Army and dispatched it north to reinforce 5th Guards Army's success. After joining 5th Guards Army and 7th Mechanized Corps, the combined force swept southwest, enveloped Kirovograd, and linked up with 5th Guards Tank Army, which had

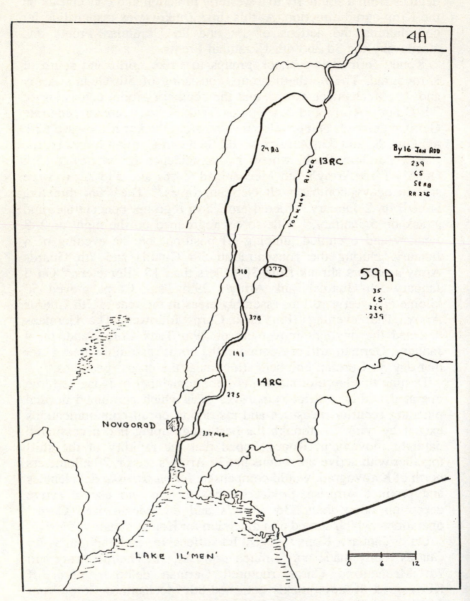

101. Leningrad–Luga, German intelligence assessment, Novgorod sector,
     13 January 1944

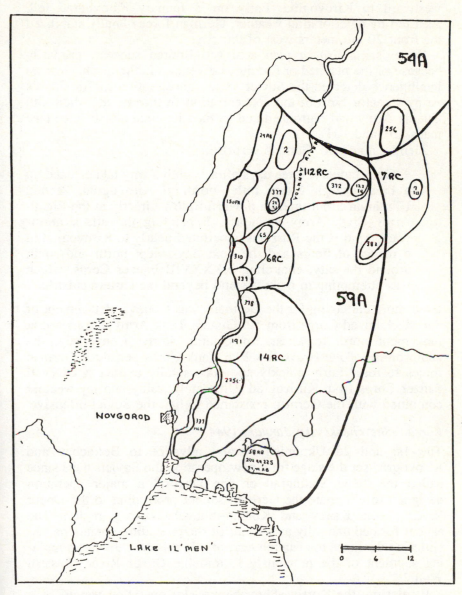

102. Leningrad–Luga, Soviet dispositions, Novgorod sector, 13 January 1944

310   *Soviet Military Deception in the Second World War*

finally broken the stalemate on 7th Guards Army's front, and thrust westward to Kirovograd. Early on 8 January Kirovograd fell. Assisted by deteriorating weather, German forces finally stabilized the front 20 kilometers west of the city.

Konev's *maskirovka* plan achieved limited success, primarily because of the planned or fortuitous diversion in the north. German intelligence detected the Soviet force concentration in 7th Guards Army's sector but not the concentration further north, where 5th Guards Army had regrouped and formed its main attack force (see maps 103 and 104).

Ziemke noted the German surprise:

> On 5 January, three days after Eighth Army had cleaned up a breakthrough fifteen miles north of Kirovograd, Second Ukrainian Front threw a powerful blow directly at the Eighth Army–Sixth Army boundary. Expanding the attack northward rapidly, the Russians penetrated nearly to Kirovograd in a matter of hours and the next day swept north and south around the city, encircling XXXXVIII Panzer Corps, which was attempting to make a stand beyond the eastern suburbs.[31]

Even more damaging for the Germans was Konev's detachment of 8th Mechanized Corps from 5th Guards Tank Army and its secret movement north to assist 5th Guards Army. Conversely, the compromise of *maskirovka* by 29th Tank Corps permitted German forces to react fairly quickly and successfully extract XXXXVIII Panzer Corps from Kirovograd. Ultimately, rainy and icy weather combined with the German resistance to halt the Soviet offensive.

Korsun–Shevchenkovsky, January 1944

The 1st and 2d Ukrainian Fronts' advance to Berdichev and Kirovograd set the stage for a new operation the Soviets have since called the "new Stalingrad on the Dnepr," a major operation designed to eliminate the German salient protruding to the Dnepr River in the Kanev and Korsun–Shevchenkovsky region. The salient formed naturally as a result of the preceding operations and Hitler's reluctance to abandon territory, in this case the last remaining segment of the previously formidable Dnepr River "Eastern Wall."

By design, the Korsun–Shevchenkovsky operation was to be a classic envelopment of the exposed salient occupied by two army corps of German First Panzer and Eighth Armies. The German command had every reason to expect an attack on the salient, thus the Soviet task to mask offensive intent was a difficult one. They could, however, conceal the direction and timing of the attack, for after the two preceding operations Soviet forces were exhausted; and the Germans expected them to regroup and reequip before mounting a new offensive. For the Germans the question was how long would the regrouping take, and where would the next attack fall? It was reasonable to assume it would be along the Kirovograd approach. Because of the depleted condition of Soviet armored forces, it was also reasonable to expect a substantial period of refitting before the next blow struck.

In late December, the *STAVKA* formulated a concept for the joint 1st and 2d Ukrainian Front operation; but, because of delays associated with the Kirovograd operation, it repeatedly amended the concept. Finally on 12 January a *STAVKA* directive ordered the two *fronts* to "encircle and destroy the enemy group in the Zvenigorodka–Mironovka salient by closing the left flank units of the 1st Ukrainian Front and the right flank units of the 2d Ukrainian Front somewhere in the Shpola region, because only such a union of 1st and 2d Ukrainian Front forces could produce the capability of developing the shock force necessary to reach the Southern Bug River."[32] The 1st Ukrainian Front was to attack on 26 January and the 2d Ukrainian Front on 25 January because of the different distances to their objectives.

Although the Soviets do not speak openly of it, the plans probably involved diversionary activity by other *fronts*, in particular the 3d and 4th Ukrainian Fronts. On 11 January 3d Ukrainian Front conducted unsuccessful attacks north of Krivoi Rog. From 16 to 18 January 3d Ukrainian Front regrouped 8th Guards and 6th Armies for an operation planned to begin on 31 January. This certainly helped confuse German intelligence which sought to identify when and where Soviet forces would next launch their main effort.[33]

In the days prior to the offensive the *STAVKA* reinforced both *fronts* for the upcoming operation by assigning 47th Army, 2d Tank Army, 6th Guards Cavalry Corps, and 5th Mechanized Corps to the 1st Ukrainian Front and 5th Guards Cavalry Corps to the 2d Ukrainian Front. As Vatutin and Konev conducted planning, they prepared *maskirovka* plans to conceal regrouping and concentration for the attack.

Vatutin had no need for an elaborate *maskirovka* plan for he was already engaged in heavy combat with counter-attacking German forces north of Uman and east of Vinnitsa. Vatutin subordinated 2d and 3d Guards Tank Armies to 38th Army and ordered them to

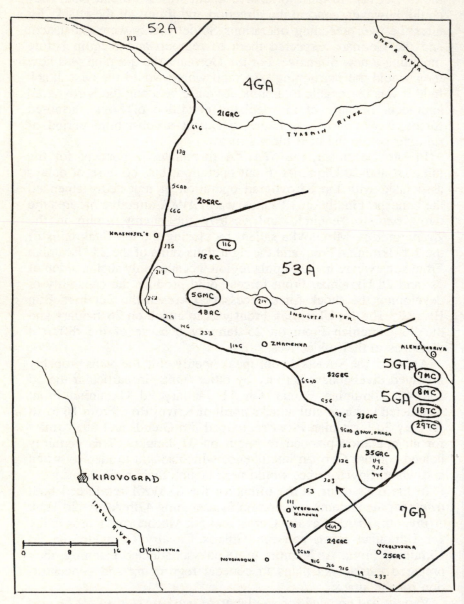

103. Kirovograd, German intelligence assessment, 4 January 1944

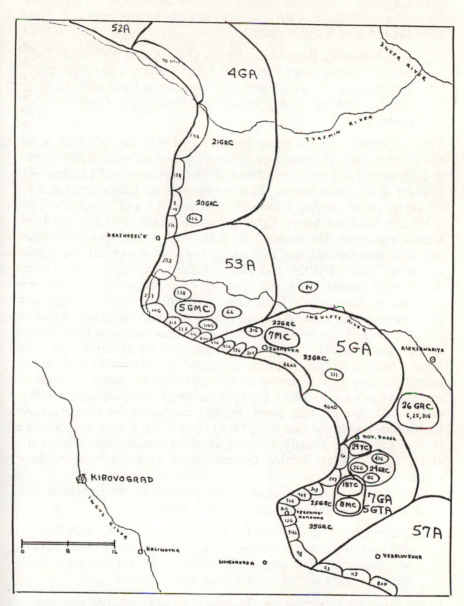

104. Kirovograd, Soviet dispositions, 4 January 1944

defend against the counter-attacks while he orchestrated a regrouping of forces to his left flank to conduct the new operation.[34] The *STAVKA* order to Vatutin read:

> 1. 1 Ukrainian Front main forces of 27 Army, 5 Gds TK and part of 40 Army are to secure the line Tal'noye, Zvenigorodka with subsequent movement of mobile units to Shpola. In this instance it is necessary to use the 104th Rifle Corps in the operation.[35]

Vatutin created a shock group consisting of 40th Army's 47th and 104th Rifle Corps (four rifle divisions), the two right flank divisions of 27th Army, and the newly formed 6th Tank Army of Lieutenant General A. G. Kravchenko. This group was to attack from a 27 kilometer sector eastward toward Zvenigorodka and Shpola.

Vatutin used the heavy fighting east of Vinnitsa to conceal his intention to attack. He assigned the bulk of his *front* forces defensive missions and formed the new tank army to spearhead the new operation. The *STAVKA* had ordered the creation of 6th Tank Army on 20 January 1944, just six days before the attack.[36] The army consisted of 5th Guards Tank Corps, which had been engaged in almost continuous combat since 3 November, and the newly arrived 5th Mechanized Corps. The sudden appearance of a new tank army in the snowy weather was bound to surprise the Germans. By 25 January the tank army had concentrated its 210 tanks and self-propelled guns near Tinovka in the rear of 40th Army. The two mobile corps were to attack the next day in close coordination with two of 40th Army's rifle corps. Further confusing the situation for the Germans was the fact that 5th Guards Tank Corps' motorized rifle brigade was already fighting in the German rear, encircled about 30 kilometers behind German lines as a result of earlier operations.

Simultaneously Konev planned his portion of the operation in accordance with a *STAVKA* order which read:

> 2 Ukrainian Front's main force of 52 Army, 4th Guards Army and part of 52 Army and not less than two mechanized corps will secure the line Shpola, Novomirgorod and link-up in the Shpola region with 1st Ukrainian Front forces.[37]

Konev planned to penetrate German defenses in a 19 kilometer sector with the joined flanks of 4th Guards and 53d Armies and then introduce Rotmistrov's 5th Guards Tank Army to develop the attack westward to Shpola. To tie down and distract German forces

19. Marshal I. S. Konev, 2d Ukrainian Front commander (right) and his chief of staff, General M. V. Zakharov, during the Korsun–Shevchenkovsky operation, February, 1944

Konev ordered 5th Guards and 7th Guards Armies, deployed further south, to attack on 23 January, one day prior to his main attack. On the right flank 52d Army would support the *front* main attack.

To cover his extensive regrouping for the operation, Konev devised a deception plan involving both active and passive measures. He created a false tank army concentration area to simulate the intention of attacking with 5th Guards and 7th Guards Armies and 5th Guards Tank Armies from the region west of Kirovograd (see map 105). While the simulation proceeded, 5th Guards Tank Army would secretly move northward to Krasnosilka, its real offensive assembly area.

Konev ordered 5th Guards Army, in whose sectors the false concentration of 5th Guards Tank Army was to occur, to create the disinformation plan. 5th Guards Army used the local forests and population points west of Kirovograd as false assembly areas. From 19 to 22 January it created 17 false concentration areas for tanks and artillery and emplaced 126 mock-up tanks, 36 false guns, 17 dummy fuel and ammunition warehouses and 200 mock-up soldiers. Trucks and tanks moved to and fro using poor *maskirovka* procedures, and

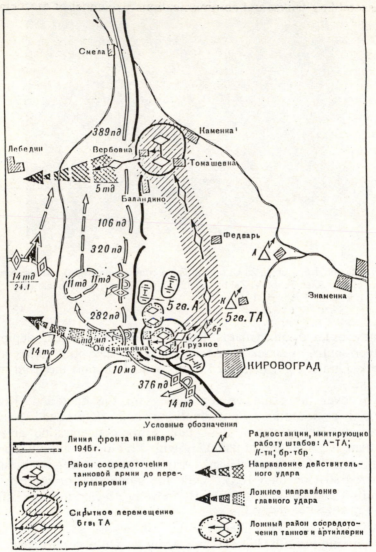

Схема 24. Замысел оперативной маскировки войск 2-го Украинского фронта (январь 1944 г.)

105. Korsun–Shevchenkovsky, 2d Ukrainian Front deception plan

troops lit bonfires to animate the area. Tractors simulated the noise of assembling tanks, and communications personnel of 5th Guards Army established radio nets complete with false messages provided by 5th Guards Tank Army personnel to simulate the radio nets of a normal tank army.[38] Artillery units simulated occupation of offensive firing positions and conducted intensive registration fires, and engineer units of the 14th Assault Engineer Sapper brigade and the 25th Separate Maskirovka Company worked to prepare the simulated concentration area, including construction of mock-up tanks, artillery, and troops.[39]

Meanwhile, both 5th Guards and 7th Guards Armies' front line units engaged in offensive preparations and conducted intensive reconnaissance. As a final measure, on 23 January the 97th Guards and 13th Guards Rifle Division of 5th Guards Army began a diversionary assault after a heavy artillery preparation.[40] At the time 5th Guards Tank Army was moving 100 kilometers northward at night under strict *maskirovka* discipline into its real concentration area near Krasnosilka. To mask the sounds of the night march, movement routes were kept 20–30 kilometers from the forward area. 4th Guards and 53d Armies also regrouped secretly and occupied their new attack concentration areas.

Vatutin's and Konev's *maskirovka* plans achieved considerable success despite the obvious exposed position and the apprehension of German forces in the area. German intelligence correctly identified Army Group South as the principal Soviet target but was uncertain as to where the new blow would fall. It noted the danger of an attack from the Belaya Tserkov' and Kirovograd areas but did not detect Vatutin's regrouping or the existance of 6th Tank Army (see maps 106 and 107). The Germans detected increased Soviet activity after 21 January, noting:

> It cannot be excluded that there might develop a fresh Russian thrust against the Zvenigorodka–Uman area, in particular if, by eventual enemy success northwest of Kirovograd, a cut off of the German front bend which projects to the northeast of the Dnepr River should come to fruition.[41]

German intelligence failed to detect the major Soviet regrouping and concentration of 4th Guards and 53d Armies southwest of Kamenka. It also assessed heavy Soviet infantry concentrations west of Kirovograd (see maps 108 and 109).

German Eighth Army, however, finally detected the 5th Guards Tank Army ruse on 21 January when German radio reconnaissance

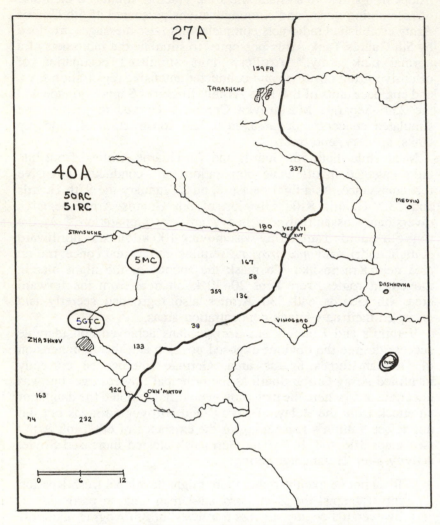

106. Korsun–Shevchenkovsky, German intelligence assessment,
Zhashkov sector, 25 January 1944

picked up signs of dummy tank activity west of Kirovograd. The
German report read:

> In the Kirovograd region we noticed today a shifting of the
> main attack north to the area east of Novo–Mirograd.
> Therefore, in a resumption of offensive operations here we

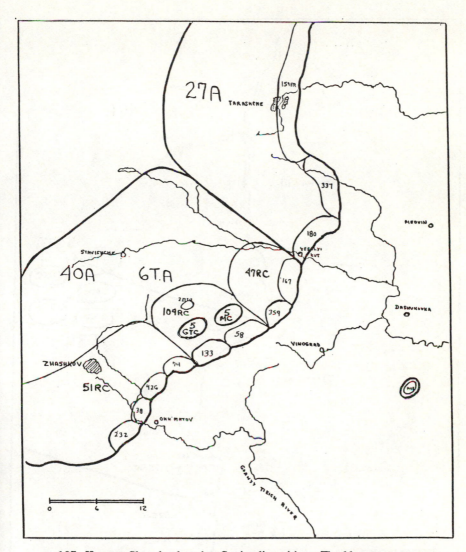

107. Korsun–Shevchenkovsky, Soviet dispositions, Zhashkov sector,
25 January 1944

would expect first of all to see an introduction into operations
of strong units for a penetration to Novo–Mirgorod. According to a report of radio reconnaissance, the staff of 5 Guards
Tank Army and sapper units are displacing northward: mine
removal is occurring in the central sector of XXXXVIII Panzer

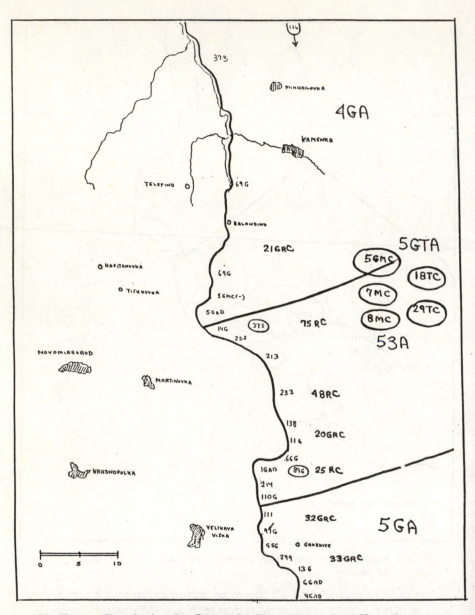

108. Korsun–Shevchenkovsky, German intelligence assessment, Kamenka sector, 23 January 1944

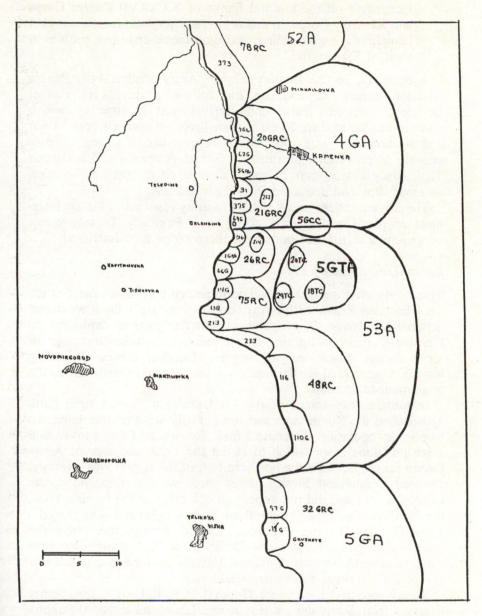

109. Korsun–Shevchenkovsky, Soviet dispositions, Kamenka sector, 23 January 1944

Corps and on the internal flanks of XXXXVII Panzer Corps and XI Army Corps; in that region artillery and multiple rocket launchers are assembling, and tank mock-ups have been built west of Kirovograd.[42]

Consequently, on 22 January Eighth Army shifted 14th Panzer Division northward; and, on the following day, 11th Panzer Division followed. Those units arrived just in time to launch counter-attacks against 2d Ukrainian Front attacking forces. Their arrival, however, was too late to re-establish a strong defense capable of preventing an ultimate Soviet penetration. 5th Guards Tank Army's deception, although unsuccessful, cost the Germans precious time and detracted from their defense.

The Soviet attacks of 24 and 26 January resulted in the encirclement of two German army corps by 3 February. In subsequent operations a significant portion of these corps was destroyed.

Rovno–Lutsk, January 1944

Three days after operations had commenced on the left flank of the 1st Ukrainian Front, 13th Army, on the *front* right flank went into action near Rovno. The operation was designed to capitalize on German fixation on fighting to the east and to take advantage of local terrain conditions to surprise German forces defending Rovno. Operational *maskirovka* on a local scale contributed to the attainment of surprise.

In mid-January forces of the 1st Ukrainian Front's right flank approached the Rovno area and temporarily went on the defensive to plan an operation to secure Lutsk, Rovno, and Shepetovka and seize positions from which to strike the flank and rear of Army Group South. Because the northern part of the region was swampy, forested terrain and Soviet forces there were overextended, the German command did not expect an offensive in the region. Thus, the 1st Ukrainian Front's right flank armies (13th and 60th) faced a weak German defense organized around strongpoints along the main roads manned by Corps Detachment "C," containing remnants of several German divisions. Vatutin planned to take advantage of the terrain and German weakness.

Vatutin ordered Lieutenant General N.P. Pukhov's 13th Army to attack from Sarny toward Rovno and Lutsk and assigned Pukhov two cavalry corps (1st Guards and 6th Guards) to spearhead his advance. To achieve surprise Pukhov concentrated the bulk of his forces 20 kilometers from the forward area and planned to launch his attack from the march.[43] His left flank units (76th and 24th Rifle Corps) were to strike frontally and then envelop Rovno, while neighboring 60th Army units attacked German positions further south at Shepetovka. Pukhov's 77th Rifle Corps covered the northern flank of the army to the Pripyat marsh region, and his two cavalry corps formed behind 76th Rifle Corps. Pukhov ordered elements of 76th Rifle Corps and the two cavalry corps to advance secretly into the German rear through the swampy region around Sarny and outflank German units at Rovno from the north and west.

On 27 January 13th and 60th Armies began their assault toward Rovno against heavy resistance. Simultaneously, on 13th Army's right flank, 1st Guards and 6th Guards Cavalry Corps conducted a secret night march with the 143d Rifle Division through the scattered German defense and, by morning on 27 January, reached positions west of Sarny well into the German rear. On 27 January, while the 76th and 24th Rifle Corps advanced only 5–6 kilometers into the main German defenses east of Rovno, the two cavalry corps remained concealed and prepared for a nighttime advance to the Styr River. After dark on 27 January the two corps raced west and secured river crossings while German attention remained riveted on the Rovno and Lutsk areas. Early on 28 January Vatutin ordered Pukhov to wheel his two cavalry corps south against the left flank of German forces defending Lutsk and Rovno. In response, Pukhov ordered 1st Guards Cavalry Corps to advance southward along the eastern bank of the Styr River toward Lutsk and 6th Guards Cavalry Corps to do likewise further east against Rovno. 1st Guards Cavalry Corps was to seize Lutsk by 31 January, and 6th Guards Cavalry Corps was to cooperate with the rifle corps attacking Rovno frontally.[44]

The cavalry corps maneuver which began early on 29 January:

> was fulfilled secretly and exactly. The German command, as before, did not have a notion about either the size of our forces introduced into the operation or the scale of their actions. They mistook the movement of large columns through the forests into their rear for a partisan raid. To verify reports received the Germans sent out reconnaissance aircraft but Soviet forces shot them down.[45]

German intelligence detected the Soviet concentration north of Shepetovka but did not identify the units as belonging to 60th Army (see maps 110 and 111). Moreover, they did not detect the full

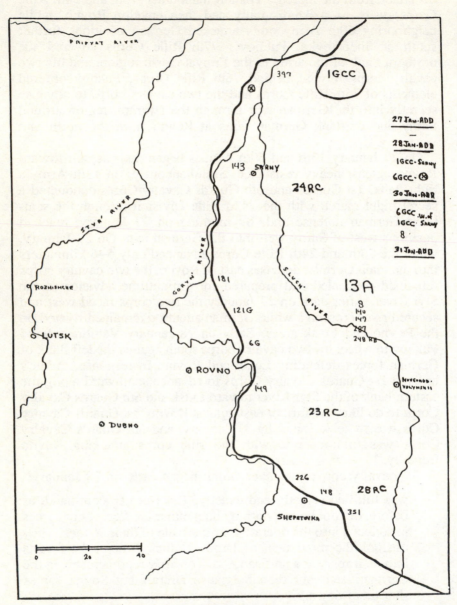

110. Rovno–Lutsk, German intelligence assessment, 26 January 1944

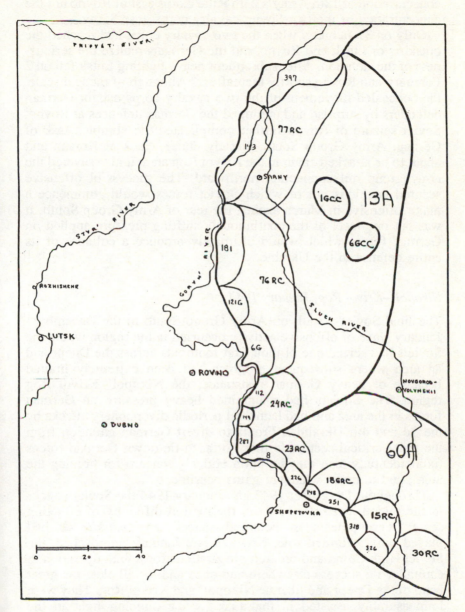

111. Rovno–Lutsk, Soviet dispositions, 26 January 1944

concentration of 13th Army's 24th Rifle Corps east of Rovno nor the concentration of the two Soviet cavalry corps near Sarny.

Only on 31 January, when the two cavalry corps had reached the outskirts of Lutsk and Rovno, did the Germans realize the seriousness of the situation. After subsequent heavy fighting Lutsk fell on 2 February and Rovno shortly thereafter.[46] Although of tactical scale, the concealed movement of the two cavalry corps caught German defenders by surprise and unhinged the German defenses at Rovno. Soviet seizure of Rovno further complicated the complex task of German Army Group South, already under attack at Korsun and about to be attacked again in the Krivoi Rog area. It also severed the army group rail connection northward. The successful offensive secured positions out of which Soviet forces would commence a major offensive in March against the rear of Army Group South. It was but one facet of the continuously shifting pressure applied on German forces which would ultimately produce a collapse of its entire defense in the Ukraine.

Nikopol'—Krivoi Rog, January 1944

The final Soviet assault on Army Group South in the December– January wave of offensive activity occurred in the region where the Soviets had seized one of their first footholds across the Dnepr and an area where subsequent progress had been extremely limited because of heavy German resistance, the Nikopol'—Krivoi Rog region. The Soviets had maintained heavy pressure on German forces in the area and had launched periodic diversionary attacks by the 3d and 4th Ukrainian Fronts to divert German attention from the more critical sectors further north, to tie down German forces (coincidentally also playing upon Hitler's concern for holding the area), and to make whatever gains possible.

Throughout December 1943 and January 1944 the Soviet attacks in the region had suffered from the natural difficulty of effecting secret regroupments in confined spaces, and *maskirovka* had played only a limited role. Now, as late January approached, the Soviet High Command ordered preparations for a final operation to capitalize on success elsewhere and once and for all clear the great bend of the Dnepr and liberate Nikopol' and Krivoi Rog. They were immeasurably assisted in that task by the ongoing fight in the Korsun area, which drew German reserves from the Nikopol' and Krivoi Rog regions.

The inter-relationship of all operations south of the Dnepr was apparent from a message which Vasilevsky sent to the *STAVKA* on 29 December:

> The successful development of the operation of the front forces of Nikoleyev [Vatutin], and chiefly — the serious defeat of the main enemy group on that direction and our fundamental decision to direct the main forces of Stepin [Konev] on Kirovograd and further to Pervomaisk — forces us to reconsider the plan of operations of the Third and especially the Fourth Ukrainian Front.[47]

Vasilevsky concluded that German forces were likely to begin withdrawing from the Nikopol' area and therefore urged renewed attacks on the area on 10–12 January. The *STAVKA* approved his proposal, but the attacks achieved only minimal gains and were halted by 17 January. Vasilevsky submitted a new plan for an attack on 30 January along the same lines as the first. This time, however, the *STAVKA* reinforced the 3d Ukrainian Front with 37th Army (from 2d Ukrainian Front), 4th Guards Mechanized Corps (from 4th Ukrainian Front), and 31st Guards Rifle Corps (from *STAVKA* reserve) (a situation analogous to the August 1943 reinforcement of the Southwestern Front prior to the Donbas operation).

Vasilevsky's new concept required Malinovsky's 3d Ukrainian Front to attack with 46th and 8th Guards Armies backed up by 4th Guards Mechanized Corps toward Apostolovo and the Dnepr River to link up with 4th Ukrainian Front whose 3d Guards, 5th Shock, and 28th Armies and 2d Guards Mechanized Corps were to crush German forces defending the Nikopol' bridgehead. To deceive the Germans regarding the location of the main attack Malinovsky planned to begin his operation on his flanks in 37th and 6th Armies' sectors.[48]

Preparation for the attack involved a major force regrouping including the concentration of 8th Guards Army, the truncation of its sector west of the Dnepr, and the movement of 6th Army divisions across the Dnepr into 8th Guards Army's old positions. 46th Army concentrated adjacent to 8th Guards Army, and 37th Army deployed forward on 46th Army's right flank. 4th Guards Mechanized Corps moved from south of the Dnepr to reinforce the joined flanks of concentrated 46th and 8th Guards Army forces. The extensive regrouping took place over three nights from 16 to 18 January.[49] Konev realistically assessed his plan noting: "It was impossible to achieve surprise fully in the offensive first of all because the Hitlerite Command expected our offensive, and certainly in his most vulnerable direction – toward Apostolovo."[50]

Chuikov, 8th Guards Army commander, used a new technique to achieve surprise, employment of what was later called an "*osobyi eshelon*" [special echelon]. Rather than conducting reconnaissance with one or two battalions per corps one to three days before the operation, Chuikov conducted reconnaissance with one battalion from each first echelon rifle division as the first phase of his actual attack, immediately preceding the artillery preparation and the actual attack (on the same day).[51]

On 30 January 37th and 6th Armies began their diversionary assaults to draw German reserves into their sector (two panzer divisions). The next day the *front* main force struck. Chuikov's new technique worked. His forces penetrated German defenses and, at 1200 1 February, 4th Guards Mechanized Corps advanced into combat. By 5 February Soviet forces had advanced 45–60 kilometers and secured Apostolovo. Heavy fighting ensued up to 24 February when Soviet forces finally secured Krivoi Rog.

The Soviet offensive at Korsun certainly did not totally mask Soviet intent to attack in the Krivoi Rog–Nikopol' sector. But the distraction on the German left flank at Korsun had a major effect on the German defensive posture at Krivoi Rog. A Sixth Army report noted:

> The combat capability of Sixth Army was affected in a definitely decisive manner when on the 28th of January, two days before the beginning of the Soviet breakthrough attack, 24th Armored [Panzer] Division was called away and sent off on a 310 kilometer march because of a change in situation on the right wing of the First Panzer Army. As a result, the strongest link in the chain of the army reserve was removed without its being possible to replace it in time with another of anywhere near equal strength. In addition to this, the road conditions were such that this movement could only be carried out at speeds of about 10 miles per hour. In the case of 24th Armored Division there was no guarantee that it would arrive at its destination in time with all of its elements.[52]

Further:

> When the Soviets 4th Guards Mechanized Corps broke through on 1 February it would have been squarely in front of the guns of 24th Panzer Division without the latter having had

to move a foot in the deep mud. As a result of the forced removal of 24th Panzer Division and of two other smaller units two days before the beginning of the attack, the backbone of the army's northern front was broken at the decisive point.[53]

When 24th Panzer Division and other units finally returned to Sixth Army's sector the damage was done, and the units had been debilitated by their long futile march.

Malinovsky's *maskirovka* plan concealed his regrouping to a considerable extent. German intelligence detected Soviet concentration in 37th, 8th Guards, and 3d Guards Armies' sectors (see maps 112 and 113). However, it did not discover the full extent of 8th Guards Army's concentration. Nor did it realize the Soviets had shifted 4th Guards Mechanized Corps north of the Dnepr River. Malinovsky's deception, by attacking first in the army secondary attack sector, deprived German forces on the main attack direction of their precious reserves. Chuikov's new tactics further exacerbated the situation and produced success in place of earlier failures.

Proskurov–Chernovitsy, March 1944

By mid-February the first phase of what has come to be known as the Right Bank of the Ukraine operation had been completed. German forces had been driven back from the Dnepr River from the Pripyat marshes to south of Nikopol'; and the 1st, 2d, and 3d Ukrainian Fronts were poised along a front running from Lutsk through Dubno, Shepetovka, Zvenigorodka, Kirovograd, Krivoi Rog, and the lower stretch of the Dnepr River. The *STAVKA* consulted Zhukov and Vasilevsky and the *front* commanders concerning upcoming operations. In previous years it had been at this point that operations had ground to a halt mired in the mud of the spring *razputitsa* [thaw]. The Germans had every reason to believe and hope that this would be the case in 1944. But it was not to be the case. Vasilevsky summed up the *STAVKA* position, stating:

> Analysis of strategic conditions on the front, the condition of enemy forces, and the continuous growth of the nation's resources provided the *STAVKA* with the basis to conclude that it would be possible and expedient to continue the offensive of the Ukrainian Fronts without any pause in order to dismember German-Fascist forces by simultaneous powerful blows on a broad front from Poles'ye to the mouth of the Dnepr and, having destroyed them piecemeal, complete the liberation of the Ukraine.[54]

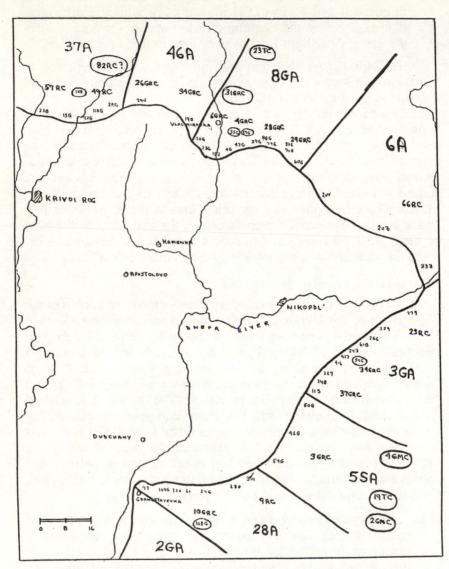

112. Nikopol'–Krivoi Rog, German intelligence assessment, 29 January 1944

The *STAVKA* ordered the 1st Ukrainian Front to strike south-ward through Chertkov to Chernovitsy, the 2d Ukrainian Front to advance through Uman and Rudnitsa to Bel'tsy and Yassy, and the 3d Ukrainian Front to advance through Nikolayev to Odessa (see

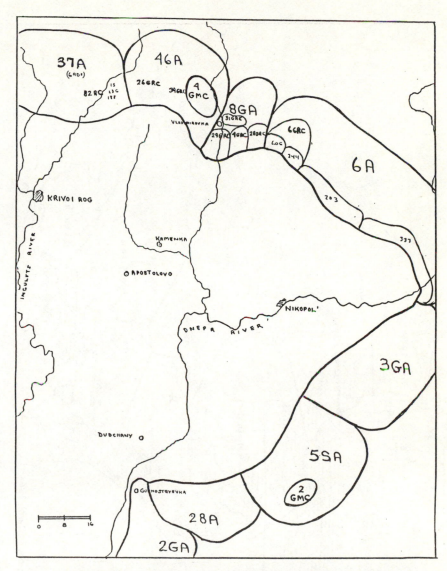

113. Nikopol'–Krivoi Rog, Soviet dispositions, 29 January 1944

map 114). The *STAVKA* reinforced Vatutin's *front* with 4th Tank Army and shifted forces from 4th to 3d Ukrainian Front. In the growing gap between Rokossovsky's Belorussian Front and the 1st Ukrainian Front it created the new 2d Belorussian Front (on the

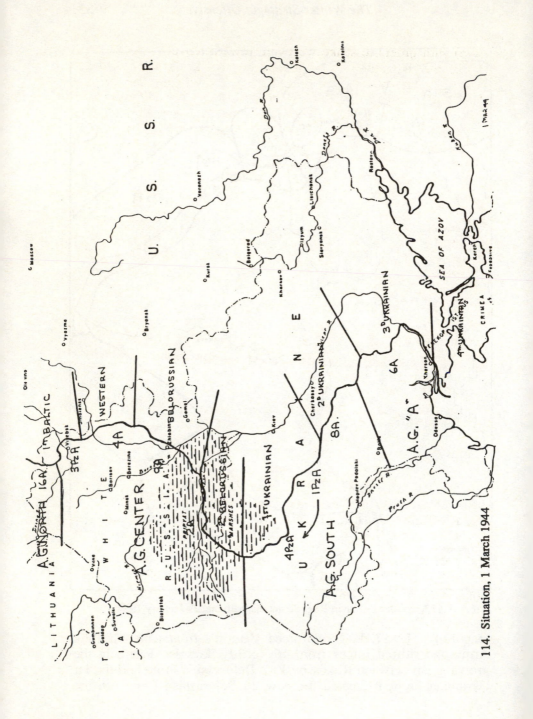

114. Situation, 1 March 1944

basis of the older Northwestern Front staff, then in *STAVKA* reserve) with orders to strike westward toward Kovel'.

Unlike the first phase of operations in the Ukraine, during the second phase the *fronts* would attack almost simultaneously on 4 March (1st Ukrainian), 5 March (2d Ukrainian), and 6 March (3d Ukrainian). On the northern flank 2d Belorussian Front would join the offensive on 15 and 16 March. The *STAVKA* assigned *fronts* their missions on 18 February, and in the last five days of February the *fronts* assigned missions to subordinate armies. The *STAVKA* directive included a *maskirovka* plan to mislead the Germans concerning the principal strategic direction of advance. Since November the main strategic attack direction had been toward Kiev, Berdichev, and Vinnitsa. That had been the case in the Kiev and Zhitomir–Berdichev operations. Now the *STAVKA* shifted the main attack to the right wing of the 1st Ukrainian Front toward the Dnestr River and Chernovitsy on the Prut River. To conceal the westward regrouping of forces the *STAVKA* ordered *maskirovka* measures to simulate a continuation of the main effort toward Vinnitsa. This task fell to Vatutin as he formulated his *front* plan.

The 18 February *STAVKA* order to Vatutin, in part, read:

> ... 1 Ukrainian Front ... prepare an offensive operation including in the *front* shock group forces of 13, 60, 1 Gds Army, 3 Gds TA and 4 TA.
>
> Strike a blow from the front Dubino, Shepetovka, Lyubar to the south with the mission of destroying German groups in the Kremenets, Staro–Konstantinov, Ternopol' areas and secure the line Berestechko, Brody, Ternopol', Proskurov, Khmel'niki.
>
> Subsequently, have in view, while firmly securing your flank toward L'vov, attacking in the general direction of Chertkov to cut off the southern group of Germans from their path of retreat to the west in the sector north of the Dnestr River.[55]

After meeting, on 23 February, with *STAVKA* representative Zhukov, Vatutin formulated a plan to strike with 13th, 60th, and 1st Guards Armies, backed up by 3d Guards and 4th Tank Armies, from the sector Torgovitsa–Shepetovka–Lyubar southward toward Ternopol' and Chertkov. 18th and 38th Armies, on the *front* center and left flank, would launch supporting attacks. 3d Guards and 4th Tank Armies were to go into action in 60th Army's sector. 1st Tank Army would remain in *front* reserve at Pogrebishchenkii on the *front's* left flank. Vatutin's *maskirovka* plan called for active measures to simulate preparations for a main attack in 38th Armies sector and measures to mask the massive regrouping required by the operation (see map 115).

On 27 February Moskalenko's 38th Army received the important mission of disinformation regarding the main attack. 18th Army, on 38th Army's right flank, was to assist.[56] Moskalenko was to simulate the concentration of 3d Guards Tank Army and a rifle corps in the center and on the left flank of his army's sector. 38th Army forces established a false concentration region, repaired bridges and roads into and through the area, prepared aircraft landing strips, and built and emplaced 400 mock-up tanks. The army moved troops, artillery, and vehicle convoys through the region and conducted extensive combat reconnaissance to its front. The member of the military council put false materials in the army newspaper regarding an upcoming offensive. Radio disinformation involved the establishment of radio nets using 3d Guards Tank Army call signs followed by a sharp cut-off in transmissions and subsequent heavy use of land lines. Moskalenko supervised the preparation and issuance of false orders, issued troops two days worth of dry rations, filled up unit ammunition reserves, and concentrated the combat formations of his army. On Moskalenko's right flank 18th Army conducted active offensive demonstrations, reconnaissance attacks, commanders' personnel reconnaissance, and artillery registration.[57]

The Germans responded to this activity by reinforcing their defenses, increasing aerial reconnaissance, regrouping to create reserves, and by shifting 6th Panzer Division to the Nemirov sector opposite 38th Army. However, despite the *maskirovka* measures, Moskalenko noted: "The German-Fascist command apparently succeeded in obtaining information about our preparations."[58]

It was even more important to maintain a cloak of secrecy around the massive regrouping of forces within the 1st Ukrainian Front, at least long enough to gain a time advantage over the Germans at the Soviet point of main effort. The bulk of 1st Ukrainian Front forces were on the left flank near Berdichev and Vinnitsa where heavy fighting had raged until mid-February. Thereafter these units were moved westward. 3d Guards Tank Army had to move 120 kilometers from the Berdichev area between 26 and 29 February. The army's motorized infantry moved over three nights, and the tank brigades and regiments over two nights. By the morning of 29 February the army, with 276 tanks, concentrated in its new assembly areas.[59] 4th Tank Army moved 350 kilometers from west of Kiev

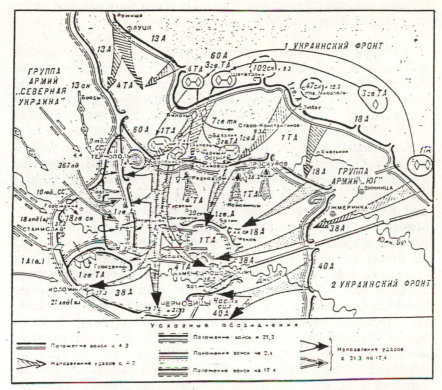

Схема 1. Проскуровско-Черновицкая операция 1-го Украинского фронта

115. Proskurov–Chernovitsy, Soviet regrouping, 26 February–20 March 1944

into its concentration area adjacent to that of 3d Guards Tank Army.

60th Army's regrouping was more complicated for it had to displace its units westward a considerable distance laterally and, at the same time, advance 30 kilometers to secure more favorable attack positions on the south bank of the Goryn' River. From 26 February to 2 March the army drove German forces south of the river and finally occupied a bridgehead of sufficient size to hold 3d Guards and 4th Tank Armies.

Although most regrouping had been completed by 1 March, there were notable exceptions. All of 60th, 1st Guards, and 3d Guards Tank Armies were forward in the new concentration area. 4th Tank

Army, however, was still short 70 tanks and one mechanized brigade, still en route from Kiev. The fuel situation was more serious, for reserve supplies were not yet available for the operation.[60]

While regrouping was in progress, Vatutin was mortally wounded by Ukrainian partisans while on an inspection visit to 13th and 60th Armies. The *STAVKA* designated Zhukov to take personal command of the 1st Ukrainian Front during the operation. Zhukov retained most of Vatutin's plan but withdrew 13th Army from the shock group and gave it essentially a flank security mission.

Soviet *maskirovka* efforts achieved considerable success. In late February German Army Group South, already fearful over its weakened left flank, detected some Soviet movements westward.[61] On 2 March Soviet 60th Army took Yampol', vividly underscoring the threat to Fourth Panzer Army. Hence, in late February Manstein began a regrouping of his own, moving units from First Panzer and Eighth Armies' sectors south of Cherkassy westward to the Proskurov area. III Panzer Corps, with four panzer divisions (1st, 11th, 16th, 17th) moved to Proskurov. Two other panzer divisions (7th and SS "Leibstandarte") under XXXXVIII Panzer Corps' control and three newly re-formed infantry divisions from OKH (68th, 357th, 359th) went to Fourth Panzer Army. In early March Manstein shifted the boundaries between his armies westward to give responsibility for defending the Shepetovka–Proskurov sector to First Panzer Army and the sector west of Ternopol'–Shepetovka to Kovel' to Fourth Panzer Army.[62] The risk Manstein took rested in his limited ability to move these major forces through the spring mud before the Soviets had regrouped and struck. The greater risk was that Manstein weakened Eighth and Sixth Armies, which were soon faced by the renewed assaults of the 2d and 3d Ukrainian Fronts.

Although German intelligence had detected some Soviet movements westward, it was unaware of the magnitude of those moves (see maps 116 and 117). It failed to identify the concentration of 13th, 60th, and 1st Guards Armies east and west of Shepetovka. It also missed the redeployment of 3d Guards Tank Army and 4th Tank Army. On the other hand, it did note the false nature of Soviet concentrations in 18th and 38th Armies' sectors.

Zhukov won the race to regroup. On 4 March his force struck, and within days 3d Guards and 4th Tank Armies had ripped a major hole through the German front. By 7 March the tank armies were approaching Proskurov. While Soviet attacks developed, the regrouping went on. Between 6 and 14 March 1st Guards Tank Army shifted 250 kilometers and concentrated southwest of Shepetovka, also under strict security.[63]

On 7 March the Germans commenced heavy counter-attacks with III and XXXXVIII Panzer Corps northwest of Proskurov and north of Ternopol' which ended the rapid progress of the Soviet offensive. Consequently, Zhukov proposed to the *STAVKA* a new plan to continue the offensive south toward the Dnestr River using 1st Guards and 60th Armies spearheaded by 4th Tank Army and the newly regrouped 1st Guards Tank Army.[64] Zhukov's aim was to capitalize on the success achieved further east by 2d Ukrainian Front by reaching Kamenets–Podolsk and cutting off the withdrawal routes of German First Panzer Army. He proposed the new phase begin on 20 March. The *STAVKA* agreed but changed his *front* objective to the city of Chernovitsy.

Zhukov's new attack was to begin on 15 March with a diversionary thrust by 13th Army toward Brody and L'vov on the right flank to conceal his intent to thrust south with his main force.[65] Meanwhile 1st Guards Tank Army would secretly deploy forward and join the regrouped *front* main forces near Proskurov.

13th Army attacked on 15 March, seized Dubno on 17 March, and by 20 March approached Brody. The attack tied down German forces, distracted German attention from the Proskurov sector, and drew one German reserve division (361st) into combat. Manstein later noted that on 16 March: "It was doubtful whether Fourth Panzer Army could in the long run prevent the enemy from advancing on L'vov or turning off to the south."[66] In conversations with Chief of the General Staff Zeitzler and Hitler, Manstein evidenced the degree to which 13th Army's attack had increased his concern about the L'vov direction.

On 21 March, Zhukov's main thrust toward the south began, ending German speculation as to where the main Soviet attack would be directed. 1st and 4th Tank Armies plunged into the German rear, ultimately cutting off First Panzer Army. 1st Tank Army reached the Dnestr River on 24 March. Meanwhile Zhukov regrouped 3d Guards Tank Army and 1st Guards Army and on 22 March commenced another sudden attack northwest of Proskurov.

In the ensuing weeks Zhukov and Manstein played a game of chess with their forces, with the fate of encircled First Panzer Army at stake. Ultimately, by the end of the month, First Panzer Army successfully broke out westward and joined German relief forces dispatched from southern Poland. Manstein's plan for the breakout

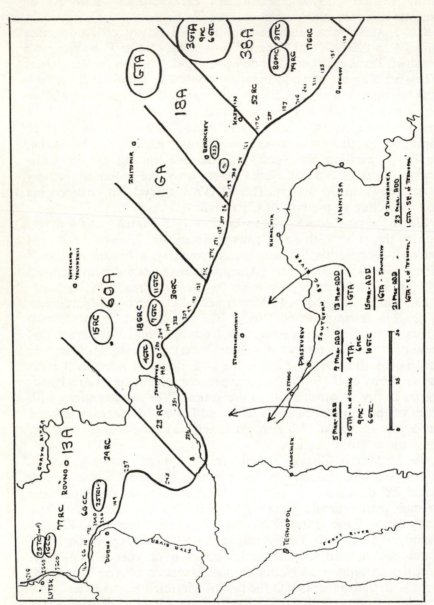

116. Proskurov–Chernovitsy, German intelligence assessment, 3 March 1944

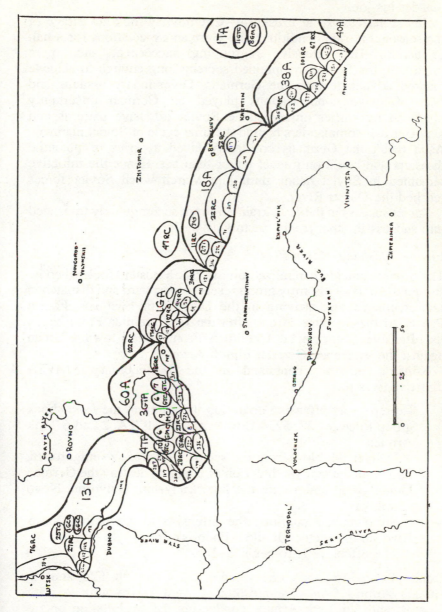

117. Proskurov–Chernovitsy, Soviet dispositions, 3 March 1944

succeeded, but disputes with Hitler cost the Army Group commander his job.

Soviet *maskirovka* at Proskurov–Chernovitsy took advantage of the seasonal terrain conditions and German expectations for a halt in action. The extensive regrouping succeeded; and, more important, the Soviets maintained secrecy long enough to achieve marked advantage over the Germans. Diversionary assaults and fake offensive concentrations played on German uncertainty produced by earlier unpredictable Soviet offensive patterns and kept German commanders behind the time cycle of Soviet planners. As a result the Germans constantly faced a series of potential disasters and could only react rather than act. Hence the initiative remained in Soviet hands until late March when Soviet forces reached the Dnestr River.

Soviet success in the 1st Ukrainian Front sector quickly translated into success in other *fronts'* sectors as well.

Uman–Botoshany, March 1944

The Soviets quickly capitalized on the risk Manstein took when he shifted the bulk of his army group reserves westward and dispatched reinforcements just arriving in the Ukraine to First and Fourth Panzer Armies' sectors. A day after the 1st Ukrainian Front began its offensive, Konev's 2d Ukrainian Front struck toward Uman against the weakened German Eighth Army.

Konev's mission, contained in the 18 February *STAVKA* directive, was to:

> prepare an offensive operation including in the *front* shock group forces of 27, 52, 4 Gds. Army, 5 Gds TA, 2 and 6 Tank Armies.
>
> Deliver the blow from the sector Vinograd, Zvenigorodka, Shpola in the general direction of Uman to destroy the German Uman group and secure the line: Ladyzhin, Gaivoron, Novo Ukrainka.
>
> Subsequently continue the offensive to reach the Dnestr River in the sector Mogilev–Podol'sk–Yagorlyk.
>
> The offensive is to begin 8–10.3[67]

Konev decided to conduct his main attack with 27th, 52d, and 4th Guards Armies from Zvenigorodka toward Uman with 2d, 5th Guards, and 6th Tank Armies conducting the exploitation operation. 7th Guards and 5th Guards Armies would launch supporting attacks on the left flank toward Novo–Ukrainka, and 40th Army would cover the right flank. Konev's offensive would emanate from the southern portion of the Korsun–Shevchenkovsky battlefield.

Extensive regrouping was required prior to the new attack to sort out units which had been engaged in reducing the two German corps encircled in the Korsun pocket. 27th and 52d Armies moved into forward positions, 4th Guards Army concentrated in a new attack sector, and the tank armies assembled to the rear. All regrouping occurred at night. *Maskirovka* was difficult, however, because of the open nature of the terrain. On 4 March units conducted reconnaissance throughout the entire *front* sector.[68]

Soviet sources mention no major active *maskirovka* measures used to cover the 2d Ukrainian Front attack. The Soviets likely relied on the 1st Ukrainian Front attack a day earlier to distract German attention and on the rapid regrouping of forces which produced a significant assault force so soon after the bitter Korsun fighting, to generate a degree of surprise. German transfer of reserves westward had, in fact, conditioned Soviet success and negated the necessity for major Soviet deception in the 2d Ukrainian Front sector.

German intelligence had not expected such a rapid Soviet resumption of the offensive after the heavy fighting of February. Most of the Soviet concentration went undetected (see maps 118 and 119). German intelligence noted the concentration of 52d, 4th Guards, and 5th Guards Army but did not detect 27th Army's occupation of forward positions or 53d Army's concentration on 4th Guards Army's left flank. In addition, German intelligence identified only five of seven Soviet mobile corps.

The 5 March Soviet assault quickly penetrated German defenses. Shortly thereafter the Germans initiated a long fighting withdrawal westward toward the Southern Bug River and ultimately the Dnestr River.

Bereznegovatoye–Snigirevka, March 1944

3d Ukrainian Front offensive planning went on while the *front's* forces widened their bridgehead across the Dnepr west of Nikopol' and fought to seize a bridgehead over the next major water obstacle defended by German Sixth Army, the Ingulets River. While the Soviets speak of no major *maskirovka* plan, the circumstances of changing plans worked to their benefit.

The original *STAVKA* order of 28 February required the *front* to gain a foothold over the Ingulets River by 2 March and insert 6th Army and 5th Shock Armies into the bridgehead to outflank

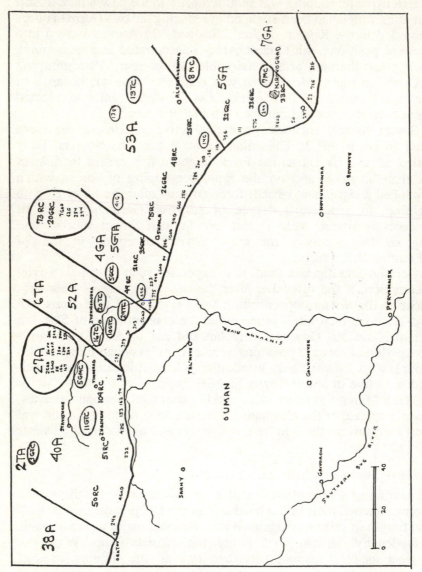

118. Uman–Botoshany, German intelligence assessment, 4 March 1944

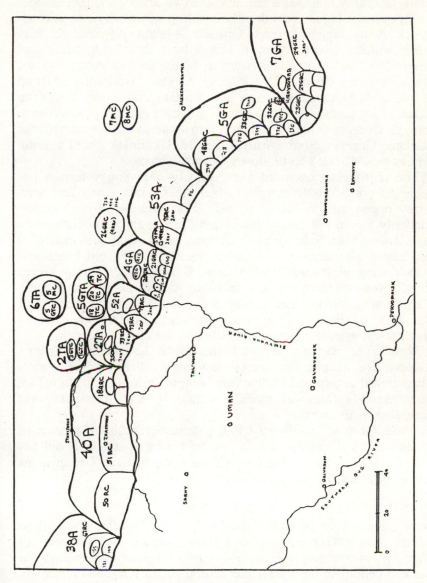

119. Uman–Botoshany, Soviet dispositions, 4 March 1944

German defenses from the south.[69] Events, however, turned out differently. 46th Army and 8th Guards Armies' advance developed more favorably than expected, and the two armies secured bridge-heads over the Ingulets south of Krivoi Rog while 6th Army and 5th Shock Army lagged behind. Quickly, Malinovsky ordered 46th Army and 8th Guards Army to attack from their bridgeheads and moved 23d Tank Corps northward to exploit in 46th Army's sector and Lieutenant General I. A. Pliyev's Cavalry-Mechanized Group (4th Guards Mechanized Corps and 4th Guards Cavalry Corps) to attack in 8th Guards Army's sector.[70] Pliyev's group would advance through German defenses and then turn south in the German rear to outflank German Sixth Army. The 3d Ukrainian Front's flank armies would attack to tie down German forces.

The regrouping occurred very quickly over soggy terrain but achieved considerable surprise when 8th Guards Army and 46th Army began their 6 March assault. That evening Pliyev's group suddenly joined the slowly developing attack and drove deep into the German rear. Subsequently German Sixth Army was encircled and began a tortuous process of extracting itself from battle and withdrawing westward. Within days, German Sixth Army joined Eighth Army to the north in a delaying action westward across the Ukraine which would not stop until late April along the borders of Rumania. In the course of that withdrawal Soviet forces would conduct yet another operation to liberate the city of Odessa.

Maskirovka played a minimal role in the 3d Ukrainian Front's success, for despite the secret movement of Pliyev's Cavalry-Mechanized Group and Malinovsky's rapid shift of his main effort, Sixth Army's fate was already settled by events which were unfolding in the north.

While German intelligence had a basically accurate picture of Malinovsky's dispositions prior to the 6 March attack, it did not detect the assembly of Pliyev's Cavalry-Mechanized Group in its assembly areas (see maps 120 and 121).

Postscript

During the winter offensive the Soviets continued to focus their efforts on the German southern flank. Unlike the summer–fall offensive, when they had mounted major operations against the German center, in the winter the central sector remained relatively stable while the Soviets conducted a major thrust around Leningrad. The degree to which this was dictated by future Soviet strategic planning for operations against German forces in Belorussia in the summer of 1944 or by the difficulty of fighting in the center is conjecture. It is clear that Soviet resources were sufficient only to assure success in the south. While the Soviet offensive unfolded in the Ukraine, diversionary activity occurred in the center in the form of the Belorussian Front's operations at Mozyr and Rogachev in January and February 1944.[71] These operations tied down German units but threatened no serious consequences. Creation of the 2d Belorussian Front in February and its subsequent operations around Kovel' also fell into the category of a diversion and measures designed to improve the Soviet position for future offensives.[72]

The Soviets used *maskirovka* with good effect in the Right Bank of the Ukraine operation, in particular during its first phase. The timed, staggered nature of the operations, somewhat reminiscent of Soviet practices during the Kursk period, kept the Germans off balance and prevented them from detecting the main Soviet strategic attack direction and from shifting reserves to counter the Soviet thrusts.

Initially the Soviets secretly shifted large strategic reserves into the Kiev bridgehead and rent German defenses on the left flank of Army Group South, thus attracting German reserves to that region. Subsequently, the Soviet offensive focus shifted slightly eastward toward Korsun and Kirovograd where the Soviets exploited secret regroupings within the 1st and 2d Ukrainian Fronts to damage German Eighth Army and First Panzer Army. No sooner had German reserves adjusted to the new Soviet thrust than Soviet forces capitalized on the weakness of the German flanks by striking at Rovno, Krivoi Rog, and Nikopol'. In the process, planning secrecy and *maskirovka* to conceal large regroupments played a significant role. Moreover, in the trying weather and terrain conditions, where *maskirovka* failed to conceal fully the Soviet regroupings, the Germans simply could not move forces rapidly enough to stave off initial defeats. German response timing lagged behind the timing associated with Soviet planning and implementation of plans and never caught up. Unable to anticipate, the Germans forever reacted, in most cases, too late.

In phase two of the operation, the Soviets concealed a major strategic regrouping for a sufficient period to mount a devastating attack on Army Group South's left flank near Shepetovka. This sealed the fate of German forces throughout the Ukraine. It also demonstrated the beneficial effects of *maskirovka* in the hands of a force whose numerical superiority was steadily growing.

Although the Soviets engaged extensively in operational and

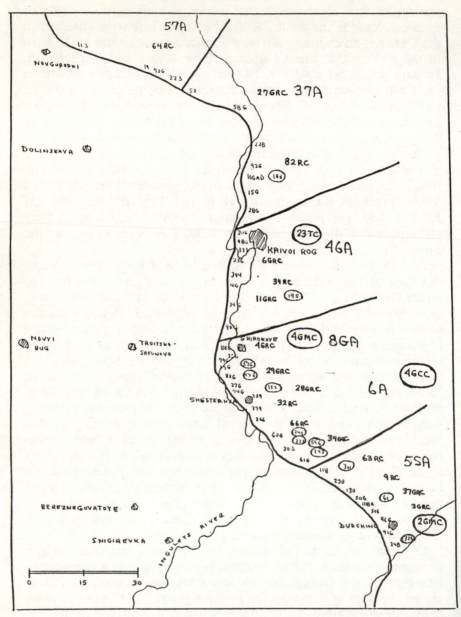

120. Bereznegovatoye–Snigirevka, German intelligence assessment, 5 March 1944

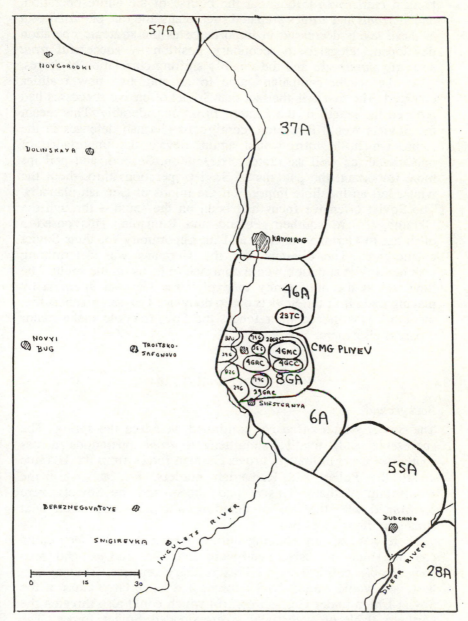

121. Bereznegovatoye–Snigirevka, Soviet dispositions, 5 March 1944

tactical *maskirovka* throughout the course of the entire operation, and all *fronts* and armies prepared such plans; the role of *maskirovka* at these levels decreased in importance as the strategic operation developed, relegated to secondary position by successful *front* strategic *maskirovka* and the steadily shifting correlation of forces.

As the winter campaign came to an end, two new realities emerged. The first was the fact that Soviet offensive successes had reduced the length of the Eastern Front considerably. This meant the Soviets would face more contiguous German defenses in the future which, in turn, would again elevate the importance of operational, as well as strategic deception. Second, and perhaps more important, the patterns of Soviet operations throughout the winter left an indelible imprint on the minds of German planners. The Soviet offensive focus had been on the south – through the Ukraine, toward southern Poland and Rumania. This posed a dilemma to German planners and an opportunity for their Soviet counterparts. The dilemma for the Germans was determining whether Soviet attention would continue to focus on the south. The Soviets had the opportunity to exploit the German dilemma by playing upon it. If the Soviets could convince German planners that the south was indeed their focus, the Soviets could make major progress elsewhere.

SUMMER OFFENSIVE, 1944

Background

The Soviet winter offensive continued well into the spring. The successive and, finally, simultaneous *front* operations across southern Russia ultimately drove German forces from the Ukraine up to the Polish and Rumanian borders. By late April the momentum of that offensive had ebbed, and the Soviets were confronted with the task of deciding where to focus their next strategic offensive efforts.

There were several enticing options (see map 122). They could continue their offensive southward into the Balkans and reap considerable political as well as military rewards. This option, however, would extend Soviet forces and leave large areas of the Soviet Union under German control which could also threaten the northern flank of potentially over-extended Soviet forces. The Soviets could also launch a major offensive from the northern Ukraine across central and eastern Poland to the Baltic Sea,

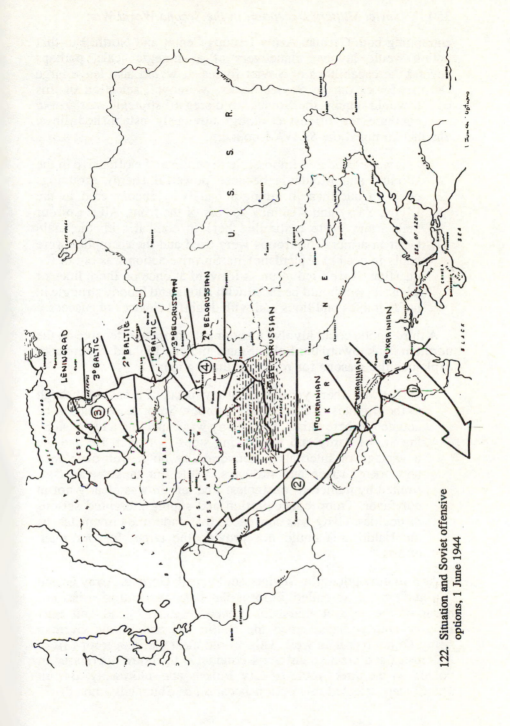

122. Situation and Soviet offensive options, 1 June 1944

entrapping both German Army Groups Center and North. But that option would involve maneuvers of a strategic scale, perhaps beyond the capabilities of Soviet forces. It would also leave large German forces on the Soviet flanks. Moreover, selection of this option would require the Soviets to disregard strategic *maskirovka* and continue the offensive along previously established lines. Shtemenko noted the *STAVKA* concern:

> It was considered impossible to continue the offensive in the Ukraine and Moldavia because powerful enemy groupings equal to our own in strength had been encountered in the L'vov, Yassy and Kishinev sectors of the front. All six of our tank armies were embroiled here in combat with the main German armor. The troops were tired and their supplies were badly in need of replenishment. Surprise action was out of the question. If we tried to press forward at once on these lines of advance, we should be faced with a long and bloody struggle in unfavorable conditions and with doubtful chances of success.[73]

A third option could involve a continuation of the offensive on the northern flank toward the Baltic States and into Finland. Shtemenko explained the reasons for rejecting that option:

> Nor were there yet any great prospects of breaking through to the frontiers of the Baltic republics. Surprise was not to be counted on here either. The enemy was expecting a big push by the Soviet Army and was taking steps to stop it. He had the advantage of internal maneuverability on a well-developed network of roads and railways, while our tanks were confronted by numerous obstacles. The terrain was clearly not in our favor. Troop concentration and supply presented serious difficulties. GHQ was convinced that under the circumstances the Baltic area could not provide the target for our main efforts.[74]

As a fourth option, the Soviets could crush German Army Group "Center" in the so-called Belorussian balcony (jutting westward north of the Pripyat marshes); penetrate into Poland and East Prussia; and, perhaps, reach the Baltic Sea and isolate German Army Group North as well. This would clear German troops from Belorussia and create conditions conducive to future operations in Poland on the direct route to East Prussia and, ultimately, Berlin. The Soviets selected this option because, as Shtemenko noted:

Analysis and re-analysis of the strategic situation gave us the growing conviction that success in the summer campaign of 1944 was to be sought in Belorussia and the western Ukraine. A major victory in the area would bring Soviet troops out on the vital frontiers of the Third Reich by the shortest possible route. At the same time more favorable conditions would be created for hitting the enemy hard on all other sectors, primarily, in the south, where there was already a strong build-up of our forces.[75]

In planning this strategic offensive the Soviets sought to capitalize on the deception potential of the other options by employing an extensive strategic *maskirovka* plan, by organizing extensive re-grouping of their forces, and by carefully time-phasing all offensive activities.

During April the *STAVKA*, general staff, and *STAVKA* representatives worked on a concept of operations in close consultation with *front* commanders. By 12 April the *STAVKA* had decided to give priority to an offensive along the Belorussian direction and then, by 28 April, had worked out the sequencing of the summer's operations.[76] The offensive would begin in early June with the Leningrad Front attacking toward Vyburg on the Karelian Isthmus. Soon after, the Karelian Front would commence operations north of Lake Ladoga. When German attention had turned north Soviet forces would strike in Belorussia, and after German reserves had sped north from eastern Poland to deal with these Soviet attacks, Soviet forces in the northern Ukraine would attack toward L'vov and the Vistula River in eastern Poland. Simultaneously the 2d Baltic Front would attack to tie down German Army Group North forces in the Baltic. After defeat of German forces in Belorussia and eastern Poland, the Soviets would cap their success with an advance into Rumania, which by then should have been denuded of German reserves.

As the offensive unfolded it would cover five distinct operations as follows (see map 123):

Karelian Isthmus–south Karelia – 10 June–9 August 1944
Belorussia – 23 June–29 August 1944
L'vov–Sandomierz – 13 July–29 August 1944
Lublin–Brest – 18 July–2 August 1944 (technically part of the Belorussian operation, but in reality a link between that operation and the L'vov–Sandomierz operation)
Yassy–Kishinev – 20 August–7 September 1944

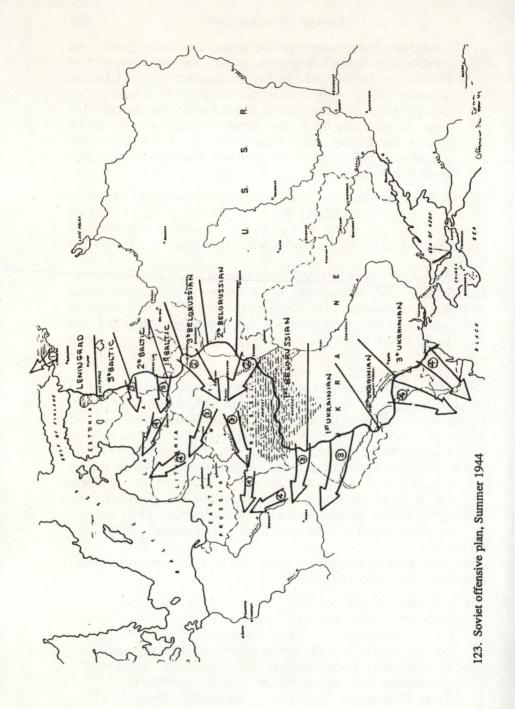

123. Soviet offensive plan, Summer 1944

Each operation would take advantage of conditions created by earlier operations, a principal feature of any strategic operational plan.

During preliminary planning the *STAVKA* re-organized the structure of its operating *fronts* so that they matched the requirements of the upcoming offensive. The Western Front, operating on the Vitebsk, Orsha, and Mogilev directions was subdivided into the 2d and 3d Belorussian Fronts; and the Belorussian Front, operating on the Rogachev and Mozyr direction, became the 1st Belorussian Front and, in so doing, absorbed the three Soviet armies of the former 2d Belorussian Front in the Kovel' area .[77] This reorganization created three *fronts* which would cooperate with a fourth (1st Baltic) in the critical Belorussian operation. Subsequently, elements of two *fronts* (1st Belorussian left wing and 2d Ukrainian) would conduct the operations through central and southern Poland: and two *fronts* (2d and 3d Ukrainian)would advance into Rumania. The successive summer strategic offensives would be far more powerful than those which had occurred in the winter across the Ukraine.

Soviet success in the upcoming operations depended to a large degree on their ability to move and concentrate strategic reserves secretly between strategic directions and transfer armies between *fronts*. The strategic plan required the movement of 5th Guards Tank Army from the southern Ukraine to Belorussia, movement of 2d Guards and 51st Armies from the Crimea to Belorussia, transfer of 28th Army from the southern Ukraine to Belorussia, shifting of 8th Guards Army and 2d Tank Army from Moldavia to the northern Ukraine, and the lateral transfer of 6th Guards Army from the 2d to the 1st Baltic Front. These regroupings would provide the force necessary to carry out the projected offensives. It was, however, absolutely necessary for the Soviets to conceal these movements, for their strategic *maskirovka* plan required German identification of these armies elsewhere.

Both the earlier offensive successes of Soviet forces and the strategic positioning of those forces in late spring facilitated Soviet use of strategic deception on an unprecedented scale. Very simply, the Soviet's strategic *maskirovka* plan sought to play upon German fears about future Soviet offensive operations against central and southeastern Europe (see map 124). By capitalizing on the situation which had persisted from January to May 1944, the Soviets actively advertised their intent to continue operations along previous lines into southern Poland and Rumania. Shtemenko described Soviet intent, writing:

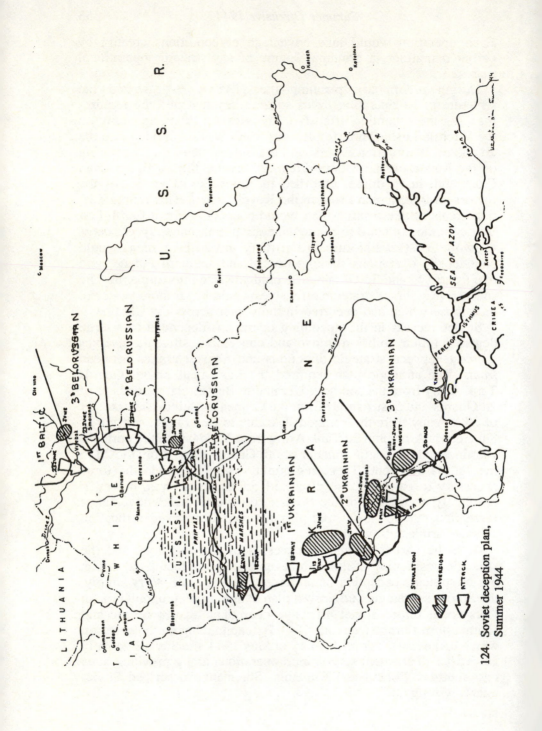

124. Soviet deception plan, Summer 1944

During the preparations for the Belorussian operation the General Staff wanted to somehow convince the Hitlerite command that the main Red Army attacks in the summer of 1944 would come in the south and the Baltic. Already, on 3 May, the 3d Ukrainian Front commander had been given the following order: You are charged with conducting operational *maskirovka* measures for the purpose of misinforming the enemy. It is necessary to show a concentration of eight–nine rifle divisions, reinforced with tanks and artillery, beyond the right flank of the front .... The false region of concentration should be animated, showing the movement and disposition of separate groups of men, vehicles, tanks and guns, and the equipping of the region; anti-aircraft guns should be placed at the locations of tank and artillery mock-ups, simultaneously designating the air defense of the entire region by the installation of anti-aircraft systems and patrolling by fighters.

The visibility and plausibility of the false objectives would be verified by observation and photographing from the air .... The period of conduct of operational *maskirovka* is from 5–15 June of this year.[78]

In accordance with this order the 3d Ukrainian Front created a false concentration area on the Kishinev direction of eight to nine rifle divisions, two artillery divisions, one tank corps, and a complete army rear area. From 29 May to 14 June forces were moved from four rail stations to the appointed area. From 15 June to 5 July the *front* simulated concentration of these forces and attack preparations. All concentration areas were animated with mock-ups, false radio nets and unit numbers and even air cover.[79]

A similar order went to the 3d Baltic Front. In addition, the *STAVKA* ordered all *fronts* in the south to remain as active as possible and demonstrate the presence of the bulk of Soviet tank armies in that region. Vasilevsky later wrote:

In order to reinforce the German opinion [that we would attack in the south], we demonstratively "left in the south" the majority of our tank armies. During daytime in the central sector of the .. front we conducted feverish "defensive" work (on the southern sector defensive work went on at night) and so forth.[80]

In addition the *STAVKA* ordered forces in the eastern and southern Ukraine to conduct limited objective attacks during May, in accordance with earlier operational objectives, to convince the German command that this was the region of continuing Soviet strategic interest. Consequently, on 1 May Konev (2d Ukrainian Front) launched an attack with 27th and 2d Tank Armies across the Prut River, toward Yassy, which culminated in a Soviet defeat at Tyrgu–Frumos.[81] The fact that the operation to this day has been considered a major Soviet effort attests to the success of the Soviet *maskirovka* plan. It, in fact, perpetuated German concerns for their position in Rumania and kept German reserves rooted to Rumania. The Soviets undertook similar efforts along the front in the southern Ukraine. In actuality, the large concentration of forces in the 1st Ukrainian Front sector had a dual purpose: to deceive the Germans regarding an attack in June and, thereafter, to conduct a real attack in July. The *STAVKA* itself adopted strict security measures to insure planning secrecy which Shtemenko later described:

> Precautions were taken to keep our intentions secret. Only a very narrow circle of people were directly engaged in working out the plans of the summer campaign as a whole and the Belorussian operation, in particular. They were, in fact, fully known only to five people: the Supreme Commander's First Deputy, the Chief of the General Staff and his deputy, the Chief of the Operations Department and one of his deputies. All correspondence on this subject as well as telephone conversations or telegraph messages were strictly forbidden and a very strict check was kept on this. Proposals from the fronts concerning operations were also dealt with by only two or three people, were usually written by hand and reported, as a rule, by the commanders in person. The troops were set to work on perfecting their defences. Front, army and divisional newspapers published material only on defence matters. All talks to the troops were about maintaining a firm hold on present positions. Powerful radio stations were temporarily closed down. Only low-power transmitters not less than 60 kilometres from the front-line and using shortened aerials under special radio control were used for the training radio network.[82]

Meanwhile the Soviets prepared to undertake the massive job of redeployment – concealed from German observation. A *STAVKA* directive of 29 May required that *front* commanders move all troops and equipment at night, observing strict light and march discipline. Daytime movement of small groups was permitted only during inclement weather or outside the range of enemy air observation. During pauses in troop movements, all forces were to be dispersed and camouflaged and kept isolated from contact with the civilian population. In general, road movement was kept to a minimum, and rail was used whenever possible. Of particular importance was the concealment of the relief of front line units. This was done at night as close to the time of attack as feasible without interfering with last-minute attack preparations.[83]

To conceal regroupment northward by rail and road, the Soviets simulated heavy rail and road movements to the south and south-west, using false dispatcher transmissions, and some actual movements. Meanwhile, traffic to real concentration areas was cloaked in maximum secrecy. Unloading of units and equipment occurred at numerous stations up to 100 or more kilometers from the front, and all unloading took place at night. *STAVKA* reserve units moved to assembly areas no closer than 50–100 kilometers from the front. Movement of units to forward positions occurred 5–7 days before the offensive to heavily concealed areas 12–20 kilometers from the front. Final deployments occurred one or two nights prior to the attack.[84]

By the end of April the *STAVKA* had ordered all *fronts* to go on the defense (except those specifically conducting deception) and had completed the outline for the summer offensive. Now work began on detailed planning to realize the basic concept of the operation, the first task of which was to plan the Belorussian operation.

Thus, the Soviet concept for the 1944 summer offensive was grander in scale than that of 1943. First, it was offensive in nature from the very start. Rather than involving a strategic offensive on one primary direction it envisioned the conduct of a series of powerful multi-*front* strategic offensives, successively along several strategic directions with the objective of destroying several German army groups. The strategic *maskirovka* plan was also more ambitious. In 1943 the Soviets had sought to conceal portions of one *front* (Steppe) in strategic reserve and then use that *front* to launch a counter-offensive. Elsewhere, the Soviets had sought to regroup secretly individual armies within *fronts* to maintain the momentum of the attack. In 1943 they had achieved mixed success. In 1944, however, the Soviets sought to regroup large strategic reserves between *fronts* and strategic directions as well. Simultaneously, the Soviets frequently would attempt to regroup armies within *fronts*. *Maskirovka* plans at *STAVKA* level and within *fronts* and armies were far more sophisticated in 1944 than they had been in 1943, as events would bear out.

Vyborg, June 1944

The opening act of the impending summer drama played out north of Leningrad where combat had stabilized since late 1941. As if by tacit agreement, in the first months of war Finnish troops had advanced to the northern outskirts of Leningrad; and, then, to the Germans' consternation, they had halted along the former 1939 borders. For almost three years the Finns had stood by as the Germans sought in vain to seize the city. As pleased as the Soviets were over the Finnish inactivity, the very presence of the Finns had tied down Soviet forces. Moreover, the Soviets were intent on retaking the territory they had seized in the Russo–Finnish War of 1939–1940 but lost in 1941.

The operations against Finnish forces were designed to drive Finland from the war as well as divert attention from Soviet offensive preparations in the critical sectors to the south. Coincidentally the operations had the potential of creating political embarrassment for the Germans if one of their allies could be driven from the war. In a sense, the northern operations would be analogous to the January 1944 offensive around Leningrad which had preceded major Soviet operations in the south, although the new operations would occur on a lesser scale.

The *STAVKA* ordered the Leningrad and Karelian Fronts to secure the Karelo–Finnish region and the Karelian isthmus northwest and north of Leningrad. General L. A. Govorov, the Leningrad Front commander, issued his operational directive on 3 May which defined the *front* mission and provided initial missions for subordinate armies, the fleet, and specialized forces participating in the operation.[85] Govorov's concept called for the 21st Army on the *front* left flank to make the main attack on 10 June through Beloostrov to secure Vyburg on the 9th or 10th day of the operation. 23d Army, on the right flank, would join the offensive after 21st Army had reached the Sestra River. Baltic Fleet units were to support 21st Army's advance and be prepared to conduct amphibious operations. The Ladoga Naval Flotilla would support 23d Army.

Finnish defenses on the Karelian isthmus were elaborate and the Soviets painfully recalled their difficulties in 1939 when numerically inferior Finnish forces had frustrated Soviet attackers for almost four months. Consequently, Govorov planned carefully for the new offensive and incorporated extensive *maskirovka* measures into his operational plan. Govorov's *maskirovka* plan called for 23d Army to conduct diversionary operations and simulated offensive preparations to draw Finnish attention and forces from the Soviet main attack sector (21st Army). In addition, he ordered offensive preparations in the Narva sector further south to simulate an intent to continue operations into Estonia.[86]

To complement these active deception measures the *front* developed plans to conceal the extensive regrouping of forces necessary to conduct the offensive. Regrouping of forces from the *STAVKA* reserve and from the left wing of the Leningrad Front began in late February and continued throughout the spring. Engineer forces engaged in extensive work to conceal these movements.[87] By the end of May these forces had concentrated south and southwest of Leningrad. The largest concentration was that of 21st Army located in assembly areas southwest of Leningrad and 65–115 kilometers from its ultimate offensive sector.

Movement of 21st Army and supporting forces forward began after mid-May. From 17 to 23 May the army rear services deployed forward by ground transport followed from 22 May to 3 June by army artillery and tank units. Regimental and battalion artillery deployed forward from 1 to 4 June; and wheeled and tracked vehicles of the rifle divisions did so between 4 and 6 June. Rifle forces moved forward by a variety of means. 97th Rifle Corps traveled by rail from 5 to 7 June and the 30th Guards and 109th Rifle Corps were transported by Baltic Fleet ships between 4 and 9 June. The Soviets used extensive *maskirovka*, radio silence, and smoke to conceal the move. Troops and artillery of 21st Army replaced 23d Army units over a period of three nights prior to the offensive in phased sequence. Simultaneously the 70th and 92d Rifle Divisions of 23d Army left their former positions and shifted eastward into their new army sector. Late on 9 June 21st Army units completed concentration and conducted reconnaissance for the attack the next day.[88]

The *maskirovka* plan required all movements to be made at night, in blackout conditions in covered vehicles and boats. Traffic regulators supervised all movements, and 13th Air Army provided fighter cover to discourage enemy aerial reconnaissance. The *front* chief of engineers assigned the *maskirovka* work in the forward area to five sapper battalions of 23d Army which conducted mine clearing work, repaired roads, and physically masked 37 kilometers of roadway to conceal the forward movement of 21st Army.[89]

Govorov also required his army commanders to prepare elaborate *maskirovka* plans including active and passive measures. Lieutenant General D.N. Gusev, 21st Army commander, and Govorov prepared a plan to concentrate secretly the bulk of *front* forces on the extreme left flank and then commit them to combat successively to develop the initial penetration into the depths.[90] The 109th, 30th Guards, and 97th Rifle Corps would initiate the assault in an 18 kilometer sector on the *front* left flank. Meanwhile the 108th and 110th Rifle Corps in *front* reserve south of Leningrad simulated deployment to the Narva sector but actually moved north, to join 21st Army's assault, and develop the offensive toward Vyborg.

Thus Govorov's plan evolved sequentially: a simulated attack by 23d Army and creation of an offensive concentration in the Narva sector south of Leningrad; the rapid and secret forward deployment and attack by 21st Army's three rifle corps; secret movement of the 108th and 110th Rifle Corps into 21st Army's sector; and exploitation by the two fresh rifle corps. To conceal these active measures and regrouping Govorov and his army commanders employed extensive passive *maskirovka*.

The offensive began on 10 June and developed according to plan. By 20 June Soviet forces had secured Vyborg. On 21 June Meretskov's Karelian Front commenced operations north of Lake Ladoga, ultimately forcing the Finns to sue for peace. The Vyborg and Karelian operations were clearly peripheral and had only limited effect on the more important operations which, on 23 June, began to unfold further south.

Belorussia, June 1944

Planning for the Belorussian operation was complete by 14 May, and on 20 May the General Staff approved the plan. After further negotiations and a decision to commit a tank army and several *STAVKA* reserve armies in Belorussia, on 30 May the *STAVKA* approved the plan. The next day directives for the offensive went to each *front*. Thereafter, *STAVKA* representatives began coordinating the detailed planning for the operation which was to begin between 15 and 20 June. The *STAVKA* appointed Vasilevsky to coordinate the 1st Baltic and 3d Belorussian Fronts, and Zhukov to do so in the 1st and 2d Belorussian Fronts.

The *STAVKA* concept for the Belorussian operation required simultaneous penetration of German defenses in six sectors, the encirclement and destruction of flank enemy groups in the Vitebsk and Bobruisk regions, and the destruction of the Orsha and Mogilev groups. Subsequently, the main group of Army Group "Center"

20. Marshal A.M. Vasilevsky, Chief of the Red Army General staff (left) and General I.D. Chernyakhovsky, commander, 3d Belorussian Front, Summer 1944

was to be encircled and destroyed by the converging blows of three *fronts* in the direction of Minsk, and Soviet forces would then advance to the western borders of the Soviet Union.[91] When Soviet success against Army Group Center was assured, the 2d and 3d Baltic Fronts would expand the offensive to the north with attacks against Army Group North toward Riga and the Belorussian Front's left wing would advance into central Poland.

During the first phase of the strategic operation the 1st Baltic and 3d Belorussian Fronts would operate against German Third Panzer Army defending the Vitebsk sector, the 3d Belorussian Front would strike German Ninth Army at Bobruisk, and the 2d Belorussian Front would attack German Fourth Army at Mogilev and Orsha. Subsequently the three *fronts* would march on Minsk to encircle German Fourth Army. After Minsk had fallen, the left wing of the 1st Belorussian Front would commence the Lublin–Brest operation to the south, and the 1st Ukrainian Front would begin a major operation toward L'vov and the Vistula River in eastern Poland.

Success in the first phase of the operation depended largely on the secret movement into the region of 6th Guards Army to reinforce the 1st Baltic Front, 28th Army to reinforce the 1st Belorussian

Front, 5th Guards Tank Army to exploit in 3d Belorussian Front's sector, and numerous other units.

The destruction of Army Group Center was no small task. In late May elements of the four Soviet *fronts* (1st Baltic, 1st, 2d, and 3d Belorussian) confronted the four armies of Army Group Center (Third Panzer, Fourth, Ninth, and Second). Approximately 1 million Soviet forces confronted about 850,000 Germans, a ratio not to Soviet planners' liking. To establish requisite ratios necessary for success would involve a massive strategic redeployment of forces to reinforce the four Soviet *fronts*. Specifically, it was necessary to move into Belorussia five combined arms armies, two tank and one air army, the 1st Polish Army, plus five tank, two mechanized, and four cavalry corps, a force of over 400,000 men, 3,000 tanks, and 10,000 guns and mortars (as well as 300,000 tons of fuel and lubricants, and 500,000 cans of rations) (see map 125).[92] Hiding such a massive redeployment from German view posed serious problems and required extensive *maskirovka* at the strategic as well as at the operational level. The Soviets drew upon their vast wealth of experience in their attempts to deceive German planners (see Appendix 2). Even so, the scope of redeployments necessitated measures exceeding those used before. In his memoirs Vasilevsky noted:

> Measures associated with forthcoming regrouping and the shifting from the depths of the country of all necessary for the Belorussia operation demanded great work and attention of the Party Central Committee, the General Staff, and the central administration of the People's Commissariat of Defense. All that colossal work had to be conducted in conditions of strict secrecy in order to hide from the enemy the huge complex of preparatory work for the forthcoming summer offensive.[93]

Ultimately, movement difficulties forced Stalin on 14 June to postpone the date of the attack to 23 June.[94]

Each *front* prepared a *maskirovka* plan in accordance with the overall *STAVKA* plan and the guidance of Zhukov or Vasilevsky. Bagramyan, in coordination with his army commanders, prepared the 1st Baltic Front *maskirovka* plan to conceal the concentration of Lieutenant General I.M. Chistyakov's 6th Guards Army and Lieutenant General A.P. Beloborodov's 43d Army in the forests northwest of Vitebsk (see map 126). Besides using normal security measures and camouflage, he ordered Beloborodov to simulate

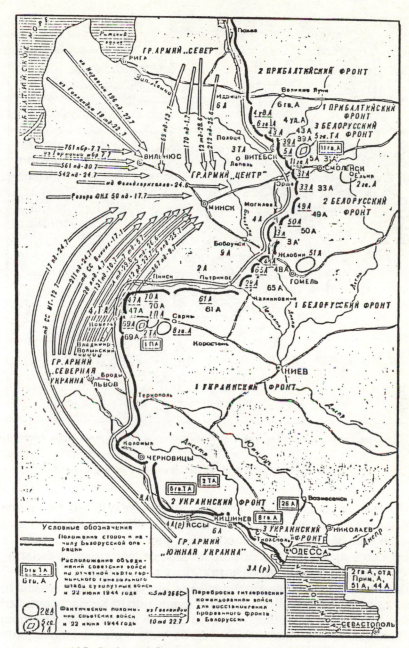

125. Soviet and German regrouping, June–July 1944

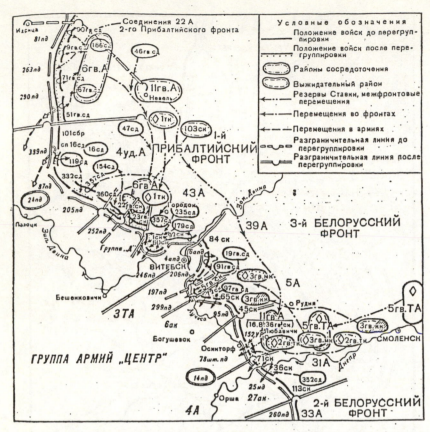

126. Belorussia, 1st Baltic and 3d Belorussian Front regrouping

offensive preparations for a direct attack on Vitebsk along the Western Dvina River from the northeast, a difficult task in an area which had been stable for a considerable period.[95] Beloborodov's plan was also designed to hide the large scale regrouping to the army right flank (75 percent of army forces concentrated in a 6–7 kilometer sector on the right flank). Chistyakov's plan sought to mask his army's 110 kilometer night march into its new concentrated attack sector, a movement covered by the 154th Rifle Division, which itself did not know of 6th Guards Army's planned move (only the division commander was informed).[96]

Rokossovsky's 1st Belorussian Front staff prepared a *maskirovka* plan to conceal the forward deployment of 28th Army and the concentration of that army and 65th Army in a narrow sector south of Bobruisk, while 3d Army prepared both a simulated and real attack near Rogachev, east of Bobruisk (see map 127). Chernyakhovosky's 3d Belorussian Front undertook similar measures to conceal attack preparations south of Vitebsk, while 39th Army simulated attack preparations adjacent to those of 43d Army along the Western Dvina River. Finally, Zakharov's 2d Belorussian Front employed its *maskirovka* plan to simulate false offensive preparations in the area south of Orsha and at Mogilev.

To guarantee secrecy, Soviet planners at all levels, drawing upon lessons of earlier operations, limited the number of persons actively involved in planning, and severely controlled the production of written documents. The immediate planning circle included only the Deputy of the High Command and the Chief of the General Staff and his deputy. Only these figures knew the full scope of the plan. Two or three staff officers in each *front* headquarters developed the *front* operational plans. In accordance with accepted practice, documents were not reprinted but rather reported personally to the respective commanders.[97] Virtually no correspondence relating to the attack was permitted. The required planning documents were revealed only to those who would sign them. The Soviets prohibited all wire and radio communications and carefully monitored the operations of all communications centers. Although the Soviets again engaged in sequential planning, the longer duration of the process permitted lower headquarters greater preparation time for their segments of the plans. Even so, the time of the offensive was kept secret until virtually the last moment. The Military Councils of the *fronts* announced the major offensive to troop units only hours before the attack began.

All activities in the front lines were maintained at a constant and normal level to mask the choice of main attack sectors. Routine communications traffic continued, and all artillery units fired in normal patterns and intensity. Registration of forward deploying artillery units was done by single pieces already in the forward area according to a carefully planned schedule to maintain the air of normality. Reconnaissance occurred on a broad front and was limited to units already in the forward area. Soviet commands prohibited newly deployed units from conducting ground reconnaissance. Air army activity also continued at normal levels and air reconnaissance by new units was severely restricted.[98]

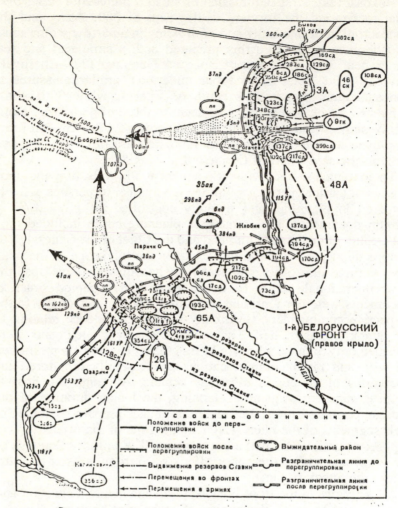

Перегруппировка войск правого крыла 1-го Белорусского фронта

127. Belorussia, 1st Belorussian Front regrouping

Throughout the planning phase, the Soviets emphasized defensive measures in main attack sectors. They constructed false minefields, improved defensive positions, and emphasized defense in all segments of the military press.

Rigorous daily command staff inspections enforced strict adherence to all required *maskirovka* measures. These included both air and ground inspection by members of *front* and army staff directorates. Representatives of operations sections of *fronts* and armies supervised regrouping and camouflage and verified the fulfillment of all aspects of the plan. They dispatched the results of their inspections at 2200 hours each day to the General Staff.[99] Vasilevsky reported:

> The *front* headquarters, staff, and political administration were giving serious attention to camouflage of rifle, tank, and artillery formations and other special troop units and all sorts of military cargoes arriving at the front. The officers of the front staff met the troops at the unloading station and escorted them to the region of concentration prescribed for them, requiring the strictest camouflage measures .... The troops' combat training was also periodically organized on well-equipped ranges and training fields in the rear, where divisions and special units earmarked for the penetration were sequentially and covertly withdrawn into second echelons.[100]

As the date of the offensive neared, *maskirovka* measures intensified. This included a major effort to simulate attack preparations in other regions of the front. On 16 June, the *STAVKA* ordered the 2d and 3d Baltic and 1st Ukrainian Fronts to:

> organize and conduct reconnaissances in force during the period of 20–23 June 1944 in a number of sectors of the front with detachments from a reinforced company up to a reinforced battalion in strength.[101]

This occurred simultaneously with similar reconnaissance measures in the actual attack region by forces of the 1st Baltic and 1st, 2d, and 3d Belorussian Fronts. Consequently, 60 advanced detachments operated at the same time along a front of over 1,000 kilometers, the most extensive use of reconnaissance up to this time.

The *front* commands responded to *STAVKA* guidance by undertaking major *maskirovka* programs at every level of command. These programs emphasized covert preparations for the operation and use of measures to disorient the enemy. The 1st Baltic Front on

30 May published an extensive document detailing *maskirovka* measures and their implementation to lower-level units.[102] The *front* also organized *maskirovka* on a territorial basis, with controllers appointed to oversee such work in each region. The *front* designated three distinct regions, at *front*, army, and troop level, each with distinct boundaries (generally measured from the front to the rear). The *front* chief of staff was responsible for *maskirovka* in the *front* region, the Military Council of each army was responsible for *maskirovka* in army regions, and rifle corps commanders supervised such activities at the troop level.

Controllers had at their disposal special engineer units to assist in physical *maskirovka* preparations, special staffs to assist them, and traffic control units to assist in the efficient movement of arriving troop formations. In the case of the 1st Baltic Front, such organization was necessary to mask the forward deployment of a complete army (6th Guards) into a sector between 4th Shock and 43d Armies which had previously been occupied by only one rifle division (the 154th).

The secret regrouping of 6th Guards Army was made possible by a well-prepared *maskirovka* plan which included: a detailed plan of regrouping; precisely delineated march routes, times, and order and priority for the movement of each division; timely reconnaissance and preparation of march routes; strictly enforced night movement in blacked-out conditions; careful concealment of supply activities; use of an extensive and efficient commandant's service for traffic control; strict *maskirovka* discipline of troops on the march and in concentration areas; systematic control of ground and air movements; and efficient measures to eliminate *maskirovka* violations.[103]

The 1st Baltic Front undertook its own plan to deceive the Germans as to the location of its main attack by preparing for a surprise assault in a heavily wooded sector northwest of Vitebsk. It moved 6th Guards Army with 12 rifle divisions, one tank corps, and almost 100,000 men secretly over a period of three nights from the right flank of the *front* sector, a distance of 120 kilometers, into the sector of the 154th Rifle Division on the *front's* left flank.[104]

The 1st Belorussian Front undertook similar deception measures which required extensive and efficient *maskirovka* in order to succeed. The *front* planned to launch two main attacks to envelop German Ninth Army in the Bobruisk area. The first main attack was to occur from the Rogachev area westward (where the Soviets had attacked as recently as May 1944). The second would occur in the wooded and marshy area south of Bobruisk. The Soviets wanted the Germans to note some of the attack preparations at Rogachev, but hoped to keep the attack south of Bobruisk secret – a difficult task, for a newly deployed army (the 28th) and a newly arrived tank corps (1st Guards) would participate in the assault. The *front* developed an elaborate *maskirovka* plan (approved on 30 May) which included night movement, stringent controls over road movement, the creation of extensive false troop and tank concentrations, and deceptive artillery fire and reconnaissance procedures. According to the *front* commander, Rokossovsky:

> We required that staffs at all levels maintain constant control from the ground and the air over careful camouflage of everything associated with *front* forces. The Germans could see only that which we wanted to show them. Units were concentrated and regrouped at night, and railroad trains ran from the front to the rear in daytime with mock-ups of tanks and guns. In many locations, false crossings were prepared and roads built for visibility. Many guns were concentrated on secondary axes, they conducted several sudden shellings, and then were transported to the rear, leaving mock-ups in the false firing positions. The *front* chief of staff, General Malinin, was inexhaustible in this regard ...[105]

On the secondary attack direction opposite Orsha and Mogilev the left wing of the 3d Belorussian Front and the 2d Belorussian Front conducted diversionary and imitative activity to distract German attention from the main attack sectors around Vitebsk and Bobruisk. The two *fronts* created false concentrations, conducted visible troop movements and conducted active ground and air reconnaissance in their sectors.[106]

The success of Soviet deception measures in the Belorussian operation can best be measured against the judgements of German intelligence, and the reaction of German Army Group Center, before the attack. In general, the Soviet strategic *maskirovka* plan achieved its goals. Throughout May and June, Eastern Intelligence Branch of OKH clung tenaciously to its early May judgement that:

> the Soviet main effort would continue in the South toward the Balkans, where it would take advantage of the clearly shaky state of Germany's allies and finally establish the long-coveted Soviet hegemony in southeastern Europe. North of the Pripyat Marshes, the Eastern Intelligence Branch predicted the front would stay quiet.[107]

By mid-May the branch, the OKH in general, and the involved army groups also recognized the threat of attack into southern Poland and adjusted forces accordingly. These high-level assessments continued even after some signs of a Soviet build-up in Belorussia were detected in June. Eastern intelligence dismissed such action in Army Group Center's sector as "apparently a deception," and German force dispositions continued to reflect these estimates.[108]

After 1 June, Army Group Center noted some changes in Soviet force deployments but did little to alter their previous estimates or reconfigure the Third Panzer, Fourth, and Ninth Armies' defenses. Increased attack indicators after 16 June "aroused no excitement and only routine interest."[109] A war journal entry of 20 June noted stepped-up partisan activity and said such activity "makes it appear that an early start of the offensive cannot be ruled out."[110]

The complacency at army group and OKH level was a reflection of the intelligence picture as these headquarters saw it, as well as ingrained self-delusion. In the face of deteriorating German reconnaissance capabilities, the intelligence picture was inaccurate at best.[111] The Germans assessed that all six Soviet tank armies were deployed in the southern sector with only slight indications that 5th Guards Tank Army was in the central sector. Intelligence maps of German Eighth Army in Rumania identified 5th Guards Tank Army adjacent to its defenses until 26 June. The following day it noted the army's possible movement north. In reality, two full tank armies were in the central sector (2d Tank Army and 5th Guards Tank Army). Intelligence failed to locate three armies which had formerly been involved in the Crimean operation (2d Guards Army, 51st Army, Coastal Army [two of which deployed after the offensive commenced]) and also missed the redeployment of 28th Army (moved 200 kilometers from the south into the Bobruisk area) and 6th Guards Army into the region northwest of Vitebsk. The Germans noted the growth of Soviet frontal aviation strength both in the south and center but determined that the main effort of long-range aviation (six of eight air armies) remained in the south. In general, German intelligence failed to detect the scope of Soviet reinforcement. By 22 June it had identified about 140 Soviet division equivalents and three tank corps facing Army Group Center. Actually, by that time, the Soviets had assembled 168 division equivalents, eight tank or mechanized corps, and two cavalry corps (which had significant armored strength within them) for use in the forthcoming offensive. The Germans assessed Soviet armored strength at between 400 and 1100 tanks, far below the over 5,000 tanks the Soviets ultimately used in the offensive.[112]

Within the army headquarters of Army Group Center, indications of an impending Soviet attack were far clearer than at higher levels of command. By mid-June "all four armies assessed enemy intentions to the effect that an attack was impending."[113] After 19 June, Third Panzer Army regarded an attack as being possible at any time, although it incorrectly assessed that the main attack would occur southeast of Vitebsk. As late as 24 June, the second day of the Soviet assault, Third Panzer Army failed to identify 6th Guards Army as a participant although it had, by that time, identified two to three divisions of that army's 12 divisions (see maps 128 and 129). German Fourth Army expected an attack at any time after 11 June, and on 19 June pinpointed the time of attack as being within two to three days. Fourth Army also correctly assessed the location of the Soviet main attack against its sector (see maps 130 and 131). German Ninth Army after 13 June assessed an attack as pending and became more exact in its assessments as the actual time of the attack approached. By 13 June Ninth Army noted a Soviet build-up in both the Rogachev areas and the area south of Bobruisk. However, up to the time of the attack, it had failed to detect the threatening presence on its front of Soviet 28th Army, 1st Guards Tank Corps, or the Cavalry-Mechanized Group (see maps 132 and 133).[114]

Warnings of the impending attack sent by the armies to Army Group Center were heeded only after 20 June when it began almost passively referring to a possible Soviet offensive. Although informed of this information, OKH attached little importance to it. Earl Ziemke in his work *Stalingrad to Berlin* captured the essence of German intelligence problems when he wrote that:

> As the often-repeated slogan 'nur keine schema' implied, a cardinal principle of German general staff doctrine was the avoidance of rigid or schematic tactical or operating conceptions. In June 1944 on the Eastern Front that rule was forgotten. To a Soviet deception, the German commands added an almost hypnotic self-induced delusion: the main offensive would come against Army Group North Ukraine because that was where they were ready to meet it.[115]

Soviet planning for and conduct of the Belorussian operation included the most ambitious *maskirovka* program they had ever attempted. It spanned all levels: strategic, operational, and tactical. Its overall success depended on careful orchestration of measures

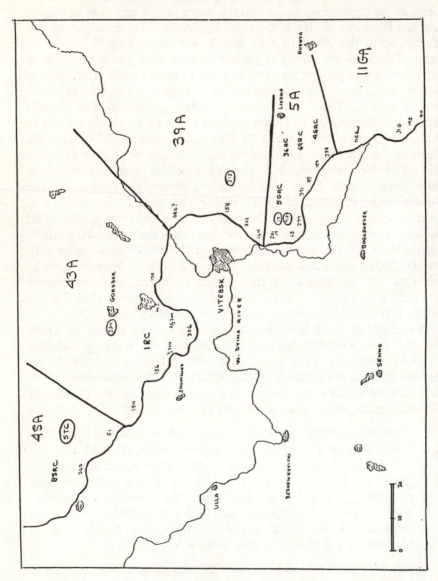

128. Belorussia, German intelligence assessment, Vitebsk sector, 22 June 1944

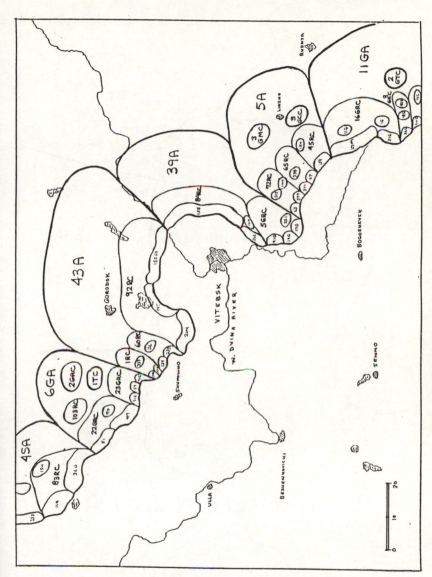

129. Belorussia, Soviet dispositions, Vitebsk sector, 22 June 1944

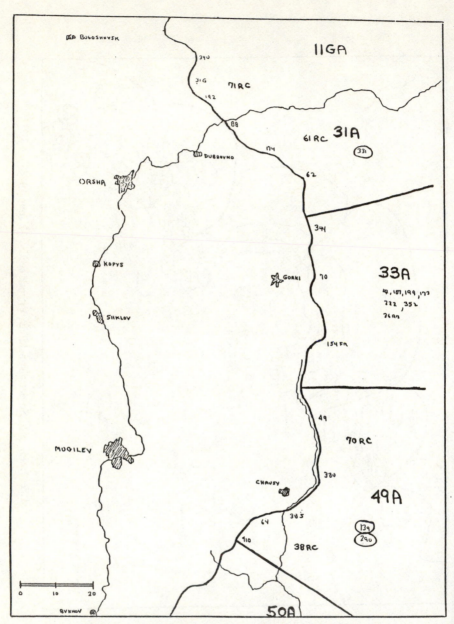

130. Belorussia, German intelligence assessment, Orsha–Mogilev
     sector, 22 June 1944

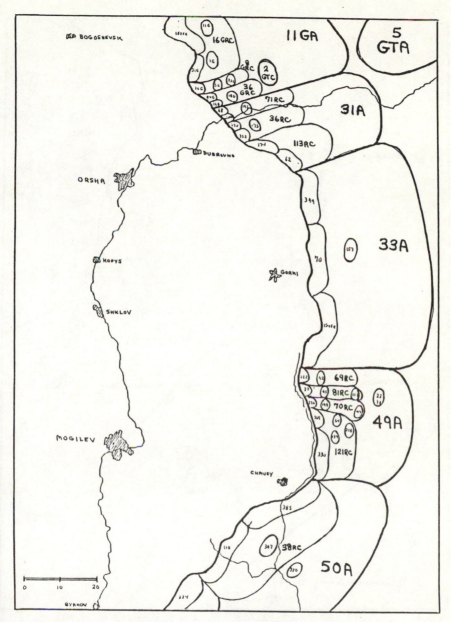

131. Belorussia, Soviet dispositions, Orsha–Mogilev sector, 22 June 1944

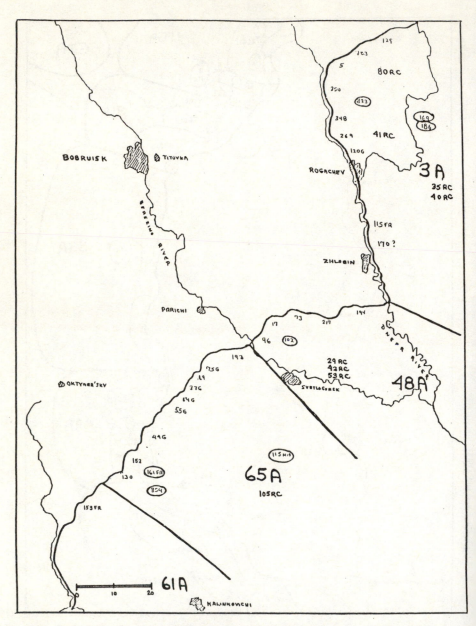

132. Belorussia, German intelligence assessment, Bobruisk sector, 22 June 1944

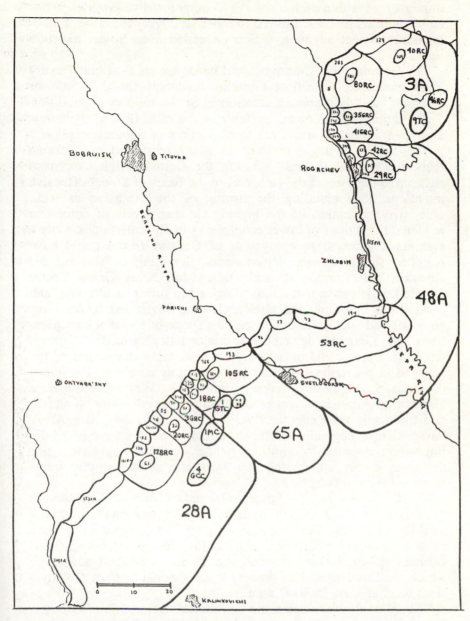

133. Belorussia, Soviet dispositions, Bobruisk sector, 22 June 1944

implemented within each level. As a comprehensive program it was an unqualified success, attested to most vividly by the ensuing 400-kilometer Soviet advance, which exceeded even Soviet expectations.

The German High Command and headquarters at virtually every level continued to reflect German contempt for the "inferior Russians" and their underestimation of Soviet military capabilities. These attitudes, reinforced by faith in the reliability of their own intelligence, conditioned them to be victims of Soviet deception.

The Soviet strategic *maskirovka* plan capitalized on German fears and misconceptions, blinding the German High Command right up to the time of the attack as to the focus of Soviet offensive intentions, thus clouding the timing of the offensive as well. Obviously, deception of the highest German levels of command rendered the actions of lower echelons virtually superfluous. Only a significant strategic redeployment of German forces could have matched similar Soviet deployments, thwarting or slowing the advance. This German strategic failure left Army Group Center exposed, vulnerable, and almost destined to suffer its ultimate fate.

At the operational and tactical levels, Soviet *maskirovka* was sophisticated enough to cover the vast scope of the attack preparations. The Germans detected few major redeployments of armies from other areas, and noted only separate tactical vestiges of the large-scale operational regrouping occurring within and between the four Soviet *fronts* making the attack. While the separate German army headquarters recognized Soviet intentions to attack, and ultimately the general timing of the attack, they, like Army Group Center, appreciated neither the scope nor the strength of the impending assaults. In addition, neither Army Group Center nor the four armies anticipated the form the offensive that overwhelmed them would take.

The skill with which the Soviets planned and executed *maskirovka* at every level of war during the Belorussian operation showed how well Soviet commanders and staff officers had digested the lessons of their earlier experience. Successful Soviet *maskirovka* and German self-deception accorded the Soviets a marked advantage which the Soviets used to destroy three German armies (28 divisions) and at least 350,000 men.

Within two weeks after the successful Belorussian operation began, Soviet forces to the south benefited from the same strategic *maskirovka* plan, this time in a location where the German High Command had originally expected the Soviet offensive. The

Germans, in light of what had occurred in Belorussia, were unable to deal with the new thrust.

L'vov–Sandomierz, July 1944

The Soviet L'vov–Sandomierz operation, which commenced on 13 July 1944, must be considered within the context of the Belorussian operation, which had begun on 23 June, and the Lublin–Brest operation, which would begin on 18 July. All three massive operations formed a unity tied together by a mutual strategic *maskirovka* plan and simple timing. Each was conditioned by the other; and each, in turn, had its effect on the other.

The overall strategic *maskirovka* plan served all three operations but gave first priority to the Belorussian operation (see map 134). Initially the plan called for creating offensive concentrations in the western Ukraine (opposite L'vov) in 1st Ukrainian Front's sector and in the southern Ukraine (opposite Rumania) in the 2d and 3d Ukrainian Front's sectors. The *STAVKA* deployed three tank armies (1st, 3d Guards, 4th) to the western Ukraine and three (2d, 5th Guards, 6th) to southern Ukraine. Then it secretly moved 2d Tank Army and 8th Guards Army into the Kovel' area behind the left wing of the 1st Belorussian Front and 5th Guards Tank Army northward to Smolensk. While German forces concentrated against perceived threats to southern Poland and Rumania, the Soviets struck in Belorussia. By 11 July the Soviets had destroyed German Army Group Center, taken Minsk, and drawn German reserves northward from southern Poland (4th, 5th, 7th Panzer Divisions). Then, on 13 July Konev's 1st Ukrainian Front attacked toward L'vov, using internal *maskirovka* to feign an attack from its left flank but actively attacking from its center and right flank. When German reserves shifted to halt this new Soviet penetration, on 18 July the left wing of the 1st Belorussian Front struck further north using its secretly deployed 8th Guards Army and 2d Tank Army to spearhead an advance toward Lublin. All three thrusts, in Belorussia and then subsequently toward L'vov and Lublin, were the product of a single strategic *maskirovka* plan, which wrought havoc on German defenses from Vitebsk to the Carpathian Mountains.

Orchestrating the second major offensive was the task of Konev's 1st Ukrainian Front. On 24 June 1944 the *STAVKA* directed Konev to:

> prepare and conduct an offensive operation to destroy enemy groups on the L'vov and Rava–Russkaya direction ... and

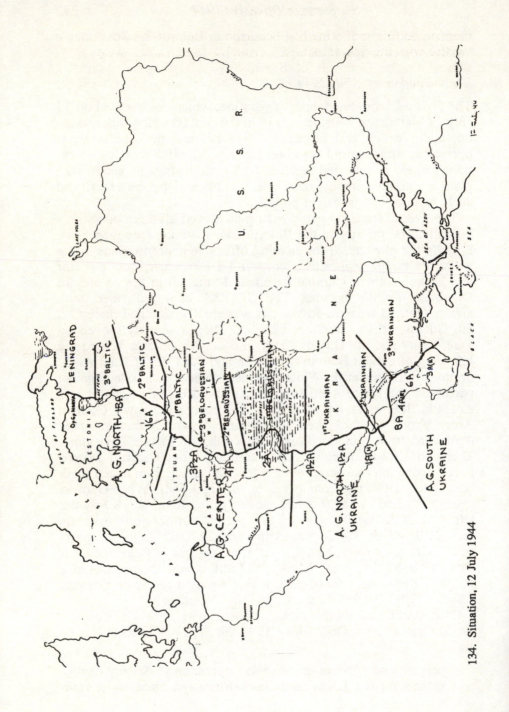

134. Situation, 12 July 1944

reach the line Khrubeshuv–Tomashuv–Yavorov–Galich, by delivering two blows: the first – from the region south-west of Lutsk in the direction of Sokal'–Rava–Russkaya and the second – from the Ternopol' region to L'vov. In order to secure the blow on the L'vov direction, an offensive was outlined by a portion of the front left wing on Stanislov.[116]

Konev decided to attack in two sectors of the front, 60–70 kilometers apart.[117] The northern attack from the Lutsk region toward Rava–Russkaya would be mounted by General V.N. Gordov's 3d Guards Army and General N.P. Pukhov's 13th Army, both concentrated in a 13-kilometer sector, backed up by General M.E. Katukov's 1st Guards Tank Army and General V.K. Baranov's Cavalry-Mechanized Group, which consisted of 25th Tank and 1st Guards Cavalry Corps. To conduct the southern attack, from the Ternopol' region toward L'vov, Konev concentrated General P.A. Kurochkin's 60th Army and General K.S. Moskalenko's 38th Army in a 14 kilometer sector supported by General P.S. Rybalko's 3d Guards Tank Army, General D.D. Lelyushenko's 4th Tank Army and a second Cavalry-Mechanized Group, commanded by General S.V. Sokolov, and consisting of 31st Tank and 6th Guards Cavalry Corps. 2d Air Army would support the two attacking forces.

Konev deployed General A.A. Grechko's 1st Guards Army and General E.P. Zhuravlev's 18th Army on the 220 kilometer front southward to the foothills of the Carpathian Mountains. He ordered Grechko to form a shock group of five rifle divisions, supported by 4th Guards Tank Corps, on his extreme right flank and use it to attack in coordination with the attack of 38th Army to cover the flank of the *front's* southern attack force and seize Galich on the Dnestr River. The remainder of 1st Guards Army and 18th Army were first to defend and then prepare for an advance toward Stanislov. The 1st Ukrainian Front's reserve consisted of 5th Guards Army, transferred from the 2d Ukrainian Front and 47th Rifle Corps detached from 1st Guards Army.

The most challenging task Konev faced was to carry out secretly the required massive regrouping of forces. In the north, 13th and 3d Guards Armies had to concentrate their forces into a narrow attack sector west of Lutsk. In the south both 60th and 1st Guards Armies also had to concentrate, and 38th Army had to move from the *front* left flank southwest of Stanislav 200 kilometers northward to the region west of Ternopol' to concentrate in a sector of 60th Army's front. *Front* mobile forces had to move considerable distances before they could deploy for the attack. 1st Guards Tank Army, located near Dubno, had to move over 500 kilometers while 4th Tank Army had to displace over 250 kilometers from the south. 3d Guards Tank Army, although already in the forward area, still had to move 60–70 kilometers into new assembly areas.[118] This regrouping involved movement of 1300 tanks/self-propelled guns, 1910 guns and mortars, and 7200 vehicles. The total number of regrouped units amounted to 37 rifle divisions, 32 tank and mechanized brigades, and 87 artillery regiments.[119]

To conceal this regroupment and mask his offensive preparations, Konev developed a *front maskirovka* plan which simulated the concentration of two tank armies and one tank corps on the *front* left flank, in 1st Guards and 18th Army's sectors (see Appendix 3 and maps 135 and 136). The plan was developed by the *front* staff and the *front* Chief of Engineers and was approved by the *front* council.[120]

The plan required that *maskirovka* measures be used during the period 2–20 July "to create in the enemy the impression of a long presence of 1st Guards Tank Army and 4th Tank Army on the Stanislov direction, at the same time that the armies were actually regrouping to the L'vov and Rava–Russkaya directions."[121] By using radio deception and other *maskirovka* measures the Soviets hoped to simulate deployment of 1st Guards Tank Army and one tank corps into 1st Guards Army's sector and 4th Tank Army into 18th Army's sector. To assist Konev, Rokossovsky's 1st Belorussian Front was to conduct an operation from 6 to 10 July in the Kovel' sector to distract the Germans from Konev's preparations.[122]

1st Guards and 18th Armies each formed an operational group, under the army's chiefs of staff, consisting of a representative from each branch of forces and the army political department, to implement the *maskirovka* plan. Each army assigned forces to carry out specific deception measures required by the plan.

Grechko of 1st Guards Army created a false concentration area for 1st Guards Tank Army in the Chertkov, Bazar, and Tluste region east of Stanislov and north of the Dnestr River, and a false tank corps assembly area near Tyshkovtsy, south of the Dnestr River (see Appendix 4). The former region coincided with the real assembly area of the reserve 47th Rifle Corps which helped animate the simulation. 1st Guards Army prepared a detailed plan which included the following *front* order:

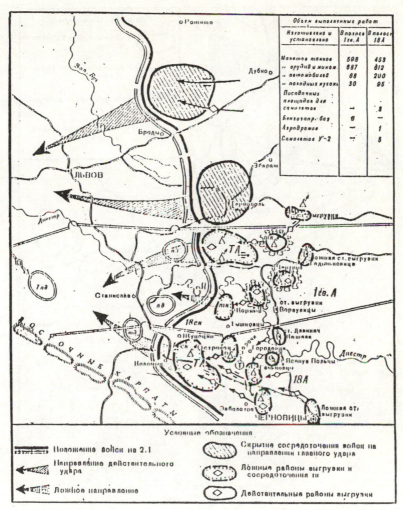

135. L'vov–Sandomierz, Soviet deception plan, 1st Guards and
    18th Armies' sectors

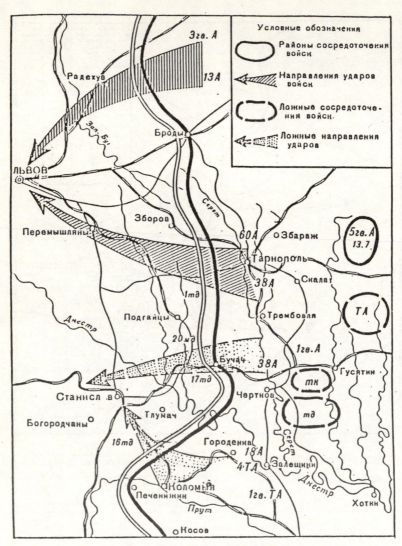

7. Замысел оперативной маскировки войск 1-го Украинского фропта
(2—20 июля 1944 г.)

136. L'vov–Sandomierz, Soviet deception plan

1. In the region of Gadyn'kovtse Station create a false tank army unloading region. The simulation will be conducted from 3 to 10 July 1944. The actual region for unloading – Vorvulints Station.
2. From the unloading region create the outward appearance of the movement of tank columns to concentration areas; assemble the dummy tank corps in the regions: the forest east of Byaly Popot; the forest east of Yagel'notsy; the forest of Chagor; Mikhal'che, Repuzhinitsy.
3. From 17 to 20 July simulate the moving up of forces into jumping-off positions; for the tank army – Slobudka Dzhurayns'ka, Polovtse; for the tank corps – Voronov Gavrilyak. Prepare a false blow of the tank army toward Buchach from the Slobudka Dzhurayns'ka and Polovtse region; and of the tank corps – in the direction of Klumach.[123]

Grechko assigned engineers, transport units, and line units to carry out tasks required by the plan. The sapper battalions built and emplaced simulations; the rifle and artillery units animated the false concentration area; the tanks and tractors prepared tracks and produced noise in the false concentration areas and near the front; and, on occasion, fired on enemy positions. The anti-aircraft units organized air cover over the deception.

Radio deception measures, developed and supervised by the *front* chief of communications, included the establishment of false radio nets and misleading radio traffic during loading and concentration. Before 8 July the dummy stations were located near the railroad unloading stations. Thereafter, they displaced forward to concentration areas.

The operational group responsible for the deception operation appointed a single officer to direct efforts in each false concentration area, and it coordinated the work of all forces involved in the operation. Specially designated signal officers supervised communications deception. Prior to 16 July these forces assembled 154 prefabricated dummy tanks, built 299 tanks and 568 guns from local materials, and emplaced 68 vehicles, 30 field kitchens, and six fuel supply points, while rifle units provided security for the area.[124]

From 17 to 19 July a portion of these simulations were transported at night to the jumping-off positions near the front (a total of 145 dummy tanks and 179 dummy guns). Chemical defense units masked the area with smoke to conceal it from German aerial reconnaissance. Simultaneously, infantry and vehicles simulated heavy movement into the forward area by marching forward during the day, returning at night, and again moving forward the following morning. Tanks, scattered along the road and in the jumping-off positions, were moved only during the daylight hours. Groups of staff officers accompanied the tanks and infantry, arranged for billeting along the way, and conducted personal reconnaissance in the forward area.

As a final step, the army staff organized and conducted extensive combat reconnaissance throughout the forward area adjacent to the dummy concentration while sappers cleared lanes through mine-fields. The Germans responded to these measures by intensifying aerial reconnaissance after 12 July and then by bombing the false concentration areas. The Soviets claim:

> Prior to 16 July the enemy did not alter his entire grouping of forces in the 1st Guards Army's sector, although already by 5 July a considerable part of our forces had castled [moved laterally] from the left flank to the right.[125]

18th Army developed a similar *maskirovka* plan to simulate the concentration of 4th Tank Army in its sector (see Appendix 5).[126] From 4 to 20 July the army chief of staff, assisted by an operational group of his deputy for operations and eight officers, simulated concentration of the tank army in the Ostrovets, Zabolotov, and Gan'kovtsy sector. On 5 July the operational group began work in the Soroki area, the simulated headquarters of the tank army, and established the radio net for the army. Army and *front* units assigned to the operational group prepared and animated simulations which extended from the concentration area forward into jumping-off positions. Trains were used to simulate transport and unloading operations while dummy tanks added realism to the simulation. Rifle forces provided security for the operation while the equipment created sounds, laid tracks and simulated activity throughout the unloading area and various concentration areas.

From 4 to 15 July 23 trains unloaded 468 mock-up tanks. The numbered codes of the trains and all communications matched those used for real tank armies. The tank corps moved to their false concentration areas consecutively (one from 4 to 9 July and one from 9 to 15 July) guided by special reconnaissance parties of officers and traffic controllers who arranged for detours and deliberately spoke to the local population about the movement. The self-propelled guns and tank destroyers "animated" the movement during daylight, and the Soviets arranged for placement of damaged vehicles at appropriate points along the route. These units returned to the railhead at night under real *maskirovka* procedures only to begin the process anew each day. Teams of troops deployed along the route with flashlights to violate light discipline of fake units moving forward, and these units used loudspeakers to enhance movement noise.[127]

The 18th Army commander established 10 false brigade and corps regions in the tank army assembly area to simulate concentration of six tank brigades, a heavy tank regiment, two self-propelled artillery regiments, 14 artillery regiments, eight tank destroyer regiments, three anti-aircraft regiments, three U-2 aircraft landing strips, and a support airfield. In these regions engineer units built 453 tank and self-propelled artillery pieces, 612 guns of all types, 200 vehicles, 95 field kitchens, and six U-2 aircraft.[128]

Radio deception was an especially complicated task. The Soviets used new radio sets to simulate tank army communications at Soroki and tied them in with tank corps radio nets operating out of Dzurkiv and Kobylets. Radio stations first established communication on 8 July with radio checks. From 9 to 11 July they avoided transmissions, and then, after 13 July, they resumed transmissions. On 18 July, when simulated concentrations were complete, the radio stations moved forward and made random transmissions using the tank armies' real codes. Radio stations used normal procedures and changed call signs and passwords every 24 hours. Frequencies were changed twice during the period of the simulation.[129]

In conjunction with the simulated movement and concentration of the tank armies, 18th Army prepared for the offensive by conducting reconnaissance in the 226th, 24th, and 271st Rifle Divisions sectors, and by launching a limited attack on 13 July with the 226th and 24th Rifle Divisions in cooperation with the 161st Rifle Division of 1st Guards Army. On 18 July the concentration simulation ended, and the following two nights 18th Army simulated forward movement of units into jumping-off positions again extensively using mock-up tanks and guns.[130]

While the active disinformation plan unfolded, front line units secretly regrouped, and the tank armies deployed into their assigned concentration areas. Of the redeploying rifle armies 38th Army had the most complicated task. It had to regroup 200 kilometers from southwest of Stanislav northward across the Dnestr River to just west of Ternopol', where it was to occupy a new sector on the left flank of concentrated 60th Army.[131] Moskalenko and his staff prepared a movement plan and a *maskirovka* plan to conceal the movement. The plan required organized night movement along roads and bridges prepared by army engineers. Heavy equipment was transported by rail. Between 23 and 27 June 38th Army turned its sector over to 1st Guards Army's 18th Guards Rifle Corps, and on 28 June it crossed the Dnestr River and headed north. Moskalenko gave high marks to the move, writing:

> 38th Army up to 7 July was already located in its new sector, but the enemy only on the following day discovered its departure from its former positions.[132]

Moskalenko, however, qualified the success of the whole regrouping effort to the Rava–Russkaya and L'vov regions adding:

> All of the large force movements along the front and their concentration in specified sectors was not concealed from his [enemy] attention. This permitted the enemy command to conclude that the offensive of our forces was soon to occur and to undertake additional counter-measures.[133]

Soviet rifle forces on the Rava–Russkaya direction also conducted large scale regroupings involving the concentration of Lt. Gen. V.N. Gordov's 3d Guards and Lt. Gen. N.P. Pukhov's 13th Army into a very narrow attack sector. 3d Guards Army had to concentrate its 76th, 21st, and 22d Rifle Corps (nine rifle divisions) in an 8 kilometer sector on the army left flank, and 13th Army had to concentrate its 24th and 27th Rifle Corps in a 5 kilometer sector on its right flank. Gordov left one rifle corps (three divisions) to cover the remaining 62 kilometers of his army's front and Pukhov's 102d Rifle Corps deployed along the remaining 66 kilometers of his front. During this regrouping more than 10 divisions had to move up to 70 kilometers into their new positions.[134]

Gordov's *maskirovka* plan concealed the regrouping and hid the actual army main attack sector by simulating preparations for an attack in the Vladimir–Volynsk sector on his right flank. At the end of June and in early July, elements of the 218th Rifle Division and 150th Tank Brigade

> conducted demonstrative movements. In daylight columns moved without *maskirovka* measures and at night tanks and vehicles moved with glaring headlights. In the false position (northeast of Torchin) mock-ups of tanks, guns, and other material were placed in position. Enemy aircraft repeatedly bombed the region .... As a whole the operational *maskirovka* measures attracted the attention of the fascist command to the

secondary direction and forced them to take forces from the Torchin salient.[135]

In addition, the combat which commenced on 6 July, further north, in the Kovel' sector also distracted German attention. 13th Army's regrouping was even more difficult because six of its divisions had to concentrate on the army right flank in the same region in which 1st Guards Tank Army had been ordered to assemble, a swampy area on the west bank of the Styr' River.[136]

Meanwhile, Konev's tank armies carried out an extensive, difficult, and critical regrouping. If the Soviet simulation of tank army assembly areas to the south was to be effective, the actual movement of the armies had to be accomplished with the greatest care. 3d Guards Tank Army had the easiest task, for it was already located in the Ternopol' region, only 60–70 kilometers from its concentration areas. The Germans were already well aware of its presence. Late on 2 July the army moved north to its new assembly area 10–12 kilometers from the front, and by 10 July its attack preparations were complete.[137] German intelligence maps indicate failure to detect the relatively short regrouping.

4th Tank Army had a more difficult regrouping. After the April fighting, 4th Tank Army had left its 10th Guards Tank Corps south of the Dnestr River near Kolomyya in support of 18th Army as a deception measure, while the remainder of the army had moved north to positions east of Ternopol'. 4th Tank Army reached its new assembly areas between 25 and 29 June and soon brought 10th Guards Tank Corps up from the south.[138] *Maskirovka* measures did not conceal the presence of part of 4th Tank Army in the Ternopol' area, but German intelligence continued to identify 10th Guards Tank Corps in the region south of the Dnestr on the Stanislov direction until after the Soviet offensive had begun.

The most extensive regrouping was that of 1st Guards Tank Army, which had to move over 300 kilometers from the region northwest of Dubno to its new assembly areas on the *front's* left flank. Army personnel traveled on trucks, and the army's tanks, SP guns, tractors, and heavy equipment traveled by rail. The army left Dubno on the evening of 24 June under stringent *maskirovka* conditions described as follows:

> regrouping occurred under the strictest observance of *maskirovka* measures. Auto transport moved only at night or in limited visibility. The army extensively used forest masses for daytime stops. Combat equipment, following by rail, was

concealed by covers, tarpaulins, and camouflage nets. The numbers of all vehicles were altered, and the signs of 1st Guards Tank Army – the rhombus on tank turrets and on the vehicle bodies – were painted over. All personnel were forbidden to wear tanker helmets and emblems. Radio stations observed silence.[139]

1st Guards Tank Army closed into new assembly areas 80–120 kilometers from the front by the evening of 29 June. There the army made preparations for its final move to combat concentration areas south of Lutsk, only 15 kilometers from the front. The Army completed that leg of the regrouping on the nights of 10–12 July.

Konev completed his extensive regrouping on schedule. More important, his, and others' *maskirovka* plans at the operational and tactical level achieved considerable success, in particular in the north. Konev later noted:

> Unfortunately, we did not fully succeed in deceiving the enemy, in spite of our *maskirovka* measures. However, the regrouping of 1st Guards Tank Army into the region south of Lutsk and 4th Tank Army into the Ternopol' region remained a secret, and that was very important for the operation.[140]

The imitative concentration of two tank armies on the Stanislov direction attracted the Germans' attention, but did not fully conceal the concentration east of L'vov (see maps 137 and 138). According to one Soviet critic:

> The reason for this was that the enemy consistently showed a preference for the L'vov direction, in as much as a thrust by Soviet forces on the Stanislov direction led to the Carpathians and could not be further developed. A thrust in the L'vov direction provided a possibility to develop the offensive in the depths.[141]

Nevertheless, the deception forced the Germans to strengthen their defenses opposite 18th Army's sector by dispatching to that area from reserve the Hungarian 2d Panzer and 7th Infantry Divisions, which remained there until after the Soviet attack on the L'vov direction.

In the L'vov sector, Konev blamed rear service units for giving away the concentration. In particular, he noted the conversation of German reconnaissance pilots who continually cited the northern drift of Soviet forces toward Ternopol'.[142] Konev, in his critique, went on to say:

> German reconnaissance revealed the positioning and com- position of the combined arms armies operating in the first line, the place of concentration of 1st and 6th Guards Cavalry Corps, 25th and 31st Tank Corps, and 3d Guards Tank Army. Regarding the regrouping of 38th Army, it was also discovered by German reconnaissance, but somewhat late. That army, in relation to the organization of regrouping, was one of the best. The enemy detected the initial departure of 38th Army forces on 8 July, and on only 12 July German intelligence discovered the 305th and 121st Rifle Divisions in the offensive sector of the army west of Ternopol'. At that time German intelligence did not succeed in discovering the regrouping of 11th Guards Tank Corps of 1st Guards Tank Army and 10th Guards Tank Corps of 4th Tank Army. 10th Guards Tank Corps, as a whole, could be called one of the best in all respects, including the questions of organized fulfillment of the march, discipline and the conduct of battle. The German command considered that that corps on 13 July still continued to remain in the Kolomyya region, while already on 7 July it was located in the new concentration area.[143]

German intelligence identified both 10th Guards Tank Corps and 1st Guards Tank Army in the region south of the Dnestr River on the Stanislov direction until after 10 July and did not note their presence elsewhere until well after the attack on L'vov had begun (see maps 139 and 140). German intelligence similarly missed the regrouping of 38th Army and the full concentration of 60th Army forces. It also did not identify the presence of 5th Guards Army, which was carried on German Eighth Army intelligence maps into mid-July.

The secret deployment of 1st Guards Tank Army to the north was extremely successful. The Germans finally detected the presence of 1st Guards Tank Army on the Rava–Russkaya direction several days after the operation had begun.

The Germans did detect some activity associated with the regroupment of 13th and 3d Guards Armies in the Rava–Russkaya sector, but they interpreted this activity as a part of Soviet activity in the Kovel' sector further north. A Soviet critique noted:

> Although the enemy in the course of 10–12 July succeeded in discovering concentrations of our artillery in the Oshcheva

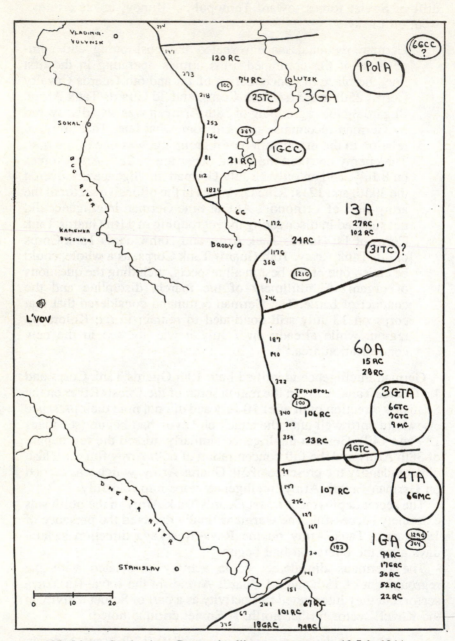

137. L'vov–Sandomierz, German intelligence assessment, 12 July 1944

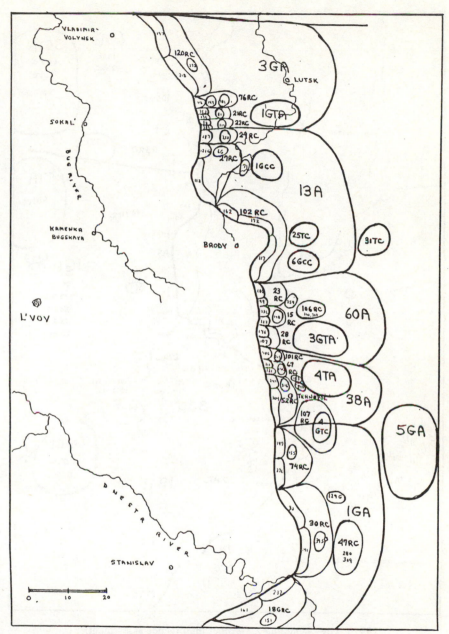

138. L'vov–Sandomierz, Soviet dispositions, 12 July 1944

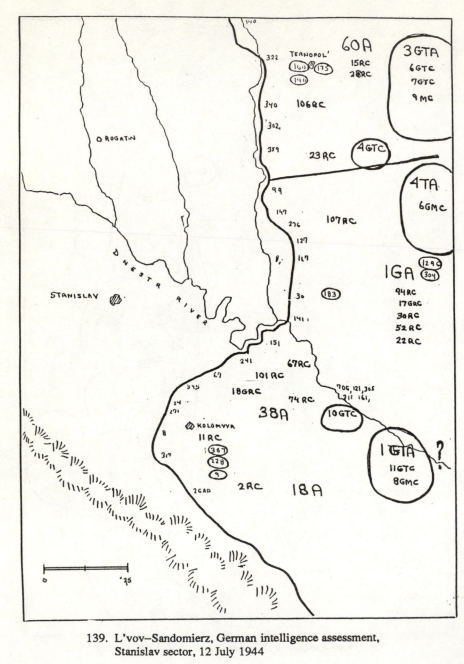

139. L'vov–Sandomierz, German intelligence assessment,
Stanislav sector, 12 July 1944

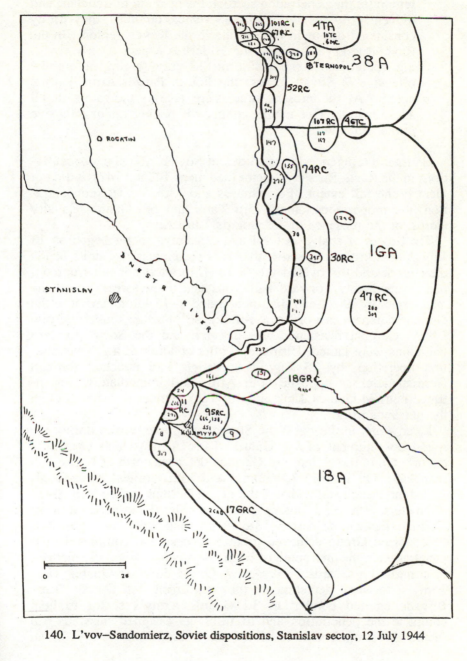

140. L'vov–Sandomierz, Soviet dispositions, Stanislav sector, 12 July 1944

region [in the penetration sector], the opening of trenches, and movement of separate tank and vehicle columns, they firmly considered our main force to be in the Kovel' region. On the Rava–Russkaya direction the Hitlerites expected only covering operations. As a result on 12 July (a day before the offensive of Soviet forces) the Fourth Panzer Army journal noted, "At the present time there are no indicators at all attesting to the fact that the enemy will begin a major offensive in the near future."[144]

German intelligence failed to detect Soviet offensive concentrations in the Rava–Russkaya sector (see maps 141 and 142). It did not identify the full extent of 3d Guards and 13th Armies' concentration, the proper location of 25th Tank and 6th Guards Cavalry Corps, or the presence of 1st Guards Tank Army.

The Soviet offensive in the Rava–Russkaya sector began on 13 July, when 3d Guards and 13th Army reconnaissance units began their work and discovered the German forward positions unmanned. Immediately, forward battalions and main forces joined the attack and, by day's end, had penetrated 8–15 kilometers into the German defenses east of Rava–Russkaya.[145] Further south, opposite L'vov, German resistance was heavier, and the Soviet forward battalions were halted. Ultimately, after conduct of a full penetration operation, by 15 July, the Soviets had punched through German defenses opposite 60th Army and immediately concentrated both 3d Guards Tank and 4th Tank Armies to drive through the narrow corridor.

Meanwhile, in the north the Soviets used *maskirovka* during the initial commitment of 1st Guards Tank Army which ultimately contributed to the collapse of German defenses north of L'vov (see map 143). On 13 July 3d Guards and 13th Armies' main forces joined the assault and widened the gap in German defenses to 10–12 kilometers. While 3d Guards Army completed the penetration of German tactical defenses, 13th Army and Sokolov's Cavalry-Mechanized Group achieved greater success and completed their penetration in the area south of where Konev had originally planned to commit 1st Guards Tank Army. On 15 July 1st Guards Tank Army's forward detachment, the reinforced 1st Guards Tank Brigade entered combat in 3d Guards Army's sector to help complete the penetration and to fulfill its assigned mission – to secure the commitment of all of 1st Guards Tank Army for an advance on Porytsk (toward Vladimir–Volynsk).[146] German Army Group North Ukraine detected the move and recorded:

> Since the presence is established of 8th Gds Mech Corps and the 6th Motorized Rifle Regt in the penetration in the Porytsk sector one can assume that the enemy has committed to action in that sector 1st Tank Army in full complement, having received its deep operating mission.[147]

Konev allowed 1st Guards Tank Brigade to continue its attack toward Porytsk, but ordered the remainder of Katukov's tank army to advance through 13th Army's penetration to the south. Meanwhile German reserves, consisting of 16th and 17th Panzer Divisions moved north to block the anticipated Soviet advance to Porytsk. 1st Guards Tank Army began to shift its attack direction late on 16 July, its movements concealed by bad weather and poor visibility. The next morning Katukov's army thrust southwest through 13th Army positions into the German rear north of L'vov.

The subsequent development of the operation demonstrated the impact of 1st Guards Tank Army's success. Under pressure from the north, German resistance also broke east of L'vov, 3d Guards and 4th Tank Armies penetrated into the depths, bypassed L'vov and, together with 1st Guards Tank Army, began a race toward the Vistula River. Subsequently, on several occasions the Soviets used forward detachments to confuse the Germans regarding where Soviet thrusts were really aimed.

Judgements concerning the success of Soviet deception in the L'vov–Sandomierz operation must be made within the context of the strategic deception plan which emphasized concealing preparations for the Belorussian operation. According to that plan the Soviets intended to display offensive intent against German forces in southern Poland, intent also designed to help conceal offensive preparations in the Kovel' region. While the plan contributed to successful deception in Belorussia it made deception in southern Poland that much more difficult. Despite these difficulties, Konev orchestrated an ambitious operational *maskirovka* plan to confuse the Germans regarding the attack location. The geographical location and military significance of L'vov made it impossible to hide offensive intent in that sector. Yet Soviet deception on the Stanislov direction marginally assisted Soviet forces attacking toward L'vov by concealing the scale of the assault. Soviet deception in the north, on the Rava–Russkaya direction achieved

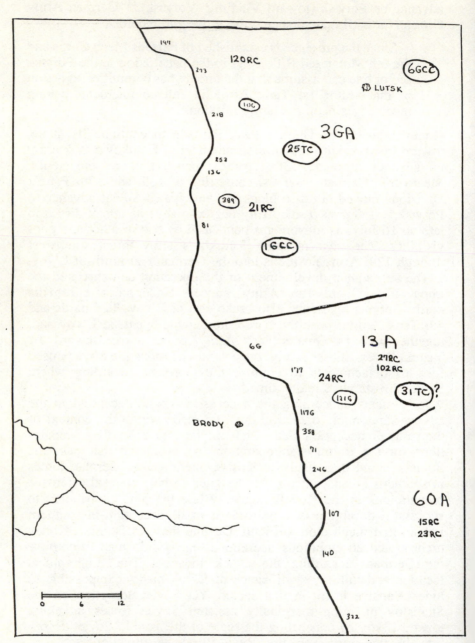

141. L'vov–Sandomierz, German intelligence assessment, Rava–Russkaya
     direction, 12 July 1944

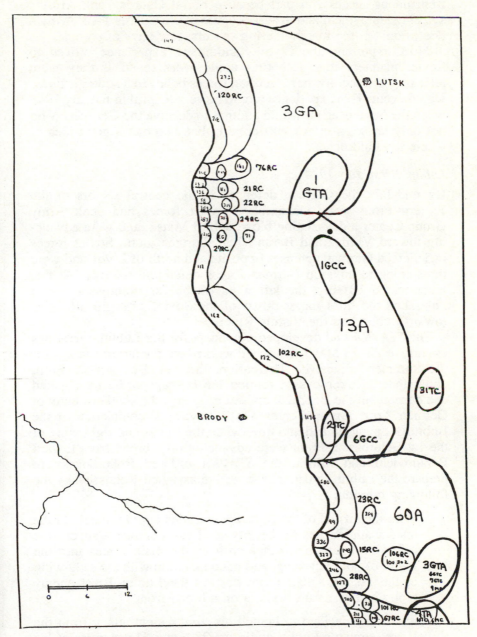

142. L'vov–Sandomierz, Soviet dispositions, Rava–Russkaya direction, 12 July 1944

tremendous success, in part because of 1st Guards Tank Army's secret redeployment and in part because of 1st Guards Tank Army's deception "on the march" during the first few days of combat.

Most important, the L'vov–Sandomierz experience proved to Soviet planners that deception could work, even if they were attacking in a sector where German forces believed a strategic thrust would occur. This experience would be very helpful in January 1945 when the Soviets again would attempt to deceive the Germans, who not only knew an attack was coming but also had a good idea of where it would occur.

Lublin–Brest, July 1944

By mid-July the German defenses in the central sectors of the Eastern Front were a shambles. Soviet forces had dealt Army Group Center a devastating blow, seized Minsk, and were advancing toward Vilnius and Baranovichi. Further south, Soviet forces had pierced German defenses opposite and north of L'vov and were threatening to envelop German forces defending the city. At this juncture, on 18 July, the left wing of the 1st Belorussian Front unleashed the third major thrust of the Soviet strategic offensive toward Lublin and the Vistula River.

The *STAVKA* had developed a concept for the Lublin operations as early as 22–23 May when it had worked out the larger concept for the summer offensive. Thereafter, the 1st Belorussian Front commander, Rokossovsky, refined the concept while he planned and carried out the Bobruisk operation against the southern flank of German Army Group Center. On 7 July, after completion of the Bobruisk operation and at a time when the center and right wing of the 1st Belorussian Front were advancing on a broad front toward Baranovichi and Minsk, the *STAVKA* ordered Rokossovsky to prepare the Lublin thrust. The directive assigned Rokossovsky the following mission:

> With the arrival of the right flank armies approximately to the distant approaches to the city of Brest, conduct a successive offensive operation with a shift of the main forces into the sector of your left wing, and in cooperation with the right wing of the 1st Ukrainian Front destroy the Lublin–Brest enemy group and reach the Vistula on a broad front.[148]

Rokossovsky decided to launch his *front's* main attack from the Kovel' area towards Lublin while the 28th and 61st Armies of his *front's* main force would advance on Brest, catch German forces

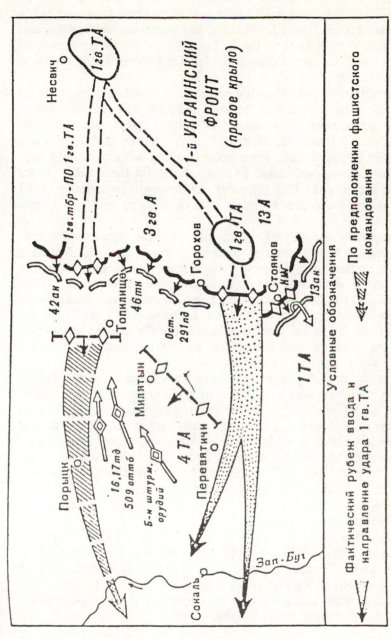

Схема № 1. Перенос рубежа ввода главных сил танковой армии (обстановка к исходу 16.7.1944 г.)

143. L'vov-Sandomierz, 1st Guards Tank Army deception

withdrawing from southern Belorussia in a pincer, and destroy them. Rokossovsky designated 69th and 47th Armies' sectors as his main attack sector. There he planned to concentrate 69th, 47th, and 8th Guards Army backed up by 2d Tank Army, 1st Polish Army, 2d and 7th Guards Cavalry Corps and 11th Tank Corps for an attack to begin on 18 July.

Organization of the offensive required a massive regrouping of forces within the left wing of the *front* and an equally massive influx of strategic reserves (see map 144). 8th Guards and 2d Tank Armies, plus 2d and 7th Guards Cavalry Corps and 11th Tank Corps, had to move from other sectors along with numerous supporting units previously used to support the 1st Belorussian Front attack in Belorussia. This required the strategic regrouping of 13 rifle divisions, three tank corps, two cavalry corps, and 18 artillery regiments.[149]

Rokossovsky's *maskirovka* plan relied on the operational situation to the north and south to distract German attention from his offensive preparations. However, since most major reinforcements would have to move into the region before the 1st Ukrainian Front launched its 13 July attack, strict *maskirovka* procedures were necessary to conceal the deployments. Between 13 and 17 July, while Soviet forces on Rokossovsky's left flank were advancing toward the Western Bug River, his *maskirovka* task eased somewhat.

The major redeployment of forces into Rokossovsky's sector began in mid-June and continued to the very eve of the attack. Chuikov's 8th Guards Army was to occupy a first echelon position in the center of Rokossovsky's main attack sector between 47th and 69th Armies. On 5 June 5th Shock Army took over 8th Guards Army's sector of the 3d Ukrainian Front (opposite Rumania) and Chuikov's army moved into *front* reserve. While Chuikov dispatched his chief of staff to Moscow to receive his new orders, on 12 July he began moving his army on its long trek from the Rumanian border to the northern Ukraine.[150]

To keep his movements orderly, Chuikov created a special operational group under his deputy commander to plan and conduct the regrouping. Chuikov himself, his political officer, and chief of artillery traveled to Rokossovsky's headquarters to coordinate the move. Later, while reflecting on the regrouping in the circumstance of a rapidly shrinking front, Chuikov wrote:

Therefore each new offensive required of us increased

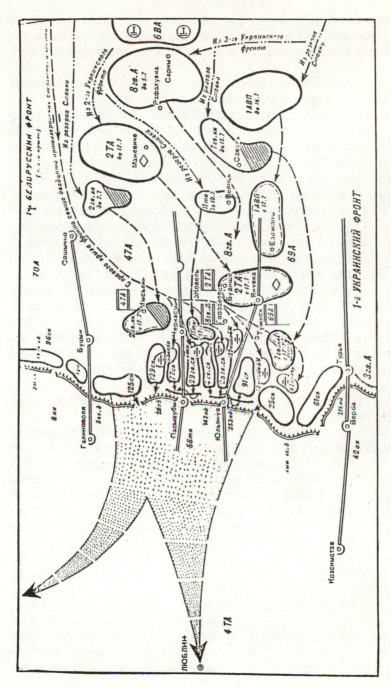

Создание ударной группировки при подготовке Люблинско-брестской наступательной операции

144. Lublin–Brest, Soviet regrouping

maneuverability and rapid and concealed concentration of considerably superior forces in one sector, so rapid that the enemy could not succeed in achieving a reciprocal maneuver.[151]

After 12 June Chuikov's army moved northward 800 kilometers and on 21 July began concentrating in its new positions near Sarny and Rafaluvka, 120 kilometers east of Kovel'. Although deep in the Soviet rear Chuikov ordered all units to observe strict *maskirovka* while unloading and moving to assembly areas. All movement was at night, under blackout conditions. The chief of the army rear and his staff supervised traffic control and unit *maskirovka*. Communications silence reigned throughout the entire assembly area.[152] After receiving precise attack orders on 9 July, Chuikov used the remaining eight days for offensive preparations and movement into forward positions between 69th and 47th Armies. Between 6 and 12 July, by night marches, 8th Guards Army moved into its forward assembly areas, and on the nights of 13 and 14 July took over the positions of the 125th and 91st Rifle Corps of 47th and 69th Armies. Simultaneously 47th and 69th Armies concentrated their forces on their left and right flanks respectively. The 11th Tank Corps, assigned to Chuikov's army, moved from *STAVKA* reserve and concentrated on 7 July just south of Kovel'.[153] On 8 July the corps participated in an attack by 47th Army toward Lyuboml' as a diversion for 1st Ukrainian Front's impending L'vov operation. Two days later the corps assembled west of Kovel' under control of 8th Guards Army.

Meanwhile, 2d Tank Army conducted an extensive regrouping after its diversionary battles along the Rumanian border in May and early June. On 12 June Bogdanov's army reverted to *STAVKA* reserve and from 15 June to 3 July moved over 650 kilometers from the Rumanian border to assembly areas near Manevichi, 50 kilometers north of Lutsk.[154] There it came under command of the 1st Belorussian Front, and for fourteen days prepared for the upcoming offensive while observing the provisions of Rokossovsky's *maskirovka* plan. 2d Tank Army and 2d and 7th Guards Cavalry Corps occupied their final jumping-off positions on the nights of 16 and 17 July.

In addition to 8th Guards and 2d Tank Armies, a huge mass of 1st Belorussian Front artillery regrouped from the *front* right flank to the left flank. The 4th Artillery Penetration Corps, the 4th Corps Artillery Brigade, the 122d and 124th High Powered Artillery Brigades and 20 more artillery divisions, brigades, and regiments moved from 450 to 650 kilometers.[155] To transport this force, Rokossovsky's rear service units employed 107 railroad trains (an average of seven trains per day for 15 days), which were assigned the task of moving the artillery as well as elements of 8th Guards, 2d Tank, and 1st Polish Armies.

As a result of this regrouping, Rokossovsky concentrated 8th Guards Army in a 9 kilometer penetration sector flanked on the left by 69th Army in a 30 kilometer sector and on the right by 47th Army in a 20 kilometer sector. Each flanking army in turn concentrated in 4–5 kilometer sectors adjacent to that of 8th Guards Army. 2d Guards Cavalry Corps, 11th Tank Corps, and 7th Guards Cavalry Corps deployed to the rear, each supporting one of the forward armies. Finally 2d Tank Army formed behind 8th Guards Army to complete the immense concentration of forces. On the *front's* extended 120 kilometer right flank, 70th Army deployed virtually all its forces in a 20 kilometer sector on the left center leaving weak forces covering the remaining 100 kilometers. In the 18 kilometer *front* penetration sector Rokossovsky concentrated 70 percent of his rifle forces, 80 percent of his artillery, and all of his armor.[156]

Rokossovsky's most imposing task was to conceal the deployment of his forces into the *front* penetration sector. His *maskirovka* plan and those of his armies contained the usual provisions for planning security, careful reconnaissance and traffic control over march routes, night movements, radio silence and radio deception, aerial verification of *maskirovka*, and air cover against German reconnaissance and air attack.[157] As an active diversionary measure, Rokossovsky ordered 70th Army to conduct an assault north of Kovel' on 17 July to draw off German reserves and distract German attention from the Kovel' area, a measure which caused the Germans to move elements of the 168th Infantry Division northward.

On 18 July Rokossovsky's main assault force, led by 8th Guards Army, which again used reconnaissance battalions to initiate its main attack (as at Krivoi Rog), struck at the German forces defending the Kovel' direction. Within hours the German tactical defenses had been ripped apart. On 20 July, while rifle forces approached the Western Bug River, 2d Tank Army moved forward and the next day began an operational exploitation which propelled it to the outskirts of Warsaw as 8th Guards Army was breaching the line of the Vistula River at Magnushev.

How well had Rokossovsky's *maskirovka* plan succeeded? German intelligence failed to detect the presence of 8th Guards

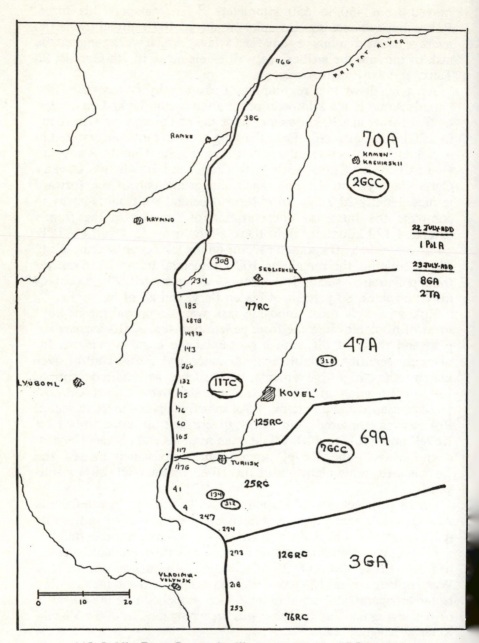

145. Lublin–Brest, German intelligence assessment, 17 July 1944

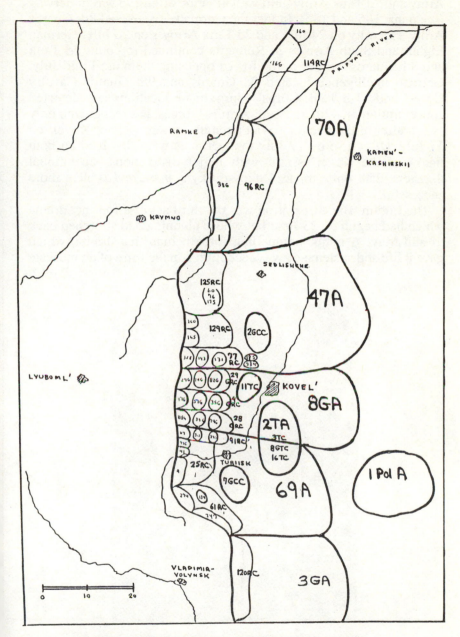

146. Lublin–Brest, Soviet dispositions, 17 July 1944

Army and 2d Tank Army until well after the offensive was underway (see maps 145 and 146). In fact the Germans discovered 8th Guards Army's identity on 24 July and 2d Tank Army's on 26 July. German Eighth and Sixth Armies in Rumania continued to count 2d Tank and 8th Guards Armies in the forces opposing them until mid-July. German intelligence located 2d Guards and 9th Guards Cavalry Corps' and 11th Tank Corps' approximate locations and detected concentration on 47th and 69th Armies' forces, but recognized only one quarter of the overall Soviet strength present west of Kovel' on 17 July. Of course by 17 July the Germans were involved on both flanks of the Kovel' sector with major distractions, operational disasters that only made Rokossovsky's *maskirovka* plan more successful.

The Lublin–Brest operation was the third act of a four act drama which had begun on 23 June but whose planning had stretched back to mid-May. A major compelling force behind that drama, which gave it life and sustenance was deception – in the form of an intricate

21. German prisoners from the Belorussian operation being paraded through Moscow, July, 1944

mosaic of operational and tactical measures unified and given meaning by firm strategic intent. The *STAVKA* strategic plan envisioned the delivery of powerful consecutive strategic blows which, taken together, would produce strategic collapse of German defenses from Vitebsk to the Carpathian Mountains. This had required the Soviets to shift massive strategic reserves from one sector to another, conceal these regroupings, and blur German appreciations concerning where attacks would occur, in what sequence, and in what strength. Obviously somewhere on the front operational and tactical simulations at one stage would become real offensives at another. Within this context German detection of offensive preparations at the operational and tactical level in some sectors were a small price to pay for Soviet achievement of strategic success overall. The Soviet strategic deception plan worked well, in particular in Belorussia and in the Kovel' sector. At L'vov German fixation on a probable Soviet offensive stubbornly remained and confounded part of Konev's deception planning but in doing so conditioned Soviet success in Belorussia. 1st Guards Tank Army's fortuitous secret attack at Rava–Russkaya moderated Konev's frustration over his failure to deceive at L'vov and ultimately rendered German defenses at L'vov untenable. While the Soviet strategic deception plan unfolded as planned, frustration compounded German defeat, for to an increasing extent the Germans realized that it was beyond their means to detect every diversion and simulation. And even if they could discern Soviet intentions, there was no guarantee they could counter the real Soviet assaults. In this depressed state, the German High Command tried to manage wholesale disaster as it waited for the next Soviet blow to land.

Yassy–Kishinev, August 1944

The five Soviet *fronts* which had smashed German strategic defenses between Vitebsk and the Carpathian Mountains, by early August struggled along an extended front from the Northern Dvina River to the upper Vistula River. The roster of cities reconquered by Soviet armies – Vitebsk, Mogilev, Bobruisk, Minsk, Vilnius, Grodno, Bialystok, Brest, Lublin, L'vov – provided mute testimony to the scale of the German disaster. By early August Soviet forces had thrust into Lithuania, crossed the Neiman River to the borders of eastern Prussia, and fought bitter battles for bridgeheads across the Narev and Vistula Rivers north and south of Warsaw.

As in 1943, as the main thrust grew in scale (see map 147), Soviet *fronts* on the flanks joined battle to capitalize on German losses on the main strategic direction. On the northern flank of the Belorussian operation the Baltic Fronts attacked in time-phased sequence from south to north to commence what has come to be called the Baltic strategic offensive. The first force to attack was the remainder of Bagramyan's 1st Baltic Front which went into action north of the Northern Dvina River on 4 July. In short order, Yeremenko's 2d Baltic Front (10 July) and Maslennikov's 3d Baltic Front joined battle as the three *fronts* drove toward the Baltic coast and Riga against heavy German resistance. This series of operations endured well into the fall – an unspectacular, slow, broad *front* advance measured in kilometers per week. Considered alongside the fighting in western Belorussia and in eastern Poland it provided sufficient distraction for the Germans regarding what was about to occur in the south.

In the south, along the Rumanian borders, the front had been relatively quiet since early May when the Germans had considered it

22. General I. Kh. Bagramyan, 1st Baltic Front commander, August, 1944

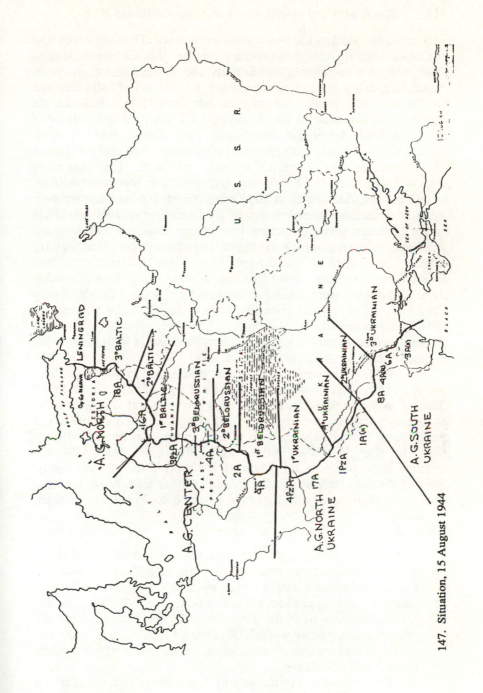

147. Situation, 15 August 1944

to be a prime location for a new major offensive. That offensive had not materialized. On the contrary, while the Germans waited expectantly for an attack, the Soviets had thinned out their front, dispatching army after army northward. By the end of July, German intelligence was finally aware that 5th Guards and 8th Guards Armies, and the bulk of the 2d and 3d Ukrainian Fronts armored force (2d Tank Army and 5th Guards Tank Army), had departed, leaving the two *fronts* with only one tank army (6th) and a depleted complement of rifle forces. Of course, by then the Germans were also well aware of the havoc wrought by these forces elsewhere, which, in turn, had forced Army Group South Ukraine to part with the bulk of its operational reserves. In the course of July, on OKH orders, the army group dispatched six panzer divisions, two infantry divisions, and two assault gun brigades northward to stiffen sagging defenses elsewhere on the Eastern Front. The German command, nevertheless, remained confident that Army Group South Ukraine could avoid a disaster similar to those which befell virtually every other German army group on the Eastern Front in the summer of 1944. Unknown to the Germans, however, the *STAVKA* had chosen German forces in Rumania as its final target in the fourth act of the summer strategic offensive drama.

Planning for the projected Soviet operation in Rumania had begun on 15 July 1944 when the Assistant Chief of the General Staff, General A.I. Antonov, directed Malinovsky and Tolbukhin to prepare concepts for the operation and bring them to Moscow at the end of July. On 31 July the two *front* commanders presented their plans to the *STAVKA*. After some discussion the *STAVKA* accepted their plans as the basis of a directive to the two *fronts*, ordering them to destroy enemy forces in the Yassy, Kishinev, and Bendery regions and subsequently advance to Fokshany, Galats, and Ismail.

Specifically, the *STAVKA* directed:

1. 2 Ukrainian Front to penetrate the enemy defense, by striking a blow with the forces of 27, 52, 53 Armies and 6 Tank Army in the general direction of Yassy, Vaslui, and Felchiul. In the first phase of the operation secure Bakeu, Vaslui, and Khushi, seize crossings over the Prut River in the Khushi, Felchiul sector and, together with 3 Ukrainian Front forces, crush the enemy Kishinev group, and do not permit their withdrawal to Byrlad and Fokshany.

   After destruction of the enemy Kishinev group, develop the

offensive in the general direction of Fokshany while securing the right flank of the shock group toward the Carpathians, south ot P'yatra. 5 Gds Cavalry Corps is to be used for forcing the Seret River and securing the right flank of the front from the west.

2. 3 Ukrainian Front to penetrate the enemy defense south of Bendery and strike a blow with the forces of 57, 37 and the right wing of 46 Army toward Opach, Selemet and Khushi, while firmly securing the front shock group from the south.

In the first phase of the operation, in cooperation with the 2 Ukrainian Front, crush the enemy Kishinev group and secure the line Leovo, Tarutino, and Moldavka. Subsequently, develop the offensive in the general direction of Reni and Ismail while not permitting the withdrawal of enemy forces across the Prut and Danube Rivers.[158]

The Black Sea Fleet was to cooperate with the 3d Ukrainian Front and conduct amphibious landings along the Rumanian Black Sea coast.

The *STAVKA* concept required the two *fronts* to conduct their main attacks in the most vulnerable enemy sectors: the 2d Ukrainian Front between the Tyrgu–Frumos and Yassy strongpoints of German Eighth Army, a region defended largely by Rumanian troops; and the 3d Ukrainian Front south of Bendery at the junction of German Sixth and Rumanian Third Armies.

Malinovsky planned to conduct his main attack with 27th and 52d Armies in an 18 kilometers sector backed up by 6th Tank Army and 18th Tank Corps. On the *front* right flank 7th Guards and 40th Armies would launch a secondary attack supported by a Cavalry-Mechanized Group consisting of 5th Guards Cavalry Corps and 23d Tank Corps. On the *front* left flank 4th Guards Army would concentrate east of the Prut River and, after the fall of Yassy, it would advance up the Prut to sever the communications between German Eighth and Sixth Armies. 4th Guards Army would leave only two divisions on its extended front east of the Prut River.[159] Thus Malinovsky would concentrate over 50 percent of his infantry, 85 percent of his artillery, and 76 percent of his armor in five percent of his 330 kilometer front.[160] 53d Army was in *front* second echelon and 27th and 57th Rifle Corps served as *front* reserves.

Tolbukhin planned his main attack in an 18 kilometer sector on the west bank of the Dnestr River using 57th, 37th, and half of 46th Armies backed up by 4th Guards and 7th Mechanized Corps. 5th

Shock Army would first simulate a main attack and then conduct a secondary attack on the *front* right flank toward Kishinev while the remainder of 46th Army on the *front* left flank would cooperate with the Black Sea Fleet in encircling and destroying Rumanian Third Army. Tolbukhin's plan required concentration of 80 percent of his infantry, 97 percent of his artillery, and all of his armor in seven percent (less than 40 kilometers) of his *front's* sector. By virtue of this concentration, an overall Soviet superiority of 2:1 became 8:1 in the main attack sectors.[161]

Massive regrouping, most of which was internal, was necessary to create these dense force concentrations, for the *STAVKA* had few reserves available for use in the operation. During the 17 days of regrouping the two *fronts* had to redeploy 45 rifle divisions (86 percent of the total), 15 tank and mechanized brigades (100 percent of the total), and 96 artillery regiments (85 percent of the total) a distance of from 20 to 110 kilometers.[162] Regrouping was of varied nature and:

> included displacement of forces and equipment from the flanks to the center of the front where they could deliver the main attack. Armies and corps, moved out of the second echelon or *front* reserve in the process of regrouping, shifted to new regions; divisions and corps transferred from one army to another; and within the armies, forces regrouped into the penetration sectors.[163]

When the boundary between 2d and 3d Ukrainian Front was shifted westward, 53d Army, located on the left flank of the 2d Ukrainian Front, was withdrawn from forward positions and concentrated in second echelon behind 52d Army. 7th Mechanized Corps, located in 4th Guards Army sector (2d Ukrainian Front), was assigned to 3d Ukrainian Front and moved into 37th Army's sector. In 3d Ukrainian Front's sector, 5th Shock Army replaced 57th Army in the sector from Speya to Bendery and received from the 2d Ukrainian Front 26th Guards Rifle Corps deployed on a broad front from Bravechiny to Dubossary. 57th Army then shifted to a sector south of Bendery where it replaced 37th Army forces, which in turn concentrated in a 9–10 kilometer sector on its south flank. 46th Army moved its 31st Guards Rifle Corps from second echelon and concentrated it and 37th Rifle Corps on the army's right flank. 4th Guards Mechanized Corps, located 80 kilometers from the front, moved by 0300 20 August to positions in the rear of 37th Army.[164] While the *fronts* regrouped between 10 and 19 August, the armies regrouped and occupied their jumping-off positions in one night – the evening of 17 August.[165] To conceal all of this movement required complex *maskirovka* measures.

Both Malinovsky and Tolbukhin developed complex *front maskirovka* plans, which included active and passive measures to conceal regrouping and confuse the Germans regarding Soviet attack intentions and locations (see map 148).[166] To assist in this work, the *STAVKA* assigned an average of 18 engineer companies to each 3d Ukrainian Front army and 10 to each army of the 2d Ukrainian Front.[167] The 2d Ukrainian Front's *maskirovka* plan focused on concealing offensive preparations in the center by creating false concentrations on the left and right flanks. In 7th Guards Army's sector north of Roshan, where the front was severed by a main road and rail line, Malinovsky simulated a heavy troop concentration using 60 dummy tanks and 400 mock-up guns to animate the concentration. On 7th Guards Army's right flank, in 40th Army's sector, the Soviets simulated artillery fire with exploding smokepots and intensified vehicle movement by moving vehicles with headlights on toward the front. In 7th Guards Army's rear area false fuel and repair stations functioned, and radio stations conducted false communications and radio checks.[168]

On 2d Ukrainian Front's left flank, in 4th Guards Army's sector, Malinovsky created another false concentration area near Telenesht and Pepen' where the Soviets emplaced 120 mock-up tanks. On the nights of 13–14 August the Soviets simulated vehicle movement, and the 25th Maskirovka Company and 14th Assault Engineer Brigade set up 350 mock-up tanks and about 1000 simulated guns and mortars (this region was 60–100 kilometers forward of 6th Tank Army's original assembly areas).[169] 6th Tank Army, located 70 kilometers northeast of its final assembly area, also built mock-up tanks (150) in its old concentration area before moving to its new assembly area on the evening of 16 and 17 August.[170] 7th Mechanized Corps, after its transfer to 3d Ukrainian Front, also left mock-up tanks in its old positions.

In the 2d Ukrainian *front* main attack sector of 52d and 27th Armies, where the terrain was fairly open, engineer units constructed physical covers to conceal road movement. Over a five day period, in the 20 kilometer sector, sappers built 125 linear kilometers of vertical masking and 250,000 square meters of horizontal masking to cover an area of 90,000 square meters.[171] To facilitate secret movements, engineers implaced underwater bridges across the Seret and Prut Rivers which Malinovsky later declared: "The

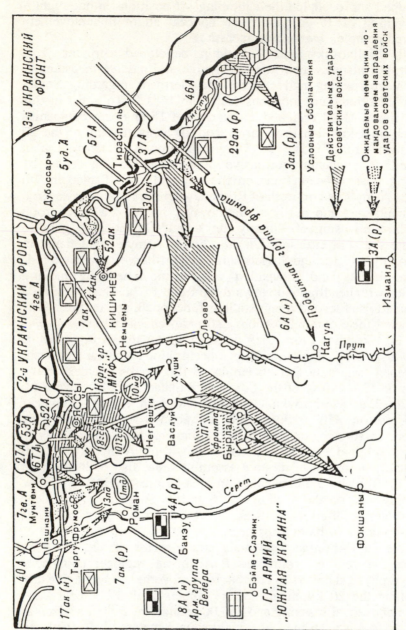

8. Ясско-Кишиневская операция (август 1944 г.)

148. Yassy–Kishinev, Soviet deception plan

enemy did not discover."[172] All units moved only at night under blackout conditions supervised by traffic regulators functioning under *front* and army staff supervision. Staff officers used aircraft to check the efficiency of *maskirovka* measures and made adjustments when necessary.

When assessing the effectiveness of 2d Ukrainian Front *maskirovka* measures the Soviets note that the Germans bombed secondary regions but not the main attack sector until the evening of the 19th when they finally detected preparations and sent 100 planes on bombing missions against the rear area of 52d Army.[173] By this time, however, it was too late to make any adjustments in their defensive posture.

Tolbukhin's *maskirovka* task was more difficult, for his forces were to attack from restricted bridgeheads on the west bank of the Dnestr River south of Bendery. Experience had shown that such bridgeheads naturally attracted both enemy attention and enemy reserves and seldom did *maskirovka* plans succeed. Nevertheless, Tolbukhin and his staff devised a plan incorporating both active and passive measures. The active measures included creation of simulated concentrations and attack preparations in 5th Shock Army's sector on the *front* right flank on the secondary *front* attack direction toward Kishinev. Specifically, Tolbukhin attempted to simulate assembly of a rifle corps, a mechanized corps, and an artillery penetration division in Karmanova, Rimerovka, Grigoriopol', and Tashlyk.[174]

Extensive sapper work in the false concentration areas resulted in construction of 5305 physical camouflage covers of various sorts, 104 warehouses, and 514 mock-up tanks, guns, mortars, and vehicles.[175] Extensive vehicular traffic between the real and the simulated concentration area during the daytime and at night deliberately observed poor *maskirovka* discipline. The units then returned at night observing proper *maskirovka* procedures. A reserve rifle regiment, an engineer brigade, and two engineer construction battalions remained in the false concentration area to help construct decoys and animate the area. False radio nets contributed to the ruse. The *front* also extensively used smoke generators to simulate attack preparations in 5th Shock Army's sector and to conceal construction of bridges across the Dnestr River in 46th Army's sector.

Since the deception in 5th Shock Army's sector was particularly important, the army commander, General N.E. Berzarin, developed a thorough *maskirovka* plan. The plan simulated a false *front* main attack and, after the offensive had begun elsewhere, covered the real army attack.[176] On 18 August, two days before the date of the offensive, 5th Shock Army conducted heavy artillery fire on German positions and intensified preparations for an infantry and tank attack. As a result, prior to 20 August, German Sixth Army did not transfer a single unit from its sector opposite 5th Shock Army to the real Soviet attack sector south of Bendery.

Tolbukhin surrounded all planning and deception with strict secrecy. He assigned false unit designations to all regrouping units, established special communications codes, shifted radio stations on a daily basis, and restricted contact of military units with the civilian population. Special groups of officers deliberately spread false rumors to reinforce the deception plan.[177]

The Black Sea Fleet and Danube Flotilla, in cooperation with 46th Army, also developed a deception plan. Naval forces planned conduct of amphibious operations across the mouth of the Dnestr River and then operations to secure positions around the mouth of the Danube River. To conceal the real location of the amphibious assaults, the Black Sea Fleet prepared simulated amphibious operations across the lower Dnestr with elements of 1st Guards Fortified Region.[178]

To conceal the actual amphibious operation the task force commander planned no artillery preparation. Instead, the landing force commander would call for fires when they were required. The first echelon of the amphibious forces, led by assault groups and accompanied by sappers, would land from rowboats and assault boats. Fifteen to twenty minutes later the follow-on echelon would land in powerboats towing anti-tank artillery and mortars. Heavy equipment would follow on larger ships after the bridgehead had been established. Throughout the operation Black Sea Fleet ships and aviation would distract German attention with naval bombardment and air attacks on German and Rumanian shore installations at Constanza and elsewhere along the coast.[179]

In the 3d Ukrainian Front's main attack sector, Tolbukhin's *maskirovka* plan and those of 37th and 57th Armies forbade any movement on main roads from Tiraspol' across the Dnestr River and into the bridgehead. All movement occurred off the roads under stringent control and verification by the army staff. In jumping-off positions deploying troops entered a dense complex of dugouts and field and communication trenches which provided cover from observation or attack (19 kilometers of trench per kilometer of front).[180] Units used bridges across the Dnestr only at night; and, by day, the bridges were taken down and concealed. All movement into the bridgehead and into attack position was timed to occur secretly at night under direct supervision by the traffic control (commandant's) service. The *front* chief of staff, General S.S. Biryuzov, later recorded:

> All was accomplished very subtly .... We were able to confirm that the operational maskirovka measures fully justified themselves. The enemy continued to expect the main attack on the Kishinev direction, not only at the moment his defense was being penetrated, but even on the second day of our offensive .... Only at the end of the second day of heavy battle did the enemy understand the whole tragedy of his situation.[181]

The Soviets cite German documents to corroborate Biryuzov's judgement. The Sixth Army war diary on 7 July noted, "The summer offensive of the Red Army against Army Group 'Center' and the concentration of enemy forces against Army Group 'Northern Ukraine' ... confirms that the enemy has postponed his planned offensive in the Balkans."[182]

German intelligence records and maps attest to the effectiveness of Soviet *maskirovka* prior to the Yassy–Kishinev operation. On 4 August 1944 a Foreign Armies East assessment lamented the deterioration of intelligence and provided as a reason Soviet use of radio silence, the fast-moving nature of military operations, and shortages of reconnaissance aircraft, all of which restricted German abilities to look deep. The same assessment recognized Soviet emphasis on the central position of the front but relegated the southern sector to secondary status, stating, "The situation opposite AG 'Sud Ukraine' makes a larger enemy attack operation unlikely for the near future .... The offensive against Rumania, however, even today plays an undoubtedly important role in Soviet intentions."[183] The report added parenthetically, "Local attacks are always possible."

On 15 August Foreign Armies East reiterated their earlier view, writing:

> The development of the enemy situation opposite AG 'Sud Ukraine' since the beginning of the summer operations has been marked by the withdrawal of enemy forces in strength for employment against the Army Groups 'Nord Ukraine' and 'Centre' (overall, 2–3 tank armies, 8–10 mobile corps, 3 inf

armies, 28 rifle divisions). It cannot be determined clearly if this shifting of forces is still going on, but …. it seems probable. An attack operation of larger size with far-reaching objectives against AG 'Sud Ukraine' appears therefore to be unlikely.[184]

The Germans, however, were realistic enough to realize the effect of these transfers, and operations to the north on German forces in Rumania, stating:

> The adversary will have recognized that the German forces withdrawn from Rumania have essentially contributed in stabilizing the fronts of Army Groups 'Nord Ukraine' and 'Centre.' The enemy must be interested, therefore, in preventing the withdrawal of further German forces. According to air reconnaissance it seems probable that attack forces are being formed with 2nd as well as 3rd Ukrainian Fronts south of Tiraspol' and north of Jassy. Both groups could be engaged on short notice.[185]

German intelligence began picking up movement in the Soviet rear, in particular in the Tiraspol' area and north of Yassy, on 16 August but stuck to the prediction of only local attacks. The next day, however, their concern began to increase as they recorded:

> The reinforcements by night … have increased in the area of Yassy. One has therefore to anticipate strong attacks, which will have more than local importance.[186]

On 18 August German intelligence noted augmentation of artillery units and counted 190 tanks north of Yassy, noted as probably from 18th Tank Corps. Only on 19 August did German intelligence recognize the likelihood of assaults in the area south of Tiraspol', "but Fremde Herre Ost refused to assess the enemy objectives …. They did not feel they had enough information." Instead they noted intensified rail activity and night traffic between the Prut and Seret Rivers, and regrouping of 5th Air Army west of the Prut. The big question remained, "Where are the tanks?"[187]

German intelligence maps on 20 August, the day of the attack, recognized some Soviet concentration north of Yassy and south of Tiraspol' (see maps 149 and 150). They did not, however, record the concentration of 52d Army west of the Prut River or 53d Army's westward move into second echelon behind 27th Army. Nor did German intelligence realize that 6th Tank Army had deployed forward from positions far to the rear around Bel'tsy. Thus, on the Yassy approaches, German intelligence underassessed the threat by about 40 percent (see maps 151 and 152). In the Tiraspol' area the Germans detected concentration of 37th and part of 57th Army south of Tiraspol' but held the bulk of 57th Army to be located north of the city (see maps 153 and 154). They also failed to detect 46th Army's concentration and the forward deployment of 31st Rifle Corps. Both 4th Guards and 7th Mechanized Corps were unlocated but presumed well to the rear. 5th Shock Army's front looked as threatening as that in the south with 53d Army poised in second echelon. As in the Yassy sector, German intelligence underestimated the threat south of Tiraspol' by about 40 percent.

On 20 August the Soviet assault commenced, rapidly penetrating German and Rumanian defenses in both sectors. By 22 August the breach in those defenses had become irreparable and compounded by the surrender of many Rumanian units. A German assessment that day finally matched reality, stating:

> The deployment of the enemy armor forces makes the objective of the adversary recognizable: to cut off the Sixth Army from crossing the Pruth River, and to defeat its forces still east of the Pruth in order to exclude the *German* units of the AG from participation in the later battle for the defile of Galaz. In doing so the opponent, above all, takes advantage of the superiority in numbers of his mobile units which are engaged in out-flanking movements (south of Tiraspol' at least two, around Jassy at least three) ....[188]

Within one week Army Group South Ukraine had suffered a fate similar to that of Army Group Center – the destruction of Sixth Army and two Rumanian armies and the utter collapse of the German front in Rumania. An Axis retreat ensued which would not halt until Soviet forces had penetrated Bulgaria and swung west to enter the plains of Hungary.

Postscript

During the summer offensive the Soviets sought to destroy three German army groups deployed on the central and southern portions of the Eastern Front in successive strategic operations. In May the *STAVKA* had developed the concept of a summer campaign which would commence in June with diversionary attacks north of Leningrad which had significant objectives in their own right. Then, after feigning offensive intentions in the northern and southern

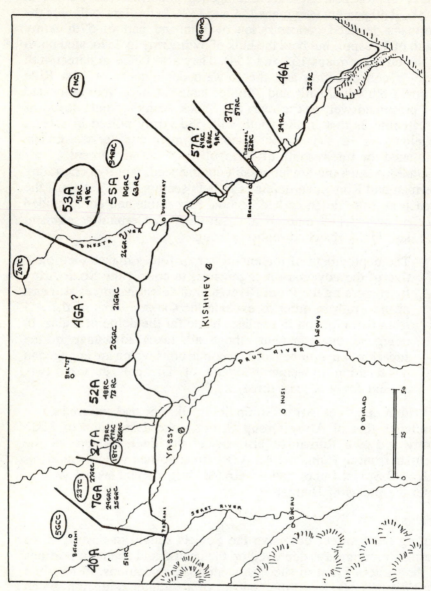

149. Yassy–Kishinev, German intelligence assessment, 19 August 1944

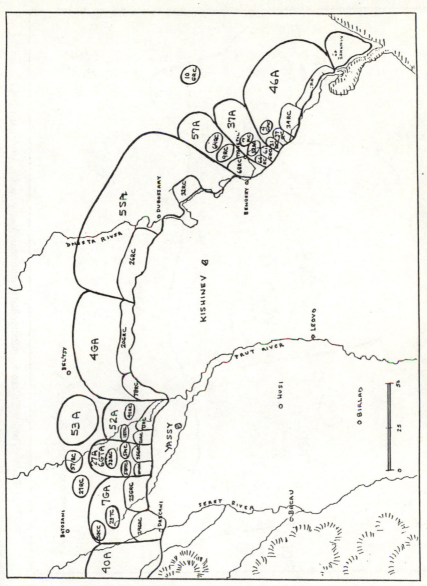

150. Yassy–Kishinev, Soviet dispositions, 19 August 1944

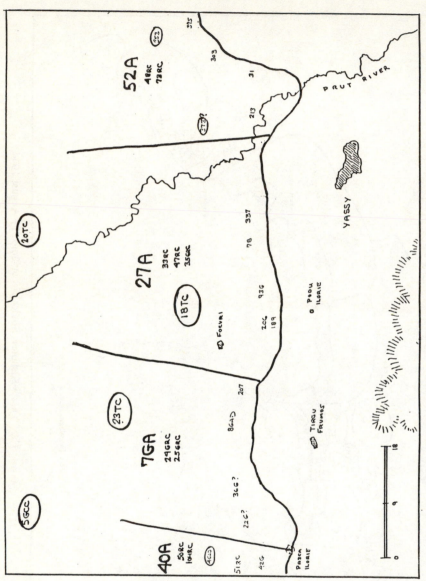

151. Yassy–Kishinev, German intelligence assessment, Yassy sector, 19 August 1944

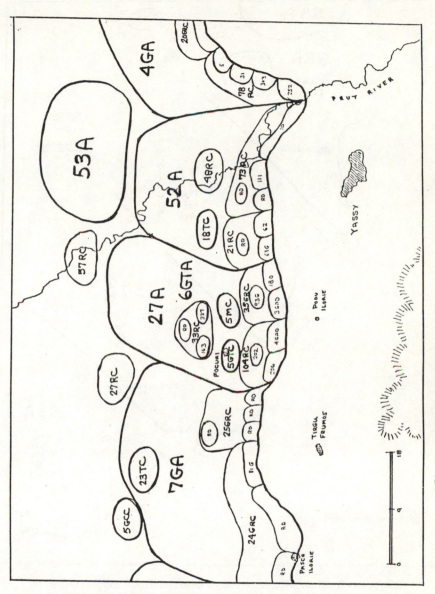

152. Yassy–Kishinev, Soviet dispositions, Yassy sector, 19 August 1944

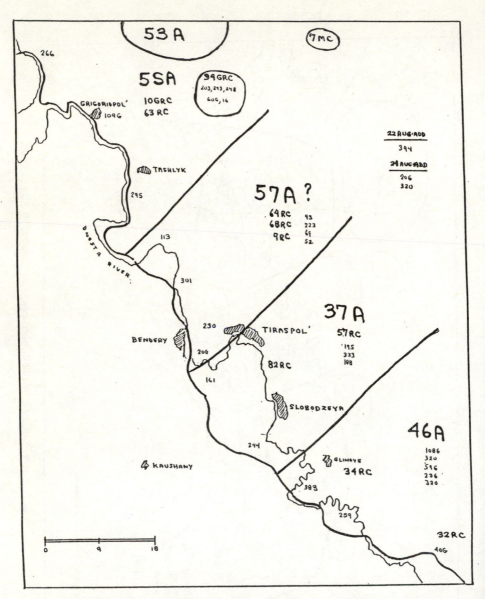

153. Yassy–Kishinev, German intelligence assessment, Tiraspol' sector, 19 August 1944

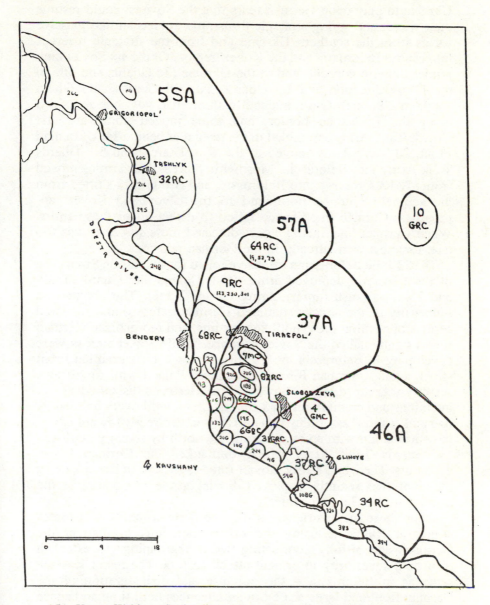

154. Yassy–Kishinev, Soviet dispositions, Tiraspol' sector, 19 August 1944

Ukraine to play upon German fears that the Soviets would resume their winter and spring strategic thrust, the Soviets shifted massive forces from the southern Ukraine and from the strategic reserves into central Belorussia and the Kovel' region. Of the six Soviet tank armies hitherto concentrated in the Ukraine (3d Guards and 4th on the L'vov direction and 1st Guards, 2d, 5th Guards, and 6th in southern Ukraine), two remained to threaten L'vov, one remained along the Rumanian border, and three moved northward. 1st Guards Tank Army assembled in the deep rear behind 1st Ukrainian Front, 2d Tank Army moved to the Kovel' area, and 5th Guards Tank Army into Belorussia. Meanwhile, three other armies moved from *STAVKA* reserve into Belorussia, and two armies shifted from the southern Ukraine northward to the L'vov and Kovel' approaches. German intelligence failed to detect all of these shifts. When German intelligence again detected these forces it was too late, for most were already in the German rear area.

The 23 June Belorussian offensive relied for success on Soviet use of three secretly deployed armies (6th Guards, 5th Guards Tank, and 28th) to crush rapidly Army Group Center. The unexpected immensity of the attacks shattered German defenses and rendered serious opposition futile until space, time, and reorganized German forces finally halted the Soviet advance. While Soviet attacks were developing in Belorussia, on 13 July Konev's 1st Ukrainian Front struck against German forces in southern Poland with forces also secretly regrouped. Here, however, the Germans discerned Soviet intentions and credibly resisted east of L'vov until overwhelmed by two tank armies' assaulting in a narrow sector directly toward L'vov in coordination with an attack from the north by secretly deployed 1st Guards Tank Army which outflanked the German L'vov defenders. Then, on 18 July, Soviet forces struck from Kovel', using the final two secretly deployed Soviet armies to complete the disaster in the German center.

When these major offensives reached their zenith, Soviet forces struck in Rumania, using the other operations to distract the Germans and artfully conducting secret regroupings to establish menacing superiority in critical attack sectors. The result was the same as in Belorussia – the collapse and disintegration of the German front and large scale Soviet advances until time and space ended the Soviet drive.

Strategic *maskirovka* played a decisive role in the summer offensive. Faced with the growing Soviet force superiority of over two to one strategically, the Germans could ill afford to lose track of

Soviet strategic reserves. Soviet freedom to move their units with impunity, and without detection and German countermeasures, permitted the Soviets to create operational force superiority of up to five to one. The more serious German problem in 1944 was their inability to detect redeploying Soviet operational and tactical reserves. They did so adequately only in the single sector where they concentrated all their attention (L'vov) but failed to do so elsewhere. Germans could, on occasion, detect tactical shifts but only after several days' delay, when it was too late. Consequently, the Soviets could convert operational superiorities of five to one into tactical superiorities of more than eight to one with impunity. No defense could withstand such an onslaught, especially since each onslaught normally contained an armored nucleus which, after penetration of the tactical defenses, often went as far as its logistical umbilical permitted it to go. By the summer of 1944 this averaged a depth of 250 kilometers.

Thus, by late August 1944, Soviet armies had penetrated to the Baltic States, East Prussia, the Vistula River line, and into southeastern Europe. Successful deception had conditioned the scale of this advance in all sectors. By late August the *STAVKA* had ordered its *fronts* to consolidate their positions and occupy positions favorable for the launching of a new strategic offensive in the winter. This period of consolidation, reminiscent of the fall period of 1943 when Soviet forces reached the Dnepr, was characterized by bitter fighting for bridgeheads along the Narev and Vistula Rivers where the Soviets strove to enlarge the bridgeheads against German armored thrusts designed to eliminate them. By mid-October, as if from sheer exhaustion, the lines in the central region stabilized with the bridgeheads still in Soviet hands. Now the attention of both sides shifted to the flanks where fighting flared anew, in reality a prelude to the forthcoming winter offensive.

THE FALL INTERLUDE

Background

By the end of August 1944, the Soviet summer strategic offensive had run its course. In the central sector of the Eastern Front the three Belorussian Fronts fought along the East Prussian borders, approached the Narev River north of Warsaw, and clung to tenuous bridgeheads across the Vistula River south of the Polish capital city (see map 155). During July and August German reserves gravitated

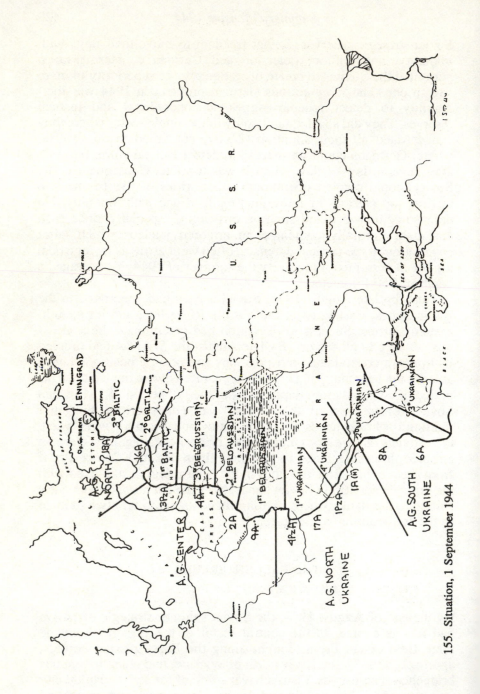

155. Situation, 1 September 1944

to the central sector to contest every kilometer of ground and, if possible, hold Soviet forces out of the German heartland of East Prussia and east of the Narev and Vistula barriers. Bitter fighting raged throughout September and into October, as worn-down Soviet forces at the end of frayed logistical umbilicals sought to improve their position for another winter offensive against equally worn and heavily attrited German forces who now fought more out of desperation than conviction. Soviet forces fought their way into the Augustov forests west of the Neiman River, to the very gates of Warsaw where 2d Tank Army, after its victorious march through Lublin to the Vistula, suffered heavy damage at the hands of Model's counter-attacking panzers, and into bridgeheads over the Vistula River at Magnushev, Pulavy, and Sandomierz. In the Narev and Vistula bridgeheads the Soviets dug in and fended off counter-attack after counter-attack by German panzer forces trying to drive them back across the rivers. By mid-October quiet had set in on the Warsaw—Berlin axis as both sides licked their wounds and prepared for the inevitable resumption of the Soviet offensive.

Meanwhile the Soviet attention shifted to the flanks where fighting raged throughout the fall. In the Baltic region the three Baltic *fronts* launched offensive after offensive and slowly drove German forces back from their "Panther" line toward Tallin and Riga. The well-constructed German defenses and the shrinking size of the front combined to thwart any hope for a rapid Soviet advance. The city of Riga became a magnet, attracting the offensive efforts of the Soviets until mid-October when a sudden secret Soviet maneuver shifted the focus of battle and propelled Soviet forces to the Baltic coast, cutting off Army Group North in the Courland pocket.

In the south, the Soviet capitalized on their August destruction of the bulk of Army Group South Ukraine by seizing Bucharest and forcing Rumania to switch her wartime allegiance. Soon after, Soviet forces crossed the Danube into Bulgaria and, in October, forced the Bulgarians to join the Allied cause. In mid-October the 2d Ukrainian Front swung west across the Carpathians into eastern Hungary, and the 3d Ukrainian Front poised for a thrust into southern Yugoslavia to seize Belgrade and destroy Germany's position in the Balkan peninsula.

The Soviet advances in the Baltic and into southeastern Europe represented strategic diversions, although with definite concrete objectives of their own, in the transitional period between the summer offensive of 1944 and the winter offensive of 1945. A thrust into the Danube Basin threatened not only Germany's military position but also its already weakened political and economic state. Germany's last ally (Hungary) would certainly abandon her should Budapest fall, and the Balaton oil fields and food supplies of the Hungarian plain were essential for continuation of the German war effort. Hitler knew this and had long stressed the value of the southern peripheral (in fact, since 1942). The Soviets knew he would defend it.

More importantly, continued Soviet attacks into the Danube basin would inexorably draw German reserves from the central portion of the front and weaken the Germans there, thus improving Soviet chances for a decisive drive during the winter along the main strategic approach to the Oder River and Berlin. Thus Soviet operations on the flanks in the fall of 1944 were necessary pre-conditions for what would occur in the center in January 1945. Zhukov, in his memoirs, noted:

> In the opinion of the General Staff, the offensive would have to be started by our Southern Front in the direction of Vienna. This would inevitably compel the German command to take considerable forces off our Western Fronts in order to rein-force their South-Eastern strategic sector crucial for defense of south and southeast Germany.[189]

In late October, the *STAVKA* surveyed the situation along the Eastern Front, especially regarding Soviet offensive capabilities in the central sector, and concluded further offensives without re-fitting and rest would be futile. Thus, as Shtemenko recorded, "On the night of 4 November 1944 a directive was issued ordering the 3d and 2d Belorussian Fronts to go over to the defensive. A few days later similar instructions were sent to the right wing of the 1st Belorussian Front."[190]

At the same time the *STAVKA* formulated the general phasing of its upcoming winter offensive without yet delineating when the main attack would occur. Clearly, however, the first stage would involve continuation of what Shtemenko called the "old line of advance – the southern flank of the Soviet–German front in the Budapest area."[191] Shtemenko affirmed Zhukov's judgement, writing:

> We well knew that the enemy was particularly sensitive in East Prussia and Hungary. If hard pressed he would be sure to throw in reserves and troops from sectors that were not under attack.

This would lead to a serious weakening of the whole Western sector, where the decisive events were to take place.[192]

Within this context, in October Soviet forces in the Baltic region prepared operations to isolate German Army Group North, while in the Balkans, Malinovsky's 2d Ukrainian Front planned operations to secure the Hungarian plains and Budapest.

Memel', October 1944

By the end of September 1944, the Leningrad Front had cleared virtually all of Estonia of German forces except the Baltic coastal islands. The 3d and 2d Baltic Fronts had reached the close approaches to Riga, and the 1st Baltic Front had seized Elgava and Dobele and threatened Riga from the South. German resistance, however, had stiffened, bolstered by extensive prepared defenses covering the approaches to Riga.

Shtemenko, then working with Bagramyan, the 1st Baltic Front commander, later noted:

> Progress was slow, however, on the main line of advance. Once again it proved impossible to split up the enemy's grouping, which made a fighting withdrawal to prepared positions 60–80 kilometers from Riga. Our troops had to gnaw their way methodically through the enemy defenses, driving him back meter by meter.
>
> With the operation going like this there could be no quick victory, and we were becoming involved in heavy losses ....
> The enemy was even counterattacking ...
>
> Everything indicated that the enemy was determined to maintain Army Group North's link with East Prussia at all costs, so that they would be able to withdraw their troops from the Baltic area by land if necessary.[193]

In these circumstances, the *STAVKA* decided to change the direction of attack of its *fronts*, in particular the 1st Baltic Front. On 24 September a *STAVKA* directive spelled out the new tasks, prompting Bagramyan to later write:

> The *STAVKA* at that time marvelously seized upon the most convenient moment for a surprise maneuver of the main forces of our *front* with the aim of attacking on a new, more favorable direction for us.[194]

The new direction was toward Memel' and the Baltic sea coast.

The *STAVKA* ordered the Leningrad Front and Baltic Fleet to complete the liberation of Estonia and the 3d and 2d Baltic Fronts to seize Riga and clear the Baltic coast of Germans. The 1st Baltic and part of the 3d Belorussian Front were:

> to prepare and conduct a powerful blow on the Memel' direction and cut off the entire enemy Baltic group from East Prussia, and also create the prerequisites for successive blows against him to destroy fully all German Fascist forces on the Baltic direction.[195]

The *STAVKA* ordered the 2d Baltic Front to shift its 10th Guards and 42d Armies southward to replace 3d Shock and 22d Armies, which, in turn, would move south of Riga and replace 4th Shock and 51st Armies of the 1st Baltic Front which Bagramyan then intended to shift southward to participate in the Memel' operation. 4th Shock and 51st Armies were to assemble in the Shyaulyai area where they would join 5th Guards Tank Army, 1st and 19th Tank and 3d Guards Mechanized Corps redeployed from the Dobele area, and two rifle corps (44th and 90th) transferred from 2d Baltic to 1st Baltic Front control.

Bagramyan planned to make his main attack in a 19 kilometer sector west of Shyaulyai with 6th Guards, 43d, 51st, and 5th Guards Tank Armies and a secondary attack in a 72 kilometer sector southwest of Shyaulyai with 2d Guards Army and 1st Tank Corps in cooperation with the 3d Belorussian Front's 39th Army. This required concentration of 50 percent of Bagramyan's force in his main attack sector.[196] Bagramyan recognized his greatest problem was to conceal so large a regrouping and his new main attack sector. He later wrote:

> We had to extract units from battle secretly, turn over our positions to the 2d Baltic Front, and regroup a distance of 80 to 240 kilometers the forces of five combined arms and one tank army as well as two tank, one mechanized and two rifle corps which had been transferred to our front from the 2d Baltic Front. Besides that, we had to shift the bases of aviation units to the new direction. The regrouping and transport involved (including 2d Baltic Front forces) 500,000 men, more than 9,000 guns and mortars, more than 1300 tanks and SP guns, and a mass of various material resources.[197]

In the period from 24 September to 4 October Bagramyan had to regroup 4th Shock, 43d, 51st, 6th Guards and 5th Guards Tank

Armies and supporting units along the front from his right to his left flank (see map 156). He planned the regrouping in two stages. First, 4th Shock and 51st Armies would take over 6th Guards and 43d Armies' sectors, permitting the latter to move south. Then 4th Shock and 51st Armies would move south after replacement by the 2d Baltic Front's 3d Shock and 22d Armies. In scale the regrouping involved movement of 50 rifle divisions, 15 tank brigades and 93 artillery regiments, or 89 percent of rifle forces, all of the armor, and 95 percent of front artillery units.[198] While conducting this regrouping Bagramyan had to convey to the enemy the false intention to continue his assaults toward Riga.

Bagramyan's *maskirovka* plan was designed to conceal the large-scale regrouping and the new main attack positions, and incorporated active disinformation measures to simulate the intention of attacking toward Riga (see Appendix 6). The plan incorporated normal strict security measures and limited participation in the planning process. The chief of staff and commandant's service supervised the regrouping. On 24 September Beloborodov's 43d Army began regrouping concealed by *maskirovka* measures developed by his chief of staff. Beloborodov turned one rifle corps over to 4th Shock Army and began moving his remaining nine divisions south. Six divisions were already underway by midnight on 24 September. By traveling 30–35 kilometers per night, at first light on 28 September 43d Army's divisions assembled near Shyaulyai, 30 kilometers from the front. In strict radio silence Beloborodov's force then occupied positions on the right flank of 2d Guards Army's sector, using 2d Guards Army's command and observation posts as well as that army's artillery positions.[199] While 43d Army redeployed, an army operational group conducted reconnaissance in the new region. The following night Chistyakov's 6th Guards Army completed its regrouping and occupied an offensive sector on Beloborodov's right flank.

6th Guards Army had conducted a 130–140 kilometer march from the Riga area also at night after its relief by 61st Army. To conceal the transfer, Chistyakov left some artillery and heavy equipment in his old sector for 61st Army to use. Chistyakov's forces moved at a rate of 30–35 kilometers per night over a period of six nights with the motorized equipment leading his march at an even more rapid rate (50–60 kilometers per night). Good weather materially assisted Chistyakov's move.[200]

Meanwhile 2d Guards Army truncated its sector and shifted its units to make room for 6th Guards and 43d Armies. Regrouping of

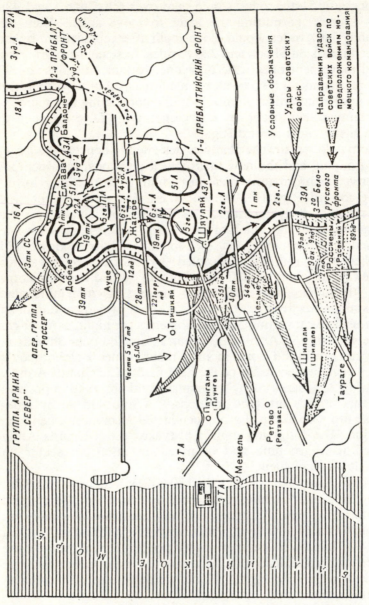

9. Мемельская операция (октябрь 1944 г.)

156. Memel', Soviet regrouping

2d Guards Army took place from 26 through 30 September and shortened the army sector by half to 35 kilometers. On the night of 30 October army units quietly occupied their new assault positions.[201]

While the initial regrouping progressed, 4th Shock and 51st Armies simulated offensive preparations for an attack on Riga together with 3d Shock and 22d Armies which were sent to relieve them.[202] These newly arriving forces conducted unconcealed daytime movements while the relieved units moved to the rear under cover of darkness. Between 28 September and 3 October bonfires blazed in the rear of 4th Shock and 51st Armies, and a system of antiaircraft fires covered the entire area. 51st Army divisions (346th, 347th, 267th, and 204th) simulated forward movement of units as did their parent 1st Guards, 10th, and 63rd Rifle Corps. Radio stations of 4th Shock and 51st Armies, as well as those of 43d Army and 5th Guards Tank Armies, the 1st and 19th Tank, and 3d Guards Mechanized Corps continued transmitting in normal patterns. 51st and 4th Shock Army units intensified combat reconnaissance and commanders' reconnaissance throughout the army sector from 0200 to 0500 between 28–30 September.[203] 4th Shock Army conducted an even heavier reconnaissance by reinforced battalions and roving guns in the army rear fired from false artillery positions.

Engineers assisted in the deception by building and emplacing 334 mock-up tanks in 51st Army's rear area, and the Soviets increased vehicular traffic and concentrated equipment in the false concentration area up to 2 October.[204] As the date of the real attack neared, engineers cleared lanes through minefields south of Riga and assembled assault bridging to support the final drive. At the same time 3d Air Army units intensified bombing of German positions opposite the simulated offensive sector.

Radio disinformation in 4th Shock and 51st Armies' sectors reinforced the other deception measures. Between 20 September and 3 October pre-arranged radio nets exchanged coded signals concerning offensive preparations using an RB radio for the staffs of each army, corps, and division. Wire communications messages verified the radio traffic.[205] All the while the Soviets simulated a defensive posture near Shyaulyai by digging more extensive defensive positions (which were subsequently used to bring new forces secretly forward), by intensifying mine laying (while replacing real mines with false ones), and by camouflaging all artillery positions.

These simulated measures were designed to cover the second

stage of Soviet regrouping, when 4th Shock and 51st Armies were to pull out of line south of Riga and move into Bagramyan's new *front* assembly area. Both armies, and regrouped 5th Guards Tank Army, would occupy *front* second echelon positions to the rear of 6th Guards Army ready to exploit 6th Guards Army's penetration of the German tactical defenses.

On 28 September Lieutenant General P. F. Malyshev's 4th Shock Army turned its sector over to 22d Army and regrouped southward, picking up 84th Rifle Corps as reinforcement to cover the *front* shock group's right flank. The remainder of 4th Shock took up second echelon positions on the right flank of 6th Guards Army. 3d Guards Mechanized Corps, displacing south at the same time, reinforced the 84th Rifle Corps.[206]

Lieutenant General Ya. G. Kreizer's 51st Army received its marching orders on 1 October and immediately began turning its position over to 3d Shock Army. Traveling by forced march, Kreizer's army closed into its new assembly areas on 4 October and prepared to develop the offensive of 6th Guards Army.[207]

Bagramyan's principal exploitation force, Lieutenant General V. T. Vol'sky's 5th Guards Tank Army, began moving from Dobele in the Riga area late on 29 September. After turning over a tank brigade and a self-propelled artillery regiment to 43d Army, Vol'sky's army marched 100 kilometers and, by the morning of 30 September, concentrated near Grudzhaya, north of Shyaulyai.[208] A strict *maskirovka* plan governed the conduct of the army's march; and to facilitate the movement of heavy equipment, Vol'sky's rear services used tank transporters to carry those tanks which had excessive hours of engine usage. By ferrying tanks to and fro on the wheeled transporters, the duration of the move was shortened, and more tanks made it to the new assembly area. A former officer of Vol'sky's rear services later wrote:

> For two nights our 5th Guards Tank Army completed an echeloned 100 kilometer march almost parallel to the front. While observing strict maskirovka measures, it regrouped in the waiting area Dyrzhi Maly–Grudzhai–Dymshi–Bovoini. Only the heavy tanks and self-propelled artillery traveled by rail. Part of the medium tanks, having limited reserves of motor hours, were transferred by trailers.[209]

On 1 October 5th Guards Tank Army conducted reconnaissance and marked out routes to the forward area, 30 kilometers to the west. Late on 5 October, after rifle forces had penetrated the

German defenses, Vol'sky's army moved forward and entered combat. At the time "the main force of Army Group North as before remained in the Riga region and 60 kilometers to the east of the city."[210]

In fact, Bagramyan's *maskirovka* plan paid off, in particular the simulated offensive gestures south of Riga where the Germans intensified their reconnaissance efforts. Northwest of Dobele the Germans moved SS "Netherlands" Division forward and placed 7th Panzer Division in reserve.[211] The German Ninth Army war journal throughout September and into early October voiced expectations of a renewed Soviet attack near Dobele and Elgava. On 26 September, General Schoener of Ninth Army reported, "The enemy is removing troops from separate directions as infantry reinforcements for the attack sectors of his tank units west of Elgava, in order to switch to a general offensive in the near future."[212] The next day Sixteenth Army began reporting heavy traffic going southwest away from the front.[213]

On 28 September Schoener discussed with Hitler an Army Group North counter-stroke which was to be conducted from both south of Shyaulyai and west of Riga on about 3 November. Two days later the chief of staff of Army Group North discounted the likelihood of the counter-thrust because the Russians would probably strike first. Earlier that day Third Panzer Army had reported it had identified the headquarters of 4th Shock Army northwest of Shyaulyai and said all radio traffic in the area had abruptly stopped.[214]

By 2 October Schoener was finally alarmed by the reported Soviet movement. The commander of Third Panzer Army now predicted a Soviet attack in several sectors west of Shyaulyai, probably within 14 days, but likely to be preceded with smaller-scale attacks in the near future.[215] Schoener agreed and reported as much to OKH.

The belated discovery of Soviet attack preparations did little to improve the German position. As Ziemke has recorded:

> Although the signs were clear, the Army Group North staff as late as the morning of 5 October did not believe *First Baltic Front* could finish redeploying its armies in less than ten days. It was therefore inclined to tailor its regroupment to the schedule for its own projected attack on the assumption that this would also bring enough forces into the right place in time to stop the Russians. Several panzer divisions had moved into the Shaulyay–Raseynyay area by the 5th, but Third Panzer Army was still woefully weak in infantry. The 551st Grenadier

Division west of Shaulyay was holding a 24-mile line that it could man only at strongpoints. The first infantry reinforcement for the army was not expected until 16 October.[216]

German intelligence reports confirmed that the Germans knew of Soviet movements, but not their full scope (see maps 157 and 158). On the evening of 4 October the Germans realized that 6th Guards, 4th Shock, and 43d Armies were moving southward; but they were unaware of their destination. They also detected 5th Guards Tank Army's departure from the Dobele area, but not the movement of 51st Army. Nor did the Germans identify the new Soviet concentrations in their main attack sectors northwest and southwest of Shyaulyai.

On 5 October Bagramyan's forces struck, and by evening 5th Guards Tank Army was exploiting into the depths of the German defenses. By 9 October 5th Guards Tank Army had overrun Third Panzer Army headquarters and reached the Baltic coast north and south of Memel', irrevocably severing contact between Army Groups North and Center. Within days Soviet forces commenced operations on the Gumbinnen approach into East Prussia ending all German hopes of restoring the situation in the Memel' area and re-establishing contact with Army Group North.

After months of tedious combat, through a skillful deception, Soviet forces of the 1st Baltic Front had regrouped massive forces, broken a virtual stalemate in the north, and reached the Baltic Sea. On 6 October, one day after the Memel' operation began, Malinovsky's 2d Ukrainian Front struck westward into Hungary, thus forcing the German High Command to add to its concern about the situation in the north new concerns for the viability of its southern flank.

Hungary, October 1944

By the end of September, Tolbukhin's 3d Ukrainian Front had completed its sweep of Bulgaria and neared the Yugoslavian border, and Malinovsky's 2d Ukrainian Front had occupied the passes through the Carpathians on an 800 kilometer front and prepared to advance into Hungary. At the time, Malinovsky's *front* consisted of 40th, 7th Guards, 27th, 53d, and 46th Armies, 6th Guards Tank Army, 18th Tank Corps, a cavalry-mechanized group, and the 4th and 1st Rumanian Armies just incorporated into the Soviet fold. The *STAVKA* ordered Malinovsky "to destroy the enemy group in Hungary and at the same time remove the country

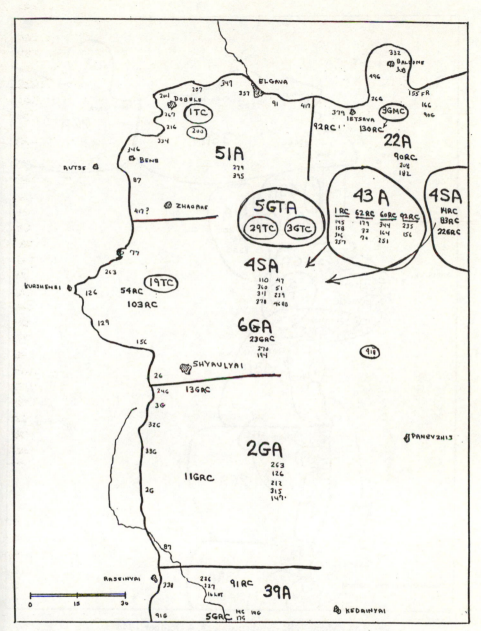

157. Memel', German intelligence assessment, 4 October 1944

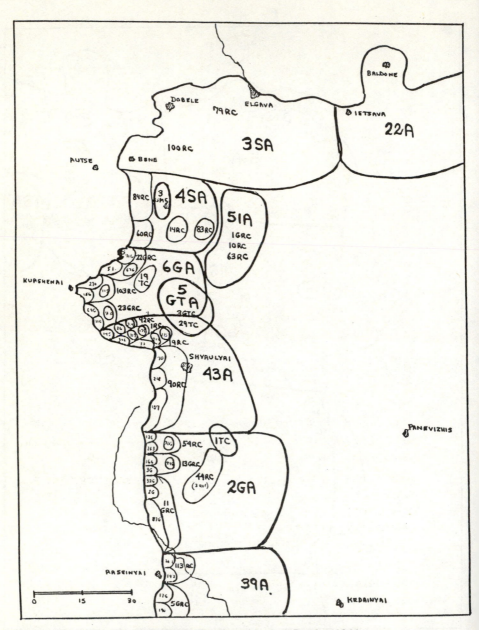

158. Memel', Soviet dispositions, 4 October 1944

23. R. Ya. Malinovsky, 2d Ukrainian Front commander, Fall 1944

from the war on the side of Germany" in cooperation with the 4th Ukrainian Front which had deployed from the Crimea to the northern Carpathian region.[217] 2d Ukrainian Front was to:

> destroy the enemy in the Cluj, Oradea, Debrecen region and, while developing the offensive to the north toward Nyiregyhaza and Chop, cooperate with the 4th Ukrainian Front in the destruction of the eastern Carpathian enemy group and secure the Uzhgorod–Mukachevo region.[218]

The *STAVKA* reinforced Malinovsky's *front* with 46th Army and 7th Mechanized Corps from 3d Ukrainian Front. 7th Mechanized Corps joined with the 4th and 6th Guards Cavalry Corps to form Lieutenant General I. A. Pliyev's Cavalry-Mechanized Group. To develop the offensive on the Budapest direction, the *STAVKA* moved its reserve 4th Guards Army into position to fill the gap between the 2d and 3d Ukrainian Fronts as the operation developed.

Since the 2d Ukrainian Front was deployed on an exceedingly broad front, its operational force densities remained low throughout the operations; and logistical sustainment was tenuous at best. Temporary force concentrations and routine resupply produced periodic advances in given sectors but could not result in decisive deep operations such as occurred in other sectors. Consequently Malinovsky's *front* ended up conducting a series of successive army or multi-army operations, each preceded by a short operational pause and limited regrouping of forces, in particular *front* mobile elements. Throughout October and November the *front maskirovka* plan for each operation generally involved the secret redeployment of tank, mechanized, and cavalry corps, singly or in combination. During the first stage in early October, and during December, 6th Guards Tank Army played an active role in the secret deployments.

The Soviets have written very little of a specific nature concerning *maskirovka* in these operations, with one notable exception, the 20 December assaults near Budapest. However, a comparison of German daily intelligence reports and the actual combat situation shows a clear gap between what German intelligence saw at any given time and the actual Soviet force present on the battlefield. A day-by-day comparison of this data reveals a clear pattern of Soviet tactical, and on occasion operational, *maskirovka*, in particular during each tactical or operational pause as the Soviets prepared for operations along new directions. These intelligence and situation reports are the primary source for subsequent judgements concerning Soviet *maskirovka* in Hungary supplemented by occasional but sketchy Soviet descriptions of their *maskirovka* planning.

Once reinforcements arrived, Malinovsky developed plans for the first phase of his operation in Hungary, known since as the Debrecan operation. Malinovsky's operational concept required 53d, 6th Guards Tank, and 1st Rumanian Armies and Cavalry-Mechanized Group Pliyev to attack from south of Oradea, in the center of the *front* sector toward Debrecan. On the *front* right flank 40th and 7th Guards Armies would attack toward Surduk, 27th and 4th Rumanian Armies toward Cluj, and Cavalry-Mechanized Group Gorshkov toward Satu–Mare. On the left flank 46th Army would clear northern Yugoslavia and advance to the Tisza River line where it was to seize bridgeheads at Szeged and south of the Hungarian–Yugoslav border.[219]

By attacking to the northwest, Malinovsky sought to catch all German forces in eastern Hungary in a pincer between the 2d and

4th Ukrainian Fronts. Thereafter, he intended to shift his direction of attack westward toward Budapest. *Maskirovka* played only a slight role in the operation. Instead, the Soviets relied on the weakness of German and Hungarian forces to achieve decisive results in this broad front attack. At the outset of the Debrecan operation, German intelligence had only a sketchy picture of 2d Ukrainian Front dispositions. It recognized strong Soviet armored concentrations south of Debrecan but did not detect the movement of Cavalry-Mechanized Group Pliyev into its attack positions. In fact, German intelligence identified Pliyev's force only on 7 October, after it had penetrated German defenses.

The Debrecan operation began on 6 October; and, within three days, 53d Army and Cavalry-Mechanized Group Pliyev had advanced 100 kilometers northwest to the Tisza River. 6th Guards Tank Army, however, failed to take Oradea, south of Debrecan. Malinovsky reacted by quickly shifting Pliyev's group eastward to assist 6th Guards Army. Together Kravchenko's tank army and Pliyev's group took Oradea (12 October) and then Debrecan (20 October). Subsequently, Cavalry-Mechanized Groups Pliyev and Gorshkov sped north and seized Nyiregyhaza on 22 October, only to be struck by a coordinated German counter-stroke which severed the cavalry-mechanized groups' communications and forced them by 27 October to abandon much of their equipment and withdraw south.

With the exception of Pliyev's initial drive to the Tisza River, German intelligence, in general, kept track of Soviet force movements well, although unable to identify specific units until after 16 October.

With both German and Soviet forces tied down in heavy combat north of Debrecan, the *STAVKA* and Malinovsky decided to take advantage of German weakness to the southwest, east of the Danube River, to mount a drive on Budapest from the 2d Ukrainian Front's left flank. The *STAVKA* ordered Malinovsky to:

> not later than 29 October go on the offensive between the Tisza and Danube Rivers with the forces of 46th Army and 2d Guards Mechanized Corps. The aim — to break up enemy defenses on the west bank of the Tisza and secure the crossing there of 7th Guards Army; subsequently, 46th Army, reinforced by 4th Guards Mechanized Corps was to strike German forces defending Budapest. Remaining *front* armies (except

40th and 4th Rumanian) were to force the Tisza and secure bridgeheads on its west bank.[220]

Malinovsky's maneuver was designed to take advantage of the fact that the weak Hungarian Third Army defended the section along the lower Tisza to the Danube. There Malinovsky planned to concentrate 46th Army forces and reinforce them, first with 2d Guards Mechanized Corps, and then with an additional rifle corps (23d) and 4th Guards Mechanized Corps. His *maskirovka* plan sought to conceal the regrouping sufficiently for Soviet forces to take Budapest before German reserves arrived in the area. Malinovsky was concerned over the *STAVKA* requirement to launch the assault within two days, on 29 October, for he preferred to wait longer to assemble a larger force. Overruled by the *STAVKA*, he finally acquiesced to a 29 October attack. By that date 46th Army and 2d Guards Mechanized Corps had concentrated. However, the follow-on 23d Rifle Corps and 4th Guards Mechanized Corps would not be assembled and ready to join the attack until 1 November.

German intelligence had an accurate picture of 46th and 7th Guards Armies' dispositions on 28 October but had not detected the movement of 2d Guards Mechanized Corps north from Szeged (see maps 159 and 160).[221] Nor did it record the approach of 4th Guards Mechanized Corps or 23d Rifle Corps, the force which was to make the final thrust on Budapest. Since the Germans had detected enough Soviet movement to realize Malinovsky's intent, they began shifting forces southwest to the Budapest area but not in enough time to forestall Malinovsky's attack, whose strength they continued to underestimate until the Soviet force was well on its way to Budapest.

On 29 October 46th Army and 2d Guards Mechanized Corps attacked and immediately penetrated Hungarian defenses and advanced to Kiskoros and Kecslemet. German 24th Panzer Division learned of 2d Guards Mechanized Corps' presence by blindly counter-attacking into it. On 1 November 4th Guards Mechanized and 23d Rifle Corps joined the Soviet assault, the same day that Kecslemet fell. By that time German intelligence was aware of 2d Guards Mechanized Corps' presence but still had not detected 4th Guards Mechanized and 23d Rifle Corps. German resistance stiffened south of Budapest and brought the Soviet advance to a halt in the southern suburbs of the city on 3 November. Late that day the Germans identified 4th Guards Mechanized Corps and 23d Rifle Corps (see maps 161 and 162). By that time they had successfully parried the assault, and Malinovsky looked elsewhere to achieve success.

Ordered by the *STAVKA* on 4 November to cease his attacks on Budapest from the south, Malinovsky now planned to regroup his forces and strike again on 10 November. He ordered forces on his right flank and center to move across the Tisza River for a general attack on Budapest from the north and northeast. 40th Army was to strike toward Miskolc; 27th and 53d Armies with Cavalry-Mechanized Group Gorshkov toward Eger; and 7th Guards and 46th Armies reinforced by 2d Guards Mechanized Corps, 4th Guards Mechanized Corps, and Cavalry-Mechanized Group Pliyev would regroup and strike north between Cegled and the Tisza River.[222] Malinovsky's attempt to conceal the movement aborted as German counter-attacks southeast of Budapest on 4 and 5 November encountered and tied up 2d and 4th Guards Mechanized Corps as they were moving to their new attack locations near Cegled. Moreover, by 6 November German intelligence had detected two of Pliyev's cavalry corps (4th and 6th Guards) near Szolnok, west of the Tisza (although not his 23d Tank Corps) (see maps 163 and 164). When the Soviet attack began on 10 November, its severity was greater than the Germans had expected (since they still held 2d and 4th Guards Mechanized Corps to be southeast of Budapest), but the Germans had begun deploying IV Panzer Corps into the area, thus Soviet progress was slow.[223] A grinding, painstaking Soviet advance resulted, which by 20 November had pushed German troops to the Hatvan, Gyongos, Eger line, where localized fighting lasted to 5 December.

Malinovsky's *maskirovka* plan, while not achieving total success, reaped some benefits. For when the German command reacted to the detected movement, it shifted forces from its left flank to the Cegled sector, thus permitting Soviet 27th and 40th Armies to make serious inroads toward Miskolc and Eger.

On 20 November the Soviets successfully masked the movement of the 37th Guards Rifle Corps from 46th Army's right flank to the left flank where it deployed on the Danube River opposite several critical islands south of Budapest. Late on 20 November the corps' three divisions assaulted across the river and, by day's end on 22 November, had seized the key islands as launching sites for future offensives across the river.[224] German intelligence noted 37th Guards Rifle Corps' absence on the 46th Army's right flank on 22 November but identified its new location only after 25 November.

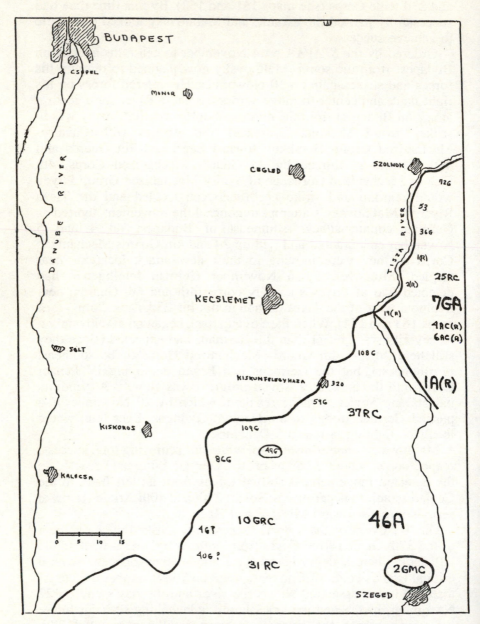

159. Budapest, German intelligence assessment, 28 October 1944

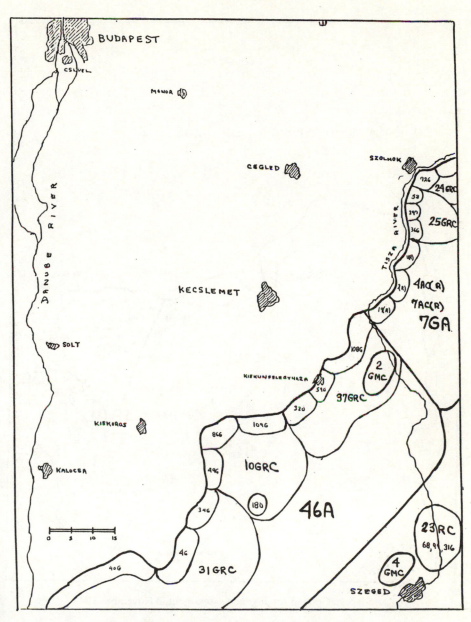

160. Budapest, Soviet dispositions, 28 October 1944

TDAE—P*

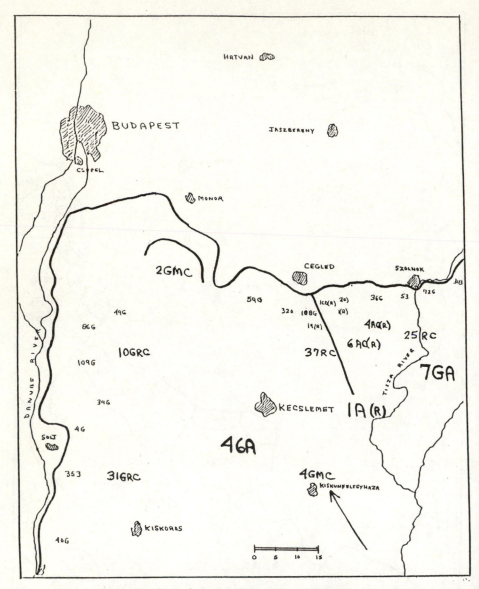

161. Budapest, German intelligence assessment, 3 November 1944

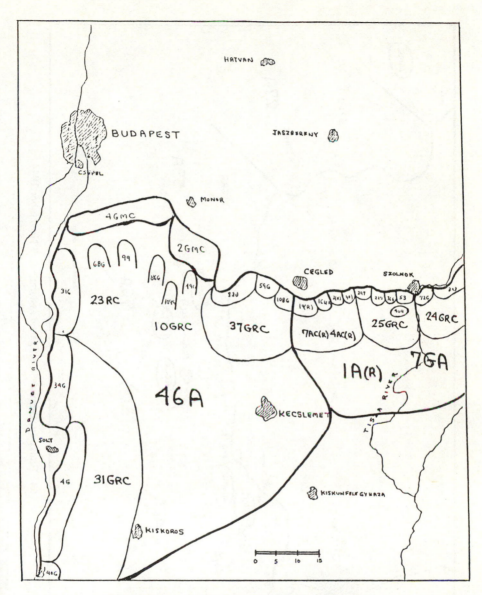

162. Budapest, Soviet dispositions, 3 November 1944

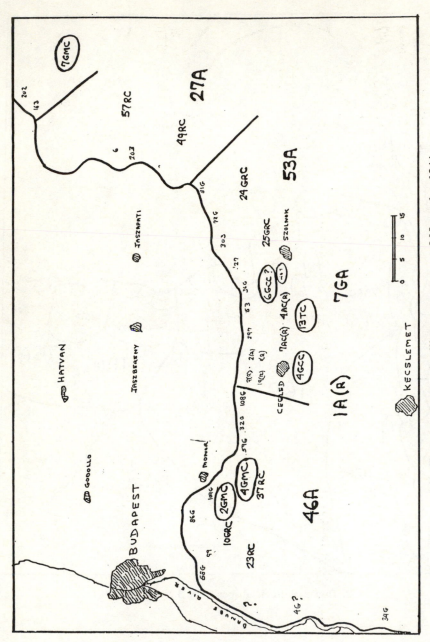

163. Budapest, German intelligence assessment, 9 November 1944

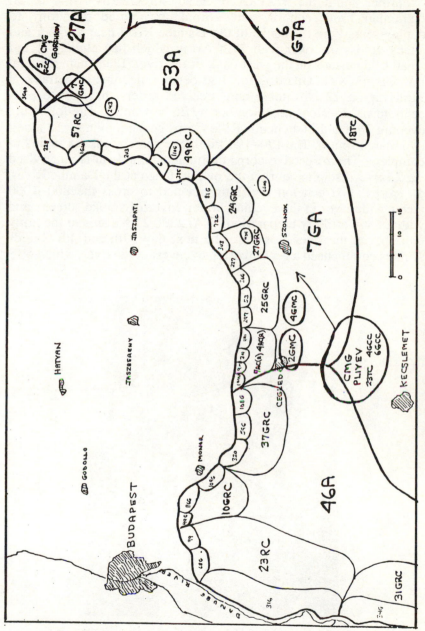

164. Budapest, Soviet dispositions, 9 November 1944

Further south the *STAVKA* released 4th Guards Army to 3d
Ukrainian Front control, and Tolbukhin ordered the army to
deploy secretly to the banks of the Danube River near Sombor and
attack across the river with 57th Army which had already seized
small bridgeheads on the west bank of the river. Lieutenant General
I. V. Galinin's 4th Guards Army had begun unloading from trains at
Timisvar on 12 November and received orders that day to concentrate six divisions near Sombor by 26 November. The following
evening 20th and 21st Guards Rifle Corps began moving west along
two march routes. The 170–190 kilometer march took six nights to
complete. The respective corps commanders and staffs supervised
maskirovka discipline during the march. Once at the Danube River,
the corps' first echelon divisions planned to cross the 800–1000
meter wide river in the evening under cover of smoke screens and
without any artillery preparation.[225] At 2300 27 November the army
units began the river crossing. The next day 57th and 4th Guards
Armies commenced a general offensive west of the river, which by 3

24. Marshal F.I. Tolbukhin, 3d Ukrainian Front commander and his *front*
commissar, General A.S. Zheltov, Fall 1944

December brought Soviet forces to the shores of Lake Balaton, southwest of Budapest.

The secret move of 4th Guards Army had taken German intelligence by surprise (see maps 165 and 166). It knew of 57th Army's presence west of the river, but only on 30 November did it note the possible arrival of 4th Guards Army east of the river. The Soviet thrust had serious consequences elsewhere, for as German Army Group Fretter-Pico (Sixth Army) shifted forces from the north (1st and 23d Panzer Divisions), the Soviet 27th Army promptly seized Miskolc.

In late November Malinovsky proposed a new plan to the *STAVKA* which involved a large scale regrouping and the commencement of a two-pronged attack to envelop and seize Budapest. The new attack, planned to begin on 5 December, would be spearheaded by 7th Guards Army (reinforced by one rifle corps) concentrated northwest of Hatvan. 6th Guards Tank Army and Pliyev's Cavalry-Mechanized Group would exploit and advance north and northwest of Budapest to envelop the city. 53d Army would attack on 7th Guards Army's right flank; and, on 7th Guards Army's left flank, 46th Army and 2d Guards Mechanized Corps would attack across the Danube River from Csepel Island to seize Estergom west of Budapest to isolate the Hungarian capital. 4th Guards Army would continue its advance northward west of the Danube River to secure Szekesferhervar and support 46th Army in its encirclement of Budapest.[226]

While Malinovsky's plan called for all rifle armies to operate on former lines, considerable regrouping was necessary, in particular to move Kravchenko's 6th Guards Tank Army forward and to reinforce 7th Guards Army with 30th Rifle Corps, which had just completed a long regrouping from the Carpathian region. 7th Guards Army concentrated its divisions near Hatvan, and 53d Army assembled on its right flank. Pliyev's Cavalry-Mechanized Group assembled to the rear of 7th Guards Army on 6th Guards Tank Army's right flank. Further south 46th Army's 23d Rifle Corps joined the 37th Guards Rifle Corps in assault positions on Csepel Island.

Soviet critics claim Malinovsky failed to achieve any measure of surprise, writing:

> Thus, without a doubt, the enemy in the course of November systematically strengthened his grouping on the Budapest direction. Besides that, having detected our concept, in

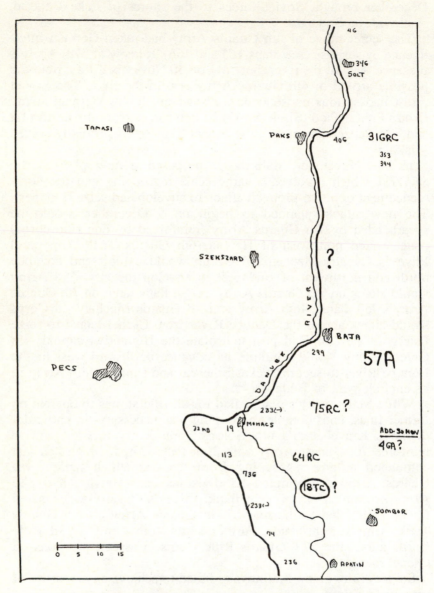

165. Budapest, German intelligence assessment, Mohacs sector,
26 November 1944

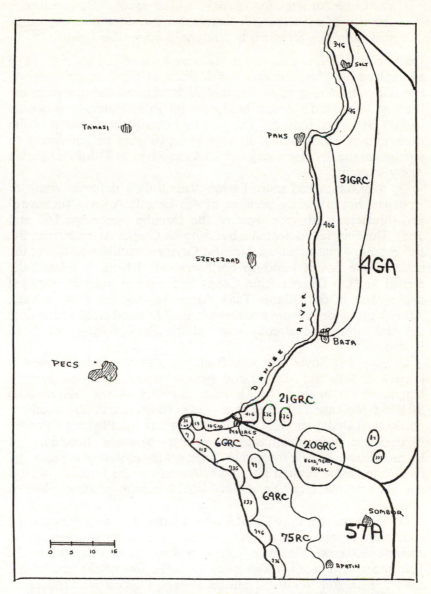

166. Budapest, Soviet dispositions, Mohacs sector, 26 November 1944

particular our intention to strike a blow south of Budapest with
the aim of enveloping it from the west, he undertook timely
measures to strengthen his defenses across the Danube.[227]

On 28 November, one day after Malinovsky received his orders and
announced his plan, General J. Friessner, of German Sixth Army,
noted the regrouping of Soviet mobile forces and the change in the
Russian command's operational concept to an intent to penetrate
toward Budapest, noting: "The possible change in direction of the
main enemy attack demands a rapid regrouping of our forces to
strengthen the defense along the Danube River in Third Hungarian
Army's sector."[228]

German forces had indeed strengthened their defenses south of
Budapest but primarily because of 4th Guards Army's successful
and threatening advance west of the Danube (see maps 167 and
168). The Germans detected a build-up on Csepel Island but not the
full extent of that build-up. Nor did German intelligence detect the
scale of the Soviet build-up northwest of Hatvan. It missed the
arrival of 30th Guards Rifle Corps and did not note the forward
deployment of 6th Guards Tank Army. In fact, 6th Guards Tank
Army's presence became known only on 7 December, at which time
the tank army had already reached the Danube River north of
Budapest.[229]

Despite this Soviet success Budapest did not fall, nor was it
encircled. 46th and 4th Guards Armies' attack south of the city
bogged down against the German defenses of the Margareithe
Stellung [defense line] between Lake Balaton and the southern
outskirts of Budapest. 6th Guards Tank Army and Pliyev's Cavalry-
Mechanized Group smashed German defenses northeast of
Budapest; and, as rifle forces cordoned off the city from the east, the
mobile forces penetrated into the hills north of the Danube, but did
not encircle the city. To do so would require another planned
operation.

On 12 December the *STAVKA* issued a directive to the 2d and 3d
Ukrainian Fronts to plan and conduct yet another operation to
encircle Budapest. Planning for this one was to be more thorough.
The directive ordered Malinovsky to strike from Sahy southward
toward Estergom on the Danube River to block withdrawal of
German forces from Budapest to the northwest. Other *front*
elements would strike Budapest from the east. Tolbukhin's forces
(which now included 46th Army, south of Budapest) were to
concentrate east and west of Lake Velencei and attack toward

Szekesferhervar and Bickse and beyond to Estergom on the Danube, there to link up with 2d Ukrainian Front forces to encircle German forces in Budapest. The coordinated assault was to commence on 20 December.[230]

On 18–19 December Malinovsky ordered 7th Guards, 53d, and 6th Guards Tank Armies to penetrate enemy defenses west and south of Sahy and develop the offensive to the northwest, west, and southwest to link up with 3d Ukrainian Front near Komarom. East of the Danube the 30th Rifle Corps and Rumanian 7th Army Corps of 7th Guards Army, and 18th Guards Rifle Corps were to occupy Pest by 23 December. 40th, 27th, and Rumanian 4th Armies, on the *front* right flank, were to penetrate into German defenses in the Matra Mountains of Czechoslovakia. To insure rapid movement to the Danube River, Malinovsky placed 6th Guards Tank Army in first echelon.[231] He also ordered Pliyev's Cavalry-Mechanized Group to move west from Szecseny to support 6th Guards Tank Army.

Tolbukhin planned to penetrate the Margareithe Line east and west of Lake Velencei with 4th Guards and 46th Armies, supported by 2d Guards and 7th Guards Mechanized, 18th Tank, and 5th Guards Cavalry Corps. 46th Army was to concentrate two rifle corps in an 8 kilometer sector east of Lake Velencei and attack toward Biscke. 2d Guards Mechanized and 18th Tank Corps would exploit, the former toward Buda and the latter toward the Danube near Estergom. 4th Guards Army was to concentrate three rifle corps in a 7 kilometer sector between the Sharviz Canal and Lake Velencei and attack toward Szekesferhervar. Thereafter, 7th Mechanized Corps and 4th Guards Army units would advance to form an outer encirclement line west of Budapest.[232]

Operational planning in both *fronts* required large scale regrouping of forces under stringent *maskirovka* measures. Within the 3d Ukrainian Front, General G.F. Zakharov's 4th Guards Army had to shift its 20th Guards Rifle Corps from the army left flank to the right flank, there to concentrate with 31st Guards, and 135th Rifle Corps, backed up by 7th Guards Mechanized and 5th Guards Cavalry Corps. The 20th Guards Rifle Corps commander, General N.I. Biryukov, later wrote:

> 20th Corps, on the night of 13 December, handed over its sector to 21st Rifle Corps and then, moving at night 80 kilometers parallel to the front, by the morning of 16 December concentrated in the Sarosd area southeast of

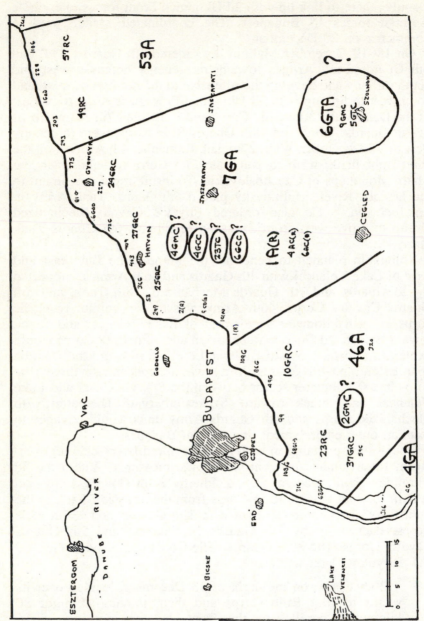

167. Budapest, German intelligence assessment, 4 December 1944

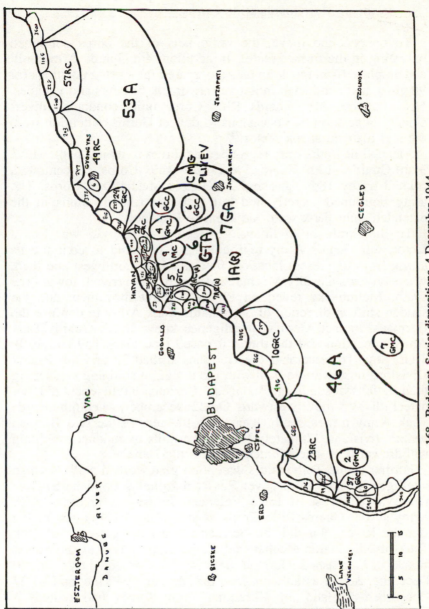

168. Budapest, Soviet dispositions, 4 December 1944

Szekesferhervar. Here we accepted part of the defensive sector of 31st Guards Rifle Corps.[233]

To conceal the move, the radio nets of the corps continued operating in the former sector. In addition, 4th Guards Army built and emplaced 150 mock-up tanks, prepared false firing positions for 90 guns, and conducted imitative movement of tanks and vehicles. Near Polgardi 21st Guards Rifle Corps units conducted diversionary attacks on two occasions to deflect German attention from the real planned attack sector.[234]

Meanwhile 46th Army regrouped its forces to its left flank where 37th Guards, 10th Guards, and 23d Rifle Corps concentrated, backed up by 18th Tank and 2d Guards Mechanized Corps. The army regrouped secretly and left just two rifle divisions in the extended right flank sector adjacent to Budapest.

To the north, in Malinovsky's sector, *maskirovka* was less a factor. 6th Guards Army regrouped and prepared to continue its attack from its present location, first attacking northwest and then, when Pliyev's Cavalry-Mechanized Group had arrived, toward the south. Malinovsky relied on Pliyev's secret movement and the sudden shift in direction of 5th Guards Tank Army to confuse the Germans. In fact, German intelligence knew of 6th Guards Tank Army's location and the threat it posed (see maps 169 and 170). Thus, after 18 December the Germans shifted 3d and 6th Panzer Divisions northward to deal with the threat, in so doing weakening their defenses south of Budapest. German intelligence did not detect Pliyev's move westward. On 22 December, when 6th Guards Tank Army turned south, it cut into the rear of the two German panzer divisions, ultimately forcing the units to conduct a fighting withdrawal from encirclement back to the Danube.

Further south, Tolbukhin's deception plan worked well. German intelligence failed to discover Soviet regrouping opposite Szekesferhervar and east of Lake Velencei. In fact, it recorded 46th Army's 10th Guards Rifle Corps as still being located east of the Danube River. Nor did the Germans detect the presence of 18th Tank or 7th Guards Mechanized Corps until well after the Soviet attack had smashed German defenses.[235] Consequently, the 20 December Soviet assault smashed the Margareithe Line; and by 27 December, 2d and 3d Ukrainian Front forces had united at Estergom, encircling large German and Hungarian forces in the Budapest region.

Soon the larger purpose of the Budapest operation began bearing fruit. In late December IV SS Panzer Corps, consisting of SS Panzer Divisions "Totenkopf" and "Viking," began arriving in the region west of Budapest. This corps had been involved in defensive operations along the Vistula, but now the threat in Hungary had drawn it away from the central sector of the front. Within weeks, its presence along the Vistula would be sorely missed.

At the strategic level, Soviet operations in Hungary had their intended impact – to draw German attention and forces from the central portion of the front. As early as 7 October Gehlen's Foreign Armies East had noted the shifting Soviet emphasis. An assessment of that date read in part:

> After we succeeded in stopping the Soviet Russian offensive, which was directed with strong forces against the General Government [Poland] and against Eastern Prussia, the main thrust has changed to the outer flanks of the army ...[236]

The assessment, however, reiterated the main Soviet priority of striking through central Poland toward the Oder and Berlin.

As the situation in Hungary deteriorated, a 10 November assessment stated:

> Independently of the current operations of the R[ed] A[rmy] against the German flanks [Hungary and 'Kurland'] [which means mainly Estonia], the preparations for large-scale attack operations against the center of the German Front between the Carpathian Mountains and the Memel River are still in progress. It seems that they will soon come to an end. The original intentions were obviously based on a number of assumptions: a. political breakdown of Hungary and thereby the opportunity to destroy Southern Army Group using only relatively small forces and to thrust forward against the 'Porta Viennensis'.
>
> Because of the consolidation of the political situation in Hungary; the suppression of the rebellions in Warsaw and in Slovakia; the German defense successes in the Battle of Debrecen, around Warsaw and in Kurland; and finally in consequence of his heavy casualties, the enemy was forced to delay considerably his planned operations and also to change the foreseen deployment of forces. The scale of the planned operations, however, has basically not been altered. From the preparations we have observed, one can see two main operations which are unchanged and will begin soon:

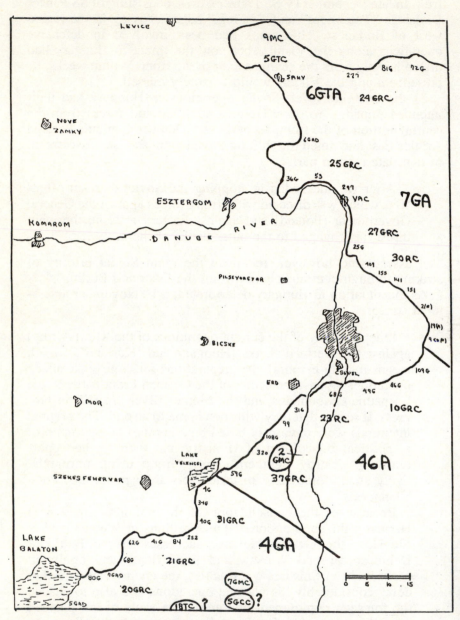

169. Budapest, German intelligence assessment, 19 December 1944

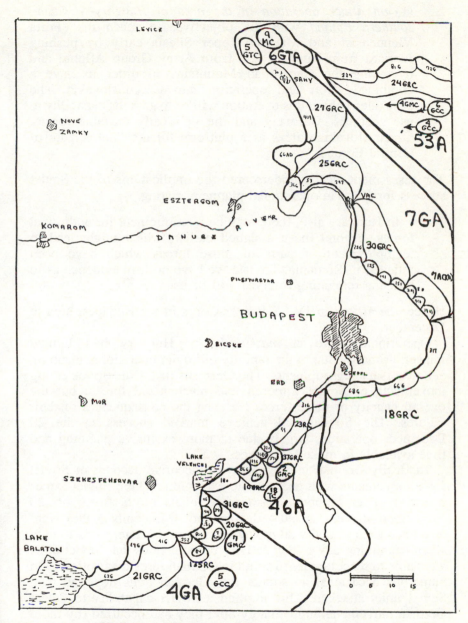

170. Budapest, Soviet dispositions, 19 December 1944

(1) *an attack operation in the area of Hungary–Slovakia–
southern Poland* with the objective: to reach the 'Porta
Viennensis' and Maehren/Upper Silesia early by pushing
forward from Hungary and from Army Group A[lpha] and
bypassing the Carpathian Mountains in order to have a
combined effort and operation into Czechoslovakia. The
basic idea behind this operation will be to gain the capability to
use southeast Germany and the politically unstable former
Czechoslovakian areas as a platform for the final seizure of
Central Europe.[237]

The assessment clearly underscored the implications of the Soviet
success for German operational planners, stating:

In Hungary also, there may be a requirement for additional
forces, beyond those assigned earlier, which might lead to
reemployment of parts of those forces which have been
relieved in Romania. To date we have no firm evidence as to
how the remaining reserves will be used ....[238]

Hence, the arrival of IV SS Panzer Corps in the Budapest area in
December.

Operationally, Soviet *maskirovka* in Hungary had limited
impact, primarily due to the rapidity of Soviet operational planning
and necessary regroupments. The Germans had difficulty detecting
movements of Soviet armored and mechanized forces, but the
overall paucity of these forces lessened the consequences of their
failures. The Soviets did achieve marked success in the 20
December operation, largely due to more extensive planning and
time available to make the moves.

Tactically German intelligence kept accurate account of Soviet
force movements with one notable exception. Where Soviet forces
operated under elaborate *maskirovka* plans (46th Army on 20
November; 4th Guards and 46th Army on 20 December), they were
able to conceal virtually all movements. It is also interesting to note
when examining day-to-day activity on both sides that Soviet units
were able to react rapidly to shifts in German force dispositions. On
numerous occasions, no sooner had German units departed than
Soviet units attacked. This implied a Soviet capability to detect
German movements immediately after they had occurred (by radio
intercept or by reconnaissance). The Soviets say nothing about this
capability. When IV SS Panzer Corps arrived, however, it was able
to mount several major counter-attacks which caught the Soviets by

surprise indicating a Soviet inability to track the progress of the SS units. Again the Soviets give no reason for this contradiction.

Postscript

The operations along the German flanks, in the Baltic and in southeastern Europe, clearly achieved their intent. While the Soviets made important gains, they also achieved their greater purpose – to deflect German attention and resources from the central sector of the front. Although Gehlin and others continually stressed the ultimate importance of the direct approach to Berlin, troops flowed to sectors where combat was the most intense, in particular if other interests in those combat areas were threatened. The Soviets realized German political and economic sensitivities over the Baltic and Danubian Basin regions, and they played on those sensitivities. Bagramyan's, Malinovsky's, and Tolbukhin's forces successfully threatened the German position in both areas; and, in fact, if reinforcements had not been sent, the situation could have become even more critical. This, combined with inactivity in November and December along the Narev and Vistula Rivers, inevitably drew German forces to the flanks. Hitler's preoccupation with the counter-offensive in the west (Ardennes) only exacerbated the situation in Poland as events in January would confirm.

CONCLUSIONS

During 1944 the Soviet capability for conducting strategic *maskirovka* matured. In 1943 the Soviets had been able to conceal their operational intent on numerous occasions; but the Germans were able to discover where Soviet strategic priorities lay. Soviet strategic offensives were more difficult and more costly in terms of Soviet losses. In 1944, however, the Soviets were able to capitalize on strategic patterns formed in 1943, as well as on German pre-conceptions and political notions (mostly Hitler's) to conceal their strategic priorities.

In the winter the Soviets conditioned the Germans into expecting a year-long drive through the Ukraine into Poland and Rumania by constantly conducting operations in that direction. Then, in the spring, the Soviets implemented an elaborate strategic *maskirovka* plan to conceal a strategic redeployment of forces and prepare a secret strategic strike against German forces in Belorussia. As had been the case before Kursk, the Soviets planned in advance an outline for all stages of the summer offensive, and all of those stages were based on the premise that the initial strategic deception would accomplish its aims. And it did.

In June the success of the strategic offensive against Army Group Center exceeded all Soviet expectations. As German reserves moved north to stabilize the situation, the 1st Ukrainian Front struck Army Group Northern Ukraine in coordination with a 1st Belorussian Front attack toward Lublin. As both forces reached the Vistula River, Soviet forces struck in the Baltic and in Rumania, driving back Army Group North and shattering Army Group South Ukraine. By late fall continued Soviet operations on both flanks had drawn German reserves from the center and created new German vulnerabilities in Poland and southern East Prussia, thus paving the way for future Soviet successes in the forthcoming winter offensive.

These Soviet successes were made possible by improved Soviet capabilities to shift large strategic reserves secretly across the front and move them into the forward area without the Germans detecting their presence. The Soviets timed and concealed these regroupings so well that the Germans were unable to counter them, even if portions of the strategic *maskirovka* plan failed. In addition, to a greater extent than before, the Soviets engaged in active disinformation on a strategic scale to exploit German perceptions and economic and political concerns.

Soviet operational *maskirovka* planning was more thorough and efficient in 1944 than it had been in 1943, in part because of improved staff efficiency, more thorough planning procedures, better tactical *maskirovka* training on the part of lower level units, and more thorough supervision of the actual conduct of *maskirovka*. In 1943 the Soviets occasionally had moved armies from one sector to another secretly. By 1944 such practices were routine as evidenced by the Belorussian, L'vov–Sandomierz, Lublin–Brest, and Memel' operations. Even when Soviet operational redeployments were detected by the Germans, it was usually too late to avoid all the tragic consequences (as at Korsun, Proskurov, and Yassy). Only on a few occasions were the Germans able to discern the full scope of Soviet redeployment (such as in the Ukraine and Baltic), and there bad weather and poor terrain hindered Soviet secret movements. Even on these occasions the Germans, although detecting movement, were hard-pressed to match the pace of those movements. In general, during 1944 the Germans gradually lost the ability to track Soviet units regrouping in the operational depths.

Even more alarming for the Germans was their increasing inability to detect Soviet tactical regrouping of forces. In 1941 and 1942 German intelligence knew the position of Soviet tactical units literally the day they arrived in sector. By 1943 this capability had weakened somewhat, but still the Germans seldom "lost" Soviet tactical units for more than one or two days. In 1944, however, when the Soviets wished to deceive the Germans tactically, they could. This normally required extensive Soviet planning and preparation; but, nevertheless, in sectors where they made the necessary effort they could deceive the Germans concerning the presence of many divisions for several days. (For example, 6th Guards and 28th Armies in Belorussia or 4th Guards Army at Budapest.)

At all levels of command the Soviets regrouped faster and in more efficient fashion than in earlier years, in part due to the more efficient Soviet logistical and rail services. Conversely, the Soviets were better able to construct and "animate" false concentrations of forces because they had developed more thorough procedures for such ruses and allocated sufficient trained forces to carry out simulations skillfully. In 1943 most simulations had either failed or only partially succeeded (Belgorod). In 1944 they usually achieved some success (Korsun, L'vov, Vitebsk, Bobruisk, Yassy) by drawing German forces from the main attack region and obscuring the location of the Soviet main attack.

Prior to 1944 the Soviets had concentrated on *maskirovka* prior to an offensive and paid little attention to similar measures after an offensive was underway. In 1944 the Soviets began effecting secret regrouping within a force during the offensive. Thus the Soviets tried to deploy 1st Guards Tank Army forward secretly during the Proskurov operation and used 1st Guards Tank Brigade of 1st Guards Tank Army to deceive the Germans regarding that tank army's direction of attack in the L'vov operation. Although the Soviets were only occasionally successful with these techniques in 1944, they attempted such deception on a larger scale in 1945, in part to compensate for the diminished space in which to conduct maneuver.

Diminished space would be the special factor that altered the nature and form of Soviet *maskirovka* in 1945. During 1944 the front still extended from the North Cape to the Black Sea. The extended front offered the Soviets the opportunity to exploit *maskirovka* in a variety of circumstances and locales. By December 1944 the front ran from the Baltic Sea to the Danube River. As it shortened, Soviet opportunities to conceal their offensive intent also diminished. This provoked them to achieve the same effect, only with different methods.

Soviet success with *maskirovka* in 1944 was, in part, also a product of deteriorating German intelligence capabilities. In August 1944 a Foreign Armies East assessment noted, "The productiveness of the essential elements of the assessment of the enemy situation, signal intelligence, human intelligence, and air reconnaissance, has decreased considerably recently," and attributed this intelligence decline to Soviet use of radio silence, the fast-moving operations which decreased the value of intelligence obtained from human sources and the decrease in German air reconnaissance, in particular in the depths.[239] As defeat followed defeat, German apprehension contributed to the intelligence confusion, for the Germans began to treat every attack indicator with greater seriousness. This further conditioned the Germans to active deception on the Soviets' part. Too much emphasis, however, should not be placed on deteriorating German intelligence, for, as the Germans withdrew westward, signal facilities increased in density. German records show a wealth of intelligence material of all types used to assess Soviet intent to attack and the prospective location of the attack. As late as mid-January 1945, German order of battle on the Soviets was superb; and, after a Soviet offensive commenced, the intelligence picture became clear down to Soviet division and separate brigade level — even in a sector of the front where German defenses had been obliterated.

CHAPTER SEVEN

THE PRACTICE OF *MASKIROVKA*
The Third Period of War, 1945

The simultaneous offensive on the entire Soviet–German front in 1945 by several *fronts* – was unexpected for the enemy. The German command, disoriented concerning strategic conditions .... threw his reserves from one sector of the front to another .... In 1945 the shifting of reserves in general did not achieve its goal, since the attacks followed on all fronts.

> M.M. Kir'yan,
> *Vnezapnost' v nastupatel'nykh operatsiyakh Velikoi Otechestvennoi voiny* [Surprise in Offensive Operations of the Great Patriotic War], 1986

INTRODUCTION

General planning for the 1945 winter strategic offensive began in late October 1944 while Soviet forces on the main direction of advance, along the Vistula and Narev Rivers, were fighting to extend the offensive deeper into Poland. The Soviets assessed the condition of their forces and concluded, at Zhukov's urgings, that Soviet forces needed a rest before resuming the offensive. Consequently, while operations continued on the flanks, after 3 November Soviet forces in the central sector of the front went over to the defensive.

In late October the *STAVKA* and general staff developed the general concept for an offensive to end the war. The concept involved a two-stage campaign commencing in November with the following aims:

- to rout the East Prussian grouping and occupy East Prussia;
- to defeat the enemy in Poland, Czechoslovakia, Hungary and Austria;
- to advance to a line running through the Vistula mouth,

Bromberg (Bydgoszcz), Poznan, Breslau (Wroclaw), Moravska Ostrava and Vienna.

The Warsaw–Berlin line of advance – the zone of the 1st Byelorussian Front – was to be the direction of the main effort. Routing the Courland enemy grouping (the 16th and 18th Armies) was assigned to the 2d and 1st Baltic Fronts and the Baltic Fleet. They were also to prevent the enemy forces pressed to the Baltic Sea from being transferred to other fronts.[1]

Shtemenko later explained the rationale for a two-stage campaign:

It was assumed from the start that the last campaign of the war against Hitlerite Germany would be carried out in two stages. In the first stage, operations were to continue mainly on what might be described as the old line of advance – the southern flank of the Soviet–German front in the Budapest area. It was calculated that a break-through could be achieved here by inserting the main forces of the Third Ukrainian Front between the River Tisza and the Danube, south of Kecskemet. From there they would be able to assist the Second Ukrainian Front with thrusts to the north-west and west .... We had no doubt that the grave threat to their southern flank would force the German command to transfer some of their forces from the Berlin sector, and this in its turn would create favourable conditions for the advance of our main forces – the Fronts deployed north of the Carpathians. The General Staff firmly believed that by the beginning of 1945 the Soviet Army on the lower Vistula would reach Bromberg, capture Poznan and take over the line running through Breslau, Pardubice, Jihlava and Vienna, in other words, advance a distance of between 120 and 350 kilometers. After that would come the second stage of the campaign, which was to culminate in Germany's surrender.[2]

During November and December, the Soviet assaults in the Baltic region and in Hungary confirmed the *STAVKA's* judgement concerning how the Germans would react to threats against their flanks. As the Germans weakened their center, the Soviets began detailed planning for the January strategic offensive. To complete stage one of the campaign, the *STAVKA* planned two large scale operations, both focused on the western strategic direction (see map 171). The first, conducted by the 3d and 2d Belorussian Fronts, would strike the heavily entrenched German East Prussia group. 3d

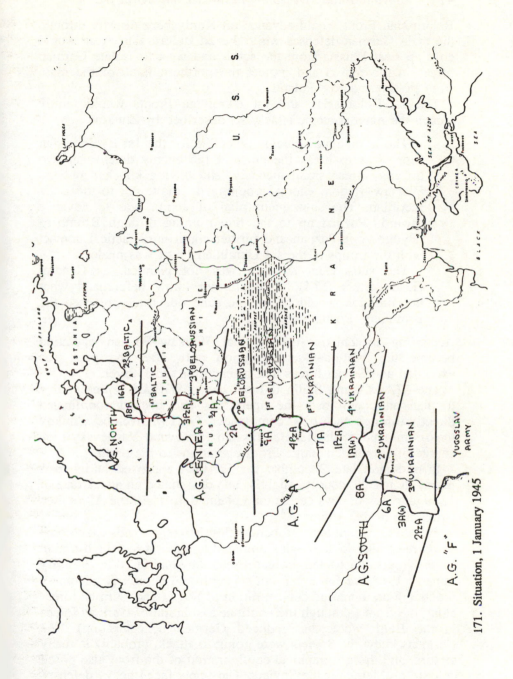

171. Situation, 1 January 1945

Belorussian Front would advance on Konigsberg directly through the main German defenses while the 2d Belorussian Front would envelop East Prussia from the south and west to isolate German forces in the region and protect the northern flank of the main strategic thrust across Poland.

The 1st Belorussian and 1st Ukrainian Fronts would jointly launch the main strategic attack. As described by Zhukov:

> The immediate strategic objective for the 1st Byelorussian Front was to break the crust of the enemy defense in two different areas simultaneously, and having knocked out the Warsaw–Radom enemy grouping, to move out to the Lodz meridian. The subsequent plan of action was to advance towards Poznan up to the line running through Bromberg (Bydgoszcz)–Poznan and further south until tactical contact with the troops of the 1st Ukrainian Front was made.
>
> The subsequent advance was not planned, as General Headquarters [*STAVKA*] could not know beforehand what the situation would be by the time our forces reached the Bromberg–Poznan line.[3]

According to Zhukov the original Warsaw–Poznan operation became the Vistula–Oder operation only after the plan was exceeded and Soviet forces had reached the Oder River.

The *STAVKA* and Stalin did not use a *STAVKA* representative to plan and coordinate the operations and instead coordinated directly through each *front* commander. On 15 November Zhukov took command of the 1st Belorussian Front, and Vasilevsky took charge of 1st and 2d Baltic Front operations to the north.

In mid- and late December the *STAVKA* approved initial *front* plans, altered the concept slightly, and designated an attack date of 12 January, eight days earlier than planned, to assist the Allies then struggling in the Ardennes.[4]

From the standpoint of conducting strategic and operational *maskirovka*, the Soviet High Command and *fronts* faced a different set of circumstances and problems than they had faced in 1944. By January 1945 the Eastern Front's length had shrunk considerably producing an increased concentration of Soviet and German forces along the front (although the continued isolation of German forces in the Baltic somewhat reduced German concentration). The Germans knew the Soviets were going to attack, probably in many sectors; and the geographical configuration of the front also posed definite problems for the Soviets. They now faced heavy defenses on the East Prussian–Konigsberg direction and heavy German concentrations on the western outskirts of Budapest. Soviet forces were mired in mountain fighting across the width of the Carpathian Mountains; and, on the western direction, they occupied restrictive bridgeheads across the Narev and Vistula Rivers from which they would have to launch their new offensive. Thus, the Soviets would have difficulty masking their intent to attack and the attack's location, strategically and operationally. Continued operations in Hungary could distract the Germans but only regarding the scale of offensives elsewhere.

To solve these problems, Soviet planners sought to develop a *maskirovka* plan which concealed primarily the scale of the attack rather than its location, timing, or their overall offensive intent. While doing so, they implemented operational and tactical deception measures which could possibly blur the German perception of attack timing and location. In general, this required strenuous *STAVKA* efforts to conceal regrouping and concentration of forces on the critical western direction. All the while the Soviets planned to continue operations in Hungary to fix German reserves in that region and posture forces on the western direction to distract German attention away from the key Königsberg approach and the Narev and Vistula bridgeheads.

VISTULA–ODER, JANUARY 1945

The *STAVKA* ordered the 1st Belorussian and 1st Ukrainian Fronts to conduct the winter offensive on the main western direction. By early December 1944 it had established the direction and zones of attack and the depth of immediate and subsequent objectives and had assigned *front* commanders who would coordinate directly with the *STAVKA* while preparing and conducting the operation. On 16 November Zhukov took command of the 1st Belorussian Front. Konev retained command of the 1st Ukrainian Front. Although, by mid-November, the offensive plan was complete with the attack date set for 20 January, to maintain secrecy the *STAVKA* did not issue detailed directives to the *fronts* until late December.[5]

The *STAVKA* concept required the 1st Belorussian Front to launch three attacks. It would launch its main attack from the Magnushev bridgehead, using three combined arms armies (61st, 5th Shock, and 8th Guards) to penetrate German defenses; and two tank armies (1st Guards and 2d Guards) and one cavalry corps (2d Guards) to conduct the exploitation toward Poznan. The 69th and

33d Armies, backed up by 9th and 11th Tank Corps and 7th Guards Cavalry Corps, would conduct a secondary attack from the Pulavy bridgehead toward Lodz; and the 47th Army, cooperating with the 1st Polish Army, would launch another secondary assault to envelop Warsaw. 3d Shock Army was in *front* reserve.[6]

Konev's 1st Ukrainian Front would conduct one powerful assault from the Sandomierz bridgehead. 6th, 3d Guards, 5th Guards, 13th, 52d, and 60th Armies, supported by the 25th, 31st, and 4th Guards Tank Corps, would penetrate German defenses; and the 3d Guards and 4th Tank Armies would conduct the exploitation. 21st and 59th Armies, in *front* second echelon, would join the attack shortly after it had begun. Konev's *front* was to attack toward Radomsko and subsequently develop the offensive toward Breslau.

The two *fronts* would attack in time-phased sequence. Konev's forces would initiate the attack on 12 January from the Sandomierz bridgehead and two days later Zhukov would commence his assaults from Pulavy and Magnushev.[7]

The geographical position of the two Soviet *fronts* made *maskirovka* extremely difficult. The Germans knew an attack was likely and had been predicting precise attack dates since late November. Repeated failure of the attack to materialize, however, dulled the credibility of these predictions. They also knew the attack would have to come from the bridgeheads across the Vistula or from the area south of the Vistula to the Carpathian Mountains. The primary indicator of an imminent attack would be the obligatory build-up of Soviet forces along the front, in particular within the bridgeheads. To continue confusing the Germans regarding the time of attack, the Soviets would have to keep secret the build-up of forces while attempting, in so far as possible, to deceive the Germans regarding attack location.

The *STAVKA* realized Zhukov's and Konov's *fronts* required large scale reinforcement before they could mount decisive offensives which could be sustained through the depths of Poland. This meant increasing the strength of Soviet forces in central Poland by as much as 50 percent by the assignment and movement into the area of significant strategic reserves. Consequently, the *STAVKA* reinforced the 1st Belorussian Front with three combined arms armies (33d, 61st, and 3d Shock), one tank army (1st Guards), and numerous supporting units. 1st Ukrainian Front received four combined arms armies (6th, 21st, 52d, 59th), one tank army (3d Guards), and one tank corps (7th Guards). Total reinforcements amounted to almost sixty rifle divisions, four tank corps, one mechanized corps, and over 120 artillery regiments.[8] Regrouping of these forces had to be accomplished secretly if the Soviets were to achieve any degree of surprise.

The *maskirovka* plan required by the *STAVKA* and implemented by Zhukov and Konev sought to achieve two distinct aims. First, it sought to conceal the size of the regrouping effort and the timing and the scale of the offensive. Second, the Soviets sought to focus German attention on secondary sectors, in particular on the region south of the Vistula River. The Soviets had no misconceptions concerning the German belief that an attack would occur in the near future. Their overall intent was to weaken the German capability to resist the attack, principally by concealing its scale.

Both *fronts* drew upon planning experience of earlier operations and used every conceivable method to insure planning secrecy. In November and December a limited number of senior officers developed initial *front* plans. In late December the planning circle expanded when army commanders and select staff officers joined the process. No written orders were prepared, and all instructions were given orally. *Front* commanders gave army commanders their orders personally in early January. Regimental commanders received their orders 4–5 days before the attack; battalion and company commanders, 2–3 days prior to the attack; platoon leaders, one day; and soldiers, hours before the attack.[9] In the 1st Belorussian Front's tank armies, only the chief of staff and chiefs of the operations section and artillery were familiar with attack plans. All other orders went to individual responsible persons only when required. Tank corps commanders received their orders orally five days prior to the offensive and mobile brigade commanders three days before the attack. Rear service commanders received only individual orders and were kept uninformed of the overall offensive scheme. Both *fronts* placed command and observation posts as far forward as possible and prepared wire communications to the forward area but did not use them until the assault commenced.

Within this atmosphere of strict secrecy Zhukov and Konev prepared *maskirovka* plans which incorporated active measures to disinform the Germans about the location of the attack and passive measures to conceal the arrival of reserves and concentration of attack forces in the bridgeheads. Zhukov created a simulated force concentration on the extreme left flank of the 1st Belorussian Front near Joselow and on the army right flank north of Warsaw to attract German reconnaissance and reserves. Near Joselow the *front* emplaced 1000 mock-up tanks, SP guns, and vehicles to simulate a

478   Soviet Military Deception in the Second World War

concentration of armored, mechanized, and rifle units. Rail and road traffic into the area increased, and radio sets from 1st Guards and 2d Guards Tank Armies established radio nets in the region using real unit call signs and frequencies. Real tanks and vehicles animated the false concentration, while engineers constructed and repaired bridges and roads throughout the region. Frontal aviation intensified activity in the sector, installed new forward airfields, and flew reconnaissance and aerial photograph missions over this sector of the front. All of this activity was closely coordinated with the real regrouping and concentration of forces in the Magnushev and Pulavy bridgeheads.[10]

Meanwhile, in the *fronts'* actual attack sectors, troops continued defensive work and maintained strict *maskirovka* discipline. All incoming transport was camouflaged to resemble loads of hay or building materials. Combat equipment (tanks, artillery) was unloaded at night and camouflaged by day, tank tracks were obliterated, and empty rail cars dispersed throughout the *front* rear area. All engineer work associated with offensive preparations occurred at night. Army and *front* staff officers inspected the quality of *maskirovka* by air. The respective *front* and army commandant's service prepared and supervised the plan of movement for all forces into assembly and jumping-off positions. Attack preparations on the *front's* right flank in 47th Army's sector, although deceptive in nature during the early stage of the operation, were also real, for 47th Army was to attack on 15 January, one day after the *front* assaults from the Magnushev and Pulavy bridgeheads.

Regrouping and concentration of 1st Belorussian Front forces in the two restrictive bridgeheads and east of the Vistula River was heavily masked according to strict plan. The limited size of the bridgeheads and their open terrain restricted the number of forces which could occupy them. Zhukov concentrated the bulk of 8th Guards Army and 5th Shock Army plus one corps of 61st Army in the bridgehead. He deployed the remainder of 61st Army and 1st Guards and 2d Guards Tank Armies in concealed positions on the east bank of the river.

Zhukov's reinforcing forces from *STAVKA* reserve moved into the area in staggered sequence. 33d Army arrived after 18 October and occupied positions on the extreme *front* left flank where it participated in the simulated offensive build-up. Ultimately, it shifted the bulk of its forces to a narrow sector on its right flank within the Pulavy bridgehead, where 69th Army likewise concentrated 90 percent of its forces. 61st Army arrived in the area from

STAVKA reserve in late December, assembled east of the Vistula, and then in early January moved one rifle corps into a narrow sector on the right flank of the Magnushev bridgehead. After 19 November Katukov's 1st Guards Tank Army moved by rail and road 300 kilometers from its refitting area west of L'vov and concentrated in the forests 30 kilometers northwest of Lublin on 30 November where it remained concealed until ordered forward to new assembly areas just east of the Vistula River.[11] Tanks and artillery moved by rail, and the forces moved by road along numerous roads at night, all the while avoiding population centers and using forested areas for daytime halts. Security on the march was strict. According to Soviet critics, "The organs of SMERSH [Chekists] successfully liquidated enemy agents" who tried to locate 1st Guards Tank Army.[12] In December 1st Guards Tank Army conducted training and war games near Lublin in an atmosphere of secrecy described by one corps commander as follows:

> The preparation of forces for the offensive was conducted in deep secrecy. The 1st Belorussian Front staff directive, which specified the missions of 1st Guards Tank Army, was revealed to a limited circle of the command staff: the members of the military council, the assistant commanders, and the chief of the operations section. It was forbidden to type documents of the operational plan, and orders for preparing troops for the offensive were given orally. It was prohibited to conduct telephone conversations on matters pertaining to offensive preparations; and radio stations, as before, were silent. Brigades received their orders five days before the offensive.[13]

Between 11 and 14 January 1st Guards Tank Army moved at night into positions on the east bank of the Vistula River, concealed in forested areas and heavily camouflaged. Only then did low-level commanders receive their orders and conduct their reconnaissance. Commanders conducted their reconnaissance dressed in the uniforms of rifle forces accompanied by 8th Guards Army commanders already in the bridgehead.[14]

The *front's* reserve army, 3d Shock, had to move almost 1000 kilometers from its positions in 2d Baltic Front's sector to new assembly areas east of Warsaw. On 2 December the army turned its positions over to 10th Guards Army and began entraining for the long trip south. On 10 December rail movement began using 23 trains for each of the army's three rifle corps. All trains were heavily camouflaged and moved only at night under radio silence. Once in the new concentration area trains unloaded over a 17 day period outside of populated areas. The last unit of 3d Shock Army completed its unloading on 10 January 50 kilometers east of Warsaw. The move had required a total of 117 trains and one month to complete. The depth of the move prevented the Germans from either seeing or disrupting it.[15]

While this extensive regrouping progressed, 8th Guards and 5th Shock Armies, in the bridgehead, and 2d Guards Tank Army, east of the Vistula, also regrouped into concentration areas for the attack, almost literally under German eyes. 8th Guards Army's task was formidable, for it was to concentrate eight rifle divisions into a sector less than 10 kilometers wide. General Chuikov described how he attempted to do this secretly:

> In order to distract the attention of the enemy from our preparations, I suggested implementation of a plan of gradually concentrating forces and weaponry in jumping-off positions. The movement of troops and equipment occurred only at night and in a proportion which could be masked by morning. In the daytime forces, located in trenches in view of the enemy, had to carry on 'household' work intensively: the enemy thought that we were preparing not for an offensive but for a firm defense, in accordance with the use of troop and equipment resources. We tried to use widely loudspeaker broadcasting stations: even music sounded over our positions, entertaining our soldiers and lulling the attentiveness of the enemy.[16]

5th Shock Army had to concentrate three rifle corps of nine rifle divisions into its narrow bridgehead sector of 10 kilometers. The army had been assigned to 1st Belorussian Front in October (from 3d Ukrainian Front) and had occupied assembly areas east of the Vistula River opposite the Magnushev bridgehead. Beginning on 28 December the army moved at night along two routes and across two bridges into the bridgehead. The 100 kilometer march by 100,000 men and equipment was heavily masked.[17] A division commander in the army later wrote:

> The troops entered the bridgehead while observing strict *maskirovka* measures. A dense network of traffic control posts was deployed to control observation of march discipline. Preparation of artillery positions occurred only at night, at first light work ceased, and open trenches were camouflaged with snow or white camouflage nets. All of this permitted us to

concentrate in the bridgehead a large mass of people and equipment and prepare for the offensive without being noticed by the enemy.[18]

The engineers contributed to the *maskirovka* efforts in the Magnushev bridgehead by building 13 one kilometer bridges capable of carrying 16–60 ton loads across the Vistula River. Some of the bridges served the *maskirovka* plan. For example, three bridges crossed into 8th Guards Army's sector. Two of the bridges entered forested areas, and the third terminated in an open region. The Soviets used the two bridges into forested areas to convey troops and equipment into the bridgehead, while the open bridge carried return traffic.[19] Zhukov and his army commanders used similar measures to concentrate 69th and 33d Armies in the Pulavy bridgehead.

Konev's *maskirovka* plan was far more elaborate that Zhukov's, in part because it had to be, given that Konev's attack would occur from only one bridgehead and also because Konev could use the region south of the Vistula River as a part of his deception plan. Konev realized the difficulties he faced and later modestly wrote:

> I do not maintain that our deceptive measures enabled us to achieve a complete tactical surprise in the direction of our main attack from the Sandomierz bridgehead, although I can vouch for the fact that they were helpful.[20]

These helpful measures included a major active simulation on the *front's* left flank and Draconian measures to conceal the concentration of resources and the build-up in the Sandomierz bridgehead.[21] On 21 December Konev ordered preparations of a simulated offensive concentration on the *front's* left flank in 60th Army's sector (see map 172). The order read:

1. Prior to the commencement of active operations for breaching the enemy defense, create a false concentration of a tank army and a tank corps on the left wing of the front in the sector of 60th Army, in the Ropchitsa, Otseka and Dembitsa region.
2. Conduct operational *maskirovka* with army forces in the shortest possible period (no more than 5–7 days), for which use the 4th Guards Tank Corps for 2–3 days in the sector of 60th Army, with subsequent lateral movement of it into the region of actual concentration, and leave behind mock-ups of tanks and artillery in the region of temporary disposition of the tank corps.
3. *Maskirovka* measures should be distinguished by exceptional

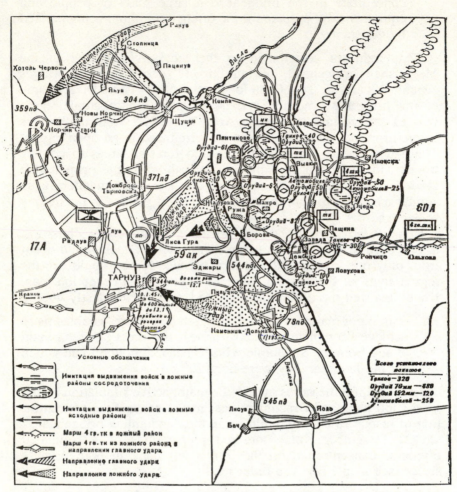

Схема 23. Замысел оперативной маскировки в Висло-Одерской операции 1-го Украинского фронта и
выполнение плана оперативной маскировки войсками 60-й армии

172. Vistula–Oder, 1st Ukrainian Front deception plan

plausibility for which it is necessary to enlist tank corps for short
periods, utilizing their movements.
4. The demonstration of false concentrations should be combined
with, and directly associated with, the actual concentration.[22]

Accordingly, 60th Army formulated a plan to implement Konev's
order and established an operational group to supervise preparation and conduct of the *maskirovka* operation. The group consisted

of representatives from each force branch (artillery–tank and mechanized–communications–engineers–political section) headed by the deputy chief of the operations section. It assigned to the group *front* forces to perform the *maskirovka* work including: the 77th and 78th Engineer Battalions/16th Separate Assault Engineer-Sapper Brigade and 22d Separate Maskirovka Company, and 60th Army forces consisting of a combat engineer battalion; two battalions of the 177th Army Reserve Rifle Regiment; a rifle battalion of the 908th Rifle Regiment, 246th Rifle Division; 10 vehicles from the 106th Rifle Corps; two army MGUs; 15 officer billeting party members; 200 collapsible tank mock-ups; a fighter aircraft element; two–three artillery batteries; two high-power artillery batteries for simulating adjusting fire; up to three small caliber anti-aircraft artillery batteries; and officer reconnaissance parties from defending army regiments.[23]

The *maskirovka* operation was subdivided into three periods: the preparatory period from 21 to 31 December; the demonstration period from 1 to 12 January; and the wrap-up period from 12 to 15 January. During the preparatory period the local population and road units built roads and constructed unloading stations while groups of officers, dressed in tankers' uniforms, conducted reconnaissance on the march routes, gave building instructions, and gave out false information to the population. From 22 December to 3 January roads were repaired between Ropchitsa, Otseka and Domb'ye; bypasses were built for tanks around several towns; and secret unloading routes were created through the forests near unloading sites. All preparations were organized to resemble similar measures for a real offensive. During the preparatory period, engineer units prepared mock-ups of 320 T-34 tanks, 250 ZIS-5 trucks, 480 76mm guns, and 120 152mm guns, all assembled in three general areas.[24]

On 1 January the *front* staff ordered the demonstration to begin. 60th Army, while continuing to defend its front, now implemented a regrouping plan to shift its forces to its right flank. Since bad weather prevented German aerial reconnaissance, the plan to demonstrate tank transport by rail and unloading was cancelled. Instead, all *maskirovka* measures now only sought to misinform enemy agents in the Soviet rear.

Early on 27 December 4th Guards Tank Corps arrived in 60th Army's sector where it stayed for two days. Then, late on 29 December, it moved secretly northwest toward its actual concentration area in the Sandomierz bridgehead. As the corps moved through the region, on the route from Zheshuv, through Ropchitsa, to Dembitsa, engineers emplaced mock-up tanks and guns. By 3 January, in place of the departed corps were 462 mock-ups of tanks, guns, and vehicles in three assembly areas; and more were emplaced later to a total of 600. Special commands then animated the false assembly areas using troop and vehicle movements and bonfires. The operational group supervised the commands with three *front* staff officers. On the seventh day of the demonstration the special commands simulated the forward positioning of artillery and used roving guns to simulate the adjustment of artillery fire. These measures were noted by enemy reconnaissance or agents, for, on the fourth day of the demonstration, German artillery fire struck one of the false concentration areas.[25]

Meanwhile the officer billeting parties operated in the region from 3–6 January, warning the population of the influx of units and dangers of the new offensive. From 1 to 4 January roving guns and mortars adjusted fire on enemy positions from false gun positions while insuring that all calibers of weapons participated. Then from 3 to 6 January, while adjusting went on, artillery units simulated forward movement. This involved transport forward of 550 gun mock-ups. Simultaneously the 336th, 148th, and 100th Rifle Divisions conducted night reconnaissance and raids in their sectors. From 4 to 6 January forward units intensified reconnaissance to simulate final attack preparations. The reconnaissance determined that the Germans had detected the concentration and were strengthening defenses in 60th Army's sector. As a consequence, the Germans moved the 344th Infantry Division into the Tarnow sector; and two days later the 359th Infantry Division moved from Tarnow into front line positions opposite 60th Army.[26]

Konev also ordered a smaller scale *maskirovka* operation to be conducted on the *front's* right flank to conceal the forward deployment of two artillery divisions and two tank destroyer brigades. 6th Army, on the right flank of the Sandomierz bridgehead, constructed false artillery firing positions and animated them with roving guns to cover the displacement of the larger artillery units. The Germans continued firing on the original gun positions long after the artillery had displaced to the main penetration sector.[27]

While Konev's active disinformation program unfolded, *STAVKA* reserves moved forward into the *front* sector and, together with in-place forces, occupied concentration areas in the bridgehead or assembly areas east of the Vistula River. During December and January Konev received three armies (21st, 52d,

59th), one army headquarters (6th) and 3d Guards Tank Army from the *STAVKA*, and most had to move considerable distances to arrive in sector. 21st Army, which in November had been part of 3d Belorussian Front on the Königsberg direction (and was still held to be there by German intelligence), in late December moved south and assembled in early January east of the Vistula River. 52d Army, which had operated in Rumania until early December, shifted north that month into *STAVKA* reserves near Vladimir–Volynsk. At the end of December it came under 1st Ukrainian Front control and deployed forward across the Vistula to occupy a sector in the Sandomierz bridgehead between 13th and 5th Guards Armies. In late December the *STAVKA* released 6th Army headquarters to Konev. He assigned to it several divisions of 3d Guards and 13th Armies and a wide sector on the right flank of the Sandomierz bridgehead and along the east bank of the Vistula River to serve as a holding force on the right flank of his main shock group and to assist in Zhukov's offensive simulation.

Konev's second reserve army, the 59th, had to travel from the Vyborg area into its new offensive sector. On 26 November 59th Army gave its sector to 23d Army and entrained for the south over 1000 kilometers. The army commander described the move:

> The transfer of army forces by railroad took place with the maintenance of great secrecy. No one at all knew the destination of the army, the route of movement or the unloading regions. Only when passing through Moscow, the army commander was given an orientation in the General Staff, that 59th Army was being included in the 1st Ukrainian Front and would concentrate on the eastern bank of the Vistula in the Zhushyv region.[28]

In early December the army commander, his operational group, and lead troop elements arrived in their assembly areas. The remaining forces followed by early January.

On 4 January 59th and 21st Armies moved forward to occupy positions in close proximity to the river, all the while concealing their move as efficiently as possible. 59th Army approached the river at night and occupied concealed assembly areas 60 kilometers from the front lines. By 8 January both armies were poised to cross the river and join the attacking Soviet forces.

Konev's two tank armies, under cover of his simulated tank army concentration south of the Vistula, prepared to move into the Sandomierz bridgehead where they would attack on the first day of the offensive. 3d Guards Tank Army, under *STAVKA* control since its August battles on the Sandomierz bridgehead, returned to 1st Ukrainian Front control on 20 October and concentrated south of the town of Sandomierz where it conducted exercises in preparation for the next offensive. On 8 December Rybalko received his army's mission in a meeting with Konev at Demba, and on 24 December he briefed his corps commanders on their missions. During the nights of 2–5 January 3d Guards Tank Army deployed forward into the Sandomierz bridgehead. There, on 9 January, brigade and regimental commanders received their missions and briefed subordinate battalion and company commanders.[29] Throughout the entire preparation period 3d Guards Tank Army remained in relatively close proximity to the front line.

4th Tank Army also prepared for combat close to the front. It phased forward in the same fashion as 3d Guards Tank Army. On the evening of 11 January both armies advanced to jumping-off positions 10–12 kilometers behind the deployed rifle forces.

Within the Sandomierz bridgehead massive regrouping occurred as the forces of five combined arms armies concentrated in a sector less than 50 kilometers wide where elements of only three armies had hitherto been deployed. Konev's Chief of Front Engineers established *maskirovka* requirements and supervised their fulfillment. Since German observation posts could observe to a depth of 5–8 kilometers beyond Soviet forward positions, all movement had to be concealed as much as possible by earthworks, trenches, forests, or simple night blackout movement. Where the terrain was open, engineers installed camouflaged vertical masking to hide movement on roads and other communications routes. By 12 January engineers had built 73 kilometers of vertical masking and had dug 121 kilometers of communications trenches.[30]

Since forests were small and scattered throughout the bridgehead engineers erected vertical masks formed from vegetation which extended from within the forests well into open areas. Shelters made of branches and vegetation hid vehicles and tanks, and watchmen insured units did not cut down precious timber to further denude the already open area. A total of 240 kilometers of vertical vegetation masks were erected, and 180 kilometers of cross country roads were carved through the forests.

Front staff designated nine distinct regions within the bridgehead, each formed around patches of forest and each containing its own road network. These regions were used to effect the final concentration of troops during late December, and each unit passed through or deployed into a specific coded region. Units deployed forward in measured order so as to not strain the concealment capacity of each region. That amounted to one or two rifle divisions per night. Divisions moved in battalion columns supervised by an extensive commandant's (traffic control) service which directed each division to its proper location. Only these thorough preparations permitted the concentration of about 500,000 men and their equipment in so limited a bridgehead without substantial detection by the Germans.[31]

Despite these *maskirovka* measures the Soviets were under no illusion about the German expectation of an attack from the Vistula bridgeheads. Thus they incorporated into their offensive scheme new attack forms and procedures – often ones tested before but not widely employed since. 5th Guards Army used one such technique that it had used before at Stalingrad and Krivoi Rog. The new technique involved initiating the attack with a platoon assault force from each first echelon rifle battalion. Each platoon was reinforced by two tanks, one SP gun, and several mock-up tanks. These platoons simulated attacks across the entire front 30 minutes prior to the planned artillery preparation to draw German forces into their defensive positions so that they would be then subject to the devastating preparatory fires. 5th Guards Army also used smoke screens to cover the deceptive platoon attacks and the main attack when it occurred.[32]

The two *front* commanders changed their patterns of artillery preparations to deceive the Germans. Instead of firing an extensive preparation, Zhukov planned a 25 minute barrage at first light, followed by the assaults of forward battalions (a special echelon). On the heels of the forward battalions, division main forces would advance in force. If its forward battalions were halted, a 70 minute heavy artillery preparation would ensue. Konev intended to fire a short, violent 15 minute artillery barrage at 0445, after which forward battalions would attack. Then, at 1000, a 107 minute artillery preparation would occur. 45 minutes before its end the simulated platoon attacks would begin, forcing the Germans to open fire and reveal their positions. The last 15 minutes of the long preparation would be barrage fire which would intensify as it reached its conclusion.[33]

Throughout the period of these intensive preparations, the Soviets supplemented their active and passive *maskirovka* measures with intensive security activity conducted by the NKVD in the rear to uncover agents and counter German diversionary activity. Only one example is cited by the Soviets, who wrote:

> In the beginning of January 'Abwehrkommand 202' alone dispatched behind the front lines more than 100 diversionary reconnaissance groups. Their liquidation was the basic task of the NKVD, all of whose activity occurred in accordance with the orders of the front military councils. They maintained close ties with the local party and democratic organizations, which helped expose the enemy and his agents. The security organ of the staffs and rear services played an important role in the search for diversionary forces.[34]

The increased efficiency of Soviet rear security services (NKVD), which were employed in greater and greater number, partially explained the deterioration of German human intelligence sources in this as well as in previous operations.

To what degree did Soviet *maskirovka* succeed? The most extensive Soviet critique states:

> As a result of the measures conducted for operational maskirovka the enemy was disoriented as to the strength and, partially, the direction of the main attack of the 1st Ukrainian Front. Expecting the offensive of the Soviet troops from the bridgehead, the Hitlerites formed their reserves there. Knowing about the concentration of tanks and equipment on the left wing of the front they simultaneously kept a strong force (about five reinforced divisions) in this sector prior to the very commencement of the penetration.
>
> Through their plausibility and completeness, the set of maskirovka measures conducted by the Soviet troops during the preparation of the Vistula—Oder operation disoriented the German fascist command as to the composition of our forces, the time of the offensive, and partially about the direction of the main attack. Preparation of the Sandomierz bridgehead regarding maskirovka made it possible to concentrate and accommodate covertly the troops arriving for the offensive.
>
> The false grouping of our forces on the east bank of the Vistula and the simulation of a direction of attack toward Krakow riveted the enemy motorized and tank units designated for countering our attack.
>
> The 4th Guards Tank Corps, as well as 21st Army

concentrated somewhat north of it, played a large role in the creation of the plausibility of the force and its animation.[35]

An examination of German intelligence documents clearly indicates that the Germans expected an attack throughout the central sector of the front from the Neiman River to the Carpathians. In fact, the Germans had expected the attack to occur since late October and had continuously revised their estimates when the offensives did not occur. A 5 January assessment by Fremde Heere Ost [Foreign Armies East] stated:

> The large scale Soviet winter offensive, for which definite dates (26 Oct, 7 Nov, end of Nov, 10 Dec, 19 Dec, 1 Jan) were determined during recent months on the basis of reliable reports, was again postponed because of unfavorable weather conditions and also, apparently, for political reasons. At present, the middle of January can be considered the next possible date of attack.[36]

Although the report reflects German concern for an attack, it also displays an air of uncertainty. Repeated postponements and frustrated expectations cast doubt on the 5 January prediction.

Regarding the direction of the Soviet offensive, the estimate indicated Army Group A in Poland was the target, stating:

> The main effort of the entire operation is still obviously in the sector of Army Group A. The directions of the main effort, which from previous reports led by way of Crakow into the Czech region, has apparently been transferred to the north-west into the Silesian area, by way of the Upper Silesian industrial region.[37]

Even here, there is evidence of German uncertainty regarding precisely where the main attack would occur – a tendency which forced the Germans to recognize credible threats on every axis of Soviet advance. In annex 2 to the report, Gehlen assessed that Konev's 1st Ukrainian Front would make the main attack from the Baranov [Sandomierz] bridgehead with the first objective being the Kattowitz–Tschenstochau region. This attack would be accompanied by strong forces operating south of the Vistula toward Krakow.[38] This assessment is in direct response to Konev's deception plan. Gehlen went on to describe the 1st Belorussian Front mission, which he assessed was to envelop Warsaw by pushing out of the Warka [Magnushev] bridgehead, first to the southwest and then

to the west and northwest direction.[39] Here Gehlin recognized
Zhukov's deception operation on 1st Belorussian Front's right flank
sector north of Warsaw.

To complicate the picture Gehlen cites intelligence collection
problems and their impact, stating:

> The fact that on the one hand all reports from agents
> designate the western and northwestern part of the Baranov
> bridgehead as the area of special importance, but on the other
> hand all other evidence (air reconnaissance, artillery recon-
> naissance, interrogation of POWs) points to the northern
> front, leaves us for the time being with the question as to
> whether this is due to extremely good camouflage measures in
> the western and northern parts of the bridgehead or due to
> agents' reports not being fully exploited.
>
> In any case one must take into account that the enemy in the
> first instance, might try to clear the Great Vistula salient by
> pushing from the Vistula bridgeheads of Baranow, Pulawy and
> Warka — possible under timely echeloning ahead of the main
> operations of the 1st Ukrainian and White Russian Fronts in
> order to enlarge the space necessary for deployment west of
> the Vistula River.[40]

In addition to testifying to the effectiveness of Soviet *maskirovka*,
this passage raises the possibility of a limited objective Soviet attack
from the Vistula bridgehead aimed at creating a larger, more
continuous bridgehead on the west bank of the river.

In conclusion Gehlen recognized the impact of earlier Soviet
offensives in Hungary, in particular regarding the shift of German
reserves to the south:

> Since the enemy has been successful, through the develop-
> ment of the situation in Hungary, in forcing the withdrawal of
> strong German reserves from the main effort sector of Army
> Groups A and Center, it is necessary, from the standpoint of an
> estimate of the enemy, to point out the importance of
> corresponding German strategic reserves, which will make it
> possible to prevent great initial successes by the enemy, i.e. to
> defeat the enemy by not permitting him to take the initiative.[41]

German Army Group "A" assessed that it was opposed by two
large Soviet groupings (see maps 173 and 174). It estimated the
southern group, the 1st Ukrainian Front, would conduct its main
effort from the Baranov [Sandomierz] bridgehead and from the

San–Vistula triangle. It added that strong attacks would also occur between Debica and the Vistula in connection with the Baranov attack. Thus Army Group "A" also believed Konev's deception plan. Army Group "A" calculated that it was opposed by four rifle armies and six mobile (tank and mechanized) corps of the 1st Ukrainian Front, with one additional army and three more mobile groups available for reinforcement (see maps 175 and 176). At the time the 1st Ukrainian Front fielded nine rifle armies, six tank corps, and three mechanized corps. Army Group "A" assessed the 1st Belorussian Front to contain three rifle armies, one Polish Army, and three tank corps with two rifle armies and three mobile corps available as reinforcements (see maps 177 and 178). At the time 1st Belorussian Front actually possessed eight rifle armies, five tank corps, and two mechanized corps. Regarding the imminence of the Soviet attack, the army group stated that although the enemy assembly phase had been completed, there was no evidence yet that the units and their supporting artillery were deploying forward into immediate assembly areas and prepared firing positions.[42]

While the Soviets achieved only limited success in confusing the Germans regarding the location and timing of the attack, they had immense success in masking the scale of the attack when it did occur. The Germans missed the Soviet redeployment of 61st, 3d Shock, 33d, 52d, 21st, and 59th Armies from the *STAVKA* reserve. They assessed that these armies were either in their former sectors up to a thousand kilometers distant or were deep in the Soviet rear area. The Germans detected the possible presence of 6th Army head-quarters but the Soviets probably intended the army to be detected as a part of their deception plan on the right wing of the 1st Ukrainian Front. The Germans detected 5th Shock Army but believed it was assembled east of the Vistula, when actually it was concentrated in the Magnushev bridgehead. The Germans assessed that 2d Guards Tank Army was 100–150 kilometers east of the Magnushev bridgehead when it was actually concentrated on the east bank of the river. 1st Guards Tank Army was located on German intelligence documents to the southwest of L'vov, when, in fact, it had also moved to concentration areas east of the Vistula River opposite the Magnushev bridgehead. 3d Guards Tank Army was depicted as being southeast of the Vistula River east of Debica, thus positioned to attack either toward Krakow or from the Sandomierz bridgehead. German intelligence was more accurate regarding the location of 4th Tank Army. It assessed one corps as being in the Sandomierz bridgehead and the second corps as prepar-

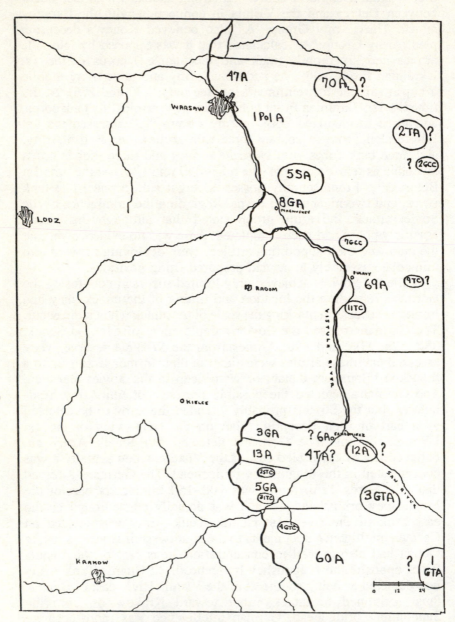

173. Vistula–Oder, German intelligence assessment, 11 January 1945

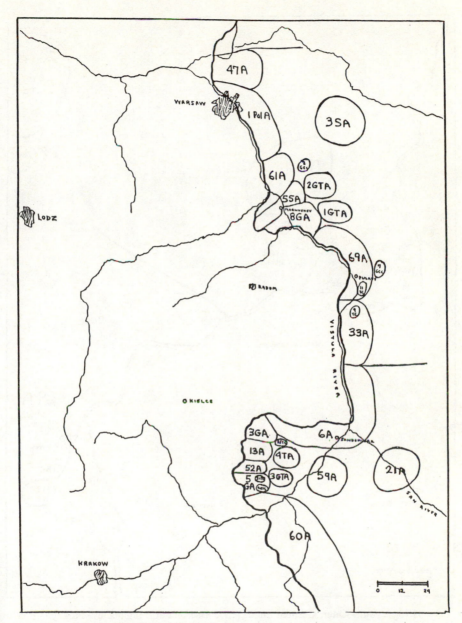

174. Vistula–Oder, Soviet dispositions, 11 January 1945

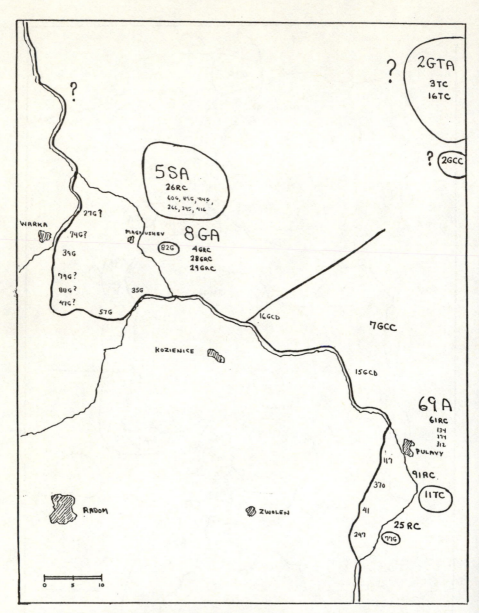

175. Vistula–Oder, German intelligence assessment, Magnushev–Pulavy
sectors, 12 January 1945

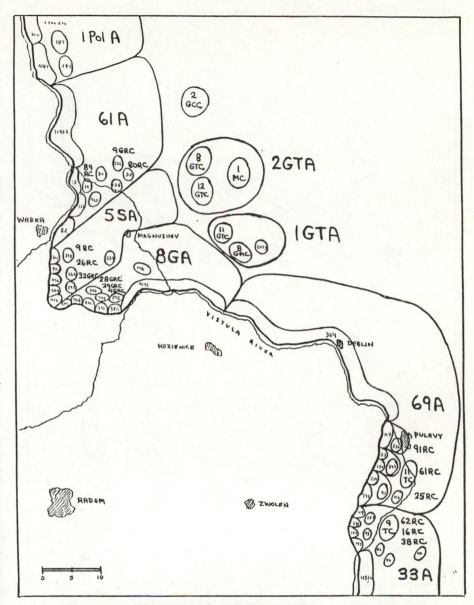

176. Vistula–Oder, Soviet dispositions, Magnushev–Pulavy sectors,
12 January 1945

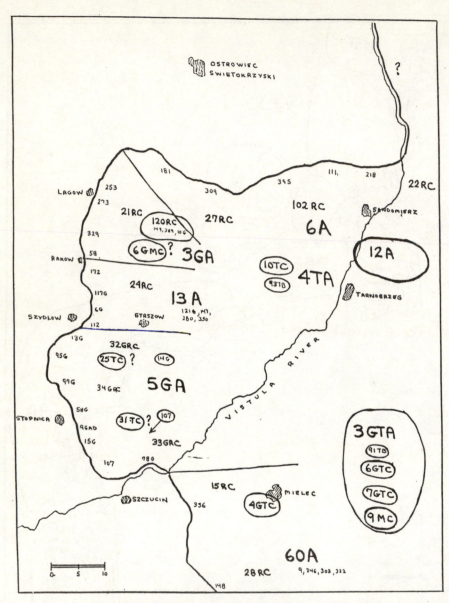

177. Vistula–Oder, German intelligence assessment, Sandomierz sector,
11 January 1945

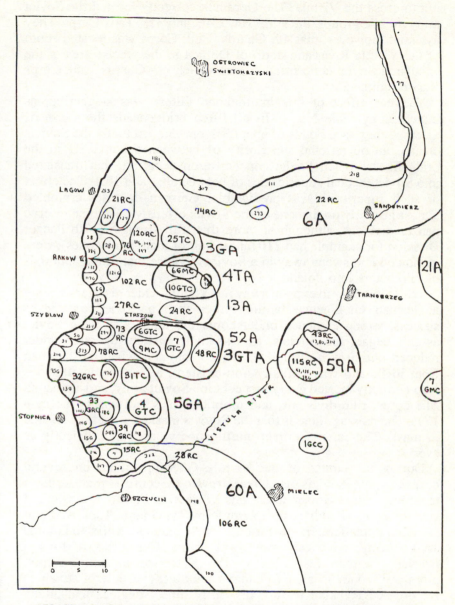

178. Vistula–Oder, Soviet dispositions, Sandomierz sector, 11 January 1945

ing to cross the Vistula. The Germans correctly located the Soviet army mobile groups, the 9th, 11th, 25th, and 31st Tank Corps. They assessed, however, that 4th Guards Tank Corps was located south of the Vistula River and north of Debica in the precise area of the simulated Soviet concentration area which 4th Guards Tank Corps was to animate.[43]

The net effect of this intelligence failure was staggering, as indicated by table No. 1. In all three bridgeheads the Germans assessed they faced odds of about 3:1 or 3.5:1. Actually the Soviets created an operational superiority of between 5:1 and 7:1 in the bridgeheads. When Soviet concentration occurred, that translated into Soviet tactical superiorities of between 8:1 and 16:1. The effect of such superiority was predictable. German defenses crumbled almost instantly on day one of the Soviet offensive. German reserve panzer divisons, although at more than full strength (17th Panzer Division for example had 210 tanks, half of them heavy ones), were inundated and swept away in a Soviet advance that drove hundreds of kilometers into Poland.

While it is easy to explain away the Vistula–Oder disaster as being a German intelligence failure rather than a Soviet *maskirovka* success, strong evidence underscores the latter. Once the Soviet assault began, the Soviets, as was their custom, operated under reduced *maskirovka* discipline. On 26 January, when the German front in Poland was virtually non-existent, a German intelligence map correctly located every first echelon Soviet army, and almost all rifle corps, rifle divisions, and mobile armies and corps (see map 179). The message here is that the Soviets masked what they wished to mask. Thereafter German intelligence worked as efficiently as ever.

During the course of the Vistula–Oder operation, on several occasions the Soviets used *maskirovka* to confuse the Germans regarding future Soviet intentions. This was but an extension of techniques used earlier (for example by 1st Guards Tank Army in the L'vov–Sandomierz operation). On 20 January while 3d Guards Tank Army advanced westward from Czestochowa toward Breslau, German resistance in the Katowice industrial region prompted Konev to alter Rybalko's tank army's route of advance. He ordered Rybalko to turn his army ninety degrees and attack southeast of the Oder River toward Ratibor into the rear of the German Katowice group. Rybalko used his corps forward detachments to simulate a continuation of the offensive toward Breslau and then wheeled his army south in a surprise attack which reached

TABLE 1

GERMAN INTELLIGENCE FAILURE VISTULA RIVER BRIDGEHEADS

Soviet Forces

	Magnushev Assessed	Magnushev Actual	Pulavy Assessed	Pulavy Actual	Sandomierz Assessed	Sandomierz Actual
Rifle Armies	2	3	1	2	4–5	7–8
Rifle Divisions	15	29	8	20	30	63
Tank Corps	0–2	3	1–2	2	2–5	6
Mechanized Corps	0	1	0	0	2	3
Cavalry Corps	0–1	0	1	1	0	1
Division Equivalents						
Rifle	15	29	8	20	30	63
Mobile	0–3	4	2–3	3	4–7	10
Total	15–18	33	10–11	23	34–37	73

German Forces

Division Equivalents			
Infantry*	3.5x2=7	2x2=4	7x2=14
Mobile	2	0	3.5
Total	9	4	17.5

Correlation of Forces

	Assessed	Actual
Strategic	1.5:1	3:1

	Assessed	Actual	Assessed	Actual	Assessed	Actual
Operational	1.7–2:1	3.6:1	2.5:1	5.7:1	2:1	4.2:1
Tactical	3:1	6–9:1	3:1	6:1	3:1	5–7:1

*German infantry divisions were twice as large as Soviet rifle divisions.

the German rear and ultimately forced the Germans to abandon the Katowice area.

Late in the operation, on 1 February Soviet forces reached the Oder River between Küstrin and Frankfurt. At the time there was increasing Soviet concern over a growing concentration of German units (principally SS units) in eastern Pomerania on the Soviet right flank. Zhukov formulated a plan to halt his *front's* force on the Oder and strike northward in conjunction with the 2d Belorussian Front to destroy the eastern Pomeranian enemy group. To conceal his

179. Vistula–Oder, German intelligence assessment, 26 January 1945

intentions, Zhukov developed a *maskirovka* plan to conceal the
necessary regrouping of forces which called for the following
measures:

– disengagement of forces from the enemy and conduct of only
  night marches;

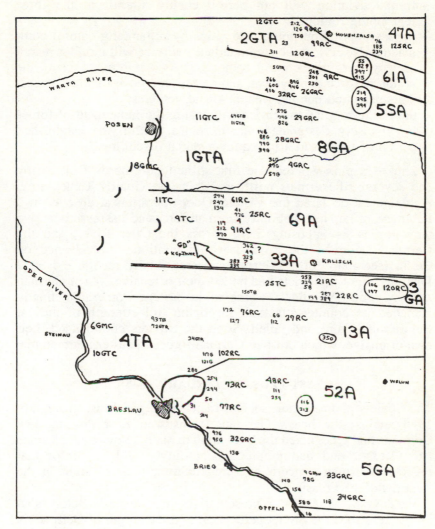

179a. Detail of map 179

- in order that the German-fascist command be convinced that previous units still operate against them, it is decided to leave in contact with the enemy for some time part of the tank army's forces with radio stations and radio nets;
- units completing the march are categorically forbidden to use radio stations [all radio stations were to be silent];

- frontal aviation will not permit enemy aircraft in the force regrouping region;
- bypass population points and cities by organizing careful commandant's service; the commandant's service will monitor march secrecy, carefully control camouflage of equipment, secure the region of force deployment, and gather and move forward to their units detached people, weapons, and vehicles;
- the traffic regulation service will ensure the movement of forces by precisely designated march routes, within the established period of time, and also required march discipline.[44]

Zhukov's plan worked. He first shifted 2d Guards Tank Army and several rifle armies north and then 1st Guards Tank Army. Although he declared the Vistula–Oder operation at an end on 2 February, as late as 6 February German forces still assessed the two tank armies as opposing them across the Oder River, and the Germans believed the Soviets would continue the advance on Berlin (see map 180).[45] German sources finally recognized on 7 February that the Soviets had halted their offensive. When German Army Group "Vistula," assembled in eastern Pomerania, finally launched its counter-attack, it faced the full strength of the 1st Belorussian Front and failed. Soon the Soviets commenced their own offensive, which crushed German forces in eastern Pomerania.

EAST PRUSSIA, JANUARY 1945

The Soviets planned their second major strategic thrust in January 1945 against the heavy German defenses in East Prussia. The Germans had recognized the likelihood of such a Soviet attack since late October and had prepared accordingly with an ardor that reflected German concern over maintaining their position in the "heartland" of Prussia.

Vasilevsky, *STAVKA* representative for the 3d Belorussian Front, described the Soviet perception of the strength of Germany's East Prussia bastion:

> Throughout the duration 1941–1945 East Prussia had important economic, political, and strategic meaning for the German High Command. Hitler's *STAVKA*, called by the fascists the Wolfsschranze, was located here in an underground sanctuary near Rastenburg up to 1944. The conquest of East Prussia – the citadel of German militarism – formed an important page of the final stage of war in Europe. The fascist

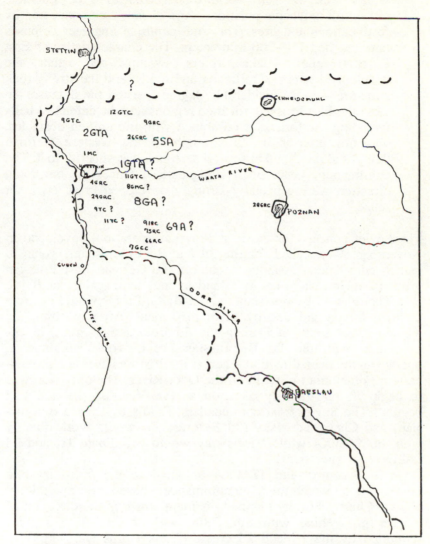

180. Vistula–Oder, German intelligence assessment, 6 February 1945

command attached great significance to retaining Prussia. It
firmly covered the approaches to Germany's central region.
On its territory and the associated adjacent region of the
northern part of Poland were erected a series of fortifications,
strongly fortified frontal and lateral positions and also large
defensive strongpoints, saturated with permanent defensive

works. The old forts were modernized to a considerable extent; all defensive positions were closely interconnected by fortifications and fires. The total depth of engineer defenses here reached 150–200 kilometers. The characteristics of East Prussian relief – lakes, rivers, swamps, and canals, the developed system of railroads and roads, and the strong rock structure – to a considerable degree assisted the defense. To 1945 the East Prussian fortified regions and the defensive belts including the fortresses combined with the unified obstacles, was not inferior in its strength to the western German "Siegfried line," and in several sectors it was superior to it. The Gumbinnen, Insterburg, Königsberg defenses on our main direction were especially strongly developed in an engineer sense.[46]

The Soviet concept for the East Prussian operation, developed in November 1944, called for the 3d and 2d Belorussian Fronts to launch coordinated assaults to cut off the German East Prussian group from German forces in Poland and pin them against the Baltic Sea. Then the 3d Belorussian and 1st Baltic Fronts would encircle German forces and destroy them piecemeal. After reaching the Vistula River south of Danzig the 2d Belorussian Front, in co-ordination with the 1st Belorussian Front, would continue to operate on the main direction – across the Vistula River and through eastern Pomerania to Stettin on the Oder River. The operation was to begin in mid-January as soon as the Vistula operation had begun.[47] The Soviet *front* commanders, Rokossovsky (2d Belorus-sian) and Chernyakhovsky (3d Belorussian) would work directly with the *STAVKA* while Vasilevsky would coordinate 1st and 2d Baltic Front operations.

On 3 December the *STAVKA* assigned to the *fronts* specific missions upon which the *front* commanders based their operational plans.[48] Chernyakovsky planned his main attack in the direction of Insterberg, Wehlau with 5th, 28th, and part of 39th Armies supported by the 1st and 2d Guards Tank Corps and with 11th Guards Army in *front* second echelon. 2d Guards Army would conduct a secondary attack on the left flank toward Darkomen, and 31st Army would defend in an extended sector on the *front's* left flank and prepare to attack once German defenses had begun to crumble. The remainder of 39th Army and the 43d Army of the 1st Baltic Front would defend along the *front* right flank to the Neiman River and west along the Neiman to the Baltic Sea.

Rokossovsky planned to conduct his main attack with 3d, 48th, 2d Shock, and 5th Guards Tank Army from the Rozan bridgehead across the Narev River toward Mlava and Marienburg. 49th Army in second echelon would develop the attack toward Ortelsburg, and 50th Army would first defend and then attack on a broad sector on the *front's* right flank. 65th and 70th Armies would conduct the *front* secondary attack from the Pultusk bridgehead on the *front's* left flank toward Drobin and Grudziaga on the Vistula River.

Regrouping of forces for the East Prussian operation was less extensive than for the Vistula–Oder operation. Most of the armies to participate in the offensive had fought German forces in the area as recently as early November 1944. Internal movements involved the concentration of 5th, 28th, and 2d Guards Armies in the north and concentration of 3d, 65th, and 48th Armies in the south. 2d Shock Army, assigned to the 2d Belorussian Front on 16 October (from the Baltic region), arrived in assembly areas east of the Narev River near Pultusk on 30 October and subsequently had to occupy first echelon positions on the left flank of the Rozan bridgehead. 70th Army, in *front* reserve since 19 November had to move from east of Warsaw into the left flank sector of the Pultusk bridgehead.

The most important move involved the 2d Belorussian Front's exploitation force, General Vol'sky's 5th Guards Tank Army. On 30 November 1st Baltic Front released the tank army to *STAVKA* reserve. By 13 December it had moved south to Bran'sk south of Belostok. There the army dug in, concealed itself, and awaited orders to move forward. On 10 January orders arrived informing Vol'sky and his chief of staff of their army's assigned missions. Three days later, on the evening of 13 January, 5th Guards Tank Army began its 150 kilometer march westward and on 15 January assembled in concentration areas northwest of Wyszkow, more than 24 hours after the Soviet assault had commenced out of the Narev bridgeheads.[49]

The limited regrouping required for the operation underscored the Soviet problem when attempting to use *maskirovka* to achieve surprise. German forces, in essence, knew in general where the bulk of Soviet forces were located. This fact made it extremely important for the Soviets to mask successfully those limited regroupings, in particular the movement of 5th Guards Tank Army. That army's performance and impact on combat would, in large measure, determine Soviet success or failure in 2d Belorussian Front's sector. Hence the Soviets took extraordinary measures to hide its presence, including the decision to move it into the forward area only after the offensive had begun.

The 3d Belorussian Front *maskirovka* plan included passive measures to conceal force regrouping and an active simulation of offensive preparations on the *front* left flank.[50] Between 1 and 10 January 31st Army postured itself to create the false impression of preparations for an assault toward Troiburg (Margerabowa) where Soviet forces had been active in late October and November. 31st Army, with engineer assistance, simulated the concentration of two tank regiments and one tank brigade northwest of Filipov and a similar concentration at and southeast of Filipov. Two railroad trains transported to the region mock-up tanks and vehicles which were then emplaced throughout the dummy concentration area by trucks (a total of 120 mock-up tanks and 20 mock-up vehicles). The 7th Separate Maskirovka Company animated the region with usual measures. The assembly of 11th Guards Army units north of the false concentration areas lent credence to them, and local units from 31st Army helped in the animation process. Rokossovsky employed similar measures in the Augustow region on his *front's* right flank.

Meanwhile units of both *fronts* attempted to conceal regrouping and concentration by usual *maskirovka* measures and by simulating attack preparations in army secondary attack sectors.[51] In most cases, army supporting armor had the greatest success concealing their movements because many of these tank and mechanized corps deployed from out-of-sector. 1st Tank Corps successfully concealed its movement from the 1st Baltic Front sector to 5th Army's sector of Chernyakhovsky's *front*. 3d Guards Cavalry Corps, which the Soviet *maskirovka* plan showed to be north of Augustow, deployed secretly into 3d Army's sector. So also did 8th Guards Tank Corps and 8th Mechanized Corps designated to support 48th and 2d Shock Armies.[52]

All in all, however, by Soviet admission, "operational *maskirovka* was unsuccessful. The enemy conducted combat reconnaissance and seized the mock-up tanks and guns. The German-Fascist command exposed the direction of the main attack of the 3d Belorussian Front."[53] Clearly this statement applied as well to the 2d Belorussian Front's main attack.

Fremde Heere Ost's 5 January assessment noted, "In the operation intended from the Narev front against East Prussia, a decision was made to carry out the attack in the direction Thorn–Graudenz." In an annex Gehlen was more specific concerning Soviet *front* missions stating:

The main effort of the attack against East Prussia lies unchanged with the 2nd White Russian Front, of which it seems Marshal Rokossovski who is well known as a highly qualified leader has been made Commander in Chief. In addition there will be operations by the 2nd White Russian Front from the Narew bridgeheads towards the lower Vistula (Thorn–Graudenz), whose northern flank will have to be covered by the advance of a task force from the area around Scharfenwiese in the direction of Ortelsburg, and attacks by the 3rd White Russian Front against the Prussian eastern border in a west-southwesterly direction in general. There is some evidence that the prominent front salient between Lomsha and Sudauen will gain increased importance. This is underlined by the fact that the 3rd Baltic Front is likely to be introduced here.[54]

The last points evidenced some German concern engendered by Rokossovsky's and Chernyakhovsky's deception operations on their flanks. In fact the Germans placed important reserve units opposite Soviet 31st Army's sector, the 18th Panzer Grenadier Division and, at a greater depth, Panzer Grenadier Division "Brandenburg." Before the Soviet assault, however, the latter moved south in reaction to the 12 January Soviet attack out of the Sandomierz bridgehead.

Although the Soviet active *maskirovka* plans had limited effect on the Germans, the passive measures caused the Germans to underestimate the forces opposing them, in particular in the 2d Belorussian Front's sector (see maps 181 and 182). On the day of the assault (14 January) the Germans had not detected the full concentration of 3d, 48th, and 65th Armies (see maps 183 and 184). Nor had they picked up the forward deployment of 2d Shock and 70th Armies. Most important, the Germans did not discover the presence of 5th Guards Tank Army until after it had joined the attack on 17 January.[55] By that time it was in the German operational rear, where it would remain until it reached the Baltic coast on 24 January. This underestimation by the Germans along the Narew River had the same effect on force ratios as it did in central Poland. German expectations of an overall ratio of 3:1 were dashed as the actual ratio was 5:1 or higher. Within three days German defenses were irrevocably smashed.

In the north the Soviet force met German expectations (see maps 185 and 186). Thus, even with the transfer of reserves southward,

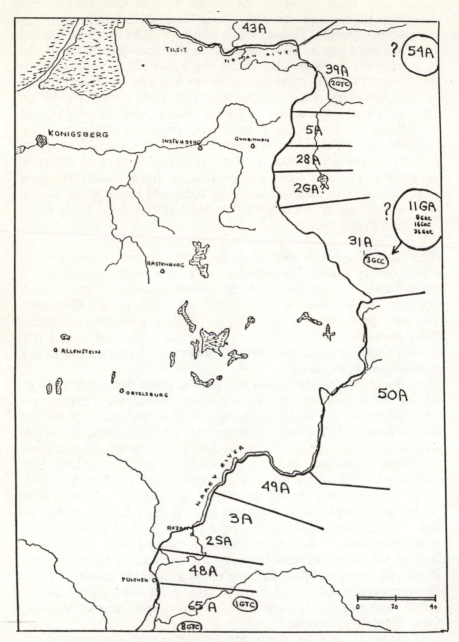

181. East Prussia, German intelligence assessment, 12 January 1945

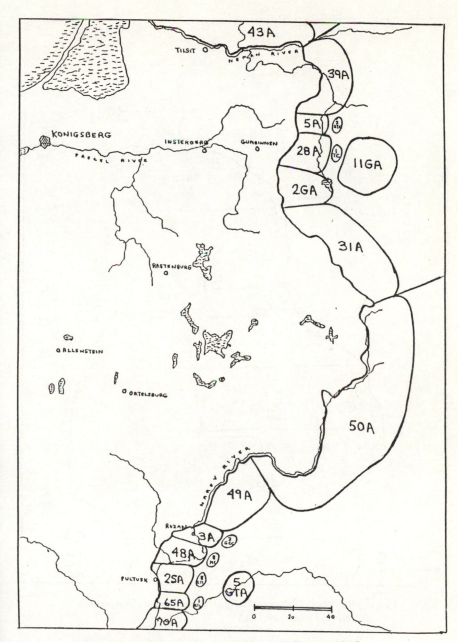

182. East Prussia, Soviet dispositions, 12 January 1945

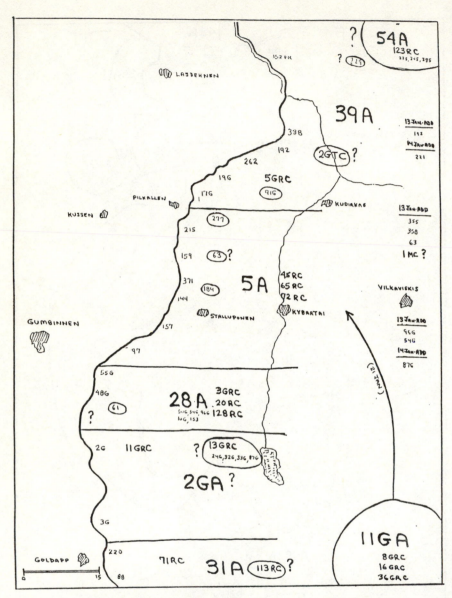

183. East Prussia, German intelligence assessment, Gumbinnen
direction, 12 January 1945

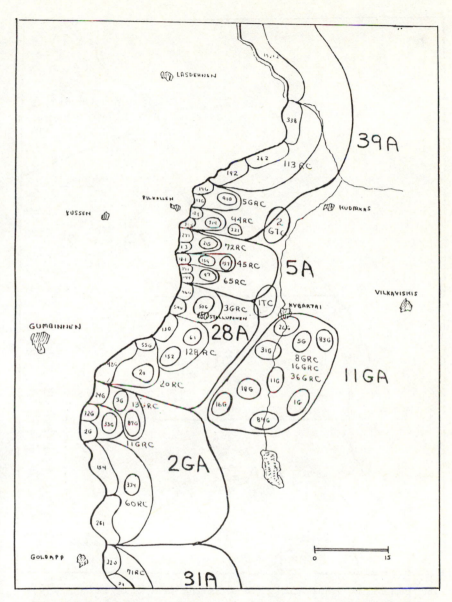

184. East Prussia, Soviet dispositions, Gumbinnen direction, 12 January 1945

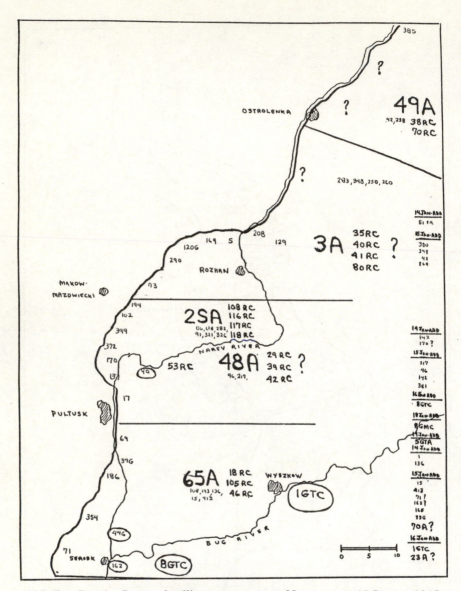

185. East Prussia, German intelligence assessment, Narev sector, 12 January 1945

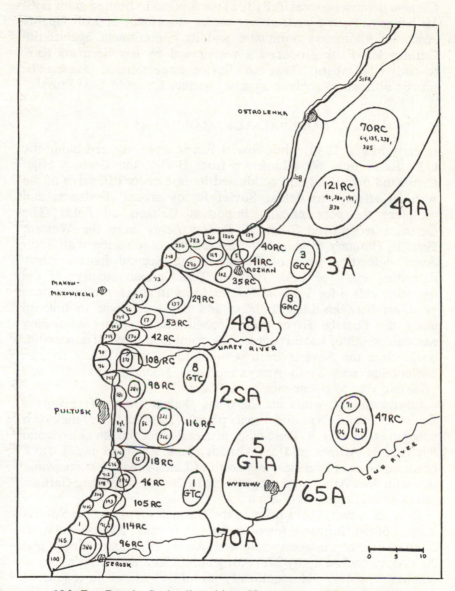

186. East Prussia, Soviet dispositions, Narev sector, 12 January 1945

German defenses successfully held the Soviets to limited gains until 19 January. Then a sudden and secret movement of 11th Guards Army 25 kilometers northward and its commitment against the German left flank produced a withdrawal by the Germans back toward Königsberg. True to Soviet expectations, *maskirovka* proved difficult to achieve against German forces in East Prussia.

LAKE BALATON, MARCH 1945

In early March 1945, while Soviet forces were engaged along the Oder River only 60 kilometers from Berlin, the German High Command organized and conducted its last major offensive of the war, an attempt to defeat Soviet forces around Budapest and recapture the economically important Balaton oil fields. The Germans redeployed Sixth SS Panzer Army from the Western Front to Hungary to launch the assault in coordination with Sixth Army defending west of Budapest and Second Panzer Army defending south of Lake Balaton. The German concept of the operation called for Sixth SS Panzer Army to attack southeast from positions between Lake Balaton and Szekesfehervar to link up along the Danube River with Second Panzer Army advancing eastward south of Lake Balaton. The combined force, if successful, could clear the Soviets from west of the Danube River and, in conjunction with Sixth Army, reoccupy Budapest. The German offensive was to commence on 6 March.[56]

Coincidentally, while the Germans planned their offensive, the Soviet 2d and 3d Ukrainian Fronts planned an offensive of their own to begin on 15 March. The Soviet plan called for the 4th Guards and 9th Guards Armies and 6th Guards Tank Army to attack from positions west of Budapest and north of Lake Velencei in coordination with 46th Army on the right flank to destroy defending German forces and advance on Vienna.

More than two weeks prior to the German offensive the Soviets learned of the Germans' intent and began forming a dense and deep defense west of Budapest using 46th Army, 4th Guards Army, and 26th Army backed up by 27th Army in 3d Ukrainian Front's second echelon. The *STAVKA* specifically prohibited use of those reserve forces designated to conduct the Soviet offensive, 9th Guards Army and 6th Guards Tank Army, and directed that offensive preparations continue even during the impending defensive operation.

By 20 February Tolbukhin had developed his concept for the Balaton defense. He decided to erect a dense defense based on current defensive positions designed to grind up attacking German forces principally using dug-in infantry, an elaborate network of anti-tank strongpoints, and the maneuver of armored and mechanized reserves positioned in key locations behind the front. After German forces were sufficiently worn down in defensive combat, Tolbukhin would launch his own offensive using *front* forces not involved in the defensive battle and *STAVKA* reserves.[57]

Tolbukhin concentrated his main force in the defensive sectors of 4th Guards and 26th Armies where he expected the German main attack to occur. 27th Army, in *front* second echelon, deployed two rifle corps west of the Danube and one on the east bank of the river to bolster first echelon defenses and establish new defensive positions as required. Tolbukhin's reserve consisted of the 18th and 23d Tank; 1st Guards Mechanized; 5th Guards Cavalry Corps; one rifle division; and several artillery brigades, including one self-propelled artillery brigade. In organizing the defense Tolbukhin focused on doing so without disrupting concurrent offensive preparations. Thus:

> The aim of the defensive battle was to retain occupied positions without the delivery of front and army counterstrokes. Counter-attacks would be conducted only in exceptional cases, based on their success.[58]

The *front* was to be prepared for the defense on 3 March, and all regrouping was complete by late on 5 March.

Regrouping was extensive and took place at night under strict *maskirovka* conditions. 26th Army assumed responsibility for the sector from Lake Balaton to 8 kilometers west of Lake Velencei and deployed the 104th, 135th, and 30th Rifle Corps in that sector. This required a shift of 104th Rifle Corps from the army right to the left flank. 26th Army took over control of 135th Rifle Corps units from 57th Army. Meanwhile 4th Guards Army picked up 31st Guards Rifle Corps from 46th Army and placed it in army second echelon behind 20th and 21st Guards Rifle Corps deployed in defensive positions north of Lake Velencei. Tolbukhin positioned the 23d Tank Corps behind 4th Guards Army, the 18th Tank Corps behind 26th Army's right flank and 1st Guards Mechanized Corps in reserve behind 26th Army. 5th Guards Cavalry Corps' three divisions deployed further to the rear behind the center of 26th Army's sector.

3d Ukrainian Front's main defensive belt extended to a depth of 7 kilometers, the second defensive belt to 15 kilometers, and the rear defensive belt to 30 kilometers. Engineers extensively prepared all defensive positions. Wherever possible the Soviets concealed the defenses and forces regrouping into them. They paid particular attention to hiding the main and reserve unit command posts.

East of the Danube River near Kecslemet the Soviets positioned the nine full-strength divisions of 9th Guards Army, a special army formed from airborne troops which the *STAVKA* had created as a purely offensive force. The *STAVKA* retained control of the army throughout the defensive phases of the Balaton operations and worked hard to conceal its presence.

Soviet *maskirovka* had some success in concealing the nature and depths of these defenses, particularly in the operational realm (see maps 187 and 188). German intelligence records indicate they had a fairly accurate picture of Soviet tactical deployments in the German main attack sector. They were able to identify the armies, rifle corps, and some of the Soviet rifle divisions in the tactical defenses. Their picture of the operational situation was considerably weaker. The Germans detected 37th Guards Rifle Corps of 27th Army but not that army's 133d or 35th Guards Rifle Corps. Nor did the Germans discover the repositioning of 1st Guards Mechanized Corps or 5th Guards Cavalry Corps behind 26th Army. Most important, German intelligence did not discover 9th Guards Army, concentrated menacingly near Kecslemet.[59]

The German offensive commenced on 6 March with III Panzer, II SS Panzer, I SS Panzer and I Cavalry Corps assaulting Soviet positions between Lakes Velencei and Balaton. The German advance continued through 15 March by which time German forces had penetrated 10 kilometers east of the Sarvizh Canal and up to 25 kilometers west of the canal. Judiciously using its reserves, the 3d Ukrainian Front absorbed the shock of the German offensive, and its defenses bent but did not break.

While the German attacks developed, the Soviets implemented their plans for the Vienna operation. On 9 March, during the defensive battles, the *STAVKA* provided the 2d and 3d Ukrainian Fronts with revised missions. The 3d Ukrainian Front was to continue to defend south of Szekesferververar with 26th and 27th Armies and launch the *front* main attack on 15–16 March north of Lake Velencei with 9th Guards and 4th Guards Armies which would strike the rear of the attacking German force. The 2d Ukrainian Front's 46th Army, supported by 6th Guards Tank Army, was to attack on 17 or 18 March westward along the south bank of the Danube River.[60] Later 2d Ukrainian Front forces north of the

Danube River and 3d Ukrainian Front forces south of Lake Balaton were to join the offensive. The offensive would begin as soon as German Sixth SS Panzer Army's offensive was halted, which the Soviets assumed would occur on 15 or 16 March.

Both Malinovsky's and Tolbukhin's offensive planning included *maskirovka* measures. Rather than plan active diversions from Soviet offensive preparations, the two *front* commanders relied on German preoccupation with their attack and passive *maskirovka* to distract the Germans' attention from and conceal offensive preparations. In particular, the *front* commanders regrouped their forces in maximum secrecy.

46th Army had to concentrate four rifle corps on its extreme left flank including one division from 7th Guards Army north of the Danube. This involved the movement, resubordination, and concentration of eleven rifle divisions and the supporting 2d Guards Mechanized Corps – all done at night. Malinovsky also moved 6th Guards Tank Army to positions west of Budapest to support 46th Army. On 10 March he ordered 6th Guards Tank Army, then refitting in assembly areas north and northwest of Sahy, to move almost 60 kilometers south across the Ipel and Danube Rivers to new positions west of Budapest. 6th Guards Tank Army began moving late on 11 March having dispatched in advance two tank brigades to reinforce 27th Army defenses. Immediately after arriving in its new position, on 16 March the *STAVKA* decided to resubordinate the army to 3d Ukrainian Front to support 9th Guards Army, thus necessitating another shift of forces.[61]

Meanwhile Tolbukhin undertook the immense task of regrouping 4th Guards Army and moving 9th Guards Army into 4th Guards Army's right flank sector. Between 8 and 14 March General Glagolov moved 9th Guards Army's nine rifle divisions from Kecslemet across the Danube into the Zamoly sector.[62] Simultaneously *front* artillery units shifted to the north to support the *front* main attack. On 13 March, as 9th Guards Army units assembled in its rear area, 4th Guards Army received its attack orders and that evening began moving the 20th and 21th Guards Rifle Corps laterally to new positions on the left flank of the former army sector. Its orders read, "The withdrawal of artillery and mortar units from positions in the sector being given to 9th Guards Army will occur only at night, within one day after the shift of rifle formation, according to the basic plan and will be completed not later than 3.00 14.3.45."[63] 4th Guards Army's history recorded its *maskirovka* plan, stating:

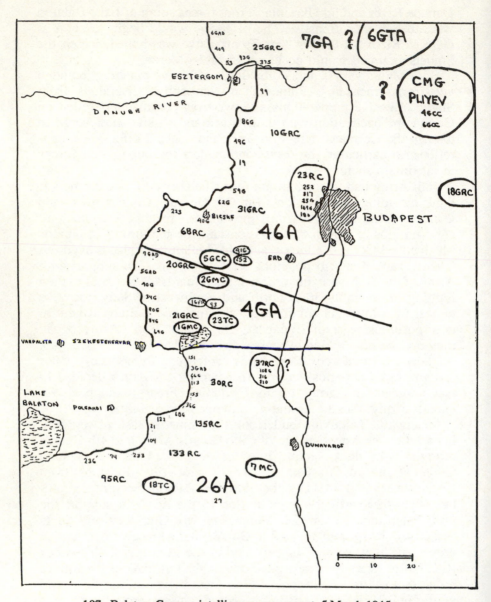

187. Balaton, German intelligence assessment, 5 March 1945

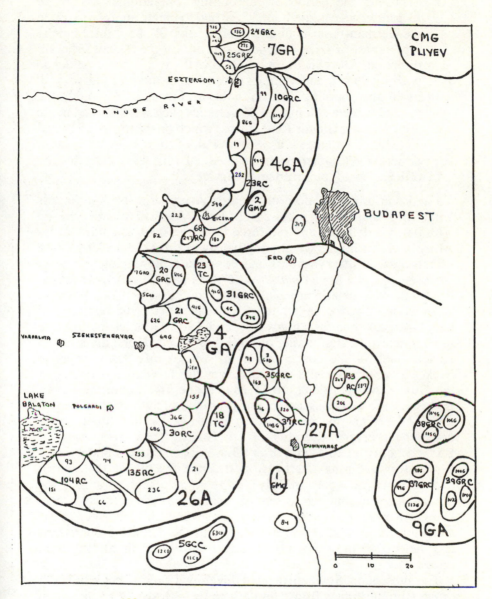

188. Balaton, Soviet dispositions, 5 March 1945

During the period of regrouping, operational *maskirovka* measures were carried out. They had to create an impression in the German-Fascist command of the arrival of our forces in the region east of Lake Velencei, and not on the Szekesferhervar direction. All vehicles traveling from the rear to the front did so with lights off, and vehicles returning to the rear did so with headlights burning and in column formation. In addition, special vehicle columns of 25 vehicles each were formed in the 20th and 21st Guards Rifle Corps, which on the nights of 14 and 15 March simulated a withdrawal of troops in an eastern direction by numerous troops. All of this was controlled by officers post [commandant's service].[64]

To assist in this deception 4th Guards Army kept its 31st Guards Rifle Corps in assembly areas east of Lake Velencei to both back-up 27th Army's defenses and reinforce the impression that 4th Guards Army was shifting its weight southeastward. By the evening of 15 March most of the two *fronts* had completed regrouping.

Because of the Soviet *maskirovka* plans and German preoccupation with their deteriorating offensive southeast of Lake Balaton, German intelligence failed to detect the Soviet regrouping and attack preparations (see maps 189 and 190). German intelligence did not detect the regrouping of 46th Army's corps and divisions to its left flank or the concentration of 4th Guards Army opposite Szekesferhervar. Nor did they discover the forward movement of 9th Guards Army. In fact, on 16 March, the first day of the Soviet offensive, the Germans noted the presence of two of that army's divisions but not the parent corps or army. German intelligence noted the probable assembly of 6th Guards Tank Army west of Budapest only on 16 March after the Soviet attack was underway.[65]

Maskirovka during the Balaton defense resembled that which had occurred at Kursk in July 1943, in particular regarding the Soviet intent to integrate offensive action into the defensive plan. Unlike Kursk, however, the Soviets were able to keep their attacking forces entirely uninvolved with the defensive operations and fielded them forward into attack positions in almost total secrecy.

The subsequent Soviet offensive developed slowly, but ultimately drove German forces from Hungary to the gates of Vienna, which fell, after only desultory resistance, by 15 April.

BERLIN, APRIL 1945

In retrospect, the Battle for Berlin in April appears somewhat anticlimactic after the bitter fighting which had occurred since 1943. So long had the Soviets been on the offensive and so large were the earlier German disasters that one could dismiss the Berlin operation as being the pitiful end of a once proud and mighty Germany. True, the results of the operation were foreordained. Allied victory was but weeks away, for someone was going to seize Berlin, and soon, after April 1945. The only question was which army, the Soviets or that of the western allies, would engage the remnants of the German military establishment in the final *Götterdämmerung*. It was only fitting that this task fell to the Soviets, as Roosevelt and Churchill had earlier ordained. The soundless cries of 10 million military dead compelled the Soviets to undertake the last great operation of her Great Patriotic War.

The Soviets did not undertake the task lightly. As astute students of history, they recalled the fate of earlier Russian armies at the gates of Berlin in 1760 and at the gates of Warsaw in 1920 when Russian hopes had been dashed by over-optimism and unfortunate circumstances. The Soviets saw to it that history would not repeat itself. The Soviet command estimated the Germans would field a force of one million – the desperate remnants of the German Army; and, deep down, they were unsure of how many Germans in the west would join their comrades along the Oder to face the more dreaded and feared Soviet Army. Experience had demonstrated that a force of one million men could render credible resistance along a formidable river barrier (the Oder), even against a force twice its size.

Thus the Soviets prepared an offensive fitting the task – an offensive that would leave little in doubt – an offensive whose conduct would do the Soviets credit in the eyes of her allies who approached Berlin from the west.

Planning for the Berlin operation commenced on 1 April, the day after the completion of 1st Ukrainian Front's Upper Silesian operation and three days prior to the completion of the 1st and 2d Belorussian Front's operations to clear German forces from eastern Pomerania. That day Zhukov (1st Belorussian Front commander) and Konev (1st Ukrainian Front commander) met in Moscow with Stalin, the *STAVKA*, and Antonov and Shtemenko of the General Staff to formulate plans for the Berlin operation. (Rokossovsky of 2d Belorussian Front coordinated with the *STAVKA* in Moscow on

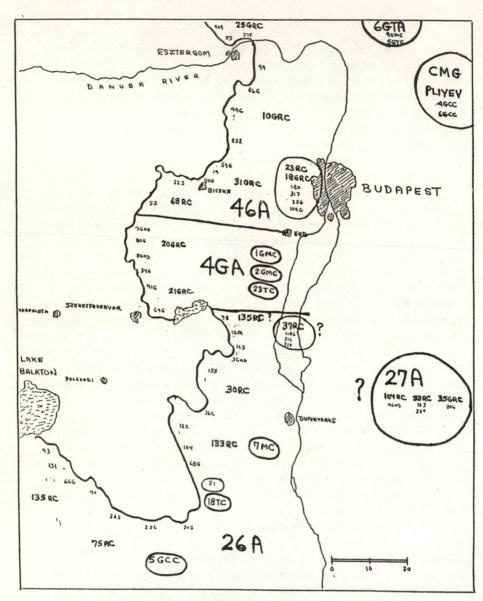

189. Balaton, German intelligence assessment, 14 March 1945

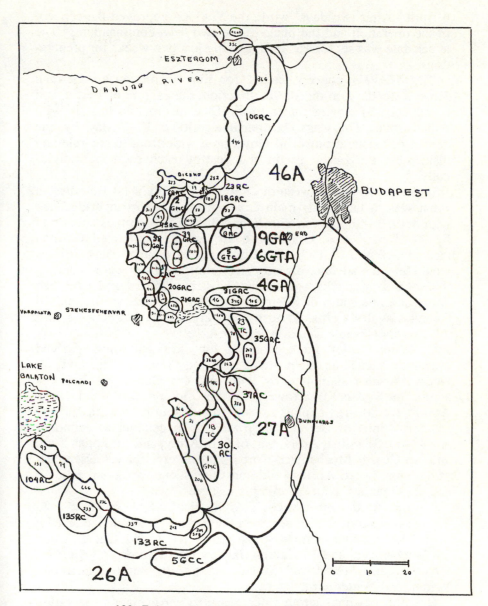

190. Balaton, Soviet dispositions, 14 March 1945

6 April.) After two days' work, the *STAVKA* approved the concept of the operation and the plans of the two *front* commanders.[66] The attack date was set for 16 April, leaving just two weeks for preparations.

The *STAVKA* concept called for the destruction of German forces defending on the Berlin direction, the capture of Berlin, and an advance by Soviet forces to the Elbe in order to link up with Allied armies. This was to be done in a period of 12–15 days by "the delivery of several powerful blows on a wide front to encircle and dismember the Berlin group and destroy each segment individually."[67]

In the center of the western direction, Zhukov's 1st Belorussian Front was to launch its main attack from the Küstrin bridgehead with 47th, 3d Shock, 5th Shock, and 8th Guards Armies supported by 9th Tank Corps. Once these armies had penetrated German tactical defenses, 1st Guards Tank and 2d Guards Tank Armies would lead the advance directly on Berlin. The *front* would conduct two secondary attacks, one north of Küstrin with 61st and 1st Polish Army and one south of Küstrin with 69th and 33d Armies and 2d Guards Cavalry Corps. 3d Army was in *front* second echelon, and 7th Guards Cavalry Corps in *front* reserve.

On Zhukov's left flank, Konev's 1st Ukrainian Front received orders to launch its main attack with 3d Guards, 13th, and 5th Guards Armies supported by 25th and 4th Guards Tank Corps across the Neisse River toward Cottbus. 3d and 4th Guards Tank Armies would then exploit toward Brandenburg, Dessau, and the southern limits of Berlin. The *front* was to conduct a secondary attack with 2d Polish Army, part of 57th Army, and 1st Polish Tank and 7th Guards Mechanized Corps. 28th Army, not yet assembled in the area, by 16 April would constitute Konev's second echelon and 1st Guards Cavalry Corps his reserve.

To the north, on Zhukov's right flank, Rokossovsky's 2d Belorussian Front was to attack in the Stettin–Schwedt sector with 65th, 70th, and 49th Armies, supported by 1st, 3d, 8th Guards Tank, 8th Mechanized, and 3d Guards Cavalry Corps, to destroy German forces around Stettin and advance to occupy Anklin, Demmin, Waren, and Wittenburg.

Creation of shock groups necessary to carry out the operation required extensive regrouping of all three *fronts*, which had to move from positions they occupied at the end of previous operations into new positions along the Oder River. A total of 28 armies had to regroup, 15 of them a distance of up to 385 kilometers and three between 530 and 800 kilometers (see map 191). All these movements had to be accomplished in 15 days (compared with 22 to 48 days available to move forces prior to the Belorussian, East Prussian, and Vistula–Oder operations).[68]

On 1 April the bulk of Konev's forces were deployed west of the Oder River from Leignitz to Ragow, south of Breslau. Leaving 52d, 21st, and 59th Armies to cover his extensive center and right flank from Goerlitz south past Breslau (in which a German garrison would hold out until 6 May) to Kronov, Konev shifted 5th Guards and 2d Polish Armies to his left flank along the Neisse River. 3d Guards Tank Army had to move from the Goerlitz area 80 kilometers north. 4th Guards Tank Army faced the most extensive move, from the Neustadt area on the *front* extreme left 250 kilometers northward to the right flank.

Zhadov's 5th Guards Army, between 5 and 10 April, regrouped at night from the region west of Breslau 150–200 kilometers to the left flank of Konev's main attack sector on the Neisse River.[69] Simultaneously, 2d Polish Army moved at night 150 kilometers from positions north of Breslau to new assault positions on 5th Guards Army's left flank. Rybalko's 3d Guards Tank Army displaced at night on 11 April and moved 100 kilometers north to occupy positions 20 kilometers to the rear of 13th Army on 13 April.[70] Lelyushenko's 4th Guards Tank Army, which had just completed intense operations in Upper Silesia, traversed the 250 kilometers from the Rogow area to new positions behind 5th Guards Army in five days of day and night movement, all by road.[71]

The reserve armies assigned to Konev conducted the longest marches and, in fact, arrived only after the offensive had begun. Lieutenant General A. A. Luchinsky's 28th Army and Lieutenant General P. G. Shafranov's 31st Army moved from the area southwest of Königsberg, but a shortage of rolling stock and the poor condition of the rails delayed their rail movement. It took 14 days to transport 28th Army 700–800 kilometers and 13 days to move 31st Army 600–775 kilometers.[72] Both armies had to complete the final 80–100 kilometers by vehicle or on foot, which required three additional days and made the *maskirovka* task more challenging.

Zhukov had to regroup the bulk of his *front* forces, including 3d Shock, 1st Polish, 61st, and 47th Armies, from his right flank north of Stettin and along the Baltic coast, where they were located on 4 April, to new assault positions south of Schwedt. He also had to concentrate 5th Shock and 8th Guards into assault positions near Küstrin while 69th and 33d Armies covered the *front* left flank past

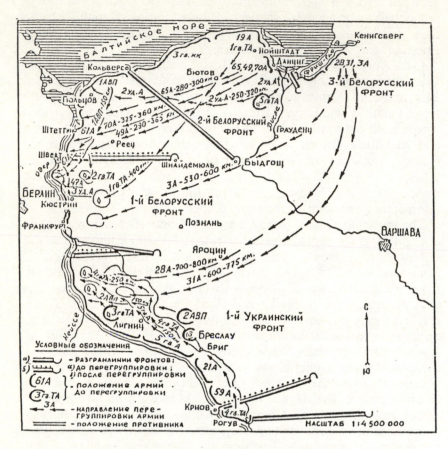

Перегруппировка армий (апрель 1945г.)

191. Berlin, Soviet regrouping, 1–16 April 1945

Frankfurt on the Oder River. 3d Shock Army, which had operated near the mouth of the Oder River in early March, began its 150 kilometer move on 20 March and after 8 April assembled east of Küstrin where it began intensive preparation for its new offensive.[73] 1st Polish, 61st, and 47th Armies conducted shorter regroupings in the same period as did 2d Guards Tank Army which completed operations in the Altdamm area on 20 March and subsequently moved to assembly areas northeast of Küstrin.[74]

1st Guards Tank Army had a more difficult regrouping, as did

Zhukov's reserve army, the 3d. Katukov's army had participated in the scizure of Gdynya, north of Danzig, an operation which it had completed on 26 March. That evening it turned its positions over to 19th Army and began the 400 kilometer trip west toward the Oder. Tanks and heavy artillery traveled by rail and the remainder of the army on vehicles. By 30 March the army concentrated at Landsberg, 40 kilometers east of Küstrin, where it began preparations for the upcoming offensive.[75] 3d Army traveled the required 530–600 kilometers from southwest of Königsberg in a period of 12 days by both road and rail and experienced the same delays as had 28th and 31st Armies. It unloaded only 10–30 kilometers from its assembly area and required only one day of subsequent movement.[76]

Rokossovsky, whose *front* would attack on 20 April, four days after Zhukov's and Konev's forces, had to move all of his armies (19th, 2d Shock, 65th, 70th, and 49th) between 250 and 360 kilometers from the area north of Danzig to new assault positions north and south of Stettin. This regrouping encompassed 86 percent of his rifle forces, 70 percent of his armor and 96 percent of his artillery.[77] Batov's 65th Army completed operations near Danzig on 4 April and, for the next two days, covered the westward deployment of 49th and 70th Armies. Batov later wrote:

> According to the initial plan, the rifle corps were to travel by march column and reach their assigned region on 17 April. However, on 6 April the *front* staff provided us 500 trucks; and the army moved by a combined march. Some divisions traveled on trucks and others on foot, then the vehicle columns returned and picked up those traveling by foot – and so on until the end of the march. Part of the equipment was transported by rail.[78]

The army columns traveled at night and concealed themselves during the day. Using multiple march routes, one per division, the army completed the movement of up to 300 kilometers in just over 5 days. Likewise, 49th and 70th Armies completed their moves in 5 days. The centralization of 2d Belorussian transport planning and rigid control by the *front* staff of all rolling stock and march routes facilitated efficient movement. 2d Shock Army thus completed its 320 kilometer movement from south of Danzig in six days rather than the planned eight days. 2d Shock also made extensive use of captured German trucks to accelerate the movement.[79]

All three *front* commanders went to great lengths to conceal the scale of movement and the destination of each major unit and used virtually all standard *maskirovka* practices, including the deliberate detachment of small army units with signal equipment to remain in the original army positions. The strict time constraints associated with the regrouping forced main units, in particular 4th Guards Tank Army and 2d Belorussian Front forces, to travel during daytime as well as at night. Moreover, the German command well realized that the Soviets would assemble along the Oder for the final drive on Berlin. The only remaining question was, "When and where?"

It was obvious to the Soviet High Command that they would have to eschew achieving strategic surprise in the Berlin operation, so a strategic *maskirovka* plan would be of little utility (although the *STAVKA* ordered the four Ukrainian *fronts* to commence operations simultaneous to operations on the Berlin direction). The *STAVKA* did direct all three *front* commanders and their subordinates to prepare operational and tactical *maskirovka* plans to conceal the time and location of the attacks. One of the *STAVKA's* principal aims was to reduce Soviet casualties in so far as possible, for at this stage of the war Soviet divisions numbered from 2500 to 5500 men; and Soviet manpower reserves had dwindled to a low ebb.

Zhukov's 1st Belorussian Front's *maskirovka* plan sought to distract German attention from the central (Küstrin) sector of the front by simulating attack preparations on the *front* left flank near Guben and on the right flank south of Stettin during the period 9–15 April (see maps 192 and 193).[80] Meanwhile units in the center would portray a defensive posture. In the Guben area the plan simulated concentration of 1st Guards Tank Army southwest of Grünberg and south of the Oder by tank and vehicle movement from an unloading station at Schwebus and by the construction of additional bridging over the Oder River near Oderek and Grossen. In the forward area the Soviets constructed false bridges across the Oder near Fürstenberg and Guben and intensified reconnaissance.

Simultaneously, south of Stettin, Zhukov simulated offensive preparations by 5th Shock and 2d Guards Tank Armies. Here the *front* staff supervised emplacement of 110 tanks, 62 vehicles, and 100 gun mock-ups, conduct of engineer reconnaissance, adjustment of artillery gunfire, and other camouflage means. In the *front* central sector other *front* armies intensified defensive preparations, including the deployment of armor and artillery mock-ups into defensive positions within the Küstrin bridgehead, the circulation of defensive orders and dissemination of rumors voicing dissatis-

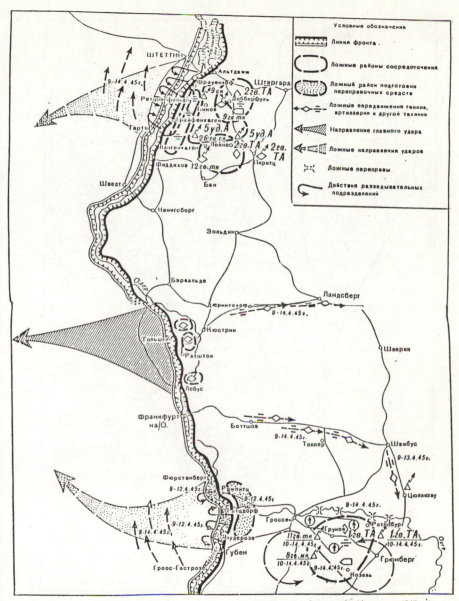

11. Замысел оперативной маскировки в полосе 1-го Белорусского фронта (9—14 апреля 1945 г.)

192. Berlin, 1st Belorussian Front deception plan

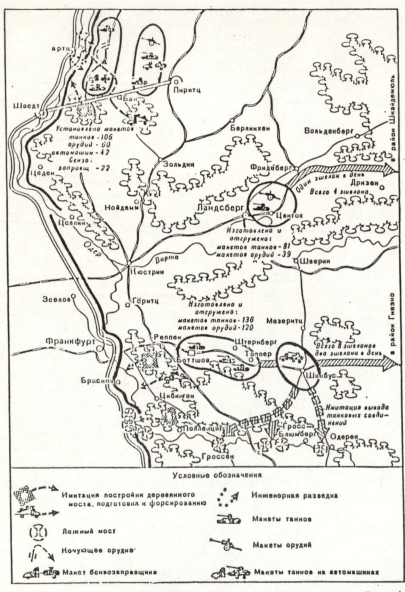

12. Оперативная маскировка в полосе 1-го Белорусского фронта
(апрель 1945 г.)

193. Berlin, 1st Belorussian Front deception measures

faction with the defensive posture. All commands in the central sector distributed instructions on conducting defensive operations and the *front* published an order to the troops announcing Zhukov's replacement as *front* commander by General V.D. Sokolovsky (the *front* chief of staff).

The 1st Belorussian Front staff supervised the general *maskirovka* plan, assigned specific tasks to subordinate units, and designated specific engineer units to conduct the *maskirovka* work. The 1st Separate Maskirovka Company arranged, through use of mock-ups and trains, to simulate routine movement of forces toward the front. Near Landsberg, east of Küstrin, a battalion of the 25th Engineer-Sapper Brigade prepared trains with flat cars loaded with mock-up tanks and guns and dispatched one train eastward per day over a four day period to simulate withdrawal of armored units from the Küstrin area. At Butzov, Sternberg, and Topper stations, east of Frankfurt, the 17th Engineer-Sapper Brigade prepared 136 T-34 and 120 76mm gun mock-ups and dispatched them eastward on eight trains (two per day) toward Gnezno, also away from the central sector. At the same time the 17th Brigade simulated vehicle and tank movement southward to the false concentration area east of Guben.

To the north 61st Army engineers erected 106 tank, 42 vehicle, and 22 fuel truck mock-ups in 2d Guards Tank Army's false assembly area southeast of Stettin and gun mock-ups in 5th Shock Army's simulated concentration area south of Stettin. Army troops animated the area with roving artillery pieces, by assembling bridging assets, and by conducting extensive engineer reconnaissance in the area.

As the real assault date approached, engineer units moved simulation activities closer to the front. Late on 11 April the 7th Front Defensive Construction Administration and a battalion of the 34th Engineer-Sapper Brigade built three false bridges into a 33d Army bridgehead south of Frankfurt. The Germans responded with a heavy artillery preparation and ground assaults on 13 April to eradicate the bridgehead, but in vain. They also intensified air reconnaissance and bombing activity in both 1st Belorussian Front false concentration areas.

Konev's *maskirovka* plan was less elaborate than Zhukov's and focused on simulating offensive preparations on the *front's* center and left flank sectors. It included active measures and a massive smoke generation operation along the 400 kilometer *front* sector to conceal the simulation and real offensive preparations along the east bank of the Neisse River. Konev employed his active deception measures three to five days before the 16 April attack date. Five chemical defense battalions (26th, 53d, 32d, 94th, and 39th) used 25 smoke generators to mask movement of troops from troop unloading sites at Oppelow, Melanane, Vossovka, Gross-Strelitz, and Gross-Steinau and river crossing sites across the Oder near Breig, Oppeln, and Kramnitz while other units simulated heavy troop movements toward Namslau, Ohlau, Karlsruhe and other locations on the *front* right flank and center. Engineer units conducted extensive offensive preparations west of the Oder River in the same region.[81] On the day of the actual attack heavy smoke screens, laid by chemical defense battalions, concealed virtually all of 3d Guards and 13th Armies' sectors; and smoke activity continued along the entire 1st Ukrainian Front. Smoke operations would continue throughout the entire 1st Ukrainian Front operation toward Berlin.

Although Rokossovsky's assault was to occur on 19 April, three days after Zhukov's and Konev's attack, he also developed an elaborate *maskirovka* plan (see map 194). The main attack of the 2d Belorussian Front was to occur south of Stettin, between Altdamm and Schwedt, near where Zhukov had conducted his simulated offensive preparations. Because of Zhukov's simulation and natural circumstances, German defenses were strongest in this area. Thus Rokossovsky's staff devised a *maskirovka* plan which would unfold between 13 and 19 April but intensify on 16 April after the 1st Belorussian Front's assault had begun.

The plan simulated concentration of 2d Shock, 49th, and 5th Guards Tank Armies north of Stettin poised for an attack across the Oder River. 19th and 2d Shock Army troops, under cover of smoke, simulated the concentration by establishing false radio nets for 5th Guards Tank, 2d Shock, and 49th Armies, conducting unmasked vehicle movements, organizing air defenses, and by simulating concentration of two artillery penetration corps in the region. 2d Shock Army animated the region with vehicle movements, roving guns, intensified armored movement, and the conduct of officer and combat reconnaissance. Army engineer units emplaced 500 mock-up guns in the process, and one battery from each army artillery battalion animated false firing areas and conducted registration fires. They also built 350 tank mock-ups and simulated tank concentrations with the assistance of army tank brigades and regiments.

Divisional engineer units closer to the front assembled assault boats along the Oder, improved approach routes to potential

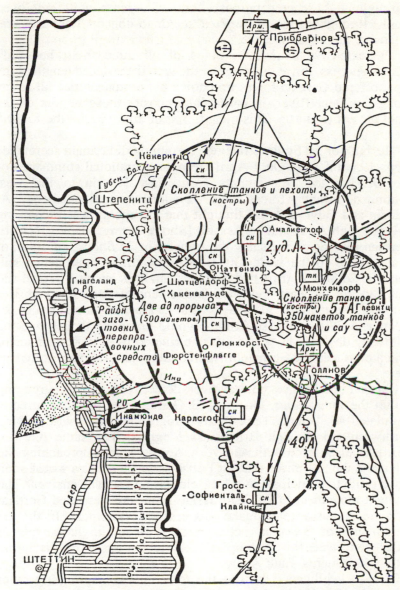

13. Замысел оперативной маскировки в полосе 2-го Белорусского
фронта (13—19 апреля 1945 г.)

194. Berlin, 2d Belorussian Front deception plan

crossing sites, and built a dense network of forward supply facilities. Throughout these preparations chemical defense units employed smoke throughout the entire *front* sector to conceal false and real offensive preparations alike.[82]

The extensive *maskirovka* plans of all three *fronts* had only limited success, for, at this stage of the war, the reduced length of the front offered German forces no choice but to concentrate all assets along the Oder River, in particular opposite those sectors of the front closest to Berlin. This meant, first of all, opposite the Küstrin area.

The bulk of the Soviet strategic regrouping did remain secret (see maps 195 and 196). On 4 April German operational summaries of the OKH noted "movements from East Prussia to the west continued. Infantry forces have advanced ... to Landsberg." At Danzig and Gdynya it was thought that the enemy was employing only the 19th Army and 2d Assault [Shock] Army.[83] Up to 16 April German records do not show the transfer of 2d Shock, 3d, 28th, or 31st Armies to the west. On 19 April German intelligence still believed 2d Shock Army had been at Danzig as late as 11 April and still had not detected westward movement of 3d, 28th, and 31st Armies.[84] At that time 3d Army was in its assembly areas east of the Oder, and 28th and 31st Armies would complete their move the following day. 2d Shock had left one rifle corps in its former sector which produced the German misperception that the entire army was there.[85]

German intelligence did, however, detect some of the regrouping within the three *fronts*. On 8 April German intelligence correctly postulated 4th Guards Tank Army's regrouping as it was moving northwestward through Brieg and Liegnitz. The same day the Germans discovered 49th and 70th Armies were approaching the Oder, and they surmised that 1st Polish and 61st Armies would soon move south to participate in a 1st Belorussian Front offensive.[86] The daylight movement of 2d Belorussian Front units enabled German aerial reconnaissance to make this correct assessment. In the 1st Ukrainian Front's sector, better *maskirovka* and night movement better concealed the regrouping despite the lapse of discipline within 4th Guards Tank Army.

German intelligence tracked the *front* internal regrouping more efficiently. On 12 April it predicted offensive activity along the Oder River within two days, and the next day it singled out Küstrin, Frankfurt, and Zehden (south of Stettin) as likely Soviet main attack sectors (see maps 197–202). Two of the three locations were correct, although the threat from 1st Ukrainian Front's sector was noticeably not singled out.[87]

In the 1st Belorussian Front sector, German intelligence correctly estimated the Soviet force opposing them with the exception of the newly arrived Soviet 3d Army. However, the Germans did not detect the final Soviet regrouping into assault positions. Further south, in the 1st Ukrainian Front sector, Konev's deception plan worked well. German intelligence failed to note the arrival of 5th Guards and 3d Guards Tank Armies and the Soviet concentration for the new offensive. South of Stettin, German intelligence assessed a threat from Soviet 70th and 61st Armies and noted the probable redeployment of 49th Army into that region but failed to detect the arrival of 65th Army.

Soviet critics later commented on the 1st Belorussian Front's problems, asserting:

> The forces of 5th Shock and 8th Guards Armies, however, operating on the direction of the main attack, in spite of extensive engineer work, did not succeed in creating in the enemy the impression of preparation of units for a lengthy defense. During the conduct of deceptive measures the troops

25. Soviet tanks entering Berlin, April–May, 1945

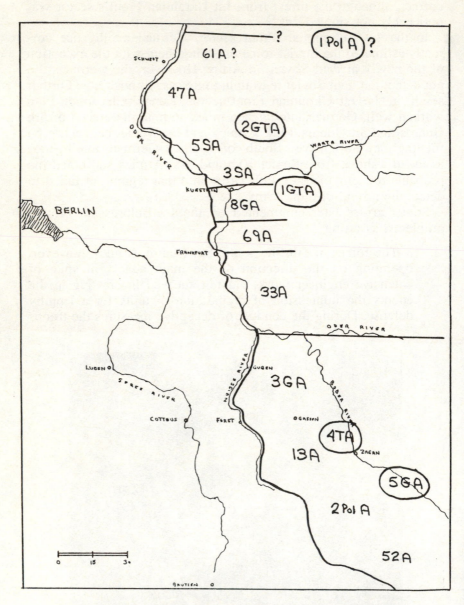

195. Berlin, German intelligence assessment, 15 April 1945

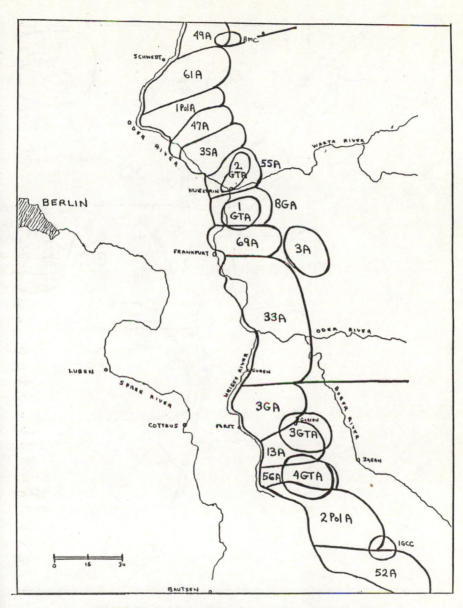

196. Berlin, Soviet dispositions, 15 April 1945

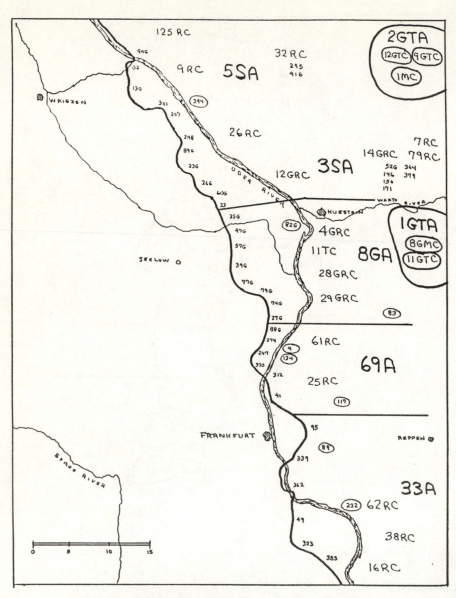

197. Berlin, German intelligence assessment, Küstrin–Frankfurt sector,
     15 April 1945

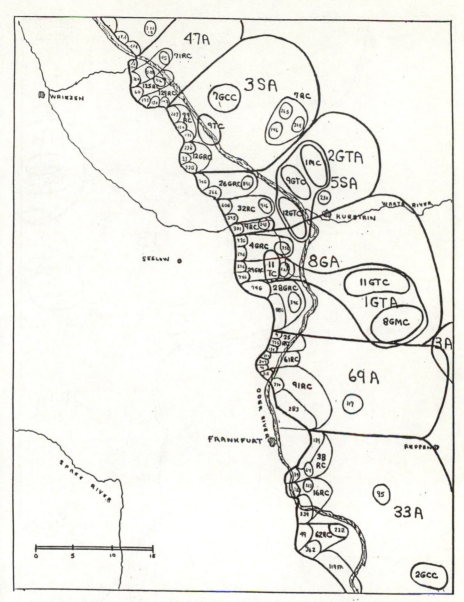

198. Berlin, Soviet 1st Belorussian Front dispositions, Küstrin–Frankfurt sector, 15 April 1945

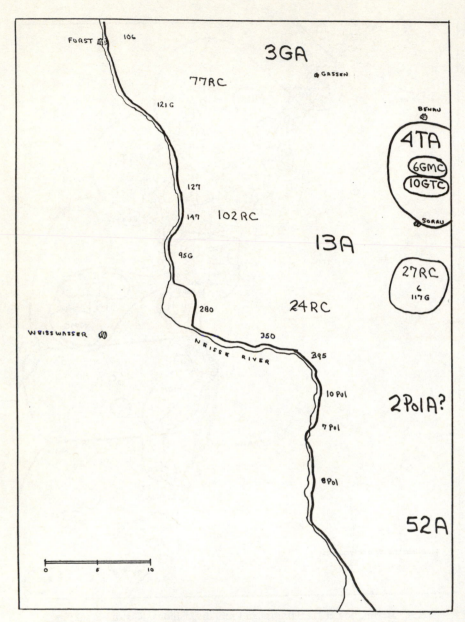

199. Berlin, German intelligence assessment, Neisse sector, 15 April 1945

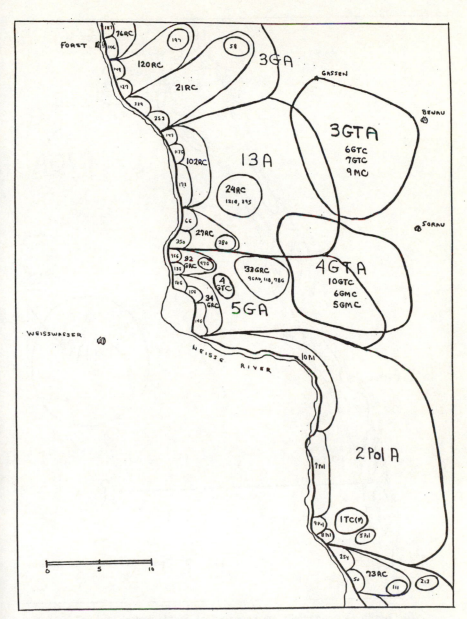

200. Berlin, Soviet 1st Ukrainian Front dispositions, Neisse sector, 15 April 1945

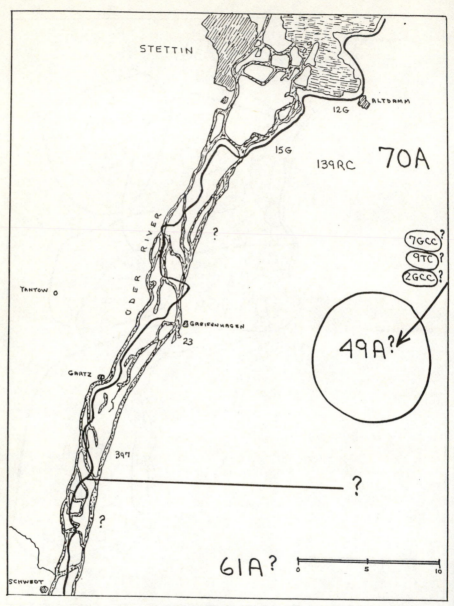

201. Berlin, German intelligence assessment, Stettin sector, 15 April 1945

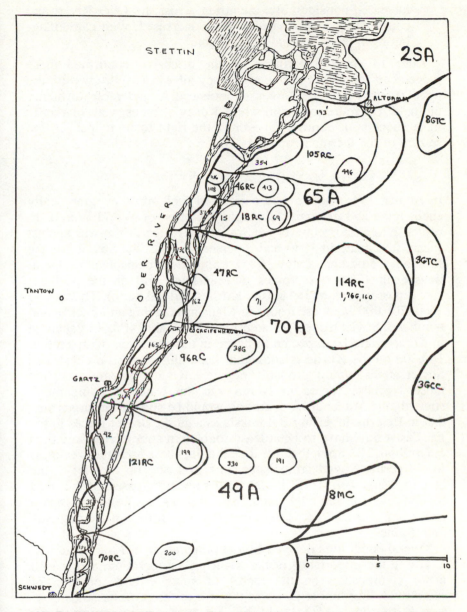

202. Berlin, Soviet 2d Belorussian Front dispositions, Stettin sector, 15 April 1945

committed a series of revealing actions: movement of vehicles increased considerably, including across the Oder River; and construction of observation posts increased, with camouflaging from enemy aerial observation.[88]

After 15 April the course of the offensive confirmed these judgements concerning the efficiency of *maskirovka* within the three *fronts*. Zhukov's forces experienced considerable difficulty on the direct route to Berlin while Konev's forces were markedly more successful, earning for Konev the right to participate in the seizure of the German capital.

MANCHURIA, AUGUST 1945

In August 1945 the Soviets conducted their most geographically challenging and extensive strategic operation of World War II. In response to allied requests for Soviet assistance in the war against Japan, first made in 1944 and repeated in 1945, the Soviets, at the Potsdam Conference (May 1945), committed themselves to operations against Japanese forces in Manchuria and on the northern island possessions of Japan (the Kuriles and Sakhalin). There were about 700,000 Japanese troops in Manchuria facing an almost equal number of Soviet troops. An additional 300,000 to 400,000 Japanese in Korea might be expected to figure in the operation, with another 100,000 on the Kurile Islands and Sakhalin.[89] A well-orchestrated Soviet attack would probably negate the requirement to engage those Japanese forces in Korea. On the basis of comparative strength, the Manchurian operation would be somewhat larger than that in Belorussia. Using Belorussia as a guide, Soviet forces in the Far East would have to be at least doubled in strength to more than 1.5 million. The Soviets did realize that Japanese armored weakness would permit Soviet armor superiority, making up for part of the lack in manpower. Thus, initial Soviet planning assessed the need for about 1.5 million men and at least one tank army and one to two tank or mechanized corps to defeat Japanese forces in the requisite time frame.

Several conditions delayed Soviet preparations for the operation, increased the importance of the Manchurian operation, and placed major significance on the factor of surprise and the role of *maskirovka*. The first reality was the size of the projected theater of operations (roughly 600 by 1,000 kilometers) and, more important, the distance of the theater from European Russia. To raise Soviet force strength to over 1.5 million men would require moving almost

700,000 men over 9,000 kilometers along the limited umbilical of the Trans-Siberian Railroad from the European theater to the Far East. Even more significant was the necessity of moving large armored forces (one tank army and one tank corps) and the massive quantity of necessary equipment and supplies. To maintain strategic surprise, this movement would have to be kept as secret as possible. Once deployed for the offensive, those forces would have to advance through the difficult and varied terrain of Manchuria to a depth of almost 900 kilometers. Terrain problems also necessitated deceiving Japanese forces about actual routes of the Soviet advance.

The second reality was the degree of fanatical resistance the Japanese had displayed in earlier operations against US forces. In two months of intense fighting on Okinawa, 110,000 American troops had suffered 49,000 casualties defeating about 60,000 Japanese. There was no reason to assume more passive Japanese reception of a Soviet advance into Manchuria. This made necessary skillful operations, using the best operational and tactical techniques developed in the European war. Thus, the Soviets had to send experienced forces and commanders secretly to the Far East. The final reality confronting the Soviets on the very eve of the offensive was that of time constraints. American use of the nuclear bomb, and possible ensuing Japanese collapse, made it imperative that the offensive should achieve its goals in a matter of days, rather than weeks or months. The Soviets determined that Manchuria had to be secured within 30 days and the main entrances into central Manchuria within one week. This was as much a political as a military decision.

From virtually every perspective, *maskirovka* would make the difference between success and failure. To a greater extent than in the west, successful strategic *maskirovka* was important, while operational and tactical *maskirovka* had to be perfect if the overall operational plan was to be realized.

Unlike the earlier years of war, in August 1945 the Soviet Army sought to employ *maskirovka* and achieve surprise in the initial phases of a new war. This required political finesse to dull Japanese apprehensions over possible Soviet war intentions and the creation and application of a *maskirovka* plan outside the context of ongoing combat. The Soviets could not rely on the "noise" of war to assist them in their task.

The Soviets understood the difficulty in masking their overall offensive intentions. General S.M. Shtemenko noted:

Our striving for surprise in our operation was complicated very much by the fact that the Japanese had long and steadfastly believed in the inevitability of war with the Soviet Union. The achievement of strategic surprise was hardly a practicable matter. Nevertheless, after pondering this problem, we returned more than once to the first days of the Great Patriotic War. Our country had also expected the war and prepared for it; however, the German attack proved unexpected. Consequently, it was not necessary to prematurely repudiate surprise in the current case.[90]

Surprise in the Manchurian operation depended first on maintaining the secrecy of the operational plan and the nature and scope of Soviet offensive preparations. Also, to an extraordinary degree, surprise would depend on the form of the attack, which had to be conducted in a manner guaranteed to pre-empt Japanese defenses or paralyze the Japanese command and control structure. This meant the use of unorthodox operational and tactical techniques, tested earlier but never before relied upon to such a major extent.

The first task was to secure planning for the operation.[91] The Soviets followed procedures developed in previous operations and severely restricted the number of planners and of planning documents. A Far East Command directive restricted full participation in planning to the *front* commander, the member of the *front*

26. From left to right, Marshal K. A. Meretskov, 1st Far Eastern Front commander; Marshal P. Ya. Malinovsky, Trans-Baikal Front commander; and Marshal A. M. Vasilevsky, commander of Soviet forces in the Far East, August, 1945

Military Council (political officer), the chief of staff, and the chief of the operational directorate. *Front* chiefs of troop branches and services participated in developing only their functional portions of the plan and were not familiar with overall *front* missions. The directive read:

> The army commander will be assigned missions personally and verbally, without the delivery of written directives from the front. The participation in the development of the army operational plan will be established on the same basis as within the front. All documents concerning the plans of troop operations will be kept in the personal safes of the front and army commanders.[92]

The most sensitive aspect of offensive preparations was the problem of masking the extensive force and materiel build-up in the Far East. This effort would take considerable time to complete, and would rely on a limited transportation network already highly vulnerable to Japanese observation. This concentration, regrouping, and deployment of forces and materiel, and the movement of commanders and staffs required to lead the forces were carried out under the cloak of a host of *maskirovka* measures. High level commanders and their staffs traveled to the Far East (normally by air) under assumed names, wearing bogus badges of rank, branch, and service.[93] Movement by rail of materiel began as early as January 1945; and, whenever possible, the Soviets relied upon indigenous stocks and production to equip their forces. Movement of men and materiel occurred only at night under strict camouflage conditions. Hundreds of kilometers of artificial covers were built to physically mask the rail line from Japanese observation (especially along the Amur and Ussuri Rivers where the rail line was under direct observation by Japanese forces on the far bank).

During June and July the Soviets used 136,000 rail cars to move the requisite number of men and materiel to launch the offensive (22–30 trains per day).[94] While the Japanese noted the increased volume of traffic, Soviet camouflage probably concealed from Japanese eyes 50 percent of the volume of men and materiel moved.

Once in the Far East, the *fronts* placed arriving units and materiel in widely dispersed camps and depots in positions distant from the front, but accessible for quick deployment forward, needing only limited use of forward assembly areas and jumping-off positions. During these movements, troops conducted exercises which made it possible for units to train, adapt to local conditions, and prepare for the attack while maintaining their concealment. One to two days before initiation of the attack, where necessary, forces moved into their initial positions; in which movement of any kind, food preparation, and wood-cutting was strictly forbidden. All newly arrived units maintained strict radio silence. Similar measures covered the extensive redeployment of forces already stationed in the Far East and Trans-Baikal regions.[95]

The Far East Command and the *front* headquarters published detailed directives and instructions concerning general and specific *maskirovka* plans to govern their forces. For example, the 1st Far Eastern Front (previously the Primor'ye group and 25th Army) issued extensive instructions calling for the creation of false troop concentrations, a decoy offensive sector, active defense preparations in other sectors, and activation of bogus reconnaissance. Troops performing these missions were not informed about the false nature of their activities.

Meanwhile, all activity in *front* sectors was kept at normal levels. The population carried on normal activities, military units followed usual routines, and radio traffic continued with no change. Newly arriving units moved only at night and rested in forests and villages out of the enemy's view. Where cover was unavailable (as in the steppes), tanks, vehicles, and personnel dug in and concealed themselves with camouflage materials or nets. The Soviets prepared unit command posts in advance, either digging them in or using existing structures which blended in with the surroundings. All communications nets lines were dug in as well as artillery firing positions prepared in advance by specially designated engineer units. Though these and other measures did little to alter Japanese judgements about ultimate Soviet offensive intentions, they did conceal the timing, scope, and location of the impending attack (see maps 203 and 204).

The extensive secrecy and *maskirovka* measures were but one aspect, albeit an important one, concerning preparations for the operation. Equally important were techniques used by the Soviets to surprise the Japanese regarding the form of the attack. Most of these techniques were by no means new, having been used on various occasions in the German war, when the Soviets had been able to judge their effectiveness. However, in Manchuria the Soviets used a wide array of these techniques on a grander scale than ever before.

As in 1939, Japanese attitudes toward likely Soviet performance conditioned the Japanese for being surprised.[96] The Japanese apparently stereotyped Soviet combat performance on the basis of German reports of how the Soviets had operated early in the war (1941–1942). Thus, they underestimated the ability of the Soviets to employ armor skillfully and coordinate combined arms forces in poor terrain. They underestimated their logistical capability to effect and support large troop concentrations in terrain they (the Japanese) considered unsuited for large-scale military operations, particularly the areas adjacent to western Manchuria. The skill of Soviet combat performance far exceeded Japanese expectations.

The form and location of the Soviet attack at the strategic, operational, and tactical levels also surprised the Japanese.[97] The Soviet two-front strategic envelopment through both eastern and western Manchuria contradicted Japanese expectations and deployments. Soviet units routinely crossed terrain the Japanese considered impassable, leaving it virtually undefended. Moreover the Japanese were unable to counter the Soviet's conscious decision to use every possible avenue of approach in their attack. Soviet use of armor in first echelon at every level of command – initially, or shortly after the beginning of the attack – also caught the Japanese off guard. Having discounted the threat of armor in such difficult terrain, they could not deal with it. The Soviet tendency to bypass fortified positions confounded Japanese commanders and rendered most Japanese defenses useless.

27. Soviet forces begin the assault, Manchuria, August, 1945

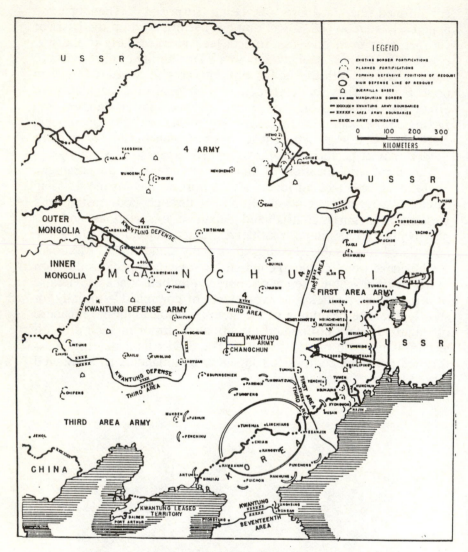

203. Manchuria, Japanese intelligence assessment and expected enemy
axes of advance, August 1945

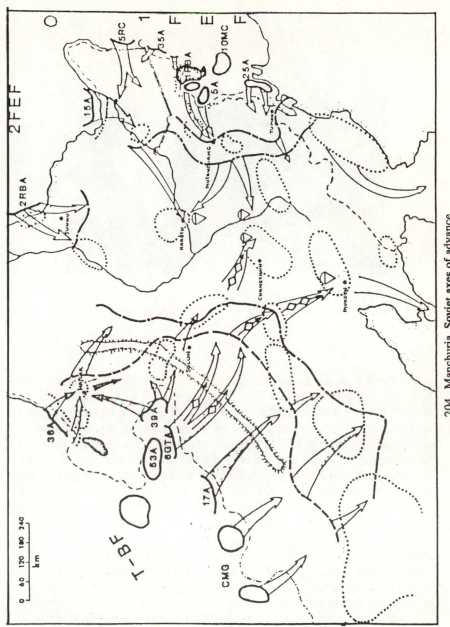

204. Manchuria, Soviet axes of advance

28. General A.I. Antonov, Chief of the Red Army general staff (right) with
General S.M. Shtemenko, Chief of the general staff's operational
department

Tactically as well, the Japanese were unprepared to deal with
Soviet combat techniques. The Soviet use of small, task-organized
assault groups with heavy engineer and firepower support clashed
with the image of human waves of infantry in the assault. Perhaps
most unexpected for the Japanese was Soviet reliance on forward
detachments to probe Japanese defenses, bypass them, and attack
deep into the Japanese operational rear. The Soviet commanders'
display of initiative at all levels did not fit Japanese preconceptions
of Soviet performance. In fact, the scope of Soviet use of rapid
maneuver surprised and confused the Japanese, resulting in a
general paralysis of their command and control. To a greater extent
than at any time before, in Manchuria the Soviets followed the
advice found in all of their earlier regulations, specifically to achieve
maskirovka by "employing methods of fighting that are new for the
enemy and weapons unknown to him."

Soviet *maskirovka* measures achieved marked success. Certainly
in mid-1945 the Japanese anticipated that the Soviet Union
ultimately would join the war against Japan. The Soviet attack,

29. Tanks of 6th Guards Tank Army cross the Grand Khingan Mountains,
    Manchuria, August, 1945

when it did occur, however, "caught the Japanese totally unprepared for an invasion they expected."[98]

Strategic indicators of Soviet intent to go to war against Japan
were present and predictable. In late January 1945, the Japanese
Army Vice Chief of Staff had predicted the Soviets would abrogate
the Japanese–Soviet Neutrality Pact and would enter the war
against Japan in the latter half of 1945.[99] It happened in April. After
the German surrender in May, the Japanese High Command
(JGHQ) had assessed that Soviet entry into the war was unlikely
until the spring of 1946, when Japan would be closer to surrender.
They conceded, however, that Soviet attack preparations could be
complete by August or September 1945; but thought weather
conditions in that period were not conducive for an attack.[100] All
these assessments were based on a political judgement that Soviet
war losses would force them to await an American invasion of Japan
before they would join the war. Moreover, in August Manchuria
was subject to heavy, often torrential monsoon rains which turned
Manchuria's few roads into morasses.

After Yalta, the Japanese had estimated it would take at least three months after the German surrender for the Soviets to move necessary forces to Manchuria for an offensive. By July Japanese estimates of Soviet reinforcements had put Soviet strength at about 1.3 million men. By August or September the Japanese estimated the Soviets would have 40–50 rifle divisions and 4,000 tanks ready to employ but considered they would not attack until they had amassed a force of at least 55–60 divisions.[101]

The Japanese did detect large-scale Soviet rail movements into the Far East. From February to August the Kwangtung Army counted 800–1,000 trains of 40 cars each and deduced the movement of 20–25 Soviet divisions. Thus, Japanese intelligence "underestimated between 30 to 50 percent the 40 Soviet divisions actually deployed eastward."[102] This caused them to believe "that they still had time to prepare their defenses against the Soviet invasion in the spring of 1946."[103] Interestingly enough, while undercounting military units and incorrectly estimating deployment, the Japanese kept a fairly accurate count of overall Soviet manpower strength in the Far East.

Based on these optimistic estimates, the Japanese were slow to implement changes in force disposition associated with their 1944 alteration of overall Kwangtung Army planning from an offensive to a defensive posture. Many units had not completed their redeployment by the time of the Soviet invasion.

As was often the case in earlier operations, there was a dichotomy between intelligence assessments at lower-level and high-level headquarters, with the lower level taking a more realistic view. At a 4 August conference at 3d Area Army the Kwangtung Army operations section said no invasion could be expected until September. If the attack did not begin then, the Kwangtung Army believed it would probably begin in the spring.[104] High level optimism muffled warnings from below, starved lower level units of meaningful intelligence information on the Soviets, and stifled the war preparations of low level units. "In short, the Japanese were unprepared strategically, operationally, or tactically for the massive Soviet blow which fell on 9 August 1945."[105] The captured deputy chief of staff of the Kwangtung Army, General M. Tomokatsu, declared that the specific dates of the entry of the USSR into the war remained unknown, despite the fact that the Kwangtung Army had detected the Soviet build-up. Hence, he declared that the declaration of war by the Soviet Union on 8 August was completely unexpected.[106] General Semizu, commander of Japanese Fifth Army stated, "We did not expect that the Russian Army would go through the taiga, and the offensive of Russian forces from almost inaccessible regions proved a complete surprise for us."[107] To a great extent, the combat performance of the Kwantung Army during the Manchurian operation attested to the degree of surprise the Soviets achieved by using new operational and tactical techniques enabling them to achieve objectives in half the time. An operation optimistically judged to last at least 30 days was, in fact, completed within 15 days.

Manchuria represented a sterling effort for the Soviets regarding the wartime use of *maskirovka*. More important, it was one of their few experiences of employing *maskirovka* in the initial stages of war and has, therefore, become a major focal point for Soviet study of the nature of the "initial period of war." Specifically, the Soviets have investigated the role of *maskirovka* in that increasingly sensitive period of a transition from peace to war.

Soviet *maskirovka* measures at the strategic, operational, and tactical levels achieved greater success in Manchuria than in any previous operation. They were able to confuse the Japanese regarding the timing, scope, location, and form of the offensive. Hence, Manchuria has become a textbook case for the Soviets on how to conduct strategic *maskirovka*. The time and special considerations of the offensive seemed to create conditions and requirements somewhat analogous to theater offensives in a modern nuclear context. That fact has prompted even more intense Soviet study.

CONCLUSIONS

Confronted with the task of organizing strategic *maskirovka* in the circumstances of a truncated, more concentrated front, Soviet planners drew on the experiences of three years of war and shifted the focus of *maskirovka*. Concealing offensive intent in the climactic stages of war was clearly impossible. Geographical considerations, principally the more restricted length of the front and the growing number of natural barriers to a broad front advance along many directions inhibited Soviet concealment of main strategic and operational attack directions. Faced with these altered circumstances, Soviet planners still attempted to use deception to conceal offensive intent and location but now placed primary emphasis on concealing the timing and scale of the offensive.

The Soviets increased the scale and improved the secrecy of strategic regrouping and concentration of forces by shifting multiple armies between *fronts* and from *STAVKA* reserve into projected attack positions. Prior to the summer campaign of 1944 the Soviets had strategically regrouped two tank armies and five combined armies. In the late fall of 1944 they had done so with three tank and ten combined armies. Then, prior to the April Berlin offensive, the Soviets regrouped 28 armies, of which 18 conducted moves of strategic proportion. Between June and August 1945 the Soviets transported one *front*, one tank army, three combined arms armies, and almost 700,000 men the breadth of the continent into the Far East.

The secrecy with which it was accomplished was even more important than the scale of the strategic regrouping. In virtually all cases the Soviets were able to conceal between 50 and 100 percent of the forces regrouped. That resulted in a proportionate German and Japanese underestimation of the force opposing them. In every case it turned prospective operational defeat on the part of the deceived into a strategic disaster.

The Soviets continued seeking to deceive their opponents regarding attack timing, but in terms of days rather than weeks or months. Because they possessed clear superiority, and the enemy perceived overwhelming opposition, the Soviets could launch feints and conduct offensive preparations at will in multiple sectors to produce constant apprehension on the part of the enemy. German and Japanese inability to see deep into the Soviet rear reinforced that apprehension and created the impression that offensives could occur at any time, in virtually any location. The inability of enemy intelligence to differentiate between threats generated multiple false predictions (as along the Vistula in late fall and along the Oder in April) and eventually an inability to precisely say when an offensive would begin.

While they focused on concealing the timing and scale of their offensives, the Soviets still developed elaborate plans to conceal attack location; and, although these plans were not as successful as they had been in 1944, they still detracted from their opponents' ability to resist. By continuing operations in Hungary from October to December 1944, the Soviets attracted significant reserves from the central sector of the front, reserves which did not return to Poland in time to halt the January disaster. Soviet operations in the Baltic prevented reinforcement of the critical central sector as well; and when forces were finally shifted southward from Courland in early February, the damage had already been done. As late as March 1945, the Germans dispatched their last large reserve force

(Sixth SS Panzer Army) to Hungary rather than to the critical Oder River front. Soviet operations against Pomerania and Silesia in February and March surprised the Germans, lulled them into a false sense of security along the Oder River, tied down or eliminated large German forces, and finally detracted from the German defense along the Oder River in April. In Manchuria, as well, the Soviets reinforced Japanese perception that an attack would occur along traditional axes (the north and east), conditioning them to be unable to cope with the ensuing major attacks from the west and in other areas the Japanese had ruled out as viable attack directions.

Soviet operational and tactical *maskirovka* in 1945 was characterized by a scope, diversity, and thoroughness born of years of practice. It involved new forms of disinformation, reconnaissance, artillery preparations, use of "special echelons," night operations, extensive employment of smoke, and a host of techniques used earlier in the war. The comprehensiveness and ubiquitousness of these measures only reinforced the Soviet ability to conduct strategic *maskirovka* and compounded the harm done to enemies in both the East and the West.

CHAPTER EIGHT

PATTERNS OF DECEPTION

Reflections on Soviet Second World War *Maskirovka* Experiences

Analysis of Great Patriotic War experiences demonstrates that the most important means for achieving surprise is *maskirovka* – one of the basic means for protecting the combat actions of forces. Without qualitative and efficacious resolution of that problem, the most original decisions and new means of achieving secret preparation and conduct of surprise attacks on the enemy cannot achieve the required result.

> M.M. Kir'yan
> *Vnezapnost' v nastupatel'nykh operatsiyakh Velikoi Otechestvennoi Voiny* [Surprise in Offensive Operations of the Great Patriotic War], 1986

The experience of the Great Patriotic War vividly demonstrates that secretly prepared operations occur as a surprise for the enemy. Operational surprise continually stuns the enemy and deprives him of the capability of rendering organized resistance. However, operations in which participate all types of forces and weapons, possessing contemporary means of reconnaissance, are very difficult to hide from the enemy. It demands great skill, initiative, and creativity on the part of the organizers of the operation and impeccable fulfillment of all measures, spelled out in the operational *maskirovka* plan.[1]

> Marshal G.V. Zhukov, 1977

These simple comments and those of General Kir'yan capture the essence of what the Soviets have learned from their Second World War experiences with deception at the strategic as well as the operational and tactical levels. The war has broadened Soviet appreciation of the utility of *maskirovka* and generated an understanding of the immense complexity of undertaking such a task. It is significant that Zhukov and Kir'yan used the present tense when describing the scope of those experiences. Soviet study of *maskirovka* today rests upon a foundation of the study of *maskirovka* in the past. To the Soviets, the scope, duration, and complexity of combat in those four years of war have yet to be surpassed. Thus, a mastery of those experiences remains a prerequisite for sound study of deception in a contemporary context.

The Soviets derived from the war an understanding of the ubiquitousness of *maskirovka*, which simply reinforced their natural ideological tendency to avoid distinguishing between normal peacetime deception and wartime military deception. The events of August 1939 (Poland); May 1940 (France); and, in particular, those of June 1941 and August 1945 proved the unity of peacetime and wartime deception, even to those in the military who had focused on *maskirovka* as primarily a wartime phenomenon. *Maskirovka* before or during "the initial period of war" emerged after Stalin's death as a major subject of Soviet concern made even more urgent by the likely quickened pace and enhanced destructive power of war in the nuclear age.

War experiences also proved the essential unity of deception relative to all levels of war and all types of *maskirovka* employed. It was simply impossible to separate strategic, operational, and tactical deception measures since all were inter-related and inter-dependent. While one could undertake tactical deception without planning great operational or strategic deception measures, it was impossible to do the reverse. Successful strategic deception depended entirely on the thoroughness of similar measures at the lower levels. Throughout the war the ability to deceive the Germans concerning overall Soviet strategic offensive plans depended on the successful secret redeployment of multiple armies and corps. That secrecy depended on the efficient conduct of movement security, which in turn depended on the rather mundane requirement to hide the individual tank and vehicle from prying German eyes. Similarly, the most elaborate deception plans would fall prey to sloppy camouflage or slipshod radio security. It was no good hiding major troop concentrations if they could be detected from analysis of radio traffic. Unimaginative reconnaissance techniques or artillery registration procedures could compromise the most carefully orchestrated *maskirovka* plan. It took failure, often on numerous occasions, for a talent for *maskirovka* to emerge. By the middle of 1943 that talent was evident.

Since it depended on the most extensive successful procedures and techniques, strategic deception took the longest time for the Soviets to master. Moreover, because of its broad focus, it usually involved a wide geographical area and depended on skillful conduct of *maskirovka* measures by a vast array of units deployed in different sectors. Hence, its success depended not only on the skill of the high command, but also on the proficiency of the Red Army in general. Only after the extensive regulations and instructions on *maskirovka* generated by war experiences had been absorbed and mastered by lower level units could the Soviet High Command expect to master strategic deception.

Soviet attempts at strategic deception during the Moscow operation were crude and limited in scope. Their purpose was simply to hide from German intelligence the scope and location of the counter-offensive, a task which involved the masking of movements and deployment of three relatively small armies. Soviet success in that endeavor resulted as much from the chaos of the general situation and fortunate bad weather as from Soviet skill at *maskirovka*. German failure to detect those large units was merely a continuation of earlier German failures, only now on a larger scale. Throughout the summer and fall of 1941, the Soviets had continually surprised the Germans by their ability to mobilize and field a series of new reserve armies, many of which appeared in unexpected locations. Often this German failure resulted from the prejudice produced by their pre-war estimates of Soviet wartime mobilization potential. These estimates failed to predict the huge scale of Soviet mobilization, consequently German intelligence neither expected nor detected the deployment of numerous reserve armies. In subsequent operations after December 1941, the Germans continued to miss the deployment of Soviet reserve armies. This recurring failure became a more serious problem throughout the war as those undetected armies became stronger and more numerous and as German reserves dwindled.[2]

The Soviet strategic plan for operations during the spring and summer of 1942 incorporated measures to deceive the Germans concerning where they would focus their main efforts. The Soviets stressed the Moscow direction where Zhukov was in command and hoped to resume the offensive which had failed during the previous winter. To distract the Germans, the Soviets organized the May Khar'kov offensive which itself incorporated an operational *maskirovka* plan. German strategic deception, which concealed their offensive preparations in southern Russia, frustrated Soviet aims and rendered Soviet *maskirovka* measures at Khar'kov superfluous. A Soviet operational disaster resulted, and the ensuing success of the German strategic offensive toward Stalingrad and the Caucasus negated the original Soviet strategic plan. It did, however, enhance Soviet chances for conducting *maskirovka* in support of their Stalingrad counter-offensive.

At Stalingrad in November 1942, the Soviets embarked on an even more deliberate attempt to conduct strategic deception. The plan involved several planned troop concentrations in other regions of the front (at Moscow, for example) as well as the usual practice of deploying masked forces into hidden concentration areas. While the threatened Soviet strategic feints had limited effect on German strategic deployments, the Soviet local redeployments and resulting secret concentrations worked well, producing the German disaster of November 1942. Here the Soviets demonstrated markedly improved skills which paid significant dividends.

During the course of 1943 Soviet strategic deception matured. The frenetic nature of the winter campaign and Soviet over-optimism concerning its outcome precluded creation of a comprehensive plan. In the summer, however, the Soviet *maskirovka* plan for the Kursk strategic defense and counter-offensive was comprehensive and effective. By employing a series of diversionary attacks on the Northern Donets and Mius Rivers, the Soviets concealed their intent to strike on the Belgorod–Khar'kov–Poltava direction and drew German reserves away from the most critical sector. Subsequently the Soviet counter-offensive rent a huge hole in the front and chewed up German operational reserves in piecemeal fashion as they redeployed to the threatened sector. Then the Soviets began offensive actions along the entire front to fix German forces and cover the main Soviet advance to the Dnepr River between Kiev and Kremenchug. Once they had reached the Dnepr River line the Soviets feinted along its entire course, secretly regrouped forces north of Kiev, and broke out west of the river, establishing a bridgehead of such a size the Germans were unable to deal with it.

Soviet strategic *maskirovka* in 1943 involved only limited regrouping and concentration of *STAVKA* reserves, the most notable examples of which were deployment and use of the Steppe Front at Kursk and the shift of forces between *fronts* during the advance to the Dnepr. Most regrouping was restricted to single or, in a few cases, multiple armies within operating *fronts*. Unlike 1942, the Soviets began to emphasize active *maskirovka* by simulating false regions of concentration (Belgorod–Khar'kov) and engaging in planned disinformation.

Throughout 1943 the Soviets centralized strategic *maskirovka* planning within the *STAVKA* and General Staff. This produced greater unity of purpose and more thorough coordination among the *fronts*. The regulations of 1943 set standards and responsibilities for *maskirovka* planning at all levels; and, as a consequence, that planning became more ubiquitous and effective. At all levels of command, Soviet planning security improved through the employment of Draconian security measures and adherence to a tight process of sequential planning.

In 1944 Soviet strategic *maskirovka* capitalized on Soviet maintenance of the strategic initiative. The expanded scope of strategic *maskirovka* included: the conduct of reconnaissance on a broad front, simultaneous offensive preparations in numerous sectors, large-scale offensive simulations, and actual commencement of operations on secondary directions both to divert German attention and make gains in their own right. By summer secret strategic redeployments reached major proportions.

In the winter offensive the Soviets focused on combat in the south but conducted minor diversions elsewhere. Implicit in the Soviet strategic plan was the attaining of surprise by operating at a time of year and in regions where terrain conditions hitherto had prohibited such operations. Soviet forces, advancing on a broad front, constantly shifted the focus of the offensive and regrouped armies between *fronts* at will. This offensive also conditioned the Germans for the even larger scale strategic *maskirovka* planned for the summer of 1944.

The Soviet strategic *maskirovka* plan for the summer of 1944 was the most successful of the war, involving as it did the secret preparation and conduct of sequential strategic offensives in Belorussia, against southern Poland, and into Rumania. The Soviet strategic *maskirovka* plan involved a large scale, concealed strategic redeployment of forces followed by simulation of a strategic offensive against German forces in southern Poland and Rumania. While the Germans were preoccupied by those simulations, Soviet forces struck in Belorussia in June and destroyed German Army Group Center. Then, in mid-July, covered by operational *maskirovka* simulations and diversions, in rapid sequence Soviet forces broke into southern and central Poland and advanced to the Vistula River. As German forces attempted to halt the disasters in the northern and central regions of the front, in August the Soviets struck in Rumania, almost destroying German Army Group South Ukraine.

While Soviet *maskirovka* worked well in the summer campaign and achieved significant results in virtually every phase, the 1944 Belorussian operation was the first occasion when Soviet strategic deception achieved virtually all of its aims. The elaborate measures undertaken to simulate hostile intent elsewhere distracted German attention and significant German forces from deployment into Belorussia. The ensuing Soviet strategic regrouping of forces progressed undetected by the Germans. Successful Soviet deception of the Germans regarding intent, scale, scope, and location of the offensive produced spectacular, but utterly predictable, Soviet results. The Soviets capitalized on their numerous successes in the fall by shifting their strategic emphasis to the flanks, in so doing setting up German forces for further defeats in the winter of 1945.

In 1944 the Soviets expanded the scope of their strategic *maskirovka* efforts and incorporated *maskirovka* plans into virtually every strategic, *front*, and army offensive operation. These plans were tailored to suit the varied conditions of each strategic, operational, and tactical sector. Noteworthy during 1944 was the Soviets' ability to regroup and concentrate secretly multiple armies between *fronts* and from *STAVKA* reserve. Unlike previous years, they were also able to move these armies into forward positions with less chance of detection. German intelligence problems; improved Soviet intelligence; the growing inflexibility of German operations caused by Hitler's active involvement in defensive planning; and the tendency of German commanders to operate in accustomed patterns, when faced by Soviet offensives, produced considerable Soviet *maskirovka* success and, hence, operational success.

Soviet strategic *maskirovka* in 1945 had to adjust to the changing nature of their offensive operations. Whereas in 1944 *maskirovka* plans had focused on masking one strategic offensive after another in separate sectors, in 1945 the plans sought to solve the more difficult problem of masking simultaneous strategic offensives in several sectors. In these circumstances Soviet planners primarily stressed masking the scale of operations and placed secondary emphasis on concealing the location and time of the attack. Better developed and managed strategic movement capabilities, tighter rear area security, and declining German ability to see deep permitted massive and secret Soviet movement of strategic reserves constituting more than 60 percent of the attacking force. The simultaneous nature of the offensives and the truncation of the front allowed the Soviets to continue to conceal the precise time of attack and even blur its real location.

In August 1945 circumstances arose whereby the Soviets could apply their talents to a theater offensive against a nation with which they were not at war. Successful strategic deception of the Japanese in Manchuria proved that the techniques learned in four years of war could be applied to the initial phase of war. Soviet success with deception in Manchuria partially compensated for the similar deception of the Soviets in June 1941, providing another case for study in the post-war years.

From their war experiences with strategic deception the Soviets learned several valuable lessons. First, they learned that it is virtually impossible to conceal totally an intent to attack. This is true in the "initial period of war" as well as during the course of war itself. That difficulty increases in direct proportion to one's strength relative to the enemy. Experience indicates, however, that it may not be necessary to mask intent. Successful masking of the scale, scope, location, or timing of the attack can produce results as satisfactory as could be produced by covering one's intent. In fact, there may be an advantage in not deceiving the enemy regarding one's overall offensive intent. Very simply, an expectant enemy tends to have a more active imagination. He is more receptive to false indicators, in particular if his intelligence collection is un-discriminating or inept.[3] A partially warned enemy can definitely be deceived regarding the other aspects of *maskirovka* such as the scale, scope, location, and timing of the attack.

Of those four other aspects of *maskirovka*, timing of the offensive is the most difficult to mask. Yet even timing need not be masked perfectly to achieve its desired ends. Specifically, the enemy need only be deceived to that point when it is impossible for him to make necessary redeployments to thwart the attack. And, if deception works regarding offensive scale and location, even a small time miscalculation by the enemy can spell disaster, for a force can be struck in the midst of redeployment. Thus throughout the war the Soviets were satisfied if they deceived the Germans by at least a factor of several days. By 1943 they normally achieved this aim.

In the Soviet view, perhaps scale, scope, and location were the most important and achievable aspects of strategic deception. Certainly these were more easily achieved than intent and timing. The results were usually sufficient to ensure defeat of the enemy, even if he knew of the general time of the attack. In virtually every strategic operation the Soviets successfully deceived the Germans in scale and scope, even if the general location of the main attack was known. As the war progressed and the correlation of forces shifted significantly to the Soviet's benefit, their ability to mask their advantage improved. At Moscow, Stalingrad, Kursk, Belorussia, Vistula–Oder, Berlin, and Manchuria, enemy underestimation of Soviet strength progressively increased. By 1944 and 1945 Soviet *maskirovka* routinely confounded enemy intelligence, resulting in the enemy missing well over 50 percent of the Soviet offensive build-up and, hence, underestimating the Soviet force by between 25 and 40 percent. This, the Soviets learned, was sufficient enemy miscalculation to accord the Soviets huge, if not decisive, battlefield advantage.

At the strategic level, Soviet deception achieved increasing success as the war progressed. Strategic deception contributed significantly to the pace of Soviet victory, while providing a wealth of experience for Soviet theorists to analyse and draw upon in postwar years.

The Soviets experienced increased success in deception within the operational and tactical realms. The Soviets recognize that their success with deception was largely a function of officer education, individual and unit training, and a variety of conditions reflecting the stage of war. During the first period of war Soviet commanders were ill-prepared to consider, prepare, or conduct *maskirovka*; and units were handicapped by the same deficiencies. German seizure and maintenance of combat initiative placed Soviet forces in a reactive posture. Experience amassed from costly defeats demonstrated the utility of *maskirovka*, and basic survival instincts compelled the Soviet Army to improve in this regard. Limited offensive planning time and frequent shortages of forces also inhibited Soviet use of *maskirovka*. Even where planning time was adequate, successful operational *maskirovka* failed when faced with more effective German planning for strategic surprise (Khar'kov, May 1942).

The education took place slowly as the Soviet High Command issued directives and regulations distilling operational and tactical experience. The extent of that education became evident at Stalingrad where effective *maskirovka* (and adequate planning time) paved the way for the first major Soviet strategic success.

The Soviets experimented with numerous new *maskirovka* techniques during the first period of war including: moving shock groups to the rear of the front (Rostov, Stalingrad) or along unexpected directions (Toropetz–Kholm, Moscow); regrouping at night; moving forces forward in one–two nights; following established routines prior to offensives; employing reconnaissance along the entire front; countering enemy air reconnaissance; attacking from the march (Moscow, 10th Army); and simulating concentration over 20–30 kilometers from the main attack sector.[4] Seldom, however, did the Soviets systematically combine enough of these measures to conceal offensive force concentrations routinely. On numerous occasions flawed headquarters planning security aborted planned *maskirovka* measures.

In 1943 standardization of *maskirovka* practices improved Soviet performance at the operational and tactical levels. In addition, German resort to deeper and more complex defenses forced the Soviets to experiment with and adopt a variety of active *maskirovka* techniques to conceal the point of main attack and to spread out German forces. Regulations specified the content of *front* and army *maskirovka* plans and designated those responsible for their conduct. Commanders formed operational groups composed of representatives from all types of arms to organize *maskirovka* measures. The Soviets began to experiment with the use of smoke to conceal preparations, formed false simulated concentration regions, and organized disinformation in consonance with higher level headquarters plans. Planning security improved as NKVD units implemented extensive anti-agent activity in 25 kilometer sectors to the rear of the front and routinely cleared the civilian population from the region.

As a result of these and other measures, the efficiency of Soviet operational and tactical *maskirovka* immeasurably improved. At Kursk they employed their first large scale offensive simulation and repeated the process at Bukrin prior to the Kiev operation. The Soviets routinely regrouped armies within *fronts* (Belgorod–Khar'kov, Bryansk, Chernigov–Pripyat, Kiev, Mishurin–Rog) and conducted numerous *front* diversionary assaults (Northern Donets and Mius Rivers). Increasingly, they moved regrouped armies forward without detection (Belgorod–Khar'kov, Bryansk, Kiev) and attacked with secretly regrouped forces from the march (Belgorod–Khar'kov, Chernigov–Pripyat).

With the initiative clearly in Soviet hands, during the third period of war all limits on ingenuity evaporated; and *maskirovka* was tailored to the precise enemy situation and to terrain and weather circumstances. Soviet commanders employed varied reconnaissance techniques and imaginative artillery preparations (including, in some cases, no preparation at all). *Front* and army plans included simultaneous offensive preparations in many sectors, larger scale simulations and numerous diversions, and the commencement of offensives on secondary directions. Soviet *front* commanders regrouped armies at will (Ukraine), and army commanders extensively shifted corps and divisions (Hungary) assisted by improved rail transport and increased motorization of the Soviet Army. Commanders consciously used bad weather and forbidden terrain to conduct offensive operations (Ukraine, Belorussia, Manchuria).

At all levels the Soviets learned some significant lessons. First, *maskirovka* had to be a well-organized venture. The army as a whole had to be well trained in its conduct, and *maskirovka* measures had to be carefully coordinated on a centralized basis by the headquarters anticipating its use in an operation. Zhukov wrote:

> In the Great Patriotic War operational *maskirovka* produced good results, because it was planned, prepared, and carried out on the basis of the centralized direction of the *STAVKA*. The principle of organizing operational *maskirovka* remained the most important and was unswervingly fulfilled in all operations on all fronts.[5]

Coordination of *maskirovka* at all levels produced vivid examples of the ideal coherency necessary for overall success. In the summer offensive of 1944 the Soviets developed a perceptive strategic *maskirovka* plan attuned to German misconceptions and combined

30. Soviet *Front* commanders near war's end. First row left to right – Marshals I.S. Konev, A.M. Vasilevsky, G.K. Zhukov, K.K. Rokossovsky and F.I. Tolbukhin. Second row from left to right Marshals K.A. Meretskov, R. Ya. Malinovsky, L.A. Govorov and Generals A.I. Yeremenko and I.Kh. Bagramyan

this with strategic and operational simulations, operational and tactical diversions, concealed strategic and operational regroupings, and efficient tactical *maskirovka* to produce a series of major strategic offensive successes. In 1945 the Soviets played on general German apprehension to effect massive strategic regroupings and still achieve a measure of surprise regarding the timing and location of offensive operations. In August 1945 the Soviets combined astute strategic *maskirovka* with concrete operational and tactical measures to achieve paralyzing surprise over the Japanese in Manchuria.

Throughout the war the *STAVKA* and General Staff supervised the education of the army in *maskirovka* measures, just as it did in other operational and tactical areas. It orchestrated the program for compiling, analysing, and disseminating information on *maskirovka*; developed the regulations, directives, and instructions; and, more important, monitored the degree to which units absorbed and capitalized on that experience. Within operating headquarters, chiefs of staff and operations sections performed the same function. *Maskirovka* became an integral part of Soviet operational planning. By 1943 the *maskirovka* plan was a distinct section of all Soviet *front* and army operational plans, a portion accorded the highest concern.

Time was of primary importance in deception planning. Sufficient time was essential to develop *maskirovka* concepts successfully. Conversely, planners had to have a good grasp of the time needed to implement specific measures that would produce the desired effect. A careful balance had to be maintained between the sophistication of *maskirovka* measures and the time necessary to implement them. Simple plans and measures often fit the circumstances better than elaborate schemes.

The Soviets paid particular attention to the size of forces and quantity of weapons used to produce the desired effect of *maskirovka*. Allocation of too many resources could detract from obtaining the very results that *maskirovka* was designed to produce. Accordingly, "decoy" forces and weapons also had to be used in timely fashion; or they would be unavailable to contribute their own weight to overall decisive combat.

Of critical importance to successful deception was the maintenance of secrecy around operational and tactical planning. Early in the war, loss or careless transmission of planning documents compromised Soviet operations in general, and *maskirovka* plans in particular. Hence the Soviets surrounded planning with Draconian security measures that severely restricted the circle of planners and the number of written planning documents.

Forces assigned *maskirovka* missions had to be well prepared to carry out their tasks. Often the Soviets solved this dilemma by not informing the units that their mission was, in fact, a feint. In other instances, actions had to be performed with the same care and vigor that was applied to usual offensive tasks. Forces engaged in *maskirovka* missions had to be provided with requisite specialized support (engineer, for example) to perform their tasks. The complexity of these missions, in part, necessitated drafting separate detailed deception plans to ensure proper attention was given to every detail of the complex mission.

Maskirovka measures had to be tailored to meet special conditions of terrain, weather, and equipment availability. The Soviets had to struggle against the ever-present tendency to apply fixed-pattern solutions to a wide variety of operational and tactical cases. What worked in the forested regions of north Russia would not necessarily work in the steppes of the Ukraine. Likewise the assignment of a unit, which lacked bridging equipment, to a mission of conducting a feint river crossing would have been folly. The Soviets circumvented this common problem by relying heavily on use of dummy and mock-up equipment deliberately revealed to enemy observation.

One of the deadliest weaknesses of deception planning was lack of knowledge about what the enemy knew concerning one's own *maskirovka* techniques. While routine methods would probably achieve success against a new and unsuspecting enemy, they could spell disaster when used against an experienced one. The Soviets learned this on numerous occasions early in the war when rigid practices yielded predictable patterns which the Germans then capitalized on. Attempts at reconnaissance *maskirovka* designed to deceive the enemy as to the location of main attacks actually tipped off where the attack would occur (Middle Don, December 1942). From 1943 on, Soviet directives urged Soviet commanders to use imaginative, innovative, and flexible techniques to preclude the establishment of predictable stereotypes. The same could be said of excessive or clumsy use of radio silence which, in fact, could be recognized as an indicator of impending offensive action.

Perhaps most important was the requirement that *maskirovka* measures capitalize on enemy perceptions, self-delusions, or misconceptions (essentially on his psychological state). This required subtlety in high-level planning and skill in low-level

TDAE—T

implementation. It also demanded imagination in the planning of deception and realism and plausibility in the execution of *maskirovka* plans. This exhortation to exploit the believable became a hallmark of Soviet deception. Even in 1941, and certainly in 1942, Soviet planners used this technique to good ends in their strategic planning. After 1943 the Soviets continued to do so at the strategic level, exploiting German and Japanese perceptions at the operational and tactical level with notable frequency.

On the basis of these war experiences, the Soviets emerged from war with a more mature appreciation for the role of deception in combat. One critic asserted:

> According to the experience of conducting operations, *maskirovka* includes a complexity of organizational, engineer-technical, and operational-tactical measures and actions, interconnected with one another, subject to the general concept of the operation and directed toward the achievement of surprise in the use of forces and equipment and the successful fulfillment by them of combat missions with minimal losses.[6]

The Soviets single out the concealment of operational concepts and force deployments as the principal purpose of *maskirovka*. They cite the following measures as essential for achieving *maskirovka* and surprise:

— *secrecy* of force deployment and operational intent;
— *demonstrative actions* to deceive regarding one's actions;
— *simulations* to confuse the enemy regarding intent and location of real forces;
— *disinformation* by technical means, false orders, or rumor.

They have concluded that these measures achieve success only if they are comprehensive and developed and implemented under the centralized control of the *STAVKA* and General Staff.

All of these lessons and conclusions underscore the theme that education in wartime is an unending process. As their voluminous writings on war experience (both official writings and post-war works) indicate, the Soviets believe the quality of performance in war directly reflects the study of war. Their detailed study progressed until the end of the war, persisted throughout the postwar years, and goes on today; probably in the same organized fashion as before. Education in *maskirovka* has been, and is, a part of this process.

CHAPTER NINE

IMPLICATIONS FOR THE FUTURE

War experience demonstrates that operational-strategic *maskirovka* has an exceptionally great importance. The achievement of surprise and consequently, to a large degree, success in an operation depends on skillful conduct of measures to realize it. In contemporary conditions this dependence has become ever more noticeable. However, the difficulties connected with the conduct of such *maskirovka* have grown. In comparison with the Great Patriotic War the saturation of forces with diverse weapons and military equipment has increased considerably. Hence, the volume of *maskirovka* work necessary during the preparation and conduct of an operations has grown. Besides that, it is necessary to realize that intelligence units have received the newest technical means of reconnaissance, that esssentially broaden their capabilities, and the conditions for the conduct of operational *maskirovka* have become considerably more complex. Nevertheless, there is no doubt that the growing capabilities do not rule out but only considerably complicate the achievement of secrecy in preparations and of surprise in operations and require greater material expenditures and continuous perfection of the means for achieving surprise.

M.M. Kir'yan
Vnezapnost' v nastupatel'nykh operatsiyakh Velikoi Otechestvennoi voiny [Surprise in Offensive Operations of the Great Patriotic War], 1986

IMPLICATIONS FOR THE FUTURE

The Soviets have consistently believed that the nature, means, and potential impact of *maskirovka* evolves in consonance with the changing conditions of changing times. This is consistent with, if not an inevitable product of, their dialectical view of history. Changes in national attitudes (political, social) and mores, although difficult to measure, are part of the dialectical process and have an effect on the atmosphere in which *maskirovka* is employed and its effectiveness.

More easily understood is the effect that changing technology has on prospects of using *maskirovka*. It is in this area that the potential effects of *maskirovka's* future use have been most pronounced. The introduction of new weapons systems, nuclear weapons, computer technology, and a wide variety of technological innovations has produced an enormous series of new problems for military planners to solve. The Soviets certainly consider the basic intent, method, technique, and perhaps the basic principles of *maskirovka* derived from a study of experience to pertain to the modern era. These basics must, however, be constantly and carefully reconsidered in the light of technological change, ensuring their continual utility in contemporary or future war. The Soviets have striven to keep abreast of those changes, as their post-war writings have indicated.

During the immediate post-war years, while Stalin retained the helm of the Soviet state, doctrine developed during the Second World War, in particular during the last two years of war, remained dominant in Soviet military art and science. As such, the subject of *maskirovka* remained an important aspect of war as defined in late wartime directives. As before, the Soviets studied *maskirovka* within the overall context of the nature and utility of surprise in war. During this period the Soviets characterized war as, "predominantly a war of maneuver, a war involving the exertion over long periods of time of great pressure, and a war which cannot be decided in a single crushing blow."[1] This view argued against a nation's ability to achieve strategic decisions in one grand battle, hence relegated strategic deception to the function of helpful adjunct to the achieving of advantage in the initial stage of a war (a means of achieving surprise) – the same role it performed in the Second World War. In describing combat, the Soviets contended that:

> The mass saturation of armies with technical equipment has made it possible to give to operations a quality of maneuver, to give them an exceptionally decisive impact and an ability to move rapidly and in great depth. It has made it possible to carry out complicated maneuvers at the same time that the scale of operations themselves has continued to grow.[2]

The prospective quickening pace of war gave added importance to surprise. This description of combat at the operational and tactical level recognized both the promise and the complexity of successful *maskirovka*, but did not accord it the decisive role on the battlefield over other factors (such as correlation of forces).

Recent historians have discounted Soviet concerns for *maski-rovka* during the Stalinist post-war years. A representative view asserted:

> Although theories on deception and surprise had been incorporated into Soviet military doctrine during Stalin's time, the extent of their usefulness was still not fully appreciated. The full integration of deception and strategic surprise into Soviet military doctrine came about only after Stalin's death in 1953. During the 1940s and early 1950s discussion of the topic of surprise and deception was not permitted by Stalin, who reserved for himself the role of chief military and political strategist in the U.S.S.R.[3]

While it is true that Stalin was publicly reluctant to accord to strategic deception a pre-eminent role in the outcome of war, at that time it was expedient for the Soviets to adopt such a stance. In the face of short-lived US nuclear monopoly, it was prudent to devalue the impact of the weapons and stress the importance of Soviet massive land power. This in itself represented a deception, for, while denigrating the impact of these weapons, the Soviets worked feverishly to add them to their arsenal. In addition, Stalin shied away from the delicate and embarrassing events of 1941, study of which would naturally cast a pall around his performance in the year of catastrophe. Instead Stalin dwelled on the resilience and strength of the Soviet nation and its tenacious strategic defense which had negated the effects of *blitzkreig*, a concept which had personified surprise in all its varied forms.

Behind the façade of public posturing, the Soviets maintained a healthy appreciation for the value of surprise and deception as evidenced by frequent references to the subject in published materials. In early 1945 one theorist labelled surprise as "one of the important conditions for achieving success in combat actions."[4] Surprise, as a temporary operating factor whose results were transitory, "paralyzes the enemy's will, depresses the morale of his troops, and stuns them to a greater or lesser degree for a varying length of time."[5] The author recognized that technological progress had increased the significance of surprise, in particular at the tactical level. Characteristically, he warned against exaggeration of the role of surprise in relationship with other factors while asserting that "all the commanders and staffs which plan and direct battle must think out thoroughly all the questions connected with surprise actions and strive to employ surprise throughout the battle, taking advantage of all possibilities for this purpose."[6]

Lieutenant General Z. Zlobin, writing late in 1945, stressed the role of armored and mechanized forces in contemporary *front* offensive operations, ascribing to them the ability to impart "impetus, swiftness, an element of surprise, and a force of thrust" into military operations.[7] Zlobin cited the wartime secret regrouping of forces between *fronts* and from *STAVKA* reserve and exhorted commanders and staffs to plan skillful operational *maskirovka*, stating, "Operational maskirovka should strive for one basic objective, namely the achievement of surprise."[8] *Maskirovka*, Zlobin asserted, should conceal the actual direction of the main thrust, its time of launching, and the forces assigned to carry out the operations. "A well-thought-out and well-prepared complex of mutually interconnected operational and technical camouflage measures are indispensible ... carried out according to a rigidly uniform plan."[9]

The following year another observer, writing on strategic offensive operations, reiterated the importance of timely regrouping of forces and the positive impact of employing strategic reserves in critical operational phases, citing as ideal cases the secret employment of strategic reserves at Moscow, Stalingrad, and in the L'vov–Sandomierz operations. In assessing the factors which contribute to strategic victory, the author cited "secrecy in the preparation of the blows" as secondary in importance only to the achievement of "absolute superiority in strength and materiel at the point of main effort."[10] A 1949 article on Soviet operational art characterized the strategy of the Soviet Supreme Command and the critical role of surprise:

> by the enormous scale of the operations, by exceptional concentration of effort, by an ability to develop new forms and means of combat, and at the same time to adjust its procedures most exactly to the particular requirements of the type of combat involved, and to take full advantage of circumstances as they developed and generally to achieve surprise in its operations.[11]

The same year Major General M. Smirnov criticized the planning of offensive operations, faulting German *blitzkreig* for its inability to convert temporary achievement of surprise into lasting victory. While denigrating the Germans' inability to capitalize on surprise, primarily because of their habitual over-estimation of their own strengths and enemy weaknesses, Smirnov outlined measures required for constructive realization of surprise's rewards. Of foremost importance was selection of the proper place to deliver the main blow. Smirnov asserted, "It is extremely important to consider the element of surprise ..." by attacking against the boundaries of enemy units or areas where the enemy could not bring up reserves, by concealing the concentration and deployment of massed shock groups, by organizing subsidiary diversionary or secondary attacks, and often by "striking the main blow on a sector where the enemy least expects it because the terrain seems to him unfavorable for the offensive."[12] Finally, Smirnov emphasized the importance of operational, tactical, and political security surrounding the planning of all phases of an operation.

A capstone work of the Stalinist years, written in 1953 by Maryganov, incorporated Stalin's assertion that "atomic bombs cannot decide the fate of war, since there are too few bombs for that to occur."[13] Having deceptively discarded the utility of nuclear surprise, Maryganov, in his description of contemporary war, paid more than passing interest to surprise, in particular at the operational and tactical level, stating:

> Operations of Soviet forces were distinctive by their decisive aims, by the full accordance of the concept with existing conditions, by the use of new forms of combat, by surprise, by the great depth of delivered blows, and by careful all-round security.[14]

These representative works, and others of the late Stalinist years, attested to continuing Soviet interest in, and concern for, surprise and the principal means of achieving it — deception. The subject was muted and discussed only in controlled works unavailable in the West, hence the Western impression of an absence of concern for the matter.

After Stalin's death in 1953, Soviet military theorists, while continuing their studies of all aspects of battle, were more free to investigate themes which could not be discussed while Stalin lived. Foremost among these was an investigation of the occurrences of June 1941, which permitted the devastating German attack on the Soviet Union. Examination of this question became a catalyst for studying a broader question relating to the nature of the initial period of war and its relationship to success or failure. Obviously the question of deception (strategic) became central to this study. Ultimately the Soviets focused attention on other initial periods of war, including France in May 1940 and Manchuria in August 1945. The threatening presence of growing nuclear arsenals lent urgency, if not an entirely new dimension, to the study of this problem.

The first series of articles investigating the initial period of war appeared after 1959, the year in which the Soviet *Military-Historical Journal* began publication. In the ensuing years Soviet theorists analysed the theme by studying the conditions surrounding the events of June 1941 noting that "questions connected with the role of surprise in the initial period of war were not worked out."[15] In these studies the topic of surprise and *maskirovka* played a large role, and obviously much of the work touched upon the relevance of those earlier experiences to the nuclear age.

Nevertheless, Soviet attitudes toward surprise and *maskirovka* before 1960 remained heavily rooted in judgements derived from the war experiences. Specifically, the Soviets considered surprise and *maskirovka* to be important factors in achieving offensive success, but not necessarily the only decisive factors. The Soviets developed a greater appreciation of the defensive aspects of *maskirovka* than before, particularly at the strategic level. They also developed a heightened respect for the impact of nuclear weaponry on modern combat.

After 1960, Khrushchev's rise to power signaled a significant change in Soviet military theory. The Soviets accepted that indeed a "revolution" had occurred in military affairs. Nuclear weapons and delivery systems took a pre-eminent position on the battlefield. Battlefield expansion encompassed virtually the entire depth of warring nations. The new Soviet view was based on the premise that "the massive use of nuclear rockets substantially alters the nature of war and methods for waging it; it imparts to war a drastically decisive and destructive character."[16] As a consequence:

> the waging of war by the above-mentioned ways and means [nuclear] may fundamentally alter the former notions of the development of armed combat according to periods or stages of war. It simultaneously attests to the extraordinary increase in the role of *the initial period of war* ... the initial period of a contemporary nuclear-rocket war will obviously be the main and decisive period, and will predetermine the development and the outcome of the entire war. Armed combat in this period will obviously be the most violent and destructive.[17]

By accepting this stark view of war, Soviet theorists were

compelled to recognize the increased and even critical importance of surprise.

> The most probable and, at the same time, most dangerous means for the unleashing of a war by the imperialist bloc against the socialist camp would be a surprise attack. Soviet military strategy takes into account the features of a real aggressor and considers that in contemporary circumstances, even a large war might arise suddenly, without the traditional threatening period characteristic of the past.[18]

These views, written by the most articulate and thorough Soviet theorist of the 1960s, Marshal V. D. Sokolovsky, summed up Soviet fixation on strategic nuclear issues during the period. Consequently, conventional operational and tactical concerns clearly became secondary to concerns for strategic nuclear war. The Soviets focused on questions of strategic surprise (and *maskirovka*) in a nuclear arena to the detriment of more traditional *maskirovka* concerns. The time factor became a pre-eminent Soviet concern along with their fixation on the issue of parrying (or achieving) a potential first strike. Thus:

> the main problem is the development of methods for reliably repelling a surprise nuclear attack as well as methods of frustrating the aggressive designs of the enemy by the timely infliction of a shattering attack on him.[19]

Behind these judgements rested a growing Soviet understanding of the consequences of strategic surprise derived from their, by now, extensive study of the circumstances of June 1941.

It is now clear that, by the late 1960s, shadowed by Khrushchev's demise, the Soviets began to question their preoccupation with strategic nuclear matters. As a result of the emerging nuclear balance world-wide and within potential theaters of war, the inevitable use of these weapons became less clear. Mutual inhibitions (political and moral) concerning their use emerged. There was growing evidence that perhaps defenses could be erected to deter their use or lessen their effects.

The net effect of this complex and subtle Soviet reassessment was a slow but perceptible shift away from sole concern for nuclear war to a growing acceptance that war was possible in either a nuclear or conventional context. Sokolovsky's 1968 edition of *Strategy* showed evidence of this shift. Victory must be attained within "the shortest possible time, in the course of a rapidly moving war." He added:

> But the war may drag on and this will demand the protracted and all-out exertion of army and people. Therefore we must also be ready for a protracted war and get the human and material resources into a state of preparedness for the eventuality.[20]

To his comments that nuclear war was likely to begin with a devastating surprise attack, he appended:

> However, the possibilities of averting a surprise attack are constantly growing. Present means of reconnaissance, detection, and surveillance can opportunely disclose a significant portion of the measures of direct preparation of a nuclear attack by the enemy .... Thus the possibilities exist not to allow a surprise attack by an aggressor.[21]

While qualifying his earlier statements about the nature of war, Sokolovsky did not definitely answer the question, "What will be the nature of modern war?" Theorists did give a partial answer. While continuing to recognize the possibility for and dangerous consequences of nuclear war, they focused again on conventional operations within and outside a nuclear context. They maintained an appreciation for surprise in a nuclear context, but also returned to the study of surprise – *maskirovka* – in a more traditional context, within the scope of theater, *front*, or army operations. While the reality of nuclear war remained, the study's substance, more often than not, was conventional *maskirovka* techniques within a theater of operations.

An important 1972 work on operational art by Colonel Savkin exemplified this renewed concern with the operational level of war. He recognized the increased complexity and importance of surprise produced by the existence of nuclear weapons, but his judgements rested clearly within the context of Second World War experiences.

> The ways and methods of achieving surprise are very diverse. In 1954–1960 they were developed in great detail in the works of Soviet authors. Depending on the concrete conditions of the situation, surprise may be achieved by leading the enemy astray with regard to one's intentions, by secrecy in preparation and swiftness of troop operations, by broad use of night time conditions, by the unexpected employment of nuclear weapons and other means of destruction, by delivering a forceful attack when and where the enemy does

not expect it, and by employing methods of conduct of combat operations and new means of warfare unknown to the enemy.[22]

This is a prescription for the requirements of *maskirovka*. Savkin artfully wove into his description all of the traditional elements of *maskirovka*. It was a restatement of appropriate passages of the 1944 regulations with the nuclear issue adroitly inserted within it. It represented a return to the more balanced appreciation of the potential nature of war evidenced in the period before 1960. According to Savkin:

> Thus, the appearance of new means of warfare has immeasurably broadened the possibilities of achieving surprise. However there is now new, albeit very sophisticated, technology which of itself is capable of having a surprise effect on the enemy. It is necessary, above all, to have a technically correct and tactically competent employment in order to deliver surprise attacks with any weapons. In other words, there is a requirement for a scientifically based military theory providing the most expedient recommendations for the effective surprise employment of ever more complex means of warfare in an operation or battle.[23]

Savkin stated that, "Other paths [exist] concerning the attainment of surprise along with searches for new weapons and their sophistication."[24] These paths are: a secret build-up in numbers of available weapons, which in due course may lead to the attainment of surprise with their mass employment on the most important axes; a search for the most skillful and original method for the unexpected use of available weapons; and the employment of methods which are new or unexpected for the enemy in the organization and conduct of an operation or battle. All of these measures required successful *maskirovka*. Savkin liberally laced his analysis with Second World War examples, and reaffirmed, "The experience in achieving surprise acquired by Soviet troops in the past war has largely retained its value and instructiveness. Therefore, one must not forget it, but study it attentively."[25] For balance Savkin added a usual qualification: "However, the critical use of experiences of past wars is far from sufficient. One must have a constant creative search for contemporary new methods of achieving surprise in an operation or battle."[26] Savkin's description of war, markedly different from that of Sokolovsky, typified the renewed Soviet concern for a balanced, traditional approach. That attitude has persisted and broadened since the early 1970s. In a practical vein the Soviet government and military exercised their *maskirovka* talents in 1956 and 1972 as they crushed incipient rebellion in Hungary and Czechoslovakia.

Parallel to the renewed Soviet concern with operational matters, military theorists have accelerated their study of the initial period of war. A plethora of articles were capped in 1974 by General S.P. Ivanov's major work detailing the circumstances of May 1940, June 1941, and August 1945. He derived from those cases relevant lessons for contemporary theorists.[27] Ivanov's work concentrated on the conventional, but noted the heightened danger posed by nuclear weapons. Above all, Ivanov answered Sokolovsky's call for study of the nature of war, providing a basis for current Soviet judgements on the initial period of war, and the role of surprise and *maskirovka* in particular. In his study Ivanov analysed the initial period of war within the context of Germany's attack on France in 1940, her attack on the Soviet Union in 1941, and the only case of the Soviet Union initiating war – the August 1945 Manchurian operation. He grudgingly praised the German methods of 1940 and 1941 when they had struck surprise massive blows, but he faulted them for failing to understand the necessity to unite front and rear while organizing a nation to conduct sustained war and for underestimating the strategic potential of the Soviet Union. He reserved particular praise for the form of the offensive with massive forces deployed forward to generate tremendous initial destructive power and momentum, a lesson not lost on the Soviets in 1945. Critiquing the Manchurian offensive, he noted,

> The campaign of Soviet forces in the Far East was a large contribution to the development of Soviet military art, most of all in the art of preparing and delivering a first shattering blow on the enemy at the beginning of war.
>
> A decisive factor in the achievement of rapid success in the campaign was surprise in the delivery of the first blow. The Soviet command succeeded in maintaining secret the concept of the offensive, the time of attack, and the place and power of the initial main attack. The means of going over to the offensive at night, without an aviation and artillery preparation strengthened the effect of the first blow's surprise and was unusual for the Second World War.[28]

Ivanov generalized from his study of the initial period of war to make the judgement (couched in terms of an aggressor state):

The beginning period of war shows the desires of aggressor governments to commit maximum force and means into the initial blow to achieve immediate strategic aims, including superiority in the air, on the seas, and command of the seas in oceanic theaters. The initial operations once again underscore the tendency of powers, undertaking upon themselves the initiative in unleashing war, to strike from the beginning, not only with maximum power, but also with surprise blows on the enemy. Experience demonstrates that to secure surprise blows, the government and military command organs of aggressor states mobilize all methods and means of influencing the enemy, including political, diplomatic, and military acts only to conceal from them the secret concept and timing of unleashed aggression.[29]

Although couched in terms of a warning and call for vigilance, the passage reflects Soviet lessons well learned throughout the war, applied to a full extent in Manchuria, and applicable in the future. Ivanov's prescription for attaining surprise by maximum application of offensive power initially in war has remained a cardinal tenet of Soviet military theorists for success in initial operations.

Subsequent Soviet military theorists have elaborated upon Ivanov's seminal work and have reached the following conclusions regarding the initial period of war:

- the tendency for the massive use of new means of armed struggle to have increasing importance in the initial period of war;
- the tendency for the results of the initial period to have increasing influence over the subsequent course of hostilities;
- the tendency for the scale of military operations to increase;
- the tendency of both sides to use surprise as the most important factor;
- the tendency for the initial period to shorten as a result of improved weaponry;
- the tendency for the role of maneuver to increase in importance.

As a result of Ivanov's and other theorists' work the Soviets now have a better understanding of the nature and dangers of the initial period of war and deception's role in it. M.M. Kir'yan has asserted:

The experience of the Second World War underscores the tendency for the initial period of war to shorten .... It also underscores the tendency for an increased scale and decisiveness of combat operations, and the desires of warring sides to achieve considerable results in the initial period of war in order to be able to exercise greater influence over the future course of war.

From the experiences of earlier wars, it is clear that up to this time no one has fully achieved victory over the enemy in the initial period. However, the presence of nuclear weapons and large groupings of armed forces located in a high state of readiness, in the case of their surprise use at the present time, as in no earlier time, permits one to achieve in the very beginning of war those results which have a decisive influence on the course and even outcome of war.[30]

Having studied the changing nature of war in its initial phases, Kir'yan pondered the role of surprise in this new context and noted that nuclear weapons could be used either at the beginning or in the course of a war. Whether or not such weapons were used:

The aggressor will try to unleash war by surprise. In this regard the development of the means for achieving strategic surprise is allotted exceptionally great attention. The experience of war has demonstrated that the aggressor, unleashing war by surprise, usually achieves considerable success.[31]

Kir'yan qualified this statement by noting elsewhere that: "The development of the technical means of reconnaissance [such as radio-electronic] makes the achievement of surprise difficult."[32] Consequently, he emphasized the importance of careful planning and execution of *maskirovka* measures if one sought to capitalize on surprise at all levels of war.

The theoretical discussions concerning the nature of war have intensified Soviet concern for deception and their understanding of the importance and complexity of *maskirovka* measures necessary to achieve the critical element of surprise in war.

Contemporary Soviet theorists accord surprise a dominant position in the litany of the principles of war, describing it as: "unexpected action which leads to the achievement of success in battle, operations and war."[33] Surprise, an exploitable and potentially decisive factor at all levels of war, "consists of the selection of time, methods, and means of combat actions which permit the delivery of a blow when the enemy is least prepared to repulse it in order to paralyze his will for organized resistance."[34] Surprise accords a force an advantage which, along with the exploitation of other factors, can produce victory. The stated prerequisites for achieving surprise today echo earlier prescriptions for success. Specifically, surprise is achieved by:

- misleading the enemy as to one's intentions [disinformation]
- maintaining the secrecy of one's own plans
- hiding combat preparations
- the use of new weapons, techniques, and forms of combat
- correct choice of the direction of the main blow and correct timing for its delivery
- unexpected air, artillery, and armor attacks and the surprise use of all types of forces
- rapid maneuver and the decisive actions that forestall enemy response and countermeasures
- conduct of fraudulent actions and deception [dummies, false installations, etc.]
- skillful use of terrain, weather, time of year, and season.[35]

Maskirovka, in its broadest definition, directly applies to five of these nine prescribed measures and tangentially affects the success of all. The tone of these means remains markedly conventional and traditional.

The Soviets cite three prerequisites for the conduct of successful *maskirovka* and the achievement of surprise. First, planning secrecy is essential and particularly challenging, since time constraints on contemporary operations rule out reliance on the time consuming process of sequential planning. Today most offensive planning must be simultaneous, making secrecy and control of information more critical. To this end, the Soviets rely more heavily on automation of planning and command and control. Second, as in the past, successful offensive action requires secret assembly and concentration of forces and masking of main attack directions. Last, in a period of increased weapon lethality (non-nuclear as well as nuclear) *maskirovka* measures are necessary to assure reasonable survivability of forces, prior to and during combat.

To achieve these prerequisites, Soviet theorists recommend employment of a variety of means whose worth had been proven in past combat. Communications discipline contributes to planning security and secrecy during the operation, and also provides a basis for communications deception prior to and during the operation. The nature of command and control of forces should also be concealed before and during war. This requires masking the initial organization of attacking forces, providing security of command and control posts, and concealing regroupment of forces during an operation. Skillful use of demonstrations, simulations, and diversionary attacks on false and secondary directions are essential to confuse enemy intelligence regarding the real attack sector. Disinformation of all types provides the atmosphere for successful development of the *maskirovka* plan at all levels. Disinformation should play on enemy preconceptions of one's force, methods of attack, and offensive intentions. In general, disinformation can operate against the enemy psychologically and condition him to being surprised, as the Egyptians demonstrated in 1973. In particular, disinformation in service of a specific plan can help conceal intent, timing, location, and scale of an offensive.

In a practical contemporary sense these judgements translate into a wide range of *maskirovka* practices the Soviets are likely to employ prior to or during any future conflict. The Soviets have always been adroit at the game of political deception, particularly the use of disinformation to exact political gains. In a potential nuclear context, this assumes greater importance, especially against an opposing coalition whose members lack a definite consensus. Pre-war deception efforts will include sophisticated political efforts to exploit dissenting views and weaken the opposing coalition. These measures will continue into the initial stages of war. Soviet pre-hostility force positioning and selection of military objectives will also seek to divide their enemies politically, as well as ultimately defeat them militarily.

The Soviets will exploit enemy stereotypes regarding their likely manner of initiating hostilities. Specifically, this means encouraging an enemy to believe that mobilization of the massive Soviet military and economic structure for war will require an extensive time period, during which any opponent can marshal adequate defensive forces. While encouraging this perception, the Soviets will streamline their war-making machinery and prepare for the sort of rapid, paralyzing war which, above all, aims at denying the enemy the will, if not the means, to resist. In this regard, they have drawn heavily on those experiences that involved surprise, surgical strikes which either accomplished or came near to accomplishing their ends (France, 1940; Russia, 1941; Vistula–Oder, 1945; Manchuria, 1945).

As they did in 1939 against Japan and against Germany and Japan in 1944 and 1945, the Soviets will both encourage and exploit enemy stereotypes regarding how they operate in war. Detailed Soviet study of their opponents, then and now, reveal the stereotype; and now, as before, the Soviets will seek to take maximum advantage of the stereotype to produce surprise and advantage over their opponent. In part, this explains the gap between bland, routine descriptions of combat practices found in general Soviet military works for foreign comsumption and actual, more bold and imaginative, wartime practices revealed in actual combat and written about in detailed Russian language works.

Thus, the Soviets continue to recommend use of new operational and tactical methods not anticipated by the enemy. This capitalizes on enemy misconceptions and stereotypical views of the Soviets and implies thorough study by the Soviets of how their opponents view them. In a specific sense, this requires careful study of techniques suited to each and every offensive situation and selection of those which are both useful and unconventional (such as Soviet exploitation of the Japanese stereotypical view of the Soviets in the Manchurian operation).

The ever-present threat of nuclear weapons' use has compelled the Soviets to address the nature of deception prior to and during the initial period of war. This means, in particular, the use of measures to lessen the importance of traditional indicators of impending war, particularly mobilization. In the Soviet view, mobilization means war, almost in the sense that it did in 1914. Therefore, they have examined measures to prepare forces for war without resort to large-scale preliminary mobilization. This includes measures for rapid, secret, selective pre-war mobilization using a variety of new technical means to reinforce forward-deployed forces; such as air, tank transporters, or more imaginative use of rail nets.[36] Observation of NATO practices indicates the potential for forward stocking of unit equipment that can be quickly manned in a pre-war period by hastily and secretly transported forces. This, combined with a Soviet propensity for retaining older equipment in theater after its replacement with newer versions, provides but one means for avoiding the massive movement of manpower and equipment forward on the eve of war. The Soviet system, often used in the past, to generate new units from existing units by use of pre-positioned cadre and weapons, can also marginally increase forward deployed forces without resort to classic mobilization and massive movements. High peacetime manning levels within major headquarters can similarly provide required headquarters personnel for newly created major headquarters to command and control the expanded wartime force. All of these measures can generate requisite Soviet force superiorities in the initial period of war, particularly in a war with only limited preparation time. In this regard, the Soviets have concluded it is necessary to increase initial wartime force levels by between 50 and 100 percent before hostilities and to mask at least 50 percent of that increase. As preparation times decrease, this requirement also proportionately decreases.

The Soviets have long understood the necessity for masking actual wartime force configuration, as well as strength. Hence, it is likely that the peacetime structure serves both administrative functions and the function of *maskirovka*. By shifting force subordination on a geographical and functional basis, a more useful and streamlined wartime organization will emerge. This organization will be somewhat larger than its peacetime predecessor and will be tailored to conduct wartime operations in concert with Soviet views on the nature of initial offensive operations. The requirements of wartime *maskirovka* dictate that the peacetime structure itself periodically change to reflect evolving Soviet force structure but not enough to raise doubt in the mind of the enemy concerning its wartime appearance. For example, most Western observers believe the 19 division- and five army-Group of Soviet Forces, Germany (GSFG) would produce a single wartime *front*. Study of past Soviet *maskirovka* practices indicate that such a force, with resubordination of units on a more rational geographical and functional basis and with minimal reinforcement, could actually form two *fronts* of at least three armies each (four armies each if some Warsaw Pact allies are added). With more extensive use of existing pre-positioned equipment and imaginative pre-hostility reinforcement, this two *front* force could rise significantly in strength. In either case the Soviets would be far better able to achieve requisite force superiorities, in particular for an attack after more limited preparation time, against a less prepared enemy coalition.

Thus, the changing nature of war has forced the Soviets to combine new *maskirovka* techniques at the strategic level with time-tested experiences that have not lost their current applicability.

Certainly modern technology has had an impact on deception on lower levels as well. To the traditional means of *maskirovka* such as masking, camouflage, radio deception, feints, demonstrations, and disinformation have been added the more technical means of optical, radio-technical, sound, hydro-acoustic, and radio deception measures – each with a well-defined function and role in the overall deception of the enemy.

All of these *maskirovka* means, and others, vary with the conditions of the area of operations and are interdependent. Above all, the means must be suited to the end. What is undisputed is the importance of these measures in contemporary combat, for "in contemporary conditions the huge destructive power of weaponry so increases the importance of surprise in armed struggle that its achievement can not only secure successful resolution of assigned missions, but in certain conditions can also decide the outcome of the operation."[37]

Throughout the Soviet military experience there has been a basic continuity in their treatment of military *maskirovka*. Certainly Soviet intent to use *maskirovka* has remained a constant. Lenin's remonstrance that, "in warfare one does not inform the foe when an attack will occur," and, "one must try to catch the enemy unaware and seize the moment when his troops are scattered," seem to epitomize Soviet concerns for *maskirovka*.[38] The Soviets have long understood the inter-relationship of political (peacetime) and wartime deception, an understanding only heightened by recent study of the initial period of war. Soviet study and conduct of *maskirovka* has been characterized by a practical concern, and much of their experience has focused on determining what can realistically be achieved in war by *maskirovka*, rather than what might be achieved in the ideal. That study goes on today with increased intensity, driven by the firm belief that "the role and importance of operational *maskirovka* measures in contemporary conditions have grown considerably." Consequently "the problem has an exceptionally great practical significance, and its future theoretical elaboration is one of the actual missions of Soviet military science."[39]

Throughout their experience, the Soviets have adhered to the dialectical approach. True to this methodology, they strive to understand both the factor of what has occurred (experience) juxtaposed against the imperative of what is occurring (changing technology) to arrive at a better understanding of what will occur in future war. (The dialectical process of understanding both thesis and antithesis to better comprehend the resulting synthesis.) Such a process demands a thorough understanding of past practices and implies that the best be retained today. A nation hoping to compete successfully with the Soviets in the military realm must understand the Soviet approach, what they study, and their conclusions from that study. In a dangerous world, this applies particularly to the realm of *maskirovka* or deception in war, lest we fall victim to history we have failed, or been unwilling, to comprehend.

NOTES

CHAPTER 1

1. I have used *maskirovka* and deception synonymously throughout this paper. Lesser included aspects of *maskirovka* are described by their own terms such as camouflage, disinformation, etc.
2. V.A. Yefrimov, S.G. Chermashentsev, "Maskirovka" [Deception], *Sovetskaya voennaya entsiklopediya* [Soviet military encyclopedia], 5, (Moskva: Voenizdat, 1978), 175. Hereafter cited as *SVE* with appropriate volume, date, and page.
3. Ibid.
4. M.M. Kir'yan, ed., *Vnezapnost' v nastupatel'nykh operatsiyakh Velikoi Otechestvennoi voiny* [Surprise in Offensive Operations of the Great Patriotic War] (Moskva: "Nauka," 1986), 9. Hereafter cited as Kir'yan, *Vnezapnost'*.
5. Yefrimov, Chermashentsev, "Maskirovka," 175.
6. Ibid.
7. S.P. Ivanov, *Nachal'nyi period voiny* [The initial period of war], (Moskva: Voenizdat, 1974), 350.
8. Marx derived his concept of the dialectic from the German philosopher Hegel, who argued that all historical development emanated from the operation of the dialectic which in essence described a process of inevitable change. According to Hegel, at any time in history all aspects of man's development were governed by a dominant ideal or spirit [*Zeitgeist*]. In each distinct period of history all social, economic, and political institutions as well as man's intellectual state was a product of and reflected that dominant spirit. Over time, Hegel maintained, counter-forces emerged to challenge the dominant "idea," in essence an antithesis that began to struggle with the original thesis. This struggle of thesis and antithesis ultimately would produce a new dominant "spirit" which would be a synthesis of the two originally conflicting "spirits." This new dominant idea or synthesis would then become a new thesis with its whole new set of resultant institutions and a new antithesis would arise to challenge it and renew the process of change. Hegel implied that as this dialectic operated, each new synthesis would contain the best aspects of the old struggling thesis and antithesis. Hence, ultimately, perfection would result as an end to this metaphysical concept of the nature of change.

    Marx accepted the validity of the dialectical process but challenged Hegel's belief in the "idea" or "spirit" as being the dominant element of it. Instead Marx turned Hegel's dialectic on its head. He argued that economic realities dominated man's development and all other aspects of that development (social, political, intellectual) were mere reflections of these economic realities. According to Marx, the key economic reality was the means of production and those who controlled them. Since primeval times those means of production had been ripped from mankind's grasp and been passed from dominant class to dominant class in a dialectical manner. Ultimately, Marx argued, the alienation of man from the fruits of his labor would be complete. At that point that very alienation would produce a new awareness among the exploited mass who would then rise in revolution; overthrow the capitalistic class; and restore to man (labor) the means of production (hence the fruits of his labor), thus creating the end result of genuine socialism.

    Marx specifically identified the stages of history which were in reality stages in the development of the dialectic, each with a dominant economic system (slave holding, feudal, capitalistic), and described the inevitable end of the process, the last stage, that of socialism. Marx implied that by the end of the nineteenth century the world would be ripe for revolution and the creation of socialism. When early twentieth century developments contradicted Marx's predictions, Lenin updated Marx by discovering a new stage of economic development, that of imperialism or "the highest stage of capitalism," which man would suffer through before revolution would occur. For contemporary Marxists and Marxist-Leninists the dialectic process remains valid although there are variations in tactics, methods of change, and the nature of the end (socialism).

CHAPTER 2

1. For example, see M.V. Frunze, "Osnovnye voennye zadachi momenta" [The fundamental military missions of the time], *Izbrannye proizvedeniya* [Selected works], (Moskva: Voenizdat, 1984), 93.
2. P. Mel'nikov, "Operativnaya maskirovka" [Operational *maskirovka*], *Voenno-istoricheskii zhurnal* [Military history journal], No. 4 (April 1982), 18. Hereafter cited as *VIZh* with appropriate volume, date, and page.
3. Kir'yan, *Vnezapnost'*, 6.
4. *Polevoi ustav RKKA, 1929* [Field regulations of the Red Army, 1929], (Moskva: Voenizdat, 1929), translation by JPRS, March 1985, 4–5.
5. Ibid., 41.
6. Kir'yan, *Vnezapnost'*, 6.
7. *Vremennyi polevoi ustav RKKA, 1936* [Temporary field regulations of the Red Army, 1936], (Moskva: Voenizdat, 1937), translation by Translation Section, the Army War College, Washington, DC, September-October 1937, 52.
8. Ibid., emphasis added by author.
9. A. Vol'pe, "Vnezapnost'" [Surprise], *Voennaya Mysl'* [Military thought] No. 3 (March 1937), 3. Hereafter cited as *VM* with appropriate volume, date, and page.
10. Ibid., 4.
11. Ibid., 10.
12. Ibid., 28.
13. Ibid., 31.
14. Ibid., 31–32.
15. Ibid., 34.
16. Gr. Pochter, "Operativnaya maskirovka i vnezapnost'" [Operational maskirovka and surprise], *VM*, No. 7 (July 1937), 47.
17. Ibid., 64.
18. Ibid., 65.
19. Ibid., 74.
20. Ibid., 76.
21. M.R. Galaktionov, *Tempy operatsii* [Tempos of operations], (Moskva: Voenizdat, 1937), reprinted in *Voprosy strategii i operativnogo iskusstva v sovetskikh voennykh trudakh (1917-1940 gg)* [Questions of strategy and operational art in Soviet military works (1917-1940)], (Moskva: Voenizdat, 1965), 541. Hereafter cited as *Voprosy strategii*.
22. For specifics, see I.F. Kuz'min, *Na strazhe mirnogo tryda (1921–1940 gg)* [On guard for peaceful work], (Moskva: Voenizdat, 1959), 212. The consequences of Soviet deception are vividly related in Edward J. Drea, *Nomonhan: Japanese–Soviet Tactical Combat, 1939*, Leavenworth Papers No. 2 (Fort Leavenworth, KS: Combat Studies Institute, U.S. Army Command and General Staff College, January 1981).
23. A.I. Belov, ed., *Voennye svyazisti v boyakh za rodinu* [Military signalmen in battles for the homeland], (Moskva: Voenizdat, 1984), 80. Disinformation

included radio and wire communication of false orders and false messages concerning engineer work, defensive configurations, and troop movements.

24. G.K. Zhukov, *Vospominaniya i razmysheniya* [Memoirs and reflections], T.1 [Vol 1], (Moskva: Izdatel'stvo Agentstva pechati Novosti, 1974), 172–173. Hereafter cited as Zhukov, *Vospominaniya.*
25. Ibid., 172.
26. Kir'yan, *Vnezapnost'*, 7.
27. Ibid.
28. S.K. Timoshenko, *Zakyuchitel'naya rech' narodnogo komissara oborony soyuza SSR geroi i marshal sovetskogo soyuza S. K. Timoshenko na voennom soveshchanii, 31 dekabrya 1940g* [Concluding speech of the Peoples' Commissar of Defense of the Soviet Union, Hero and Marshal of the Soviet Union S.K. Timoshenko at a military conference, 31 December 1940], (Moskva: Voenizdat, 1941), 27, 30, 46.
29. A. Kononenko, "Boi vo flandrii (Mai 1940 gg)" [The Battle in Flanders (May 1940)], *VIZh*, No.3 (March 1941), 10, 20.
30. Ibid., 20,22.
31. A.I. Starunin, "Operativnaya vnezapnost'" [Operational surprise, *VM*, No. 3 (March 1941), 27.
32. Ibid., 28.
33. Ibid.
34. Ibid., 29.
35. Ibid., 32.
36. Ibid., 35.
37. S.N. Krasil'nikov, *Nastupatel'naya armeiskaya operatsiya* [The army offensive operation], (Moskva: Voenizdat, 1940), reprinted in *Voprosy strategii*, 490.
38. Ibid., 493.
39. Ibid., 493–494.
40. Ibid., 495.
41. A. Radzievsky, "Dostizhenie vnezapnost' v nastupatel'nykh operatsiyakh" [The achievement of surprise in offensive operations], *VIZh*, No. 4 (April 1974), 12. Hereafter cited as Radzievsky, "Dostizhenie vnezapnost'."

CHAPTER 3

1. Mandated in *Directive of the General Staff Concerning the Study and Application of War Experience, 9 November 1942*, No. 1005216, translated by U.S. Army General Staff, G-2.
2. The Soviets employed two methods of planning – sequential and parallel. In the former each headquarters completed its planning before the lower headquarters received its orders and began its planning. While this system provided for better planning security, often lower headquarters (corps and below) were allotted insufficient time in which to plan the operation. Parallel planning involved simultaneous work at all levels. Since it required early issuance of basic orders to units at all levels, a much wider planning circle knew the operational objectives, time, and force concentrations. Hence security was more difficult to maintain. Throughout the war the Soviets relied heavily on sequential planning.
3. V. Matsulenko, "Operativnaya maskirovka sovetskikh voisk v pervom i vtorom periodakh voiny" [Operational *maskirovka* of Soviet forces in the first and second periods of war], *VIZh*, No.1 (January 1972), 12. Hereafter cited as Matsulenko, "Operativnaya maskirovka ... v pervom i vtorom periodakh".
4. Kir'yan, *Vnezapnost'*, 53.
5. Matsulenko, "Operativnaya maskirovka ... v pervom i vtorom periodakh," 12.
6. Kir'yan, *Vnezopnost'*, 56.

7. Such as the surprise Soviet use of the medium T-34 and heavy KV-1 tanks in the initial stage of war. German intelligence had no knowledge of these tanks' existence; and, even when discovered, the Germans were slow to spread the word of the tanks' existence and take countermeasures. Introduction by the Soviets in late 1941 of the new multiple rocket launchers (the *Katyushas*) also came as a surprise for the Germans.

8. Kir'yan, *Vnezapnost'*, 18.

9. Zhukov, *Vospominaniya*, 418.

10. The widespread Soviet deception detailed in V. Morozov, "Pochemu ne zavershilos' nastuplenie v Donbasse vesnoi 1943 goda" [Why the offensive in the Donbas was not completed in the spring of 1943] *VIZh*, No. 3 (March 1963). See also D. M. Glantz, *From the Don to the Dnepr: A Study of Soviet Offensive Operations, December 1942–August 1943* (Carlisle, PA: US Army War College, 1984), unpublished manuscript, 122–124.

11. Kir'yan, *Vnezapnost'*, 21–22.

12. Ibid., 23–24.

13. Ibid., 22.

14. Matsulenko, "Operativnaya maskirovka ... v pervom i vtorom periodakh ...," 18–19. German Fourth Panzer Army intelligence maps do not reflect the false unit locations of *major* Soviet units. German force deployments, however, indicated a degree of Soviet success in deceiving the Germans with regard to the location of the Soviet offensive.

15. A thorough description of Soviet deception measures associated with the secret deployment of 3d Guards Tank Army is found in V.A. Matsulenko, *Operativnaya maskirovka voisk* [Operational *maskirovka* of forces]. (Moskva: Voenizdat, 1975), translation by U.S. Army Foreign Science and Technology Center, Charlottesville, VA, 1977, 98–103. Hereafter cited as Matsulenko, *Operativnaya*.

16. P.P. Tovstukha, R.M. Portugal'skii, *Upravlenie voiskami v nastuplenii* [Command and control of forces on the offensive], (Moskva: Voenizdat, 1981), 80–81 outlines the form and content of formal *maskirovka* planning and the agencies designated to accomplish it.

17. *Nastavlenie po proryv pozitsionnoi oborony* [Regulations for penetration of a positional defense], (Moskva: Voenizdat, 1944), 147.

18. *Polevoi ustav krasnoi armii, 1944* [Field regulations of the Red Army, 1944], (Moskva: Voenizdat, 1944), translation by the Office of the Assistant Chief of Staff G-2, GSUSA and published by JPRS, 1985, 10.

19. Ibid., 44.

20. Ibid.

21. Ibid.

22. Kir'yan, *Vnezapnost'*, 61.

23. At the least, Soviet strategic *maskirovka* succeeded in Hitler's view. Although German military figures correctly assessed the likelihood of a Soviet drive through East Prussia and Poland, they underestimated the strength of that effort and, to some degree, were mistaken as to its focus.

CHAPTER 4

1. Details of the Rostov offensive operation are found in *Istoriya Velikoi Otechestvennoi Voiny Sovetskogo Soyuza 1941–1945*, T-2 [History of the Great Patriotic War of the Soviet Union, 1941–1945, Vol 2], (Moskva: Voenizdat, 1967), 220–224; I.Kh. Bagram'yan, *Tak nachinalas' voina* [How war begins], (Kiev: Izdatel'stvo politicheskoi literatury Ukrainy, 1984), 391–435, hereafter cited as *Tak nachinalas'*; K. Kirichenko, "V boyakh pod Rostovom-na-Donu (oktyabr-dekabr' 1941g)" [In battles at Rostov on the Don (October-December 1941)]

VIZh, No. 12 (December 1983), 12–17.
2. Bagram'yan explains the conflict between Timoshenko and Cherevichenko, which ultimately led to the latter's replacement by General Malinovsky.
3. Antonov was later 1st Assistant Chief of the General Staff (1942), Chief of the General Staff's operations directorate, and then Chief of the General Staff (1945).
4. Bagram'yan, *Tak nachinalas'*, 426.
5. Ibid., 421.
6. Franz Halder, *The Halder Diaries: The Private War Journals of Colonel General Franz Halder*, (Boulder, Colo: Westview Press, 1977), 1303.
7. Ibid., 1306.
8. Ibid., 1307.
9. Ibid., 1321.
10. Franz Halder, *War Journal of Franz Halder*, VII, typescript translated copy, (Carlisle, PA: US Army War College, undated), 168–169.
11. Ibid., 198.
12. Soviet preparations for the Moscow counter-offensive described in D.Z. Muriyev, *Proval operatsii "Taifun"* [The failure of Operation Typhoon], (Moskva: Voenizdat, 1966), 142–159; A.M. Samsovov, *Porazhenie vermakhta pod Moskvoi* [Defeat of the Wehrmacht at Moscow], (Moskva: Moskovskii Rabochi, 1981), 247–258; *Bitva za Moskvu* [The battle for Moscow], (Moskva: Moskovskii Rabochi, 1968), 1–97.
13. *Maskirovka* measures associated with the forward deployment of 10th Army are detailed in F. Golikov, "Rezervnaya armiya gotovitsa k zashchite stolitsy" [A reserve army prepares to defend the capital] *VIZh*, No. 5 (May 1966).
14. Matsulenko, *Operativnaya*, 11–12.
15. G.I. Berdnikov, *Pervaya Udarnaya: Boevoi pyt' l-i udarnoi armii v Velikoi Otechestvennoi voine* [1st Shock: The combat path of 1st Shock Army in the Great Patriotic War], (Moskva: Voenizdat, 1985), 23–29.
16. F.I. Golikov, *V Moskovskoi Bitve* [In the battle of Moscow], (Moskva: Izdatel'stvo "Nauka," 1967), 46–51.
17. Ibid., 51.
18. Halder, 184.
19. Ibid., 188.
20. D. Muriyev, "Nekotorye voprosy sovetskoi voennoi strategii v Moskovskoi bitve" [Some questions concerning Soviet military strategy in the battle of Moscow], *VIZh*, No. 11 (November 1971), 17.
21. A. Seaton, *The Battle for Moscow*, (New York: Playboy Press Paperbacks, 1971), 198.
22. Berdnikov, 24.
23. Halder, 208.
24. V.D. Sokolovsky, ed., *Pazgrom nemetsko-fascistskikh voisk pod Moskvoi* [The destruction of German-Fascist forces at Moscow], (Moskva: Voenizdat, 1964), 317–330.
25. I.A. Yeremenko, *V nachale voiny* [In the beginning of war], (Moskva: "Nauka," 1965), 402–403. Hereafter cited as Yeremenko, *V nachale voiny*.
26. Ibid.
27. Ibid., 404.
28. Ibid., 409–410.
29. Kir'yan, *Vnezapnost'*, 15.
30. Ibid., 37; Yeremenko, *V nachale voiny*, 413–414.
31. G. Semenov, "Iz opyta organizatsii i vedeniya nastupatel'noi operatsii 3-i udarnoi armiei zimoi 1942 goda" [From the experience of organizing and conducting the offensive operation of 3d Shock Army in the winter of 1942] *VIZh*, No. 1 (January 1977), 86.
32. Halder, 1384.
33. Ibid., 1382–1385.

34. Ibid., 1392.
35. Matsulenko, *Operativnaya*, 11–12.
36. Ibid., 12; Kir'yan, *Vnezapnost'*, 53–54.
37. Kir'yan, *Vnezapnost'*, 56.
38. Ibid.
39. M. Khozin, "Ob odnoi maloissledovannoi operatsii" [Concerning one little investigated operation] *VIZh*, No. 2 (February 1966), 35.
40. *Na volkhovskom fronte 1941–1944 gg* [On the Volkhov Front 1941–1944], (Moskva: Izdatel'stvo "Nauka," 1982), 24–25.
41. K.A. Meretskov, *Serving the People*, (Moscow: Progress Publishers, 1971), 184; S.P. Platonov, ed., *Bitva za Leningrad* [The battle for Leningrad], (Moskva: Voenizdat, 1964), 137.
42. *Na volkhovskom fronte*, 29.
43. Platonov, 140.
44. Meretskov, 186.
45. Halder, 1382.
46. Bagramyan, *Tak shli my k pobede* [How we marched to victory], (Moskva: Voenizdat, 1977), 4. Hereafter cited as Bagramyan, *Tak shli*.
47. Ibid., 8.
48. K.S. Moskalenko, *Na yugo-zapadnom napravlenii 1941–1943* [On the Southwestern Direction 1941–1943], (Moskva: "Nauka," 1973), 134–136.
49. Bagramyan, *Tak shli*, 8.
50. V.S. Golubovich, *Marshal R. Ya. Malinovsky*, (Moskva: Voenizdat, 1984), 64–65; A. Radzievsky, "Dostozhenie vnezapnosti v nastupatel'nykh operatsiyakh" [The achievement of surprise in offensive operations] *VIZh*, No. 4 (April 1974), 13, cites Soviet use of radio imitation to simulate the assembly of five rifle divisions on the left flank of the Southern Front. Radzievsky claimed the ruse failed because physical measures did not reinforce the radio deception.
51. Bagramyan, *Tak shli*, 10.
52. Golubovich, 69.
53. A.F. von Bechtolzheim, "German Army Operations," *Address Before the Army War College*, (Carlisle Barracks: PA, 26 January 1954), 3.
54. Halder, 1388.
55. Ibid., 1390.
56. E.F. Ziemke, "Operation Kreml: Deception, Strategy, and the Fortunes of War" *Parameters*, Vol 9, No.1 (March 1979), surveys opposing strategies in 1942 and focuses on German deception plans implemented in late spring to cover the conduct of plan "Blau."
57. G.K. Zhukov, *The Memoirs of Marshal Zhukov*, (New York: Delacorte Press, 1971), 364–365.
58. Ibid., 365.
59. A.M. Vasilevsky, *Delo vsei zhizni* [Life's work], (Moskva: Politizdat, 1983), 185.
60. Bagramyan, *Tak shli*, 65.
61. Ibid., 67.
62. Ibid., 69–71.
63. Ibid., 75–76.
64. Moskalenko, 186.
65. Ibid., 186–189.
66. Bagramyan, *Tak shli*, 82.
67. Halder, 1433.
68. Ibid., 1435–1437.
69. Ibid., 1439.
70. W. Goerlitz, *Paulus and Stalingrad*, (New York: The Citadel Press, 1963), 176.
71. Ibid., 178.
72. Halder, 1442–1443.
73. Von Bechtolzheim, 9.

74. Kir'yan, *Vnezapnost'*, 38.
75. L.M. Sandalov, *Pogorelo–gorodishchenskaya operatsiya* [Pogorelo–Gorodishche operation], (Moskva: Voenizdat, 1960), 13. Hereafter cited as Sandalov, *Pogorelo*.
76. Ibid., 14. See also L.M. Sandalov, *Na moskovskom napravlenii* [On the Moscow direction], (Moskva: "Nauka," 1970), 276–305. Hereafter cited as Sandalov, *Na moskovskom napravlenii*.
77. Matsulenko, *Operativnaya*, 15–16.
78. Ibid., 16.
79. Radzievsky, "Dostizhenie vnezapnosti," 13.
80. Sandalov, *Pogorelo*, 16–18.
81. Ibid., 17.
82. Halder, 1487.
83. Ibid., 1489.
84. Ibid., 1496.
85. Ibid., 1497–1501.
86. K. Tippelskirch, *Istor'iya vtoroi mirovoi voiny* [History of the Second World War], (Moskva: Voenizdat, 1956), 241, as quoted in Radzievsky, "Dostizhenie vnezapnosti," 14.
87. Kir'yan, *Vnezapnost'*, 39.
88. Meretskov, 229.
89. Platonov, 163.
90. Meretskov, 230; Platonov, 163.
91. Platonov, 164.
92. Ibid., 232–234.
93. Platonov, 177–182.
94. Halder, 1516.
95. Ibid., 1517.
96. *Sbornik Materialov po izucheniyu opyta voiny No. 2 Sentyabr-Oktyabr 1942* [Collection of Materials for the Study of War Experience No. 2 Sept-Oct 1942), (Moskva: Voenizdat, 1942). This is one of more than 60 volumes produced during the war on virtually every aspect of operations. This volume pertained to operations in the winter of 1941 and 1942.
97. Ibid., 45.
98. Ibid., 46.
99. Ibid., 65.
100. Ibid., 138.
101. Ibid., 266.
102. Matsulenko, *Operativnaya*, 17–18.
103. Ibid, 18; P. Mel'nikov, 19–20.
104. Kir'yan, *Vnezapnost'*, 16.
105. Ibid., 21.

CHAPTER 5

1. Matsulenko, "Operativnaya maskirovka ... v pervom i vtorom periodakh," 14–15.
2. Soviet planning for the Stalingrad counter-offensive described in A.M. Samsonov, *Stalingradskaya bitva* [The Battle of Stalingrad], (Moskva: Izdetel'stvo Akademii Nauk SSSR, 1960), 438–463; *Stalingradskaya Epopeya* [The Stalingrad Epic], (Moskva: Izdatel'stvo "Nauka," 1968); K.K. Rokossovsky, ed., *Velikaya pobeda na Volga* [Great victory on the Volga], (Moskva: Voenizdat, 1965), 207–259. Hereafter cited as *Velikaya pobeda*.
3. Vasilevsky, 220.

4. Kir'yan, *Vnezapnost'*, 18.
5. *Dvesti ognennykh dnei* [Two hundred days of fire], (Moskva: Voenizdat, 1968), 60, 62.
6. V. Matsulenko, "Operativnaya maskirovka voisk v kontranastuplenii pod Stalingradom" [Operational *maskirovka* of forces at Stalingrad], *VIZh*, No. 1 (January 1974), 12. Hereafter cited as Matsulenko, "Operativnaya maskirovka ... pod Stalingradom." See also N. Orlov, G. Tvardovskii, "Sposoby obespechen-iya skrytnosti podgotovki operatsii i vnezapnosti deistvii voisk v gody voiny" [The means of providing for secrecy in the preparation of operations and surprise in the operations of forces in the war years], *VIZh*, No. 9 (September 1981), 20.
7. Matsulenko, *Operativnaya*, 33–35.
8. E. Ziemke, *Stalingrad to Berlin*, (Washington, D.C.: Center for Military History, 1968). 46. Hereafter cited as Ziemke, *Stalingrad*.
9. Vasilevsky, 223.
10. Zhukov, *Memoirs*, 397.
11. Tippelskirch, 241 as quoted in Sandalov, *Na moskovskom napravlenii*, 307.
12. Ziemke, *Stalingrad*, 48.
13. David Kahn, "An Intelligence Case History: The Defenses of Osuga, 1942," *Aerospace Historian*, December 1981, 245. This excellent article thoroughly covers German estimates in Ninth Army sector in the late summer and fall of 1942. Kahn demonstrates that the Germans were deceived but does not credit the Russians with a deliberate deception plan.
14. Ibid., 248.
15. Moskalenko, 354.
16. Matsulenko, *Operativnaya*, 34.
17. Matsulenko, "Operativnaya maskirovka ... pod Stalingradom," 13–14. See also A.D. Tsirlin et al, *Inzhenernye voisk v boyakh za Sovetskuyu rodinu* [Engineer forces in the battles for the Soviet homeland], (Moskva: Voenizdat, 1970), 138–147. Hereafter cited as Tsirlin, *Inzhenernye*.
18. Matsulenko, *Operativnaya*, 32, 40.
19. K.K. Rokossovsky, *Soldatskii dolg* [A soldier's duty], (Moskva: Voenizdat, 1968), 152. Hereafter cited as Rokossovsky, *Soldatskii*.
20. *Dvesti ognennykh dnei*, 139.
21. Ziemke, *Stalingrad*, 48.
22. Alan Clarke, *Barbarossa: The Russian–German Conflict 1941–45*, (New York: Signet Books, 1965), 272.
23. W. Goerlitz, *Paulus and Stalingrad*, (New York: The Citadel Press, 1963), 196–197.
24. Ziemke, *Stalingrad*, 48.
25. Ibid., 49.
26. H. Schroeter, *Stalingrad*, (New York: Ballentine, 1958), 52–53.
27. Ziemke, *Stalingrad*, 49.
28. Matsulenko, *Operativnaya*, 33.
29. Goerlitz, 229.
30. Quoted in Tsirlin, *Inzhenernye*, 141.
31. Zhukov, *Vospominaniya* [Vol 2], 291.
32. Soviet planning details in Vasilevsky, 227–232.
33. K.K. Rokossovsky, *Velikaya pobeda* , 340.
34. *Sbornik materialov po izucheniyu opyta voiny No. 8 Avgust-Oktyabr' 1943g* [Collection of materials for the study of war experience, No. 8 August-October 1943], (Moskva: Voenizdat, 1943), 23, translated by Directorate of Military Intelligence, Army Headquarters, Ottawa, Canada. Hereafter cited as *Sbornik materialov* with appropriate volume and page.
35. Rokossovsky, *Velikaya pobeda*, 336–341.
36. *Sbornik materialov*, No. 8, 24.
37. Moskalenko, 376; Vasilevsky, 269–272.

38. Ibid.
39. Erich von Manstein, *Lost Victories*, (Chicago: Henry Regnery Company, 1958), 331.
40. Ibid., 329–347; G. Doerr, *Podkhod na Stalingrad* [Approach to Stalingrad], (Moskva: Voenizdat, 1957), 88–98, translated from German.
41. Rokossovsky, *Velikaya pobeda*, 370.
42. Ibid., 380–381.
43. Ibid.; V.M. Domnikov ed., *V Nastuplenii gvardiya: ocherk o boevom puti 2-i gvardeiskoi armii* [Guards on the offensive: A sketch about the combat path of 2d Guards Army], (Moskva: Voenizdat, 1971), 27–34.
44. Domnikov, 30–33; Matsulenko, *Operativnaya*, 37.
45. Matsulenko, *Operativnaya*, 37.
46. Manstein, 346.
47. This analysis found in *Sbornik materialov* No. 6.
48. Ibid., 80.
49. Ibid.
50. Ibid.
51. Ibid., 81.
52. Ibid., 83–84.
53. V.P. Morozov, *Zapadnee voronezha* [West of Voronezh], (Moskva: Voenizdat, 1956), 24–27. Hereafter cited as Morozov, *Zapadnee*.
54. Ibid., 37.
55. A.M. Zvartsev, *3-ya gvardeiskaya tankovaya* [3d Guards Tank], (Moskva: Voenizdat, 1982), 30–32.
56. Morozov, *Zapadnee*, 51.
57. Matsulenko, *Operativnaya*, 48–49.
58. Ibid., 47–48.
59. Moskalenko, 377.
60. Ibid., 378.
61. Ibid., 379.
62. Morozov, *Zapadnee*, 34–35.
63. Moskalenko, 379.
64. Matsulenko, *Operativnaya*, 49.
65. Vasilevsky, 275–276.
66. Sandalov, *Na moskovskom napravlenii*, 320–322; Morozov, *Zapadnee*, 90–96.
67. Ziemke, *Stalingrad*, 84. German forces withdrew from the Voronezh bridgehead on 25 January. The following day they were just beginning a further withdrawal westward when 40th Army's offensive began.
68. P.M. Simchenkov, "Dostizhenie skrytnosti" [The achievement of secrecy], *VIZh*, No. 6 (June 1986), 17–18.
69. I.Ya. Vyrodov, ed., *V srazheniyakh za Pobedu: boevoi put' 38-i armii v gody Velikoi Otechestvennoi voiny 1941–1945* [In battles for victory: the combat path of the 38th Army in the Great Patriotic War 1941–1945], (Moskva: "Nauka," 1974), 167–168.
70. Moskalenko, 404–405.
71. Details of Soviet intelligence failure in the Donbas contained in V. Morozov, "Pochemu ne zavershilos' nastuplenie v Donbasse vesnoi 1943 goda" [Why the offensive in the Donbas was not completed in the spring of 1943], *VIZh*, No. 3 (March 1963), 16–32.
72. For details on German planning see Ziemke, *Stalingrad*, 124–125.
73. G. Zhukov, "Na Kurskoi duge" [In the Kursk bulge], *VIZh*, No. 8 (August 1967), 73. Hereafter cited as Zhukov, "Na Kurskoi duge".
74. S.M. Shtemenko, *The Soviet General Staff at War 1941–1945*, (Moscow: Progress Publishers, 1970), 154.
75. Zhukov, "Na Kurskoi duge," 76.
76. Ibid., 81.

77. K. Rokossovsky, *Soldier's Duty*, (Moscow: Progress Publishers, 1985), 184, 188, 185 echoes the Russian version of *Soldatskii dolg* and states:

> From the character of the enemy's activities, supplemented by intelligence data, we surmised that [the offensive] ... would be undertaken on the Kursk Bulge ...

Further:

> The Soviet Command had managed correctly to surmise the enemy's plan, the likely directions of his main effort, and even the deadlines of the offensive ...

Finally:

> On July 2, GHQ alerted us to the possibility of the enemy's launching an offensive at any moment. This was the third such warning, the two previous ones having been issued on the 2d and 3d of May.

Hereafter cited as *Soldier's Duty*. Other sources echoed Rokossovsky's view. No good answer exists regarding where the Soviets obtained their intelligence. It could have come from Ultra materials passed by the British or from internal Soviet intelligence sources or, more likely, a combination of the two.

78. Matsulenko, *Operativnaya*, 50–51.
79. Ibid., 51.
80. Ibid.
81. Ibid., 55–56.
82. Ibid., 56. See also I.M. Chistyakov, *Sluzhim otchizne* [Serving the fatherland], (Moskva: Voenizdat, 1975), 140–144. Hereafter cited as Chistyakov, *Sluzhim*.
83. I.S. Konev, *Zapiski komanduyushchego frontom 1943–1945* [Notes of a *front* commander], (Moskva: "Nauka," 1972), 10–11. Hereafter cited as Konev, *Zapiski*.
84. Matsulenko, *Operativnaya*, 56.
85. Konev, *Zapiski*, 11.
86. Quoted in B.G. Solov'ev, *Vermakht na puti k gibeli* [The Wehrmacht on the path to destruction], (Moskva: "Nauka," 1973), 249.
87. F.W. von Mellenthin, *Panzer Battles*, (Norman, OK: University of Oklahoma Press, 1956), 228–231.
88. Zhukov, "Na Kurskoi duge" [In the Kursk Bulge], *VIZh*, No. 9 (September 19678), 85. Continuation of earlier article.
89. Ibid.
90. D.M. Glantz, "Soviet Defensive Tactics at Kursk, July 1943," *CSI Report No. ll*, (Ft. Leavenworth, KS: Combat Studies Institute, 1986).
91. Matsulenko, *Operativnaya*, 57–58.
92. L. Sandalov, "Bryanskii front v Orlovskoi operatsii" [The Bryansk Front in the Orel Operation], *VIZh*, No. 8 (August 1963), 66.
93. I.Kh. Bagramyan, "Flangovyi udar 11-i gvardeiskoi armii" [The flank blow of llth Guards Army], *VIZh*, No 7 (July 1963), 89; I.Kh. Bagramyan, "Proryv sil'no ukreplennoi oborony protivnika i razvitie uspekha v khode kontranastupleniya pod Kurskom" [Penetration of a strongly fortified defenses and development of success in the counter-offensive at Kursk], *Bitva na Kurskoi duge* [Battle of the Kursk bulge], (Moskva: "Nauka," 1975), 54.
94. V.I. Chuikov, *Ot Stalingrada do Berlina* [From Stalingrad to Berlin], (Moskva: Voenizdat, 1980), 347. Hereafter cited as Chuikov, *Ot Stalingrada*.
95. A.G. Yershov, *Osvobozhdenie donbassa* [Liberation of the Donbas], (Moskva: Voenizdat, 1973), 98.
96. V.I. Chuikov, *V boyakh za Ukrainu* [In battles for the Ukraine], (Kiev: Izdatel'-stvo politicheskoi literatury Ukrainy, 1972), 50. Hereafter cited as Chuikov, *V boyakh*.
97. Ibid., 53.
98. Ibid.
99. Chuikov, *Ot Stalingrada*, 350.

100. Ibid., 351–353.
101. Chuikov, *V boyakh*, 53.
102. Ibid.
103. Ziemke, *Stalingrad*, 137.
104. Yershov, 110–112.
105. Domnikov, 108.
106. "6th Army, Russia," *MS #C-078*, Historical Division European Command, Foreign Military Studies Branch. Undated, but late 1940s. Contains all the subsequent details on German intelligence in the Mius River defense of July 1943.
107. G. Utkin, *Shturm "Vostochnogo vala"* [Storm of the Eastern Wall] (Moskva: Voenizdat, 1967), 241. Hereafter cited as Utkin.
108. G. Zhukov, "In the Kursk Bulge," *The Battles of Kursk*, (Moscow: Progress Publishers, 1974), 53–55; details on all aspects of planning for the Belgorod–Khar'kov operations found in D.M. Glantz, *From the Don to the Dnepr: Soviet Offensive Operations December 1942–August 1943*. Manuscript to be published.
109. Ziemke, *Stalingrad*, 151.
110. Tsirlin, *Inzhenernye*, 171.
111. Matsulenko, *Operativnaya*, 66; for confirmation see *Small Units Actions During the German Campaign in Russia*, DA Pamphlet No. 20–269, Washington, D.C.: Department of the Army, July 1953), 220–228.
112. Matsulenko, *Operativnaya*, 61.
113. Kir'yan, *Vnezapnost'*, 58.
114. Vyrodov, 234–235.
115. Kir'yan, *Vnezapnost'*, 56.
116. Z. Al'shits, "Dostizhenie vnezapnosti v nastupatel'nykh operatsiyakh Velikoi Otechestvennoi voiny" [The achievement of surprise in offensive operations of the Great Patriotic War], *VIZh*, No. 11 (November 1964), 20.
117. Kir'yan, *Vnezapnost'*, 56–57.
118. Matsulenko, *Operativnaya*, 64–65.
119. N. Orlov, G. Tvardovskii, 21.
120. Quoted in Matsulenko, *Operativnaya*, 65, from the German article in *Wehrwissenschaftliche Rundschau*, No. 10, 1965, 599.
121. Ibid., 66.
122. Vasilevsky, 312.
123. Zhukov, *Memoirs*, 481–482; Shtemenko, 184–185.
124. Vasilevsky, 313.
125. V.P. Istomin, *Smolenskaya nastupatel'naya operatsiya (1943g)* [Smolensk offensive operation (1943)], (Moskva: Voenizdat, 1975), 19.
126. Ibid., 23.
127. Ibid., 24–25, 33–34, 47.
128. A.I. Yeremenko, *Gody vozmezdiya 1943–1945* [Years of retribution 1943–1945], (Moskva: "Finansy i statistika", 1985), 30. Yeremenko was Kalinin Front commander. Hereafter cited as Yeremenko, *Gody vozmezdiya*.
129. Kir'yan, *Vnezapnost'*, 41.
130. Ibid.
131. Ibid.
132. Ibid., 23; Istomin, 19.
133. Istomin, 49.
134. Ibid.; V.P. Boiko, *S dumoi o rodine* [With thought about my homeland], (Moskva: Voenizdat, 1982), 87–88. Boiko was the member of the military council (political commissar) of 39th Army.
135. Istomin, 89–90.
136. N.N. Voronev, *Na sluzhbe voennoi* [In military service], (Moskva: Voenizdat, 1963), 387–388.
137. Istomin, 105.
138. Ibid.

139. Ibid., 108; Kir'yan, *Vnezapnost'*, 165.
140. Kir'yan, *Vnezapnost'*, 166.
141. Istomin, 120–128.
142. Yeremenko, *Gody vozmezdiya*, 45.
143. V.T. Evdokimov, "Boevye deistviya 184-i strelkovoi divizii v dukhovshchinsko-demidovskoi operatsii" [Combat action of the 184th Rifle Division in the Dukhovshchina-Demidov operation], *VIZh*, No. 2 (February 1986), 54–55.
144. Yeremenko, *Gody vozmezdiya*, 46.
145. S. Malyanchikov, "Manevr i udar 50-i armii pod Bryanskom" [Maneuver and the attack of 50th Army at Bryansk], *VIZh*, No. 10 (October 1969), 28.
146. A.S. Galitsan, "Bryanskaya operatsiya 1943" [The Bryansk Operation of 1943], *SVE* 1:1976, 609.
147. F.D. Pankov, *Ognennye Rubezhi: boevoi put' 50-i armii v Velikoi Otechestvennoi voine* [Lines of Fire: the combat path of 50th Army in the Great Patriotic War], (Moskva: Voenizdat, 1984), 140.
148. Malyanchikov, 28.
149. Pankov, 142.
150. Malyanchikov, 31.
151. Ibid., 32.
152. Utkin, 23–24; A.S. Galitsan, "Chernigovsko–pripyatskaya operatsiya" [The Chernigov–Pripyat operation], *SVE* 8:1980, 454–456.
153. I. Glebov, "Manevr voisk v Chernigovsko–Pripyatskoi i Gomel'sko–Rechitskoi nastupatel'nykh operatsiyakh" [Maneuver of forces in the Chernigov–Pripyat and Gomel'–Rechitsa offensive operations], *VIZh*, No. 1 (January 1976), 13.
154. Kir'yan, *Vnezapnost'*, 58.
155. Glebov, 14.
156. Kir'yan, *Vnezapnost'*, 59.
157. Utkin, 27.
158. Rokossovsky, *A Soldier's Duty*, 209.
159. Glebov, 14.
160. M.A. Kozlov, ed., *V plameni srazhenii: boevoi put' 13-i armii* [In the flames of battle: the combat path of 13th Army], (Moskva: Voenizdat, 1973), 129.
161. Utkin, 86–88; for details on the later stages of the Belgorod–Khar'kov operation see Glantz, *From the Don to the Dnepr*, draft manuscript.
162. Konev, *Zapiski*, 48.
163. A.P. Riyazansky, *V ogne tankovykh srazhenii* [In the fire of tank battles], (Moskva: "Nauka," 1975), 95.
164. Konev, *Zapiski*, 53; Utkin, 94.
165. Utkin, 203.
166. Konev, *Zapiski*, 69.
167. Utkin, 204–210; S. Pechenenko, "Gvardeiskaya strelkovaya diviziya v boyakh za Dnepr" [A guards rifle division in battles of the Dnepr], *VIZh*, No. 9 (September 1968), 54; M. Sharokhin, "Forsirovanie Dnepra armiei s khodu" [The forcing of the Dnepr by an army from the march], *VIZh*, No. 9 (September 1963), 54–56.
168. Vasilevsky, 313; Utkin, 242.
169. Yershov, 120.
170. Chuikov, *Ot Stalingrada*, 353–354.
171. Yershov, 135.
172. Chuikov, *Ot Stalingrada*, 354–355.
173. Ibid., 355.
174. Ibid., 357.
175. Manstein, 456.
176. Utkin, 315–316.
177. Kir'yan, *Vnezapnost'*, 167.
178. Utkin, 326.
179. Matsulenko, *Operativnaya*, 44–45; A.A. Grechko, *Bitva za Kavkaz* [Battle for

the Caucasus], (Moskva: Voenizdat, 1973), 264–267. Hereafter cited as Grechko, *Bitva*.

180. Grechko, *Bitva*, 405–413.
181. Ibid., 406–407.
182. Ibid., 411.
183. Ibid.
184. Matsulenko, *Operativnaya*, 47.
185. L. Kozlov, "Nekotorye voprosy voennogo iskusstva v Novorossiiskoi operatsii" [Some questions concerning military art in the Novorossiisk operation], *VIZh*, No. 10 (October 1981), 73–74.
186. Ibid., 74.
187. Ibid., 73.
188. A.A. Grechko, ed., *Istoriya vtoroi mirovoi voiny 1939–1945 T-7* [A history of World War II], Vol 7, (Moskva: Voenizdat, 1976), 253. Hereafter cited as *IVMV* with appropriate volume and date.
189. Ibid.
190. Ibid.
191. Ibid., 373; N.A. Svetlishin, "Nevel'skaya operatsiya," *SVE*, 5:1978, 560–561.
192. Yeremenko, *Gody vozmezdiya*, 76; V.K. Pyatkov, K.S. Belov, S.S. Frolov, *Tret'ya udarnaya: boevoi put' 3-i udarnoi armii* [3d Shock: combat path of 3d Shock Army], (Moskva: Voenizdat, 1976), 73; K.N. Galitsky, *Gody surovykh ispytanii 1941–1944* [Years of rigorous ordeals 1941–1944], (Moskva: "Nauka," 1973), 304. Hereafter cited as Galitsky, *Gody surovykh*.
193. Galitsky, *Gody surovykh*, 306–307.
194. Ibid., 315.
195. A. Gazin, "28–ya strelkovaya diviziya v boyakh na Nevel'skom napravlenii" [28th Rifle Division in battles on the Nevel' direction], *VIZh*, No. 9 (September 1981), 27–28.
196. Pyatkov, 75; Galitsky, *Gody surovykh*, 315–316.
197. G. Semenov, "Vnezapnyi udar po vragu" [A surprise attack on the enemy], *VIZh*, No. 10 (October 1969), 79–80.
198. Ziemke, *Stalingrad*, 199.
199. Glebov, 198.
200. G.A. Koltunov, "Gomel'sko–rechitskaya operatsiya" [The Gomel'–Rechitsa operation], *SVE*, 2:1976, 600–602.
201. A. Gorbatov, M. Ivashechkin, "Nastuplenie 3-i armii severnee Gomelya" [The offensive of 3d Army north of Gomel'], *VIZh*, No. 8 (August 1962), 32. Gorbatov was 3d Army commander, and Ivashechkin was his chief of staff.
202. Rokossovsky, *Soldier's Duty*, 220.
203. Gorbatov, 32.
204. Rokossovsky, *Soldier's Duty*, 220.
205. P. Batov, "Na gomel'skom napravlenii" [On the Gomel' direction], *VIZh*, No. 12 (December 1968), 78. Hereafter cited as Batov, "Na gomel'skom napravlenii".
206. Batov, *Na pokhodakh i boyakh*, 315.
207. Batov, "Na gomel'skom napravlenii," 79.
208. Batov, *Na pokhodakh i boyakh*, 316.
209. Gorbatov, 34.
210. Ziemke, *Stalingrad*, 192.
211. Rokossovsky, *Soldier's Duty*, 221–22.
212. Ibid., 222; I.I. Fedyuninsky, *Podnyatye po trevoge* [Raising the alarm], (Moskva: Voenizdat, 1964), 163.
213. Glebov, 17.
214. Batov, *Na pokhodakh i boyakh*, 361.
215. Ziemke, *Stalingrad*, 195.
216. A. Grechko, "V boyakh za stolitsu Ukrainy" [In battles for the capital of the Ukraine), *VIZh*, No. 11 (November 1967), 4. Hereafter cited as Grechko, "V

boyakh za stolitsu". At the time Grechko was deputy *front* commander of the 1st Ukrainian Front.

217. Ibid., 5.
218. K. Krainyukov, "Osvobozhdenie Kieva" [The liberation of Kiev], *VIZh*, No. 10 (October 1963), 68–69; Utkin, 352–353. Krainyukov was 1st Ukrainian Front member of the military council.
219. Yu.D. Zakharov, *General armii N. F. Vatutin* [Army General N. F. Vatutin], (Moskva: Voenizdat, 1985), 146. Hereafter cited as Zakharov, *Vatutin*.
220. Moskalenko, 152.
221. Kir'yan, *Vnezapnost'*, 106, 131.
222. Vyrodov, 277.
223. Ibid., 278.
224. S. Alferov, "Peregruppirovka 3-i gvardeiskoi tankovoi armii v bitve za Dnepr (oktyabr' 1943g)" [The regrouping of 3d Guards Tank Army in the battle for the Dnepr (October 1943)], *VIZh*, No. 3 (March 1980), 16–17.
225. Ibid., 17.
226. Matsulenko, *Operativnaya*, 78–79.
227. Alferov, 19–21.
228. Ibid., 23; Zvartsev, 111–113; N.G. Nersesyan, *Kievsko–Berlinskii: boevoi put' 6-go gvardeiskogo tankovogo korpusa* [Kiev–Berlin: combat path of 6th Guards Tank Corps], (Moskva: Voenizdat, 1974), 80–82.
229. Matsulenko, *Operativnaya*, 79.
230. Tsirlin, 191–193; Moskalenko, 155.
231. H. van Nes, "German Intelligence Appreciation November 1943", *A Transcript of Proceedings 1985 Art of War Symposium, From the Dnepr to the Vistula: Soviet Offensive Operations – November 1943–August 1944* (Carlisle Barracks, PA: Center for Land Warfare, 1985), 57. Hereafter cited as van Nes, "German Intelligence Appreciation November 1943".
232. Zakharov, *Vatutin*, 147.
233. Van Nes, "German Intelligence Appreciation November 1943," 58.
234. Ibid., 59.
235. Ibid.
236. Manstein, 486.
237. N. Shekhovtsov, "Nastuplenie voisk Stepnogo fronta na krivorozhskom napravlenii v oktyabre 1943 goda" [The offensive of Steppe Front forces on the Krivoi Rog direction in October 1943], *VIZh*, No. 10 (October 1968), 28–29.
238. Utkin, 223.
239. Konev, *Zapiski*, 72.
240. Ibid., 79.
241. Manstein, 481.
242. Ibid., 485.
243. V.K. Krainyukov, *Ot dnepra do visly* [From the Dnepr to the Vistula], (Moskva: Voenizdat, 1971), 98–100. Hereafter cited as Krainyukov, *Ot dnepra*.
244. A.N. Grylev, *Dnepr-karpaty-krym: Osvobozhdenie Pravoberezhoi Ukrainy i Kryma v 1944 gody* [Dnepr–Carpathians–Crimea: the liberation of the right bank of the Ukraine and Crimea in 1944], (Moskva: "Nauka." 1970), 38–39.
245. Grylev, 40; Krainyukov, *Ot dnepra*, 100–101.
246. G. Koltunov, "Udar voisk 1-go Ukrainskogo fronta na zhitomirskom napravlenii zimoi 1943/1944 goda" [The attack of 1st Ukrainian Front forces on the Zhitomir direction in the winter of 1943/1944], *VIZh*, No. 2 (February 1967), 16; Moskalenko, 217, provides the *front* order which read:

To the commanders of 13,60 [armies] With the aim of deceiving the enemy regarding our intentions the commander of the *front* orders: the commander of 13 and 60 to conduct demonstrative actions in the regions:

1. Commander of 13 Army in the region Khodaki, Khotinovka, Lipyany,

Medynovo Sloboda, Sarnovichi.
2. Commander of 60 Army in the region of Peremoga, Meleni, Chepovichi, Ksavorov.
3. In these regions show: a) the preparation of a large operation with attacks west and southwest to display a large concentration of infantry, artillery, and tank forces; b) demonstrate up to 20 false division radio nets (10 per army); c) demonstrate the concentration of Rybalko's tank army [3d Guards Tank Army] in the Khodaki, Stremingorod, Medynova Sloboda region. Radio stations will arrive from Rybalko in Kalenskoe by morning 19.12.43; d) spread rumors that along the entire front we will go over to a firm defense; e) conduct continuous reconnaissance on the front Korosten, Kholosno, Shershin.
4. This deception operation will be conducted in the period from morning 19.12.43g to the morning of 26.12.43g.

"Bogolyubov"

Bogolyubov was chief of staff of the 1st Ukrainian Front. German operational records show 3d Guards Tank Army just where the Soviets wished them to see it – at its false concentration area. German intelligence also recorded the presence of about 10 false divisions.

247. Mellenthin, 263.
248. A.Kh. Babadzhanyan, N.K. Popel', M.A. Shalin, I.M. Kravchenko, *Lyuki otkryli v berline: boevoi put' 1-i gvardeiskoi tankovoi armii* (They opened the hatchway in Berlin: combat path of 1st Guards Tank Army], (Moskva: Voenizdat, 1973), 100 (hereafter cited as Babadzhanyan, Lyuki); M.I. Povalii, ed., *Vosemnadtsataya v srazheniyakh za rodinu: boevoi put' 18-i armii* [The 18th in battles for the homeland: combat path of 18th Army], (Moskva: Voenizdat, 1982), 328–333.
249. Moskalenko, 214.
250. Ibid., 218.
251. Manstein, 496–497.
252. Ibid., 497.
253. Matsulenko, *Operativnaya*, 66–67.
254. Solov'ev, 254.
255. Van Nes, "German Intelligence Appreciation November 1943," 60.

CHAPTER VI

1. A.M. Shtemenko, *General'nyi shtab v gody voiny* [The general staff in the war years], (Moskva: Voenizdat, 1968), 201 (hereafter cited as *General'nyi shtab*).
2. Ibid.
3. Ibid., 200–202; Vasilevsky, 336–338; Zhukov, *Vospominaniya* Vol 2, 212–213.
4. Shtemenko, *General'nyi shtab*, 202.
5. Ibid.
6. A. Rakitsky, "Udar pod Leningradom" [Blow at Leningrad], *VIZh*, No. 1 (January 1974), 26.
7. A.S. Galitsin, "Leningradsko–Novgorodskaya operatsiya" [Leningrad–Novgorod operation], *SVE*, 4:1977, 617–619.
8. S.P. Platonov, ed., *Bitva za Leningrad 1941–1944* [The battle of Leningrad 1941–1944], (Moskva: Voenizdat, 1964), 302–303 (hereafter cited as Platonov, *Bitva*).
9. I.T. Korovnikov, P.S. Lebedev, Ya.G. Polyakov, *Na trekh frontakh: boevoi put' 59-i armii* [On three fronts: the combat path of 59th Army], (Moskva: Voenizdat, 1974), 91 (hereafter cited as Korovnikov, *Na trekh frontakh*).

10. P. Yegorov, "Na novgorodsko–luzhskom napravlenii" [On the Novgorod–Luga direction], *VIZh*, No. 2 (February 1974), 68. Yegorov was the senior officer of the *front* directorate during the operation.
11. Platonov, *Bitva*, 307.
12. A.I. Belov, ed., *Voennye svyazisty v boyakh za rodinu* [Military signalmen in combat for its homeland], (Moskva: Voenizdat, 1984), 182.
13. Rakitsky, 31–32; Fedyuninsky, 174; L. Zaitsev, A. Borshchov, "Taktika nastupatel'nogo boya pri proryv blokady Leningrada" [Tactics of offensive combat during the penetration of the Leningrad blockade], *VIZh*, No. 1 (January 1983), 21.
14. V. Matsulenko, "Operativnaya maskirovka voisk v tret'em periode voiny" [Operational *maskirovka* of forces in the third period of war], *VIZh*, No. 6 (June 1972), 30.
15. I.T. Korovnikov, *Novgorodsko–Luzhskaya operatsiya: nastuplenie voisk 59–i armii (yanvar'–fevral' 1944g)* [The Novgorod–Luga operation: the offensive of 59th Army forces (January–February 1944)], (Moskva: Voenizdat, 1960), 36–38 (hereafter cited as Korovnikov, *Novgorodsko–Luzhskaya operatsiya*). Korovnikov was 59th Army commander.
16. Yegorov, 68.
17. Korovnikov, *Novgorodsko–Luzhskaya operatsiya*, 62–63.
18. Meretskov, *Serving the People*, 275–276.
19. Platonov, *Bitva*, 328.
20. Ibid., 330.
21. Matsulenko, *Operativnaya*, 87.
22. Ziemke, *Stalingrad*, 250.
23. Ibid.
24. Ibid., 253.
25. Grylev, 49.
26. P.Ya. Yegorov, I.V. Krivoborsky, I.K. Ivlev, A.I. Rogalevich, *Dorogami pobed: boevoi put' 5-i gvardeiskoi tankovoi armii* [By the road of victory: combat path of 5th Guards Tank Army], (Moskva: Voenizdat, 1969), 130–132 (hereafter cited as Yegorov, *Dorogami pobed*).
27. A.S. Zhadov, *Chetyre goda voiny* [Four years of war], (Moskva: Voenizdat, 1978), 157. Zhadov was 5th Guards Army commander.
28. I.A. Samchuk, P.G. Skachko, Yu.N. Babikov, I.L. Gnedoi, *Ot Volgi do El'by i Pragi* [From the Volga to the Elbe and Prague], (Moskva: Voenizdat, 1970), 144.
29. Yegorov, *Dorogami pobed*, 143.
30. Grylev, 50.
31. Ziemke, *Stalingrad*, 226.
32. Konev, *Zapiski*, 98.
33. Chuikov, *V boyakh*, 123–127.
34. Zakharov, *Vatutin*, 167.
35. Grylev, 59.
36. G.T. Zavizion, P.A. Kornyushin, *I na Tikhom okeane* .... [To the Pacific Ocean], (Moskva: Voenizdat, 1967), 9. Hereafter cited as Zavizion, *I na Tikhom okeane*.
37. Grylev, 59.
38. Yegorov, *Dorogami pobed*, 164.
39. For details on all aspects of *maskirovka*, see Matsulenko, *Operativnaya*, 89–91; Kir'yan, *Vnezapnost'*, 60–61; Tsirlin, *Inzhenernye*, 202; A. Tsirlin, "Inzhenernye voiska 2-go Ukrainskogo fronta v Korsun'–Shevchenkovskoi operatsii" [Engineer forces of the 2d Ukrainian Front in the Korsun'–Shevchenkovskii operation], *VIZh*, No. 2 (February 1974), 76; A.I. Radzievsky, ed., *Armeiskie operatsii* [Army operations], (Moskva: Voenizdat, 1977), 150–152. Hereafter cited as Radzievsky, *Armeiskie*. Tsirlin was chief of engineers of the 2d Ukrainian Front.

40. Zhadov, 162.
41. H. van Nes, "The Korsun–Shevchenkovskii Operation: A German Intelligence Appraisal," *A Transcript of Proceedings, 1985 Art of War Symposium, From the Dnepr to the Vistula: Soviet Offensive Operations – November 1943–August 1944*, (Carlisle Barracks, PA: Center for Land Warfare, 1985), 179. Hereafter cited as van Nes, "The Korsun–Shevchenkovskii Operation."
42. Ibid.; Kir'yan, *Vnezapnost'*, 60.
43. Details on the operation in I.M. Belkin, *13 armiya v Lutsko–Rovenskoi operatsii 1944g* [13th Army in the Lutsk–Rovno operation 1944], (Moskva: Voenizdat, 1960).
44. Kozlov, 188–196; Ziemke, *Stalingrad*, 246.
45. Grylev, 97.
46. Kozlov, 183–201.
47. Grylev, 104–105.
48. Grylev, 110–111; V.M. Ivanov, "Nikopol'–Krivorozhskaya operatsiya 1944," *SVE*, 5:1978, 599–601.
49. Chuikov, *V boyakh*, 124–125.
50. Ibid., 126.
51. Ibid., 126–127.
52. F. von Senger und Etterlin, "24th Panzer Division Operations in the Southern Ukraine, November 1943 to June 1944," *A Transcript of Proceedings, 1985 Art of War Symposium, From the Dnepr to the Vistula: Soviet Offensive Operations – November 1943–August 1944*, (Carlisle Barracks, PA: Center for Land Warfare, 1985), 222. Von Senger served as an officer in 24th Panzer Division.
53. Ibid.
54. Vasilevsky, 356.
55. Grylev, 130.
56. Moskalenko, 280.
57. M.I. Povaly, *Vosemnadtsataya v srazheniyakh za rodinu: boevoi put' 18-i armii* [The 18th in battles for the homeland: the combat path of 18th Army], (Moskva: Voenizdat, 1982), 371.
58. Moskalenko, 281.
59. Zvartsev, 153–154.
60. Moskalenko, 282–283.
61. Grylev, 135; Manstein, 527, states, "Although the weather prevented our air reconnaissance from telling what movement or troop concentrations were taking place on the other side, the Army Group was able to assess the enemy's intentions ... by the end of February." Manstein does not elaborate on how he made the assessment.
62. Manstein, 526.
63. Babadzhanyan, *Lyuki*, 131.
64. Grylev, 137.
65. Moskalenko, 285; Grylev, 138–139.
66. Manstein, 531.
67. Grylev, 160; for some details see V.M. Ivanov, "Umansko–botoshanskaya operatsiya 1944," [The Uman–Botshany operation 1944], *SVE*, 8:1980, 195–196.
68. Grylev, 161.
69. Ibid. 179; for some details see F.D. Vorob'ev, "Bereznegovato–snigirevskaya operatsiya 1944" [The Bereznegovatoye–Snigirevka operation 1944], *SVE*, 1:1976, 450–451.
70. Chuikov, *V boyakh*, 141–153; I.A. Pliyev, *Pod gvardeiskim znamenem* [Under guards banners], (Ordzhonikidze: Izdatel'stvo "IR," 1976), 100–104.
71. V.M. Ivanov, "Rogachevsko–zhlobinskaya operatsiya 1944" [The Rogachev–Zhlobin operation 1944], *SVE*, 7:1979, 135–136; Grylev, 205–217.
72. Grylev, 200–205.
73. Shtemenko, *General'nyi shtab*, 291–292.

74. Ibid., 292.
75. Ibid.
76. Zhukov, *Memoirs*, 516–518.
77. Vasilevsky, 388–389.
78. Shtemenko, *General'nyi shtab*, 300–301.
79. Kir'yan, *Vnezapnost'*, 61–62; A. Shimansky, "O dostizhenii strategicheskoi vnezapnosti pri podgotovke letne-osennei kampanii 1944 goda" [Concerning the achievement of strategic surprise during preparations of the summer–autumn campaign of 1944], *VIZh*, No. 6 (June 1968), 19.
80. Vasilevsky, 389.
81. F.I. Vysotsky, M.E. Makukhin, F.M. Sarychev, M.K. Shaposhnikov, *Gvardeiskaya tankovaya* [Guards tank], (Moskva: Voenizdat, 1963), 103.
82. Shtemenko, *General'nyi shtab*, 301–302; Vasilevsky, 389.
83. Shimansky, 18.
84. Ibid., 22.
85. Platonov, *Bitva*, 428.
86. Ibid., 438.
87. Tsirlin, *Inzhenernye*, 247.
88. Platonov, 443.
89. Tsirlin, *Inzhenernye*, 247.
90. V. Zubakov, "21-ya armiya v Vyborgskoi nastupatel'noi operatsii (10–20 iyunya 1944g.)" [21st Army in the Vyborg offensive operation (10–20 June 1944)], *VIZh*, No. 6 (June 1971), 25–26. Contains planning details of 21st Army.
91. Zhukov, *Memoirs*, 524–525; Vasilevsky, 389–390.
92. Matsulenko. *Operativnaya*, 113. The scale of redeployments covered in detail in N. Yakovlev, "Operativnye peregruppirovki voisk pri podgotovka Belorusskoi operatsii" [Operational regrouping of forces during the preparation of the Belorussian operation], *VIZh*, No. 9 (September 1975).
93. Vasilevsky, 415.
94. Ibid., 402.
95. S.P. Kiryukhin, *43-ya armiya v vitebskoi operatsii* [43d Army in the Vitebsk operation], (Moskva: Voenizdat, 1961), 52–54.
96. I.M. Chistyakov, 217–218.
97. Matsulenko, *Operativnaya*, 117–118.
98. Ibid., 115–116.
99. V. Chernyayev, "Operativnaya maskirovka voisk v Belorusskoi operatsii" [Operational *maskirovka* of forces in the Belorussian operation], *VIZh*, No. 8 (August 1974), 13.
100. Vasilevsky, 424–425.
101. Matsulenko, *Operativnaya*, 118.
102. Chernyayev, 14. This article also reprints detailed tactical *maskirovka* instructions the 1st Belorussian Front issued to all of its subordinate commands.
103. Matsulenko, *Operativnaya*, 97.
104. The scope of this redeployment detailed in Yakovlev, 92, and in Chistyakov, *Sluzhim*, 216–220. German Third Panzer Army intelligence maps clearly show the Soviet 154th Rifle Division sector but up to 24 June do not evidence any awareness of the extensive Soviet redeployments into that sector. See text for sample map.
105. K.K. Rokossovsky, "Na napravlenii glavnogo udara" [On the direction of the main blow], in A.M. Samsonov, ed., *Osvobozhdenie Belorussii, 1944* [The liberation of Belorussia, 1944], (Moskva: Izdatel'stvo "Nauka," 1974), 143. Hereafter cited as Samsonov, *Osvobozhdenie Belorussii*. For an army level view (65th Army) see P.I. Batov, *V pokhodakh i boyakh* [In campaigns and battles], (Moskva: Voenizdat, 1966), 405–416.
106. Matsulenko, *Operativnaya*, 100.
107. Ziemke, *Stalingrad*, 313.
108. Ibid., 315.

109. Ibid.
110. Ibid., 315–316.
111. For an excellent overall assessment of German intelligence capabilities, see H. van Nes, "Bagration: Study of the Destruction of Army Group CENTRE during the Summer of 1944 as Seen From the Point of View of Military Intelligence," *1985 Art of War Symposium, From the Dnepr to the Vistula: Soviet Offensive Operations, November 1943–August 1944, A Transcript of Proceedings*, (Carlisle Barracks, PA: US Army War College, 1985), 245–293. Hereafter cited as van Nes, "Bagration". An OKH perspective is found in Graf von Kielmansegg, "A View from the Army High Command (OKH)," *1985 Art of War Symposium*, 293–297.
112. Soviet order of battle and strength figures found in Samsonov, *Osvobozhdenie Belorussii*, 741–785 and "Belorusskaya operatsiya v tsifrakh" [The Belorussian operation in figures], *VIZh*, No. 6 (June 1964).
113. Van Nes, "Bagration," 267.
114. Ibid., 270–272.
115. Ziemke, *Stalingrad*, 316.
116. *Istoriya Velikoi Otechestvennoi voiny Sovetskogo Soyuza 1941–1945* [A history of the Great Patriotic War 1941–1945], (Moskva: Voenizdat, 1962), 4:206–207.
117. Konev, *Zapiski*, 231–232. Contains full planning details.
118. S. Petrov, "Dostizhenie vnezapnost' v L'vovsko–Sandomirskoi operatsii" [The achievement of surprise in the L'vov–Sandomirsk operation], *VIZh*, No. 7 (July 1974), 31.
119. B. Petrov, "O nekotorykh tendentsiyakh v sozdanii i ispol'zovanii udarnykh gruppirovok po opytu frontovykh nastupatel'nykh operatii Velikoi Otechestvennoi voiny" [Concerning some tendencies in the creation and use of shock groups based on the experience of *front* offensive operations of the Great Patriotic War"], *VIZh*, No. 11 (November 1983), 17. Hereafter cited as B. Petrov, "O nekotorykh tendentsiyakh."
120. Konev, *Zapiski*, 232–233; Matsulenko, *Operativnaya*, 106–121; Radzievsky, *Armeiskie*, 141–147. Contains details of the *maskirovka* operations.
121. Matsulenko. *Operativnaya*, 108.
122. B. Panov, S. Anov, "K voprosu o proryve na Rava–Russkom napravlenii" [Concerning the question of the penetration on the Rava–Russkaya direction], *VIZh*, No. 2 (February 1970), 95.
123. Matsulenko. *Operativnaya*, 108–109. *Maskirovka* units included: 114th Engineer-Sapper Battalion, 6th Engineer-Sapper Brigade; 583d Separate Sapper Battalion, 280th Rifle Division; 558th Separate Sapper Battalion, 309th Rifle Division; 197th Separate Sapper Battalion, 151st Rifle Division; 325th Rifle Regiment, 129th Rifle Division; 957th Rifle Regiment, 309th Rifle Division; Training Battalion, 113th Army Depot Rifle Regiment; one battalion, senior lieutenant's course; two battalions, 840th Artillery Regiment, 280th Rifle Division; separate anti-aircraft machine gun company, 309th Rifle Division; 2 chemical defense companies; six T-34 tanks; 36 trucks of the 522d automobile battalion; two platoons of the 22d Separate Maskirovka Company; 150 mock-up tanks; two powerful loudspeakers; three radio stations [R. B.]; and nine vehicles of the 7th Automobile Company.
124. Ibid., 110.
125. Ibid., 112.
126. Ibid, 112–119; Povaly, 390–391. Units involved in *maskirovka* included the 132d, 133d, and 135th Separate Engineer Battalions, 9th Separate Engineer-Sapper Brigade; two battalions, 145th Rifle Regiment, 66th Guards Rifle Division; 71st Separate Tank Destroyer Battalion, 66th Guards Rifle Division; two batteries, 1448th Self-propelled Artillery Regiment, 9th Rifle Division (10 SAU-76 SPs); one anti-aircraft regiment, 37th Anti-Aircraft Division; 20 vehicles, 590th Automobile Company; two railroad trains; three tractors, 146th Gun Artillery Brigade; one radio company, one cable company, and other elements, 188th Separate Signal Regiment; MGU-12, MGU-39 broadcast stations; 200 men, 23d Defensive

Construction Administration; one platoon, 23d Maskirovka Company; two platoons, 30th Separate Sapper Battalion; and 126 assembled and disassembled mock-up tanks.
127. Radzievsky, *Armeiskie*, 144–145.
128. Matsulenko, *Operativnaya*, 116.
129. Ibid., 117.
130. Povaly, 391–392.
131. Vyrodov, 370–371.
132. Moskalenko, 385–386.
133. Ibid., 386.
134. A. Rakitsky, "Nastupatel'naya operatsiya 3-i gvardeiskoi armii (iyul'' 1944g)" [The offensive operations of 3d Guards Army (July 1944)], *VIZh*, No. 9 (September 1978), 70–72.
135. Ibid., 73–74.
136. Sekirin, 217.
137. Zvartsev, 166–168.
138. D.D. Lelyushenko, *Moskva–stalingrad–berlin–praga* [Moscow–Stalingrad–Berlin–Prague], (Moskva: "Nauka," 1985), 247.
139. Babadzhanyan, *Lyuki*, 182.
140. Konev, *Zapiski*, 233.
141. Radzievsky, *Armeiskie*, 147.
142. Konov, *Zapiski*, 244.
143. Ibid.
144. Panov, 95–96.
145. Ibid., 96–98.
146. 1st Guards Tank Brigade action described in S. Petrov, 33–36.
147. Ibid, 33; Matsulenko, *Operativnaya*, 119–120.
148. B. Petrov, "O sozdanii udarnoi gruppirovki voisk v lyublinsko–brestskoi nastupatel'noi operatsii" [Concerning the creation of the shock group of forces in the Lublin–Brest offensive operation], *VIZh*, No. 3 (March 1978), 83. Hereafter cited as B. Petrov, "O sozdanii."
149. B. Petrov, "O nekotorykh tendentsiyakh," 13.
150. Chuikov, *Ot stalingrada*, 430–431.
151. Ibid., 431.
152. Ibid., 435.
153. I.I. Yushchuk, *Odinnadtsatyi tankovyi korpus v boyakh za rodinu* [The 11th Tank Corps in battles for the homeland], (Moskva: Voenizdat, 1962), 59.
154. Vysotsky, 109.
155. B. Petrov, "O sozdanii," 84.
156. Ibid., 86.
157. Ibid., 86–88.
158. M.M. Minasyan, *Osvobozhdenie narodov Yugo–Vostochnoi Evropy* [Liberation of the peoples of South-Eastern Europe], (Moskva: Voenizdat, 1967), 114.
159. V. Matsulenko, "Nekotorye osobennosti voennogo iskusstva v Yassko–Kishinevskoi operatsii" [Some features of military art in the Yassy–Kishinev operation], *VIZh*, No. 8 (August 1969), 16.
160. F. Gaivoronsky, "Sovetskoe voennoe iskusstvo po opytu Yassko–Kishinevskoi operatsii" [Soviet military art based on the experience of the Yassy–Kishinev operation], *VIZh*, No. 8 (August 1983), 12.
161. Ibid.; S.S. Biryuzov, *Sovetskii soldat na balkanakh* [Soviet soldiers in the Balkans], (Moskva: Voenizdat, 1963), 80.
162. B. Petrov, "O nekotorykh tendentsyakh," 17.
163. M.V. Zakharov, ed., *Osvobozhdenie yugo–vostochnoi i tsentral'noi evropy voiskami 2-go i 3-go ukrainskikh frontov 1944–1945* [The liberation of south-eastern and central Europe by forces of the 2d and 3d Ukrainian Fronts 1944–1945], (Moskva: "Nauka," 1970), 81.

164. Biryuzov, 83–84.
165. Zakharov, 82.
166. Gaivoronsky, 12–14; Zakharov, 82–86; Matsulenko, *Operativnaya*, 122–131.
167. Tsirlin, *Inzhenernye*, 263.
168. Matsulenko. *Operativnaya*, 122.
169. Ibid., 123–124.
170. Zavizion, 62.
171. Tsirlin, *Inzhenernye*, 264.
172. Matsulenko, *Operativnaya*, 125.
173. P.Ya. Malinovsky, ed., *Yassko–Kishinevskie Kanny* [Yassy–Kishinev Cannae], (Moskva: "Nauka," 1964), 91. Cannae was a battle between Hannibal of Carthage and the Romans in 216 B.C. The Carthaginians won by a classic double envelopment which resulted in one of the most complete victories in history.
174. Biryuzov, 81.
175. Ibid., 265; Matsulenko, *Operativnaya*, 126.
176. D. Zherebin, "Pyataya udarnaya v boyakh za Moldaviyu" [5th Shock in battles for Moldavia], *Oni osvobozhdali moldaviyu, oni shturmovali berlina* [They liberated Moldavia, they stormed Berlin], (Kishinev: Kartya moldovenyaske, 1984), 24.
177. Matsulenko, *Operativnaya*, 127.
178. Ibid., 128; details in G.I. Vaneyev, *Chernomortsy v Velikoi Otechestvennoi voine* [Black Sea sailors in the Great Patriotic War], (Moskva: Voenizdat, 1978), 346–350.
179. Matsulenko. *Operativnaya*, 129.
180. Ibid.
181. Biryuzov, 81–82.
182. Matsulenko. *Operativnaya*, 130.
183. H. van Nes, "The Yassy–Kishinev Operation: An Intelligence Appraisal," *A Transcript of Proceedings 1985 Art of War Symposium, From the Dnepr to the Vistula: Soviet Offensive Operations – November 1943–August 1944)*, (Carlisle Barracks, PA: Center for Land Warfare, 1985), 453. Hereafter cited as van Nes, "The Yassy–Kishinev Operation."
184. Ibid., 454.
185. Ibid.
186. Ibid., 455.
187. Ibid., 456.
188. Ibid., 455–456.
189. Zhukov, *Memoirs*, 557.
190. Shtemenko, *General'nyi stab*, 374.
191. Ibid.
192. Ibid., 376.
193. Ibid., 362–363.
194. Bagramyan, *Tak shli*, 433.
195. K.L. Orlov, et al. ed., *Bor'ba za sovetskuyu pribaltiku v velikoi otechestvennoi voine, T.2.: K. Baltiskomu moryu* [Struggle for the Soviet Baltic in the Great Patriotic War, Vol. 2: To the Baltic Sea], (Riga: Izdatel'stvo "Liesma," 1967), 175.
196. Bagramyan, *Tak shli*, 435.
197. Ibid., 437.
198. B. Petrov, "O nekotorykh tendentsiyakh," 17.
199. A.P. Beloborodov, *Vsegda v boyu* [Always in battle], (Moskva: Voenizdat, 1978), 332–333.
200. Chistyakov, *Sluzhim*, 249–250.
201. Domnikov, 246.
202. Bagramyan, *Tak shli*, 438.
203. Matsulenko, *Operativnaya*, 134; S.M. Sarkis'yan, *51-ya armiya (boevoi put')*, [51st Army (combat path)], (Moskva: Voenizdat, 1983), 267.
204. Matsulenko, *Operativnaya*, 135.

205. Ibid.
206. Orlov, 180.
207. Sarkis'yan, 267.
208. Yegorov, *Dorogami pobed*, 266.
209. F.I. Galkin, *Tanki vozvrashchayutsya v boi* [Tanks return to combat], (Moskva: Voenizdat, 1964), 153.
210. Bagramyan, *Tak shli*, 443.
211. Matsulenko, *Operativnaya*, 136.
212. Ibid.
213. Ziemke, *Stalingrad*, 406.
214. Ibid., 407.
215. Matsulenko, *Operativnaya*, 136–137.
216. Ziemke, *Stalingrad*, 407.
217. P.Ya. Malinovsky, *Budepesht–Vena–Praga* [Budapest–Vienna–Prague], (Moskva: "Nauka," 1965), 42.
218. M.M. Malakhov, "Debretsenskaya operatsii 1944" [Debrecan operation 1944], *SVE*, 3:1977, 119.
219. Malinovsky, 47–48.
220. Ibid., 79. For details on this and subsequent operations see D. Glantz, ed., "Operations in Hungary, 26 October–31 December 1944," *A Transcript of Proceedings 1986 Art of War Symposium, From the Vistula to the Oder: Soviet Offensive Operations – October 1944–March 1945*, (Carlisle Barracks, PA: Center for Land Warfare, 1986), 99–279. Hereafter cited as Glantz, "Operations in Hungary."
221. Glantz, "Operations in Hungary," 128.
222. Minasyan, 318.
223. Glantz, "Operations in Hungary," 147.
224. A.M. Samsonov, ed., *Osvobozhdenie Vengrii ot fashizma* [The liberation of Hungary from fascism], (Moskva: "Nauka," 1965), 109. Hereafter cited as Samsonov, *Osvobozhdenie Vengrii*. This segment is by 46th Army commander, Lieutenant General I.T. Shlemin.
225. S. Alferov, "Nastuplenie 4-i gvardeiskoi armii v Budapeshtskoi operatsii" [The offensive of 4th Guards Army in the Budapest operation], *VIZh*, No. 9 (September 1982), 14; I. Biryukov, "Na podstupakh k Budapeshty" [On the approaches to Budapest], *VIZh*, No. 3 (March 1965), 87. Lieutenant General Biryukov was commander of 20th Guards Rifle Corps.
226. Malinovsky, 89.
227. Minasyan, 325.
228. Ibid.
229. *Lagenkarte, Hr. Gp. Sud* 4.12.44 (original).
230. Malinovsky, 95.
231. Ibid., 86; Minasyan, 345.
232. Minasyan, 348.
233. Samsonov, *Osvobozhdenie Vengrii*, 121. This account is by Biryukov of 20th Guards Rifle Corps.
234. T.F. Vorontsov, N.I. Biryukov, A.F. Smekalov, *Ot volzhskikh stepei do avstri-iskikh Al'p: boevoi put' 4-i gvardeiskoi armii* [From the Volga steppes to the Austrian Alps: the combat path of 4th Guards Army], (Moskva: Voenizdat, 1971), 132; Alferov, 16–17.
235. Glantz, "Operations in Hungary," 186.
236. H. van Nes, "German Intelligence Appreciation," *A Transcript of Proceedings 1986 Art of War Symposium, From the Vistula to the Oder: Soviet Offensive Operations – October 1944–March 1945*, (Carlisle Barracks, PA: Center for Land Warfare, 1986), 103.
237. Ibid, 108.
238. Ibid, 109.

239. Van Nes, "The Korsun–Shevchenkovskii Operation: A German Intelligence Appraisal," 178.

CHAPTER VII

1. Zhukov, *Memoirs*, 556.
2. Shtemenko, *Generalnyi shtab*, 374.
3. Zhukov, *Memoirs*, 560.
4. Shtemenko, *Generalnyi shtab*, 381.
5. Zhukov, *Memoirs*, 558.
6. Ibid., 561; *front* missions delineated in N.A. Svetlishin, "Vislo–oderskaya operatsiya 1945" [The Vistula–Oder operation 1945], *SVE* 2:1976, 147–148.
7. Ibid.
8. B. Petrov, "O nekotorykh tendentsiyakh," 14.
9. Kir'yan, *Vnezapnost'*, 31.
10. Matsulenko, *Operativnaya*, 140–141.
11. Babadzhanyan, *Lyuki*, 223; M.E. Katukov, *Na ostrie glavnogo udara* [At the point of the main attack], (Moskva: Voenizdat, 1976), 336. Katukov was commander of 1st Guards Tank Army.
12. Babadzhanyan, *Lyuki*, 233.
13. Ibid, 228.
14. I.F. Dremov, *Nastupala groznaya bronya* [Formidable armor attacks], (Kiev: Izdatel'stvo politicheskoi literatury, 1981), 88.
15. G.G. Semenov, *Nastupaet udarnaya* [Shock attacks], (Moskva: Voenizdat, 1970), 180–185.
16. V.I. Chuikov, *Konets tret'ego reikha* [The end of the Third Reich], (Moskva: "Sovetskaya Rossiya," 1973), 100. Hereafter cited as Chuikov, *Konets*.
17. F. Bokov, "Nastuplenie 5-i udarnoi armii s magnushevskogo platsdarma" [The offensive of 5th Shock Army from the Magnushev bridgehead], *VIZh*, No. 1 (January 1974), 66.
18. I.P. Roslyi, *Poslednii prival – v berline* [The last halt – in Berlin], (Moskva: Voenizdat, 1983), 236.
19. V. Matsulenko, "Operativnaya maskirovka voisk v Vislo–Oderskoi operatsii" [Operational *maskirovka* of forces in the Vistula–Oder operation], *VIZh*, No. 1 (January 1975), 12. Hereafter cited as Matsulenko, "Operativnaya maskirovka v Vislo–oderskoi operatsii."
20. I. Konev, *Years of Victory*, (Moscow: Progress Publishers, 1984), 16. A good translation of *God pobedy* [Year of victory], (Moscow: Voenizdat, 1966).
21. Radzievsky, *Armieskie*, 147–149.
22. Matsulenko, *Operativnaya*, 142–143.
23. Matsulenko, "Operativnaya maskirovka v Vislo–oderskoi operatsii," 14.
24. Ibid.
25. Matsulenko, *Operativnaya*, 148.
26. Ibid., 149.
27. Matsulenko, "Operativnaya maskirovka v Vislo–oderskoi operatsii," 16.
28. Korovnikov, *Na trekh frontakh*, 184.
29. Zvartsev, 196–199.
30. Matsulenko, *Operativnaya*, 150; I. Galitsky, "Iz opyta operativnoi maskirovki pri podgotovke nastupleniya fronta" [From the experience of operational *maskirovka* in preparation of a *front* offensive], *VIZh*, No. 5 (May 1966), 40–48. Galitsky was 1st Ukrainian Front chief of engineers.
31. Matsulenko, *Operativnaya*, 151.
32. I.P. Galitsky, *Dorogu otkryvali sapery* [Sappers open the roads], (Moskva:

Voenizdat, 1983), 233; M.M. Kir'yan, *S sandomirskogo platsdarma* [From the Sandomierz bridgehead], (Moskva: Voenizdat, 1960), 77.

33. Kir'yan, *Vnezapnost'*, 33.
34. Ibid., 33.
35. Matsulenko, *Operativnaya*, 152.
36. "Fremde Heere Ost (I) No. 81/45 SECRET, Estimate of the Overall Enemy Situation: 5 Jan. 1945," *The German G-2 Service in the Russian Campaign* (Ic-Dienst Ost) (United States Army, 22 July 1945), Appendix A, 181. Hereafter cited as Fremde Heere Ost (I) No. 81/45.
37. Ibid.
38. Ibid., H. van Nes, "German Intelligence Appreciation – The Vistula–Oder Operation," *A Transcript of Proceedings 1986 Art of War Symposium, From the Vistula to the Oder: Soviet Offensive Operations – October 1944–March 1945*, (Carlisle Barracks, PA: Center for Land Warfare, 1986), 492. Hereafter cited as van Nes, "German Intelligence Appreciation – The Vistula–Oder Operation."
39. Ibid.
40. Ibid.
41. Fremde Heere Ost (I) No. 81/45, 182–183.
42. Van Nes, "German Intelligence Appreciation – The Vistula–Oder Operation," 495–496, quoting document Army Group "A" Chief of Staff Br. B. Nr. 1 c/AO Nr. 17/45 gKdos. "Short Assessment of the Enemy Situation in Front of Army Group 'A'," HQ 3 Jan 1945.
43. Derived from original of Fremde Heere Ost *Lage Ost* (map) 13.1.45.
44. Matsulenko. *Operativnaya*, 153–154.
45. See Army Group Vistula situation maps, 3–4 February 1945; Ziemke, *Stalingrad*, 442, reports 17 February as the date 1st and 2d Guards Armies turned away from the Oder to the north, whereas this move began on 2 February. See also Babadzhanyan, *Lyuki*, 260, and M.D. Solomatin, *Krasnogradtsy* [Men of Krasnograd], (Moskva: Voenizdat, 1963), 157–159.
46. Vasilevsky, 438–439.
47. Ibid., 440.
48. M.A. Alekseyev, "Vostochno–prusskaya operatsiya 1945" [East Prussian operations 1945], *SVE* 2:1976, 379–381.
49. Yegorov, 289–297.
50. Matsulenko, *Operativnaya*, 154–155.
51. For details of *maskirovka* within 28th Army see A.D. Kharitonov, *Gumbin-nenskii proryv* [Gumbinnen penetration], (Moskva: Voenizdat, 1960), 46–47. Kharitonov was 28th Army commander.
52. E.F. Ivanovsky, *Ataku nachinali tankisty* [Tankers begin the attack], (Moskva: Voenizdat, 1984), 204, speaks of 8th Guards Tank Corps' regrouping.
53. Matsulenko, *Operativnaya*, 156.
54. Fremde Heere Ost (I) No. 81/45, 182; van Nes, "German Intelligence Appreciation – The East Prussian Operation," *Transcript 1986 Art of War Symposium*, 287. Quoting Abt Fremde Heere Ost (I) No. 81/45, 351 (original).
55. Fremde Heere Ost *Lage Ost* 5.1.45.
56. For details of the Balatan operation see D. Glantz, ed., "Operations in Hungary, January–March 1945," *A Transcript of Proceedings, 1986 Art of War Symposium, From the Vistula to the Oder: Soviet Offensive Operations – October 1944–March 1945*, (Carlisle Barracks, PA: Center for Land Warfare, 1986), 663–789.
57. M.M. Malakhov, *Osvobozhdenie vengrii i vostochnoi avstrii (oktyabr' 1944g-aprel' 1945g)* [The liberation of Hungary and eastern Austria (October 1944–April 1945)], (Moskva: Voenizdat, 1965), 175.
58. Ibid., 176.
59. See map O.K.H. *Lagenkarte, Hgr. Sud*, Stand 6.3.45.
60. S. Ivanov, "Na venskom napravlenii," [On the Vienna direction], *VIZh*, No. 6

(June 1969), 26.
61. Zavizion, 156–160.
62. Ivanov, 27.
63. Vorontsov, 190–195.
64. Ibid. 191.
65. See maps *Lage H. Gp. Sud.* Stand: 15–20.2.1945, 06^{00} Uhr.
66. Konev, *Year of Victory*, 87–89.
67. G.K. Zhukov, "Berlinskaya operatsiya 1945" [The Berlin operation 1945], *SVE* 1:1976, 457.
68. N.M. Ramanichev, "Iz opyta peregruppirovki armii pri podgotovke Berlinskoi operatsii" [From the experience of regrouping an army during the preparation of the Berlin operation], *VIZh*, No. 8 (August 1979), 9.
69. Zhadov, 257.
70. Zvartsev, 241.
71. Ramanichev, 14.
72. Ibid., 19.
73. V.K. Pyatkov, K.S. Belov, S.S. Frolov, *Tret'ya udarnaya: boevoi put' 3-i undarnaye armiya* [3d Shock: the combat path of 3d Shock Army], (Moskva: Voenizdat, 1976), 174.
74. Ramanichev, 9–16, contains details of all regroupings.
75. Babadzhanyan, *Lyuki*, 287–288.
76. Ramanichev, 12.
77. B. Petrov, "O nekotoriykh tendentsiyakh," 17; P.I. Batov, *Operatsiya "oder": boevye deistviya 65-i armii v Berlinskoi operatsii, aprel'-mai 1945 goda* [Operation Oder: combat operations of 65th Army in the Berlin operation, April–May 1945], (Moskva: Voenizdat, 1965), 13–27, contains all details of that army's regrouping. See also Konev, *Year of Victory*, 315–316.
78. Batov, *V pokhodakh*, 469–470.
79. Ramanichev, 13.
80. Matsulenko, *Operativnaya*, 160–161.
81. Ibid., 165–166.
82. Ibid., 166–189.
83. MS C-029 *OKH War Diary*, 561.
84. Ramanichev, 13.
85. Ibid., 13.
86. Ibid., 14.
87. MS C-029 *OKH War Diary*, 571.
88. Matsulenko, *Operativnaya*, 163.
89. "Kampanii sovetskikh vooruzhennikh sil na dal'nem vostoke v 1945 g (facti i tsirfry)" [The campaign of the Soviet armed forces in the Far East in 1945: facts and figures], *VIZh*, No. 8 (August 1965), 64–74; Saburo Hayashi and Alvin Coox, *Kogun: The Japanese Army in the Pacific War*, (Quantico, VA: The Marine Corps Association, 1959).
90. Shtemenko, *Generalnyi shtab*, 413.
91. Planning details found in L.N. Vnotchenko, *Pobeda na dal'nem vostoke* [Victory in the Far East], (Moskva: Voenizdat, 1971), 64–168.
92. Shtemenko, *Generalnyi shtab*, 420.
93. Ibid. 419. See also Meretskov, *Serving the People*, 337–338; Chistyakov, 271–273.
94. M.V. Zakharov, ed., *Finale*, (Moscow: Progress Publishers, 1972), 71.
95. Matsulenko, *Operatinaya*, 172–175.
96. Those Japanese attitudes portrayed in Drea, *Nomonhan*.
97. A detailed account of Soviet operational and tactical techniques is found in D.M. Glantz, *August Storm: The Soviet 1945 Strategic Offensive in Manchuria*, Leavenworth Papers No. 7, (Fort Leavenworth, KS: Combat Studies Institute, 1983); D.M. Glantz, *August Storm: Soviet Tactical and Operational Combat in Manchuria, 1945*, Leavenworth Papers No. 8, (Fort Leavenworth, KS: Combat

Studies Institute, 1983).

98. E.J. Drea, "A Japanese Pearl Harbor: Manchuria 1945," (Fort Leavenworth, KS: Combat Studies Institute, 1984), manuscript, 1.
99. E.J. Drea, "Missing Intentions: Japanese Intelligence and the Soviet Invasion of Manchuria, 1945," *Military Affairs*, April 1984, 67.
100. Ibid., 67–68.
101. Ibid.
102. Ibid.
103. Ibid., 69.
104. Ibid., 70.
105. Ibid.
106. Matsulenko, *Operativnaya*, 172.
107. Ibid., 177.

CHAPTER VIII

1. G. Zhukov, "Organizatsiya operativnoi maskirovki" [The organization of operational *maskirovka*], *VIZh*, No. 5 (May 1977), 48. Hereafter cited as Zhukov, "Organizatsiya maskirovki."
2. The German ability to detect Soviet tactical units (corps and below) also deteriorated as the war progressed. From 1941 to early 1943 German intelligence could usually identify newly deployed Soviet divisions within 24 hours of their arrival in front line positions. By early 1944 the detection time lengthened to 2–3 days, and in late 1944 and early 1945 detection took 3–4 days and often did not occur at all prior to a major attack. This deterioration attested to both reduced German reconnaissance capability and improved Soviet *maskirovka* at the lowest levels.
3. This should be of particular concern to contemporary intelligence agencies who tend to be inundated by voluminous, but often uncollated and unanalysed, data gathered by a variety of sophisticated technological collection means. Experience shows that too much information can be as confusing as too little, and it can paralyze operations by even the best analysts.
4. Kir'yan, *Vnezapnost'*.
5. Zhukov, "Organizatsiya maskirovki," 48.
6. Kir'yan, *Vnezapnost'*, 192.
7. Ibid., 194.

CHAPTER IX

1. L. Vetoshnikov, "Operativnoye iskusstvo i ego mesto v Sovetskom voennom iskusstve" [Operational art and its place in Soviet military art], *VM*, April 1949, translation by Eurasian Branch, G-2, US Army General Staff, 9.
2. Ibid.
3. J. Valenta, "Soviet Views of Deception and Strategic Surprise: The Invasion of Czechoslovakia and Afghanistan," *Strategic Military Deception*, (New York: Pergamon Press, 1982), 337. The author goes on to stress recent Soviet appreciation of strategic deception and detail its use in the Czechoslovakian and Afghan invasions.
4. B. Zlatoverov, "Tactical Surprise and Methods for Achieving It," *VM*, February 1945, translation by Eurasian Branch, G-2, US Army General Staff, 1.
5. Ibid.
6. Ibid., 24.
7. Z. Zlobin, "Modern Army Group Operations," *VM*, April 1945, translation by

Eurasian Branch, G-2, US Army General Staff, 6.

8. Ibid., 29.
9. Ibid., 24.
10. N. Pavlenko, "Concerning the Scale of Strategic Offensive Operations," *VM*, September 1946, translation by Eurasian Branch, G-2, US Army General Staff, 28.
11. Vetoshnikov, 17.
12. M. Smirnov, "Some Questions Concerning the Planning of Offensive Operations," *VM*, April 1949, translation by Eurasian Branch, G-2, US Army General Staff, 28–29.
13. I.V. Maryganov, *Peredovoi kharakter sovetskoi voennoi nauki* [The advanced nature of Soviet military science], (Moskva: Voenizdat, 1953), 125.
14. Ibid., 101.
15. V.A. Semonov, *Kratkii ocherk razvitiya sovetskogo operativnogo iskusstva* [A short survey of the development of Soviet operational art], (Moskva: Voenizdat, 1960), 260. See also a general article by P.A. Rotmistrov. "Vnezapnost'" [Surprise], *VM*, No. 2 (February 1955), 14–26.
16. V.D. Sokolovsky, *Voennaya Strategiya* [Military Strategy], (Moskva: Voenizdat, 1962, 1963, 1968), translation for the Foreign Technology Division, by H.F. Scott, 200. Contains an excellent textual comparison of all three Russian editions of Sokolovsky's book.
17. Ibid., 211.
18. Ibid., 193.
19. Ibid., 218.
20. Ibid.
21. Ibid., 288.
22. V.E. Savkin, *Osnovye printsipy operativnogo iskusstvo i taktiki* [The basic principles of operational art and tactics], (Moskva: Voenizdat, 1972), translation by the United States Air Force, 235.
23. Ibid., 236.
24. Ibid.
25. Ibid., 238.
26. Ibid.
27. S.P. Ivanov, *Nachal'nyi period voiny* [The initial period of war], (Moskva: Voenizdat, 1974).
28. Ibid., 299.
29. Ibid., 350.
30. M.M. Kir'yan, *Problemy voennoi teorii v sovetskikh nauchno-spravochnykh izdaniyakh* [The problems of military theory in Soviet scientific reference publications], (Moskva: "Nauka," 1985), 123–124.
31. Ibid., 113.
32. M.M. Kir'yan, "Vnezapnost'" [Surprise], *SVE*, 2, 1976, 163.
33. Ibid., 161.
34. Ibid.
35. Ibid.
36. K.M. Keltner, G.H. Turbiville, Jr., "Soviet Reinforcement in Europe," *Military Review*, April 1987, 34–50, contains an excellent description of Soviet views on and capabilities for rapid reinforcement.
37. Kir'yan, *Vnezapnost'*, 199.
38. Savkin, 230.
39. Kir'yan, *Vnezapnost'*, 195.

APPENDIX 1

Gomel'–Rechitsa, 65th Army Smokescreen Plan

PLAN OF CONDUCT OF SMOKE SCREENING FOR SUPPORT OF CROSSING OF SOZH AND DNEPR RIVERS BY 65TH ARMY

In zone of which corps	Purpose and Location of smoke screen	Outlay of Smoke Equipment	Readiness	Executors
19th Rifle Corps	Covering of bridge across Sozh at Nov. Tereshkovich from effect of enemy aviation	1000 cannisters	In operation	Chief of chemical service of 19th Rifle Corps
246th Rifle Division	Covering of bridge across Sozh 1 km southwest of hill with marker 118.4 from effect of enemy aviation	500 cannisters	In operation	Chief of chemical service of 246th Rifle Division
27th Rifle Corps	Covering of construction of bridge across Dnepr in region of Loev Sea	500 hand smoke grenades, 2 tons smoke compound	With beginning of construction of bridge	Chief of chemical service of 27th Rifle Corps
	Covering of crossing of *chasti* [regiments] across Dnepr in region of Kamenka; false smoke screen at discretion of corps commander	500 cannisters, 500 hand smoke grenades	By 0500 on 10–13	Chief of chemical service of 27th Rifle Corps
	Covering of crossing of *chasti* across Dnepr 2 km southwest of Kamenka; false smoke screen at discretion of corps commander	700 cannisters, 2 tons smoke compound	By 0500 on 10–13	Chief of chemical service of 27th Rifle Corps
	Covering of crossing of *chasti* across Dnepr in region of hill with marker 107.5; false smoke screen at discretion of corps commander	500 cannisters, 1 ton smoke compound	By 0500 on 10–13	Chief of chemical service of 27th Rifle Corps

18th Rifle Corps	Covering of crossing of *chasti* across Dnepr 2.5 km north-east of Shittsa; false smoke screen at discretion of corps commander	500 cannisters, 250 hand smoke grenades, 2.5 tons smoke compound	By 0500 on 10–13	Chief of chemical service of 18th Rifle Corps
	Covering of crossing of *chasti* across Dnepr 1 km south of Shittsa; false smoke screen at discretion of corps commander	600 cannisters, 250 hand smoke grenades, 1.5 tons smoke compound	By 0500 on 10–13	Chief of chemical service of 18th Rifle Corps
	Covering of crossing of *chasti* across Dnepr 1 km north of Radul' Sea; false smoke screen at discretion of corps commander	400 cannisters, 500 hand smoke grenades, 1 ton smoke compound	By 0500 on 10–13	Chief of chemical service of 18th Rifle Corps

APPENDIX 2

Belorussia: *STAVKA* Directive on *Maskirovka*

From a Directive of the Headquarters of the Supreme High Command
To Front Commanders:

To insure concealment of activities going forward on all fronts, I order:

1. All movements of troops and equipment are to be done only at night, strictly observing night march discipline. Movement during the day is to be authorized only in weather when flying is absolutely impossible, and only for individual groups that cannot be observed by the enemy on the ground. At daytime halting places and new assembly regions, troops and equipment are to be dispersed and carefully camouflaged. Personnel must not communicate with the local population and movement of groups and subunits along open roads and terrain sectors must be minimized.

   Direct special attention to concealment when replacing first-line troops.

2. During the entire period of regrouping and preparation for action keep up the existing fire situation. Establish a procedure for ranging artillery and mortar weapons that guarantees concealment of the artillery grouping in the primary axis.

3. Prohibit newly arrived formations from conducting ground reconnaissance.

4. Do not conduct commander's reconnaissance in large groups simultaneously. To conceal the true sectors of action organize the work of commander's reconnaissance groups on a broad front, including the passive sectors.

   In necessary cases, command personnel on commander's reconnaissance are authorized to wear the uniforms and gear of privates. Tank soldiers are categorically forbidden to appear on commander's reconnaissance in their special uniforms
   ...

13. Organize careful daily checks on execution of all orders relating to concealment. Make daily checks from the air of the concealment of headquarters and troop

positions, for which purpose special officers from the front and army staffs must be appointed ...

Report on orders issued by 1 June 1944.

Zhukov
Antonov

1900, 29 May 1944

Source: (TsAMO SSSR [Central Archives of the USSR Ministry of Defense], fund 48–80, inventory 1795, file 3, sheets 3–5. Original.)

From the 30th May 1944 Directive of the Military Council of the 1st Baltic Front

To insure concealment during preparations and to achieve surprise in conduct of the operation

I Order:

...A. Concerning Concealment of Troops and Maintenance of Military Secrecy

1. All movements of troops and rear services are to be done only at night between 2200 and 0400 with an exactly determined travel distance. Do not try to travel long distances. End marches in forested, sheltered regions. Do not permit columns to stretch out or lagging subunits to move during daytime.

   No matter where troops and their rear services may be when light comes, all roads must be perfectly still; all movement must stop.

2. Motor vehicles can travel only at night with headlights out. Set up white signs that are plainly visible at night on the roads. Paint the front part of the hood and rear sides of vehicles white. Traveling at high speed or passing vehicles on the march is categorically forbidden.

   The movement of troops, transports, motor vehicles, and combat equipment must follow strictly routes that are planned and scouted in advance, with no diversion to parallel roads and trails ...

5. When single enemy planes or small groups appear antiaircraft weapons and troop units on the march and at unit lines must not open fire. It is permitted to fire at enemy aircraft operating in large groups and threatening troops on the march and at unit lines ...

8. During the entire period of regrouping and preparation for action maintain the existing fire conditions. Establish a procedure for ranging artillery and mortar weapons that insures concealment of the artillery grouping in the main axis.

9. When enemy aircraft appear during tactical exercises subunits and units must take cover immediately and, according to predetermined signals, quickly deploy and simulate defensive construction on natural lines.

10. Establish rigorous control at communications centers and do not permit discussion, especially open discussion of activities on wire communications.

11. Make defensive subjects paramount in the Red Army press, and categorically forbid running any articles and notices that in any way treat questions of preparation for upcoming actions.

12. No activity (troop movement, hauling supplies, commander's reconnaissance, and so on) can be permitted or carried out before steps have been taken to conceal this activity.

    For this purpose:

    – Select one assistant chief of staff at all unit and formation headquarters to be assigned to work out instructions for camouflaging troops in all types of combat activity and to see that specially designated officers monitor this closely:

- Army and corps commanders must establish an order for commander's reconnaissance which precludes clustering of such groups. Commander's reconnaissance groups may only travel on roads and trails where defensive forces ordinarily travel:
- In zones scheduled for vigorous actions, step up defensive works, paying special attention to the quality (convincingness) of construction on dummy minefields and the like.

B. Concerning Discipline on the March and at Unit Lines

1. Raise standards demanded of subordinate commanders and troops, and continuously explain to them the rules of troop behavior on the march, at unit positions, and on the job.

2. Persistently explain to troops and demand that they increase vigilance, especially on the march, and (maintain – editor) military secrecy.

3. Establish constant checks by officers on the behavior of troops on the march and at unit lines.

4. Prohibit familiarization flights over territory occupied by the enemy for the personnel of new units joining the air army. Only the leaders can be authorized to make such flights, a day or two before the start of action. In this case establish an overflight zone whose depth guarantees that the plane can land in our territory if damaged by enemy fire ...

C. Concerning the Provost Service

1. The entire front region should be broken into the following zones for purposes of more precise organization of the provost service:

   a. The front zone, from the line of front bases (city of Nevel') to the line of army bases (Zheleznitsa, Bychikha). The organization of provost work in this zone is assigned to the chief of staff of the front;

   b. Army zone, from the line of army bases (Zheliznitsa, Bychikha) to the line of division exchange points;

   c. Troop zones, from the line of division exchange points to the forward edge of defense.

   Organization of provost service in the army and troop zone and in the unit areas should be assigned to the military councils of the armies and commanders of the corps ...

3. Provost and security service must be organized and carried out strictly on all front, army, and troop roads beginning at 1800 of 2 June 1944 ...

   Each provost must be given a group of officers from the army and front reserve and entire rifle subunits and units to perform provost duty on the roads and in troop areas.

   Determination of the composition of the group of officers and subunits for provost service must be based on the following considerations:

   a. One provost officer post with two officers for each 3–5 kilometers of road and one two-man post operated by soldiers and sergeants for every 1–2 kilometers of road;

   b. Two officers and 3–5 two-man posts for each battalion in the troop unit area ...

5. Front and army signal chiefs must insure constant wire communication and telephones on all routes, at every officer provost post and every provost office. Provost officers in charge of roads and regions must be given the necessary mobile equipment for this purpose ...

7. To insure concealed movement of troops, trains, vehicle transport, combat equip-

ment, and individual groups of soldiers and officers and to camouflage engineer work to prepare the spring board for the offensive, immediately determine the ground enemy's fields of vision in the forward zone (troop zone) and organize the strictest provost and security service. Take steps to establish vertical screens. Prohibit daytime travel by all motor vehicles (including cars) through fields of visibility and set markers at the boundaries of fields of visibility with especially rigorous provost officer posts.

8. Determine the limit for truck traffic in a day figuring 100 trucks for each army and front unit.

   The front chief of rear services should make up and issue special passes to armies and front units for daytime vehicle traffic within the established limit.

9. Categorically forbid written communications relating to activities being carried on. Only the restricted circle of scheduled persons should be permitted to see the content of essential documents, and documents must not go beyond the headquarters that prepared them.

10. Prohibit direct submission of requests from directorates, staffs, and chiefs of the arms of troops to the corresponding directorates of the fronts, sending them only through the army and front staffs.

11. In reports to front headquarters at 2100 each day report the results of the concealment inspection.

Do not put this Directive in written or printed form; disseminate it to the commanders of regiments and detached battalions by personal communication and instruction of subordinate commanders.

Guards Army Gen I. Bagramayan, commander of the 1st Baltic Front

Lt. Gen Leonov, member of the Military Council of the 1st Baltic Front

Lt Gen Kurasov, chief of staff of the 1st Baltic Front

30 May 1944

(TsAMO SSSR, fund 235, inventory 2074, file 75, sheets 2–10).

Source: A. Izosimov, "On the 35th Anniversary of the Belorussian Operation," *VIZh*, No. 6 (June 1979), 49–52. Translated by JPRS.

APPENDIX 3

L'vov–Sandomierz, 1st Ukrainian Front Deception Plan

Document No 1   "APPROVED"

Commander of 1st Ukrainian Front   Member of Military Council of 1st
Mar SU Konev   Ukrainian Front Lt Gen Kraynyukov

11 June 1944

Plan of Measures for Operational Camouflage,
Concealment and Deception in the 1st Ukrainian Front Zone

Missions	Area Where Measures Conducted	Time Periods	Persons Responsible	Total Forces and Means	Note
1	2	3	4	5	6
/1st Gds Army/ Demonstrate a tank army concentration					
/18th Army/ Demonstrate a tank army concentration:	Vinograd, Kolomyya, Zabolotuv, Rudna Station	Beginning and end of work and demonstration by special order	Cmdr 18th Army	Rif .bns: 2 Engr bns: 2 Arty batteries: 3 AAA regts: 1	Responsible staff officer of 1st Ukrainian Front Engr-Maj Momotov
a. Arrival and unloading of tanks on railroad			Chief of 18th Arm Engr Trps	Tank co: 1 Ftr avn flt: 1 Radio co: 1 Chem co: 1 Tank mock-ups: 500	
b. Tank movement to assembly area	Over roads: Rudna Station...		Cmdr of armd and mech trps of 18th Arm	Vehicle mock-ups: 200 Gun mock-ups: 600 Train mock-ups: 2	
c. Occupation of initial areas	Locations for special ground recon	"	Chief of 18th Arm Engr Trps	Field kitchen mock-ups: 100 Smokepots: 5,000 Sound units: 2	
d. Trp bivouacking	"	"	"	Tractors: 4 Vehicles: 15 Motorcycles: 10	

Document No 1 [Continued from previous page.]

1	2	3	4	5	6
e. Deception of local populace by special measures	In movement and concentration areas	"	Chief of 18th Arm Engr Trps and political department		200 persons of 23d uo[o?] [possibly special sections directorate] of RGK [High Cmd Res]
f. Screening concentration from the air	"	"	18th Arm arty cmdr, cmdr of 10th iak [ftr corps]		
g. Radio deception	Army RBS [probably type of radio] ... Corps ...	"	18th Arm sig officer		
h. Blanketing initial positions on day of attack	By special order	"	18th Arm chief of chem serv		

Chief of staff of 1st UF   Deputy commander and chief of engineer
[Ukrainian Front]   troops of 1st UF
Arm Gen Sokolovskiy   Lt Gen Engr Trps Galitskiy

From Ministry of Defense Central Archives, stack 236, list 2698, file 353, sheets 24-26

APPENDIX 4

L'vov–Sandomierz, 1st Guards Army Deception Plan

PLAN OF OPERATIONAL CAMOUFLAGE MEASURES IN ZONE
OF OPERATIONS OF TROOPS OF 1ST GUARDS ARMY IN
L'VOV–SANDOMIERZ OPERATION (7–4–44 – 7–20–44)

Date	Simulation in regions of unloading: Vygnanka st., Vorvulintsa st.	Date	Simulation in regions of concentration: forest east of Byaly Potok; forest south-east of Yagel'nitsy; forest east of Slobudka Koshylovetska, Repushintsa, Kolyanka, Korolyuvka, Rashkov	Date	Simulation in regions of initial positions on boundaries: Slodubka, Dzhuryn'ska, Polovtse; Voronov, Gavrilyak
7-7 - 7-10	1. Unloading of arriving echelons with tank mock-ups in Army rear, transfer of mock-ups to simulation regions of unloading for demonstration of false disposition of tank *chasti* (*podrazdelenlya* of 22nd Detached Camouflage Company, infantry platoon) 2. Sound simulation of unloading of tanks using MGU units 3. Covering of regions of unloading with smoke 4. Anti-aircraft artillery covering of unloading regions (2 batteries of 47th Rifle	7-7 - 7-10	1. Assembly and set up of mock-ups of tanks, fuel trucks, vehicles; equipping of fuel and lubricant base (two in each region) 2. Staking-out of march routes from unloading station to regions of concentration (5 groups each of 5 tankers and 15 combat engineers) 3. Simulation of movement of tanks into region of concentration; show of "lagging" tanks on march route	7-19	1. Reconnaissance of forward edge in zone of divisions of 30th Rifle Corps and 18th Guards Rifle Corps (1 group from division) 2. Reconnaissance of initial positions (3 groups of 7-8 men each) 3. Building of march routes from region of concentration to initial positions 4. Show of "lagging" tank mock-ups on march routes 5. Placement of tank mock-ups in initial positions 6. Preparation in smoke screen on a 6-8 km front 7. Demonstration of
		7-12 - 7-15	4. Sound simulation of tank movement with MGU units		
		7-12	5. Commander's		

Corps)

5. "Animation" of unloading regions:

a) daily shifting of mock-ups to simulate arrival and departure of tanks

b) conduct of intense fire with tracer bullets from small arms upon appearance of enemy aircraft;

c) daily shifting of tanks and tractors (platoon of T-34 tanks, 2 tractors from rear staff of 1st Guards Army)

0800-
1900
7-12-
7-15
reconnaissance of populated areas

6. Simulation of repair of materiel

7-15,
0600-
2000
7. Demonstration of increased vehicle movement on basic march routes in daytime

8. Demonstration of concentration of artillery and its advance into position regions in the sector of the 30th Rifle Corps

9. Conduct of at least 2 searches for taking prisoners daily in the zone of each division (according to orders on reconnaissance departments)

7-13-
7-20
10. Conduct of reconnaissance in force in regions of Stadnitsa, Trybukhovtse, Khatymnyva, Gubina, Luka, Bogordychina, Intela.

7-10-
7-14
11. Railroad operations,
a) construction of network of graded roads of light type – Chertkov, Tluszcz; Byaly Potok, Rydodyby, Slobudka Dzhurny'ska; Yagel'-nitsa, Polovtse; Marylyuvka, Slobudka, Koshylovetska; Koshilovtse;
b) preparation of bridges and paving on creeks and rivers which will be crossed

increased transport

7-17-
7-19
of ammunition into regions of combat disposition of infantry, and to artillery firing positions

8. Adjusting fire of guns according to plans of commanders

7-18-
7-19,
0800-
1900
of artillery corps

by graded roads;
c) equipping of
roads with markers
and road signs

Forces and equipment
Engineer battalion of the 6th Combat Engineer Brigade
Two combat engineer battalions of the 47th Rifle Corps
Road construction battalion of Army road department
Two platoons of the 22nd Detached Camouflage Company from the Front Staff
Two chemical protection companies of the 47th Rifle Corps
Five rifle battalions of the 47th Rifle Corps
Two anti-aircraft batteries of the 25th Anti-Aircraft Artillery Division

RB Radios	3
Vehicles	40
Tractors	6
Fuel and Lubricants	as per request
Smoke Cannisters	20,000
T-34 Tanks	6
Rifle Cartridges (tracer)	40,000
MGU	2

APPENDIX 5

L'vov–Sandomierz, 18th Army
Deception Instructions

Document No 2

To carry out instructions and in conformity with the plan of the 1st Ukrainian Front commander

I ORDER:

1. Perform simulation of tank army concentration in vicinity of Vinograd, Kolomyya, Zabolotuv in the period from 4 through 20 July 1944.

2. For immediate direction of all simulation measures assign an operations group made up of the following: chief of operations group – deputy chief of army staff operations department Col Soloveykin, Col Stopog from engineer troops staff, Lt Col Yakovlev from artillery staff, Col Pisarikhin from staff of BT i MV [armored and mechanized troops], Lt Col Fiktor from communications department, Lt Col Shcherbak from political department, Engr-Maj Nikul'chenko from VOSO [military transportation] department, and Lt Col Barten'yev from the chemical department.

3. Subordinate operations group directly to army chief of staff and provide it with means of transportation from the 201st Motor Transport Platoon.

4. My deputy for engineer troops Col Comrade Zhurin is to ensure the building of 500 tank mock-ups, 200 vehicle mock-ups, 600 gun mock-ups, and 100 field kitchen mock-ups using resources of two engineer battalions and two rifle battalions from the 66th Guards Rifle Division by 20 July 1944, placing them in areas according to the plan ...

5. The artillery commander is to place three gun batteries on mechanical traction and one AAA regiment for screening assembly areas at the disposal of the chief of the operations group.

6. The commander of BT i MV is to place two batteries at the operations group chief's disposal from the 1448th sap [Self-Propelled Artillery Regiment] and five motor-cycles for use in unloading and assembly areas.

7. Army signal officer Maj Gen Comrade Murav'yev is to arrange a dummy radio link according to the plan of the front signal officer for deception of the enemy, having the army RSB in Soroki and corps RSB's in the areas of Vinograd and Kobylets.

8. Political department chief Col Comrade Brezhnev is to place one MGU [powerful loudspeaker] sound broadcasting station at the disposal of the operations group chief and together with the chief of the army staff intelligence department organize deception of the local populace with respect to the concentration of major tank forces and offensive being prepared in the army sector. Use 15 officers for spreading false information among the populace.

9. VOSO chief Col Comrade Zelenin is to support through the front VOSO the measures being carried out by rolling stock (a locomotive, 30 flatcars and 3 boxcars). Arrange the train's progress according to the schedule of the operations group chief.

10. My deputy for rear services Maj Gen Comrade Baranov is to support uninterrupted operation of motor transport for the entire period of the activities, releasing fuel on requisitions of the army chief of engineer troops with my approval.

11. Chief of the army chemical service is to provide blanketing in vicinity of Stefaneshti Station, Yasunuv Pol'ny Station, 1–2 km west of Dzurkuv and 1–2 km south of Venyava, assigning the chemical company of 66th Guards Rifle Division and 5,000 smoke pots for this purpose.

12. Engr-Maj Momotov, representative of 1st UF staff, provides consultation on matters of operational camouflage, concealment and deception.

13. Report daily to operations group chief on progress of simulation work ...

Commander of 18th Army   Member of Military Council of 18th Army
Lt Gen Zhuravlev   Maj Gen Kolonin
                            Chief of Staff of 18th Army
                            Lt Gen Ozerov.

APPENDIX 6

Memel', 1st Baltic Front Deception Plan

PLAN OF DECEPTION OF ENEMY IN THE ZONE OF THE 1ST
BALTIC FRONT IN THE PERIOD OF REGROUPING AND
PREPARATION FOR THE MEMEL' OFFENSIVE
(FROM 9–24–44 THROUGH 10–3–44)

Measures	Forces and Equipment	Executors	Responsible Leader
1. Measures conducted in the zones of the 4th Assault and 51st Armies			
1. Simulation of reinforcement of Front troops:			
a) daily movement of troops of 1st Baltic Front to advanced positions of 4th Assault and 51st Armies	Troops of 2nd Baltic Front	Commander of 22nd and 3rd Assault Armies	Front chief of staff
b) lighting of fires in forests northwest of Baldone and northeast of Dobele	Troops of 4th Assault and 51st Armies	Corps commanders	Commanders of 4th Assault and 51st Armies
c) daily launching of balloon at set time south of Bausk	Balloon	Commander of artillery of 4th Assault Army	Commander of Front artillery
d) laying out of firing positions in zones of 4th Assault and 51st Armies	1 battery each from the 102nd and 103rd Howitzer Artillery Brigades, and 2 each M-31 rocket launchers	Commanders of artillery of 4th Assault and 51st Armies	Commander of Front artillery
e) organization of radio operations in regions of actual disposition of the 3rd Guards Mechanized Corps, and 1st and 19th Tank Corps of the 5th Guards Tank Army	Corps radios by instruction of Front communications chief	Army communications chiefs	Front communications chief
2. Demonstration of preparation of troops for the offensive			

a) conduct of reconnaissance in regions: Baldone, Yelgava, Bersmuizha, Gardene station	Reconnaissance groups from 4th Assault and 51st Armies	Corps and division commanders	Commanders of 4th Assault and 51st Armies
b) increase in reconnaissance activity in indicated regions	Reconnaissance department of armies	Same persons	Same persons
c) increase in adjusting fire	According to Army plans	Same persons	Same persons
d) false removal of mines on forward edge and construction of passages in minefields	Combat engineer companies of rifle divisions	Chiefs of Army engineer troops; commanders of rifle corps and rifle divisions	Same persons
e) placement of gun mock-ups in firing positions and organization of fire of roving guns from these positions	100 mock-ups for each Army (4th Assault and 51st Armies)	Chiefs of engineer troops, corps and division commanders	Same persons
f) placement of tank mock-ups	100 mock-ups for each Army (4th Assault and 51st Armies)	Same persons	Same persons
g) simulation of movement of tank *chasti*, on the basis of 3 tank mock-ups for one real tank or tractor, into the region of concentration southwest of Baldone and northeast of Dobele	15 tanks each from Armies (4th Assault and 51st Armies)	Commanders of armored and mechanized troops of 4th Assault and 51st Armies	Commanders of 4th Assault and 51st Armies
h) demonstration of concentration of pontoon facilities in regions southwest of Baldone and Mitava	37th and 60th Pontoon Battalions of 9th Pontoon Bridge Brigade	Chief of staff of Front engineer troops	Chief of Front engineer troops
i) organization of radio misinformation of enemy about offensive of 51st and 4th Assault Armies	By designation of Army chiefs of staff	Chiefs of staff of 4th Assault and 51st Armies	Commanders of 4th Assault and 51st Armies
j) increase in combat activity of aviation at enemy strong points and closest supply lines; bomb Tekava, Sloka.	By designation of commander of 3rd Air Army	Chief of staff of 3rd Air Army	Commander of 3rd Air Army

2. Measures conducted in zone of the 43rd Army and 2nd and 6th Guards Armies

1. Maintenance of rigid camouflage discipline in regions of troop disposition		Corps and division commanders	Commanders of 43rd Army and 2nd and 6th Guards Armies
2. Organization of controller's service in regions of troop concentration		Corps and division commanders	Commanders of 43rd Army and 2nd and 6th Guards Armies
3. Development and reinforcement of defense of 43rd Army and 2nd and 6th Guards Armies			
a) dig supplementary trenches in depths of regimental defenses	Troops of 43rd Army and 2nd and 6th Guards Armies	Corps and division commanders	Same persons
b) conduct false mining of forward edge of defense	29th, 30th, and 28th Combat Engineer Brigades	Chiefs of engineer troops of 43rd Army and 2nd and 6th Guards Armies	Same persons
c) install wire obstacles on forward edge	Troops of 43rd Army and 2nd and 6th Guards Armies	Corps and division commanders	Same persons

APPENDIX 7
Map Sources

German intelligence assessment maps in the text are based primarily on the following sources. Maps depicting actual Soviet dispositions are based on sources cited in the text and a multiplicity of Soviet memoirs and unit histories. German archival intelligence maps, prepared subsequent to the beginning of each Soviet offensive, confirm the accuracy of Soviet sources.

Map   Source

2. *Lagenkarten vom Kriegstagebuch*, 1. Pz. Armee, Lage:17.11.41.

4. Muriyev, 16.

5. *O.K.H., Lage Ost*, Stand:4-8.12.41 abds.

7. Herresgruppe Mitte/Ia, *Anlagen zum Kriegstagebuch: Lagekarten, eigene und Feindlage*. Lage am 4.1.42. Hereafter cited as Heeresgruppe Mitte/Ia. *Lagekarten*.

9. Heeresgruppe Mitte/Ia, *Lagekarten*. Lage am 8.1.42.

12. A.O.K.16, *Feindlage vor 16 Armee*, Stand: 9-15.1.42; Heeresgruppe Nord/Ic, *Entwicklung der Lage 1.1.-12.1*, Feindlage 12.1.

14. A.O.K.17, *Feindlage vom 18.1* morgens vor dem Antreten; Pz. A.O.K.1, *Lagenkarten zum K.T.B.*, Stand:18.1.42.

17. Pz. A.O.K.1, *Lagenkarten zum KTB*, Stand:10-11,12-13.5.42; A.O.K.6, *Lagenkarte zum KTB*, Lage:9-12.5.1942; A.O.K.17, *Feindlage vor 17. Armee*: 11.5. Anderungen am 11.5.

20. Heeresgruppe Mitte/Ia, *Lagenkarten*, Lage am 3.8.43.

22. Heeresgruppe Nord/Ic, *Entwicklung der Lage*, Feindlage 30.8.

25. Heeresgruppe Sud, *Kräfte Raum Don*, Stand 17.11.42; *Hgr. B*, Gen Std H Op Abt 111b. Stand:18.11.42 abds.

27. Heeresgruppe Don, *Feindlage vom Kriegstagebuch*, Stand 14.12.42; Rum. AOK 3 Ic, *Feindlage* am 17.12.1942.

29. Heeresgruppe Don, *Lagenkarte vom Kriegstagebuch*, Stand:20-23.12.42; *Hgr. B*, Gen Std H Op Abt 111b. Stand:23.12.42 abds.

32. A.O.K.2, *Lagenkarte vom Kriegstagebuch*, Stand 11-13.1.43; *Hgr. B*, Gen Std H Op Abt 111b. Stand:12.1.43 abds.

34. A.O.K.2, *Lagenkarte vom Kriegstagebuch*, Stand 24.1.43.

38. Pz. A.O.K.2; *Chefkarte u Abendlage*, Lage vom 5.7.43 bezw. 4.7.43; A.O.K.2, *Lagenkarten vom Kriegstagebuch*, Lage vom 5.7.43.

40. Pz. A.O.K.4, *Lagenkarten vom Kriegstagebuch*, Feindlage am 5.7.43; Armee-Abt. Kempf, *Feindlage*, Stand:5.7.

42. Pz. A.O.K.2, *Chefkarte u Abendlage*, Lage vom 13.7. bezw. 12.1.43.

44. Pz. A.O.K.1, *Lagenkarten*, Lage am 15.7.43, Ic 16.7.43.

46. A.O.K.6, Ic, *Feindlagenpausen, Anlage z. Tätigkeitsbericht*, Lage vom 16.7.43.

48. Matsulenko, *Operativnaya*, 63.

49. *Armeeabteilung Kempf*, Feindlage vom 1-4.8.43.0[00]; Pz. A.O.K.4, *Lagenkarten vom Kriegstagebuch*, Feindlage am 1-3.8.43.

52. Istomin, *Smolenskaya nastupatel'naya operatsiya*, 120-121.

53. A.O.K.4. Ia. *Kartenband zum Kriegstagebuch*, Lage der 4. Armee am 5.8.43 22[00].

55. A.O.K.4. Ia. *Kartenband zum Kriegstagebuch*, Lage der 4. Armee am 12-13.8.43 22[00].

57. A.O.K.4. Ia. *Kartenband zum Kriegstagebuch*, Lage der 4. Armee am 27.8.43 22[00].

59. A.O.K.4. Ia. *Kartenband zum Kriegstagebuch*, Lage der 4. Armee am 12.9.43 18[00].

61. A.O.K.4. Ia. *Kartenband zum Kriegstagebuch*, Lage der 4. Armee am 14-16.9.43 18[00].

63. Malyanchikov, 29.

64. *Hgr. Mitte* Gen Std H Op Abt 111b. Stand:7.9.43 abds.

66. AOK2, Ic/AO *K.T.B. Feindlagekarten*, Feindlage: 25.8.43.

68. Glebov, 15.

69. AOK2, Ic/AO *K.T.B. Feindlagekarten*, Feindlage: 10.9.43.

71. *8. Armee Ic/AO* Feindlage vom 23.9.43 0[00].

73. *8. Armee Ic/AO* Feindlage vom 29.9.43 0[00].

75. Pz. A.O.K.1, *Lagenkarten, Ic*, Lage vom 13-15.8.43.

77. A.O.K.6, Ic, *Feindlagenpausen, Anlage z. Tätigskeitsbericht*, Lage vom 19.8.43; Pz. A.O.K.1, *Lagenkarten, Ic*, Lage vom 13-15.8.43.

81. Matsulenko, *Operativnaya*, 47.

83. Panzer-A.O.K.3, ABT. Ic/A.O., *Anlagenband A/1* zum Tätigkeitsbericht-Nr. 10, Feindbild, Stand: 4-5.10.

85. Glebov, 17.

86. Heeresgruppe Mitte, Abt. 1a, *Kriegstagebuchkarten*, Lage am 14-17.10.43; 2. Armee, *Feindlage*: 14.10.43.

88. Glebov, 18.

89. 2. Armee, *Feindlage*: 9.11.43.

91. Alferov, 18.

92. *8. Armee Ic/AO*, Feindlage vom 2-6.11.43 Pz. A.O.K.4, *Lagenkarten vom Kriegstagebuch*, Feindlage am 28.10.-6.11.43.

94. *8. Armee Ic/AO*, Feindlage vom 14-15.10.43.0001.

96. Pz. A.O.K.4, *Lagenkarten vom Kriegstagebuch*, Feindlage am 23.12.43.

99. Heeresgruppe Nord, *Karte der Feind-u. eigenen Lage (einschl. Banden) im bereich der 16. u. 18. Armee* Stand:10-16.1.44.fruh.

101. Heeresgruppe Nord, *Karte der Feind-u. eigenen Lage (einschl. Banden) im bereich der 16. u. 18. Armee* Stand:10-16.1.44.fruh.

103. 8. Armee, *Feindlage im Einbruchsraum* vom 4.1.44.0^{00} A.O.K.6/Ic, *Vermütete Feindlage* Stand am 4.1.44.

105. Radzievsky, *Armeiskaya Operatsiya*, 151.

106. Pz. A.O.K.1, *Lagenkarten*, Lage am 23.1.44.

108. 8. Armee, *Feindlage im Einbruchsraum* vom 24-25.1.44.0^{00}.

110. Anlage 4 zum Ic–Tätigkeitsbericht, *Feindlagenkarten des Pz. A.O.K. 4 fur 25-26.1.44.*

112. A.O.K.6/Ic, *Feindlage vor 6. Armee* Stand:29.1.44.

115. I. Yakubovsky, "Na proskurovsko–chernovitskom napravlenii" [On the Proskurov–Chernovitsy direction], *VIZh*, No.3 (March 1969), 21.

116. *Lagenkarte 4. Pz. Armee.* Stand:3-15.3.44.19^{00}.

118. 8. Armee Ic/AO, Feindlage vom 4-5.3.44.0^{00}.

120. A.O.K.6/Ic, *Vermütete Feindlage* Stand am 2-7 Marz 44.

125. Shimansky, 20.

126. Yakovlev, 93.

127. Yakovlev, 95.

128. O.K.H., *Kriegsgeschichtliche Abteilung*, "Der grosse Durchbruch bei HGr. Mitte v. 21.6-10.8.44." Stand:22.6; Lagenkarte Hr. Gr. Mitte Ic/AO *Lage bei 3. Pz.-Armee*, 20-22 Juni 44

130. O.K.H., *Kriegsgeschichtliche Abteilung*, "Der grosse Durchbruch bei HGr. Mitte v. 21.6-10.8.44." Stand 22.6; Lagenkarte Hr. Gr. Mitte Ic/AO *Lage bei 4.- Armee*, 20-22 Juni 44.

132. O.K.H., *Kriegsgeschichtliche Abteilung*, "Der grosse Durchbruch bei HGr. Mitte v. 21.6-10.8.44." Stand:22.6; Lagenkarte Hr. Gr. Mitte Ic/AO *Lage bei 9.- Armee*, 20-22 Juni 44.

135. Matsulenko. *Operativnaya*, 107.

136. Radzievsky, 148.

137. O.K.H., *Kriegsgeschichtliche Abteilung*, "Der grosse Durchbruch bei HGr.

Nord-ukraine u. Kämpfe am grossen Weichselbruckenkopf v. 8.7-29.8.44."
Stand:12.7.44.

139. O.K.H., *Kriegsgeschichtliche Abteilung*, "Der grosse Durchbruch bei HGr.
Nord-ukraine u. Kämpfe am grossen Weichselbruckenkopf v. 8.7-29.8.44."
Stand:12.7.44.

141. O.K.H., *Kriegsgeschichtliche Abteilung*, "Der grosse Durchbruch bei HGr.
Nord-ukraine u. Kämpfe am grossen Weichselbruckenkopf v. 8.7-29.8.44."
Stand:12.7.44.

143. S. Petrov, "Dostizhenie vnezapnosti," 33.

144. B. Petrov, "O sozdanii," 87.

145. O.K.H., *Kriegsgeschichtliche Abteilung*, "Der grosse Durchbruch bei HGr.
Nord-ukraine u. Kämpfe am grossen Weichselbruckenkopf v. 8.7-29.8.44,"
Stand 17.7.44.

148. Matsulenko, *Operativnaya*, 123.

149. O.K.H., *Lagenkarte HGr. Süd-Ukraine*, Stand:19.8.44; *8. Armee* Ic/AO
Feindlage vom 19.8.44.0^{00}.

151. O.K.H., *Lagenkarte HGr. Süd-Ukraine*, Stand:19.8.44 *8. Armee* Ic/AO
Feindlage vom 19.8.44.0^{00}.

153. O.K.H., *Lagenkarte HGr. Süd-Ukraine*, Stand:19.8.44 *8. Armee* Ic/AO
Feindlage vom 19.8.44.0^{00}.

156. Matsulenko, *Operativnaya*, 132.

157. A.O.K.16 Ic/AO, *Feindlage-Karten* Stand:1.-14. Okt. 1944; Heeresgruppe
Mitte Abt. Ic/AO *Landkarten: Feinde und Eigenlage, 11 Sep-2 Dez 1944* Stand 1-
4.10.44.

159. O.K.H., *Lagenkarte, Hgr Sud* Stand:28.10.44.

161. O.K.H. *Lagenkarte, Hgr. Sud.* Stand:3.11.44.

163. O.K.H. *Lagenkarte, Hgr. Sud.* Stand:9.11.44.

165. O.K.H. *Lagenkarte, Hgr. Sud.* Stand:26.11.44.

169. O.K.H. *Lagenkarte, Hgr. Sud.* Stand:19.12.44.

172. Radzievsky, Shkema 23.

173. O.K.H. *Lage Ost* Stand:11-12.1.45 abds.

175. O.K.H. *Lage Ost* Stand:11-12.1.45 abds; Hgr A, *Gen StdH/Op Abt 111b*.
Stand:11-12.1.45 abds.

177. O.K.H. *Lage Ost* Stand:11-12.1.45 abds Hgr A, *Gen Std H/Op Abt 111b*.
Stand:11-12.1.45 abds.

179. Heeresgruppe Mitte Abt Ic/AO *Feind-Lagen-Skizze* Stand:26.1.45.

180. H.Gr. Weichsel, Ia *Lage-Karten der Heeresgruppe Weichsel* Stand:4.2.45.

181. O.K.H. *Lage Ost* Stand:12.1.45 abds. Hgr. Mitte., *Gen StdH Op Abt 111b*
Stand:12.1.45 abds.

183. Pz. A.O.K.3, Ic/AO, *Feindlage* Stand:12.1.45.

185. Hgr. Mitte, *Gen Std H Op Abt 111b* Stand:12.1.45 abds.

187. O.K.H. *Lagenkarte, Hgr. Sud.* Stand:6.3.45.

189. O.K.H. *Lagenkarte, Hgr. Sud.* Stand:14.3.45; *Lage H. Gp. Sud.* Stand:
15.2.1945 06^{00} Uhr.

191. Ramanichev, 11.

192. Matsulenko, *Operativnaya*, 159.

193. Matsulenko. *Operativnaya*, 162.

194. Matsulenko, *Operativnaya*, 167.

195. *Hgr. Weichsel*, Gen Std H Op Abt 111b Stand:15.4.45 abds.

197. *Hgr. Weichsel*, Gen Std H Op Abt 111b Stand:15.4.45 abds.

199. *Hgr. Weichsel*, Gen Std H Op Abt 111b Stand:15.4.45 abds.

201. *Hgr. Weichsel*, Gen Std H Op Abt 111b Stand:15.4.45 abds.

203. U.S. Army Forces Far East. Military History Section, Japanese Monograph No. 155, *Record of Operations Against Soviet Russia – On Northern and Western Fronts of Manchuria and in Northern Korea (August 1945)*. Tokyo, 1945.

Index